CATALOGUE OF THE EXCAVATED PREHISTORIC AND ROMANO-BRITISH MATERIAL IN THE GREENWELL COLLECTION

CATALOGUE OF THE EXCAVATED PREHISTORIC AND ROMANO-BRITISH MATERIAL IN THE GREENWELL COLLECTION

I.A. KINNES AND I.H. LONGWORTH

with contributions by D.K. Dunlop, S.P. Needham,
V. Rigby, I.M. Stead, G. Varndell and G. Wilson

Illustrations by P.K. Dean with K. Hughes

Published for the Trustees of the British Museum by
BRITISH MUSEUM PUBLICATIONS LIMITED

Frontispiece
Canon William Greenwell, 1820–1918
(Durham Cathedral Library)

Published by British Museum Publications Ltd,
46 Bloomsbury Street, London WC1B 3QQ

British Library Cataloguing in Publication Data
Kinnes, Ian
  Catalogue of the excavated prehistoric and
  Romano-British material in the Greenwell Collection.
  1. Man, Prehistoric – Great Britain   2. Great
  Britain – Antiquities
  I. Title   II. Longworth, I.H.   III. Dunlop, D.K.
  936.1'01'0216   GN805
  ISBN 0-7141-1371-9

Printed in Great Britain by
Henry Ling Ltd.,
at the Dorset Press, Dorchester, Dorset

CONTENTS

PREFACE

The excavated material in the Greenwell Collection, the bulk of which came to the British Museum in 1879 with later additions notably in 1889 and 1893, forms one of the foundation collections of British prehistory. Although many of the barrows opened were recorded and some of the finds given brief mention according to the descriptions of the time, the objects in the collection have remained to all intents and purposes unpublished. The intention of this fully illustrated catalogue is to remedy this deficiency. Although the main authors must take responsibility for the overall contents, the catalogue represents essentially a collaborative effort by the staff of the Department of Prehistoric and Romano-British Antiquities. To all those who have helped us within the Museum and to the many colleagues outside who have advised, assisted and answered so many of our problems, I offer my grateful thanks.

I.H. Longworth
Keeper of Prehistoric and Romano-British Antiquities

Acknowledgements

For assistance with the identification and analysis of material we are indebted to Dr M. Tite, Dr M.J. Hughes, D. Hook and Dr I. Freestone (Research Laboratory British Museum: metal analysis and ceramic petrology), Dr J. Clutton-Brock and staff of the Departments of Palaeontology and Zoology (British Museum Natural History: animal bones, shells, fossils), D. Britton (Pitt Rivers Museum: metal analysis), Dr P. Phillips and Dr W.A. Cummins (CBA Implement Petrology Committee: stone axe petrology) and E. Crowfoot (textiles). Photography was undertaken by W.V. Bowley (British Museum). We are grateful for access to material in other museums and collections to Dr D.V. Clarke and Dr T. Cowie (National Museum of Antiquities of Scotland: NMAS), E. Grantham (Driffield: GC), E. Owles (Moyses Hall Museum: MHM), G. Plowright (Bristol Museums), R.T. Schadla-Hall (Hull Museums: HM) and Dr A. Sherratt (Ashmolean Museum: Ashm). T.C.M. Brewster and Dr D.G. Coombs kindly provided material and information in advance of their own publications. For further assistance and information we are grateful to D. Britton, R. Miket, Dr J.N.G. Ritchie, M. Smith and I.J. Thorpe.

INTRODUCTION

This catalogue comprises the prehistoric and Romano-British material from certain or probable burial sites which was originally in the collection of Canon William Greenwell. The post-Roman material and the finds retrieved by Greenwell from the Grime's Graves flint mine have been reserved for publication elsewhere. The results of new examinations of sites and relevant material from other collections have been incorporated where accessible (see Acknowledgements).

The sites and finds have been recorded to a standard scheme (see below), and all objects are illustrated with the exception of unretouched flints and featureless potsherds from non-burial contexts. An attempt has been made to reconcile disparities in the records on the information available. The prime source remains the accession registers in the British Museum, supplemented and amended where necessary by the surviving manuscript material (*WG Mss*). The excavation accounts (especially *BB* and *RR*) are central to the record. The combination of these demonstrates that the contexts and associations for this material are substantially reliable as an information source, a circumstance unfortunately not true for the majority of nineteenth-century collections.

CATALOGUE FORMAT

Numbered barrows (1-297) are listed in the order as published by Greenwell (1877; 1890). Unnumbered barrows (UN 1-146; for definition see p.14) are listed alphabetically by county (pre-1971 boundaries).

Each entry is organised as follows:

No.   PARISH OR FAMILIAR NAME (other names)   No. of objects

Old county; new county   National grid reference

CONTEXT: description and circumstances of excavation or discovery. Primary references.

1 seq. **Burials:** in published order: form and context.
1 seq. *Associations:* numbered sequentially.
      Material registered but not identified as '*Flint flake*'.
      Material recorded but not preserved as '*flint flake*'.

A seq. **Features:** in published order: form and context.
1 seq. *Associations:* as above.

Other contexts or **Unlocated**
1 seq. *Associations:* as above.

The illustrations follow the catalogue format and numbering; all objects are at a scale of 1:2 except where otherwise specified.

Abbreviations used in the catalogue
Dimensions

B.	Base diameter (of vessel)	L.	Length
D.	Depth	M.	Mouth diameter (of vessel)
Diam.	Diameter	Th.	Thickness
H.	Height	W.	Width

Flint Tables

Where information on flint objects is tabulated the following additional abbreviations have been used.

Butt form	Btt	Colour	Col.	Cortex	Ctx
Broken	Bkn	Beige	Bge	Present	x
Corticated	Ct.	Brown	Br.		
Dihedral	Dh.	Burnt	Bt	Wear	Wr
Faceted	Fc.	Dark Grey	D. Gr.	Bilateral	Bil.
Platform	Pl.	Grey	Gr.	Distal	Dis.
Punctiform	Pnct.	Light Brown	L. Br.	Left	L.
Removed	Rem.	Light Grey	L. Gr.	Right	R.
Snapped	Sn.	Mottled Grey	M. Gr.		
Thermal	Thm.	Patinated	Pat.		
		Speckled	Sp.		

Scars	Sc.	Serrated	
Blade	Bl.	Teeth per cm	T.p.cm
Flake	Fl.		

CANON WILLIAM GREENWELL

'Never mind theories, collect facts'

This favourite and frequently cited precept might stand as an appropriate judgement on the life and work of Canon William Greenwell, a great Victorian antiquary and 'facile princeps in the archaeology of these islands' (Charles Hercules Read, Proc.Soc.Ant. London 2s 30, 36).

Greenwell's longevity was matched by his industry (Appendix 1). Prevented by ill health from a career at the bar, he was ordained into the Church of England and for over sixty years served Durham Cathedral as Minor Canon and, later, Librarian and archivist. He took his secular duties seriously also, serving as Justice of the Peace and Chairman of Petty Sessions, Poor Law Guardian, County Alderman and officer in the Durham Volunteers. The extent of his antiquarian interests is revealed by volumes on the history and architecture of Durham Cathedral and on medieval charters for the Surtees Society, and a wide range of papers, particularly in the numismatic field where he established a notable reputation as a collector and student of Archaic Greek coinage. He was a keen fisherman and devised the trout fly known as 'Greenwell's Glory'. The breadth of his interests and achievements is documented in obituary notices, notably Proc.Soc.Ant. London 2s 30, 200-4 and Arch. Aeliana 3s 15, 1-21, the latter equipped with a full bibliography.

GREENWELL AS ARCHAEOLOGIST

As with most of his contemporaries, Greenwell's interest in excavation seems to have derived from his role as collector. He accumulated antiquities throughout his life in a determined and, occasionally, unprincipled fashion (Evans 1943, 124): his motivation, apparently, to reconstruct a past and especially a prehistory for Britain. Although a shrewd bargainer in the antiquities market, profit was not his concern, and the relatively large sums that he requested for the major collections now in the British Museum went to restore the fortunes of his family, not himself. The material which he excavated or otherwise acquired forms one of the basic sources for British prehistory, and it is fortunate that he took pains to document and list the objects in a series of manuscript catalogues (now in the British Museum).

Greenwell's first barrow opening seems to have been in December 1847 at Chollerton, Northumberland (letter to Albert Way, 6 December 1847, Society of Antiquaries). However, it was not until 1862-3 that he began intensive field-work, expanding from Northumberland to North Yorkshire and thence to the Wolds in a series of annual campaigns up to 1889, with forays to Argyll, Cumbria, Suffolk, Wessex and the Cotswolds. His last recorded excavation, at Maiden's Grave, was at the age of eighty-one. In 1872 he travelled to Brittany 'where I had hoped to have had some howking of dolmens etc.... I was so ill with the horrible food that I was obliged to come away' (letter to G. Rolleston,, 10 September 1872, Ashmolean Museum). This abortive excursion must have owed its inception to his acquaintance with W.C. Lukis, an amateur of Breton megaliths, with whom he had worked in West Yorkshire. He collaborated also with other leading barrow-diggers of the period, notably John Thurnam and Llewellyn Jewitt, and was acknowledged as a mentor in the basics of excavation by General Pitt Rivers (1898, 28). In East Yorkshire he was frequently assisted by local antiquaries, such as W. Lovel and the Rev. Porter, and was often obliged by duties elsewhere to leave them in charge, leading to accusations of negligence and unprofessional conduct.

These arose primarily from a natural rivalry with J.R. Mortimer, himself an opener of over 300 barrows on the Wolds. As a local man and competing collector, Mortimer seems to have felt that the Canon was an interloper. His brother, Robert, was present at the opening of

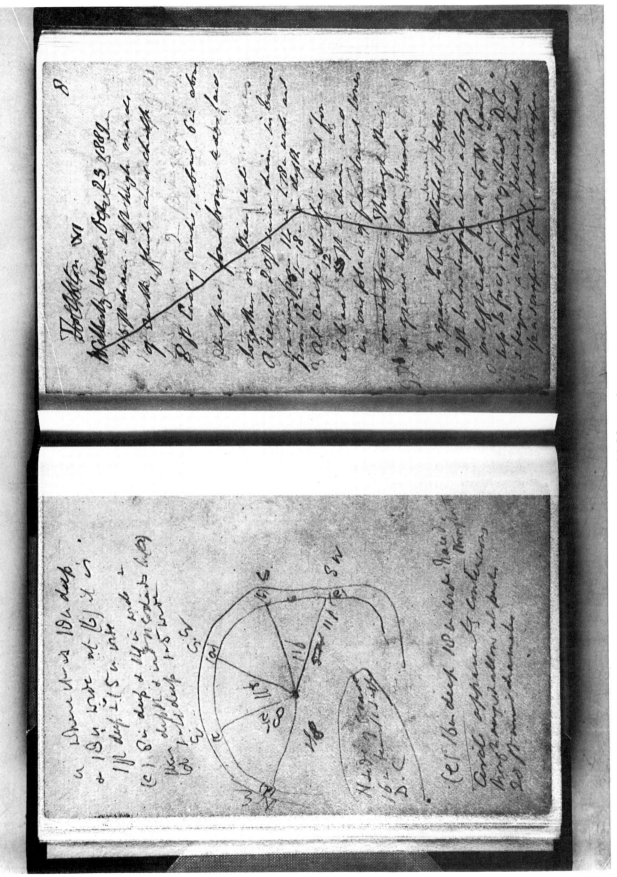

Sample pages from the surviving field note-book (WG Ms 1: Barrow 235; British Museum).

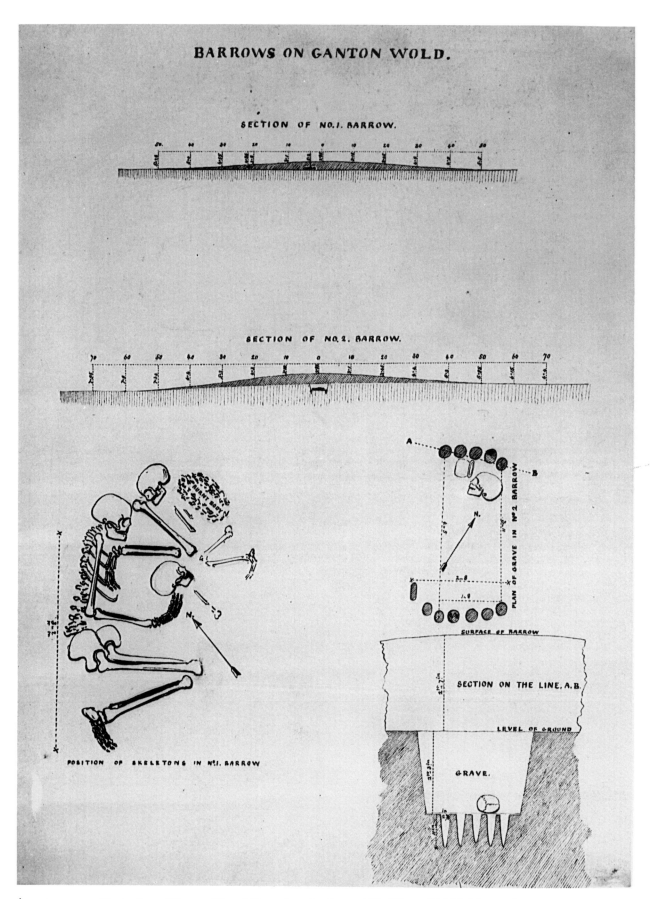

A contemporary illustration of Ganton 25 and 26, perhaps by General Pitt Rivers (British Museum).

Helperthorpe 49 and recorded that the barrow was 'being rapidly completed and unsatisfactorily explored... trenched over with four-tined forks and shovels in a hurried manner....' (Mortimer Manuscripts, Hull Museum). It was felt that Greenwell often missed burials, initially, it was said, being unaware of the existence of graves, and recovering only those on or above the old surface. Mortimer re-opened three of Greenwell's barrows (3, 49, UN 98), recording valuable additional information for two, but his own techniques were equally open to question. By 1867 there was open enmity, Greenwell asking John Evans for support against 'that scoundrel Mortimer'. In their declining years collaboration, if not friendship, was resumed, both working together at Danes Graves, and Mortimer using Greenwell's introduction to *British Barrows* as the model and basis for the preface to his own volume (1905).

Greenwell recorded little of his excavation technique: 'My practice has always been to drive a trench, the width of the barrow as it was originally constituted and before it was enlarged by being ploughed down, from South to North, through and beyond the centre. I have not always found it necessary to remove the whole of the North and West sides, as they are generally found to be destitute of secondary interments; in very many cases, however, I have turned over the whole mound' (1877, 27 n.1). The digging was done by locally hired labourers who seem to have worked in line on an advancing face from the south or south-east and sometimes in a series of parallel workman-width trenches, the intervening baulks being then taken down. The surviving long cairn at Raiset Pike (Crosby Garrett 228) has a massive trench dug along its axial line to the base of the mound. In the arable areas of East Yorkshire barrow opening was confined to the months before planting and after harvest, and the summer was therefore devoted to work on uncultivated uplands.

One field notebook survives (WG Ms 1), recording nine barrows in the Folkton area in October 1889. Observed features are noted in the order of discovery, with frequent emendations as to the size of graves and disposition of skeletons. Sketches are few and essentially repetitive of the written account. The field notes were in pencil and then written over in ink, apparently shortly afterwards since extra information and corrections were occasionally added at this stage (Plate 2).

The plans and sections of Ganton 25 and 26, opened in April 1867, are of high quality but their author is unknown (Kinnes 1977), although there is good reason to believe that they were the work of Pitt Rivers in his period of 'pupilage' (Plate 3). This drawing shows some divergence from the published account. Comparison of the Folkton notebook and the publication shows that the final reports were essentially a rationalised version of the basic notes, and in some cases a prolonged interval must have separated the two stages.

Attempts to reconstruct the ground plans and stratigraphy of the barrows suggest that Greenwell was occasionally at fault in recording dimensions or compass directions, and this is manifest in the results of modern re-excavation of certain sites (Appendix 2A). The structural complexities of the long barrows at Willerby and Kilham not surprisingly eluded Greenwell in his limited explorations (Manby 1963 and 1976). In the former instance he had not even completed excavation of the obvious crematorium deposit, perhaps in recognition of the unlikelihood of associated artefacts (Manby 1963, figs 3-4). Elsewhere re-examination has been of limited value since the mounds had been largely destroyed by a further century of cultivation, and stratigraphic re-assessment of Greenwell's finds was not possible. New burials and pits were found at Cowlam 56, Rudston 62 and Folkton 241 and 245 attesting the limited nature of the initial work. More importantly, it was shown at Weaverthorpe 47 that the burials had been missed, Greenwell having mistaken the chalk rubble core for undisturbed natural, despite having had the mound 'turned over down to the chalk rock, the labour of six men and of two hard-working volunteers having been expended on it through a period of five days' (1877, 202). At the same site he failed to record the existence of three stake-circles and, indeed, seems rarely to have paid much attention to structural features. As with most of his contemporaries, outer ditches were investigated only briefly and, as it were, by accident, although any sealed by the mound were usually noted. Most of the re-excavated sites have produced additional finds from the mound or the backfill of the original opening. Greenwell seems to have been more assiduous than most in collecting and preserving such material, but clearly much depended upon his workmen for such retrieval (compare Rudston 62).

It is not at all clear how sites were selected for publication, especially in the definitive series (1877, 1890). Mortimer observed that Greenwell 'not infrequently omitted to mention a barrow in which he found nothing'. Whilst this is partly true, as can been seen for examples in the Unnumbered series (Appendix 2B), in other cases unproductive sites were assigned a formal number (as Brimpton 294-5). Some barrows excavated by others were included in the numbered series (Appendix 2C) where Greenwell had acquired the finds but Rolleston retained the material from Market Weighton 226 and Upper Swell 282. The landowner had the finds, including grave-goods, from Goodmanham 110.

Sites are included in the Unnumbered series on two criteria: evidence for excavation by Greenwell either from published or archival sources, and the existence of finds made by others in the Greenwell Collection, acquired either by gift or purchase (Appendix 2D). The possibility exists that more sites, without surviving finds or record, were excavated by Greenwell but this cannot be demonstrated on existing evidence.

The final words in this introduction must be Greenwell's own:

> ....nor can I look back to any part of my life
> with less of regret or greater satisfaction than
> that which has been passed in an endeavour to
> revive, in however faint a form it might be, the
> almost forgotten past (1877, viii).

APPENDIX 1
A GREENWELL CALENDAR

Year	Date	Barrow	Other
1820	23 Mar.		Born Greenwell Ford, Co. Durham
1839			BA University of Durham; read for bar at Middle Temple but prevented by ill health from completion
1843			MA University of Durham (Theology)
1844			Ordained; Perpetual Curate, parish of Ovingham-with-Mickley
1847	Dec.	213	
1854			Principal, Neville Hall, Newcastle
1856			Chaplain and Censor, Cosin Hall, Durham; Minor Canon, Durham Cathedral
1862			Librarian to the Dean and Chapter and Keeper of Rolls and Charters, Durham Cathedral
	June	UN 24	
	?	187-8	
1863			With John Thurnam in Wiltshire
	Mar.	UN 114	
	June	185	
	Oct.	184	
	Nov.	190-2, 201	
	?	UN 118	
1864			With W.C. Lukis in West Yorkshire
	Mar.	221, UN 70-83	
	Apr.	124-5, 127-8, UN 115	
	June	152, 154-8	
	Sept.	138-40	
	Oct.	162, UN 134-8	
	?	228, UN 117	
1865	June	2	
	July	150	
	?	199, 222-3	
1866	Mar.	72-3	
	Apr.	153, 164	
	May	159, 200	
	June	160	
	Oct.	46	
	Nov.	49, UN 95	
1867			Pitt Rivers as 'pupil'
	Apr.	24-6, 29-30, 57, UN 107	
	Oct.	16, 18, 44, 47	
	Nov.	58-9	
	?	3, 50-6, 233	
1868			FSA; first contact with G. Rolleston
	Apr.	1	
	May	UN 50	
	June	UN 51	

Year	Date	Barrow	Other
	Dec.	224	
	?	227, 234, UN 96	
1869	Feb.	UN 52-5	
	Nov.	62	
	?	23, 63-6, 225, UN 133	
1870	Nov.	68	
	?	205	
1872	Oct.		Abortive journey to Brittany
1874	Sept.	229-30	
	Oct.	231	
	?	216-20	
1875	?	UN 65-6	
1876	Feb.	UN 5	
1877			*British Barrows*; with Ll. Jewitt in Derbyshire
	Sept.	UN3	
	?	UN 64	
1878			FRS
	Oct.	277-80, 286	
1879			First major donation to British Museum (79 12-9-)
	Nov.	282-5	
	?	287	
1883	?	296	
1887	?	252, 266	
1889	Oct.	235-6, 244-6, 248-51	
1890			'Recent Researches....'
1898	July	UN 84-9	
1901	Oct.	UN 103	
1905			'Early Iron Age Burials....'
1909			Donation by J.P. Morgan to British Museum (WG1-)
1918	27 Jan.		Died

CONCORDANCE OF BARROWS AND EXCAVATORS

A RE-EXCAVATED BARROWS

Greenwell excavation

3	J.R. Mortimer	1895
47	T.C.M. Brewster	1966–8
49	Mortimer	1868
50–4	I.M. Stead	1969–72
55–6	Brewster	1968
62	A.L. Pacitto	1968
79	D.G. Coombs	1969
81	Coombs	1969
161	Pacitto	1962
222	T.G. Manby	1958–60
234	Manby	1965–9
238	Brewster	1967–9
240–1	Brewster	1967–9
245	Brewster	1967–9
UN 54–5	A.R. Edwardson	1959
UN 95	Mortimer	1868

Other excavation

UN 100–1	Mortimer	1872	(Londesborough)
UN 108	Mortimer	1883	(Silburn)
UN 113	F. Vatcher	1960	(Londesborough)
UN 120	Coombs	1973	(Londesborough)

B UNNUMBERED SERIES: GREENWELL EXCAVATIONS

Published by Greenwell (1865, 1866, 1868, 1869, 1906; with Embleton 1862, with Rolleston 1877)

UN 5, 24, 26, 50–5, 60, 64–6, 70–90, 92, 106, 115, 117–18, 134–8

Published by others (Mortimer 1868, 1905; Trechmann 1914)

UN 3, 95–6

Unpublished

UN 19, 61, 67, 91, 97, 102–5, 107, 110, 112, 114, 119, 125, 131, 133

C NUMBERED SERIES: EXCAVATED BY OTHERS

7–9	F. Porter, C. Monkman	1866
151	I. Fish (?)	1866
189	W. Procter	1867
195–6	Mr Dennis	1863
226	G. Rolleston	1866
232	Rolleston, D. Royce	1875–6
297	Unknown	1881

D UNNUMBERED SERIES: OTHER BARROWS

Excavated by others

UN 1	W. Dewe	1861
13	F.R. Simpson	1862
15	Capt. Carpenter	1852
16	J.S. Donaldson	1838
41	J. Beatty	1863
43	G. Tate	1857
44	G. Rome Hall	1865
47	Mr Wightman	1872
62	J. Thurnam	1859
63	Thurnam	1863
68	J. Silburn	1851
93–4	Lord Londesborough	1851
99	Silburn	1851
100–1	Londesborough	1851
108–9	Silburn	1851
120	Londesborough (Conyngham)	1849
124	R. Skelton	1851
129–30	Londesborough (Conyngham)	1849
141	J. Morrison	1870
142	J. Hilson	1872

Published: primary accounts

UN 1, 4, 6, 8, 13, 16, 22–3, 33, 43–4, 47, 62–3, 69, 93–4, 100–1, 108, 113, 120, 124, 126, 129–30, 139, 141, 146

Unpublished

UN 2, 7, 9–12, 14–15, 17–18, 20–1, 25, 27–32, 34–42, 45–6, 48–9, 56–9, 68, 98–9, 109, 111, 116, 121–3, 127–8, 132, 140, 142–5

TABLE 1 BRONZE ANALYSES

	Barrow	Ref.	Cu	Sn	Pb	As	Sb	Ag	Ni	Bi	Fe	Au	Co	Cd	Zn
	Spearhead														
1	297.1 tang	B (1961) no. 50	83.1	16.4	0.38	0.12	<0.05	<0.0057	<0.01	<0.005	<0.006	nd	nd	nd	nd
	collar	B (1961) no. 51	87.8	12.1	0.096	0.22	nd	<0.105	0.025	<0.005	0.006	nd	nd	nd	nd
	Daggers														
2	39.2 blade	BBA 019	89.5	8.0	nd	0.03	0.50	0.85	0.04	0.03	0.90	nd	nd	nd	<0.1
	rivet 2	BBA 022	86.5	13.5	nd	0.25	0.10	0.25	0.045	0.01	0.30	nd	nd	nd	<0.08
3	49.1	U	82.6	17.2	<0.03	<0.1	0.14	0.23	0.019	<0.01	<0.005				0.02
4	68.1 blade	U	88.4	10.0	<0.02	0.53	0.50	0.33	0.008	<0.008	0.022				<0.04
	rivet	BBA 974	99.0	0.12	0.02	1.2	0.40	0.03	0.01	<0.01	0.02	<0.005	<0.005	nd	<0.01
5	152.2	B (1961) no. 10	93.3	6.5	nd	nd	nd	0.023	0.021	<0.004	nd				0.02
6	287.1 dagger	BBA 987	82.3	11.3	0.10	0.54	0.21	0.09	0.15	<0.01	0.03	<0.005	<0.005	<0.005	<0.04
	rivet	BBA 988	87.5	12.1	0.09	0.30	0.13	0.01	0.14	<0.01	0.06	nd	<0.005	nd	<0.04
7	297.2	B (1961) no. 23	87.0	12.6	0.063	0.17	0.044	0.024	0.20	<0.01	0.007				<0.08
8	UN 1.1	B (1961) no. 17	86.9	12.2	nd	0.44	0.22	0.22	0.075	0.0085	nd				<0.04
9	UN 16.1	U	86.0	13.8	nd	nd	nd	<0.005	0.022	0.017	0.10				
10	UN 33.1	U	88.3	10.2	0.019	0.97	0.22	0.21	0.009	<0.008	0.0087				
11	UN 69.1	B (1961) no. 9	85.9	13.0	nd	0.75	nd	0.086	0.13	0.0052	0.007				
	Knife-daggers														
12	277.2	B (1961) no. 35	85.4	13.6	0.47	0.31	<0.05	0.022	0.087	<0.004	0.0074				<0.04
13	282.1	(X) BBA 986	X	X	tr	tr	-	-	tr		tr				
14	286.1	B (1961) no. 40	85.0	14.7	nd	0.13	nd	<0.005	0.014	0.0062	0.011				<0.04
15	296.1 blade	(X) BBA 995	X	X	tr	tr	-	tr	tr	<0.01	tr				
	rivet	BB 990	85.8	6.5	<0.01	0.41	0.14	0.10	0.49	<0.01	0.03	<0.005	0.023	0.005	0.03
16	UN 101.4 blade	(X) BBA 993	X	-	-	X	tr	tr	tr	<0.01	tr				
	rivet	BBA 994	96.7	0.11	<0.01	<0.05	0.12	0.28	0.02	<0.01	0.01	<0.005	<0.005	<0.005	0.02
	Razors														
17	68.10 (rivet)	U (corroded sample)	92.6	7.1	0.03	0.54	0.1	0.042	0.056	0.01	0.005				0.1
18	216.1	U	83.1	16.6	nd	nd	nd	0.0067	0.07	<0.004	0.017				0.04
19	289.1	BBA 989	83.6	12.2	0.26	0.29	0.17	0.16	0.24	0.01	0.03	<0.005	<0.005	nd	0.02
20	UN 8.1	U	84.4	14.7	nd	0.35	0.16	0.26	0.16	<0.004	<0.012				<0.04
	Blades														
21	57.5	U	88.9	11.0	0.035	0.08	0.04	0.02	0.018	<0.008	0.0087				
22	280.1	(X) BBA 983	X	X	tr	X	tr	tr	tr	0.008	tr				<0.08
	Rivet														
23	57.6	BBA 968	86.7	12.0	0.03	<0.05	<0.05	0.03	<0.01	<0.01	0.01	<0.005	<0.005	<0.005	0.01
	Axes														
24	39.1	B no. 9	86.2	12.5	<0.02	0.85	0.16	0.22	0.026	<0.008	<0.004				<0.08
25	235.6	B no. 10	87.2	12.7	nd	nd	nd	0.0067	<0.01	<0.004	0.009				
26	235.7	B no. 11	86.0	13.8	nd	nd	nd	0.0067	0.02	<0.004	0.009				
27	235.8	B no. 12	85.9	14.2	nd	<0.1	nd	0.086	0.011	<0.004	0.0079				
28	235.9	B no. 13	85.2	14.5	nd	nd	nd	0.0054	<0.01	0.015	0.01				

| Identification | | | | | | | | | | | | | | |
Barrow	Ref.	Cu	Sn	Pb	As	Sb	Ag	Ni	Bi	Fe	Au	Co	Cd	Zn
Awls														
29 2.2	U	88.2	9.4	1.77	0.42	0.12	0.11	0.048	<0.01	<0.005				<0.1
	(corroded sample)													
30 2.3	(X) BBA 966	X	X	X	tr	tr	tr	tr		tr				
31 2.4	(X) BBA 967	X	X	X	tr	tr	tr	tr		tr				
32 39.3	U	85.7	12.8	0.03	0.86	0.24	0.32	0.026	<0.01	0.065				<0.1
	(corroded sample)													
33 62.3	(X) BBA 972	X	X	tr	X	-	tr	tr		tr				
34 62.4	(X) BBA 973	X	X	-	-	-	-	-		tr				
35 62.1	(X) BBA 971	X	-	tr	-	tr	tr	-		tr				
36 71.1	(X) BBA 975	X	X	tr	X	-	tr	tr		tr				
37 115.8	(X) BBA 978	X	X	tr	tr	-	-	-		tr				
38 115.1	(X) BBA 977	X	X	-	tr	-	-	-		tr				
39 161.4	(X) BBA 981	X	X	tr	tr	tr	tr	tr		tr				
40 280.2	(X) BBA 984	X	X	X	tr	-	-	-		tr				
41 UN 21.1	(X) BBA 992	X	X	tr	tr	tr	tr	-		tr				
Shanks														
42 103.1	(X) BBA 976	X	X	X	-	-	-	-		tr				
43 280.3	(X) BBA 985	X	X	tr	X	tr	tr	-		tr				
Pin														
44 297.3	BBA 991	83.4	11.3	0.15	0.45	0.26	0.17	0.77	<0.01	0.03	<0.005	0.017	nd	0.03
Ring														
45 250.5	BBA 982	86.4	10.0	0.01	0.09	0.23	0.03	0.01	<0.01	0.03	<0.005	<0.005	<0.005	0.02
Earring														
46 58.8	(X) BBA 969	X	X	tr	X	tr	tr	tr		tr				
47 58.9	(X) BBA 970	X	X	tr	tr	tr	tr	tr		tr				
48 115.2	(X) BBA 979	X	X	-	X	-	tr	tr		tr				
49 115.3	(X) BBA 980	X	X	-	X	-	tr	tr		tr				

Key

BBA	British Museum Research Laboratory: British Bronze Age series (Atomic Absorption Spectroscopy; Hughes *et al.* 1976)
(X) BBA	British Museum Research Laboratory: X-ray fluorescence surface analysis.
B (1961)	Britton 1961, table 1
B	Britton 1963, table 6
U	Unpublished analyses by E. E. Richards, Research Laboratory, Oxford (kindly supplied by D Britton)
nd	Not detected
X	An element present at a concentration greater than *c.* 1%
tr	An element present at a concentration less than *c.* 1%) XRF
-	An element beneath the detection limit of *c.* 0.2%)

GLOSSARY

Accessory Cup	Used in preference to 'Incense Cup' or 'Pygmy Cup' for non-specific forms of cup-sized vessels normally serving the function as accessory to a burial.
biface	flint implement with all-over bifacial intrusive retouch; function unknown; the category includes some possible rough-outs.
Bipartite Vase	Vessel having two structural divisions separated by shoulder; not immediately assignable to a recognised ceramic tradition.
Bronze Age	Sherds of fabric displaying typical oxidised outer and reduced inner walls; not assignable to a particular ceramic tradition within the Bronze Age.
Collared Urn	Collared vessel containing cremated bones, after Longworth 1961, 263.
Collared Vessel	After Longworth 1961, 263.
Food Vessel Urn	After ApSimon 1969, 38.
Plain Ware	Undecorated sherds not assignable to ceramic tradition or period.
plano-convex knife	Flint knife with plano-convex section produced by invasive retouch over dorsal face, the ventral face normally left as struck.
scraper	Classified by forms of retouch. *disc*: all round edge retouch. *end*: retouch confined to distal or proximal end of flake; both on *double-end*. *end-and-side*: retouch confined to either end and left or right side of flake. *horseshoe*: continuous edge retouch on either end and both sides of flake. *side*: retouch confined to one side of flake.
shank	Fragmentary or corroded bronze objects of a size and cross-section comparable with both awls and pins.
sponge-finger stone	After Smith and Simpson 1966.
Urn	Vessel of Bronze Age fabric and acting as container of cremated bone but not assignable to a particular ceramic tradition.
Vase:	Vessel of Food Vessel size but not assignable to a particular ceramic tradition; not associated with a burial.
Yorkshire Vase	Food Vessel with one or more grooves spanned by perforate or imperforate lugs.

BIBLIOGRAPHY

ABBREVIATIONS

ABI	Evans 1881
AHG	Witts 1881
Antiq. J.	*Antiquaries' Journal*
Arch.	*Archaeologia*
Arch. Ael.	*Archaeologia Aeliana*
Arch. J	*Archaeological Journal*
ASI	Evans 1897
BAP	Abercromby 1912
BAR	British Archaeological Reports, Oxford
BB	Greenwell and Rolleston 1877
EIABY	Greenwell 1906
Exc AR	*Excavations Annual Report* (Ministry of Public Buildings and Works)
GB	O'Neil and Grinsell 1960
GM	*Gentleman's Magazine*
Hist. Berwicks. Nat. Cl.	*History of the Berwick-shire Naturalists' Club*
J. Brit. Arch. Ass.	*Journal of the British Archaeological Association*
LBC	Crawford 1925
NPY	Newbigin 1937
PBF	Prähistorische Bronze-funde, Munich
Proc. Preh. Soc.	*Proceedings of the Prehistoric Society*
Proc. Soc. Ant. Lond.	*Proceedings of the Society of Antiquaries of London*
Proc. Soc. Ant. Scot.	*Proceedings of the Society of Antiquaries of Scotland*
QJ Suff. Inst. Arch.	*Quarterly Journal of the Suffolk Institute of Archaeology*
RR	Greenwell 1890
Trans. Cumb. Westm. Arch. Ant. Soc.	*Transactions of the Cumberland and Westmorland Archaeological and Anti-quarian Society*
TYD	Bateman 1861
Ulster J. Arch.	*Ulster Journal of Archae-ology*
VCH Wilts.	*Victoria County History of Wiltshire*, Vol. 1
WG Ms	Greenwell Manuscripts, British Museum
Yorks. Arch. J.	*Yorkshire Archaeological Journal*

Anon., 1869. 'Examination of Suffolk tumuli', *QJ Suff. Inst. Arch.* 1, 19–20 and 37–42.

Abercromby, J., 1912. A *Study of Bronze Age Pottery of Great Britain and Ireland*, Oxford.

ApSimon, A. M., 1969, 'The Earlier Bronze Age in the North of Ireland', *Ulster J. Arch.* 32, 28–72.

Bateman, T., 1861. *Ten Years' Diggings in Celtic and Saxon Grave Hills*, London.

Britton, D., 1961. 'A study of the composition of Wessex culture bronzes', *Archaeometry* 4, 39–52.

Britton, D., 1963. 'Traditions of metal-working in the Later Neolithic and Early Bronze Age of Britain: Part 1', *Proc. Preh. Soc.* 29, 258–325.

Butler, J. J., 1963. 'Bronze Age connections across the North Sea', *Palaeohistoria* 9, 1–286.

Butler, J. J., and Smith, I. F., 1956. 'Razors, urns and the British Middle Bronze Age', *Annual Report of the University of London Institute of Archaeology* 12, 20–52.

Campbell, M., and Sandeman, M. L. S., 1962, 'Mid-Argyll: a field survey of the historic and prehistoric monuments', *Proc. Soc. Ant. Scot.* 95, 1–125.

Clare, T., 1979. 'Rayset Pike long cairn in the Machell Mss.', *Trans. Cumb. Westm. Arch. Ant. Soc.* 79, 144–6.

Clark, J. G. D., 1932. 'The date of the plano-convex flint knife in England and Wales', *Antiq. J.* 12, 158–62.

Clark, J. G. D., 1934. 'Derivative forms of the petit tranchet in Britain', *Arch. J.* 91, 32–58.

Clarke, D. L., 1970. *Beaker Pottery of Great Britain and Ireland*, Cambridge.

Clifford, E. M., 1937. 'The Beaker folk in the Cotswolds, *Proc. Preh. Soc.* 3, 159–63.

Conyngham, A. D., 1849. 'Account of discoveries made in barrows near Scarborough', *J. Brit. Arch. Ass.* 4. 101–7.

Coombs, D., 1974. 'Excavation of three round barrows on Etton Wold, East Riding of Yorkshire', *Yorks. Arch. J.* 46, 1–9.

Cowie, T. G., 1978. *Bronze Age Food Vessel Urns in Northern Britain*, BAR 55, Oxford.

Crawford, O. G. S., 1925. *Long Barrows of the Cotswolds*, Gloucester.

Davis, J. B., and Thurnam, J., 1865. *Crania Britannica*, London.

Dewe, W., 1861. 'The bronze blade of a Celtic dagger', *J. Brit. Arch. Ass.* 17, 334.

Donaldson, J. S., 1838. 'Remarks on the tumulus at Cheswick', *Hist. Berwicks. Nat. Cl.* 1, 92–3.

Dymond, D. P., 1966. 'Ritual monuments at Rudston, East Yorkshire, England', *Proc. Preh. Soc.* 32, 86–95.

Edwardson, A. R., 1959. 'Further excavations on tumuli at Risby, 1959' *Proceedings of the Suffolk Institute of Archaeology* 28, 153–60.

Evans, J., 1943. *Time and Chance*, London.

Evans, J., 1881. *The Ancient Bronze Implements, Weapons and Ornaments of Great Britain and Ireland*, London.

Evans, J., 1897. *The Ancient Stone Implements, Weapons and Ornaments of Great Britain*, 2nd edn., London.

Pell, C. I., 1957. 'Middle Bronze Age urns from Furness', *Trans. Cumb. Westm. Arch. Ant. Soc.* 57, 9–12.

Fox, C., 1923. *The Archaeology of the Cambridge Region*, Cambridge.

Gerloff, S., 1975. *The Early Bronze Age Daggers in Great Britain*, PBF V1.2, Munich.

Gibson, A., 1978. *Bronze Age Pottery in the North-East of England*, BAR 56, Oxford.

Green, H. S., 1980. *The Flint Arrowheads of the British Isles*, BAR 75, Oxford.

Greenwell, W., 1862. 'An account of the opening of two barrows situated in the parish of Ford ...', *Hist. Berwicks. Nat. Cl.* 4, 390–4.

Greenwell, W., 1865. 'Notices of the examinations of ancient grave-hills in the North Riding of Yorkshire', *Arch. J.* 22, 97–117 and 241–63.

Greenwell, W., 1866. 'An account of excavations in cairns near Crinan', *Proc. Soc. Ant. Scot.* 6, 336–51.

Greenwell, W., 1868a. 'Notes of the opening of Ancient British tumuli in North Northumberland', *Hist. Berwicks. Nat. Cl.* 5, 195–205.

Greenwell, W., 1868b. 'Two stone axes', *Proc. Soc. Ant. Lond.* 2S.4, 60–1.

Greenwell, W., 1869. 'Ancient British tumuli', *QJ Suff. Inst. Arch.* 1. 8–12.

Greenwell, W., 1872. 'On two ancient interments at Wooler and Ilderton', *Hist. Berwicks. Nat. Cl.* 6, 415–20.

Greenwell, W., 1881. 'On barrows at Aldbourne, Wiltshire, and their contents', *Proc. Soc. Ant. Lond.* 8, 175–9.

Greenwell, W., 1889. 'A prae-historic cist burial at Sacriston', *Transactions of the Durham and Northumberland Archaeological and Architectural Society*, 3, 183–8.

Greenwell, W., 1890. 'Recent researches in barrows in Yorkshire, Wiltshire, Berkshire, etc.', *Arch.* 52, 1–72.

Greenwell, W., 1906. 'Early Iron Age burials in Yorkshire', *Arch.* 60, 251–324.

Greenwell, W., and Embleton, D., 1862. 'Notes on a tumulus and its contents at Grundstone Law', *Transactions of the Tyneside Naturalists' Field Club* 6, 34–9.

Greenwell, W., and Rolleston G., 1877. *British Barrows*, Oxford.

Guido, C. M., 1978. *The Glass Beads of the Prehistoric and Roman Periods in Britain and Ireland*, London.

Hardaker, R., 1974. *A Corpus of Early Bronze Age Dagger Pommels from Great Britain and Ireland*, BAR 3, Oxford.

Hardy, J., 1886. 'On urns and other antiquities found round the southern skirts of the Cheviot Hills', *Hist. Berwicks. Nat. Cl.* 11, 269–313.

Henshall, A. S., 1950. 'Textiles and weaving appliances in prehistoric Britain', *Proc. Preh. Soc.* 16, 130–62.

Henshall, A. S., 1972. *The Chambered Tombs of Scotland 2*, Edinburgh.

Hicks, J. D., 1969. 'Esh's Barrow', *Yorks. Arch. J.* 42, 306–13.

Hilson, J., 1872. 'Notes on the cist opened at Lanton Mains, Roxburghshire, in October 1870', *Hist. Berwicks. Nat. Cl.* 6, 347–9.

Jessen, K., and Helbaek, H., 1944. *Cereals in Great Britain and Ireland in Prehistoric and Early Historic Times*, Copenhagen.

Jockenhovel, A., 1980. *Die Rasiermesser in Westeuropa*, PBF VIII. 3, Munich.

Kinnes, I. A., 1977. 'British Barrows: a unique visual record?' *Antiquity* 51, 52–4.

Kinnes, I. A., 1979. *Round Barrows and Ring Ditches in the British Neolithic*, British Museum Occasional Paper 7, London.

Leeds, E. T., 1927. 'Neolithic spoons from Nether Swell, Gloucestershire', *Antiq. J.* 7, 61–2.

Londesborough, A. D., 1851. 'An account of the opening of some tumuli in the East Riding of Yorkshire', *Arch.* 34, 251–8.

Longworth, I. H., 1961. 'The origins and development of the Primary Series in the Collared Urn tradition in England and Wales', *Proc. Preh. Soc.* 27, 263–306.

Longworth, I. H., 1969. 'Five sherds from Ford, Northumberland, and their relative dating', *Yorks. Arch. J.* 42, 25–31.

Longworth, I. H., 1984. *Collared Urns of the Bronze Age in Great Britain and Ireland*, Cambridge.

Manby, T. G., 1956. 'Neolithic B pottery from East Yorkshire', *Yorks. Arch. J.* 39, 1–8.

Manby, T. G., 1958. 'Beakers from the Howardian Hills', *Yorks. Arch. J.* 39, 397–9.

Manby, T. G., 1963. 'The excavation of the Willerby Wold long barrow, East Riding of Yorkshire', *Proc. Preh. Soc.* 29, 173–205.

Manby, T. G., 1969. 'Bronze Age Pottery from Pule Hill, Marsden, WR Yorkshire, and footed vessels of the Early Bronze Age from England', *Yorks. Arch. J.* 42, 273–82.

Manby, T. G., 1974. *Grooved Ware Sites in the North of England*, BAR 9, Oxford.

Manby, T. G., 1976. 'The excavation of the Kilham long barrow, East Riding of Yorkshire', *Proc. Preh. Soc.* 42, 111–60.

Manby, T. G., 1980. 'Bronze Age settlement in Eastern Yorkshire', in J. Barrett and R. Bradley (eds), *The British Later Bronze Age*, BAR 83, Oxford.

Martin, E. A., 1981. 'The barrows of Suffolk', *East Anglian Archaeology* 12, 64–88.

Morrison, J., 1872. 'Remains of early antiquities, in and on the borders of the parish of Urquhart ...', *Proc. Soc. Ant. Scot.* 9, 250–63.

Morrison, J., 1880. 'Notes on an urn found at Kennyshillock, Urquhart, Elgin', *Proc. Soc. Ant. Scot.* 14, 109–10.

Mortimer, J. R., 1905. *Forty Years' Researches in British and Saxon Burial Mounds of East Yorkshire*, London.

Mortimer, J. R., 1911. 'Danes Graves', *Transactions of the East Riding Antiquarian Society* 18, 30–52.

Mortimer, R., 1868. 'Notice of a barrow at Helperthorpe, Yorkshire', *Reliquary* 8, 77–9.

Needham, S., 1979. 'A pair of Early Bronze Age spearheads from Lightwater, Surrey', in C. Burgess and D. Coombs (eds), *Bronze Age Hoards*, BAR 67, Oxford.

Neish, J., 1870. 'Notice of the discovery of a cist with overlying urns at Tealing, Forfarshire', *Proc. Soc. Ant. Scot.* 8, 381–4.

Newbigin, N., 1935. 'Neolithic A pottery from Broom Ridge, Ford, Northumberland', *Proc. Preh. Soc.* 1, 155–6.

Newbigin, N., 1937. 'The Neolithic pottery of Yorkshire', *Proc. Preh. Soc.* 3, 189–216.

O'Neil, H. E., and Grinsell, L. V., 1960. 'Gloucestershire barrows', *Transactions of the Bristol and Gloucestershire Archaeological Society* 89, 5–149.

Pacitto, A. L., 1969. 'The excavation of two burial mounds at Ferry Fryston', *Yorks. Arch. J.* 42, 295–305.

Pacitto, A. L., 1972. 'Rudston barrow LXII: the 1968 excavations', *Yorks. Arch. J.* 44, 1–22.

Palmer, S., 1873. 'A dagger blade...', *Proc. Soc. Ant. Lond.* 2s 5, 429.

Peake, H. J. E., 1931. *The Archaeology of Berkshire*, London.

Pierpoint, S., and Phillips, P., 1978. 'A grave–group from Levisham Moor, North Yorkshire', *Yorks. Arch. J.* 50, 43–8.

Piggott, S., 1931. 'The Neolithic pottery of the British Isles', *Arch. J.* 88, 67–158.

Piggott, S., 1938. 'The Early Bronze Age in Wessex', *Proc. Preh. Soc.* 4, 52–106.

Piggott, S., 1960. *The West Kennet Long Barrow: Excavations 1955-56*, London.

Piggott, S., 1973. 'The Wessex culture of the Early Bronze Age', *VCH Wilts* 1.2, 325–75.

Pitt Rivers, A. H., 1898. *Excavations on Cranborne Chase, IV*, privately printed.

Roe, F. E. S., 1966. 'The battle–axe series in Britain', *Proc. Preh. Soc.* 32, 199–245.

Rolleston, G., 1876. 'On the people of the long barrow period', *Journal of the Anthropological Institute* 5, 120–73.

Rome Hall, G., 1867. 'On the opening and examination of a barrow of the British period at Warkshaugh, North Tynedale', *Natural History Transactions for Northumberland and Durham* 1, 151–67.

Schmidt, P. K., and Burgess, C. B., 1981. *The Axes of Scotland and Northern England*, PBF IX.7, Munich.

Sheppard, T., 1902. 'Notes on the antiquities of Brough', *Antiquary* 38, 80–3.

Simpson, D. D. A., 1965. 'Food Vessels in south–west Scotland', *Transactions of the Dumfries and Galloway Natural History and Antiquarian Society* 42, 25–50.

Simpson, D. D. A., 1968. 'Food Vessels: associations and chronology', in J. M. Coles and D. D. A. Simpson (eds), *Studies in Ancient Europe*, Edinburgh.

Simpson, F. R., 1862. 'An account of an Ancient British grave discovered at North Sunderland', *Hist. Berwicks. Nat. Cl.* 4, 428–30.

Skelton, W., 1852. 'Yorkshire barrows', *GM* 37, 78.

Smith, I. F., and Simpson D. D. A., 1966. 'Excavation of a round barrow on Overton Hill, North Wiltshire', *Proc. Preh. Soc.* 32, 122–55.

Smith, R. A., 1931. *The Sturge Collection*, London.

Stead, I. M., 1965. *The La Tène Cultures of Eastern Yorkshire*, York.

Stead, I. M., 1979. *The Arras Culture*, York.

Tait, J., 1965. *Beakers from Northumberland*, Newcastle upon Tyne.

Tate, J., 1862. 'The antiquities of Yevering Bell', *Hist. Berwicks. Nat. Cl.* 4, 431–53.

Tate, G., 1891. 'Sepulchral remains on North Charlton', *Hist. Berwicks. Nat. Cl.* 13, 269–72.

Thomas, N. 1968. 'Note on the Carrickinab awl' *Ulster J. Arch.* 31, 23–4.

Thurnam, J., 1861. 'On the examination of a chambered long–barrow at West Kennet, Wiltshire', *Arch.* 38, 405–21.

Thurnam, J., 1864. 'On the two principal forms of ancient British and Gaulish skulls', *Memoirs of the Anthropological Society* 1, 120–68 and 459–519.

Thurnam, J., 1869. 'On ancient British barrows: Part 1, Long barrows', *Arch.* 42, 161–244.

Thurnam, J., 1872. 'On ancient British barrows: Part 2, Round barrows', *Arch.* 43, 285–552.

Trechmann, C. T., 1914. 'Prehistoric burials in the County of Durham', *Arch. Ael.* 3S.11, 119–76.

Tyndall, E., 1870. 'Recent explorations of two large barrows ... at Rudstone', *Arch. J.* 27, 71–5.

Varley, R.A., 1982. 'Two Bronze Age Collared Urns from the Hambleton Hills, North Yorkshire', *Yorks. Arch. J.* 54, 23–32.

Walker, I. C., 1966a. 'The counties of Nairnshire, Moray and Banffshire in the Bronze Age', *Proc. Soc. Ant. Scot.* 98, 76–125.

Walker, I. C., 1966b. 'Some objects from Nairnshire, Moray and Banffshire in the British Museum', *Proc. Soc. Ant. Scot.* 98, 312–15.

Watts, L., and Rahtz, P. (eds), 1984. *Cowlam Wold Barrows*, York University Archaeological Publications 3.

Witts, G. B., 1881. *Archaeological Handbook of Gloucestershire*, Cheltenham.

INDEX OF SITES

INDEX OF OBJECTS AND CATEGORIES

THE CATALOGUE

1 KIRBY UNDERDALE (Uncleby I)   1:1-6

Yorkshire E.R.; North Humberside   SE 821 594

ROUND BARROW: Diam. 29 m, H. 0.6 m, reduced by ploughing; composition not recorded; opened April 1868.
BB 135-6; *Mortimer* 1905, 118.

Burial 1: adult cremation deposit, in heap Diam. 0.3 m; on old surface 9 m S. by E. of centre.
1 *Bone ring-headed pin*: cut and polished to oval
    section; burnt and point broken.
    L. 13.0 cm; Diam. (head) 1.0 cm.   79 12-9 1

Burial 2: adult cremation deposit; between two flint blocks at base of central oval grave L. 2 m, D. 1.8 m, aligned NE.-SW.; 'two pelvic bones of a horse' at D. 1 m.

Old surface: area 8.5 m NE. of centre.
2 *Stone polished axe fragment*: greenstone; ground and
    polished; broken and roughly reworked bilaterally.
    L. 7.9 cm; W. 5.2 cm; Th. 2.9 cm.   79 12-9 2
3 *Flint end-scraper*: edge retouch on distal at 85
    degrees; platform butt; cortex remnant; mottled
    grey.
    L. 4.5 cm; W. 3.2 cm; Th. 1.4 cm.   79 12-9 1510
4 *Flint side-scraper*: edge retouch on R. at 40 degrees;
    platform butt; cortex remnant; mottled grey.
    L. 4.1 cm; W. 2.7 cm; Th. 0.7 cm.   79 12-9 1511
5 *Flint worked flake*: partial edge retouch on L., some
    inverse edge retouch on R.; platform butt; cortex
    remnant; mottled grey.
    L. 6.6 cm; W. 1.8 cm; Th. 1.1 cm.   79 12-9 1513
6 *Flint worked fragment*; edge retouch on R.; cortex
    remnant; grey.
    L. 2.4 cm; W. 1.6 cm; Th. 0.4 cm.   79 12-9 1512

2 LANGTON   2:1-16

Yorkshire E.R.; North Yorkshire   SE 820 685

ROUND BARROW: Diam. 18 m, H. 1.7 m, reduced by ploughing and levelling; oolitic rubble and earth, with extensive burning traces on old surface; internal cairn Diam. 3m, H. 0.9 m, SW. of centre, oolitic rubble with clay capping; opened 13-15 June 1865.
BB 136-40; *Times* 8 December 1866; *Kinnes* 1979, Ad 1.

Burial 1: adult male inhumation, crouched on L. with head NNW.; on old surface at centre between two sand-filled pits Diam. 0.9 m, D. 0.6 and 0.8 m, and overlain by edge of internal mound; flint behind head.
1 *Flint spall*: white.
    L. 3.5 cm; W. 0.8 cm; Th. 0.2 cm.   79 12-9 103

Burial 2: adult female inhumation, crouched on R. with head SW.; 0.2 m above old surface between two layers of slabs in charcoal-rich matrix, 4.5 m SE. by S. of centre; objects grouped at waist.
2 *Bronze awl*: Thomas Type 2B; tang of flat rectangular
    section expanding to central section with tapered
    angle facets; point of round section (Table 1.29).

    L. 2.4 cm; W. 0.4 cm; Th. 0.3 cm.   79 12-9 4
    BB fig. 95; *Thomas* 1968, 23.
3 *Bronze awl*: Thomas Type 2; central expansion with
    tapered angle facets; point of round section; tang
    broken (Table 1:30).
    L. 2.6 cm; W. 0.3 cm; Th. 0.2 cm.   79 12-9 5
    Thomas 1968, 23.
4 *Bronze awl*: point fragment of round section (Table
    1:31)
    L. 1.2 cm; Th. 0.2 cm.   79 12-9 6
5 *Belemnite fragment*   79 12-9 12
6 *Jet disc bead*: cut and polished to lentoid section;
    conical perforation.
    Diam. 1.5 cm ext., 0.7 cm int.; Th. 0.4 cm.
    BB fig. 44.   79 12-9 8
7 *Boar tusk implement*: cut splinter with narrow groove
    at point and multiple incisions at butt.
    L. (chord) 9.4 cm; Th. 0.6 cm.   79 12-9 7
    BB fig. 94.
8 *Animal tooth bead*: root only; hourglass perforation.
    L. 1.5 cm, Th. 1.1 cm.   79 12-9 9
    BB fig. 46.
9 *Fish vertebra*: species unidentifiable.   79 12-9 13
10 *Shell bead*: winkle (*Littorina obtusata*); perforation
    at base of cut slice.   79 12-9 10
    BB fig. 45.
11 *Dentalium shell fragment*: (*Antalis entalis*).
        79 12-9 11
12 *Cowrie shells*: three (*Trivia arctica*).   79 12-9 14

Burial 3: adult ?female inhumation, crouched on L. with head E.; on rough paving on old surface, 1.8 m S. of Burial 2; vessel on side at knees.
13 *Collared Vessel*: twisted cord: on collar, diagonal
    lines crossed by two roughly horizontal lines; on
    upper neck, horizontal line above arcs.
    M. 14.2 cm; H. 18.2 cm. B. 7.7 cm.   79 12-9 3
    Longworth no. 1190.

Feature A: ?mortuary house or enclosure defined by two parallel walls of 'flat stones set on their edges, and five or six deep', aligned E.-W., E. of centre; L. 2.7 m at N. and 1.8 m at S., 4.5 m apart.

Feature B: pit Diam. 0.9 m, D. 0.6 m, fill of stones and rubble, 0.6 m W. of Burial 3.

Mound material
14 *Bronze Age sherd*: heavy grit temper.   79 12-9 16
15 *Early Iron Age sherd*: flint temper.   79 12-9 16a

Not located
16 '*Antler fragment*': not identified.   79 12-9 15

3 KIRBY GRINDALYTH (Rivis; Duggleby Wold I; M291)
3:1-20

Yorkshire E.R.; North Yorkshire   SE 875 696

ROUND BARROW: Diam. 22.5 m, H. 1.8 m (D. 25 m; H. 2.1 m: GM), reduced by ploughing; core of 'very stiff clay with chalk and flints intermixed' capped by 'layers of loamy earth' (and 'burnt matter': GM); three internal mounds of chalk rubble, aligned E.-W. across centre (0.6 m apart: GM), H. 0.5 m with flat tops Diam. 1.2 m (basal Diam. 1.2 m, top Diam. 0.7 m: GM); opened 1867, re-opened Mortimer August 1895.
BB 140-1; Times 11 April 1867; GM 1867, 1:792-4; Mortimer 1905, 42-3.

Burial 1: adult ?male inhumation, crouched on R. with head W.; on charcoal layer on central mound, with four stake holes Diam. 5 cm, D. 25 cm at head; objects near head and 'close to body'; flints probably among nos 1-8 below.
   'quartz pebbles': three, not preserved.

Feature A: sub-rectangular pit L. 1.8 m, W. 1.5 m, D. 0.8 m (L. 1.5 m, W. 0.9 m, D. 0.6 m: GM), aligned NE.-SW., 7.5 m S. of centre (9 m: GM); earth and clay fill.

Feature B: pit Diam. 0.6 m, D. 0.5 m, 3.6 m S. of centre; earth and clay fill.

Burial 1 or mound material
1-8 'Flint flakes': eight; not identified.
                                        79 12-9 19 and 21-7

Mound material (1867)
9 Neolithic Bowl rim sherd: grit-tempered. 79 12-9 30
   NPY no. 23.
10 'Sandstone rubber': not identified.   79 12-9 29
11-13 'Flint scrapers': three; not identified.
                                        79 12-9 18, 20 and 28
14 Flint knife: edge retouch on R. and partial on L.; worn; mottled grey.
   L. 6.7 cm; W. 2.4 cm; Th. 0.7 cm.   79 12-9 17

Mound material (1895)
15 'Gritstone pounder': not identified.   HM
16 Flint leaf point roughout: all over bifacial invasive retouch; butt removed; cortex remnant; mottled grey.
   L. 10.7 cm; W. 5.0 cm; Th. 1.4 cm.   HM 338.42.16
   Mortimer 1905, fig. 41b.
17-19 'Flint scrapers': three; not identified.   HM
20 'Flint knife': not identified.   HM

4 HESLERTON

Yorkshire E.R.; North Yorkshire   SE 90 74
ROUND BARROW: Diam. 14.5 m, H. 0.9 m, reduced by ploughing; earth core with chalk rubble capping; previously opened.
BB 141.

Burial 1: child inhumation, crouched on R. with head NW.; at base of central oval grave L. 1 m, W. 0.7 m, D. 0.5 m, aligned SE.-NW.; at knees 'a large quantity of ... the seed of some fruit'.

Burial 2: inhumation fragments, disturbed by previous opening; at N. side.

Mound material
   'flint scraper': not preserved.

5 HESLERTON (Hall II)
5:1-14

Yorkshire E.R.; North Yorkshire   SE 90 74
OVAL BARROW: L. 25 m, W. 20 m, H. 0.8 m, aligned NNE.-SSW.; earth with some chalk and much charcoal.
BB 141-2.

Burial 1: adult male inhumation, crouched on L. with head ESE.; on layer of 'decayed leather' at E. end of central oval grave L. 2.4 m, W. 1.4 m, D. 0.9 m, aligned E.-W., chalk rubble fill; vessel at face.
1 Food Vessel: Yorkshire Vase; externally on rim and upper two-thirds, herringbone made by fine point; on lugs, vertical impressions; lower section over small area, lighter haphazard impressions; at base, row of vertical impressions; six surviving of nine horizontally perforated lugs spanning shoulder groove.
   M. 15.7 cm; H. 11.7 cm; B. 6.7 cm.   79 12-9 31
   BB fig. 70; BAP no. 154.

Mound material
2 'Neolithic Bowl rim sherd': decorated; not identified.   79 12-9 32
3 Neolithic Bowl rim sherd: grit tempered.
   NPY no. 22.   79 12-9 32a
4 Beaker sherd: corky fabric; fine twisted-cord horizontal lines.   79 12-9 32b
5 ?Food Vessel sherd: coarse rectangular tooth-comb stamped chevron.   79 12-9 32c
   'the bottom and some other portions of a vessel': not preserved.
6 Jet bead fragment: cut and polished; drilled hourglass perforation.
   L. 2.3 cm; W. 1.8 cm; Th. 1.7 cm; Diam. (perforation) 0.6 cm.   79 12-9 33
7 Flint end- and side-scraper: edge retouch on distal and L. at 80 degrees; faceted butt; mottled grey.
   L. 4.1 cm; W. 2.9 cm; Th. 0.6 cm.   79 12-9 35
8 Flint end- and side-scraper: edge retouch on distal and L. at 75 degrees; platform butt; patinated.
   L. 4.7 cm; W. 3.4 cm; Th. 1.2 cm.   79 12-9 36
9 Flint end-scraper: edge retouch on distal at 70 degrees; platform butt; cortex remnant; mottled grey.
   L. 3.4 cm; W. 2.8 cm; Th. 1.1 cm.   79 12-9 34
10 'Flint scraper': not identified.   79 12-9 38
11 'Flint knife': not identified.   79 12-9 41
12 'Flint saw': not identified.   79 12-9 40
13 Flint worked flake: partial edge retouch on distal and bilateral; mottled grey.
   L. 4.4 cm; W. 4.5 cm; Th. 1.2 cm.   79 12-9 37
14 Flint utilised flake: wear on L.; mottled grey.
   L. 4.7 cm; W. 1.9 cm; Th. 0.6 cm.   79 12-9 39

6 HESLERTON (Cordner)
6:1-7

Yorkshire E.R.; North Yorkshire   SE 91 74
ROUND BARROW: Diam. 21 m, H. 1 m, reduced by ploughing; earth and flints.
BB 142-5; Kinnes 1979, Ae3.

Burial 1: adolescent inhumation, crouched on L. with head W. by N.; at centre on clay fill of hollow D. 0.5 m.

Feature A: trench L. 4.8 m aligned NE.-SW., at SW. W. 0.9 m, D. 1.7 m, at NE. W. 0.3 m, D. 0.6 m, with extensions at SW. L. 0.9 m, W. 0.6 m, D. 0.6 m and at NE. Diam. 0.6 m, D. 1.2 m; fill of burnt earth, burnt chalk and charcoal with central row of large flints; at E. side of mound.
1 Neolithic Bowl: corky fabric.
   M. 26.2 cm; H. 12.3 cm.   79 12-9 42
   BB fig. 91; NPY no. 21.1.

Feature A or mound material

2 *Neolithic Bowl sherds*: forty-six, representing minimum two vessels; corky fabric.　　79 12-9 45
M. 29.2 cm (one vessel).
NPY no. 21.2.

3 *Neolithic Bowl sherd*: base of neck; corky fabric.
　　　　　　　　　　　　　　　　　　79 12-9 45a

4 *Neolithic Bowl rim sherd*: vesicular fabric.
　　　　　　　　　　　　　　　　　　79 12-9 45b

5 *Neolithic Bowl rim sherds*: two; corky fabric.
NPY no. 21.3.　　　　　　　　　　　79 12-9 45c

Feature B: apsidal extension to W. and at SW. end of Feature A, L. 1.8 m, W. 1.8 m, D. 0.2 m; fill of burnt earth and charcoal rising to mound surface; charred log L. 0.9 m and 0.2 m square at S. side.

Feature C: oval pit L. 0.6 m, W. 0.3 m, D. 0.5 m, aligned N.-S.; fill of burnt earth; 4.8 m E. by S. of centre.

Mound material

6 *Beaker*: rectangular tooth-comb stamped: on neck, broad zone of upright triangles filled with horizontal to diagonal lines, enclosed by narrow zones of short vertical lines bounded by pairs of horizontal lines; on body, three narrow zones as above, separated by reserved bands; corky fabric.
M. 14.0 cm; H. 18.2 cm; B. 7.5 cm.　　79 12-9 43
BAP no. 105; *Clarke* no. 1328.

7 *Flint knife*: edge retouch on distal and L. at 80 degrees; invasive retouch on R.; butt removed; mottled grey.
L. 4.7 cm; W. 3.0 cm; Th. 0.7 cm.　　79 12-9 44

7　SHERBURN (Duggleby I)　　　　　　7:1-12

Yorkshire E.R.; North Yorkshire　　　　SE 960 741

ROUND BARROW: Diam. 18 m, H. 0.5 m, reduced by ploughing; composition not recorded; opened by Porter and Monkman 15 May 1866.
BB 146-7; *Kinnes* 1979, Cc6.

Burial 1: 'broken human bones, ... not less than eight bodies"; on old surface 4.5 m E. of centre.

Burial 2: cranial fragments; on old surface near centre.
1 *Neolithic bowl sherds*: six, including rim and remains of lug; quartz temper.　　　　　79 12-9 47
2 *Neolithic Bowl*: plain.
M. c. 26.0 cm; H. c. 14.0 cm.　　　　79 12-9 61
3 *Beaker sherd*: tooth-comb stamped horizontal lines.
　　　　　　　　　　　　　　　　　　79 12-9 47a

Burial 3: adult female inhumation, crouched on L.; in central hollow; skull between two flint blocks.
4 *Flint utilised blade*: wear on R.; platform butt; cortex remnant; grey.
L. 6.3 cm; W. 1.7 cm; Th. 0.8 cm.　　79 12-9 48
5 *Flint utilised blade*: bilateral wear; platform butt; mottled grey.
L. 5.6 cm; W. 1.8 cm; Th. 0.6 cm.　　79 12-9 49
6 *Flint utilised flake*: wear on distal; platform butt; mottled grey.
L. 2.9 cm; W. 3.8 cm; Th. 0.8 cm.　　79 12-9 51

Flint flakes

	Btt	Ctx	Col	L.	W.	Th.	79 12-9
7			Gr.	5.4	2.2	0.4	50
8	Fc.	X	Gr.	2.8	3.9	0.3	52
9			Gr.	2.9	2.4	0.4	53
10			Gr.	2.6	2.2	0.2	54

Burial 4: adolescent inhumation, crouched on R.; on layer of burnt earth and charcoal on old surface at NW.; Beaker at knees.
11 *Beaker*: rectangular tooth-comb stamped: alternate zones of lattice and horizontal lines.
M. 16.2 cm; H. 21.9 cm; B. 8.3 cm.　　79 12-9 46
BAP no. 154; *Clarke* no. 1384.

Features A-C: three pits Diam. 0.5 m, to N., SE. and SW. of centre; chalk rubble fills.

Old surface

12 *Flint end- and side-scraper*: edge retouch on distal and L. at 70 degrees; platform butt, damaged; mottled grey.
L. 3.1 cm; W. 3.6 cm; Th. 0.9 cm.　　79 12-9 55

8　SHERBURN (Duggleby II)　　　　　　8:1-2

Yorkshire E.R.; North Yorkshire　　　　SE 960 741

ROUND BARROW: Diam. 15 m, H. 0.6 m, reduced by ploughing; composition not recorded; opened by Porter and Monkman May 1866.
BB 147; *Kinnes* 1979, Ae 4.

Burial 1: 'broken and scattered human bones, the remains of at least five bodies'; on layer of clay and charcoal 2.4 by 2.4m, on old surface at E. side.

Burial 2: cranial and rib fragments; with charcoal on old surface 4.5 m SE. of centre.
1 *Neolithic Bowl sherds*: three; quartz- and flint-tempered.　　　　　　　　　　　79 12-9 62
2 *Neolithic Bowl sherds*: two; quartz-tempered.
NPY no. 10.　　　　　　　　　　　79 12-9 63

Burial 3: inhumation traces; at base of central oval grave L. 1.5 m, W. 0.9m, D. 0.8m, aligned N.-S.; chalk rubble fill.

Burial 3 Grave fill
'*potsherd*': not preserved.
'*flint chippings*': two; not preserved.

9　SHERBURN (Prodham 1)　　　　　　9:1-3

Yorkshire E.R.; North Yorkshire　　　　SE 960 741

ROUND BARROW: Diam. 18 m, H. 0.6 m, reduced by ploughing; composition not recorded; opened by Porter and Monkman May 1866.
BB 147-8.

Burial 1: inhumation traces; on old surface 6.6 m SE. of centre.
'*flint chippings*': two; not preserved.

Burial 2: inhumation traces; 6 m S. by W. of centre.
1 *Flint end- and side-scraper*: edge retouch on distal and R. at 65 degrees, wear on L.; dihedral butt; mottled grey.
L. 3.8 cm; W. 2.1 cm; Th. 0.7 cm.　　79 12-9 65

Burial 3: double inhumation: adult male crouched on R. with head W., and adult female crouched on R. with head E.; in central oval grave L. 0.9 m, W. 0.6 m, D. 0.3 m, aligned E.-W.; Food Vessel at face of male.
2 *Food Vessel*: tripartite; plain.
M. 12.2 cm; H. 12.2 cm; B. 7.8 cm.　　79 12-9 64

Not located
3 '*Flint scraper*': not identified.　　79 12-9 66

10   SHERBURN (Binning)   10:1-4

Yorkshire E.R.; North Yorkshire   SE 962 740

OVAL BARROW: L. 27 m, W. 22 m, H. 0.3 m, aligned N.- S., reduced by ploughing; earth addition to natural knoll.
BB 148-9.

Burial 1: inhumation and cremation; adult crouched on L. with head SE., overlying adult cremation; on old surface. 5.4 m WSW. of centre; flint below head.
   'flint chipping': not preserved.

Mound material
1   *'Sherds'*: three; not identified.   79 12-9 74
     NPY no. 11.
2   *'Flint scraper'*: not identified.   79 12-9 72
3   *Flint utilised flake*: wear on distal; platform butt; mottled grey.
     L. 1.8 cm; W. 4.2 cm; Th. 0.6 cm.   79 12-9 72a
4   *'Flint core'*: not identified.   79 12-9 73

11   SHERBURN (Lamplough I)   11:1

Yorkshire E.R.; North Yorkshire   SE 96 74

ROUND BARROW: Diam. 12 m, H. 0.5 m, reduced by ploughing; chalk rubble.
BB 149-50.

Burial 1: triple burial: infant skull overlying child cremation deposit at feet of adult inhumation crouched on R. with head W.; on old surface 4.2 m ENE. of centre; vessel on side at feet of adult.
1   *Food Vessel*: twisted cord: on internal rim bevel, three horizontal lines; on external rim bevel, two horizontal lines; on neck, two rows of chevrons; on and beneath shoulder, two rows of horseshoes; squashed oval.
     M. 14.6-16.6 cm; H. 15.7 cm; B. 7.6 cm.   79 12-9 75
     BAP no. 213.

12   SHERBURN (Lovel)   12:1-8

Yorkshire E.R.; North Yorkshire   SE 94 73

ROUND BARROW: Diam. 17 m, H. 0.6 m, reduced by ploughing; earth and some chalk.
BB 150-2.

Burial 1: adult? male inhumation, crouched on R. with head SW.; on old surface 6.3 m NW. of centre; objects beneath head.
1   *'Flint knife or scraper'*: not identified.
                                                  79 12-9 80
2   *Flint knife*: blunting edge retouch on R., invasive retouch on proximal and L.; cortex remnant; mottled grey.
     L. 7.2 cm; W. 3.6 cm; Th. 1.0 cm.   79 12-9 81
3   *Flint utilised flake*: wear on R.; platform butt; cortex on L.; patinated.
     L. 5.2 cm; W. 1.9 cm; Th. 0.7 cm.   79 23-9 78

Burial 2: adult cremation deposit; in inverted urn on top of grave fill at centre.
4   *'Bronze awl'*: not identified.   79 12-9 83
     BB fig. 40.
5   *Collared Urn*: incised herringbone on collar and neck; corky fabric.
     M. 22.7 cm; H. 34.3 cm; B. 10.5 cm.   79 12-9 76
     BB fig. 97; *BAP* no. 118; *Longworth* no. 1252.

Burial 3: double inhumation: adolescent crouched on R. with head N. by W., and child crouched on L. with head WSW.; in central oval grave L. 2.1 m, W. 1.8 m, D. 0.5 m, aligned NE.-SW.; fill of clayey earth and some chalk;

vessel at knees and knife at chest of adolescent.
6   *Food Vessel*: twisted cord: on internal rim bevel, four to five horizontal lines; on neck irregular roughly-applied vertical and diagonal lines; in part of shoulder groove, traces of horizontal line; on body, two rows of 'knot' impressions; partially corky fabric.
     M. 15.4 cm; H. 14.5 cm; B. 7.2 cm.   79 12-9 77
     BAP no. 118a.
7   *Flint plano-convex knife*: invasive retouch on distal and bilateral; platform butt; grey.
     L. 6.0 cm; W. 1.8 cm; Th. 0.8 cm.   79 12-9 82

Not located
8   *'Flint implement'*: not identified.   79 12-9 79

13   SHERBURN (Lamplough II)   13:1-23

Yorkshire E.R.; North Yorkshire   SE 97 75

ROUND BARROW: Diam. 27 m, H. 0.8 m, reduced by ploughing; earth.
BB 152-5.

Burial 1: inhumation and cremation; adult female crouched on R. with head W., overlying adolescent cremation deposit; at base of central oval grave L. 1.4 m, W. 1 m, D. 1.2 m, aligned SE.-NW.; vessel at knees of female, knife with cremation.
1   *Food Vessel*: on internal rim bevel, three twisted cord lines; on outer edge of rim, short vertical whipped cord 'maggots'; on neck and body, horizontal twisted rope lines.
     M. 17.8 cm; H. 17.0 cm; B. c 8.7 cm.   79 12-9 84
     BB fig. 72; *BAP* no. 69.
2   *Flint plano-convex knife*: converging bifacial and bilateral invasive retouch on keeled blade; platform butt; burnt.
     L. 8.2 cm; W. 2.4 cm; Th. 1.2 cm.   79 12-9 86
     BB fig. 98.

Burial 2: adult male inhumation, crouched on L. with head SSW.; in oval grave L. 1.5 m, W. 1.3 m, D 1.2 m, aligned NE.-SW., 0.6 m SW. of Burial 1; Food Vessel at knees.
3   *Food Vessel*: on outer edge of rim, first ridge, shoulder groove and shoulder, coarse diagonal whipped cord 'maggots'; on body, one row of roughly incised vertical chevrons.
     M. 18.8 cm; H. 16.2 cm; B. 9.0 cm.   79 12-9 85
     BAP no. 70.

Mound material
4   *Beaker sherd*: tooth-comb stamped horizontal lines.
                                                  79 12-9 97a
5   *Beaker sherds*: seven, including base; tooth-comb stamped horizontal lines.   79 12-9 97b
6   *Beaker sherds*: four; one with incised lattice pattern.   79 12-9 97c
     Clarke no. 1385.
7   *Food Vessel rim sherd*: decoration blurred; on top of rim, twisted cord herringbone; on external rim bevel and internally, rows of ? cord loops set on side.
                                                  79 12-9 97d
8   *Food Vessel sherd*: short diagonal whipped cord lines.
                                                  79 12-9 97e
9   *Plain sherd*: flint-tempered.   79 12-9 97
10 *Plain sherds*: four; grit-tempered.   79 12-9 97f
11 *'Stone axe flake'*: not identified.   79 12-9 87
12 *Flint end-scraper*: edge retouch on distal at 65 degrees; on core fragment with one flake scar; faceted butt; cortex remnant; mottled grey.
     L. 5.1 cm; W. 3.8 cm; Th. 1.5 cm.   79 12-9 89

13-14 *'Flint scrapers'*: two; not identified.

79 12-9 90-91

15 *Flint serrated blade*: worn fine serrations bilaterally; cortex remnant; beige.
L. 4.5 cm; W. 1.8 cm; Th. 0.7 cm.   79 12-9 1516

16 *Flint serrated flake*: fine edge retouch on R. at five
teeth per cm; cortex on L.; burnt.
L. 5.2 cm; W. 2.1 cm; Th. 1.0 cm.   79 12-9 1519

17 *'Flint saw'*: not identified.   79 12-9 88

18 *Flint worked blade*: edge retouch on distal and
partially bilateral at 75 degrees; worn on R.;
mottled grey.
L. 5.4 cm; W. 1.7 cm; Th. 0.7 cm.   79 12-9 1515

19 *Flint utilised blade*: bilateral wear; cortex remnant; mottled grey.
L. 5.7 cm; W. 2.2 cm; Th. 0.7 cm.   79 12-9 1514

20 *Flint utilised blade*: bilateral wear; cortex
remnant; mottled grey.
L. 5.8 cm; W. 2.0 cm; Th. 0.6 cm.   79 12-9 1517

21 *Flint utilised flake*: wear on R.; faceted butt; grey.
L. 5.4 cm; W. 2.3 cm; Th. 0.6 cm.   79 12-9 1518

22 *'Antler fragment'*: not identified.   79 12-9 92

23 *'Antler tine'*: not identified.   79 12-9 93

14 SHERBURN (Lamplough III)   14:1-4

Yorkshire E.R.; North Yorkshire   SE 87 95

ROUND BARROW: Diam. 21 m, H. 0.8 m, reduced by ploughing;
earth.
BB 155.

Burial 1: adult cremation deposit; on fill of hollow 3 m
SE of centre.

Mound material

1 *Beaker sherds*: two; twisted cord horizontal lines.
79 12-9 95

2 *Beaker sherd*: horizontal lines in uncertain technique; eroded.   79 12-9 95a
Clarke no. 1386.

3 *Early Iron Age sherd*: vesicular fabric.   79 12-9 96

4 *'Flint scraper'*: not identified.   79 12-9 94

15 SHERBURN (Lamplough IV)   15:

Yorkshire E.R.; North Yorkshire   SE 97 95

ROUND BARROW: Diam. 18 m 'very slight elevation',
reduced by ploughing; composition not recorded.
BB 155.

Burial 1: child cremation deposit; in SW. side of
central irregular hollow Diam. 1.5 m, D. 0.5 m.

16 GANTON (Brough V)   16:1-5

Yorkshire E.R; North Yorkshire   SE 97 75

ROUND BARROW: Diam. 21 m, H. 0.5 m, reduced by ploughing;
earth and chalk; opened 10 October 1867.
BB 155-7.

Burial 1: double inhumation: adult crouched on L. with
head SSW. and, behind head, remains of infant on L. with
head SW.; on old surface 4.2 m E. of centre; pin behind
infant head.

1 *Bone pin*: cut longbone sliver; broken and eroded.
L. 6.4 cm; W. 1.0 cm.   79 12-9 98

Mound material

2 *Flint hollow-based arrowhead*: bifacial total edge
retouch; mottled grey.
L. 3.5 cm; W. 2.0 cm; Th. 0.5 cm.   79 12-9 102
BB fig. 28; *ASI* fig. 331.

3-4 *'Flint scrapers'*: two; not identified.

79 12-9 100-101

5 *'Flint knife'*: not identified.   79 12-9 99

17 GANTON (Brough II)   17:1-6

Yorkshire E.R.; North Yorkshire   SE 97 75

OVAL BARROW: L. 27 m, W. 15 m, H. 0.3 m, reduced by
ploughing; earth and some chalk.
BB 157-8.

Burial 1: skull fragment; in ploughsoil 2.7 m SE. of
centre.

Burial 2: adult inhumation, crouched on R. with head
SW., disturbed by Burial 3; in central grave L. 1.8 m, W.
1.5 m, D. 0.2 m, aligned SE.-NW.; vessel at head.

1 *Food Vessel*: on internal rim bevel, short vertical
incised lines; on external rim bevel, jabbed
impressions; on neck and shoulder grooves and first
ridge, vertical slashed lines; on shoulder, row of
jabbed impressions; on upper body, two rows of
vertical incised chevrons with horizontal line
beneath; on lower body, vertical and diagonal incised
lines with horizontal line beneath, all carelessly
applied.
M. 18.5 cm; H. 17.9 cm; B. *c*. 8.2 cm.   79 12-9 104
BAP no. 185.

2 *'Sherd'*: not identified.   79 12-9 1522

Burial 3: adult inhumation, crouched on R. with head
SW.; in central grave beneath large flint blocks, partly
disturbing Burial 2.

Burial 4: adult inhumation, crouched on R. with head
NW.; in hollow to E. of central grave.

Mound material

3 *Food Vessel*: Yorkshire Vase; on internal and external
rim bevels, neck and shoulder groove, impressed
herringbone split by twisted cord horizontal lines;
two surviving imperforate lugs; very distorted.
M. 14.8-16.5 cm; H. 11.5-14.1 cm; B. 6.2-6.6 cm.
79 12-9 105

4 *Flint point*: bilateral invasive retouch converging
on proximal; platform butt; mottled grey.
L. 7.5 cm; W. 3.8 cm; Th. 0.9 cm.   79 12-9 106
BB fig. 30; *ASI* fig. 243.

Not located

5 *Flint blade*: grey.
L. 1.7 cm; W. 1.2 cm; Th. 0.4 cm.   79 12-9 1521

6 *Flint core fragment*: cortex remnant; mottled grey.
L. 4.8 cm; W. 3.5 cm; Th. 2.4 cm.   79 12-9 1520

18 GANTON (Brough I)   18:1-6

Yorkshire E.R.; North Yorkshire   SE 97 75

ROUND BARROW: Diam. 18 m, H. 0.6 m; earth and chalk with
many flint blocks at E. and S.; opened October 1867.
BB 158-60.

Burial 1: adult cremation deposit, in heap Diam. 0.3m;
at D 1.3 m in central grave Diam. 1.8 m, D. 1.8 m, fill of
chalk rubble with large flints at base and over top;
inhumation fragments in fill; battle-axe beside
cremation, sherds and flint in fill.

1 *'Sherd'"* not identified.   79 12-9 1523

2 *Stone battle-axe*: dolerite Y 796; Roe IIA; all over
ground and polished; hourglass perforation; ? recent
damage on cutting-edge, abrasion on butt.
L. 13.0 cm; W. 6.3 cm; Th. 3.9 cm; Diam.
(perforation) 2.9 cm.   79 12-9 107

BB fig. 99; *ASI* fig. 126; *Roe* 1966, no. 273.
'*flint-chipping*': ? not preserved, or perhaps one of 4 to 6.

Mound material

3 *Flint end-scraper and knife*: edge retouch on distal at 60 degress, bifacial invasive retouch on L., partial edge retouch on R. at 60 degrees with some inverse invasive retouch; platform butt; cortex remnant on R.; mottled grey.
   L. 3.5 cm; W. 3.0 cm; Th. 1.1 cm.   79 12-9 108

Not located

4 *Flint worked flake*: edge retouch on R.; distal removed; platform butt; cortex remnant on L.; grey.
   L. 4.0 cm; W. 1.9 cm; Th. 0.7 cm.   79 12-9 1524
5 *Flint worked flake*: edge retouch on distal and L., some invasive retouch on proximal; platform butt; mottled grey.
   L. 3.0 cm; W. 2.6 cm; Th. 0.7 cm.   79 12-9 1525
6 *Flint blade*: snapped; grey.
   L. 2.6 cm; W. 0.9 cm; Th. 0.2 cm.   79 12-9 1526

19 GANTON (Brough IV)   19:1-4

Yorkshire E.R.; North Yorkshire   SE 986 760

ROUND BARROW: Diam. 21 m, H. 0.3 m, reduced by ploughing; earth.
BB 161.

Burial 1: adult cremation deposit; in charcoal matrix ? burnt *in situ* in central oval hollow L. 0.6 m, W. 0.5 m, D 0.2 m; urn on side over cremation, pin with bones.
1 *Bipartite Vessel*: plain; soft grog and grit-tempered; distorted.
   M. 11.1-13.3 cm; H. 15 cm; B. 10.9 cm. 79 12-9 109
   '*bone pin*': not preserved.

Mound material

2 *Flint barbed-and-tanged arrowhead*: bifacial invasive retouch; one barb broken; mottled grey.
   L. 2.6 cm; W. 1.9 cm; Th. 0.4 cm.   79 12-9 110
   Green 1980, no. A50.
3-4 '*Flint scrapers*': two; not identified.
                                            79 12-9 111-112

20 GANTON (Brough VI)   20:1-4

Yorkshire E.R.; North Yorkshire   SE 986 760

ROUND BARROW: Diam. 13 m, H. 0.4 m, reduced by ploughing; earth.
BB 161.

Burial 1: adult inhumation, crouched on R. with head S. by W.; on old surface 4.2 m SW. by W. of centre.

Burial 2: adult cremation deposit; in central hollow Diam. 0.4 m; bronze fragment 0.1 m above bones.
   '*bronze fragment*': not preserved.

Mound material

1-3 '*Flint scrapers*': three; not identified.
                                            79 12-9 113-115
4 '*Flint knife*' not identified.   79 12-9 116

21 GANTON (Brough III)   21: 1-165

Yorkshire E.R.; North Yorkshire   SE 985 760

ROUND BARROW: Diam. 18 m, H. 0.9 m, reduced by ploughing; chalk rubble and flint.
BB 161-6.

Burial 1: child inhumation, crouched on L. with head E.; 0.6 m above old surface 2.1 m SE. of centre; Food Vessel at head beneath two large flint blocks.
1 *Food Vessel*: twisted cord: on internal rim bevel, four lines; on neck, wavy line enclosed above by two and below by three horizontal lines; beneath shoulder, two horizontal lines.
   M. 12.3 cm; H. 9.9 cm; B. 5.5 cm.   79 12-9 117
   BB fig. 69; *BAP* no. 29.

Burials 2 to 4 were in the upper fill of a grave Diam. 1.7 m, D. 1 m, 0.9 m E. of Burial 1.

Burial 2: adult ?female cremation deposit, in heap Diam. 0.5 m; beneath heap of chalk and flint on top of grave fill.

Burial 3: child inhumation, crouched on L. with head NNE.; immediately E. of Burial 2.

Burial 4: adult male inhumation, crouched on L. with head E.; in charcoal-rich matrix beneath Burials 2 and 3; Beaker and knife behind head.
2 *Beaker*: rectangular tooth-comb stamped: on neck, bar chevron pattern with triangles filled by short diagonal lines enclosed by pairs of horizontal lines; on body, bar chevron pattern with triangles filled by short vertical lines enclosed by pairs of horizontal lines; on lower body, rows of finger pinching.
   M. 13.5 cm; H. 17.3 cm; B. 6.2 cm.   79 12-9 118
   BB fig. 101; *BAP* no. 130; *Clarke* no. 1283
3 *Flint knife*: invasive retouch on L.; platform butt; mottled grey.
   L. 5.9 cm; W. 3.1 cm; Th. 0.5 cm.   79 12-9 142

Burial 5: adult ?female inhumation, crouched on R. with head SW.; in hollow D. 0.6 m, 2.4 m S. of centre; Food Vessel at face, surrounded by chalk blocks.
4 *Food Vessel*: whipped cord: on internal and external rim bevels, short diagonal lines; on neck and below shoulder, single rows of herringbone.
   M. 11.8 cm; H. 11.1 cm; B. 5.9 cm.   79 12-9 119
   BAP no. 30.
5 *?Food Vessel sherds*: (preserved with above) three; one with linear incised herringbone; compact fabric.
                                            79 12-9 119a

Burial 6: adult female inhumation, crouched on R. with head SW.; in charcoal-rich fill of hollow D. 0.3 m, 4.8 m SSW. of centre.

Burial 7: double inhumation: adult male crouched on L. with head E. and, at feet, adult male crouched on R. with head NW.; at base of central oval grave L. 2.4 m, W. 2 m, D. 0.3 m, aligned E.-W.; Food Vessel at face of former, arrowhead at knees of latter.
6 *Food Vessel*: jabbed impressions: on internal rim bevel, two rows in part forming herringbone; beneath rim, two rows; above and below shoulder, single rows.
   M. 16.7 cm; H. 15.8 cm; B. 8.0 cm.   79 12-9 120
   BAP no. 28.
7 *Flint leaf arrowhead*: bifacial invasive retouch; cortex remnant; mottled grey.
   L. 4.0 cm; W. 2.1 cm; Th. 0.3 cm   79 12-9 123
   Green 1980, no. 93.

Burial 8: double inhumation: adult male crouched on L. with head S., facing and partly overlying adolescent female crouched on R. with head SE.; on fill of hollow D.

0.8 m, 4.5 m ENE. of centre; vessels between chests and hips, tusk and pebble behind shoulders of male.

8 *Miniature Food Vessel*: on rim bevel and external surface, incised herringbone.
   M. 8.0 cm; H. 5.5 cm; B. 4.0 cm.   79 12–9 121
   BB fig. 77; *BAP* no. 31.

9 *Cover*: (for above); deeply impressed pinpricks in single row around outer edge, two concentric rows on upper surface, and two rows set from these to converge on concave facets of handle; incomplete remains of two perforations for vertical suspension.
   Diam. *c.* 8.1 cm.   79 12–0 121a

10 *Accessory Cup*: on top of rim, single row of pinpricks; on external rim edge, deep horizontal groove containing irregularly spaced pinpricks; on neck, irregularly placed pinpricks; on body, reserved zone bordered above and below by deep groove and two horizontal lines of pinpricks; on base, two concentric lines of pinpricks; remains of one vertical perforation through lip.   79 12–9 1527a

11 *Cover*: (for above); on outer edge, incised line above row of deeply impressed pinpricks; on upper surface, one or two concentric rows of similar pinpricks with remains of incised double triangle pattern within; remains of one perforation for suspension.
   Diam. *c.* 7.0 cm.   79 12–9 1527
   'quartz pebble': not preserved.
   'boar's tusk': not preserved.

Burials 9 to 11 were in the fill of an irregular trench L. 4.5 m, W. 1.5 m, D. 0.6 m, aligned ENE.–WSW., and commencing 2.4 m ENE. of centre.

Burial 9: infant inhumation, with head W.; 3.3 m ENE. of centre.

Burial 10: child inhumation, crouched on L. with head E.; 3.6 m NE. by E. of centre; Beaker behind head.

12 *Beaker*: rectangular tooth-comb stamped: on neck, alternate pendant and reserved triangles, the pendants filled with short horizontal lines, enclosed above by two and below by one horizontal line; above shoulder, narrow zone of short vertical lines between single horizontal lines; on body, alternate pendant and reserved triangles bordered above by single horizontal line.
   M. 13.5 cm; H. 20.0 cm; B. 8.8 cm.   79 12–9 122
   BB fig. 83; *BAP* no. 131; *Clarke* no. 1284.

Burial 11: infant inhumation, with head ENE.; in basal hollow 6.3 m ENE. of centre.

Mound material: *c.* 80 per cent of the flints were deposited together at the SW. side of the mound, but these can no longer be distinguished from the remainder.

13 *Flint disc scraper*: edge and invasive retouch at 70 degrees; dark grey.
   L. 3.0 cm; W. 3.3 cm; Th. 1.2 cm.   79 12–9 1904

14 *Flint horseshoe scraper*: edge retouch on distal and bilateral at 50 degrees; platform butt; patinated.
   L. 3.1 cm; W. 3.6 cm; Th. 1.1 cm.   79 12–9 125

15 *Flint horseshoe scraper*: edge retouch on distal and bilateral at 55 degrees; mottled grey.
   L. 3.3 cm; W. 3.5 cm; Th. 1.3 cm.   79 12–9 126

16 *Flint horseshoe scraper*: edge retouch on distal and bilateral at 60 degrees; platform butt; mottled grey.
   L. 2.8 cm; W. 2.0 cm; Th. 0.5 cm.   79 12–9 130

17 *Flint horseshoe scraper*: edge retouch on distal and bilateral at 80 degrees; cortex remnant; mottled grey.
   L. 3.9 cm; W. 3.1 cm; Th. 1.3 cm.   79 12–9 140

18 *Flint end- and side-scraper*: edge retouch on distal and R. at 70 degrees; platform butt; mottled grey.
   L. 4.5 cm; W. 3.8 cm; Th. 0.9 cm.   79 12–9 124

19 *Flint end- and side-scraper*: edge retouch on distal and R. at 60 degrees; corticated butt; grey.
   L. 2.2 cm; W. 2.5 cm; Th. 0.5 cm.   79 12–9 127

20 *Flint end- and side-scraper*: edge retouch on distal and R. at 65 degrees; damage on L.; corticated butt; mottled grey.
   L. 2.1 cm; W. 1.8 cm; Th. 0.4 cm.   79 12–9 128

21 *Flint end- and side-scraper*: edge retouch on distal and R. at 70 degrees; cortex remnant; mottled grey.
   L. 1.8 cm; W. 2.5 cm; Th. 0.9 cm.   79 12–9 129

22 *Flint end-scraper*: edge retouch on distal at 40 degrees; platform butt; cortex remnant; mottled grey.
   L. 4.4 cm; W. 3.7 cm; Th. 1.3 cm.   79 12–9 133

23 *Flint end-scraper*: edge retouch on distal at 70 degrees; faceted butt; cortex on R.; mottled grey.
   L. 5.1 cm; W. 2.8 cm; Th. 1.0 cm.   79 12–9 138

24 *Flint end-scraper*: edge retouch on distal at 70 degrees; dihedral butt; damaged; light grey.
   L. 4.0 cm; W. 3.0 cm; Th. 0.6 cm.   79 12–9 139

25 *Flint side-scraper*: denticulated edge retouch on L. at 60 degrees; platform butt; cortex remnant; dark grey patinated.
   L. 4.7 cm; W. 4.8 cm; Th. 0.8 cm.   79 12–9 136

26 *Flint knife*: partial invasive edge retouch on L.; cortex remnant; snapped; mottled grey.
   L. 4.6 cm; 2.9 cm; Th. 0.7 cm.   79 12–9 135

27 *Flint knife*: bilateral edge retouch at 45 degrees; cortex remnant; broken; mottled grey.
   L. 4.7 cm; W. 2.3 cm; Th. 0.4 cm.   79 12–9 141

28 *Flint knife*: invasive retouch on L.; edge wear on R.; platform butt; cortex remnant; dark grey.
   L. 5.0 cm; W. 3.3 cm; Th. 1.3 cm.   79 12–9 1905

29 *Flint worked flake*: partial edge retouch on distal at 55 degrees; platform butt; cortex remnant; mottled grey.
   L. 3.5 cm; W. 4.7 cm; Th. 1.2 cm.   79 12–9 132

30 *Flint worked flake*: core rejuvenation flake struck at 90 degrees to platform; invasive retouch on R.; cortex remnant; mottled grey.
   L. 6.5 cm; W. 2.7 cm; Th. 1.4 cm.   79 12–9 134

31 *Flint worked blade*: bilateral edge retouch; punctiform butt; mottled grey.
   L. 4.8 cm; W. 1.3 cm; Th. 0.2 cm.   79 12–9 146

32 *Flint worked blade*: bilateral edge retouch; distal removed; punctiform butt; cortex remnant; mottled grey.
   L. 5.8 cm; W. 1.8 cm; Th. 0.5 cm.   79 12–9 147

33 *Flint worked flake*: partial bilateral edge retouch; platform butt; mottled grey.
   L. 4.4 cm; W. 4.6 cm; Th. 1.0 cm.   79 12–9 151

34 *Flint worked flake*: partial edge retouch on distal; edge wear on R.; platform butt; cortex remnant; mottled grey.
   L. 5.2 cm; W. 3.8 cm; Th. 1.5 cm.   79 12–9 154

35 *Flint worked flake*: partial edge retouch on distal; platform butt; cortex remnant; mottled grey.
   L. 3.9 cm; W. 6.7 cm; Th. 1.6 cm.   79 12–9 162

36 *Flint worked flake*: partial edge retouch; cortex remnant; mottled grey.
   L. 5.8 cm; W 4.1 cm; Th. 1.2 cm.   79 12–9 165

37 *Flint worked flake*: partial edge retouch on distal; platform butt; mottled grey.
   L. 4.0 cm; W. 5.2 cm; Th. 1.2 cm.   79 12–9 169

38 *Flint worked flake*: partial inverse retouch on L.; distal removed; cortex remnant; mottled grey.
   L. 3.4 cm; W. 1.6 cm; Th. 0.6 cm.   79 12–9 211

39 *Flint worked flake*: fine edge retouch on L.; corticated butt; mottled grey.
   L. 4.7 cm; W. 2.4 cm; Th. 0.5 cm.   79 12–9 220

40 *Flint worked flake*: edge retouch on distal; proximal snapped; mottled grey.
   L. 2.4 cm; W. 2.2 cm; Th. 0.4 cm.   79 12–9 221

41 *Flint worked flake*: partial edge retouch on distal;
   platform butt; cortex remnant; mottled grey.
   L. 6.4 cm; W. 3.2 cm; Th. 1.4 cm.   79 12-9 241
42 *Flint worked flake*: partial edge retouch on distal;
   platform butt; mottled grey.
   L. 4.8 cm; W. 5.2 cm; Th. 1.4 cm.   79 12-9 243
43 *Flint worked flake*: coarse bifacial invasive
   retouch; snapped; patinated.
   L. 5.3 cm; W. 2.3 cm; Th. 1.1 cm.   79 12-9 249
44 *Flint worked flake*: edge and invasive retouch on L.;
   platform butt; cortex remnant; dark grey.
   L. 3.1 cm; W. 3.3 cm; Th. 1.1 cm.   79 12-9 1903
45 *Flint worked flake*: thermal flake; partial edge
   retouch on distal and L.; cortex remnant; dark grey.
   L. 3.6 cm; W. 3.6 cm; Th. 1.0 cm.   79 12-9 1906

   Flint utilised flakes

	Wr.	Btt	Ctx	Col.	L.	W.	Th.	79 12-9
46	L.		x	Pat.	4.9	1.8	0.9	143
47	L.		x	Gr.	4.3	2.0	0.6	144
48	R.		x	Pat.	4.1	1.6	0.6	145
49	LR.	Pnct.		Pat.	6.2	1.6	0.8	148
50	LR.			M. Gr.	7.0	3.0	0.8	149
	Dist.							
51	L.	Rem.	x	M. Gr.	4.6	1.8	0.5	150
52	L.	Pl.	x	M. Gr.	4.4	2.9	1.1	153
53	L.	Pl.	x	M. Gr.	5.1	2.4	1.5	155
54	Dist.	Pl.		M. Gr.	4.5	3.2	1.0	156
55	R.	Pl.	x	M. Gr.	4.8	3.9	1.3	158
56	L.	Pl.		M. Gr.	4.8	1.9	0.9	181
57	Dist.	Pl.	x	M. Gr.	4.6	3.9	0.9	194
58	L.	Dh.	x	M. Gr.	5.5	4.3	1.0	195
59	LR.	Pl.	x	M. Gr.	5.6	3.1	0.9	219
60	LR.	Pl.		M. Gr.	3.0	3.0	0.7	226
61	R.	Pl.	x	M. Gr.	4.7	5.8	1.0	257
62	L.	Pl.	x	D. Gr.	6.3	2.3	0.9	1907

   Flint flakes

	Btt	Ctx	Col.	L.	W.	Th.	79 12-9
63	Pl.	x	M. Gr.	5.5	4.6	1.2	131
64	Pl.	x	Gr.	4.8	4.8	1.0	137
65	Pl.	x	M. Gr.	6.8	2.6	1.1	152
66	Dh.	x	Pat.	4.6	3.3	0.9	157
67	Pnct.	x	Gr.	6.8	3.8	1.3	159
68	Pl.	x	M. Gr.	4.1	4.0	1.0	161
69		x	M. Gr.	4.0	5.2	1.6	163
70	Pl.		M. gr.	4.5	5.7	1.0	164
71	Pnct.	x	M. Gr.	4.1	3.9	1.2	166
72	Pl.		M. Gr.	4.1	3.8	0.8	167
73		x	M. Gr.	5.8	4.8	1.3	168
74	Pl.	x	M. Gr.	4.2	4.4	1.0	171
75	Ct.	x	Gr.	4.1	4.2	1.1	172
76	Pl.	x	M. Gr.	4.0	3.0	0.9	173
77		x	M. Gr.	4.0	3.5	1.0	174
78	Pl.	x	Gr.	4.5	4.2	1.0	175
79	Ct.	x	M. Gr.	3.5	3.6	1.1	176
80	Pl.	x	M. Gr.	4.8	4.1	1.3	177
81	Rem.	x	M. Gr.	3.2	5.4	0.7	178
82	Pl.	x	M. Gr.	4.4	4.6	1.0	179
83	Ct.	x	M. Gr.	3.1	3.9	0.9	180
84		x	M. Gr.	4.1	4.4	0.5	182
85	Pl.	x	M. Gr.	5.0	6.6	1.4	183
86	Pl.		M. Gr.	3.6	3.2	1.1	184
87	Pl.	x	M. Gr.	5.0	5.0	0.9	185
88		x	M. Gr.	5.5	3.9	0.7	186
89		x	M. Gr.	3.7	3.6	0.5	187
90	Pl.		M. Gr.	4.3	3.2	0.7	188
91	Pl.	x	M. Gr.	5.7	2.3	1.2	189
92	Pl.		M. Gr.	4.8	2.6	0.6	190
93	Pl.		M. Gr.	3.9	3.5	0.5	191

   Flint Flakes

	Btt	Ctx	Col.	L.	W.	Th.	79 12-9
94	Pl.	x	M. Gr.	4.1	5.4	1.2	192
95	Pl.		M. Gr.	4.5	2.9	1.0	193
96	Pl.		M. Gr.	4.2	3.1	0.8	196
97	Pl.	x	M. Gr.	3.0	4.0	0.9	197
98	Pl.	x	M. Gr.	4.6	4.5	0.8	199
99	Pl.	x	M. Gr.	4.8	2.6	0.6	200
100	Pl.	x	M. Gr.	4.1	3.4	0.5	201
101	Pl.	x	M. Gr.	4.0	3.8	0.9	202
102	Pl.	x	M. Gr.	5.1	3.9	1.4	203
103	Pl.	x	M. Gr.	4.5	4.6	1.0	204
104	Pl.	x	M. Gr.	4.7	4.8	1.2	205
105			M. Gr.	2.4	3.5	1.3	206
106	Pl.	x	M. Gr.	3.5	3.7	0.7	207
107	Ct.	x	M. Gr.	3.9	4.5	0.7	208
108		x	M. Gr.	4.4	5.5	0.7	209
109	Pnct.	x	M. Gr.	5.1	5.3	1.6	210
110	Dh.	x	M. Gr.	4.1	7.1	0.9	212
111	Pl.	x	M. Gr.	4.5	4.7	0.8	213
112	Pl.	x	M. Gr.	3.1	4.1	0.9	214
113	Pl.	x	M. Gr.	4.0	3.4	1.2	216
114	Ct.	x	M. Gr.	2.9	3.8	1.0	217
115	Ct.	x	M. Gr.	3.3	4.4	1.1	218
116	Pl.	x	M. Gr.	3.2	4.5	1.0	222
117		x	M. Gr.	2.2	3.1	0.9	223
118	Pl.	x	M. Gr.	4.1	2.3	0.9	224
119		x	M. Gr.	4.2	3.3	1.2	225
120			M. Gr.	3.2	1.9	0.6	228
121	Pl.	x	M. Gr.	4.2	3.3	0.9	229
122	Pl.	x	Gr.	2.6	3.1	1.0	230
123			L. Gr.	4.1	2.0	1.3	231
124	Pl.		M. Gr.	3.5	2.8	1.2	232
125	Pl.	x	M. Gr.	5.3	4.7	1.1	233
126	Pl.	x	M. Gr.	4.2	5.1	1.0	234
127	Pl.	x	M. Gr.	4.5	5.1	0.9	235
128	Pl.	x	M. Gr.	5.2	5.8	1.1	236
129		x	M. Gr.	5.0	3.2	0.9	237
130	Pl.	x	M. Gr.	4.7	2.8	1.4	238
131	Ct.		M. Gr.	4.4	4.7	1.3	239
132	Pl.	x	Pat.	3.4	3.2	0.4	240
133	Pl.	x	M. Gr.	3.7	2.6	0.5	242
134	Pl.	x	M. Gr.	4.2	4.3	1.0	244
135	Pl.	x	M. Gr.	5.4	3.6	1.7	245
136	Pl.		M. Gr.	5.3	4.3	1.2	246
137	Pl.		M. Gr.	5.8	5.1	0.9	247
138	Pl.	x	M. Gr.	4.1	4.6	0.9	248
139	Pl.	x	Gr.	4.5	4.7	1.0	250
140	Ct.		Gr.	4.0	3.4	0.9	251
141	Pl.	x	M. Gr.	4.2	5.1	0.7	252
142	Pl.	x	M. Gr.	4.7	3.9	1.1	253
143	Pl.		M. Gr.	4.9	3.4	0.9	254
144	Ct.		M. Gr.	4.5	3.6	1.1	255
145	Ct.		M. Gr.	3.5	3.5	0.5	256
146			M. Gr.	4.8	3.9	0.8	258
147	Ct.	x	M. Gr.	5.9	4.8	1.2	259
148	Pl.	x	M. Gr.	5.7	5.8	1.1	260
149	Pl.	x	M. Gr.	4.4	3.1	1.0	262
150	Pl.	x	M. Gr.	4.7	3.3	0.9	264
151	Pl.		M. Gr.	5.8	4.5	0.6	266

152 *Flint core*: mottled grey.
    L. 3.8 cm; 3.1 cm; Th. 1.4 cm.   79 12-9 170
153 *Flint core*: single platform with irregular flake
    scars; previous platforms; re-use as hammerstone;
    cortex remnant; mottled grey.
    L. 1.5 cm; 2.8 cm; Th. 2.7 cm.   79 12-9 261
154 *Flint core*: single platform with irregular flake
    scars; previous platforms; re-use as hammerstone;
    cortex remnant; mottled grey.
    L. 4.1 cm; W. 3.7 cm; Th. 2.0 cm.   79 12-9 263

155 *Flint core*: one platform with parallel blade scars; opposed blade scar; cortex remnant; patinated.
L. 3.4 cm W. 3.3 cm; Th. 3.3 cm.   79 12–9 267

156 *Flint core fragment*: one platform with irregular flake scars; mottled grey.
L. 4.3 cm; W. 3.9 cm; Th. 2.0 cm.   79 12–9 268

157 *Flint core fragment*: mottled grey.
L. 4.0 cm; W. 3.5 cm; Th. 1.4 cm.   79 12–9 269

158 *Flint core rejuvenation flake*: one platform with parallel blade scars; cortex remnant; mottled grey.
L. 5.2 cm; W. 2.9 cm; Th. 0.9 cm.   79 12–9 198

159 *Flint hammerstone fragment*: one battered face; cortex remnant; grey.
L. 5.2 cm; W. 3.8 cm; Th. 1.5 cm.   79 12–9 265

160 *Flint fragment*: cortex remnant; patinated.
L. 5.5 cm; W. 4.6 cm; Th. 1.5 cm.   79 12–9 160

161–2 *Flint thermal flakes*: two; mottled grey.
79 12–9 215 and 227

Not located

163 *Neolithic Bowl sherd*: porous fabric; plain.
79 12–9 271a
NPY no. 7.

164 *Bronze Age sherds*: two; plain.   79 12–9 271
165 *'Pebble'*: not identified.   79 12–9 270

22 GANTON (Brough VII)   22:1–5

Yorkshire E.R.; North Yorkshire   SE 985 762

ROUND BARROW: Diam. 16 m, H. 0.3 m, reduced by ploughing; earth, chalk rubble and flint blocks; internal penannular ditch Diam. 7 m, W. 0.5–0.7 m, D. 0.8 m with SSE. causeway W. 2.4 m, chalk rubble fill.
BB 166–7.

Burial 1: adult male inhumation, crouched on R. with head S. by E.; at base of internal ditch in enlarged section, 3.9 m E. by S. of centre.

Burial 2: adolescent inhumation, crouched on L. with head E.; on old surface between two layers of flints, 1.8 m E. by S. of centre.

Burial 3: adult mandible fragment and two metacarpals; above old surface, 2.1 m ENE. of centre.

Burials 4 to 6 were in a central oval grave L. 2.6 m, W. 2 m, D. 1 m, aligned E.–W.

Burial 4: 'numerous disturbed bones of two bodies'; in grave fill.

1 *Beaker sherds*: eighteen; tooth-comb stamped: alternate zones of horizontal lines and herringbone with a single zone of open triangles enclosing fringe of short diagonal impressions.
B. 9.5 cm.   79 12–9 272–3
Clarke no. 1285.

2 *Food Vessel rim sherd*: twisted cord: internally, ?horseshoes; on rim, short diagonal twisted cord lines.   79 12–9 272a

Burial 5: adult female cremation deposit; at D. 0.4 m in grave fill, near S. side.

Burial 6: adult female inhumation, crouched on L. with head E.; at base of grave at E.

Lower grave fill

3 *Flint knife or point*: double-ended on blade; on distal, obverse retouch on R. and invasive retouch on L., worn; on proximal, converging edge retouch on L. and partially on R.; cortex remnant; grey.
L. 6.5 cm; W. 1.6 cm; Th. 0.7 cm.   79 12–9 275

4 *Antler tine*: red deer bez tine; worn and battered tip; butt broken.
L. 30.8 cm.   79 12–9 274

'a large portion of a red-deer's antler': not preserved.

Not located

5 *Flint flake*: platform butt; cortex remnant; grey.
L. 4.8 cm; W. 1.9 cm; Th. 0.3 cm.   79 12–9 275a

23 GANTON (Southwell)   23:1–23

Yorkshire E.R.; North Yorkshire   SE 99 76

ROUND BARROW: Diam. 15 m, H. 0.3 m, reduced by ploughing; earth and chalk with much burnt material; opened 1869.
BB 167–9.

Burial 1: adult male inhumation, crouched on R. with head SW. by S.; on fill of Feature A, 4.2 m SSE. of centre.

Burial 2: adolescent inhumation, crouched on R. with head S.; beneath flint blocks on old surface, -4 m ESE. of centre; Food Vessel at face.

1 *Food Vessel*: coarse twisted cord: on internal rim bevel, two to three lines; on neck, irregular traces of horizontal lines; on body, irregularly executed opposed filled triangles.
M. 14.0 cm; H. 11.5 cm; B. 7.0 cm.   79 12–9 277
BAP no. 211.

Burial 3: adolescent femur fragments; 1.5 m S. of centre.

Feature A: deposit of dark earth and burnt material (as in mound) L. 2.1 m, W. 0.6 m, aligned E.–W., beginning in slight hollow below Burial 1.

Feature A or Mound material

2 *Neolithic bowl sherds*: thirty-three, including four rims representing minimum four vessels; grit-tempered.   79 12–9 276

3 *Neolithic bowl sherds*: seven including one rim; corky fabric.   79 12–9 276a

4 *Neolithic bowl sherds*: seven including two rims; corky fabric.   79 12–9 276c

5 *Neolithic bowl sherds*: twenty-three including two rims; varying grit- and ?grog-temper. 79 12–9 276d

6 *Neolithic bowl sherd*: ?shell-tempered. 79 12–9 276e
NPY no. 6.

7 *Beaker base sherd*: tooth-comb stamped horizontal rows.   79 12–9 276f

8 *Bronze Age base sherd*: corky fabric.   79 12–9 276b

9 *Bronze Age sherd*: grit- and grog-tempered.
79 12–9 276g

10 *'Stone pounder'*: not identified.   79 12–9 291
11 *'Flint knife'*: not identified.   79 12–9 278
12–23 *'Flint flakes'*: twelve; not identified.
79 12–9 279–290

24 GANTON (Southwell V)   24:1–3

Yorkshire E.R.; North Yorkshire   TA 00 76

ROUND BARROW: Diam. 12 m, H. 0.3 m, reduced by ploughing; earth (chalk: *GM*); opened April 1867.
BB 169; *Times* 11 April 1867; *GM* 1867, 1: 792–4.

Burial 1: charred bones; on old surface in burnt earth matrix S. of centre; around vessel.

1 *Collared Vessel*: on internal moulding, rows of jabbed impressions; on collar and neck, impressed herringbone made by ?flint flake; beneath shoulder, row of diagonal impressions in same technique.
M. 13.0 cm; H. 14.6 cm; B. 7.2 cm.   79 12–9 292
Longworth no. 1147.

Burial 2: adult male inhumation, crouched on L. with head SW. (female with head SSW.: *GM*); in central oval grave L. 1.2 m, W. 0.9 m, D. 0.5 m, aligned NE.-SW; pin at face.

2 *Bone pin:* cut and polished from caprovine metatarsal to ovate section; butt damaged; eroded.
   L. 9.5 cm; W. 0.8 cm.   79 12-9 293
   BB fig. 102.

Not located

3 *'Flint core':* not identified.   79 12-9 294

25 GANTON (Southwell IV)   25:1-15

Yorkshire E.R.; North Yorkshire   TA 00 76

ROUND BARROW: Diam. 31 m, H. 0.8 m (H. 1.2 m: *GM*), reduced by ploughing; sand (and clay with chalk: *GM*); opened April 1867; surviving plan and section drawing ? by Pitt Rivers (*Plate* 2).
BB 170-1; *Times* 11 April 1867; *GM* 1867, 1:792-4: *Kinnes* 1977.

Burial 1: child cremation deposit, in heap Diam. 0.5 m; on old surface, S of centre.
   'piece of calcined flint': not preserved.

Burial 2: adult inhumation, crouched on R. with head NW.; in central oval grave L. 1.2 m, W. 1 m, D. 0.7 m, aligned SE.-NW., cut into clay and lined and floored with wooden planks braced by five stakes at NW. and six at SE., Diam. 0.4 m, D. 0.3 m; Food Vessel on side at face.

1 *Food Vessel:* on internal rim bevel, neck and halfway down body, single rows of vertical or diagonal incisions and impressions; ?seed impression near shoulder.
   M. 13.1 cm; H. 13.9 cm; B. 7.0 cm.   79 12-9 295
2 *Plaster cast of wooden stake impression:* round section cut to faceted point of sub-rectangular section.
   L. 30.5 cm; D. 9.0 cm.   79 12-9 296
3 *Plaster cast of wooden plank impression:* irregular split face.
   L. 13.6 cm; W. 19.0 cm.   79 12-9 297

Mound material

4 *Flint shouldered point or knife:* bilateral edge retouch converging on proximal; cortex remnant; mottled grey.
   L. 6.5 cm; W. 2.8 cm; Th. 0.6 cm.   79 12-9 307
5 *Flint disc scraper:* edge retouch at 85 degrees; cortex remnant; mottled grey.
   L. 3.3 cm; W. 3.8 cm; Th. 0.9 cm.   79 12-9 301
6 *Flint horseshoe scraper:* edge retouch on distal and bilateral at 80 degrees; inverse invasive retouch on proximal; cortex remnant; mottled grey.
   L. 4.5 cm; W. 4.1 cm; Th. 1.1 cm.   79 12-9 299
7 *Flint horseshoe scraper:* edge retouch on distal and bilateral at 85 degrees; platform butt; mottled grey.
   L. 4.9 cm; W. 3.9 cm; Th. 0.9 cm.   79 12-9 300
8 *Flint horseshoe scraper:* edge retouch on distal and bilateral at 70 degrees; platform butt; mottled grey.
   L. 3.8 cm; W. 3.3 cm; Th. 0.5 cm.   79 12-9 302
9 *Flint horseshoe scraper:* edge retouch on distal and bilateral at 75 degrees; proximal broken; light grey.
   L. 6.2 cm; W. 2.6 cm; Th. 0.6 cm.   79 12-9 304
10 *Flint end-scraper:* on core fragment; edge retouch on distal at 80 degrees; cortex remnant; mottled grey.
   L. 5.5 cm; W. 3.5 cm; Th. 0.8 cm.   79 12-9 303
11-12 *'Flint scrapers':* two; not identified.
                                            79 12-9 305-6
13 *'Flint flake':* not identified.   79 12-9 298
14-15 *'Flint cores':* two; not identified.
                                            79 12-9 308-9

26 GANTON (Southwell III)   26:1-7

Yorkshire E.R.; North Yorkshire   TA 00 76

ROUND BARROW: Diam. 24 m, H. 0.8 m (Diam. 28 m, H. 0.9 m: *GM*), reduced by ploughing; chalk rubble and clayey earth; opened April 1867; surviving plan and section drawing ? by Pitt Rivers (*Plate* 2).
BB 171-3; *Times* 11 April 1867; *GM* 1867, 1:792-4; *Kinnes* 1977.

Burial 1: cremation deposit, in heap Diam. 0.2 m; 0.3 m above old surface 5.7 m SSW. of centre; cup on bones at W.

1 *Accessory Cup:* bipartite; on upper body, twisted cord in vertical lines above three horizontal lines; lower body eroded.
   M. *c.* 5.9 cm; H. *c.* 4.0 cm; B. 7.4 cm.   79 12-9 310
   BAP no. 292.

Burial 2: adolescent skull, on R. with head N.; 0.3 m E. of Burial 1; arrowhead at face.

2 *Flint barbed-and-tanged arrowhead:* bifacial invasive retouch; mottled grey.
   L. 3.3 cm; W. 2.4 cm; Th. 0.3 cm.   79 12-9 312
   Green 1980, no. 324.

Burial 3: adult inhumation, crouched on L. with head WNW.; on old surface between two layers of flint blocks, at centre; scraper beneath shoulders.

3 *Flint double-ended scraper:* edge retouch on distal at 70 degrees; invasive retouch on proximal; damaged; speckled grey.
   L. 4.4 cm; W. 1.9 cm; Th. 0.7 cm.   79 12-9 313

Burials **4 to 8** were grouped on old surface, 1.5 m E. of centre: see surviving plan.

Burial 4: child inhumation, crouched on R. with head W. (N. on plan).

Burial 5: adult cremation deposit; against back of Burial 4.

Burial 6: adult ?female inhumation, crouched on L. with head ENE.; to W. of Burial 4.

Burial 7: child skull (and longbone on plan); near R. hand of Burial 6.

Burial 8: adolescent mandible (not on plan); at back of Burial 6.

Burial 9: adult skull, on L.; on old surface 2.7 m NW. of centre; Food Vessel at face.

4 *Food Vessel:* on neck and internal rim bevel, two rows of irregularly placed vertical and diagonal opposed impressions, the latter partly obliterated by later smoothing; distorted.
   M. 10.4-11.6 cm; H. 10.0 cm; B. 5.3 cm. 79 12-9 311

Mound material

5 *Stone rubber:* sandstone; pecked and smoothed; three faces ground flat; recent groove damage on one face.
   L. 6.2 cm; W. 6.1 cm; Th. 5.7 cm.   79 12-9 315
6 *'Flint drill':* not identified.   79 12-9 314
7 *'Flint flake':* not identified.   79 12-9 1528

27 GANTON (Southwell I)   27:1-5

Yorkshire E.R.; North Yorkshire   TA 00 76

ROUND BARROW: Diam. 14.5 m, H. 0.9 m; earth and flints.
BB 173-5.

Burial 1: cremated bones of male and ?female with
unburnt bone fragments; 0.5 m above old surface at
centre; disturbed.

1 *Collared Vessel sherds:* seven, mainly from collar;
   twisted cord: on top of rim, single line; externally,
   vertical lines above multiple chevrons.
   Longworth no. 1147a.   79 12-9 322

2 *Flint knife:* on blade; converging bilateral edge
   retouch at 40 degrees; punctiform butt; brown.
   L. 7.2 cm; W. 1.8 cm; Th. 1.3 cm.   79 12-9 317
   BB fig. 21.

Burial 2: adult male inhumation, crouched on R. with
head E.; on old surface below Burial 1.

Burial 3: child cranial fragments; near Burial 2.

Burial 4: adult male inhumation, crouched on R.; 0.6 m
above old surface 1.2 m W. of centre, with charcoal
beneath flint blocks; sherd(s) near head, button at
chest.

3 *'Sherd'* not identified.   79 12-9 1529

4 *Jet button:* cut and polished to conical dome bevelled
   to flat base with central drilled V-perforation.
   Diam. 2.0 cm; Th. 0.7 cm.   79 12-9 318

Burial 5: disturbed and broken bones of adult male; N. of
centre (cf. Burial 1).

Feature A: oval pit L. 1.2 m, W. 1 m, D. 0.6 m, fill of
dark earth and flints; 0.9 m E. of centre; vessel over
fill.

5 *Bucket-shaped vase:* two pairs of perforations and
   remains of third.
   M. 10.0 cm; H. 10.3 cm; B. 8.3 cm.   79 12-9 316
   BB fig. 92; *Manby* 1980, 351.

Feature B: oval pit L. 1.2 m, W. 0.9 m, D. 0.6 m, fill of
chalk rubble and earth, 0.9 m WNW. of centre.

28 GANTON (Southwell II)   28: 1-12

Yorkshire E.R.; North Yorkshire   TA 00 76

ROUND BARROW: Diam. 23 m, H. 1.2 m, reduced by ploughing;
flint rubble and dark earth.
BB 175-8.

Burial 1: adult ?female inhumation, crouched on R.; 0.3
m above old surface, 5.4 m S. by E. of centre; sherd at
chest, scraper at lower back.

   'fragment of a drinking-cup': not preserved.

1 *Flint side-scraper and notched flake:* edge retouch on
   R at 55 degrees; inverse edge retouch forming notch
   on L; cortex remnant; mottled grey.
   L. 4.1 cm; W. 3.9 cm; Th. 0.7 cm.   79 12-9 323

Burial 2: adult cremation deposit; in urn in ploughsoil,
5.4 m WNW. of centre.

2 *Collared Urn:* twenty-three sherds including rim and
   base; twisted cord: on internal surface, six
   horizontal lines; on rim, single line; on collar,
   hurdle pattern.   79 12-9 320-1
   Longworth no. 1148.

3 *Collared Vessel sherd:* incised: two horizontal lines
   beneath lattice.   79 12-9 321a
   Longworth no. 1148a.

Burial 3: adult cremation deposit, in heap Diam. 0.3 m;
0.9 m above old surface, 2.1 m SSW. of centre.

Burials 4 to 10 were in a slight hollow beneath large
flints, SW. of centre.

Burial 4: adult male inhumation, crouched on R. with
head E.; 2.1 m SW. of centre.

Burial 5: adult male inhumation, crouched on R. with
head NW.; knees near head of Burial 4; vessel behind
head.

   'plain vase' not preserved.

Burial 6: adult male inhumation, crouched on R. with
head NE; lower back near head of Burial 5.

Burial 7: adult male inhumation, crouched on L. with
head NW.; head on feet of Burial 5; legs cut away by
insertion of Burial 10; 2.1 m S. of centre.

Burial 8: 'numbers of broken bones' E. of Burial 7 and
around Burial 10; pin and sherds in area.

4 *Beaker sherds:* eleven, including rim and base; tooth-
   comb stamped: on neck, narrow zone of short diagonal
   lines enclosed by single horizontal lines; above,
   vertical lines forming panels alternately plain and
   filled with short horizontal lines.   79 12-9 319
   Clarke no. 1286.

5 *Bone pin:* splinter of bird longbone; point cut and
   ground, tip abraded.
   L. 12.9 cm; W. 0.7 cm; Th. 0.5 cm.   79 12-9 329
   BB fig. 8.

Burial 9: adult male skull and cervical vertebrae, on
L.; 2.7 m S. of centre.

Burial 10: adult male inhumation, crouched on R. with
head E.; 1.2 m SE. by S. of centre; objects at chest.

6 *'Stone rubber':* not identified.   79 12-9 324

7 *Flint utilised flake:* wear on L.; dihedral butt;
   cortex remnant; mottled grey.
   L. 5.0 cm; W. 2.3 cm; Th. 0.6 cm.   79 12-9 1530

8 *Flint blade:* platform butt; cortex remnant; mottled
   grey.
   L. 4.9 cm; W. 1.1 cm; Th. 0.5 cm.   79 12-9 326

9 *Flint flake:* platform butt; cortex remnant; mottled
   grey.
   L. 4.6 cm; W. 2.0 cm; Th. 0.6 cm.   79 12-9 327

10 *'Flint core':* not identified.   79 12-9 328

Feature A: pit Diam. 0.6 m, D. 0.5 m, 2.2 m SW. of
centre.

Not located

11 *Flint utilised flake:* wear on L.; cortex remnant;
    grey.
    L. 5.6 cm; W. 2.6 cm; Th. 0.8 cm.   79 12-9 325

12 *'Antler fragment':* not identified.   79 12-9 330

29 GANTON (Southwell VI)   29:1-3

Yorkshire E.R.; North Yorkshire   TA 01 76

ROUND BARROW: Diam 18 m, H. 0.5 m; earth; opened 5 April
1867.
BB 178-9.

Burial 1: adult cremation deposit; ?burnt *in situ*, in
central oval pit L. 1 m, W. 0.9 m, D. 0.3 m, aligned E.-
W., inserted over Burial 2; cup inverted on bones at E.,
flint at W.

1 *Accessory Cup:* on internal rim bevel, indistinct
   decoration; on upper body, point-tooth comb-stamped
   hurdle pattern; two pairs of opposed perforations.
   M. 7.2 cm; H. 4.1 cm; B. 5.3 cm.   79 12-9 331
   BB fig. 103; *BAP* no. 291.

2 *Flint flake:* platform butt; cortex remnant; burnt.
   L. 5.9 cm; W. 3.0 cm; Th. 1.1 cm.   79 12-9 332

Burial 2: adult inhumation, crouched on R. with head W.; at base of central grave L. 2.1 m, W. 1.5 m, D. 1 m, aligned SE.-NW., fill of earth, clay and flints, below Burial 1.

Not located

3 *Flint discoidal knife fragment*: incomplete all over bifacial invasive retouch; cortex remnant; snapped; mottled grey.
   L. 5.5 cm; W. 4.5 cm; Th. 1.3 cm.   79 12-9 332a

30 GANTON (Southwell VII)   30:1-2
Yorkshire E.R.; North Yorkshire   TA 01 76

ROUND BARROW: Diam. 14 m, H. 0.3 m; earth; opened 5 April 1867.
BB 179.

Burial 1: adult cremation deposit; ?burnt *in situ* in central hollow L. 0.7 m, W. 0.5 m, D. 0.2 m, aligned N.-S.; knife on bones at N.

1 *Flint knife*: bilateral converging edge retouch; platform butt; burnt.
   L. 5.5 cm; W. 3.3 cm; Th. 1.0 cm.   79 12-9 333

Mound material

2 *Flint leaf arrowhead fragment*: all over bifacial invasive retouch; mottled grey.
   L. 2.1 cm; W. 1.4 cm; Th. 0.3 cm.   79 12-9 334
   Green 1980, no. A167.

31 BINNINGTON (Puckering)   31:1-14
Yorkshire E.R.; North Yorkshire   TA 01 76

ROUND BARROW: Diam. 16 m, H. 0.5 m, reduced by levelling; earth, with large flint blocks over old surface.
BB 179-80.

Burial 1: adult cremation deposit, in heap Diam. 0.2 m; below small central cairn of large flints, on earth fill of hollow L. 1.6 m, W. 1.1 m, D. 0.5 m, aligned SE.-NW.

?Burial 2: no details; in levelled area at N.

1 *Food Vessel*: on internal rim bevel, twisted cord herringbone; on ridges, single rows of impressions.
   M. 13.5 cm; H. 12.8 cm; B. 7.0 cm.   79 12-9 335
   RAP no. 30.

?Burial 3: no details; in levelled area at N.

2 *Miniature Food Vessel*: Yorkshire Vase; on internal rim bevel, two twisted cord lines; on neck, horizontal twisted cord lines above diagonal incisions; in shoulder groove, single horizontal twisted cord line; on body, confused pattern of horizontal and short vertical twisted cord lines forming zoned decoration for part of circumference; three surviving of originally ?five imperforate lugs with pairs of round-based impressions.
   M. 7.5 cm; H. 5.6 cm; B. 3.8 cm.   79 12-9 336
   BAP no. 282.

Mound Material

3 *Stone polished axe fragment*: greenstone; ground and polished with lateral facets; blade and one edge broken; flakes detached from butt.
   L. 8.6 cm; W. 3.5 cm; Th. 1.7 cm.   79 12-9 346
4 *'Flint scraper'*: not identified.   79 12-9 341
5 *'Flint knife'*: not identified.   79 12-9 338
6-9 *'Flint flakes'*: four; not identified.
                                           79 12-9 342-5
10-11 *'Flint fragments'*: two; not identified.
                                           79 12-9 339-40

Not located

12 *Neolithic Bowl*: porous fabric.
    M. 21.0 cm; H. 9.5 cm.   79 12-9 337
13 *Neolithic Bowl sherds*: two including rim; porous fabric.   79 12-9 337a
    NPY no. 5.
14 *Bronze Age sherds*: forty-two; plain. 79 12-9 337b

32 WILLERBY (Marr III)   32:1-3
Yorkshire E.R.; North Yorkshire   TA 03 76

ROUND BARROW: Diam. 22 m, H. 0.9 m; earth.
BB 180-1.

Burial 1: adult inhumation, crouched on L. with head S. by E.; in central hollow D. 0.3m covered by two layers of flints and layer of clay and charcoal; vessel near face.
   'remains of a drinking-cup': not preserved.

Mound material

1 *Stone polished adze*: greenstone; ground and polished to high gloss; some flake scars still visible; butt broken.
   L. 15.1 cm; W. 4.4 cm; Th. 1.6 cm.   79 12-9 347
   BB fig. 11; ASI fig. 116.
2 *'Flint scraper'*: not identified.   79 12-9 349
3 *'Flint knife'*: not identified.   79 12-9 348

33 WILLERBY (Marr IV)   33:1-5
Yorkshire E.R.; North Yorkshire   TA 03 76

ROUND BARROW: Diam. 19m, H. 0.9 m; earth.
BB 181-3.

Burials 1-7 were in a central oval grave L. 2.4 m, W. 2.1m, D. 1.5 m; upper fill of earth and lower of lenses of chalk and earth.

Burial 1: child inhumation, crouched on L. with head NNE; at D. 0.6 m on layer of ?wood at base of earth fill.

Burial 2: adult female inhumation, crouched on L. with head E. by S.; at base on N. side.

Burial 3: child inhumation, part-disarticulated; at head of Burial 2.

Burial 4: child inhumation; at feet of Burial 2.

Burial 5: infant inhumation; at back of Burial 2.

Burial 6: adult ?male inhumation, crouched on R. with head WSW. and part-disarticulated; knees near feet of Burial 2.

Burial 7: child inhumation; on legs of Burial 6.

Burial 8: adult male inhumation, crouched on L. with head SE.; in hollow D. 0.5 m cut across S. edge of central grave, bones displaced by settling of fill.

Burial 9: adult female inhumation, crouched on R. with head WNW.; over SE. edge of central grave, bones displaced by settling of fill.

Burial 10: adult cremation deposit; in inverted urn 0.6 m above old surface, NE. of centre.
   'cinerary urn': not preserved.

Grave fill
   'fragment of an earthenware vase': not preserved.

1 *Flint awl*: converging edge retouch on L. and partially on R.; partial inverse invasive retouch bilaterally; broken; grey.
   L. 2.8 cm; W. 1.3 cm; Th. 0.4 cm.   79 12-9 353

2 *Flint end- and side-scraper*: edge retouch on distal at 70 degrees; invasive retouch on R.; platform butt; cortex remnant; mottled pink.
L. 4.0 cm; W. 3.5 cm; Th. 1.1 cm.   79 12-9 350

3 *Flint worked flake*: edge retouch on distal and R. at 65 degrees; partial inverse retouch on L.; broken; grey.
L. 2.1 cm; W. 3.2 cm; Th. 1.2 cm.   79 12-9 351

Not located

4 *'Flint saw'*: not identified.   79 12-9 352

5 *Flint core*: prismatic with multiple blade scars; cortex remnant; mottled grey.
L. 2.8 cm; W. 2.7 cm; Th. 1.7 cm.   79 12-9 353a

34 WILLERBY (Marr II)   34:1-3

Yorkshire E.R.; North Yorkshire   TA 03 76

ROUND BARROW: Diam. 14 m, H. 0.6 m; chalk rubble and earth.
BB 183-4; *GM* 1868, 1:84.

Burial 1: multiple inhumation: adult ?female crouched on R. with head S. facing row of child, adolescent and child all crouched on L. with heads SSW.; in area *c.* 1 m square 0.2 m above old surface, 2.4 m E. of centre; Food Vessel at face of adolescent.

1 *Food Vessel base sherd*: plain.   79 12-9 1531

Burial 2: adult male inhumation, crouched on L. with head NW.; on chalk slab paving at base of central grave Diam 1.5 m, D. 1.2 m, covered by turf below chalk rubble fill; disturbed bones in fill.

Not located.

2 *'Flint knife'*: not identified.   79 12-9 355
3 *'Flint flake'*: not identified.   79 12-9 354

35 WILLERBY (Marr I)   35:1-11

Yorkshire E.R.; North Yorkshire   TA 03 76

ROUND BARROW: Diam. 20 m, H. 1m; earth.
BB 184-5; *GM* 1868, 1:84.

Burial 1: adult inhumation, crouched on R. with head W., at base of central oval grave L. 1.8 m, W. 1.5 m, D. 0.8 m, aligned E.-W., fill of earth capped by 'very stiff clay'; Food Vessel at face and flints behind head.

1 *Food Vessel*: Yorkshire Vase; twisted cord: on internal rim bevel, horizontal lines; on outer rim bevel, short vertical lines; on neck, horizontal lines above row of short diagonal lines; in neck, diagonal lines between single horizontal lines; on body, zone of horizontal lines above split then plain herringbone bordered beneath by row of vertical chevrons above zone of horizontal lines; three surviving of four horizontal perforated lugs spanning neck groove with horizontal lines.
M. 14.2 cm; H. 11.8 cm; B 6.0 cm.   79 12-9 356
BAP no. 133.

2 *Flint side-scraper*: partial edge retouch on distal and R. at 75 degrees; platform butt; cortex remnant; mottled grey.
L. 4.8 cm; W. 2.7 cm; Th. 1.0 cm.   79 12-9 357

3 *Flint plano-convex knife*: on blade: all over invasive flaking; punctiform butt; light grey.
L. 4.8 cm; W. 1.6 cm; Th. 0.5 cm.   79 12-9 358
Clark 1932, no. 2.23.

Burial 1, clay capping or mound material
4-8 *'Flint flakes'*: five; not identified.
79 12-9 362-5 and 1532

Clay capping
'potsherds': not preserved.

Mound material
'several fragments of a vase': not preserved.
9 *'Flint saw'*: not identified.   79 12-9 361

Not located
10 *'Flint scraper'*: not identified.   79 12-9 360
11 *'Flint knife'*: not identified.   79 12-9 359

36 WILLERBY

Yorkshire E.R.; North Yorkshire   TA 03 76

ROUND BARROW: Diam. 18 m, H. 0.9 m; earth and chalk-rubble.
BB 185.

Burial 1: inhumation traces; at base of central oval grave L. 1.7 m, W. 1.4 m, D. 0.9 m, aligned NE.-SW., fill of flints, clay and earth.

37 WILLERBY   37:1

Yorkshire E.R.; North Yorkshire   TA 03 76

ROUND BARROW: Diam. 31 m, H. 1.5 m, reduced by ploughing; earth and chalk.
BB 185.

Burial 1: disturbed inhumation; in ploughsoil 4.5 m S. of centre.

Not located
1 *'Flint flake'*: not identified.   79 12-9 366

38 WILLERBY (Marr V)   38:1-14

Yorkshire E.R.; North Yorkshire   TA 03 76

ROUND BARROW: Diam. 20 m, H. 2.3 m; composition not recorded; opened March 1849 by Lord Londesborough, re-opened by WG.
BB 185-6; *Conyngham* 1849, 106-7.

Burial 1: inhumation traces; 0.5 m above old surface at centre.

Burial 2: adult male inhumation, crouched with head E.; on old surface at centre; vessel behind shoulders.

1 *Food Vessel*: whipped cord: on internal rim bevel, short vertical lines; on ridges, short diagonal lines.
M. 17.8 cm; H. 17.3 cm; B. 8.0 cm.   79 12-9 1969

Mound material
2 *'Pottery fragments'*: not identified.   79 12-9 367
3-8 *'Flint scrapers'*: six; not identified.
79 12-9 368-72 and 1976
9 *'Flint knife'*: not identified.   79 12-9 1975
10-14 *'Flint flakes'*: five; not identified.
79 12-9 1970-74

39 BUTTERWICK   39:1-16

Yorkshire E.R.; North Yorkshire   SE 978 732

ROUND BARROW: Diam. 17 m, H. 0.6 m; earth; 'rude wall of small chalk stones' H. 0.5 m, aligned ESE.-WNW., across old surface S of centre.
BB 186-91.

Burial 1: adult male inhumation, crouched on L. with head NE.; at base of central grave Diam. 3 m, D. 1.7 m, fill of chalk; line of upright chalk slabs along back, upper part of body covered by turf; wooden-sheathed dagger with ?horn handle in R. hand with point to chin, flint and awl on blade, buttons along chest, axe at hips with haft trace L. 0.6 m extending towards heels.

1 *Bronze flat axe*: Type Migdale; slight waisting at hilt; lentoid section with steep edge bevels, corroded (Table 1:24).
   L. 10.2 cm; W. 5.9 cm; Th. 1.1 cm.   79 12-9 383
   BB fig. 38; *ABI* fig. 2; *Schmidt and Burgess* 1981, no. 183.

2 *Bronze dagger*: Gerloff Type Butterwick; flat blade with concave edge bevels with traces of hammer-marks; damaged butt originally of slight trilobate outline with omega hilt line and traces of wooden haft; one rivet in hole and one loose (Table 1:2).
   L. 11.3 cm; W. 5.2 cm; Th. 0.3 cm.
   rivet L. 1.3-1.4 cm; shank Diam. 0.7 cm.
                                             79 12-9 374
   BB fig. 37; *ABI* fig. 279; *Gerloff* 1975, no. 20.

3 *Bronze awl*: Thomas Type 1B; tapered facets at central swelling; ends lacking (Table 1:32).
   L. 5.5 cm; W. 0.3 cm; Th. 0.3 cm.   79 12-9 376
   BB fig. 104; *ABI* fig. 225; *Thomas* 1968, 23.

4 *Jet button*: cut and polished to conical dome bevelled to flat base with central drilled V-perforation; recent damage.
   Diam. 4.3 cm; Th. 1.0 cm.   79 12-9 377

5 *Jet button*: cut and polished to ovate conical dome bevelled to flat base with skewed drilled V-perforation.
   L. 4.0 cm; W. 3.5 cm; Th. 0.9 cm.   79 12-9 378

6 *Jet button*: cut and polished to conical dome bevelled to domed base with central drilled V-perforation recut at one side after initial failure.
   Diam. 4.1 cm; Th. 0.9 cm.   79 12-9 379

7 *Jet button*: cut and polished to conical dome with double bevel to narrowed flat base with off-centre drilled V-perforation.
   Diam. 3.1 cm; Th. 1.0 cm.   79 12-9 380

8 *Jet button*: cut and polished to asymmetric conical dome bevelled to flat base with off-centre drilled V-perforation recut to second V-perforation near one edge.
   Diam. 3.9 cm; Th. 0.8 cm.   79 12-9 381
   BB fig. 105; *ASI* fig. 370.

9 *Stone button*: sandstone; ground and polished to conical dome bevelled to flat base with off-centre drilled V-perforation; incised irregular cross on dome, incised circle on base; recent damage.
   Diam. 3.7 cm; Th. 1.3 cm.   79 12-9 382
   BB fig. 4; *ASI* fig. 369.

10 *Flint knife*: invasive retouch on L.; wear on R.; corticated butt; mottled grey.
   L. 5.9 cm; W. 5.5 cm; Th. 1.4 cm.   79 12-9 375

Grave fill

11 *Peterborough Ware sherd*: rows of bone impressions.
   Manby 1956, fig. 4.1.   79 12-9 373b

12 *Food Vessel sherds*: two; twisted cord: above shoulder, single horizontal line; below, multiple chevron pattern filled with loops.
                                             79 12-9 373

13 *'Flint scraper'*: not identified.   79 12-9 384

Not located

14 *Beaker rim sherd*: incised: on internal rim bevel, short vertical lines; on external surface, incised bar chevron pattern filled with short vertical lines beneath two horizontal lines.   79 12-9 373a

15 *Beaker sherd*: two faint horizontal lines; porous fabric.   79 12-9 373c

16 *Bronze Age sherds*: two; plain.   79 12-9 373d

40 HELPERTHORPE (Grundon I)   40:1-48

Yorkshire E.R.; North Yorkshire   SE 94 72

ROUND BARROW: Diam. 22 m, H. 0.9 m; earth with some chalk near centre.
BB 191.

Burial 1: adult male inhumation, crouched on L. with head N.; in central oval grave L. 1.8 m, W. 1.4 m, D. 0.9 m, aligned N.-S., fill of earth and chalk rubble.

Mound material

1 *Beaker sherd*: twisted cord horizontal lines; weathered.   79 12-9 385

2 *Flint barbed-and-tanged arrowhead fragment*: bifacial invasive retouch; one barb broken and retouched, other barb and point broken; mottled grey.
   L. 1.9 cm; W. 1.5 cm; Th. 0.3 cm.   79 12-9 429a
   Green 1980, no. A48.

3-37 *'Flint flakes'*: thirty-five; not identified.
                                             79 12-9 394-428

38 *Flint core*: two platforms with single flake scars, evidence of previous platforms; cortex remnant; mottled grey.
   L. 4.0 cm; W. 4.4 cm; Th. 3.1 cm.   79 12-9 391

39 *Flint core*: single platform with flake scar, evidence of previous platforms; cortex remnant; dark grey.
   L. 2.9 cm; W. 3.0 cm; Th. 3.2 cm.   79 12-9 393

40 *'Flint core'*: not identified.   79 12-9 392

Not located

41-2 *'Stone rubbers'*: two; not identified.
                                             79 12-9 430 and 1533

43-4 *'Flint scrapers'*: two; not identified.
                                             79 12-9 386 and 389

45-7 *'Flint flakes'*: three; not identified.
                                             79 12-9 388, 390 and 429

48 *'Flint implement'*: not identified.   79 12-9 387

41 HELPERTHORPE (Grundon II)   41:1-4

Yorkshire E.R.; North Yorkshire   SE 94 72

ROUND BARROW: Diam. 21 m, H. 0.9 m; earth and some chalk.
BB 191-2.

Burial 1: double inhumation: child in front of adult, both crouched on R. with head S.; 0.7 m above old surface at centre; arrowhead at face of adult.

1 *Flint barbed-and-tanged arrowhead*: all over bifacial invasive retouch; mottled grey.
   L. 3.3 cm; W. 2.2 cm; Th. 0.6 cm.   79 12-9 431
   Green 1980, no. 92.

Burial 2: adult male inhumation, crouched on L. with head N.; at base of irregular central grave Diam. 1.2 m, D. 0.6 m, chalk fill with two child bones; knife at face, antlers at head and feet.

2 *Flint knife*: on snapped flake; invasive retouch on distal and L.; platform butt; cortex remnant; grey.
   L. 5.0 cm; W. 2.5 cm; Th. 0.7 cm.   79 12-9 432

3 *Antler tine*: red deer brow tine, sliced at butt, recent damage at tip.
   L. 16.5 cm; max. Diam. 2.9 cm.   79 12-9 433

4 *Antler tine*: red deer brow tine, tip worn, butt cut.
   L. 20.0 cm; max. Diam. 3.1 cm.   79 12-9 434

42 WEAVERTHORPE (Ford)   42:1-34

Yorkshire E.R., North Yorkshire   SE 979 689

ROUND BARROW: Diam. 18 m, H. 1.2 m; earth and some chalk.
BB 192-3.

Burial 1: disarticulated bones: cranial and some post-
cranial fragments of adolescent and skull of adult male;
on old surface, 1.5 m SSW. of centre; hammerstone near
male skull.
1 'Hammerstone': not identified.   79 12-9 438

Burial 2: adult male inhumation, crouched on L. with
head E.; on old surface at centre; Beaker behind head.
2 Beaker: tooth-comb stamped: beneath rim, two bands of
   lattice separated by three horizontal lines; beneath
   neck cordon, band of lattice above four horizontal
   lines; on belly, zone of short diagonal lines bounded
   by chevrons with four horizontal lines above and
   three below; distorted.
   M. 13.5-14.3 cm; H. 19.7 cm; B. 8.4 cm.
   BAP no. 155; Clarke no. 1403.   79 12-9 435

Burial 3: 'numerous portions of human bones'; above
Burial 2 at centre.

Feature A: deposit of 'soft black mould' L. 3.6 m, W. 1.2
m, Th. 0.5-0.15 m, aligned SE.-NW.; near centre.
   'Vessel of plain dark-coloured pottery': not
   preserved (some sherds perhaps in 4-16 below).
3 'Flint scraper': not identified.   79 12-9 436

Feature A or mound material
4 Neolithic Bowl rim sherd: porous fabric.
                                               79 12-9 1534
5 Neolithic Bowl sherds: seven, including rim; flint
   temper.   79 12-9 1534a
6 Neolithic Bowl rim sherd: flint temper.
                                               79 12-9 1535
7 Neolithic Bowl rim sherds: two; flint and quartz
   temper.   79 12-9 1535a
8-9 Neolithic Bowl rim sherds: two; quartz temper.
                                               79 12-9 1535b and c
10 Neolithic Bowl rim sherd: flint temper; weathered.
                                               79 12-9 1535d
11 Neolithic Bowl sherds: eight, including two rims from
    different vessels; porous fabric.   79 12-9 1535e
12-13 Neolithic Bowl sherds: two; flint temper.
                                               79 12-9 1535f and g
14 Neolithic Bowl sherds: three; flint temper.
                                               79 12-9 1535h
15 Neolithic Bowl sherd: imperforate lug.
                                               79 12-9 1535i
16 Neolithic Bowl sherds: eight, including four rims;
    diagonal fingertipped rilling on top of rim; porous
    fabric.
    M. c. 28.5 cm; H. c. 14.0 cm.   79 12-9 1545a
    NPY no. 13.
17-23 'Flint flakes': seven; not identified.
                                               79 12-9 1537- 1543
24 'Animal tooth': not identified.   79 12-9 1544

Mound material
25 Beaker base sherd: tooth comb-stamped vertical
    chevrons.
    B. 7.0 cm.   79 12-9 1545
    Clarke no. 1404.
26 Beaker rim sherd: tooth comb-stamped: on internal
    bevel, filled triangles; externally, zone of
    horizontal lines above triangle defined by pairs of
    lines and filled with horizontal lines.
                                               79 12-9 1545b
27 Bronze Age base sherd   79 12-9 15351
28 Early Iron Age sherds: two, including base; quartz-
    tempered.   79 12-9 1534a

29 Early Iron Age rim sherd: incised diagonal lines on
    internal rim bevel; calcareous and rock temper.
                                               79 12-9 1535j
30 Early Iron Age sherd: calcareous temper.
                                               79 12-9 1536a
31 Early Iron Age sherds: three: broad zone of round
    stabs; metamorphic rock temper.   79 12-9 15351
32 Early Iron Age base sherd: vesicular, with some rock
    temper.   79 12-9 1535m
33 'Sherd': not identified.   79 12-9 1536
34 'Flint scraper': not identified.   79 12-9 437

43 WEAVERTHORPE (Anderson)   43:1-47

Yorkshire E.R.; North Yorkshire   SE 987 686

ROUND BARROW: Diam. 16 m, H.1.2 m, reduced by ploughing;
earth with some chalk.
BB 193-7.

Burial 1: adult ?male inhumation, crouched on R. with
head W.; 0.3 m above old surface, 4.5 m S. of centre;
Food Vessel at knees.
1 Food Vessel: on internal and external rim bevels and
   neck grooves, whipped cord herringbone above row of
   twisted cord horseshoes; on lower body, band of
   irregularly placed twisted cord horseshoes; two of
   four feet survive; half surface eroded.
   M. 15.2 cm; H. 13.8 cm.   79 12-9 440
   BB fig. 74; BAP no. 113; Manby 1969, fig. 3.2.

Burial 2: child inhumation; above old surface, 4.5 m
ESE. of centre.

Burial 3: adult male inhumation, crouched on L. with
head E.; 0.8 m above old surface, 1.8 m SW. of centre;
point and knife behind head, flake at knees.
2 Flint pointed implement: converging bilateral edge
   retouch and all over bifacial invasive retouch;
   broken; patinated.
   L. 5.2 cm; W. 4.2 cm; Th. 0.9 cm.   79 12-9 443
3 Flint knife: edge retouch on R. at 65 degrees,
   invasive retouch on L; platform butt; cortex remnant;
   light grey.
   L. 6.2 cm; W. 4.9 cm; Th. 1.2 cm.   79 12-9 442
   BB fig. 20.
4 'Flint flake': not identified.   79 12-9 444

Burial 4: child inhumation; 0.5 m above old surface, 2.7
m WSW. of centre.

Burial 5: adult female inhumation, crouched on R. with
head E.; on old surface, 2.7 m E. of centre; scraper
behind head.
5 'Flint scraper': not identified.   79 12-9 445

Burial 6: adult inhumation, crouched on L. with head W.;
0.6 m above old surface, 1.5 m ESE. of centre; Food
Vessel and point at face.
6 Food Vessel: twisted cord; on internal rim bevel, two
   rows of short diagonal lines split by one horizontal
   line; on outer rim bevel and both ridges, short
   vertical lines.
   M. 14.2 cm; H. 10.6 cm; B. 7.9 cm.   79 12-9 441
   BAP no. 112.
7 Flint knife: on blade; converging bifacial edge
   retouch; point broken; punctiform butt; mottled
   grey.
   L. 5.5 cm; W. 1.8 cm; Th. 0.6 cm.   79 12-9 478

Burial 7: adult male inhumation, crouched on L. with
head E.; 0.6 m above old surface, 2.7 m ENE. of centre.

Burial 8: child inhumation, crouched on L.; 0.3 m above
old surface, 4.5 m ENE. of centre.

Burial 9: child inhumation; 0.3 m above old surface, 5.4 m NNE. of centre.

Burial 10: child inhumation, crouched on R.; 0.6 m above old surface, 2.7 m NW. of centre.

Burial 11: child inhumation, crouched on R. with head W.; 0.6 m above old surface, 3.6 m NE. of centre.

Burial 12: adult male inhumation, part-disarticulated; at base of central oval grave L. 2.7 m, W. 2 m, D. 1.5 m, aligned E.–W.; fill of chalk rubble; rubble upcast on old surface at N.; knife at knees, flake near head.

8   *Flint knife*: invasive retouch on R., invasive and edge retouch on distal, wear on L.; punctiform butt; cortex remnant; grey.
    L. 9.4 cm; W. 4.3 cm; Th. 0.7 cm.   79 12–9 446
    BB fig. 106.

9   *'Flint flake'*: not identified.   79 12–9 447

Mound material

10 *Beaker sherd*: tooth-comb stamped chevrons; porous fabric.   79 12–9 468a

11 *Food Vessel*: (on old surface 5.7 m SW. of centre) Yorkshire Vase; on internal rim bevel, row of jabbed impressions enclosed by pairs of twisted cord lines; on outer rim bevel, short vertical twisted cord lines; on neck, single horizontal twisted cord line above row of jabbed impressions, with similar row enclosed by triple horizontal twisted cord lines; below shoulder, three horizontal twisted cord lines; four surviving of five plain imperforate lugs spanning shoulder groove.
    M. 13.3 cm; H. 11.8 cm; B. 6.3 cm.   79 12–9 439
    BAP no. 114.

12 *Bronze Age sherds*: two; weathered.   79 12–9 468

13 *Clay spindle-whorl fragment*: half remaining; plain; well-smoothed.
    Diam. 4.6 cm; Th. 3.1 cm.   79 12–9 474

14 *Flint leaf arrowhead*: all over bifacial invasive retouch; point broken; patinated.
    L. 5.3 cm; W. 1.9 cm; Th. 0.5 cm.   79 12–9 476
    Green 1980, no. A45.

15–18 *'Flint scrapers'*: four; not identified.
    79 12–9 480–2, 1578

19 *Flint worked blade*: edge retouch on R. and partially on L.; platform butt; mottled grey.
    L. 5.4 cm; W. 1.7 cm; Th. 0.5 cm.   79 12–9 477

20 *'Flint implement'*: not identified.   79 12–9 479

21–41 *'Flint flakes'*: twenty-one; not identified.
    79 12–9 448–67 and 448a

Not located

42 *'Bronze ring fragment'*: not identified. 79 12–9 475

43–7 *'Sandstone fragments'*: not identified.
    79 12–9 469–73

44   WEAVERTHORPE (Smith III)   44:1–7

Yorkshire E.R.; North Yorkshire   SE 995 685

ROUND BARROW: Diam. 13 m, H. 0.5 m, reduced by ploughing; earth and chalk rubble; opened 28 October 1867.
BB 197–9.

Burial 1: adult inhumation, crouched on L. with head NNE.; on old surface, 3.6 m ENE. of centre; flints and pin at knees.

1   *Flint pointed implement*: bilateral edge retouch converging at proximal; patinated.
    L. 4.4 cm; W. 2.0 cm; Th. 0.6 cm.   79 12–9 484

2   *Flint end- and side-scraper*: edge retouch on distal and R. at 60 degrees; platform butt; cortex remnant; mottled grey.
    L. 2.6 cm; W. 4.6 cm; Th. 1.0 cm.   79 12–9 483

3   *Bone pin*: on caprovine longbone splinter; butt damaged; eroded.
    L. 7.7 cm; W. 0.7 cm; Th. 0.2 cm.   79 12–9 485

Burial 2: adult female inhumation, crouched on R. with head E.; in slight central hollow; wearing necklace, vessel behind head.

    'food vessel': not preserved.

4   *Jet necklace*: one hundred and fifteen disc beads cut and polished with drilled perforations; sub-triangular pendant cut and polished with bevelled edges and drilled hourglass perforation.
    bead Diam. 0.6–0.9 cm; Th. 0.2–0.4 cm.
    pendant L. 1.9 cm; W. 2.1 cm; Th. 0.7 cm.
    BB fig. 49.   79 12–9 486

Burial 3: adult inhumation, crouched on L. with head E.; partly-destroyed in ploughsoil, E. of centre; knife at knees.

5   *Flint plano-convex knife*: near-complete edge retouch; cortex remnant; mottled grey.
    L. 5.8 cm; W. 2.0 cm; Th. 0.9 cm.   79 12–9 487
    BB fig. 107; *ASI* fig. 241; *Clarke* 1932, no. 5.10.

Burial 4: adult male inhumation, crouched on R. with head W., with nearby adult mandible fragment; on old surface between two pits to N. and S. Diam. 0.9 m, D. 0.5 m, 1.5 m W. of centre.

Mound material

6   *Neolithic Bowl sherds*: seven, representing minimum two vessels.   79 12–9 488a

7   *'Flint chip'*: not identified.   79 12–9 488

45   WEAVERTHORPE (Smith I)   45:1–4

Yorkshire E.R.; North Yorkshire.   TA 00 68

ROUND BARROW: Diam. 16 m, H. 0.6 m; earth and some chalk.
BB 199–200.

Burial 1: child inhumation; on old surface, 3.6 m S of centre.

Burial 2: infant inhumation; in oval hollow L. 0.5 m, W. 0.3 m, D. 0.2 m, 2.7 m SW. of centre; Food Vessel on side 0.3 m to NW.

1   *Food Vessel*: Yorkshire Vase; twisted cord: on internal rim bevel, herringbone; on outer rim bevel, short vertical lines; on neck and shoulder groove, herringbone; three of four imperforate lugs surviving.
    M. 12.8 cm; H. 10.3 cm; B. 5.8 cm.   79 12–9 489
    BAP no. 38.

Burial 3: adult inhumation; at base of central oval grave L. 2.3 m, W. 1.7 m, D. 0.5 m, aligned N.–S.

2   *Food Vessel*: fine twisted cord: on internal rim bevel, herringbone; on outer rim bevel and both ridges, short vertical and diagonal lines.
    M. 15.4 cm; H. 13.4 cm; B. 7.1 cm.   79 12–9 490
    BAP no. 37.

Mound material

3   *'Flint scraper'*: not identified.   79 12–9 491

4   *Antler pick*: red deer shed antler with bez tine; butt damaged, tine eroded.
    Beam L. 21.8 cm; max. Diam. 3.3 cm; tine L. 16.9 cm.
    79 12–9 1546

46 WEAVERTHORPE (Smith II) 46:1-18

Yorkshire E.R.; North Yorkshire TA 00 68

ROUND BARROW: Diam. 21 m, H. 1.2 m; earth and chalk; opened 5 October 1866.
BB 200-1.

Burial 1: adult male inhumation, crouched on R. with head NE.; on old surface 2.7 m SE. of centre; flake at face.
   Flint flake: probably one of nos 9-17 below.

Burial 2: cranial fragment: 2.7 m S. of centre.
   Flint flake: probably one of nos 9-17 below.

Burial 3: infant inhumation; 0.5 m above old surface, 3.6 m W. by S. of centre.

Burial 4: child inhumation; 0.5 m above old surface, 3.6 m SW. of centre.

Burial 5: adult female inhumation, crouched on R.; 0.5 m above old surface S. of centre; hammerstone and flint behind head.
1 *Hammerstone*: quartzite; both ends abraded, on pebble.
   L. 5.9 cm; W. 4.0 cm; Th. 3.0 cm. 79 12-9 506
   BB fig. 15.
   Flint flake: probably one of nos 9-17 below.

Burial 6: adult inhumation; on old surface at centre but disturbed with some bones in grave fill.

Burial 7: adult male inhumation, crouched on R. with head W.; at base of central oval grave L. 2 m, W. 1.3 m, D. 0.6 m, aligned E.-W.; flint behind head.
2 *Flint worked flake*: edge retouch on R.; punctiform butt; cortex remnant; patinated.
   L. 5.8 cm; W. 2.4 cm; Th. 1.0 cm. 79 12-9 492

Burial 8: adult male inhumation, crouched; 0.3 m above old surface, 6.3 m NE. of centre.

Mound material: probably including flints from Burials 1, 2 and 5.
3 *Food Vessel*: (0.5 m above old surface, 4.5 m W. by S. of centre) plain.
   M. 15.5 cm; H. 13.9 cm; B. 7.5 cm. 79 12-9 1547
   BAP no. 176.
4 'Part of plain vase': (on old surface, below no. 3) not identified. 79 12-9 507
5-6 'Flint scrapers': two; not identified.
   79 12-9 493-4
7 'Flint implement': not identified. 79 12-9 495
8 *Flint utilised flake*: worn bilaterally; dihedral butt; mottled grey.
   L. 4.7 cm; W. 2.5 cm; Th. 0.5 cm. 79 12-9 496
9-14 'Flint flakes': six; not identified.
   79 12-9 497-502
15-17 'Flint chips': three; not identified.
   79 12-9 503-5
18 *Antler fragment*: beam fragment, broken.
   L. 16.5 cm; W. 3.5 cm; Th. 1.1 cm. 79 12-9 1548

47 WEAVERTHORPE (Smith IV; Octon Wold 1)

47:1-117

Yorkshire E.R.; North Humberside TA 004 691

ROUND BARROW: Diam. 24 m, H. 1 m, (Diam. 21 m, H. 0.8 m: 1966), reduced by ploughing; earth and chalk rubble (core of chalk rubble Diam. 6 m, H. 0.5 m with earth capping: 1966); ditch W. 1 m, D. 0.6 m (W. 2.1 m, D. 1.2 m: 1966); opened 29 October 1867, re-excavated by T.C.M. Brewster 1966-8.
BB 201-3; *Exc AR* 1966 and 1968.

Burials 1-5 and Features A-C were excavated 1966-8; Greenwell had mistaken the inner mound for natural chalk.

Burial 1: disturbed adult inhumation; in central shaft grave Diam. 1.8 m.

Burial 2: multiple inhumation; crouched adult with two separate crania at feet and one at chest, with other bones of these nearby; at base of central grave Diam. 1.2 m in oval setting of chalk blocks.

Burial 3: adolescent inhumation, crouched; in shallow grave near centre.

Burial 4: double infant inhumation; in grave cut into chalk core.
1 *Beaker sherds*: three; two with incised lines.
   P1982 1-1 2

Burial 5: adolescent inhumation, crouched; on old surface S. of centre.

Feature A: hearth, on old surface outside inner mound.
2 *Beaker sherds*: thirty-nine including rim; incised: beneath rim and at base of neck, groups of four horizontal lines; on neck and below, lattice-filled hexagons in reserved spaces. P1982 1-1 1

Feature B: double post circle Diam. 20 m.

Feature C: stake circle Diam. 10 m.

Mound material (1867)
3 *Neolithic Bowl rim sherd*: flint-tempered sandy fabric. 79 12-9 1549e
   NPY no. 12.
4 *Early Iron Age sherds*: five including three rims; fingertip impressions on rim and applied shoulder cordon; vesicular fabric. 79 12-9 1549
5 *Early Iron Age rim sherd*: vesicular fabric.
   79 12-9 1549a
6 *Early Iron Age rim sherd*: vesicular fabric.
   79 12-9 1549b
7 *Early Iron Age rim sherd*: angular basalt temper.
   79 12-9 1549f
8 *Early Iron Age base sherds*: two; vesicular fabric.
   79 12-9 1549d
9 *Romano-British rim sherd*: Huntcliff ware; vesicular fabric. 79 12-9 1549g
10 *Romano-British sherd*: Huntcliff ware; vesicular fabric. 79 12-9 1549c
11 'Pierced lug of vessel': not identified.
   79 12-9 1550
12 *Flint horseshoe scraper*: edge retouch on proximal and bilateral at 65 degrees; cortex remnant; grey.
   L. 2.1 cm; W. 2.0 cm; Th. 0.7 cm. 79 12-9 510
13 *Flint horseshoe scraper*: edge retouch on distal and bilateral at 70 degrees; platform butt; patinated.
   L. 3.1 cm; W. 3.1 cm; Th. 1.0 cm. 79 12-9 514
14 *Flint end- and side-scraper*: edge retouch on distal and R. at 60 degrees; platform butt; cortex remnant; patinated.
   L. 2.3 cm; W. 2.0 cm; Th. 0.7 cm. 79 12-9 512
15 *Flint end- and side-scraper*: edge retouch on distal and R. at 70 degrees; platform butt; cortex remnant; patinated.
   L. 2.6 cm; W. 2.7 cm; Th. 0.9 cm. 79 12-9 517
16 *Flint end- and side-scraper*: edge retouch on distal and L. at 55 degrees; corticated butt; patinated.
   L. 2.3 cm; W. 3.1 cm; Th. 0.8 cm. 79 12-9 518
17 *Flint end-scraper*: edge retouch on distal at 60 degrees; dihedral butt; patinated.
   L. 2.4 cm; W. 1.8 cm; Th. 0.5 cm. 79 12-9 511
18 *Flint side-scraper*: edge retouch on L. at 65 degrees; platform butt; cortex remnant; patinated.
   L. 3.4 cm; W. 3.0 cm; Th. 1.4 cm. 79 12-9 515

19–21 *'Flint scrapers'*: three, not identified.
                                    79 12–9 508, 519–520
22 *Flint serrated flake*: edge retouch on L. at eight
   teeth per cm; cortex remnant; grey.
   L. 3.5 cm; W. 1.9 cm. Th. 0.8 cm.   79 12–9 521
23 *Flint worked flake*: partial edge retouch on R.;
   patinated.
   L. 2.5 cm; W. 2.9 cm; Th. 0.9 cm.   79 12–9 509
24 *Flint worked flake*: invasive retouch on distal and
   R.; cortex remnant; broken; beige.
   L. 2.0 cm; W. 1.8 cm; Th. 0.5 cm.   79 12–9 513
25 *Flint worked flake*: edge retouch on bilateral at 50
   degrees; corticated butt; cortex remnant; grey.
   L. 2.2 cm; W. 2.1 cm; Th. 0.6 cm.   79 12–9 516
26–31 *'Flint implements'*: six; not identified.
                                        79 12–9 522–27

Flint flakes

	Btt	Ctx	Col.	L.	W.	Th.	79 12–9
32	Pl.		M. Gr.	4.2	2.9	0.8	1561
33	Pl.	x	M. Gr.	4.0	1.8	0.5	1562
34	Dh.		M. Gr.	2.1	2.7	0.6	1563
35	Pl.		Gr.	3.4	4.0	1.1	1565
36	Pl.		Bt	4.0	3.3	1.4	1566
37	Bkn		Bt	2.7	1.6	0.7	1557
38	Pl.	x	Gr.	6.0	2.4	0.7	1559
39	Pl.		Gr.	4.6	3.0	1.2	1560

40 *Flint core*: single platform with irregular flake
   scars; evidence of previous platform; cortex
   remnant; mottled grey.
   L. 4.8 cm; W. 3.6 cm; Th. 4.8 cm.   79 12–9 1553
41 *Flint core*: single platform with flake scars;
   evidence of previous platform; cortex remnant;
   mottled grey.
   L. 4.6 cm; W. 3.7 cm; Th. 3.6 cm.   79 12–9 1554
42 *Flint core*: one platform with two flake scars,
   opposed platform with irregular flake scars;
   evidence of previous platform; cortex remnant;
   mottled grey.
   L. 4.2 cm; W. 3.0 cm. Th. 2.9 cm.   79 12–9 1555
43 *Flint core*: single platform with flake scar; evidence
   of previous platforms; cortex remnant; patinated.
   L. 2.7 cm; W. 2.7 cm; Th. 3.0 cm.   79 12–9 1556
44 *Flint core*: single platform with parallel blade
   scars; flake scars on reverse; evidence of previous
   platforms; cortex remnant; mottled grey.
   L. 3.2 cm; W. 3.4 cm; Th. 2.7 cm.   79 12–9 1557
45 *Flint core*: single platform with parallel blade
   scars; patinated.
   L. 3.2 cm; W. 1.6 cm; Th. 2.5 cm.   79 12–9 1558
46 *Flint core*: discoidal with irregular multidirectional flake scars; patinated.
   L. 4.2 cm; W. 3.2 cm; Th. 1.5 cm.   79 12–9 1564

Mound material (1966–8)
47 *Beaker sherds*: six including rim; incised: below rim,
   horizontal lines above lattice.   P1982 1–1 3
48 *Beaker sherd*: twisted cord horizontal lines.
                                        P1982 1–1 4
49 *Beaker sherd*: rows of arcuate impressions.
                                        P1982 1–1 5
50 *Beaker rim sherd*: plain.   P1982 1–1 6
51 *Beaker sherd*: ?decorated.   P1982 1–1 7c
52 *Bronze Age sherds*: two; plain.   P1982 1–1 7a–b
53 *Plain sherds*: two.   P1982 1–1 10a–b
54 *Flint horseshoe scraper*: edge retouch on distal and
   bilateral at 60 degrees; cortex remnant; patinated.
   L. 4.1 cm; W. 3.9 cm; Th. 1.3 cm.   P1982 1–1 18
55 *Flint end- and side-scraper*: edge retouch on distal
   and L. at 60 degrees; faceted butt; mottled grey.
   L. 5.5 cm; W. 2.6 cm; Th. 0.8 cm.   P1982 1–1 16

56 *Flint end-scraper*: edge retouch on distal at 70
   degrees; platform butt; cortex remnant; mottled
   grey.
   L. 3.2 cm; W. 2.2 cm; Th. 1.0 cm.   P1982 1–1 17
57 *Flint end-scraper*: edge retouch on distal; faceted
   butt; burnt.
   L. 2.9 cm; W. 2.0 cm; Th. 0.5 cm.   P1982 1–1 22
58 *Flint scraper fragment*: edge retouch at 80 degrees;
   broken; mottled grey.
   L. 3.1 cm; W. 1.7 cm; Th. 1.0 cm.   P1982 1–1 19
59 *Flint knife*: edge retouch on distal and L. at 60
   degrees; cortex remnant; snapped; patinated.
   L. 4.6 cm; W. 2.3 cm; Th. 0.8 cm.   P1982 1–1 20
60 *Flint worked flake*: edge retouch on distal at 60
   degrees; mottled grey.
   L. 2.8 cm; W. 4.1 cm; Th. 1.1 cm.   P1982 1–1 21
61 *Flint worked flake*: partial edge retouch; mottled
   grey.
   L. 2.5 cm; W. 2.4 cm; Th. 0.4 cm.   P1982 1–1 23
62 *Flint utilised flake*: wear on L.; corticated butt;
   mottled grey.
   L. 3.7 cm; W. 3.5 cm; Th. 0.9 cm.   P1982 1–1 24
63 *Flint utilised blade*: bilateral wear; cortex
   remnant; patinated.
   L. 5.4 cm; W. 1.1 cm; Th. 0.5 cm.   P1982 1–1 25

Flint blades

	Btt	Ctx	Col.	L.	W.	Th.	P1982 1–1
64	Fc.	x	M. Gr.	7.4	2.2	0.9	35
65		x	M. Gr.	6.5	0.9	0.9	36
66			M. Gr.	4.8	1.2	0.4	37
67	Sn.		M. Gr.	2.7	1.4	0.4	38
68			Pat.	4.4	1.2	0.5	39
69	Sn.		Pat.	2.9	1.2	0.4	40
70	Pl.		M. Gr.	3.1	1.4	0.5	41
71	Sn.	x	Pat.	3.4	1.2	0.6	42
72		x	M. Gr.	3.2	1.3	0.4	43
73		x	Pat.	3.0	1.5	0.3	44
74	Pl.		M. Gr.	3.8	1.4	0.5	45
75			Pat.	3.3	1.0	0.3	46
76	Pl.		M. Gr.	3.7	1.1	0.4	47
77	Sn.		M. Gr.	3.5	1.4	0.4	48

Flint flakes

	Btt	Ctx	Col.	L.	W.	Th.	P1982 1–1
78		x	Bt	4.8	2.9	1.0	49
79		x	M. Gr.	4.3	2.7	0.9	50
80			M. Gr.	3.9	1.4	0.3	51
81	Pl.		M. Gr.	1.4	1.5	0.3	52
82	Pl.		Pat.	4.2	2.8	1.1	53
83		x	M. Gr.	4.3	2.1	0.7	54
84			Bge	2.4	1.3	0.2	55
85	Pl.	x	Br.	3.3	3.0	0.6	56
86		x	M. Gr.	4.9	2.2	1.5	57
87		x	M. Gr.	3.9	3.1	1.4	58
88	Sn.	x	Pat.	3.2	2.4	0.6	59
89		x	Bt	3.2	3.2	1.1	60
90			Pat.	3.0	2.8	0.8	61
91	Sn.		M. Gr.	2.9	1.3	0.4	62
92			M. Gr.	2.6	1.3	0.5	63
93		x	Pat.	3.3	2.5	0.4	64
94			M. Gr.	2.5	1.3	0.3	65

95 *Flint core and hammerstone*: two opposed platforms
   with irregular flake scars; evidence of previous
   platforms; edges abraded; patinated.
   L. 4.8 cm; W. 4.3 cm; Th. 3.9 cm.   P1982 1–1 66
96 *Flint core*: discoidal; one platform with flake scars;
   mottled grey to patinated.
   L. 4.2 cm; W. 3.1 cm; Th. 1.7 cm.   P1982 1–1 67

97 *Flint core*: cortical platform with irregular flake scars; patinated.
L. 4.1 cm; W. 2.5 cm; Th. 2.8 cm.   P1982 1-1 68

Old surface (1966-1968)

98 *Flint microlithic rod*: bilateral edge retouch converging on each end; mottled grey.
L. 2.9 cm; W. 0.2 cm; Th. 0.3 cm.   P1982 1-1 12

99 *Flint disc scraper*: all round edge and invasive retouch; cortex remnant; dark grey.
L. 2.5 cm; W. 2.5 cm; Th. 0.9 cm.   P1982 1-1 13

100 *Flint utilised flake*: wear on distal and L.; dark grey.
L. 2.3 cm; W. 3.5 cm; Th. 0.5 cm.   P1982 1-1 14

101 *Flint utilised blade*: wear on L.; cortex remnant; mottled grey.
L. 3.5 cm; W. 1.2 cm; Th. 0.5 cm.   P1982 1-1 15

Flint blades

Btt	Ctx	Col.	L.	W.	Th.	P1982 1-1
102		M. Gr.	5.0	1.5	0.6	28
103		M. Gr.	4.6	1.7	0.6	29
104	x	M. Gr.	2.9	0.9	0.3	30
105		M. Gr.	3.3	1.0	0.4	31

Flint flakes

Btt	Ctx	Col.	L.	W.	Th.	P1982 1-1
106 Sn.	x	M. Gr.	2.8	1.0	0.5	32
107	x	M. Gr.	2.3	1.5	0.6	33
108 (Thm.)		Bt	1.7	2.5	0.7	34

Ditch fill (1867)

109 *Antler pick*: shed red-deer antler; brow and bez tines and beam broken.
L. (beam) 36 cm; (tine) 18.3 cm; W. (beam) 5.7 cm.
79 12-9 1551

110 *Antler rake*: red-deer antler; beam broken; tines abraded at tips.
L. 41.8 cm; W. (beam) 5.7 cm.   79 12-9 2095

Ditch fill (1966-8)

111 *Beaker rim sherds*: two; plain.   P1982 1-1 8
112 *Beaker sherds*: three; plain.   P1982 1-1 9
113 *Plain sherds*: two.   P1982 1-1 11
114 *Flint horseshoe scraper*: edge retouch on distal and bilateral at 60 degrees; platform butt; mottled grey.
L. 2.1 cm; W. 2.0 cm; Th. 0.4 cm.   P1982 1-1 26

115 *Flint horseshoe scraper*: edge retouch on distal and bilateral at 80 degrees; mottled grey.
L. 3.3 cm; W. 3.0 cm; Th. 1.2 cm.   P1982 1-1 27

116 *Flint utilised flake*: wear on L.; corticated butt; broken; mottled grey.
L. 3.1 cm; W. 0.6 cm; Th. 3.1 cm.   P1982 1-1 69

Not located (1867)

117 *Stone pebble*   79 12-9 1552

48 LANGTOFT (Lamplough)

Yorkshire E.R., North Humberside   TA 00 68

ROUND BARROW: Diam. 21 m, H. 0.5 m; earth; previously opened.
BB 204-5.

Burial 1: double inhumation; adult male and adolescent, disturbed in previous opening; in slight hollow with much charcoal, 2.4 m SSE. of centre.
'*some fragments of a drinking-cup*': not preserved.

Burial 2: few disarticulated bones; in pit Diam. 0.4 m, D. 0.3 m, fill of burnt earth and charcoal, below Burial 1.

Burial 3: disturbed leg bones of three adults; 0.6 m NW. of Burial 1.

Features A-C: three pits Diam. 0.6-0.7 m, D. 0.6 m, fills of chalk rubble with charcoal, beneath deposit of burnt earth and charcoal; A. 3.6 m ESE. of centre, B. 0.9 m E. of A, C. 0.9 m ESE. of A.

Feature D: pit L. 2.3 m, W. 0.6 m, D. 0.6 m, aligned NE-SW., fill of chalk, burnt earth and charcoal; 4.5 m E. of centre and 1.2 m N. of Feature B.
'*fragment of a vase*': not preserved.

Feature E: pit L. 1.4 m, W. 1 m, D. 0.9 m, aligned NNE-SSW., fill as D., 1.8 m SSW. of centre.

49 HELPERTHORPE (Esh II)   49: 1-9

Yorkshire E.R.; North Yorkshire   SE 959 689

LONG BARROW: excavated as round barrow Diam. 16 m, H. 0.5 m, reduced by ploughing; earth and chalk; opened 1 November 1866 (supplementary ms. record by R. Mortimer), re-opened 1868 by J.R. and R. Mortimer (ms. record); ditch Diam. 19.5 m, W. 0.9 m (Moritmer).
BB 205-8; *Hicks* 1969.

Burial 1: crematorium deposit; disarticulated bones burnt *in situ*; in hollow 1 m square (Diam. 1.4 m, D. 0.4 m: RM) in burnt flint and chalk matrix, burning extending 2 m to WNW. on old surface; 5.4 m ESE. of centre.

Burial 2: adult male inhumation, crouched on L. with head NW.; on old surface, 3.9 m ESE. of centre: adolescent femur near head; bone pin and quartz pebble behind head.
'*quartz pebble*': not preserved.
'*bone pin*': not preserved.

Burial 3: three skulls with some post-cranial; adolescent with some post-cranial, adult female and adult (all children: RM); on old surface 2.2 m ESE. of centre.

Burial 4: child inhumation, 'partly disturbed'; on old surface 2.1 m ESE. of centre.

Burial 5: '*few calcined bones*'; in oval hollow L. 1 m, W. 0.8 m, D. 0.5 m, fill of burnt earth and charcoal; below Burial 3.

Burial 6: adult male inhumation, crouched on L. with head E. (SE.: RM); on old surface, 1.8 m WNW. of centre; dagger in R. hand with point to chin.
1 Bronze dagger and bone pommel
Dagger: Gerloff Type Masterton; flat blade with concave edges and hollowed edge bevels; heeled butt with central double-notch and W-shaped hilt line; two rivets in holes and three separate (Table 1:3).
L. 10.5 cm; W. 5.1 cm; Th. 0.2 cm.
Rivet L. 0.8-1.0 cm; shank Diam. 0.8-0.9 cm.
79 12-9 528
Pommel: Hardaker Group 1; cut and polished from longbone fragment; elongated oval cap with sub-rectangular socket; two opposed pairs of small perforations.
L. 4.8 cm; W. 1.8 cm; Th. 1.4 cm; socket D. 0.9 cm.
79 12-9 528
BB figs 108-9; *AB1* figs 280-1; *Gerloff* 1975, no. 79; *Hardaker* 1974, no. 3.

Burial 7: (excavated Mortimer) cremation deposit; in pit Diam. 0.8 m, D. 0.5 m, NNE. of Burial 1.

Feature A: probable post-bedding facade trench L. 12.5 m, W. 1.5 m, D. 1.4 m, aligned NNE.-SSW., at E. side of mound; central pit L. 2 m, W. 1.8 m, D. 1.5 (with vessel); trench fill of loose stones, earth and charcoal; pit fill of burnt earth and charcoal.

2 *Neolithic Bowl*: restored; flint temper.
Diam. 12.8 cm; H. 8.3 cm;   HM 119.42
NPY no. 14.1; *Hicks* 1969, fig. 2.1.

3 *Neolithic Bowl sherds*: two, including rim; flint and shell temper.   HM 120.42
NPY no. 14.4; *Hicks* 1969, fig. 2.2.

4 *Neolithic Bowl sherds*: eleven, including rim; diagonal fine fingertip fluting on internal rim; flint temper.   HM 115.42
NPY no. 14.3; *Hicks* 1969 fig. 2.3.

5 *Neolithic Bowl sherd*: flint temper.   HM 115.42

6 *Neolithic Bowl sherds*: three, including rim; corky fabric.   HM 114.42
NPY no. 14; *Hicks* 1969, fig. 2.4.

7 *Neolithic Bowl sherds*: three, including rim; gritted fabric.   HM 116.42
NPY no. 14; *Hicks* 1969, fig. 2.5.

8 *Neolithic Bowl rim sherd*: gritted fabric.   HM 116.42
NPY no. 14; *Hicks* 1969, fig. 2.6.

9 *Neolithic Bowl sherds*: twenty-five, representing minimum three vessels; flint temper.   HM No number.

50   COWLAM (Cowlam IV: Cottam B)   50:1-79

Yorkshire E.R.; North Humberside   SE 984 667

SQUARE-DITCHED BARROW: Diam. 6.5 m, H. 0.6 m (H. 0.2 m: 1969), reduced by ploughing; chalk rubble; enclosing square ditch 10 m by 10 m, W. 3 m, D. 1.2 m; opened 1867, re-excavated by I.M. Stead 1969.
BB 208-9; *GM* 1867, ii 651-3; *Stead* 1979, 99.

Burial 1: adult female inhumation, crouched on L. with head NE.; on old surface at centre; bracelet on R. arm, brooch near chin, beads at neck.

1 *Bronze bracelet*: penannular with mortise and tenon fastening; round-sectioned body thickened laterally and vertically at five spaced points, four with very worn cast relief ornament.
Diam. 5.9 cm.   79 12-9 534
BB fig. 110; *EIABY* fig. 3; *ABI* fig. 486; *Stead* 1979, fig. 27.1.

2 *Bronze and iron arched-bow brooch*: high arched bow and foot terminating in flat disc with central dot; broken four-coil spring; tip of iron pin surviving in catch-plate.
L. 4.9 cm.   79 12-9 535
BB fig. 111; *EIABY* fig. 4; *ABI* fig. 498; *Stead* 1979, fig. 23.1.

3 *Glass beads*: sixty survive of recorded seventy; blue, one with twelve impressed white annulets (white glass now missing), the remainder with white scrolls.
                                            79 12-9 536
BB fig. 112; *Stead* 1979, 80; *Guido* 1978, 105.

Mound material (1867)
4 *Early Iron Age rim sherd*: flint-tempered.
                                            79 12-9 529a
5 *Early Iron Age base sherd*: sandy fabric.
                                            79 12-9 529b
6 *Early Iron Age base sherds*: two; flint-tempered.
                                            79 12-9 529c-d
7 *Early Iron Age base sherds*: two; vesicular fabric.
                                            79 12-9 529e-f
8 *Early Iron Age sherd*: flint-tempered. 79 12-9 529g
9 *Early Iron Age sherds*: forty-two; chalk-tempered to vesicular fabric.   79 12-9 529
10 *Shale bracelet fragment*: cut and polished to plano-convex section; broken.
Diam. *c.* 10.0 cm; W. 0.9 cm; Th. 0.8 cm.
                                            79 12-9 537

11 *'Flint scraper'*: not identified.   79 12-9 530
12-14 *'Flint flakes'*: three; not identified.
                                            79 12-9 531-3

Mound material (1969)
15 *Beaker sherd*: incised parallel lines.   P1983 6-1 1
16 *Food Vessel rim sherd*: row of jabbed impressions.
                                            P1983 6-1 2
17 *Accessory Cup rim sherd*: short vertical strokes enclosed between pairs of angled incised lines, above zone of vertical slashes.   P1983 6-1 3
18 *Early Iron Age rim sherd*: vesicular fabric.
                                            P1983 6-1 4
19 *Early Iron Age shoulder sherd*: calcite-tempered.
                                            P1983 6-1 5
20 *Early Iron Age sherds*: fifty-one; calcite-tempered.
                                            P1983 6-1 6-8
21 *Early Iron Age sherds*: five, flint-tempered.
                                            P1983 6-1 9-10
22 *Romano-British sherds*: twelve, wheel-turned jars.
                                            P1983 6-1 11-15
23 *Flint barbed-and-tanged arrowhead*: all over invasive retouch on one face, inverse edge retouch on other; point snapped; mottled grey.
L. 2.3 cm; W. 2.0 cm; Th. 0.2 cm.   P1983 6-1 16
24 *Flint horseshoe scraper*: edge retouch on bilateral and distal at 80 degrees; on thermal flake; mottled grey.
L. 1.7 cm; W. 2.1 cm; Th. 0.5 cm.   P1983 6-1 17
25 *Flint side-scraper*: edge retouch on R. at 60 degrees; platform butt; cortex remnant; mottled grey.
L. 2.7 cm; W. 3.2 cm; Th. 0.5 cm.   P1983 6-1 18
26 *Flint worked flake*: edge retouch on distal; broken; mottled grey.
L. 2.8 cm; W. 2.0 cm; Th. 0.6 cm.   P1983 6-1 19
27 *Flint worked flake*: edge retouch on bilateral; faceted butt; cortex remnant; snapped; mottled grey.
L. 2.4 cm; W. 2.5 cm; Th. 0.8 cm.   P1983 6-1 20
28 *Flint worked flake*: all over unifacial invasive retouch; broken; mottled grey.
L. 1.9 cm; W. 2.9 cm; Th. 0.5 cm.   P1983 6-1 21
29 *Flint utilised flake*: wear on L; cortex remnant; mottled grey.
L. 2.9 cm; W. 1.5 cm; Th. 0.7 cm.   P1983 6-1 22

Flint blades

	Btt	Ctx	Col.	L.	W.	Th.	P1983 6-1
30			M. Gr.	3.7	1.0	0.5	23
31	Sn.		M. Gr.	4.0	1.5	0.5	24
32			M. Gr.	3.2	0.9	0.6	25
33	Pl.		M. Gr.	2.5	1.1	0.2	26

Flint flakes

	Btt	Ctx	Col.	L.	W.	Th.	P1983 6-1
34	Pl.		M. Gr.	2.3	1.3	0.5	27
35	Pl.	x	M. Gr.	2.5	1.5	0.6	28
36	Bkn		Pat.	2.2	3.9	0.9	29
37		x	M. Gr.	2.0	1.4	0.3	30
38	Pl.		Pat.	4.6	5.1	2.4	31a
39	Ct.	x	Pat.	4.0	3.7	0.7	31b
40	Pl.		M. Gr.	3.8	3.0	0.8	31c
41			M. Gr.	2.8	4.1	0.9	31d
42	Pl.		Pat.	3.5	1.8	0.7	31e
43	Ct.	x	M. Gr.	2.0	3.4	0.7	31f
44			M. Gr.	1.3	2.3	0.5	31g
45			M. Gr.	1.8	2.1	0.6	31h
46			Pat.	2.5	2.0	0.4	31i
47		x	Pat.	2.1	1.5	0.5	31j
48	Fc.		M. Gr.	2.9	2.3	0.5	32a
49	Fc.		M. Gr.	1.6	1.8	0.5	32b

Ditch fill (1969)

50 *Early Iron Age rim sherd*: finger-tipping on rim; calcite-tempered.   P1983 6-1 33
51 *Early Iron Age rim sherd*: flint-tempered.
P1983 6-1 34
52 *Early Iron Age rim sherd*: vesicular fabric.
P1983 6-1 44
53 *Early Iron Age base sherd*: calcite-tempered.
P1983 6-1 42
54 *Early Iron Age sherds*: three; flint-tempered.
P1983 6-1 36
55 *Early Iron Age sherds*: eleven; vesicular fabric.
P1983 6-1 37-39, 43
56 *Early Iron Age sherd*: rock-tempered.   P1983 6-1 39
57 *Early Iron Age sherd*: grog-tempered.   P1983 6-1 40
58 *Early Iron Age sherds*: eight; calcite-tempered.
P1983 6-1 41, 46
59 *Romano-British Samian sherd*.   P1983 6-1 53
60 *Romano-British sherds*: two; Huntcliff ware.
P1983 6-1 52
61 *Romano-British sherds*: two, including rim; Crambeck ware.   P1983 6-1 48, 53
62 *Romano-British sherds*: twenty-one, including rim and base; grey coarse ware.   P1983 6-1 47, 50-53
63 *Flint horseshoe scraper*: edge retouch on bilateral and distal at 80 degrees; broken; patinated.
L. 2.6 cm; W. 3.6 cm; Th. 0.8 cm.   P1983 6-1 55
64 *Flint horseshoe scraper*: edge retouch on bilateral and distal at 60 degrees; corticated butt; mottled grey.
L. 3.6 cm; W. 3.0 cm; Th. 1.0 cm.   P1983 6-1 56
65 *Flint horseshoe scraper*: edge retouch on bilateral and distal at 80 degrees; patinated.
L. 2.1 cm; W. 2.2 cm; th. 0.8 cm.   P1983 6-1 57
66 *Flint end- and side-scraper*: edge retouch on R. and distal at 60 degrees; platform butt; mottled grey.
L. 2.6 cm; W. 3.2 cm; Th. 1.0 cm.   P1983 6-1 65
67 *Flint end-scraper*: edge retouch on distal at 60 degrees; cortex remnant; mottled grey.
L. 2.3 cm; W. 1.6 cm; Th. 1.0 cm.   P1983 6-1 58
68 *Flint scraper fragment*: edge retouch at 80 degrees; cortex remnant; broken; patinated.
L. 3.1 cm; W. 2.3 cm; Th. 1.1 cm.   P1983 6-1 59
69 *Flint scraper fragment*: edge retouch at 40 degrees; cortex remnant; broken; mottled grey.
L. 2.5 cm; W. 2.4 cm; Th. 0.8 cm.   P1983 6-1 60

Flint utilised flakes

	Wr	Btt	Ctx	Col.	L.	W.	Th.	P1983 6-1
70	R.			M. Gr.	5.0	2.5	1.3	61
71	R.	Sn.	x	Pat.	2.5	1.6	0.7	62

Flint flakes

	Btt	Ctx	Col.	L.	W.	Th.	P1983 6-1
72			M. Gr.	2.7	1.4	0.5	63
73	Ct.	x	M. Gr.	3.0	4.9	1.3	66
74	Pl.		M. Gr.	2.7	1.2	0.5	67
75	Pl	x	M. Gr.	3.6	2.9	0.9	68
76	Fc.		M. Gr.	2.4	1.9	0.6	69
77		x	M. Gr.	2.9	2.5	1.2	70
78	Pl.		M. Gr.	2.2	1.7	0.4	71

79 *Flint core*: one platform with parallel blade scars; cortex remnant; mottled grey.
L. 2.6 cm; W. 2.3 cm; Th. 2.0 cm.   P1983 6-1 64

51 COWLAM (Cowlam II; Cottam D)   51:1-38
Yorkshire E.R.; North Humberside   SE 984 667

SQUARE-DITCHED BARROW: Diam. 7.2 m, H. 0.3 m, reduced by ploughing; chalk rubble, ditch enclosing area 12 m by 11 m; opened 1867, re-excavated by I.M. Stead 1972.
BB 209-10; *GM* 1867, ii 651-3; *Stead* 1979, 99.

Burial 1: adult female inhumation, crouched on L. with head N.; at centre on old surface; bracelet on R. arm.
1 *Bronze bracelet*: penannular knobbed; thirty-six knobs separated by body segments decorated with closely spaced grooves.
L. 6.1 cm; W. 5.8 cm; Th. 0.8 cm.   79 12-9 539
BB fig. 113; *EIABY* fig. 2; *ABI* fig. 485; *Stead* 1979, fig. 27.6.

Feature A: pit L. 2.1 m, W. 1.2 m, D. 0.9 m (D. 0.6 m: *GM*), aligned E.-W.; beneath and to W. of Burial 1.
2 *'Flint flake'*: not identified.   79 12-9 1568

Feature A backfill (1972)
3 *Early Iron Age rim sherd*: calcite-tempered.
P1983 6-1 72
4 *Early Iron Age sherds*: two; flint-tempered.
P1983 6-1 73

Feature B (1972): irregular hollow at NW.
5 *Early Iron Age rim sherd*: flint-tempered.
P1983 6-1 74
6 *Early Iron Age rim sherd*: calcite-tempered.
P1983 6-1 75
7 *Early Iron Age base sherds*: two; calcite-tempered.
P1983 6-1 76
8 *Early Iron Age cordoned sherd*: diagonal slashing on cordon; calcite-tempered.   P1983 6-1 77
9 *Early Iron Age sherds*: sixty-one; calcite-tempered.
P1983 6-1 78-81
10 *Early Iron Age sherds*: two; flint-tempered.
P1983 6-1 80, 82
11 *Flint flake*: platform butt; mottled grey.
L. 3.2 cm; W. 2.1 cm; Th. 0.6 cm.   P1983 6-1 120

Feature C (1972): irregular hollow at SW.
12 *Early Iron Age sherd*: flint-tempered. P1983 6-1 88a
13 *Early Iron Age sherd*: grog-tempered. P1983 6-1 88b
14 *Plain sherds*: thirty-one, including rim, base and cordon; calcite-tempered.   P1983 6-1 83-87

Feature D (1972): irregular hollow at NE.

Mound material (1972)
15 *Early Iron Age rim sherds*: three; calcite-tempered.
P1983 6-1 89
16 *Early Iron Age base sherd*: calcite-tempered.
P1983 6-1 90
17 *Early Iron Age cordoned sherds*: two; diagonal slashing on cordon; calcite-tempered. P1983 6-1 92
18 *Early Iron Age sherd*: notched decoration; calcite-tempered.   P1983 6-1 93
19 *Early Iron Age sherds*: sixty-seven; calcite-tempered.   P1983 6-1 91, 94
20 *Romano-British Samian sherd*: Drag. 33; Central Gaulish.   P1983 6-1 95
21 *Flint side-scraper*: edge retouch on L. at 60 degrees; patinated.
L. 2.5 cm; W. 3.0 cm; Th. 0.7 cm.   P1983 6-1 96
22 *Flint scraper fragment*: edge retouch on ?distal; snapped; mottled grey.
L. 3.5 cm; W. 1.7 cm; Th. 0.5 cm.   P1983 6-1 97
23 *Flint knife*: inverse edge retouch on R. at 40 degrees; platform butt; cortex remnant; patinated.
L. 4.2 cm; W. 2.0 cm; Th. 0.7 cm.   P1983 6-1 98

Flint flakes

Btt	Ctx	Col.	L.	W.	Th.	P1983 6-1
24		x	M. Gr.	2.1	1.5	0.3	99
25	Pl.		M. Gr.	3.6	2.7	0.8	100
26			M. Gr.	2.4	5.2	0.8	101
27			Pat.	2.3	3.0	0.7	102
28	Pl.	x	M. Gr.	3.3	1.7	1.0	103
29	Pl.		M. Gr.	2.5	1.7	0.3	104

Ditch fill (1972)

30 *Bronze globe-headed pin*: corroded.
L. 4.4 cm; Diam. (shank) 0.3 cm, (head) 0.4 cm.
P1983 6-1 105
31 *Early Iron Age sherds*: three; flint-tempered.
P1983 6-1 106
32 *Early Iron Age sherds*: three; calcite-tempered.
P1983 6-1 106
33 *Flint end-scraper*: edge retouch on distal at 60 degrees; corticated butt; mottled grey.
L. 3.4 cm. W. 2.6 cm; Th. 0.9 cm. P1983 6-1 115
34 *Flint end-scraper*: edge retouch on distal at 80 degrees; cortex remnant; mottled grey.
L. 2.9 cm; W. 2.0 cm; Th. 0.4 cm. P1983 6-1 116
35 *Flint end-scraper*: edge retouch on distal at 80 degrees; cortex remnant; mottled grey.
L. 2.9 cm; W. 2.8 cm; Th. 0.8 cm. P1983 6-1 117

Flint flakes

Btt	Ctx	Col.	L.	W.	Th.	P1983 6-1
36	Pl.	x	M. Gr.	3.7	3.7	1.2	118
37			M. Gr.	2.0	2.5	0.4	119

Not located

38 *Early Iron Age sherds*: twenty-seven, including rim; vesicular fabric.
79 12-9 538

52 COWLAM (Cowlam III; Cottam C)   52:1-51

Yorkshire E.R.; North Humberside   SE 984 667

SQUARE-DITCHED BARROW: Diam. 9.6 m, H. 0.6 m (Diam. 7.5 m, H. 0.1 m: 1969), educed by ploughing; earth and chalk, enclosing square ditch 10.5 m by 10.5 m, W. 2 m, D. 1.1 m; opened 1867, re-excavated by I.M. Stead 1969.
BB 210-1; *GM* 1867, ii 651-3; *Stead* 1979, 99.

Burial 1: adult female inhumation, crouched on L. with head NE.; on old surface at centre.

Feature A: oval pit L. 0.9 m, W. 0.6 m, D. 0.5 m (L. 3.7 m, W. 0.8 m, D. 0.7 m: 1969); 1.2 m SE. of centre.
1 *Early Iron Age rim sherd*: vesicular fabric.
P1983 6-1 122
2 *Early Iron Age rim sherds*: two; rock-tempered.
P1983 6-1 123
3 *Early Iron Age rim sherd*: flint-tempered.
P1983 6-1 124
4 *Early Iron Age rim sherd*: calcite-tempered.
P1983 6-1 125
5 *Early Iron Age base sherds*: two; vesicular fabric.
P1983 6-1 126
6 *Early Iron Age shoulder sherd*: row of diagonal strokes; vesicular fabric. P1983 6-1 126
7 *Early Iron Age sherds*: thirty-five; vesicular fabric. P1983 6-1 126-8
8 *Early Iron Age sherds*: five; flint-tempered.
P1983 6-1 126-8
9 *Early Iron Age sherds*: eighteen; calcite-tempered.
P1983 6-1 129-30
10 *Early Iron Age sherds*: nineteen; calcite-, chalk- and grog-tempered. P1983 6-1 126

Feature B: oval pit, L. 1.5 m, W. 0.9 m, D. 0.5 m; burnt material in fill; 1.2 m W. of centre.
11 *Early Iron Age sherds*: three; calcite-tempered.
P1983 6-1 131

Feature C (1969): irregular hollow at SE.

Mound material

12 *Early Iron Age rim sherd*: cabling on rim; vesicular fabric. P1983 6-1 134
13 *Early Iron Age base sherd*: vesicular fabric.
P1983 6-1 135
14 *Early Iron Age sherds*: twenty; vesicular fabric.
P1983 6-1 134, 136-43
15 *Early Iron Age sherds*: six; rock-tempered.
P1983 6-1 134, 139, 141
16 *Early Iron Age sherds*: three; calcite-tempered.
P1983 6-1 135
17 *Early Iron Age sherds*: seven; flint-tempered.
P1983 6-1 139, 141
18 *Romano-British sherd*: grey coarse ware.
P1983 6-1 144
19 *Flint leaf arrowhead fragment*: all over bifacial invasive retouch; snapped; mottled grey.
L. 2.3 cm; W. 1.7 cm; Th. 0.2 cm. P1983 6-1 146
20 *Flint plano-convex knife*: all round invasive retouch; mottled grey.
L. 3.9 cm; W. 2.1 cm; Th. 0.7 cm. P1983 6-1 147

Flint flakes

Btt	Ctx	Col.	L.	W.	Th.	P1983 6-1
21		x	M. Gr.	2.0	1.5	0.2	148
22		x	M. Gr.	1.8	2.9	0.5	149
23		x	M. Gr.	2.3	2.7	0.8	150
24			M. Gr.	2.5	2.8	0.4	179
25			M. Gr.	2.0	1.7	0.3	180

Ditch fill (1969)

26 *Early Iron Age rim sherd*: cabling on rim; calcite-tempered. P1983 6-1 151
27 *Early Iron Age rim sherd*: vesicular fabric.
P1983 6-1 152
28 *Early Iron Age base sherd*: chalk-tempered.
P1983 6-1 153
29 *Early Iron Age sherds*: twenty; vesicular fabric.
P1983 6-1 158-62
30 *Early Iron Age sherds*: three; rock-tempered.
P1983 6-1 155, 160
31 *Early Iron Age sherds*: five; flint-tempered.
P1983 6-1 154, 157-58
32 *Early Iron Age sherds*: sixty-three including three rim, calcite-tempered. P1983 6-1 156
33 *Early Iron Age sherd*: grog-tempered. P1983 6-1 160
34 *Romano-British rim sherd*: Crambeck ware.
P1983 6-1 165
35 *Romano-British sherds*: two; Crambeck ware.
P1983 6-1 165, 169
36 *Romano-British sherd*: Huntcliff ware. P1983 6-1 169
37 *Romano-British sherds*: two; grey coarse ware.
P1983 6-1 168
38 *Flint blade*: snapped; patinated.
L. 2.1 cm; W. 1.0 cm; Th. 0.2 cm. P1983 6-1 170

Flint flakes

Btt	Ctx	Col.	L.	W.	Th.	P1983 6-1
39			Pat.	2.6	1.8	0.5	171
40	Bkn	x	M. Gr.	1.6	1.8	0.3	172
41		x	M. Gr.	3.5	2.1	0.4	173
42	Pl.	x	M. Gr.	3.6	2.0	0.5	174
43	Bkn		M. Gr.	1.9	1.4	0.3	175
44	Fc.		M. Gr.	3.3	1.8	0.4	176
45		x	M. Gr.	3.9	2.1	0.4	177
46	Pl.		Pat.	3.2	2.6	1.0	178

Not located

47 *Bronze Age sherds*: two, including base.
                                          79 12-9 540a
48 *Early Iron Age sherds*: three; vesicular fabric.
                                          79 12-9 540b
49-50 *'Flint scrapers'*: two; not identified.
     BB fig. 18.   79 12-9 540-41
51 *'Flint fragment'*: not identified.   79 12-9 542
     (See also 52 or 53 Cowlam, below)

52 or 53 COWLAM   52/53:1-16

The following material derives from one or both of these barrows; precise context unknown.

1 *Neolithic Bowl rim sherd*: flint-tempered.
                                          79 12-9 544a
2 *Neolithic Bowl rim sherds*: two, sandy fabric.
                                          79 12-9 544b
3 *Neolithic Bowl rim sherd*: corky fabric.
                                          79 12-9 544c
4 *Neolithic Bowl rim sherd*: corky fabric.
                                          79 12-9 544d
5 *Neolithic Bowl sherd*: pit; chalky fabric.
                                          79 12-9 544e
6 *Beaker rim sherd*: rusticated; eroded. 79 12-9 544f
7 *Beaker sherd*: fine twisted cord lines. 79 12-9 544g
8 *Beaker sherd*: tooth-comb stamped horizontal lines; eroded.   79 12-9 544h
9 *Beaker base sherd*: plain.   79 12-9 544i
10 *Beaker sherd*: plain, eroded.   79 12-9 544j
11 *Beaker sherds*: seven; plain.   79 12-9 544k
12 *Bronze Age sherds*: six; plain.   79 12-9 544l
13 *Early Iron Age sherds*: two, including rim; on shoulder, row of finger tip impressions; vesicular fabric.   79 12-9 544m
14 *Early Iron Age base sherds*: two; vesicular fabric.
                                          79 12-9 544n
15 *Early Iron Age sherds*: one hundred and one, from several vessels; vesicular fabric. 79 12-9 544o
16 *Early Iron Age sherds*: ninety-one, from several vessels; calcite-gritted, with some flint and basaltic inclusions.   79 12-9 544p

53 COWLAM (Cowlam VIII; Cottam E)   53:1-23

Yorkshire E.R.; North Humberside   SE 984 667

SQUARE-DITCHED BARROW: Diam. 12.6 m. H. 0.3 m (Diam. *c.* 8 m: 1972), reduced by ploughing; chalk and earth, enclosing square ditch *c.* 9 m by 8 m, W. 1.5-2 m, D. 0.5 m; opened 1867; re-excavated by I.M.Stead 1972.
BB 211; *GM* 1867, ii 651-3; *Stead* 1979, 99.

Burial 1: adult female inhumation, crouched on L. with head N.; at centre on old surface.

Mound material (1867)

1 *Neolithic Bowl sherds*: three, including rim; grit-tempered.   79 12-9 543a
2 *Neolithic Bowl rim sherd*: grit-tempered.
                                          79 12-9 543b
3 *Neolithic Bowl rim sherds*: two joining; grit-tempered.   79 12-9 543c
4 *Neolithic Bowl sherds*: four; grit-tempered.
                                          79 12-9 543d
5 *Beaker sherd*: rusticated; eroded.   79 12-9 543e
6 *Beaker sherd*: finger-grooved; vesicular fabric.
                                          79 12-9 543f
7 *Bronze Age sherd*: quartz-tempered.   79 12-9 543g
8 *Plain sherds*: nine; vesicular fabric. 79 12-9 543h
9 *Plain sherd*: grit-tempered.   79 12-9 543i
10 *'Antler tine'*: not identified.   79 12-9 544

Mound material (1972)

11 *Bronze Age sherds*: two; grit-tempered.
                                          P1983 6-1 182
12 *Early Iron Age sherds*: two; vesicular fabric.
                                          P1983 6-1 181
13 *Fired clay spindle-whorl*: irregular ovate section; cylindrical perforation.
   Diam. 3.2 cm, (perf.) 0.7 cm; Th. 1.5 cm.
                                          P1983 6-1 184

Flint flakes

	Btt	Ctx	Col.	L.	W.	Th.	P1983 6-1
14	Pl.	x	M. Gr.	3.4	2.6	0.8	185
15	Fc.	x	Pat.	4.1	2.6	1.1	186

Ditch fill (1972)

16 *Early Iron Age rim sherds*: four; vesicular fabric.
                                          P1983 6-1 187-90
17 *Early Iron Age base sherds*: two; vesicular fabric.
                                          P1983 6-1 191-92
18 *Early Iron Age base sherd*: calcite-tempered.
                                          P1983 6-1 193
19 *Early Iron Age sherds*: one hundred; vesicular fabric.
                                          P1983 6-1 194-216
20 *Early Iron Age sherds*: sixteen; flint-tempered.
              P1983 6-1 194, 196-97, 208, 210, 212, 215
21 *Early Iron Age sherds*: eleven; rock-tempered.
                    P1983 6-1 210-11, 214, 218-19
22 *Flint blade*: snapped; mottled grey.
   L. 1.8 cm; W. 0.8 cm; Th. 0.2 cm.   P1983 6-1 220
23 *Flint flake*: platform butt; mottled grey.
   L. 3.1 cm; W. 3.8 cm; Th. 1.2 cm.   P1983 6-1 221
   (See also 52 or 53 Cowlam, above)

54 COWLAM (Cowlam I: Cottam A)   54:1-33

Yorkshire E.R.; North Humberside   SE 984 667

SQUARE-DITCHED BARROW: Diam. 15m, H. 0.7 m, (Diam. 10 m: 1969), reduced by ploughing; chalk and earth, enclosing square ditch 14.5 m by 14 m, W. 2 m, D. 1m; opened 1867, re-excavated by I.M. Stead 1969
BB 213; *GM* 1867, ii 651-3; *Stead* 1979, 99.

Burial 1: adult ?female inhumation, crouched on R. with head SSW.; at centre on old surface.

Mound material (1969)

1 *Early Iron Age rim sherd*: flint-tempered.
                                          P1983 6-1 222
2 *Early Iron Age rim sherd*: vesicular fabric.
                                          P1983 6-1 223
3 *Early Iron Age base sherd*: rock-tempered.
                                          P1983 6-1 226
4 *Jet bead*: cut and polished to barrel form with drilled perforation.
   L. 1.8 cm; Diam. 0.6 cm.   P1983 6-1 227
5 *Flint worked flake*: edge retouch on L.; broken; mottled grey.
   L. 2.3 cm; W. 2.0 cm; Th. 0.7 cm.   P1983 6-1 228
6 *Flint worked flake*: on thermal flake; partial edge retouch; cortex remnant; patinated.
   L. 2.6 cm; W. 3.3 cm; Th. 1.1 cm.   P1983 6-1 229
7 *Flint utilised blade*: wear on R.; snapped; mottled grey.
   L. 2.7 cm; W. 1.1 cm; Th. 0.2 cm.   P1983 6-1 230
8 *Flint blade*: mottled grey.
   L. 4.6 cm; W. 1.2 cm; Th. 0.3 cm.   P1983 6-1 231

Flint flakes

	Btt	Ctx	Col.	L.	W.	Th.	P1983 6-1 .
9	Pl.		Bge	2.7	2.7	0.4	232
10	Pl.		M. Gr.	2.2	2.3	0.6	233
11			M. Gr.	2.4	1.9	0.4	234
12			Bge	1.5	1.8	0.3	235
13		x	M. Gr.	2.5	2.5	0.7	236

Ditch fill (1969)

14 *Early Iron Age rim sherd*: cabling on rim; vesicular fabric. P1983 6-1 237

15 *Early Iron Age sherds*: twelve; vesicular fabric. P1983 6-1 238

16 *Early Iron Age sherds*: two; flint-tempered. P1983 6-1 239

17 *Glass bracelet fragment*: light blue translucent with twisted trail and bosses of opaque blue and white; ovate section; broken. Diam. 5.4 cm; Th. 1.2 cm. P1983 6-1 243

18 *Flint leaf arrowhead*: all-round edge and partial invasive bifacial retouch; mottled grey. L. 4.0 cm; W. 2.3 cm; Th. 0.4 cm. P1983 6-1 244

19 *Flint horseshoe scraper*: edge retouch on bilateral and distal at 80 degrees; cortex remnant; mottled grey. L. 3.4 cm; W. 3.1 cm; Th. 1.8 cm. P1983 6-1 245

20 *Flint horseshoe scraper*: edge retouch on distal and bilateral at 80 degrees; corticated butt; mottled grey. L. 2.8 cm; W. 3.0 cm; Th. 0.9 cm. P1983 6-1 246

21 *Flint horseshoe scraper*: edge retouch on bilateral and distal at 60 degrees; cortex remnant; mottled grey. L. 2.5 cm; W. 3.3 cm; Th. 1.1 cm. P1983 6-1 247

22 *Flint end- and-side scraper*: edge retouch on L. and distal; platform butt; patinated. L. 2.9 cm; W. 2.8 cm; Th. 0.4 cm. P1983 6-1 248

23 *Flint plano-convex knife fragment*: edge and invasive retouch; broken; mottled grey. L. 3.2 cm; W. 1.7 cm; Th. 0.7 cm. P1983 6-1 249

24 *Flint knife*: edge retouch on bilateral converging on distal: platform butt; mottled grey. L. 4.0 cm; W. 1.8 cm; Th. 0.6 cm. P1983 6-1 250

25 *Flint utilised flake*: wear on bilateral; faceted butt; mottled grey. L. 3.4 cm; W. 3.5 cm; Th. 0.4 cm. P1983 6-1 251

Flint blades

	Btt	Ctx	Col.	L.	W.	Th.	P1983 6-1
26	Bkn		M. Gr.	3.3	1.0	0.3	253
27		x	Pat.	2.6	1.3	0.3	254

Flint flakes

	Btt	Ctx	Col.	L.	W.	Th.	P1982 6-1
28	Ct.	x	M. Gr.	4.2	3.3	1.2	256
29	Ct.	x	Pat.	2.2	1.7	0.5	257
30	Pl.		Pat.	1.9	2.3	0.4	258
31	Pl.	x	Pat.	2.0	2.7	0.4	259
32	Bkn		M. Gr.	3.3	1.4	0.5	260
33	Bkn		M. Gr.	3.2	2.1	0.6	261

55   COWLAM (Cowlam V; Cottam II)   55:1-12

Yorkshire E.R.; North Humberside   SE 986 675

ROUND BARROW: Diam. 14 m, H. 0.6 m; earth; (ditch Diam. 14 m:1968); opened 1867, re-excavated by T.C.M. Brewster 1968.

BB 213-14; GM 1867, 652; Watts and Rahtz 1984.

Burials 1-3 were in a central oval grave L. 2.1 m, W. 1.2 m, D. 0.8 m, aligned SE.-NW.

Burial 1: adult inhumation, crouched on L. with head SE.; at base of grave.

Burial 2: scattered cremation deposit; in grave fill.

Burial 3: scattered bones of adult and child; in grave fill.

Grave fill

'drinking-cup sherds': not preserved.
'cinerary urn sherds': not preserved.

Grave fill (1968)

1 *Stone polished axe fragment*: greenstone; ground and polished; broken. L. 2.9 cm; W. 2.4 cm; Th. 0.4 cm. P1982 1-1 74

2 *Flint barbed-and-tanged arrowhead*: all over bifacial invasive retouch; one barb broken; mottled grey. L. 2.7 cm; W. 1.6 cm; Th. 0.5 cm. P1982 1-1 75

Mound material (1968)

3 *Beaker sherd*: traces of decoration; weathered. P1982 1-1 70

4 *Early Iron Age sherd*: flint-gritted. P1982 1-1 71a

5 *Early Iron Age sherd*: no visible temper. P1982 1-1 71b

6 *Romano-British rim sherd*: Huntcliff ware. P1982 1-1 72

7 *Romano-British rim sherd*: Crambeck ware. P1982 1-1 73

8 *Flint horseshoe scraper*: edge retouch on distal and bilateral; platform butt; mottled grey. L. 2.1 cm; W. 2.0 cm; Th. 0.5 cm. P1982 1-1 76

9 *Flint end- and-side scraper*: edge retouch on distal and partial L.; damage on R.; cortex remnant; patinated. L. 4.8 cm; W. 3.0 cm; Th. 0.7 cm. P1982 1-1 77

10 *Flint scraper fragment*: edge retouch at 60 degrees; broken; mottled grey. L. 4.4 cm; W. 2.0 cm; Th. 0.7 cm. P1982 1-1 78

11 *Flint worked flake*: partial edge retouch on R., wear on L.; platform butt; patinated. L. 3.4 cm; W. 2.2 cm; Th. 0.5 cm. P1982 1-1 79

12 *Flint utilised flake*: wear on R.; broken; mottled grey. L. 1.8 cm; W. 1.8 cm; Th. 0.3 cm. P1982 1-1 80

56   COWLAM (Cowlam VI; Cottam III)   56:1-9

Yorkshire E.R.; North Humberside   SE 986 675

ROUND BARROW: Diam. 15 m, H. 0.5 m; earth (ditch Diam. 14 m, W. 1.2 m:1968); opened 1867, re-excavated by T.C.M. Brewster 1968.

BB 214; GM 1867, 652; Watts and Rahtz 1984.

Burial 1: double inhumation: male crouched on R. with head NW. and male crouched on L. with head SE; in central grave L. 1.4 m, W. 1.2 m D. 0.3 m, with traces of ?wood beneath second male; vessel between heads.

1 *Food Vessel*: on internal rim bevel, groups of twisted cord horizontal and short diagonal lines; on upper ridge, short vertical incised lines; on lower ridge, short diagonal twisted cord lines; on body, rows of irregularly executed incised vertical chevrons; one hulled barley grain impression. M. 13.5 cm; H. 12.7 cm; B. 6.8 cm. 79 12-9 545 *BAP no. 179; Jessen & Helbaek 1944, 18.*

Burial 2: scattered bones of adult male and child; in fill of central grave.

Burials 3-5: (1968) were in a grave L. 3 m, W. 1.5 m, D. 1.4 m, N. of centre.

Burial 3: adult inhumation, crouched on R. with head W.; objects at back.
2 *'Bronze point or awl':* not received.
3 *'Bone point':* not received.

Burial 4: adult female inhumation, crouched on R. with head S.; in upper fill of grave; vessel behind shoulder.
4 *Food Vessel:* Yorkshire Vase; fine twisted cord: on internal rim bevel, two horizontal lines; on neck, shoulder groove and body, filled triangles; four imperforate vertical lugs spanning shoulder groove.
   M. 15.2 cm; H. 11.2 cm; B. 7.9 cm.   P1982 1-1 81

Burial 5: scattered bones of three adults and one child; in grave fill.
5 *Beaker sherds:* nineteen including base; rectangular tooth-comb stamped: zones of short vertical lines separated by zone of three to four horizontal lines.
   B. *c.* 8.0 cm.   P1982 1-1 82

Feature A (1968): pit L. 2.4 m, W. 1.5 m, D. 0.4 m, fill of earth with some charcoal, E. of centre.

Mound material (1968)
6 *Bronze Age sherd:* plain.   P1982 1-1 83
7 *Early Iron Age sherd:* fine calcite grit.
                                            P1982 1-1 84
8 *Early Iron Age sherds:* two, no visible temper.
                                            P1982 1-1 84
9 *Flint end-scraper:* edge retouch on distal; corticated butt; mottled grey.
   L. 3.0 cm.; W. 3.2 cm; Th. 0.7 cm.   P1982 1-1 85

57 COWLAM (Cowlam VII)   57:1-116
Yorkshire E.R.; North Humberside   SE 97 67

ROUND BARROW: Diam. 17 m, H. 1.8 m, reduced by ploughing and levelling; earth; opened 29-30 April 1867.
BB 214-21; *GM* 1867, ii: 651-3; *Manby* 1974, 121; *Kinnes* 1979, Ba5.

Burial 1: double inhumation: adult female crouched on L. with head N., facing incomplete adolescent crouched on L. with head S., with many broken bones in area; on level of old surface 4.8 m NW. of centre.
   'Fragments of pottery': probably among nos 7-18 below.
1 *Boar tusk blade:* longitudually sliced; point damaged, some flaking.
   L. 12.9 cm; W. 2.4 cm; Th. 0.5 cm.   79 12-9 550

Burial 2: adult male inhumation, crouched on R. with head WSW.; in fill of hollow Diam. 0.9 m, D. 0.3 m, below Burial 1.

Burial 3: multiple disarticulated and incomplete inhumations: at SE. adult crouched on L. with head E., in front of adult and adult male crouched on R. with head SW., adult crouched on L. with head E. over hips of first with headless adult nearby; on chalk slab paving L. 2.9 m, W. 1 m, aligned SE.-NW., and beginning 5.4 m NW. of centre.

Burial 4: adult male inhumation, partly disarticulated and incomplete, on R. with head E.; on old surface at centre; macehead at face.
2 *Antler macehead:* red deer shed antler beam, cut end polished to bevel; sub-rectangular perforation cut from both sides.
   L. 15.2 cm; W. 4.4 cm; Th. 3.8 cm; Diam. (perforation) 2.2 cm.   79 12-9 551
   BB fig. 33.

Burial 5: adolescent inhumation, crouched on R. with head SW.; 0.3 m above old surface; 1.8 m W. of centre; scraper behind head.
   Flint scraper: probably one of nos 71-82 below.

Burial 6: adult ?female inhumation, semi-disarticulated on L. with head E.; on old surface 1.8 m N. of centre; arrowhead beneath hips.
3 *Flint leaf arrowhead:* all over bifacial invasive retouch; point broken, patinated.
   L. 4.2 cm; W. 2.2 cm; Th. 0.4 cm.   79 12-9 552
   BB fig. 27; *Green* 1980, no. 91.

Burial 7: disarticulated and incomplete inhumations; adult female skull on R., on legs of incomplete adult male crouched on R. with head WSW.; on old surface in charcoal-rich matrix, 1.2 m NW. of Burial 6; pin at face of female.
4 *Bone pin:* split caprovine metatarsal, cut and polished to asymmetric fine point.
   L. 11.0 cm; W. 0.9 cm; Th. 0.4 cm.   79 12-9 553

Burial 8: double inhumation: child crouched on L. with head SSE. with remains of another with head SE.; on old surface, 0.6 m NE. of Burial 7.

Burial 9: child inhumation, crouched on R. with head E.; 0.3 m above old surface, 0.7 m N. of Burial 7.

Burial 10: adult male inhumation, crouched on R., no skull but aligned WSW.-ENE.; above old surface W. of Burial 9.

Feature A: pit Diam. 0.8 m, D. 0.5 m, fill of earth; 3 m SE. of centre.

Mound material: probably including pottery from Burial 1 and scraper from Burial 5.
5 *Bronze blade fragment:* tanged spearhead or Gerloff Type Armorico-British B dagger; stout midrib flanked by pronounced single ribs with traces of edge bevels; broken and corroded (Table 1:21).
   L. 9.7 cm; W. 4.0 cm; Th. 0.7 cm.   79 12-9 554
   Gerloff 1975, no. 134; *Needham* 1979, no. 33.
6 *Bronze rivet:* thick with eight longitudinal facets and lipped heads (Table 1:23).
   L. 2.5 cm; shank Diam. 0.8-1.0 cm.   79 12-9 555
7 *Neolithic Bowl rim sherd:* flint-temper. 79 12-9 548
8 *Neolithic Bowl sherds:* seven including rim; gritted, partly porous fabric.   79 12-9 1569
9 *Neolithic Bowl rim sherd:* corky fabric.
                                            79 12-9 1570a
10 *Neolithic Bowl sherds:* three including rim; flint-temper.   79 12-9 1570b
11 *Neolithic Bowl rim sherd:* flint-temper.
                                            79 12-9 1570c
12 *Neolithic Bowl rim sherd:* fine flint-temper.
                                            79 12-9 1570d
13 *Neolithic Bowl rim sherd:* flint-temper.
                                            79 12-9 1570e
14 *Neolithic Bowl rim sherd:* fine grit-temper.
                                            79 12-9 1570f
15 *Neolithic Bowl rim sherd:* corky fabric.
                                            79 12-9 1570g
16 *Neolithic Bowl rim sherd:* corky fabric.
                                            79 12-9 1570h
17 *Neolithic Bowl sherds:* eleven; varying grit-temper.
                                            79 12-9 1570i
18 *Neolithic Bowl sherds:* chalk-temper. 79 12-9 1570j
   NPY no. 16.
19 *Beaker rim sherd:* rectangular tooth-comb stamped reserved triangles surrounded by horizontal lines.
                                            79 12-9 549a
20 *Beaker neck sherd:* rectangular tooth-comb stamped zone of three horizontal lines separated by plain zone from second with two horizontal lines above traces of further decoration.   79 12-9 549b

21 *Beaker sherd*: rectangular tooth—comb stamped zone of two horizontal lines separated by plain zone from single horizontal line.   79 12—9 549c

22 *Beaker sherds*: three; rectangular tooth—comb stamped horizontal lines outlining reserved zone with further zones including chevron and ?filled triangles, all irregularly executed.   79 12—9 549d

23 *Beaker sherd*: rectangular tooth—comb stamped; reserved bar—chevron pattern, triangular spaces filled with horizontal lines.   79 12—9 549e

24 *Beaker sherd*: rectangular tooth—comb stamped horizontal lines.   79 12—9 549f

25 *Beaker sherd*: spatulate impressions above line.
                                                        79 12—9 549g

26 *Beaker sherd*: tooth—comb stamped three horizontal lines separating zones of chevron lattice.
                                                        79 12—9 549h

27 *Beaker sherd*: incised zone of lattice with two rectangular tooth—comb stamped horizontal lines below.   79 12—9 549i

28 *Beaker sherds*: four; finger—pinched rustication; corky fabric.   79 12—9 549j and 1570k

29 *Beaker sherd*: finger—pinched rustication.
                                                        79 12—9 549k

30 *Beaker sherd*: lines of fingernail impressions.
                                                        79 12—9 549l

31 *Beaker sherd*: rectangular tooth—comb stamped impressions.   79 12—9 549m

32 *Beaker sherd*: plain.   79 12—9 549n

33 *Beaker sherds*: four; plain.   79 12—9 1570l
   Clarke no. 1263.

34 *Food Vessel rim sherd*: twisted cord: on internal rim bevel, diagonal lines; on external rim bevel, vertical lines; on neck, diagonal lines.
                                                        79 12—9 548a

35 *Accessory Cup*: (inverted above old surface, 7.2 m SW. of centre); beneath rim, two irregular rows of comb-impressed short lines forming herringbone for part of circumference.
   M. 11.3 cm; H. 7.1 cm; B. 6.8 cm.   79 12—9 546

36 *Bronze Age sherds*: twenty—eight; plain.
                                                        79 12—9 1570m

37 *Early Iron Age rim sherds*: shouldered jar; rock—tempered.   79 12—9 1570t

38 *Early Iron Age base sherds*: two; bowl; rock—tempered.
                                                        79 12—9 1570u

39 *Early Iron Age sherds*: twenty—one, of minimum twelve jars; rock—tempered.   79 12—9 1570v

40 *Early Iron Age sherds*: three; flint—tempered.
                                                        79 12—9 1570x

41 *Romano—British base sherd*: handmade jar; grey and brown vesicular ware.   79 12—9 1569a

42 *Romano—British base sherd*: handmade jar; grey and brown vesicular ware.   79 12—9 1569a

43 *Romano—British sherds*: two, including rim; Huntcliff ware; worn.   79 12—9 1569a

44 *Romano—British rim sherd*: handmade jar; dark grey vesicular ware.   79 12—9 1570n

45 *Romano—British base sherd*: handmade jar; dark grey vesicular ware.   79 12—9 1570o

46 *Romano—British base sherd*: handmade jar; dark grey vesicular ware.   79 12—9 1570p

47 *Romano—British sherds*: thirty—two, including base, of minimum six handmade jars; dark grey vesicular ware.   79 12—9 1570q

48 *Romano—British base sherd*: handmade jar; grey and brown ware with crystalline calcite—temper.
                                                        79 12—9 1570r

49 *Romano—British sherds*: seventeen, of minimum seven handmade jars; calcareous tempered.   79 12—9 1570s

50 *Romano—British sherds*: two of rim and neck, of handmade jar; Huntcliff ware; worn.   79 12—9 1570z

51 *'Pottery fragments'*: not identified.   79 12—9 547

52 *?Crucible sherds*: two; fine—grained dense fabric.
                                                        79 12—9 1570y

53 *Stone rubber*: two polished faces; siltstone.
   L. 22.0 cm; W. 7.6 cm; Th. 3.0 cm.   79 12—9 592

54 *Stone rubber*: one polished face; sandstone.
   L. 6.0 cm; W. 5.6 cm; Th. 2.6 cm.   79 12—9 594

55 *Stone rubber*: polished edge facets and two abraded faces; sandstone.
   L. 5.7 cm; W. 4.9 cm; Th. 2.8 cm.   79 12—9 596

56 *Stone rubber fragment*: bevelled with use; quartzite.
   L. 6.2 cm; W. 5.8 cm; th. 3.2 cm.   79 12—9 600

57 *Stone rubber fragment*: polished facets; sandstone.
   L. 5.4 cm; W. 4.1 cm; Th. 4.7 cm.   79 12—9 602

58 *Stone rubber fragment*: one polished face; tufa.
   L. 5.3 cm; W. 5.1 cm; Th. 3.5 cm.   79 12—9 604

59 *Hammerstone*: abraded edges; quartzite.
   L. 8.5 cm; W. 6.0 cm; Th. 3.9 cm.   79 12—9 593

60 *Hammerstone*: abraded edges; sandstone.
   L. 5.9 cm; W. 4.9 cm; Th. 2.4 cm.   79 12—9 601

61-3 *Sandstone fragments*: three.
                                        79 12—9 597, 599 and 603

64 *Quartzite fragment*   79 12—9 598

65 *Flint leaf arrowhead*: all over bifacial invasive retouch; grey.
   L. 4.3 cm; W. 2.0 cm; Th. 0.4 cm.   79 12—9 556
   BB fig. 114; *Green* 1980, no. A46.

66 *Flint leaf arrowhead*: all over bifacial invasive retouch; point snapped; mottled grey.
   L. 2.7 cm; w. 1.6 cm; th. 0.3 cm.   79 12—9 557
   Green 1980, no. A46.

67 *Flint leaf arrowhead*: invasive retouch on L., point snapped; mottled grey.
   L. 2.8 cm; W. 2.4 cm; Th. 0.5 cm.   79 12—9 579

68-9 *'Flint drills'*: not identified.   79 12—9 570—1

70 *Flint ?piercer*: on core fragment; some bifacial edge retouch; cortex remnant; grey.
   L. 5.7 cm; W. 3.4 cm; Th. 2.6 cm.   79 12—9 591

71 *Flint horseshoe scraper*: edge retouch on distal and bilateral at 70 degrees; platform butt; patinated.
   L. 2.8 cm; W. 2.4 cm; Th. 0.7 cm.   79 12—9 566

72 *Flint end- and side-scraper*: edge retouch on proximal and L. at 60 degrees; cortex remnant; grey.
   L. 3.1 cm; W. 2.3 cm; Th. 0.8 cm.   79 12—9 563

73 *Flint end-scraper*: edge retouch on distal at 60 degrees; dihedral butt; mottled beige.
   L. 2.5 cm; W. 1.9 cm; Th. 0.9 cm.   79 12—9 600d

74-82 *'Flint scrapers'*: nine, not identified.
                                 79 12—9 559—62, 564—5 and 567—9

83 *Flint knife*: all over invasive retouch at 50 degrees; platform butt; patinated.
   L. 3.6 cm; W. 3.0 cm; Th. 1.1 cm.   79 12—9 558

84 *Flint 'polisher'*: cuboid; roughly flaked on three faces, cortex remnant on two faces, sixth face highly polished.
   L. 4.9 cm; W. 4.8 cm; Th. 4.6 cm.   79 12—9 572
   BB fig. 26; *ASI* fig. 184.

85 *Flint blade*: platform butt; mottled grey.
   L. 4.4 cm; W. 1.4 cm; Th. 0.6 cm.   79 12—9 600c

   Flint flakes

	Btt	Ctx	Col.	L.	W.	Th.	79 12—9
86	Pl.		M. Gr.	3.0	1.3	0.3	600a
87	Pl.	x	Bt	4.0	1.7	0.7	600b
88	Pl.		Gr.	2.1	1.0	0.3	600e
89	Pl.		M. Gr.	2.3	0.9	0.4	600f
90	Pnct.		D. Sp.	2.4	1.7	0.4	600g
91	Dh.	x	M. Gr.	1.5	2.3	0.5	600h
92	Pnct.		Pat.	2.9	1.1	0.5	600i
93	Bkn		M. Gr.	1.8	1.6	0.5	600j

94–112 *'Flint flakes'*: nineteen; not identified.

79 12-9 575-8, 580-9 and 1571-5

113 *Flint core*: single platform with parallel blade scars; cortex remnant; patinated.

L. 2.2 cm; W. 2.9 cm; Th. 2.7 cm.   79 12-9 595

114–5 *'Flint cores'*: two; not identified.

79 12-9 573-4

116 *'Flint fragment'*: not identified.   79 12-9 590

58 COWLAM (Cowlam IX)   58:1-34

Yorkshire E.R.; North Humberside   SE 96 66

ROUND BARROW: Diam. 20 m, H. 0.6 m; earth and chalk rubble; opened 5–6 November 1867.
BB 222–5; Greenwell 1868b.

Burial 1: adult inhumation, crouched on L. with head S.; on old surface, 1.8 m S. of centre.

Burial 2: adult cremation deposit, in heap Diam. 0.2 m; 0.2 m above old surface, 0.9 m S. of centre.
   'two potsherds': not preserved.

Burial 3: adolescent inhumation, crouched on R. with head W.; on old surface, 1.8 m SE. of centre.

Burial 4: adult cremation deposit, in heap Diam. 0.2 m; 0.2 m above old surface, 2.7 m W. of centre.

Burial 5: adult male inhumation, crouched on L. with head SE.; at SE. end of central oval grave L. 2.6 m, W. 1.8 m, D. 1.1 m, aligned SE.–NW., fill of earth including some disturbed bones; battle-axe at face with traces of wooden haft to R. hand, flint and jet behind head.

1 *Stone battle-axe*: dolerite, Y 785; Roe IIIA; all over ground and polished; cutting edge flat-bevelled; hourglass perforation.

L. 11.1 cm; W. 5.5 cm; Th. 4.4 cm; Diam. (perf.) 2.4 cm.   79 12-9 605
BB fig. 115; *ASI* fig. 135; *Roe* 1966, no. 252.

2–4 *Jet fragments*: three; split along bedding planes; unworked.

L. 3.0 cm; W. 1.3 cm; Th. 1.2 cm.   79 12-9 609
L. 3.2 cm; W. 0.9 cm; Th. 0.6 cm.   79 12-9 609a
L. 1.5 cm; W. 0.9 cm; Th. 0.9 cm.   79 12-9 609b

5 *Flint end- and side-scraper*: edge retouch on proximal and R. at 60 degrees; grey.

L. 2.1 cm; W. 2.7 cm; Th. 0.8 cm.   79 12-9 606

6 *Flint end-scraper*: edge retouch on distal at 60 degrees; cortex remnant; grey.

L. 2.9 cm; W. 2.1 cm; Th. 0.9 cm.   79 12-9 607

7 *Flint flake*: platform butt; patinated.

L. 4.0 cm; W. 1.7 cm; Th. 0.7 cm.   79 12-9 608

Burial 6: adult ?female inhumation, crouched with head NE.; on wooden flooring at NE. side of oval grave L. 1.8 m, W. 1.3 m, D. 0.9 m, aligned NE.–SW., connecting with N. side of central grave; earrings at temporals and jet behind head.

8 *Bronze earring*: basket type; broad oar-shaped body of sheet metal tapering to narrow tang of oval section with pointed end; edges of body thinned, and bordered by two splayed grooves at body-tang junction (Table 1:46).

Diam. 2.4 cm; W. 3.0 cm; tang Th. 0.3 cm.

79 12-9 611

9 *Bronze earring*: basket type; body damaged; tang of oval section tapered to missing tip; traces of grooves at body-tang junction (Table 1:47).

Diam. 2.5 cm; W. 2.8 cm; tang Th. 0.3 cm.

79 12-9 612
BB fig. 47; *ABI* fig. 490; *Butler* 1963, 190, no. 4.
'two formless pieces of jet': not preserved.

Burial 6 grave fill
   'three potsherds': not preserved.

10 *Jet button fragment*: cut and polished to conical dome bevelled to flat base with remains of central drilled V-perforation.

Diam. 1.4 cm; Th. 0.9 cm.   79 12-9 610

Mound material

11 *Stone saddle quern fragment*: sandstone; three pecked and ground faces.

L. 9.3 cm; W. 6.9 cm; Th. 6.4 cm.   79 12-9 1576

12 *Stone saddle quern fragment*: sandstone, one polished face.

L. 10.0 cm; W. 9.2 cm; Th. 3.1 cm.   79 12-9 618

13 *Quartzitic pebble fragment*   79 12-9 635

14 *Flint leaf arrowhead*: partial invasive retouch, partial inverse invasive retouch; cortex remnant; mottled grey.

L. 3.4 cm; W. 2.4 cm; Th. 0.4 cm.   79 12-9 617
Green 1980, no. A44.

15–16 *'Flint drills'*: two; not identified.

79 12-9 615-6

17 *Flint horseshoe scraper*: edge retouch on distal and bilateral at 55 degrees; platform butt; cortex remnant; grey.

L. 3.0 cm; W. 2.9 cm; Th. 0.9 cm.   79 12-9 614

18 *Flint end-scraper*: edge retouch on distal at 65 degrees; worn bilaterally; patinated.

L. 4.0 cm; W. 3.4 cm; Th. 0.8 cm.   79 12-9 613

19 *Flint flake*: platform butt; white.

L. 8.4 cm; W. 3.1 cm; Th. 1.0 cm.   79 12-9 619

20–7 *'Flint flakes'*: eight; not identified.

79 12-9 620-7

28 *Flint core*: one platform with blade scar, on reverse opposed platform with irregular flake scars; cortex remnant; mottled grey.

L. 5.0 cm; W. 2.8 cm; Th. 2.9 cm.   79 12-9 628

29 *Flint core*: one platform with flake scar forming second platform with two blade scars; cortex remnant; mottled grey.

L. 4.0 cm; W. 2.5 cm; Th. 3.3 cm.   79 12-9 633

30 *Flint pebble core*: platform preparation arrested by fault, traces of previous single platform with remnants of parallel blade scars; corticated; grey.

L. 4.3 cm; W. 3.0 cm; Th. 3.4 cm.   79 12-9 634

31–4 *'Flint cores'*: four; not identified.

79 12-9 629-32

59 COWLAM (Cowlam X)   59:1-21

Yorkshire E.R.; North Humberside   SE 96 66

ROUND BARROW: Diam. 21 m, H. 0.5 m; earth and chalk rubble; opened 7–8 November 1867.
BB 225–6; *Manby* 1974, 121.

Burial 1: adult inhumation, crouched on R. with head W.; on old surface, 4.8 m SSW. of centre.

Burial 2: child skull; 0.6 m N. of Burial 1; chisel at face.

1 *Stone chisel*: Group VI, Y 786; all over ground and polished; re-worked edge-faceted axe; cutting-edge damaged.

L. 9.5 cm; W. 2.1 cm; Th. 1.8 cm.   79 12-9 636
Manby 1974, 118.

Burial 3: adult male inhumation, crouched on L. with head E.; on old surface and with legs overlying grave of Burial 5, 1.8 m NW. of centre; flints behind head.

2 *Flint horseshoe scraper*: edge retouch on distal and bilateral at 80 degrees, all over invasive retouch; platform butt; grey.

L. 2.1 cm; W. 1.9 cm; Th. 0.7 cm.   79 12-9 637

3 *Flint knife*: bilateral invasive retouch; corticated butt; grey.
L. 4.9 cm; W. 3.1 cm; Th. 0.8 cm.   79 12-9 638

Burial 4: disturbed inhumation; on old surface, 2.7 m W. of centre.

Burial 5: adult male inhumation, incomplete and partly disarticulated on L. with head SE.; in oval grave L. 2.3 m, W. 2.1 m, D. 1.4 m, aligned SE.-NW., fill of chalk rubble around earth and chalk-filled wooden enclosure, W. of Burial 3.

Burial 5 grave-fill
4 *Flint knife*: converging bilateral invasive retouch; platform butt; cortex remnant; grey.
L. 5.1 cm; W. 3.4 cm; Th. 0.7 cm.   79 12-9 639
Clarke 1932, no. 5.4.

Mound material
5 *Flint piercer*: partial edge retouch on L., wear on R.; cortex remnant; patinated.
L. 5.0 cm; W. 3.3 cm; Th. 0.7 cm.   79 12-9 642
6 *'Flint scraper'*: not identified.   79 12-9 640
7 *Flint rod fragment*: all over coarse invasive retouch; cortex remnant; broken; mottled grey.
L. 6.3 cm; W. 3.3 cm; Th. 2.6 cm.   79 12-9 655
8 *Flint worked fragment*: bifacial edge retouch on distal and R.; cortex remnant; mottled grey.
L. 3.4 cm; W. 3.9 cm; Th. 1.3 cm.   79 12-9 641
9 *Flint worked flake*: converging bilateral invasive retouch on distal; broken; beige.
L. 3.4 cm; W. 2.0 cm; Th. 0.5 cm.   79 12-9 644
10-12 *'Flint implements'*: three; not identified.
79 12-9 643 and 645-6
13 *Flint utilised flake*: bilateral wear; platform butt; cortex remnant; mottled grey.
L. 5.8 cm; W. 2.9 cm; Th. 0.9 cm.   79 12-9 647
14 *Flint utilised flake*: bilateral wear; punctiform butt; grey.
L. 5.2 cm; W. 1.9 cm; Th. 0.5 cm.   79 12-9 650
15 *Flint blade*: punctiform butt; grey.
L. 5.1 cm; W. 1.0 cm; Th. 0.5 cm.   79 12-9 651
16 *Flint flake*: platform butt; grey.
L. 5.6 cm; W. 2.3 cm; Th. 0.7 cm.   79 12-9 648
17 *Flint flake*: punctiform butt; cortex remnant; mottled grey.
L. 6.8 cm; W. 2.4 cm; Th. 0.7 cm.   79 12-9 649
18-19 *'Flint flakes'*: two; not identified.
79 12-9 652-3
20 *Flint core*: single platform with parallel blade scars; traces of previous platform; mottled grey.
L. 2.5 cm; W. 2.3 cm; Th. 2.0 cm.   79 12-9 656
21 *'Flint core'*: not identified.   79 12-9 654

60   THWING   60:1-13

Yorkshire E.R.; North Humberside.   TA 05 72

ROUND BARROW: Diam. 21 m, H. 0.5 m, reduced by ploughing; earth; internal ditch Diam. 11 m, W. 1.2 m, D. 0.8 m.
BB 226-8.

Burial 1: adult male inhumation, crouched on R. with head N.; 0.3 m above old surface, 1.6 m E. by N. of centre.

Burial 2: adult inhumation, crouched on L. with head ESE.; above old surface, 4 m WNW. of centre; Beaker at feet.
1 *Beaker*: rectangular tooth-comb stamped: on rim, short diagonal and transverse lines; beneath rim, short diagonal lines enclosed by single lines; on neck, upper zone of bar-chevron pattern with

triangles filled with diagonal lines enclosed by vertical chevrons with single horizontal line below; on belly, two narrow zones of short diagonal lines (lower made by plain spatula) enclosed by single horizontal lines and separated by plain zone; on body, horizontal line above zone of lattice; at base, zone of vertical chevrons.
M. *c*. 16.0 cm; H. 23.0 cm; B. *c*. 9.0 cm.
BAP no. 150; *Clarke* no. 1397.   79 12-9 657

Burials 3-4 were in central grave Diam. 2.1 m, D. 1.2 m.

Burial 3: adult inhumation, crouched on L. with head ESE.; at D. 0.3 m; jet on R. arm, wood in L. hand.
2 *Jet button*: cut and polished to peaked dome bevelled to convex base with central drilled V- perforation; upper face with incised decoration: perimeter defined by two concentric circles with hatched infill, centre with four hatched pendant triangles in cruciform design, running chevron on inner circle.
Diam. 3.9 cm; Th. 0.7 cm.   79 12-9 660
BB fig. 3.
3 *Jet ring*: cut and polished to square section, incised hatched bands on both faces and perimeter; two drilled V-perforations at one side.
Diam. (outer) 2.7 cm; (inner) 1.4 cm; Th. 0.7 cm.
BB fig. 5.   79 12-9 661
4 *Wood fragments*: unidentifiable.   79 12-9 659

Burial 4: 'broken and scattered' bones of adult; at base of grave.

Burials 3 and 4 grave fill
5 *Peterborough Ware rim sherd*: Ebbsfleet; internally and on top of rim, whipped cord diagonal lines; on neck, row of vertical fingertip impressions.
79 12-9 658
6 *Peterborough Ware rim sherd*: Ebbsfleet; internally and on top of rim, whipped cord herringbone; beneath rim, whipped cord diagonal lines.   79 12-9 658a
7 *Peterborough Ware neck sherd*: Ebbsfleet; diagonal whipped cord lines.   79 12-9 658b
8 *Peterborough Ware shoulder sherd*: Ebbsfleet; diagonal whipped cord lines above and below.
79 12-9 658c
9 *Peterborough Ware sherd*: lightly incised diagonal lines.   79 12-9 658d
10 *Peterborough Ware sherd*: coarsely incised diagonal lines.   79 12-9 658e
Manby 1956, fig. 3.
11 *Beaker sherds*: two; rectangular tooth-comb stamped pair of lines with traces of lattice/lozenge above.
Clarke no. 1398.   79 12-9 1577
12 *Flint barbed-and-tanged arrowhead*: bifacial invasive retouch; patinated.
L. 2.0 cm; W. 1.9 cm; Th. 0.3 cm.   79 12-9 662
BB fig. 117, *Green* 1980, no. 326.
13 *Flint barbed-and-tanged arrowhead*: bifacial invasive retouch; one barb broken; patinated.
L. 1.8 cm; W. 1.7 cm; Th. 0.4 cm.   79 12-9 663
Green 1980, no. 326.
'flint barbed-and-tanged arrowhead': not preserved.

61   RUDSTON (Rudstone I)   61:1-50

Yorkshire E.R.; North Humberside   TA 098 658

ROUND BARROW: Diam. 20 m, H. 0.6 m; chalk rubble; extensive burning on old surface.
BB 229-32.

Burial 1: child inhumation, crouched on L. with head E.; 0.3 m above old surface, 2.5 m SSW. of centre.

Burial 2: adult male inhumation, crouched on L. with head NE.; 0.2 m above old surface, 2.5 m SE. by E. of centre; jet beneath R. tibia.

1   *Jet button*: ovate, cut and polished to dome bevelled to flat base; central V-perforation broken away at one side.
    L. 2.5 cm; W. 2.3 cm; Th. 0.7 cm.   79 12-9 667
    BB fig. 118.

2   *Shale or lignite ring*: cut and polished to rectangular section; on edge, transverse hourglass perforation cut across original V-perforation; radial incisions over both faces and edge, on one face forming double cross opposite perforation; dark brown.
    Diam. (outer) 2.8 cm; Diam. (inner) 1.6 cm; Th. 0.7 cm.   79 12-9 668
    BB fig. 119.

Burial 3: adult male inhumation, crouched on L. with head NW.; on old surface, 3 m E. by S. of centre, with partial cover of chalk blocks.

Burial 4: disturbed bones of adult male inhumation; beneath and to W. of Burial 3.
    'several fragments of broken burnt stone .... used in polishing': not preserved.

Burial 5: adult ?female inhumation, crouched on R. with head WSW.; at W. end of oval grave L. 2.2 m, W. 1.4 m, D. 0.6 m, aligned ESE.-WNW., 2.7 m E. by S. of centre; some bones in fill; Beaker behind head, antler at knees.

3   *Beaker*: on neck, zone of horizontal grooved lines; remainder rectangular tooth-comb stamped: on upper belly, zone of horizontal lines; on belly, vertical and diagonal fringing lines enhancing plain zone; on body, zone of irregularly executed horizontal lines above band of multiple vertical chevrons.
    M. 13.1 cm; H. 20.1 cm; B. 8.0 cm.   79 12-9 665
    BAP no. 144; *Clarke* no. 1366.

4   *Antler pick*: shed red deer antler; brow and bez tines broken, beam tine abraded, beam broken.
    L. (beam) 47.8 cm; L. (tine) 19.1 cm; max. Diam. 4.4 cm.   79 12-9 669
    BB fig. 34.

Burial 6: adult ?female inhumation, crouched on R. with head WNW.; on old surface 5.1 m NE. of centre; pin and flints nos 5-6, 8-9 behind hips, no. 7 at R. hand, no. 10 beneath knees.

5   *Flint side-scraper*: edge retouch on L. at 50 degrees and partial on proximal; patinated.
    L. 2.8 m; W. 4.3 m; Th. 0.7 cm.   79 12-9 671

6   *Flint worked flake*: edge retouch on distal and R.; platform butt; cortex remnant; patinated.
    L. 5.0 cm; W. 3.3 cm; Th. 0.8 cm.   79 12-9 672

7   *Flint worked flake*: fine edge retouch on distal; dihedral butt; cortex remnant; mottled grey.
    L. 6.3 cm; W. 5.3 cm; Th. 0.8 cm.   79 12-9 675

8   *Flint flake*: platform butt; broken; patinated.
    L. 3.0 cm; W. 2.0 cm; Th. 0.3 cm.   79 12-9 673

9   *Flint flake*: punctiform butt; broken; patinated.
    L. 2.2 cm; W. 1.6 cm; Th. 0.3 cm.   79 12-9 674

10   *'Flint flake'*: not identified.   79 12-9 676

11   *Bone pin*: caprovine metatarsal splinter, cut and polished to fine point; transverse fine incisions at butt.
    L. 6.4 cm; W. 1.8 cm; Th. 0.3 cm.   79 12-9 670

Burial 7: adult cremation deposit; in pit Diam. 0.4 m, D. 0.5 m, 3.6 m N. of Burial 5; flints nos 12-15, 17-19 among bones, no. 16 above bones.

12   *Flint worked flake*: edge retouch on R.; faceted butt; burnt, pitted and fragmented.
    L. 4.5 cm; W. 4.7 cm; Th. 0.8 cm.   79 12-9 680

13   *Flint worked fragment*: partial edge retouch; burnt.
    L. 2.0 cm; W. 1.4 cm; Th. 0.8 cm.   79 12-9 681

14   *Flint worked flake*: partial fine edge retouch; platform butt; burnt.
    L. 4.5 cm; W. 3.9 cm; Th. 0.6 cm.   79 12-9 677

15-6   *'Flint implements'*: burnt; not identified.
        79 12-9 678-9

17   *Flint utilised flake*: bilateral wear; corticated butt; patinated.
    L. 6.3 cm; W. 3.1 cm; Th. 1.0 cm.   79 12-9 684

18   *Flint flake*: burnt and shattered.
    L. 5.0 cm; W. 4.5 cm; Th. 0.7 cm.   79 12-9 682

19   *'Flint flake'*: burnt; not identified.   79 12-9 683

Feature A: burnt earth deposit; on old surface 4.8 m SSE. of centre.
    'Dark-coloured plain pottery': probably part of nos 21-39 below.

20   *Flint leaf arrowhead*: all over bifacial invasive retouch; patinated.
    L. 3.1 cm; W. 1.8 cm; Th. 0.4 cm.   79 12-9 666
    Green 1980, no. A517.
    'Flint chippings': probably among nos 40-5 below.

Feature B: oval pit L. 1.2 m, W. 0.6 m, D. 0.5 m, aligned ENE.-WSW., burnt fill, 6.3 m SE. of centre.
    'Potsherds': probably part of nos 21-39 below.
    'Flint chippings': probably part of nos 40-5 below.

Feature C: pit Diam. 0.3 m, D. 0.5 m, fill of earth and charcoal, below Burial 4.

Feature D: pit Diam. 0.3 m, D. 0.3 m, charcoal in fill; 4.5 m N. of Burial 5.

Feature A or B or mound material

21   *Neolithic Bowl sherds*: three including rim; coarse quartz-temper.   79 12-9 664

22   *Neolithic Bowl rim sherd*: variable grit-temper.
        79 12-9 664a

23   *Neolithic Bowl rim sherd*: light grit-temper.
        79 12-9 664b

24   *Neolithic Bowl rim sherd*: fine to medium flint-temper.   79 12-9 664c

25   *Neolithic Bowl rim sherds*: four; fine chalk-temper.
        79 12-9 664d

26   *Neolithic Bowl rim sherd*: fine to coarse grit-temper.
        79 12-9 664e

27   *Neolithic Bowl rim sherd*: medium grit-temper.
        79 12-9 664f

28   *Neolithic Bowl rim sherd*: fine grit- and sand-temper.
        79 12-9 664g

29   *Neolithic Bowl rim sherds*: two; medium quartz-temper.   79 12-9 664h

30   *Neolithic Bowl sherds*: three including rim; porous fabric.   79 12-9 664i

31   *Neolithic Bowl rim sherd*: heavy quartz-temper.
        79 12-9 664j

32   *Neolithic Bowl rim sherd*: diagonal ripple burnishing; fine grit-temper.   79 12-9 664k

33   *Neolithic Bowl rim sherd*: heavy grit-temper.
        79 12-9 664l

34   *Neolithic Bowl rim sherd*: diagonal ripple burnishing; fine grit-temper.   79 12-9 664m

35   *Neolithic Bowl sherds*: three including rim; coarse grit-temper.   79 12-9 664n

36   *Neolithic Bowl sherd*: with fragmentary lug; some quartz-temper.   79 12-9 664o

37   *Neolithic Bowl sherds*: one hundred and forty-three; coarse limestone and/or quartz-temper. 79 12-9 664p

38   *Neolithic Bowl sherds*: two hundred and eight; fine to medium grit-temper.   79 12-9 664q

39   *Neolithic Bowl sherds*: eighteen; soft chalk-temper; weathered.   79 12-9 664r
    NPY no. 3.

40 *Flint utilised blade*: bilateral wear; broken; patinated.
   L. 3.8 cm; W. 1.4 cm; Th. 0.3 cm.   79 12-9 694
41 *Flint flake*: punctiform butt; cortex remnant; mottled grey.
   L. 8.0 cm; W. 2.8 cm; Th. 1.3 cm.   79 12-9 691
42 *Flint flake*: punctiform butt; cortex remnant; patinated.
   L. 3.9 cm w. 1.5 cm Th. 0.5 cm.   79 12-9 693
43 *Flint flake*: broken; cortex remnant; beige.
   L. 2.9 cm; W. 1.5 cm; Th. 0.3 cm.   79 12-9 695
44-5 *'Flint flakes'*: two; not identified.
                                  79 12-9 690 and 692

Mound material

46 *Fired clay loomweight fragment*: plano-convex section roughly finished on exterior; light buff, no filler.
   L. 6.0 m; W. 4.7 cm; Th. 3.8 cm.   79 12-9 689
47 *Stone rubber*: gritstone; sub-rectangular, one face worn smooth, two edges ground smooth.
   L. 16.1 cm; W. 13.2 cm; Th. 4.2 cm.   79 12-9 686
48 *Stone pebble*: quartzite; broken.
   L. 12.2 cm; W. 9.0 cm; Th. 5.6 cm.   79 12-9 685
49 *'Flint scraper'*: not identified.   79 12-9 687

Not located

50 *Flint worked flake*: inverse edge retouch on R.; platform butt; cortex remnant; patinated.
   L. 4.9 cm; W. 3.4 cm; Th. 1.0 cm.   79 12-9 688

62 RUDSTON (Rudstone IV)   62:1-663

Yorkshire E.R.; North Humberside   TA 098 658

ROUND BARROW: Diam. 20 m, H. 1.4 m, reduced by ploughing; earth (turf) core with chalk capping; ditch Diam 23 m, W. 3.2 m, D. 1 m (Pacitto); opened November 1869, limited excavation by C. and E. Grantham 1960, re-excavated by A.L. Pacitto September 1968.
BB 234-45; *Tyndall* 1870; *Pacitto* 1972.

Burial 1: adult ?female inhumation, crouched on L. with head NW.; vessel at face and awl at chest.
1 *Bronze awl*: Thomas Type 2A; short wedge-shaped tang to square-sectioned swelling and round-sectioned point; damaged (Table 1:35).
   L. 3.8 cm; W. 0.3 cm; Th. 0.2 cm.   79 12-9 705
   Pacitto 1972, fig. 9.19; *Thomas* 1968, 23.
2 *Food Vessel*: whipped cord: on internal rim bevel, vertical lines; on both ridges, diagonal lines; in neck and on body, irregular horizontal to diagonal lines.
   M. 16.0 cm; H. 13.4 cm; B. c. 6.5 cm.   79 12-9 696
   BAP no. 110; *Simpson* 1968, fig. 46.4; *Pacitto* 1972, fig. 11.4.

Burial 2: adult male inhumation remnants; in ploughsoil 1.8 m NE. of centre.

Burials 3-6 and 8-11 were in a central grave cut through the turf core, Diam. 2.7 m, D. 4.2 m (3.2 m chalk-cut), fill of earth and chalk; at 1.8 m above base four large flat sandstone slabs, with two upright slabs at S. side.

Burial 3: child inhumation, crouched on L. with head E. by S.; 1 m above old surface at E. side.

Burial 4: adult ?female inhumation, crouched on L. with head ENE.; in earth fill above dished layer of charcoal above old surface at centre; flints 6-8 and awl 4 at chest, flint 9 and awl 3 behind hips, Beaker at heels.
3 *Copper awl*: ?Thomas type 1C; round section with central swelling; damaged and corroded (Table 1:33).
   L. 1.7 cm; Diam. 0.2 cm.   79 12-9 703
   Pacitto 1972, fig. 9.17; *Thomas* 1968, 23.

4 *Bronze awl*: Thomas Type 1B; both ends of round section with square-sectioned central expansion with lozenge facets; damaged and corroded (Table 1:34).
   L. 3.2 cm; W. 0.2 cm; Th. 0.2 cm.   79 12-9 704
   Pacitto 1972, fig. 9.18; *Thomas* 1968, 23.
5 *Beaker*: coarse circumferential grooves.
   M. 14.6-15.3 cm; H. 17.7 cm; B. 10.8 cm.
                                             89 12-9 697
   BB fig. 85; *BAP* no. 139; *Clarke* no. 1371; *Pacitto* 1972, fig. 11.5.
6 *Flint knife*: distal and bilateral retouch; dihedral butt; cortex remnant; grey.
   L. 5.6 cm; W. 3.2 cm; Th. 0.9 cm.   79 12-9 706
   Pacitto 1972, fig. 9.15.
7-9 *'Flint flakes'*: three; not identified.
                                             79 12-9 725-7

Burial 5: disturbed adult ?male inhumation, originally crouched on L. with head SE.; disturbed by Burial 4.

Burial 6: adult female inhumation, crouched on L. with head E.; on charcoal layer at centre; Beaker behind head, flint beneath feet.
10 *Beaker*: tooth-comb stamped: on neck, broad zone of vertical herringbone bordered above by three horizontal lines and narrow band of lozenge and below by four horizontal lines and narrow band of lozenge; on belly, narrow zone of herringbone bordered above and below by three horizontal lines and narrow band of lozenge; on lower body, narrow zone of vertical herringbone bordered above by two to three horizontal lines and narrow band of lozenge and below by three to five horizontal lines.
   M. 12.5-13.1 cm; H. 15.5 cm; B. 7.7 cm. 79 12-9 698
   BB fig. 82; *BAP* no. 138; *Clarke* no. 1370; *Pacitto* 1972, fig. 11.2.
11 *Flint knife*: invasive retouch on L; platform butt; broken; grey.
   L. 4.3 cm; W. 2.5 cm; Th. 0.6 cm.   79 12-9 708
   Pacitto 1972, fig. 9.16.

Burial 7: cranial fragments; in mound, 0.6 m above old surface, 1.2 m E. of grave edge.

Burial 8: adult male inhumation, crouched on L. with head S., and at legs, two infant inhumations; in basal cist L. 1.1 m, W. 0.6 m, H. 0.5 m, aligned SSE.-NNW.; four side-slabs, two paving slabs and capstone, at N. side of grave; Beaker behind head, stone at face.
12 *Beaker*: tooth-comb stamped: on top and outer edge of rim, short diagonal opposed lines; on neck, zone of horizontal lines bordered above and below by short diagonal lines; at base of neck and on to belly, broad zone of lozenge band with band of horizontal lines above and below bordered by short diagonal lines; on body, similar broad zone.
   M. 13.0 cm; H. 19.9 cm; B. 7.8 cm.   79 12-9 699
   BAP no. 135; *Clarke* no. 1367; *Pacitto* 1972, fig. 11.1.
13 *Stone fragments*: three; ferruginous sandstone.
                                             79 12-9 712

Burial 9: double cremation deposit: adult male with few bones of adult, in oval heap L. 0.5 m, W. 0.3 m; at centre of basal cist L. 1.1 m, W. 0.8 m, H. 0.6 m, aligned SSE.-NNW., six side-slabs, one paving slab and capstone, at S. side of grave; Beaker in SE. corner.
14 *Beaker*: tooth-comb stamped: on internal rim bevel, herringbone; on neck, broad zone of narrow band of vertical herringbone separated by three horizontal lines from band of short vertical lines, the whole enclosed above by two and below by three horizontal lines; on upper body, broad zone of narrow band of vertical herringbone separated by two horizontal

lines from band of herringbone, the whole enclosed above by three and below by two horizontal lines; on lower body, broad zone of lozenge band separated by three horizontal lines from band of herringbone separated by two horizontal lines from band of short vertical lines separated by three horizontal lines from band of lattice, the whole bordered above and below by two horizontal lines.

M. 16.1 cm; H. 22.3 cm; B. 8.8 cm.   79 12-9 700
BB fig. 120; *BAP* no. 136; *Clarke* no. 1368; *Pacitto* 1972, fig. 10.1.

Burial 10: adult male cremation deposit; 0.1 m above base between cists; Beaker at SSE.

15 *Beaker*: tooth-comb stamped: beneath rim, short vertical to diagonal lines bordered above by vertical chevrons and below by zone of incised horizontal lines; below, three zones of multiple vertical chevrons, the uppermost bordered by row of lozenges, with basal zone of bar-chevrons with upright and pendant triangles filled with multiple vertical chevrons, the main zones separated by narrow bands of horizontal lines and the whole bordered below by three horizontal lines.

M. 14.4 cm; H. 20.0 cm; B. 7.6 cm.   79 12-9 701
BAP no. 137; *Clarke* no. 1369; *Pacitto* 1972, fig. 10.2.

Burial 11: disturbed bones of adult and child; in basal fill at SW.

Burial 12: (1968) double inhumation: two adult males, both crouched on R. with heads W.; in hollow, 6 m E. of centre.

Burial 13: (1968) adult female inhumation, crouched on R. with head E.; in hollow at NE. edge of central grave.

Burial 14: (1968): adult female inhumation, crouched on R. with head N.; in grave cut through chalk capping at SE.

Shaft-grave fill

16 *Beaker sherds*: fifteen, including rim; tooth-comb stamped: beneath rim, lines above 'flag' motif; bar chevron on one sherd.   79 12-9 702
Clarke no. 1372; *Pacitto* 1972, fig. 11.3

17 *Beaker sherds*: five; coarse tooth-comb stamped: zone of horizontal lines bordering ?filled hexagon pattern.   79 12-9 702a

18 *Stone worked block*: gritstone; large flake removed from centre of concave edge.
L. 27.0 cm; W. 10.8 cm; Th. 7.2 cm.   79 12-9 709

19 *Stone worked block*: gritstone; large flakes removed from centres of opposing edges.
L. 20.4 cm; W. 12.2 cm; Th. 6.2 cm.   79 12-9 710

20 *Stone block*: gritstone.
L. 20.9 cm; W. 11.0 cm; Th. 8.5 cm.   79 12-9 711

21 *'Flint scraper'*: not identified.   79 12-9 714

22 *'Flint knife'*: not identified.   79 12-9 707

23-4 *'Flint saws'*: two; not identified.   79 12-9 718-9

25-6 *'Flint flakes'*: two; not identified.
'bone pin': not preserved.   79 12-9 723-4

Mound material (1869)

'potsherds': not preserved.

27 *Stone rubber*: quartzitic sandstone; multiple ground facets and one dished face.
L. 8.0 cm; W. 7.9 cm; Th. 5.9 cm.   79 12-9 729
BB fig. 13.

28-9 *'Flint scrapers'*: two; not identified.
79 12-9 715-6

30 *'Flint saw'*: not identified.   79 12-9 717

31-4 *'Flint flakes'*: not identified.
79 12-9 713 720-2

30 *'Flint saw'*: not identified.   79 12-9 717

31-4 *'Flint flakes'*: four; not identified.
79 12-9 713 and 720-2

35 *Flint core*: single platform with irregular flake scars on obverse and R.; evidence of previous platforms; cortex remnant; mottled grey.
L. 3.4 cm; W. 2.7 cm; Th. 2.7 cm.   79 12-9 728

Old surface and mound material (1960)

36 *Neolithic Bowl rim sherd*: no obvious temper.   GC B1

37 *Neolithic Bowl rim sherd*: externally, diagonal incised strokes; grit-tempered.   GC A8

38 *Neolithic Bowl rim sherd*   GC A2

39-41 *Neolithic Bowl rim sherds*: three; sandy fabric.
GC A2, B3

42-4 *Neolithic Bowl rim sherds*: three; grit-tempered.
GC A2, A3 and B1

45 *Neolithic Bowl shoulder sherd*: few grits.   GC

46 *Neolithic Bowl sherds*: sixty-four; grit-tempered. GC

47 *Neolithic Bowl sherds*: eighteen; sandy fabric.   GC

48 *Neolithic Bowl sherd*: vesicular fabric.   GC

49 *Neolithic Bowl*: on external rim bevel, incised vertical strokes; no obvious tempering.
M. *c.* 24.0 cm.   GC

50 *Flint polished axe fragment*: ground and polished to lenticular section; broken; patinated.
L. 5.7 cm; W. 1.4 cm; Th. 1.4 cm.   GC
Pacitto 1972, fig. 8.19.

51 *Flint leaf arrowhead*: all over bifacial invasive retouch; one end snapped and other damaged; patinated.
L. 5.4 cm; W. 2.8 cm; Th. 0.3 cm.   GC
Pacitto 1972, fig. 8.9.

52 *Flint leaf arrowhead*: fine all round edge retouch with bifacial invasive retouch at point; patinated.
L. 3.5 cm; W. 2.2 cm; Th. 0.2 cm.   GC
Pacitto 1972, fig. 8.15; *Green* 1980, no. A165.

53 *Flint horseshoe scraper*: edge retouch on bilateral and distal at 80 degrees; faceted butt; mottled grey.
L. 2.9 cm; W. 2.8 cm; Th. 0.8 cm.   GC

54 *Flint end-scraper*: edge retouch on distal at 60 degrees; platform butt; cortex remnant; mottled grey.
L. 5.1 cm; W. 3.0 cm; Th. 1.3 cm.   GC
Pacitto 1972, fig. 8.10.

55 *Flint end-scraper*: edge retouch on distal at 80 degrees; mottled grey.
L. 3.4 cm; W. 2.1 cm; Th. 0.8 cm.   GC
Pacitto 1972, fig. 8.11.

56 *Flint end-scraper*: edge retouch on distal at 80 degrees; mottled grey.
L. 3.1 cm; W. 3.2 cm; Th. 0.4 cm.   GC

57 *Flint scraper fragment*: edge retouch at 80 degrees; burnt.
L. 3.1 cm; W. 3.0 cm; Th. 0.8 cm.   GC

Flint serrated blades   GC

	T.p.cm	Btt	Ctx	Col.	L.	W.	Th.	Pacitto
58	8	Pl.	x	Br.	5.4	2.0	0.6	Fig. 8.12
59	8			M. Gr.	3.9	1.8	0.4	Fig. 8.13
60	8	Pl.		M. Gr.	5.1	1.4	0.6	Fig. 8.18
61	9	Pl.		M. Gr.	6.7	1.2	0.8	Fig. 8.17
62	10	Pl.		Bt	4.9	2.1	0.8	
63	10 (bil.)	Sn.		M. Gr.	3.6	0.8	0.2	
64	11 (bil.)			M. Gr.	4.4	1.1	0.4	
65	10		x	M. Gr.	3.8	1.0	0.3	
66	14		x	M. Gr.	3.6	0.9	0.3	
67	12	Pl.		M. Gr.	3.2	1.0	0.4	
68	9	Pl.		M. Gr.	3.8	1.6	0.4	
69	12	Pl.	x	M. Gr.	3.3	1.5	0.5	
70	10 (bil.)	Sn.		Pat.	2.7	1.4	0.2	
71	9 (bil.)	Sn.		M. Gr.	1.9	1.1	0.2	

Flint serrated flakes — GC

	T.p.cm	Btt	Ctx	Col.	L.	W.	Th.
72	9	Pl.	x	M. Gr.	5.7	4.2	1.2
73	10	Pl.	x	M. Gr.	3.8	2.5	0.6
74	10	Ct.	x	M. Gr.	3.4	2.2	0.7
75	11	Sn.		Bt	1.4	0.9	0.2

Flint utilised blades — GC

	Wr.	Btt	Ctx	Col.	L.	W.	Th.
76	LR.	Pl.		M. Gr.	6.0	1.7	0.6
77	L.	Pl.	x	M. Gr.	6.9	1.7	0.9
78	R.	Pl.	x	M. Gr.	6.0	2.0	1.5
79	LR.	Pl.		M. Gr.	3.8	1.3	0.4
80	LR.	Sn.		M. Gr.	3.6	1.5	0.2
81	LR.	Pl.		M. Gr.	4.2	1.6	0.5
82	LR.	Pl.		M. Gr.	4.2	1.7	0.5
83	L.	Sn.		M. Gr.	2.1	0.7	0.2
84	L.	Sn.		Bt	2.0	0.9	0.4
85	L.	Sn.		M. Gr.	3.0	1.8	0.5
86	L.	Sn.		M. Gr.	2.1	1.6	0.2
87	R.	Sn.		M. Gr.	2.1	0.9	0.2

Flint utilised flakes — GC

	Wr.	Btt	Ctx	Col.	L.	W.	Th.
88	R.	Sn.	x	M. Gr.	2.7	2.5	0.4
89	R.	Fc.	x	M. Gr	5.3	4.8	0.3
90	R.	Pl.		M. Gr.	4.9	2.6	0.7
91	LR.	Ct.	x	M. Gr.	4.0	2.0	0.7
92	LR..	Ct.	x	M. Gr.	3.6	1.8	0.3
93	L.	Fc.	x	M. Gr.	4.0	2.1	0.8
94	L.	Pl.		M. Gr.	3.0	1.7	0.4
95	L.	Pl.	x	M. Gr.	3.8	2.2	1.0
96	R.			Pat.	2.9	1.8	0.3
97	L.	Sn.	x	M. Gr.	3.1	1.8	0.7
98	L.	Fc.		M. Gr.	2.2	1.9	0.4
99	R.	Sn.		Pat.	2.5	1.3	0.4
100	R.	Sn.		M. Gr.	1.8	2.1	0.8

Flint blades — GC

	Btt	Ctx	Col.	L.	W.	Th.
101	Pl.	x	M. Br.	4.5	1.3	0.5
102	Pl.	x	M. Gr.	4.9	1.9	0.9
103	Ct.	x	M. Gr.	4.5	1.3	0.2
104	Pl.		M. Gr.	4.5	1.7	0.3
105	Fc.		M. Gr.	4.5	1.3	0.3
106	Sn.		M. Gr.	3.5	1.4	0.3
107			M. Gr.	3.9	1.3	0.3
108	Pl.		M. Gr.	4.0	1.3	0.5
109	Pl.		M. Gr.	3.8	1.2	0.4
110	Pl.		M. Br.	3.7	1.5	0.4
111	Pl.		Pat.	3.5	1.9	0.4
112		x	Bt	3.6	1.7	0.4
113	Sn.		M. Gr.	3.1	1.1	0.6
114	Pl.	x	M. Gr.	3.7	1.6	0.6
115	Sn.		Pat.	2.7	0.9	0.2
116	Sn.	x	M. Gr.	2.8	1.2	0.3
117	Ct.	x	M. Gr.	2.9	0.8	0.2
118	Pl.		M. Gr.	3.1	1.3	0.2
119	Ct.	x	M. Gr.	3.9	1.4	0.6
120	Sn.		M. Gr.	1.7	1.3	0.3
121			Pat.	3.3	1.1	0.2
122	Ct.	x	M. Gr.	4.0	1.4	0.7
123	Sn.	x	Pat.	2.8	1.1	0.5
124	Sn.	x	M. Gr.	2.9	1.7	0.4
125	Pl.		Pat.	3.3	1.7	0.3
126	Sn.	x	M. Gr.	2.9	1.4	0.3
127	Pl.		M. Gr.	3.5	1.1	0.2
128	Pl.	x	M. Gr.	2.5	0.8	0.2

Flint blades — GC

	Btt	Ctx	Col.	L.	W.	Th.
129			Pat.	3.3	0.9	0.3
130	Sn.		M. Gr.	3.2	0.8	0.4
131	Pl.		M. Gr.	2.4	1.4	0.4
132	Pl.		M. Gr.	2.3	0.9	0.2
133	Pl.	x	M. Gr.	3.0	1.0	0.6
134	Sn.		M. Gr.	3.0	1.1	0.5
135	Ct.	x	M. Gr.	3.1	1.2	0.4
136	Pl.	x	M. Gr.	2.8	0.8	0.3
137	Pl.		Pat.	2.7	1.0	0.2
138	Ct.	x	M. Gr.	2.3	0.8	0.4
139	Sn.	x	M. Gr.	2.5	0.8	0.3
140	Sn.		M. Gr.	3.9	1.2	0.2
141	Pl.		M. Gr.	3.2	1.1	0.4
142	Pl.		M. Gr.	2.1	1.1	0.2
143	Sn.		Pat.	2.9	0.9	0.2
144	Sn.		M. Gr.	2.6	1.2	0.2
145	Sn.		Pat.	2.8	0.9	0.2
146	Pl.		M. Gr.	2.8	1.1	0.4
147			Bt	2.3	0.9	0.3
148	Pl.	x	M. Gr.	3.0	1.0	0.4
149	Sn.		Pat.	2.0	1.0	0.1
150	Pl.		L. Br	2.1	0.7	0.2
151	Sn.		M. Gr.	2.2	1.1	0.2
152			M. Gr.	3.4	0.8	0.3
153	Pl.		M. Gr.	2.0	1.0	0.3
154	Sn.		M. Gr.	3.0	1.1	0.2
155			Bt	3.6	1.1	0.4
156	Pl.		M. Gr.	2.9	1.0	0.4
157		x	M. Gr.	2.9	0.9	0.4
158	Sn.		Pat.	2.1	1.2	0.4
159	Pl.		M. Gr.	2.8	1.0	0.3
160	Pl.		Pat.	3.0	0.9	0.2
161	Sn.		M. Gr.	2.3	0.8	0.2
162	Sn.		M. Gr.	2.3	0.9	0.3
163			Pat.	2.9	0.9	0.2
164	Pl.		M. Gr.	3.5	0.9	0.3
165	Pl.	x	M. Gr.	2.5	1.1	0.3
166	Ct.	x	M. Gr.	3.2	1.1	0.5
167			Bt	2.8	1.1	0.4
168	Fc.	x	M. Gr.	2.6	0.9	0.4
169			M. Gr.	3.0	1.3	0.2
170	Sn.		Pat.	1.6	1.0	0.2
171	Sn.		M. Gr.	2.4	1.2	0.3
172	Sn.	x	M. Gr.	1.9	0.9	0.2
173	Ct.	x	M. Gr.	2.6	0.9	0.3
174	Pl.		Pat.	2.6	1.0	0.3
175	Pl.		M. Gr.	2.1	0.9	0.3
176			M. Gr.	3.0	0.7	0.2
177	Pl.		M. Gr.	2.5	1.0	0.2
178	Sn.		Pat.	2.2	0.9	0.2
179	Sn.	x	Pat.	1.9	0.7	0.2
180	Sn.		M. Gr.	1.5	1.1	0.3
181	Sn.		Bt	1.4	1.0	0.4

Flint flakes — GC

	Btt	Ctx	Col.	L.	W.	Th.
182	Pl.	x	M. Gr.	3.4	4.1	0.8
183	Pl.	x	M. Gr.	3.7	5.0	0.9
184	Pl.		M. Gr.	4.1	3.0	1.0
185	Ct.	x	M. Gr.	4.1	2.3	0.9
186	Pl.		M. Gr.	5.0	2.5	0.5
187	Pl.		Pat.	5.0	1.7	0.8
188			Bt	4.0	2.2	0.9
189	Sn.		M. Gr.	3.4	2.4	0.6
190	Pl.		M. Gr.	4.0	2.3	0.6
191	Pl.	x	M. Gr.	2.1	3.2	0.6
192		x	M. Gr.	3.3	1.5	0.3

	Flint flakes				GC		*Flint flakes*				GC
Btt	Ctx	Col.	L.	W.	Th.	Btt	Ctx	Col.	L.	W.	Th.
193 Pl.	x	M. Gr.	3.3	1.9	0.6	261	x	M. Gr.	2.5	1.2	0.5
194 Fc.	x	M. Gr.	4.0	2.5	1.0	262 Fc.	x	M. Gr.	3.0	4.7	0.8
195 Pl.	x	M. Gr.	4.1	3.2	1.4	263 Fc.		M. Gr.	3.5	2.3	0.8
196 Pl.	x	M. Gr.	3.5	2.2	0.5	264 Fc.		M. Gr.	3.7	2.4	0.3
197 Sn.	x	M. Gr.	4.0	3.0	0.7	265 Pl.		Pat.	2.4	1.5	0.4
198 Pl.	x	Bt	4.4	2.0	0.9	266 Pl.		Pat.	1.7	1.6	0.3
199 Pl.		M. Gr.	3.0	4.2	0.3	267 Ct.	x	M. Gr.	3.9	1.7	0.7
200 Pl.		M. Gr.	3.7	2.1	0.5	268 Ct.	x	M. Gr.	5.0	1.8	0.9
201 Pl.		M. Gr.	3.9	2.4	0.9	269 Pl.		Pat.	3.0	1.3	0.2
202 Sn.	x	M. Gr.	2.7	2.9	1.1	270 Sn.		Pat.	2.8	2.0	0.9
203 Pl.	x	M. Gr.	2.0	4.0	0.5	271 Sn.		M. Gr.	2.5	1.8	0.8
204 Pl.		M. Gr.	2.6	3.3	0.7	272 Sn.	x	Pat.	3.2	1.5	0.8
205 Pl.		M. Gr.	3.4	1.7	0.5	273 Sn.	x	M. Gr.	1.9	2.6	0.3
206 Sn.	x	M. Gr.	3.0	2.3	0.4	274 Sn.		M. Gr.	2.5	1.8	0.2
207 Pl.		M. Gr.	2.3	1.6	0.2	275 Sn.		M. Gr.	2.0	1.7	0.5
208 Fc.	x	M. Gr.	2.2	3.4	0.8	276 Sn.	x	M. Gr.	2.1	1.3	0.2
209 Sn.	x	M. Gr.	2.5	3.0	0.4	277 Sn.	x	M. Gr.	1.3	1.2	0.1
210 Pl.		M. Gr.	2.9	1.9	0.6	278 Sn.		M. Gr.	1.5	1.5	0.1
211 Pl.		Pat.	2.9	2.6	0.5	279 Sn.	x	M. Gr.	2.4	1.0	0.2
212 Pl.	x	M. Gr.	4.3	2.3	0.3	280 Sn.	x	M. Gr.	1.7	1.0	0.3
213	x	Pat.	3.3	2.0	0.5	281 Ct.	x	M. Gr.	1.5	2.5	0.3
214 Pl.		M. Gr.	2.5	2.5	0.4	282 Fc.		M. Gr.	1.9	2.2	0.3
215 Pl.	x	Pat.	3.3	1.6	0.3	283		M. Gr.	2.6	3.0	0.8
216 Pl.		M. Gr.	2.0	2.5	0.3	284	x	Bt	2.0	1.5	0.4
217 Pl.	x	M. Gr.	2.9	4.2	0.6	285		M. Gr.	1.5	2.1	0.4
218		Bt	3.6	2.2	0.6	286		M. Gr.	2.3	1.4	0.3
219 Pl.		M. Gr.	2.4	2.2	0.4	287		M. Gr.	2.0	1.8	0.3
220 Pl.	x	M. Gr.	3.3	1.6	0.3	288		Bt	2.2	1.3	0.5
221 Pl.	x	M. Gr.	2.9	2.0	0.3	289 Pl.		M. Gr.	2.5	1.3	0.3
222 Pl.		Pat.	3.0	1.3	0.2	290 Pl.	x	M. Gr.	2.5	1.8	0.4
223 Ct.	x	M. Gr.	2.7	3.1	0.9	291 Pl.		M. Gr.	2.5	1.4	0.4
224		M. Gr.	3.5	2.0	0.6	292 Pl.		M. Gr.	1.6	2.2	0.5
225 Pl.		M. Gr.	2.5	1.7	0.7	293 Pl.		M. Gr.	3.1	2.1	0.5
226 Pl.		M. Gr.	3.2	1.9	0.3	294 Pl.		M. Gr.	2.2	2.0	0.5
227 Pl.		M. Gr.	2.3	1.6	0.4	295 Pl.		M. Gr.	2.4	1.7	0.4
228 Pl.	x	M. Gr.	2.6	2.5	0.5	296 Pl.	x	M. Gr.	2.8	2.2	0.9
229 Pl.		M. Gr.	3.8	2.2	0.3	297 Pl.		M. Gr.	3.4	2.3	0.6
230 Pl.		M. Gr.	1.5	2.7	0.4	298 Pl.		M. Gr.	2.2	1.8	0.3
231 Pl.	x	M. Gr.	3.6	1.6	0.5	299 Pl.		M. Gr.	3.0	2.0	0.4
232 Pl.		M. Gr.	3.0	2.8	0.6	300 Pl.	x	M. Gr.	2.3	1.6	0.4
233 Pl.		M. Gr.	4.8	2.3	0.5	301 Pl.	x	M. Gr.	2.6	1.4	0.3
234 Pl.	x	M. Gr.	4.1	3.4	1.0	302 Pl.	x	M. Gr.	2.1	1.2	0.3
235 Pl.		M. Gr.	2.9	1.8	0.4	303 Pl.		M. Gr.	2.5	1.0	0.2
236 Pl.		M. Gr.	2.7	2.0	0.6	304 Pl.		M. Gr.	2.2	1.3	0.4
237 Pl.		M. Gr.	2.5	1.8	0.2	305 Pl.	x	M. Gr.	1.7	2.0	0.6
238 Pl.	x	M. Gr.	3.9	1.2	0.9	306 Pl.		M. Gr.	1.7	2.3	0.3
239 Pl.		M. Gr.	2.8	1.4	0.4	307 Pl.		Pat.	2.8	1.8	0.3
240 Pl.	x	M. Gr.	2.5	2.6	0.8	308 Pl.	x	Pat.	2.5	1.3	0.9
241 Pl.	x	M. Gr.	2.5	1.7	0.4	309 Pl.		Pat.	3.0	1.7	0.3
242 Pl.	x	M. Gr.	2.6	2.4	0.5	310 Pl.		Bt	2.3	1.9	0.4
243 Pl.		M. Gr.	3.9	2.4	0.6	311 Pl.		Bt	2.2	1.1	0.4
244 Pl.	x	M. Gr.	2.1	2.2	0.7	312 Pl.		Bt	1.7	2.5	0.3
245 Pl.		M. Gr.	2.4	2.2	0.3	313 Pl.		Bt	2.9	1.5	0.3
246 Pl.	x	M. Gr.	3.0	2.0	0.6	314 Pl.		Bt	1.8	1.1	0.2
247 Pl.	x	M. Gr.	2.8	2.4	0.3	315 Pl.		M. Gr.	2.1	1.7	0.2
248 Pl.	x	M. Gr.	2.1	2.2	0.7	316 Pl.	x	M. Gr.	1.9	1.4	0.3
249 Pl.	x	M. Gr.	3.4	1.3	0.6	317 Pl.		M. Gr.	2.2	1.3	0.3
250 Pl.		M. Gr.	2.9	1.7	0.6	318 Pl.		M. Gr.	1.3	1.5	0.3
251 Pl.	x	M. Gr.	2.3	3.6	0.7	319 Pl.		M. Gr.	1.1	1.2	0.2
252 Sn.	x	M. Gr.	2.0	2.2	0.4	320 Pl.		M. Gr.	1.5	1.7	0.5
253 Sn.	x	M. Gr.	2.3	1.6	0.6	321 Pl.		M. Gr.	1.4	1.0	0.4
254 Sn.		M. Gr.	2.2	1.3	0.5	322 Pl.		M. Gr.	1.2	1.9	0.3
255 Sn.	x	M. Gr.	3.1	1.4	0.5	323 Pl.	x	M. Gr.	1.6	1.7	0.3
256 Sn.		M. Gr.	2.4	1.5	0.6	324 Pl.		M. Gr.	2.0	1.3	0.3
257	x	M. Gr.	2.6	2.2	0.5	325 Pl.		M. Gr.	1.5	1.2	0.2
258		Pat.	3.1	2.4	0.3	326 Pl.		M. Gr.	1.8	1.4	0.4
259	x	M. Gr.	2.4	1.1	0.7	327 Sn.	x	M. Gr.	1.7	1.3	0.5
260		Bt	2.2	1.6	0.5	328 Sn.		M. Gr.	1.6	1.5	0.3

Flint flakes   GC

	Btt	Ctx	Col.	L.	W.	Th.
329	Sn.		M. Gr.	1.8	1.3	0.3
330	Sn.	x	M. Gr.	1.7	1.4	0.2
331	Sn.		M. Gr.	1.4	1.5	0.3
332	Sn.	x	M. Gr.	2.0	1.5	0.5
333	Sn.		M. Gr.	1.2	1.2	0.3
334	Ct.	x	M. Gr.	1.4	1.4	0.4
335	Pl.		Pat.	1.3	1.7	0.2
336			Pat.	2.5	1.8	0.3
337			M. Gr.	2.5	1.5	0.3
338			M. Gr.	2.0	0.8	0.2
339			M. Gr.	1.1	1.8	0.4
340		x	M. Gr.	1.5	0.6	0.2
341			M. Gr.	1.6	1.2	0.3
342			M. Gr.	1.8	0.8	0.3
343			M. Gr.	1.8	1.2	0.3

344 *Chert flake*: platform butt; yellow-brown.
L. 4.1 cm; W. 2.2 cm; Th. 0.8 cm.

Flint core-rejuvenating flakes

	Btt	Sc.	Ctx	Col.	L.	W.	Th.
345	Pl.	Bl.		M. Gr.	2.5	1.6	0.8
346	Pl.	Bl.		M. Gr.	5.2	2.6	1.4
347	Pl.	Bl.	x	M. Gr.	5.4	2.1	1.1
348	Pl.	Bl.		M. Gr.	3.0	2.5	0.7
349	Pl.	Fl.	x	M. Gr.	5.0	4.6	2.2
350	Pl.	Fl.	x	M. Gr.	3.1	4.4	1.3
351	Pl.	Fl.	x	M. Gr.	4.9	1.4	0.9
352	Pl.	Fl.		Pat.	4.4	2.2	1.2
353	Sn.	Bl.	x	M. Gr.	5.3	1.6	0.6
354	Fc.	Fl.		M. Gr.	4.5	2.8	1.9
355	Fc.	Fl.	x	M. Gr.	3.8	5.8	2.0
356	Fc.	Fl.	x	M. Gr.	4.7	1.6	1.0
357	Ct.	Fl.	x	M. Gr.	3.3	4.9	1.6
358	Ct.	Fl.	x	M. Gr.	4.8	2.5	1.3

359 *Flint core*: single platform with multi-directional flake scars; mottled grey.
L. 4.8 cm; W. 4.1 cm; Th. 2.7 cm.   GC

360 *Flint core*: single platform with multi-directional flake scars; cortex remnant; mottled grey.
L. 4.5 cm; W. 2.9 cm; Th. 3.1 cm.   GC

361 *Flint core*: single platform with multi-directional flake scars; cortex remnant; mottled grey.
L. 5.1 cm; W. 4.3 cm; Th. 2.7 cm.   GC

362 *Flint core*: two platforms with parallel blade scars; cortex remnant; mottled grey.
L. 3.3 cm; W. 3.3 cm; Th. 2.5 cm.   GC

363 *Flint core*: two platforms with flake and blade scars; cortex remnant; mottled grey.
L. 3.4 cm; W. 2.3 cm; Th. 1.6 cm.   GC

364 *Flint core*: flake scars; burnt.
L. 4.4 cm; W. 3.6 cm; Th. 3.7 cm.   GC

365 *Bone point*: on distal end of immature bovid metacarpal; cut and polished point on transverse slice; abraded.
L. 8.5 cm; W. 4.6 cm; Th. 2.2 cm.   GC
Pacitto 1972, fig. 8.20.

Mound material (1968)

366 *Neolithic Bowl sherds*: five including rim.
                                              P1982 11-1 1
367 *Neolithic Bowl sherd*   P1982 11-1 2
368 *Neolithic Bowl sherds*: two including rim.
                                              P1982 11-1 3
369 *Neolithic Bowl sherd*:   P1982 11-1 4
370 *Neolithic Bowl rim sherd*   P1982 11-1 5a
371 *Neolithic Bowl sherds*: four including rim.
                                              P1982 11-1 5b
372 *Neolithic Bowl sherds*: two.   P1982 11-1 5c

373 *Neolithic Bowl rim sherd*: quartz temper.
                                              P1982 11-1 6
374 *Neolithic Bowl sherds*: three.   P1982 11-1 7a
375 *Neolithic Bowl shoulder sherd*   P1982 11-1 7b
376 *Neolithic Bowl sherds*: five including rim.
                                              P1982 11-1 8
377 *Neolithic Bowl sherds*: four.   P1982 11-1 9a
378 *Neolithic Bowl sherds*: eight.   P1982 11-1 9b
379 *Neolithic Bowl sherds*: four.   P1982 11-1 10
380 *Neolithic Bowl sherds*: four including rim.
                                              P1982 11-1 11
381 *Beaker sherds*: five; incised lines.   P1982 11-1 12
382 *Beaker sherds*: three; plain.   P1982 11-1 13
383 *Bronze Age sherds*: three.   P1982 11-1 14
384 *Bronze Age sherd*   P1982 11-1 15
385 *Plain sherds*: two; weathered.   P1982 11-1 16
386 *Plain sherds*: six; weathered.   P1982 11-1 17
387 *Plain sherd*   P1982 11-1 18
388 *Plain sherds*: three.   P1982 11-1 19
389 *Plain sherd*: weathered.   P1982 11-1 20
390 *Plain sherds*: three.   P1982 11-1 21
391 *Plain sherds*: four.   P1982 11-1 22
392 *Plain sherd*: weathered.   P1982 11-1 23
393 *Plain sherds*: four.   P1982 11-1 24
394 *Plain sherd*: weathered.   P1982 11-1 25
395 *Plain sherds*: two; weathered.   P1982 11-1 26
396 *Plain sherds*: seven; weathered.   P1982 11-1 27
397 *Plain sherds*: two.   P1982 11-1 28
398 *Plain sherds*: three.   P1982 11-1 29
399 *Plain sherd*.   P1982 11-1 30
400 *Flint leaf arrowhead*: all round edge and inverse retouch; patinated.
L. 2.8 cm; W. 1.9 cm; Th. 0.2 cm.   P1982 11-1 31
Pacitto 1972, fig. 9.14.
401 *Flint horseshoe scraper*: irregular edge retouch on bilateral and distal; faceted butt; patinated.
L. 5.1 cm; W. 6.4 cm; Th. 1.5 cm.   P1982 11-1 32
402 *Flint horseshoe scraper*: irregular edge retouch on bilateral and distal; corticated butt; cortex remnant; mottled grey.
L. 5.3 cm; W. 4.6 cm; Th. 1.3 cm.   P1982 11-1 33
403 *Flint horseshoe scraper*: edge retouch on bilateral and distal at 80 degrees; platform butt; cortex remnant; mottled grey.
L. 4.0 cm; W. 4.4 cm; Th. 1.0 cm.   P1982 11-1 34
404 *Flint horseshoe scraper*: edge retouch on bilateral and distal at 80 degrees; corticated butt; cortex remnant; mottled grey.
L. 3.2 cm; W. 3.0 cm; Th. 0.9 cm.   P1982 11-1 35
405 *Flint horseshoe scraper*: edge retouch on bilateral and distal at 80 degrees; platform butt; cortex remnant; mottled grey.
L. 3.7 cm; W. 3.2 cm; Th. 0.7 cm.   P1982 11-1 36
Pacitto 1972, fig. 9.13.
406 *Flint horseshoe scraper*: edge retouch on bilateral and distal at 80 degrees; corticated butt; burnt.
L. 4.1 cm; W. 3.5 cm; Th. 1.1 cm.   P1982 11-1 37
Pacitto 1972, fig. 9.4.
407 *Flint horseshoe scraper*: edge retouch on bilateral and distal at 80 degrees; faceted butt; mottled grey.
L. 4.3 cm; W. 3.9 cm; Th. 1.2 cm.   P1982 11-1 38
Pacitto 1972, fig. 9.5.
408 *Flint double-end- and side-scraper*: edge retouch on proximal, distal and R. at 60 degrees; cortex remnant; mottled grey.
L. 5.4 cm; W. 3.1 cm; Th. 0.6 cm.   P1982 11-1 39
409 *Flint end- and side-scraper*: edge retouch on distal and L. at 80 degrees; cortex remnant; mottled grey.
L. 3.6 cm; W. 3.2 cm; Th. 1.4 cm.   P1982 11-1 40

410 *Flint end- and side-scraper*: edge retouch on distal
   and partial L. at 80 degrees; faceted butt; broken;
   mottled grey.
   L. 4.4 cm; W. 3.4 cm; Th. 0.7 cm.   P1982 11–1 41
411 *Flint double-end scraper*: edge retouch on proximal
   and distal at 80 degrees; cortex remnant; patinated.
   L. 5.0 cm; W. 2.7 cm; Th. 1.4 cm.   P1982 11–1 42
   Pacitto 1972, fig. 9.11.
412 *Flint end-scraper and utilised flake*: edge retouch
   on distal at 80 degrees; wear on R.; corticated
   butt; mottled grey.
   L. 3.8 cm; W. 2.2 cm; Th. 0.8 cm.   P1982 11–1 43
413 *Flint end-scraper*: edge retouch on distal at 80
   degrees; cortex remnant; mottled grey.
   L. 3.1 cm; W. 3.3 cm; Th. 0.8 cm.   P1982 11–1 44
414 *Flint end-scraper*: edge retouch on distal at 60
   degrees; platform butt; cortex remnant; mottled
   beige.
   L. 2.8 cm; W. 2.5 cm; Th. 0.8 cm.   P1982 11–1 45
415 *Flint end-scraper*: edge retouch on distal at 80
   degrees; platform butt; cortex remnant; mottled
   grey.
   L. 6.0 cm; W. 4.4 cm; Th. 1.3 cm.   P1982 11–1 46
416 *Flint end-scraper*: edge retouch on distal; faceted
   butt; cortex remnant; mottled grey.
   L. 4.1 cm; W. 3.3 cm; Th. 1.0 cm.   P1982 11–1 47
417 *Flint end-scraper*: on thermal flake; edge retouch on
   distal; cortex remnant; patinated.
   L. 4.3 cm; W. 3.9 cm; Th. 0.9 cm.   P1982 11–1 48
   Pacitto 1972, fig. 9.12.
418 *Flint scraper fragment*: edge retouch at 60 degrees;
   broken; patinated.
   L. 3.3 cm; W. 3.0 cm; Th. 0.4 cm.   P1982 11–1 49
   Pacitto 1972, fig. 9.9.
419 *Flint scraper fragment*: edge retouch at 60 degrees;
   burnt and broken.
   L. 3.1 cm; W. 2.5 cm; Th. 0.9 cm.   P1982 11–1 50
420 *Flint scraper fragment*: edge retouch at 30 degrees;
   snapped; mottled grey.
   L. 2.6 cm; W. 1.6 cm; Th. 0.9 cm.   P1982 11–1 51
421 *Flint scraper fragment*: edge retouch at 80 degrees;
   cortex remnant; broken; mottled grey.
   L. 2.8 cm; W. 1.9 cm; Th. 0.5 cm.   P1982 11–1 52a
422 *Flint scraper fragment*: edge retouch at 80 degrees;
   broken; mottled grey.
   L. 2.8 cm; W. 2.5 cm; Th. 0.7 cm.   P1982 11–1 52b
423 *Flint scraper fragment*: edge retouch at 80 degrees;
   snapped; mottled grey.
   L. 1.4 cm; W. 2.9 cm; Th. 0.5 cm.   P1982 11–1 52c
424 *Flint scraper fragment*: edge retouch on distal and
   R.; snapped; patinated.
   L. 2.4 cm; W. 1.8 cm; Th. 0.5 cm.   P1982 11–1 52d
425 *Flint scraper fragment*: edge retouch; cortex
   remnant; broken; patinated.
   L. 4.4 cm; W. 3.2 cm; Th. 0.7 cm.   P1982 11–1 53
426 *Flint scraper fragment*: edge retouch at 40 degrees;
   broken; mottled grey.
   L. 3.7 cm; W. 3.2 cm; Th. 1.1 cm.   P1982 11–1 54
427 *Flint scraper fragment*: edge retouch; platform
   butt; cortex remnant; mottled grey.
   L. 3.5 cm; W. 3.5 cm; Th. 0.9 cm.   P1982 11–1 55
428 *Flint scraper fragment*: edge retouch at 80 degrees;
   snapped; mottled grey.
   L. 2.9 cm; W. 3.6 cm; Th. 0.6 cm.   P1982 11–1 56
429 *Flint scraper fragment*: edge retouch at 60 degrees;
   cortex remnant; broken; mottled grey.
   L. 2.6 cm; W. 2.4 cm; Th. 0.9 cm.   P1982 11–1 57
430 *Flint scraper fragment*: edge retouch at 60 degrees;
   cortex remnant; broken; mottled grey.
   L. 3.4 cm; W. 3.2 cm; Th. 0.5 cm.   P1982 11–1 58

431 *Flint knife*: edge retouch on L. and R. converging on
   distal at 30 degrees; patinated.
   L. 4.9 cm; W. 3.6 cm; Th. 1.2 cm.   P1982 11–1 59
432 *Flint knife*: edge retouch on R. at 60 degrees;
   platform butt; cortex remnant; patinated.
   L. 7.2 cm; W. 3.7 cm; Th. 1.4 cm.   P1982 11–1 60
   Pacitto 1972, fig. 9.7.
433 *Flint knife fragment*: edge retouch on R. at 30
   degrees; broken; mottled grey.
   L. 3.5 cm; W. 2.4 cm; Th. 0.6 cm.   P1982 11–1 61
434 *Flint awl*: edge retouch on R. and obliquely on
   distal with inverse retouch on L.; point snapped;
   light brown.
   L. 3.6 cm; W. 2.3 cm; Th. 0.6 cm.   P1982 11–1 62
435 *Flint serrated blade*: serrated on L. at 12 teeth per
   cm; beige.
   L. 3.3 cm; W. 1.1 cm; Th. 0.2 cm.   P1982 11–1 63
436 *Flint serrated blade*: serrated on R. at 10 teeth per
   cm; wear on L.; platform butt; snapped; mottled
   grey.
   L. 2.6 cm; W. 1.2 cm; Th. 0.3 cm.   P1982 11–1 64
437 *Flint serrated blade*: serrated on L. at 7 teeth per
   cm; wear on R.; platform butt; mottled grey.
   L. 6.1 cm; W. 1.9 cm; Th. 1.0 cm.   P1982 11–1 65
438 *Flint serrated blade*: serrated on R. at 10 teeth per
   cm; platform butt; mottled grey.
   L. 4.4 cm; W. 1.5 cm; Th. 0.8 cm.   P1982 11–1 66
439 *Flint serrated blade*: serrated on L. at 14 teeth per
   cm; platform butt; patinated.
   L. 4.4 cm; W. 2.0 cm; Th. 0.5 cm.   P1982 11–1 67
440 *Flint serrated flake*: serrated on L at 13 teeth per
   cm; platform butt; burnt and broken.
   L. 2.9 cm; W. 1.7 cm; Th. 0.5 cm.   P1982 11–1 68
441 *Flint worked flake*: edge retouch on L.; platform
   butt; broken; patinated.
   L. 3.5 cm; W. 3.9 cm; Th. 0.6 cm.   P1982 11–1 69
442 *Flint worked flake*: irregular edge retouch on L., R.
   and distal; platform butt; mottled grey.
   L. 2.6 cm; W. 3.2 cm; Th. 0.6 cm.   P1982 11–1 70
443 *Flint worked flake*: partial edge retouch on
   bilateral; platform butt, broken; mottled grey.
   L. 3.5 cm; W. 2.5 cm; th. 1.0 cm.   P1982 11–1 71
444 *Flint worked flake*: irregular edge retouch on distal
   and inverse retouch on R.; corticated butt; cortex
   remnant; mottled grey.
   L. 5.4 cm; W. 5.5 cm; Th. 1.2 cm.   P1982 11–1 72
445 *Flint worked flake*: irregular edge retouch on R. and
   partial on L.; snapped; mottled grey.
   L. 5.4 cm; W. 2.5 cm; Th. 0.6 cm.   P1982 11–1 73
446 *Flint worked flake*: edge retouch on L.; wear on R.;
   platform butt; broken; patinated.
   L. 2.8 cm; W. 1.5 cm; Th. 0.8 cm.   P1982 11–1 74
447 *Flint worked blade*: edge retouch on L.; wear on R.;
   platform butt; snapped; mottled grey.
   L. 5.1 cm; W. 1.8 cm; Th. 1.0 cm.   P1982 11–1 75
448 *Flint worked flake*: edge retouch on L. at 60
   degrees; cortex remnant; damaged; mottled grey.
   L. 8.5 cm; W. 3.1 cm; Th. 1.0cm.   P1982 11–1 76
   Pacitto 1972, fig. 9.10.
449 *Flint worked flake*: edge retouch on proximal and R.;
   inverse retouch on L.; snapped; mottled grey.
   L. 2.4 cm; W. 1.5 cm; Th. 0.5 cm.   P1982 11–1 77
450 *Flint worked flake*: edge retouch on R.; corticated
   butt; cortex remnant; broken; mottled grey.
   L. 4.5 cm; W. 2.5 cm; Th. 0.9 cm.   P1982 11–1 78
451 *Flint worked flake*: irregular edge retouch on L, R.
   and distal; mottled grey.
   L. 3.7 cm; W. 2.6 cm; Th. 0.8 cm.   P1982 11–1 79
452 *Flint worked flake*: irregular edge retouch;
   snapped; mottled beige.
   L. 2.3 cm; W. 3.2 cm; Th. 0.6 cm.   P1982 11–1 80

453 *Flint worked flake*: edge retouch on L; broken; mottled grey.
L. 3.1 cm; W. 3.8 cm; Th. 0.8 cm.   P1982 11-1 81

454 *Flint worked flake*: irregular edge retouch on bilateral; cortex remnant; mottled grey.
L. 7.4 cm; W. 3.7 cm; Th. 0.7 cm.   P1982 11-1 82

455 *Flint worked flake*: bifacial edge retouch on L.; cortex remnant; banded grey.
L. 5.5 cm; W. 5.5 cm; Th. 1.6 cm.   P1982 11-1 83

Flint utilised blades

	Wr	Btt	Ctx	Col.	L.	W.	Th.	P1982 11-1
456	R.		x	Pat.	5.8	2.1	0.5	84
457	LR.	Pl.		M. Gr.	4.8	1.8	0.4	85
458	R.		x	Pat.	3.5	1.1	0.3	86
459	R.		x	M. Gr.	6.0	1.8	0.4	87
460	R.	Pl.	x	M. Gr.	3.5	0.9	0.4	88
461	LR.	Sn.		M. Gr.	3.4	1.2	0.6	89
462	R.		x	M. Gr.	4.5	1.1	0.5	90
463	L.			M. Gr.	2.8	1.2	0.2	91a
464	LR.	Sn.		M. Gr.	2.3	1.0	0.2	91b

Flint utilised flakes

	Wr	Btt	Ctx	Col.	L.	W.	Th.	P1982 11-1
465	L.	Fc.	x	M. Gr.	2.8	2.2	0.6	92
466	R.	Pl.		M. Gr.	4.2	2.4	0.5	93
467	R.	Fc.	x	Pat.	4.7	3.8	0.9	94
468	LR.	Fc.		Pat.	3.2	3.1	0.5	95
469	Dis.	Pl.		M. Gr.	2.2	3.4	0.5	96
470	L.		x	M. Gr.	3.4	2.0	0.7	97
471	R.	Sn.	x	Pat.	2.7	1.5	0.5	98
472	L.	Fc.		Pat.	4.5	2.8	0.5	99a
473	LR.	Pl.	x	Pat.	5.5	3.6	0.3	99b
474	L.		x	Pat.	7.7	2.9	0.9	100
475	L.	Ct.	x	Pat.	3.1	1.9	0.5	101
476	R.	Fc.		M. Gr.	3.4	2.0	0.7	102
477	LR.	Pl.	x	Pat.	4.2	3.6	0.7	103

Flint blades

	Btt	Ctx	Col.	L.	W.	Th.	P1982 11-1
478			M. Gr.	3.1	1.2	0.3	104
479	Sn.		M. Gr.	3.2	1.1	0.5	105
480			M. Gr.	2.6	0.8	0.3	106a
481	Sn.	x	M. Gr.	3.8	1.4	0.5	106b
482			M. Gr.	3.8	0.8	0.3	106c
483	Sn.		M. Gr.	2.0	1.1	0.2	106d
484			M. Gr.	2.5	0.7	0.2	106e
485	Sn.		M. Gr.	2.0	0.8	0.2	106f
486			M. Gr.	3.5	1.6	0.6	107
487	Sn.		M. Gr.	2.3	1.0	0.3	108a
488			M. Gr.	2.5	1.3	0.3	108b
489	Sn.	x	M. Gr.	2.6	1.0	0.4	109a
490		x	M. Gr.	3.8	1.5	0.4	109b
491	Sn.		M. Gr.	2.5	1.5	0.3	110
492	Sn.		M. Gr.	1.5	0.5	0.1	111
493			M. Gr.	3.3	1.0	0.3	112a
494	Sn.	x	Pat.	5.0	1.3	0.8	112b
495			Pat.	3.1	1.1	0.7	112c
496			M. Gr.	2.8	1.1	0.2	113
497	Pl.		M. Bge	5.1	2.0	0.5	114
498		x	M. Gr.	3.6	1.2	0.7	115
499	Sn.	x	Pat.	3.8	1.3	0.7	116a
500	Pl.		M. Gr.	3.1	1.0	0.3	116b
501	Pl.		M. Gr.	2.6	1.2	0.4	116c
502	Sn.		M. Gr.	2.4	1.1	0.4	117a
503	Sn.	x	M. Gr.	1.8	1.3	0.3	117b
504	Sn.		Pat.	2.8	1.1	0.3	118a
505			M. Gr.	2.7	0.9	0.4	118b
506	Sn.	x	M. Gr.	3.3	1.5	0.5	118c
507			M. Gr.	3.8	1.1	0.4	119

Flint blades

	Btt	Ctx	Col.	L.	W.	Th.	P1982 11-1
508	Sn.		Pat.	2.2	1.0	0.3	120
509		x	Pat.	6.7	1.0	1.5	121a
510			M. Gr.	3.5	1.7	0.4	121b
511	Sn.		M. Gr.	3.1	1.1	0.3	122
512			M. Gr.	4.1	1.1	0.3	123a
513	Sn.		M. Gr.	2.0	1.2	0.3	123b
514		x	Pat.	3.0	1.1	0.3	124
515	Sn.		M. Gr.	1.7	0.6	0.2	125a
516			M. Gr.	3.3	1.4	0.2	125b
517			M. Gr.	3.5	1.2	0.3	125c
518		x	M. Gr.	3.3	1.0	0.3	125d
519		x	M. Gr.	2.5	0.4	0.2	125e
520	Sn.		M. Gr.	2.6	0.7	0.3	125f
521			M. Gr.	1.9	0.9	0.2	125g
522		x	M. Gr.	3.6	1.3	0.7	125h
523		x	M. Gr.	3.9	1.1	0.5	126a
524	Pl.		M. Gr.	3.5	1.4	0.4	126b
525		x	M. Gr.	4.0	1.4	0.5	126c
526	Sn.		M. Gr.	3.2	1.8	0.3	126d
527	Pl.		M. Gr.	2.9	1.2	0.4	127
528		x	M. Gr.	5.8	1.7	0.9	128
529		x	M. Gr.	4.7	1.3	0.6	129a
530			M. Gr.	4.0	1.5	0.5	129b
531			M. Gr.	2.6	1.4	0.3	129c
532	Sn.	x	M. Gr.	2.1	1.0	0.4	129d
533	Sn.		M. Gr.	3.0	1.7	0.3	129e
534	Sn.	x	M. Gr.	2.2	1.0	0.2	129f
535	Sn.		M. Gr.	2.5	1.5	0.3	129g
536			M. Gr.	3.2	1.2	0.3	129h
537	Sn.		M. Gr.	1.8	0.6	0.2	129i
538	Pl.		M. Gr.	2.3	0.6	0.2	129j
539			M. Gr.	2.5	0.8	0.1	129k
540	Sn.		M. Gr.	1.8	1.0	0.2	130a
541			M. Gr.	1.8	1.0	0.2	130b

Flint flakes

	Btt	Ctx	Col.	L.	W.	Th.	P1982 11-1
542			M. Gr.	3.9	2.1	0.5	131a
543		x	M. Gr.	3.9	2.6	0.5	131b
544	Pl.	x	M. Gr.	3.9	3.1	0.9	132a
545		x	M. Gr.	2.8	4.2	0.8	132b
546	Pl.		M. Gr.	3.4	3.4	1.0	132c
547			M. Gr.	2.0	2.3	0.3	132d
548	Fc.		M. Gr.	3.3	3.9	1.2	132e
549		x	M. Gr.	3.1	1.9	0.5	132f
550	Pl.	x	M. Gr.	2.9	2.2	0.5	133
551	Ct.	x	M. Gr.	3.4	2.9	0.9	134
552	Pl.	x	M. Gr.	3.9	2.6	0.8	135a
553		x	M. Gr.	2.6	2.1	0.4	135b
554			M. Gr.	1.5	2.5	0.4	136
555			M. Gr.	2.2	2.6	0.8	137
556			M. Gr.	3.1	3.2	0.8	138
557		x	M. Gr.	4.5	3.2	0.6	139a
558	Pl.		M. Gr.	4.3	2.2	0.5	139b
559			M. Gr.	4.3	2.5	0.4	139c
560		x	M. Gr.	1.6	1.8	0.4	139d
561			M. Gr.	2.2	1.5	0.4	139e
562		x	M. Gr.	1.9	2.4	0.4	140
563			M. Gr.	3.6	2.3	0.9	141
564			M. Gr.	2.0	2.0	0.5	142
565	Fc.	x	M. Gr.	7.3	2.2	1.9	143
566	Pl.		M. Gr.	2.2	2.2	0.3	144
567		x	M. Gr.	2.7	1.8	0.4	145
568			M. Gr.	1.6	1.3	0.5	146
569	Pl.	x	M. Gr.	4.6	3.5	0.7	147
570	Pl.	x	M. Gr.	3.2	3.0	1.1	148a
571	Ct.	x	M. Gr.	3.4	2.9	0.9	148b
572			M. Gr.	1.9	1.2	0.2	148c

Flint flakes

	Btt	Ctx	Col.	L.	W.	Th.	P1982 11-1
573	Pl.		M. Gr.	6.0	3.0	1.2	148d
574			M. Gr.	2.9	1.5	0.6	149
575	Pl.		Bge	2.4	2.4	0.6	150
576	Pl.	x	M. Gr.	2.3	2.2	0.4	151a
577			M. Gr.	3.0	1.8	0.5	151b
578	Fc.		Pat.	3.0	2.9	0.8	151c
579	Pl.		Bt	1.8	2.0	0.4	152a
580		x	M. Gr.	2.2	1.4	0.3	152b
581	Pl.	x	M. Gr.	1.7	2.1	0.5	153a
582			M. Gr.	3.6	2.0	0.8	153b
583	Pl.		Pat.	2.3	2.5	0.5	153c
584			Pat.	3.0	1.5	0.4	153d
585		x	M. Gr.	3.5	2.4	0.8	154
586	Pl.	x	M. Gr.	2.9	2.6	0.5	155a
587	Pl.		M. Gr.	3.6	3.3	1.0	155b
588			M. Gr.	2.9	1.6	0.2	156a
589			M. Gr.	2.0	1.6	0.4	156b
590			M. Gr.	1.8	3.3	0.5	156c
591			M. Gr.	2.8	2.6	0.5	156d
592	Pl.		M. Gr.	3.6	3.7	0.7	157
593	Fc.		M. Gr.	2.3	2.0	0.6	158a
594			M. Gr.	2.6	2.1	0.8	158b
595		x	Pat.	3.4	1.6	0.5	158c
596		x	Pat.	2.8	1.5	0.5	159a
597		x	Pat.	3.1	1.1	0.6	159b
598	Sn.	x	M. Gr.	2.4	1.9	0.2	159c
599	Sn.	x	M. Gr.	2.6	1.4	0.5	159d
600	Ct.	x	M. Gr.	2.3	2.0	0.7	159e
601	Pl.		M. Gr.	2.4	2.9	0.8	159f
602	Bkn		M. Gr.	4.5	2.6	0.3	160
603	Pl.		M. Gr.	4.0	3.7	1.0	161a
604	Pl.	x	M. Gr.	2.8	2.8	1.0	161b
605		x	M. Gr.	3.7	4.1	1.7	161c
606		x	M. Gr.	3.0	1.3	0.4	161d
607	Pl.		M. Gr.	3.6	1.9	0.7	162
608	Ct.	x	M. Gr.	1.3	1.3	0.3	163a
609	Pl.	x	M. Gr.	3.3	3.5	0.7	163b
610		x	M. Gr.	3.0	2.3	0.8	163c
611			Pat.	2.3	1.5	0.4	164
612		x	M. Gr.	3.0	1.4	0.2	165a
613			M. Gr.	2.0	2.0	0.2	165b
614		x	M. Gr.	3.1	1.6	0.4	165c
615		x	M. Gr.	3.6	1.9	0.5	165d
616	Ct.	x	M. Gr.	2.9	1.7	0.5	165e
617	Fc.	x	M. Gr.	2.8	1.9	0.7	165f
618	Pl.		Pat.	3.1	1.6	0.4	166
619	Pl.	x	M. Gr.	2.6	3.6	0.8	167a
620			M. Gr.	1.7	1.2	0.2	167b
621	Pl.	x	M. Gr.	3.1	2.6	0.6	167c
622	Pl.		M. Gr.	2.1	1.6	0.4	167d
623		x	M. Gr.	3.7	1.8	0.3	168a
624	Pl.	x	M. Gr.	3.0	2.1	0.8	168b
625	Ct.	x	M. Gr.	1.8	2.4	0.6	168c
626			M. Gr.	2.0	1.8	0.2	169a
627		x	M. Gr.	1.6	1.1	0.2	169b
628		x	M. Gr.	4.0	2.3	0.6	169c
629	Pl.		M. Gr.	2.4	2.4	0.9	169d
630			M. Gr.	1.9	1.5	1.0	169e
631	Pl.		M. Gr.	2.5	1.5	0.4	169f
632		x	M. Gr.	3.3	1.8	0.3	169g
633		x	M. Gr.	4.3	2.2	1.1	170a
634		x	M. Gr.	3.1	1.8	0.7	170b
635	Pl.		M. Gr.	3.5	1.7	0.8	170c
636		x	M. Gr.	5.1	2.0	0.8	170d

Flint blades

	Btt	Ctx	Col.	L.	W.	Th.	P1982 11-1
637			M. Gr.	4.2	2.9	1.0	170e
638			M. Gr.	1.5	1.5	0.3	170f
639		x	M. Gr.	3.0	1.9	0.7	170g
640		x	M. Gr.	3.5	1.8	0.8	170h
641	Sn.		M. Gr.	1.5	2.9	0.3	171a
642		x	M. Gr.	2.8	3.8	1.8	171b
643	Fc.		M. Gr.	3.5	4.0	1.0	171c
644	Pl.		M. Gr.	4.2	2.4	0.7	171d
645			Pat.	8.3	5.8	1.3	172
646	Pl.		Pat.	5.8	3.3	1.0	173

Flint core rejuvenation flakes

	Sc.	Btt	Ctx	Col.	L.	W.	Th.	P1982 11-1
647	Fl.	Pl.		Pat.	3.2	3.8	1.4	174
648	Fl.	Pl.		M. Gr.	4.0	2.8	1.3	175
649	Fl.			M. Gr.	3.7	2.3	1.2	176a
650	Fl.		x	M. Gr.	3.4	2.9	1.0	176b
651	Bl.	Pl.	x	M. Gr.	3.3	1.2	0.7	177

652 *Flint core*: one platform with parallel blade scars; cortex remnant; patinated.
L. 5.8 cm; W. 3.2 cm; Th. 2.5 cm.   P1982 11-1 178

653 *Flint core*: one platform with parallel blade scars; traces of previous platform; patinated.
L. 2.3 cm; W. 1.8 cm; Th. 2.0 cm.   P1982 11-1 179

654 *Flint core*: one platform with flake scars; cortex remnant; mottled grey.
L. 4.5 cm; W. 3.6 cm; Th. 1.8 cm.   P1982 11-1 180

655 *Flint core*: one platform with blade scars; mottled grey.
L. 3.6 cm; W. 3.5 cm; Th. 2.8 cm.   P1982 11-1 181

656 *Flint core*: one platform with flake scars; cortex remnant; mottled grey.
L. 4.2 cm; W. 3.8 cm; Th. 2.8 cm.   P1982 11-1 182

657 *Flint core*: one platform with flake scars; traces of previous platform; cortex remnant; mottled grey.
L. 6.1 cm; W. 4.6 cm; Th. 1.9 cm.   P1982 11-1 183

Ditch fill (1968)

658 *Incised sandstone fragment*: reticulated and radial pattern around hatched central figure in fine incision; on burnt and broken fragment.
L. 5.0 cm; W. 4.4 cm; Th. 3.4 cm.   P1982 11-1 184
Pacitto 1972, fig. 7.1.

659 *Incised sandstone fragment*: central double lentoid, in part coterminous, with three fringing diagonal lines at either side in fine incision; on burnt and broken fragment.
L. 2.6 cm; W. 2.3 cm; Th. 1.9 cm.   P1982 11-1 185
Pacitto 1972, fig. 7.2.

660 *Incised sandstone fragment*: central lentoid with six radial lines from one side in fine incision; on burnt and broken fragment.
L. 2.4 cm; W. 1.8 cm; Th. 1.2 cm.   P1982 11-1 186
Pacitto 1972, fig. 7.3.

661 *Incised sandstone fragment*: crows foot on flat face in fine incision; on burnt and broken fragment.
L. 5.0 cm; W. 3.9 cm; Th. 2.3 cm.   P1982 11-1 187
Pacitto 1972, fig. 7.4.

662 *Incised sandstone fragment*: two parallel lines in fine incision; on burnt and broken fragment.
L. 3.0 cm; W. 2.7 cm; Th. 1.9 cm.   P1982 11-1 188
Pacitto 1972, fig. 7.5.

663 *Incised sandstone fragment*: line with adjacent running loops in fine incision; on burnt and broken fragment.
L. 2.0 cm; W. 1.5 cm; Th. 1.0 cm.   P1982 11-1 189
Pacitto 1972, fig. 7.6.

63 RUDSTON (Rudstone V)

Yorkshire E.R., North Humberside

63:1-118

TA 098 658

ROUND BARROW: Diam. 24 m, H. 2 m, reduced by ploughing; earth and some chalk; internal mound of earth and chalk S. of centre Diam. 6.3 m, H. 0.6 m; internal causewayed ditch of oval plan radius 5.4 -9.7 m, W. 1.2 m, D. 1 m; opened 1869.
BB 245-51; *Tyndall* 1870.

Burial 1: adult inhumation, crouched on R. with head SSW.; in upper mound 9 m ESE. of centre.

Burial 2: infant inhumation, crouched on R. with head S.; in hollow Diam 0.9 m, D. 0.1 m, 4.8 m SE. by E. of centre; Beaker at face.

1 *Beaker*: rectangular tooth-comb stamp: above neck cordon, two horizontal lines; on neck, band of roughly-executed filled triangles enclosed above by two and below by three horizontal lines; on body, roughly-executed bar-chevron pattern enclosed above by five to six and below by three horizontal lines.
M. 10.0 cm; H. 14.5 cm; B. 6.5 cm.   79 12-9 730
BAP no. 110; *Clarke* no, 1373.

Burial 3: adult female inhumation, crouched on R. with head NE.; 0.3 m above old surface, 3.5 m SE. of centre; infant mandible fragment nearby; pin behind head.

2 *Bone pin*: splinter of caprovine-size longbone; butt cut and bevelled by polishing, point rubbed to oval section, tip lacking.
L. 5.3 cm; W. 0.6 cm; Th. 0.3 cm.   79 12-9 732

Burial 4: adult ?female inhumation, crouched on L. with head ESE.; in hollow cut into internal mound 0.4 m above old surface, 1.8 m SSE. of centre.

Burial 5: child or adolescent inhumation, crouched on R. with head S. by W.; 0.5 m above old surface, 2.3 m SE. by E. of centre.

Burial 6: adult male inhumation, crouched on L. with head SE. by S.; on old surface, 1.2 m S. of centre.

Burial 7: infant inhumation, crouched on L. with head N.; 0.3 m above old surface, 1.2 m S. of centre.

Burial 8: separate radius; 0.8 m above old surface, 1.2 m E. of centre.
'*some portions of a drinking-cup*': not preserved.

Burial 9: adult male inhumation; crouched on R. with head NNW.; on old surface, 1.2 m E. of centre.

Burials 10-13 were in a central grave 1.2 m, W. 1.6 m, D. 1.5 m, aligned E.-W., cut through the internal mound into the bedrock.

Burial 10: adult male inhumation, crouched on R. with head W.; in upper fill at 0.15 m above old surface level 'between two planks apparently of willow' L. 1 m and 0.5 m apart; objects at face.

3 *Food Vessel*: Yorkshire Vase; on internal rim bevel, two pairs of twisted cord lines; on external bevel, one pair of twisted cord lines; in neck, one pair of twisted cord lines above incised herringbone with a further pair of twisted cord lines in shoulder groove; on lugs, short lines of paired twisted cord; two, originally probably four, horizontally perforated lugs.
M. 15.3-16.6 cm; H. 12.4 cm; B. *c.* 7.2 cm.
79 12-9 731
BAP no. 105; *Simpson* 1968, fig. 45.3.

4 *Ammonite fragment*: outer face and terminals abraded.
L. (Chord) 5.3 cm; W. 1.9 cm; Th. 1.8 cm.
79 12-9 736

5 *Flint barbed and tanged arrowhead*: all over bifacial invasive retouch; grey.
L. 3.7 cm; W. 3.6 cm; Th. 0.5 cm.   79 12-9 735
BB fig. 29; *ASI* fig. 318; *Green* 1980, no. 323.

Burial 11: disturbed bones of adult and infant; in grave fill.
'*fragments of a drinking-cup*': not preserved.

Burial 12: cremation deposit, in heap Diam. 0.3 m; 1 m below old surface level at centre of grave.

6 '*Bone pin fragment*': not identified.   79 12-9 733

Burial 13: adult inhumation, crouched on L. with head SE.; at base of grave in charcoal-lined hollow; scraper at back.

7 *Flint horseshoe scraper*: marginal retouch at 50 degrees; punctiform butt; grey.
L. 6.2 cm; W. 4.1 cm; Th. 0.4 cm.   79 12-9 737

Burial 14: adult female inhumation, crouched on L. with head S. by E.; on old surface beneath mound of chalk Diam. 5.1 m, H. 0.9 m, 4.8 m E. by N. of centre.

Burial 15: adult female inhumation, crouched on L. with head NW.; on old surface beneath inner mound as Burial 14, 3.6 m NE. of centre.

Feature A: pit Diam. 1.8 m, D. 1.5 m with fill of chalk and charcoal, 0.3 m N. of central grave.

Mound material

8 *Collared Vessel rim sherd*: plain.   79 12-9 825
Longworth no. 757a.

9 *Food Vessel rim sherd*: plain.   79 12-9 825a

10 *Bronze Age sherds*: seven; plain.   79 12-9 825b

11 *Stone axe fragment*: section of cutting-edge broken by impact fracture; bifacially ground and polished to sharp edge with some minor abrasion; igneous rock.
L. 4.6 cm; W. 3.7 cm; Th. 0.9 cm.   79 12-9 822

12 '*Stone axe fragment*': not identified.   79 12-9 823

13 *Stone macehead*: made on naturally smoothed beach or erratic pebble; hourglass perforation, central section heavily abraded; no edge wear or damage.
L. 5.7 cm; W. 4.8 cm; Th. 2.2 cm; perforation ext. Diam. 2.1 cm, internal Diam. 0.8 cm.   79 12-9 734

14 *Hammerstone*: quartzite pebble, narrow end abraded by use as hammer.
L. 12.4 cm; W. 9.9 cm; Th. 7.5 cm.   79 12-9 738

15 *Hammerstone*: sandstone pebble, one end and opposing corner abraded by use as hammer.
L. 9.3 cm; W. 9.0 cm; Th. 5.8 cm.   79 12-9 739

16 *Hammerstone*: quartzite pebble, both ends abraded by use as hammer.
L. 7.4 cm; W. 7.3 cm; Th. 4.4 cm.   79 12-9 740

17 *Stone rubber*: eroded sandstone pebble, one face worn smooth by grinding.
L. 6.9 cm; W. 6.9 cm; Th. 6.1 cm.   79 12-9 741

18 *Pebble*: broken.   79 12-9 815

19-20 *Sandstone pebbles*: two.   79 12-9 816-7

21-22 *Quartzite pebbles*: two.   79 12-9 818-9

23 *Jet Ring*: cut and polished to regular plano-convex section.
Diam. (ext.) 6.0 cm; (int.) 4.2 cm; Th. 1.0 cm.
79 12-9 821

24 *Flint axe fragment*: ground and polished to oval cross-section; grey-white.
L. 2.5 cm; W. 1.7 cm; Th. 1.2 cm.   79 12-9 824

25 *Flint leaf arrowhead*: all-over bifacial invasive retouch; damaged; grey.
L. 3.7 cm; W. 2.2 cm; Th. 0.5 cm.   79 12-9 742
Green 1980, no. A166.

26 *Flint leaf arrowhead fragment*: all-over bifacial invasive retouch; broken; grey.
L. 2.4 cm; W. 2.3 cm; Th. 0.4 cm.   79 12-9 795

27 *Flint point*: converging bilateral edge retouch; platform butt; grey.
L. 5.3 cm; W. 2.3 cm; Th. 0.6 cm.   79 12-9 768

28 *Flint point*: on blade; bilateral edge retouch with some distal inverse invasive retouch; mottled grey.
L. 4.8 cm; W. 1.2 cm; Th. 0.6 cm.   79 12-9 790

29 *Flint disc scraper*: complete edge retouch at 65-100 degrees; cortex remnant; mottled grey.
L. 4.0 cm; W. 3.3 cm; Th. 1.7 cm.   79 12-9 830

30 *Flint disc scraper*: all-round retouch at 70 degrees; beige.
L. 3.1 cm; W. 2.9 cm; Th. 0.7 cm.   79 12-9 881
BB fig. 121.
(object marked as Rudston 65)

31 *Flint horseshoe scraper*: distal and bilateral edge retouch at 75 degrees; grey.
L. 4.6 cm; W. 4.2 cm; Th. 0.8 cm.   79 12-9 750
BB fig. 17.

32 *Flint horseshoe scraper*: distal and bilateral edge retouch at 65 degrees with some inverse invasive retouch; cortex remnant; mottled pink-white.
L. 5.9 cm; W. 5.1 cm; Th. 1.5 cm.   79 12-9 751

33 *Flint end-and-side scraper*: distal and R. edge retouch at 70 degrees; corticated butt; cortex remnant; patinated.
L. 2.9 cm; W. 2.8 cm; Th. 1.3 cm.   79 12-9 752

34 *Flint end-and-side scraper*: distal and R. edge retouch at 55 degrees; platform butt; mottled grey.
L. 4.0 cm; W. 4.0 cm; Th. 1.9 cm.   79 12-9 828

35 *Flint end-and-side scraper*: distal and partial edge retouch at 65 degrees; platform butt; cortex remnant; grey.
L. 3.9 cm; W. 4.0 cm; Th. 1.3 cm.   79 12-9 829

36 *Flint double-end scraper*: distal and proximal edge retouch at 90 degrees; cortex remnant; pink.
L. 4.2 cm; W. 3.5 cm; Th. 2.0 cm.   79 12-9 757

37 *Flint end scraper*: distal edge retouch at 70 degrees; on unclassifiable core fragment with cortex remnant; mottled grey.
L. 3.7 cm; W. 3.6 cm; Th. 1.5 cm.   79 12-9 754

38 *Flint end scraper*: distal edge retouch at 55 degrees; cortex remnant; grey; burnt.
L. 3.7 cm; W. 3.5 cm; Th. 1.0 cm.   79 12-9 759

39 *Flint end scraper*: distal edge retouch at 75 degrees; dihedral butt; cortex remnant; heavily patinated.
L. 7.5 cm; W. 4.8 cm; Th. 2.3 cm.   79 12-9 1579

40-51 '*Flint scrapers*': twelve; not identified.
79 12-9 753, 755-6, 758, 760-2, 826-7, 831-3

52 *Flint piercer*: bifacial invasive retouch on R.; dihedral butt; cortex remnant; mottled grey.
L. 4.3 cm; W. 5.4 cm; Th. 1.5 cm.   79 12-9 838

53 *Flint fabricator*: bifacial bilateral edge retouch with lateral abrasion; rectangular section; cortex remnant; broken and patinated.
L. 5.5 cm; W. 2.3 cm; Th. 1.6 cm.   79 12-9 839

54-7 '*Flint saws or knives*': four; not identified.
79 12-9 745, 747-9

58-65 '*Flint knives*': eight; not identified.
79 12-9 763-7, 770, 834, 836

66-70 '*Flint implements*': five; not identified.
79 12-9 774, 788, 791-3

71 *Flint worked flake*: edge retouch on L. and partially on R.; punctiform butt; mottled grey.
L. 5.0 cm; W. 2.0 cm; Th. 0.5 cm.   79 12-9 743

72 *Flint worked flake*: inverse edge retouch at 75 degrees on proximal; dihedral butt; cortex remnant; grey.
L. 4.9 cm; W. 4.3 cm; Th. 1.0 cm.   79 12-9 775

73 *Flint worked flake*: some inverse edge retouch on proximal; punctiform butt; cortex remnant; broken; grey.
L. 3.7 cm; W. 2.2 cm; Th. 0.6 cm.   79 12-9 776

74 *Flint worked flake*: some edge retouch on R.; platform butt; broken; grey.
L. 4.7 cm; W. 3.1 cm; Th. 1.0 cm.   79 12-9 777

75 *Flint worked flake*: invasive edge retouch on R.; platform butt; cortex remnant; grey.
L. 2.8 cm; W. 2.4 cm; Th. 0.6 cm.   79 12-9 794

76 *Flint worked flake*: inverse edge retouch on R. and partially on L.; platform butt; cortex remnant; grey.
L. 4.0 cm; W. 2.6 cm; Th. 0.9 cm.   79 12-9 835

77 *Flint worked flake*: edge retouch on proximal; cortex remnant; grey.
L. 4.4 cm; W. 3.9 cm; Th. 0.8 cm.   79 12-9 837

78 *Flint worked flake*: partial edge retouch on L.; platform butt; point broken; grey.
L. 4.2 cm; W. 4.0 cm; Th. 1.2 cm.   79 12-9 840

79 *Flint utilised blade*: edge damage on R.; punctiform butt; cortex remnant; broken; grey.
L. 5.4 cm; W. 1.8 cm; Th. 0.6 cm.   79 12-9 744

80 *Flint utilised flake*: edge damage on L.; broken; mottled grey.
L. 4.0 cm; W. 1.5 cm; Th. 0.6 cm.   79 12-9 746

81 *Flint utilised flake*: distal and bilateral edge damage; cortex remnant; grey.
L. 3.7 cm; W. 2.9 cm; Th. 0.7 cm.   79 12-9 769

Flint flakes

	Btt	Ctx	Col.	L.	W.	Th.	79 12-9
82	Pl.		M. Gr.	3.2	3.4	1.1	771
83	Pl.	x	M. Gr.	2.8	3.3	0.8	773
84	Pl.	x	M. Gr.	4.0	4.2	1.3	778
85	Pl.		Gr.	2.7	1.3	0.6	785
86	Pl.	x	Gr.	4.4	4.9	1.2	801
87	Pl.	x	Gr.	3.0	1.6	0.5	843
88	Pl.	x	Bt	3.3	2.8	0.8	787
89	Pnct.		Gr.	5.2	2.0	0.5	772
90	Pnct.	x	Gr.	3.8	1.5	0.5	781
91	Pnct.		Gr.	2.5	1.1	0.2	784
92	Dh.	x	Gr.	3.5	1.6	0.5	782
93			Bt	3.1	3.0	0.7	786

Flint blades

	Btt	Ctx	Col.	L.	W.	Th.	79 12-9
94	Pnct.	x	Gr.	5.0	1.6	0.8	780
95	Pnct.		M. Gr.	5.0	1.6	0.5	842

96 *Flint core fragment*: blade scar with previous platform trace on reverse; basal cortex; mottled grey.
L. 4.2 cm; W. 5.3 cm; Th. 2.1 cm.   79 12-9 796

97 *Flint core fragment*: parallel blade scars; cortex remnant; mottled beige.
L. 5.7 cm; W. 3.3 cm; Th. 2.1 cm.   79 12-9 797

98 *Flint discoidal core*: irregular multidirectional flake scars on one face; cortex remnant; mottled grey, patinated on reverse.
L. 3.5 cm; W. 4.9 cm; Th. 1.7 cm.   79 12-9 798

99 *Flint discoidal core*: irregular multidirectional flake scars on both faces; cortex remnant; mottled grey.
L. 4.4 cm; W. 4.4 cm; Th. 1.5 cm.   79 12-9 799

100 *Flint core fragment*: parallel blade scars with lateral flaking on reverse; traces of previous platforms; bilateral cortex; mottled grey.
L. 6.3 cm; W. 3.5 cm; Th. 1.9 cm.   79 12-9 800

101 *Flint core*: two platforms at right angles with single flake scars; traces of previous platforms; cortex remnant; dark grey.
L. 3.5 cm; W. 6.0 cm; Th. 3.9 cm.   79 12-9 802

102 *Flint discoidal core*: irregular multidirectional flake scars on both faces; cortex remnant; mottled grey.
L. 5.4 cm; W. 5.0 cm; Th. 2.3 cm.   79 12-9 803

103 *Flint core fragment*: irregular flake scars with traces of previous platforms at right angles; cortex remnant; dark grey.
L. 4.7 cm; W. 3.5 cm; Th. 2.1 cm.   79 12-9 804
104 *Flint core*: single platform with irregular blade scars; traces of previous platforms; cortex remnant on reverse; grey.
L. 4.0 cm; W. 3.5 cm; Th. 2.3 cm.   79 12-9 806
105 *Flint pebble core*: cortical; mottled grey.
L. 4.5 cm; W. 4.0 cm; Th. 2.7 cm.   79 12-9 807
106 *Flint core*: single platform with irregular flake scars; traces of previous platforms; variable patination; banded.
L. 3.6 cm; W. 2.7 cm; Th. 2.9 cm.   79 12-9 808
107 *Flint discoidal core*: irregular multidirectional flake scars on both faces; cortex remnant; mottled grey.
L. 4.4 cm; W. 4.0 cm; Th. 1.9 cm.   79 12-9 809
108 *Flint core*: cortical; mottled grey.
L. 4.8 cm; W. 4.0 cm; Th. 2.4 cm.   79 12-9 810
109 *Flint core*: mottled grey.
L. 4.2 cm; W. 3.7 cm; Th. 2.5 cm.   79 12-9 811
110 *Flint core*: single flake scar; cortex remnant; mottled pink.
L. 5.5 cm; W. 6.2 cm; Th. 4.1 cm.   79 12-9 820
111 *Flint core trimming flake*: struck from platform to remove hinge; punctiform butt; cortex remnant; mottled grey.
L. 5.9 cm; W. 1.8 cm; Th. 1.2 cm.   79 12-9 779
112 *Flint core trimming flake*: struck from platform to remove hinge; cortex remnant; mottled grey.
L. 4.9 cm; W. 1.7 cm; Th. 1.1 cm.   79 12-9 783
113 *Flint hammerstone*: terminal shattering; cortical; mottled grey.
L. 4.6 cm; W. 4.2 cm; Th. 3.0 cm.   79 12-9 805
114 *Flint hammerstone*: lateral band of shattering; cortical; mottled grey.
L. 6.2 cm; W. 6.1 cm; Th. 6.2 cm.   79 12-9 813
115 *Flint fragment*: one flake removed; cortical; grey.
L. 7.6 cm; W. 5.1 cm; Th. 1.8 cm.   79 12-9 789
116 *Flint fragment*: cortical; heavily patinated.
L. 5.9 cm; W. 4.4 cm; Th. 3.6 cm.   79 12-9 812
117 *Flint pebble fragment*: cortical; grey.
L. 3.1 cm; W. 2.2 cm; Th. 1.4 cm.   79 12-9 814
118 *Flint fragment*: cortical; mottled grey.
L. 5.4 cm; W. 4.8 cm; Th. 1.2 cm.   79 12-9 841

64 RUDSTON (Rudstone VI)   64:1-33

Yorkshire E.R., North Humberside   TA 094 655

ROUND BARROW: Diam. 21 m, H. 0.8 m; core of chalk rubble Diam. 5.4 m, H. 0.5 m, covered by earth; opened 1869.
BB 252.

Burial 1: pelvic bone; 0.3 m above old surface 3.9 m SE. of centre.

Burial 2: adult female inhumation, crouched on R. with head SE.; 0.3 m above old surface 8 m S. of centre; bronze stain on R. cheekbone.

Burial 3: adult male inhumation, crouched on R. with head SE.; at base of grave L. 3 m, W. 2.4 m, D. 2.3 m, fill of chalk rubble and charcoal including disturbed bones of adult male, 1.2 m SE. of centre; flints behind head.
1 *Flint worked flake*: invasive retouch on L.; marginal retouch on distal and part of R.; platform butt; cortex remnant; grey.
L. 4.4 cm; W. 2.7 cm; Th. 0.8 cm.   79 12-9 845
2-5 '*Flint flakes*': four; not identified.
79 12-9 846-9

Mound material
6 '*Pieces of a drinking-cup*': two; not identified.
79 12-9 844
7 '*Plain sherds*': two; not identified.   79 12-9 876
8 *Stone axe fragment*: flake struck from polished stone axe; Group VI.
L. 2.7 cm; W. 3.4 cm; Th. 0.4 cm.   79 12-9 871
9 *Pebble hammerstone*: ovoid gritstone pebble; broader end with limited abrasion.
L. 6.1 cm; W. 4.7 cm; Th. 4.4 cm.   79 12-9 872
10 *Quartzitic pebble*.   79 12-9 873
11 *Flint horseshoe scraper*: marginal retouch at 65 degrees; platform butt; mottled grey.
L. 5.0 cm; W. 4.0 cm; Th. 1.2 cm.   79 12-9 851
12 *Flint end-and-side scraper*: marginal retouch on distal and L. at 50 degrees; platform butt; cortex remnant; damaged; patinated.
L. 2.3 cm; W. 2.2 cm; Th. 0.6 cm.   79 12-9 852
13-17 '*Flint scrapers*': five; not identified.
79 12-9 850, 853, 855-7
18 *Flint knife*: all over bifacial invasive retouch; grey.
L. 5.6 cm; W. 2.4 cm; Th. 0.9 cm.   79 12-9 865
19 *Flint knife*: invasive retouch on distal; faceted butt; mottled grey.
L. 4.1 cm; W. 2.7 cm; Th. 0.9 cm.   79 12-9 854
20 *Flint knife*: invasive retouch bilaterally converging on proximal; punctiform butt; patinated.
L. 5.5 cm; W. 3.3 cm; Th. 0.7 cm.   79 12-9 864
21-2 '*Flint knives*': two; not identified.
79 12-9 866, 868
23-5 '*Flint serrated flakes*': three; not identified.
79 12-9 861-3
26 *Flint worked flake*: marginal retouch on R.; dihedral butt; cortex remnant; grey.
L. 4.2 cm; W. 3.5 cm; Th. 0.9 cm.   79 12-9 858
27 *Flint worked flake*: marginal retouch bilaterally; platform butt; broken and burnt; mottled pink.
L. 4.3 cm; W. 1.8 cm; Th. 0.6 cm.   79 12-9 867
28 *Flint utilised flake*: both sides affected; ?platform butt; grey.
L. 4.9 cm; W. 2.4 cm; Th. 0.6 cm.   79 12-9 859
29 *Flint utilised flake*: marginal wear on R.; platform butt; mottled grey.
L. 4.3 cm; W. 2.8 cm; Th. 0.8 cm.   79 12-9 860
30 *Flint discoidal core*: irregular, multidirectional bifacial flake scars; cortex remnant; mottled grey.
L. 4.6 cm; W. 4.2 cm; Th. 0.9 cm.   79 12-9 869
31 *Flint hammerstone*: cortex remnant; grey.
L. 4.2 cm; W. 5.3 cm; Th. 4.2 cm.   79 12-9 870
32 *Bone pin*: ground and polished from bovid-size longbone fragment to oval section; butt snapped and point damaged.
L. 8.4 cm; W. 0.8 cm; Th. 0.7 cm.   79 12-9 874
33 *Bone point or spatula*: caprovine tibia, proximal end removed by diagonal slice; point highly worn and polished ?by use.
L. 16.0 cm; W. 1.1 cm; Th. 0.9 cm.   79 12-9 875
BB fig. 35.

65 RUDSTON (Rudstone X)   65:1-28

Yorkshire E.R.; North Humberside   TA 09 65

ROUND BARROW: Diam. 17 m, H. 0.5 m; earth and chalk; opened 1869.
BB 252-3.

Burials 1-2 were in central grave L. 3 m, W. 1.4 m, D. 2.1 m, aligned E.-W.; chalk fill.

Burial 1: adult male inhumation, crouched on L. with

head ESE.; at centre of base of grave; worked flake at knee, flake at face.

1 *Flint worked flake*: edge retouch on R.; platform butt; mottled grey.
   L. 5.4 cm; W. 2.6 cm; Th. 0.6 cm.   79 12-9 877
   '*Flint chipping*': probably one of nos 20-26 below.

Burial 2: 'many disturbed bones' of adult ?female; in grave fill; sherds and antlers in fill.
   '*piece of a drinking-cup*': not preserved.
   '*two antler fragments*': not preserved.

Burial 3: child cranial fragment; 0.3 m above old surface, 5.4 m SE. of centre.

Mound material

2 *Flint pebble rubber*: one face worn smooth.
   L. 6.4 cm; W. 5.2 cm; Th. 3.1 cm.   79 12-9 1583
3 '*Flint axe fragment*': not identified.   79 12-9 886
4 *Flint leaf point fragment*: all over bifacial invasive retouch; patinated.
   L. 1.8 cm; W. 2.5 cm; Th. 0.4 cm.   79 12-9 887
5 *Flint hollow-based arrowhead fragment*: partial bifacial invasive retouch; patinated.
   L. 2.5 cm; W. 2.1 cm; Th. 0.3 cm.   79 12-9 894
   Clark 1934, no. G43; Green 1980, no. A164.
6 *Flint end- and side-scraper*: edge retouch on distal and R. at 80 degrees; wear on L.; punctiform butt; cortex remnant; patinated.
   L. 4.6 cm; W. 2.6 cm; Th. 0.7 cm.   79 12-9 889
7 *Flint end- and side-scraper*: edge retouch on distal and R. at 65 degrees; corticated butt; snapped; grey.
   L. 5.0 cm; W. 2.8 cm. Th. 1.1 cm.   79 12-9 890
8 *Flint end-scraper*: edge retouch on distal at 60 degrees; platform butt; mottled grey.
   L. 3.8 cm; W. 2.4 cm. Th. 1.1 cm.   79 12-9 883
9 *Flint end-scraper*: edge retouch on distal at 55 degrees; cortex remnant; patinated.
   L. 4.8 cm; W. 3.5 cm; Th. 0.9 cm.   79 12-9 884
10 *Flint scraper*: edge retouch on L. at 60 degrees; corticated butt; snapped; patinated.
   L. 4.0 cm; W. 2. 4 cm; Th. 1.0 cm.   79 12-9 882
11 '*Flint scraper*': not identified.   79 12-9 880
12 *Flint knife*: invasive retouch on distal and L.; cortex remnant; grey.
   L. 3.9 cm; W. 3.7 cm; Th. 0.6 cm.   79 12-9 892
13 *Flint knife*: edge retouch on distal and bilateral; platform butt; cortex remnant; grey.
   L. 3.4 cm; W. 2.9 cm; Th. 0.5 cm.   79 12-9 893
14 *Flint fabricator*: edge retouch on distal and bilateral; worn; triangular section; cortex remnant; patinated.
   L. 6.8 cm; W. 2.0 cm; Th. 1.4 cm.   79 12-9 885
15 *Flint serrated flake*: edge retouch on R., five teeth per cm; butt removed; cortex remnant; mottled grey.
   L. 4.6 cm; W. 2.5 cm; Th. 0.8 cm.   79 12-9 878
16 *Flint worked flake*: partial edge retouch on distal and bilateral; platform butt; worn; patinated.
   L. 4.5 cm; W. 4.2 cm; Th. 0.8 cm.   79 12-9 888
17 *Flint worked flake*: invasive retouch on R.; platform butt; cortex remnant; grey.
   L. 1.8 cm; W. 1.3 cm; Th. 0.4 cm.   79 12-9 900
18 '*Flint implement*': not identified.   79 12-9 891
19 *Flint utilised flake*: bilateral wear; platform butt; cortex remnant; mottled grey.
   L. 3.9 cm; W. 1.6 cm; Th. 0.3 cm.   79 12-9 879
20 *Flint flake*: punctiform butt; grey.
   L. 2.4 cm; W. 0.9 cm; Th. 0.2 cm.   79 12-9 901
21 *Flint blade*: punctiform butt; cortex remnant; mottled grey.
   L. 5.2 cm; W. 1.2 cm; Th. 0.6 cm.   79 12-9 1582
22-6 '*Flint flakes*': five; not identified.
                                              79 12-9 895-9

27 *Flint core*: single platform with irregular flake scars; cortex remnant; pink and grey.
   L. 3.0 cm; W. 5.3 cm; Th. 6.3 cm.   79 12-9 1580
28 *Flint discoidal core*: bifacial irregular multi-directional flake scars; cortex remnant; patchy grey.
   L. 4.0 cm; W. 3.7 cm; Th. 2.0 cm.   79 12-9 1581
   (see Rudston 63.30)

66 RUDSTON (Rudstone VII-IX)   66:1-79

Yorkshire E.R.; North Humberside   TA 099 658

CURSUS: surviving bank of square-ended S. terminal of cursus A; excavated as long mound (VII) L. 42 m, W. 12 m, H. 1.4 m (W.) and 1.7 m (E.), aligned E.-W., with long mounds (IX, VIII) attached to W. end L. 58 m, W. 15 m, H. 1.2 m and to E. end, aligned N.-S.; terminal bank of earth for 12 m at W. remainder with earth core and chalk capping; W. bank of earth; opened 1869, W. ditch sectioned by Grantham 1958.
BB 253-7; Dymond 1966.

Burial 1: adult female inhumation, crouched on R. with head W.; 0.6 m above old surface, at W. end; Beaker at R. tibia.

1 *Beaker*: tooth-comb stamped: beneath rim, two horizontal lines separated by reserved zone from deep band of five narrow zones of short vertical lines and reserved spaces in chequerboard effect, each zone separated and bordered by pairs of horizontal lines; on shoulder, narrow zone of herringbone bordered above by three and below by two horizontal lines; on body, two narrow zones of diagonal lines separated by reserved zone, upper bordered above and below by two horizontal lines, lower bordered above and below by three horizontal lines.
   M. 13.3-14.0 cm; H. 22.1 cm; B. 8.5 cm. 79 12-9 902
   BB fig. 122; BAP no. 128; Clarke no. 1374.

Burial 2: child inhumation, head ESE.; 0.2 m above Burial 1; knife near head.

2 *Flint knife*: blunting edge retouch on R.; invasive retouch on L., distal worn; faceted butt; cortex remnant; patinated.
   L. 4.6 cm; W. 3.0 cm; Th. 0.8 cm.   79 12-9 905

Burials 3-4 were in a grave L. 2.1 m, W. 1.4 m, D. 0.6 m, aligned SE. by E.-NW. by W., fill of earth around sides with chalk at centre, below Burial 1; wooden beam L. 1.7 m, W. 0.2 m, Th. 0.1 m, aligned E.-W. across fill at level of old surface with hollow space above.

Burial 3: adult inhumation, crouched on R. with head W.; at NW. end at base in chalk fill; Beaker behind head, flints nos 4, 6, 8 at chest, nos 7, 9 at knees and no. 5 at feet.

3 *Beaker*: tooth-comb stamped: on neck, zone of vertical lines enclosed above by two horizontal lines and below by four grooved lines, above row of pinpricks for part of circumference; on upper body and belly, zone of vertical lines enclosed above by five and below by four horizontal lines with fringe of short diagonal lines beneath.
   M. 13.7 cm; H. 18.8 cm; B. 8.2 cm.   79 12-9 903
   BAP no. 129; Clarke no. 1375.
4 *Flint end-scraper*: edge retouch on distal at 65 degrees; cortex remnant; broken; mottled grey.
   L. 2.9 cm; W. 2.6 cm; Th. 0.7 cm.   79 12-9 907
5 *Flint end-scraper*: edge retouch on distal at 60 degrees; corticated butt; grey.
   L. 2.9 cm; W. 1.9 cm; Th. 0.8 cm.   79 12-9 911

6 *Flint ?side-scraper*: partial edge retouch on distal and R. at 50 degrees; platform butt; broken; mottled grey.
L. 2.9 cm; W. 3.0 cm; Th. 0.9 cm.   79 12-9 906

7 *Flint side-scraper*: edge retouch on R. at 60 degrees; platform butt; cortex remnant; patinated.
L. 2.2 cm; W. 2.2 cm; th. 0.6 cm.   79 12-9 909

8 *Flint flake*: corticated butt; grey.
L. 3.2 cm; W. 3.1 cm; Th. 0.5 cm.   79 12-9 908

9 *Flint flake*: platform butt; cortex remnant; grey.
L. 2.3 cm; W. 2.5 cm; Th. 0.6 cm.   79 12-9 910

Burial 4: adult female inhumation, bones in heap; at feet of Burial 3.

Burial 5: disturbed bones of adult male and child; 1.4 m above old surface, 23 m E. of Burial 3.

Burial 6: child inhumation, crouched on L. with head ESE.; below and to S. of Burial 5.

Mound material: terminal bank (VII)

10 'Neolithic Bowl sherds': not identified.
NPY no. 1.   79 12-9 904

11 *Flint point*: edge retouch on L. and converging on proximal, some inverse invasive retouch on proximal; mottled grey.
L. 3.5 cm; W. 2.4 cm; Th. 0.7 cm.   79 12-9 915

12 *Flint end- and side-scraper*: edge retouch on distal at 55 degrees, invasive retouch on R.; platform butt; mottled grey.
L. 3.4 cm; W. 2.2 cm; Th. 0.8 cm.   79 12-9 912

13 *Flint end-scraper*: edge retouch on distal at 60 degrees; platform butt; cortex remnant; patinated.
L. 2.6 cm; W. 2.9 cm; Th. 1.0 cm.   79 12-9 913

14 *Flint end-scraper*: edge retouch on distal at 55 degrees; corticated butt; grey.
L. 2.6 cm; W. 2.8 cm; Th. 1.1 cm.   79 12-9 914

15 *Flint worked flake*: partial bifacial invasive retouch; grey.
L. 2.1 cm; W. 2.5 cm; Th. 0.4 cm.   79 12-9 916

16 *Flint blade*: punctiform butt; grey.
L. 3.8 cm; W. 1.2 cm; Th. 0.4 cm.   79 12-9 917

17 *Flint flake*: cortex remnant; beige.
L. 3.2 cm; W. 1.9 cm; Th. 0.5 cm.   79 12-9 918

18 *Flint flake*: broken; grey.
L. 2.5 cm; W. 1.5 cm; Th. 0.2 cm.   79 12-9 919

19 *Flint core*: single platform with flake scar, trace of previous platform on reverse; cortex remnant; mottled grey.
L. 3.9 cm; W. 4.0 cm; Th. 2.0 cm.   79 12-9 1584

Mound material: east bank (VIII)

20 *Flint leaf arrowhead*: unifacial all over invasive retouch, all-round inverse invasive retouch; proximal broken; grey.
L. 2.6 cm; W. 1.8 cm; Th. 0.3 cm.   79 12-9 1585

21 *Flint horseshoe scraper*: edge retouch on distal and bilateral at 65 degrees; broken; patinated.
L. 3.6 cm; W. 2.1 cm; Th. 0.7 cm.   79 12-9 921

22 *Flint end-scraper*: edge retouch on distal at 80 degrees, invasive retouch on proximal; cortex remnant; grey.
L. 2.4 cm; W. 3.0 cm; Th. 1.0 cm.   79 12-9 920

Mound material: west bank (IX)

23 *Quartzite pebble*: split; one end abraded.
L. 9.2 cm; W. 8.0 cm; Th. 3.9 cm.   79 12-9 1695

24 *Flint blade*: cortex remnant; patinated.
L. 4.2 cm; W. 1.4 cm; Th. 0.5 cm.   79 12-9 1693

25 *Flint flake*: platform butt; grey.
L. 3.2 cm; W. 1.6 cm; Th. 0.3 cm.   79 12-9 1694

26 *Flint flake*: punctiform butt; burnt.
L. 4.5 cm; W. 1.5 cm; Th. 0.7 cm.   79 12-9 1696

Ditch material (Grantham Collection)

27 *Neolithic Bowl sherd*: plain.

28 *Beaker rim-sherd*: two rows of blurred impressions; eroded.

29 *Beaker rim-sherd*: beneath rim, twisted cord horizontal lines set with twist opposed.   L9

30 *Beaker sherds*: four; horizontal incised lines.
L8, 12, 14, 15

31 *Beaker sherd*: short incised strokes.   L14

32 *Beaker sherd*: externally, blurred horizontal lines; internally, twisted cord horizontal lines.
L6

33 *Beaker sherds*: eighteen; plain or with uncertain decoration.

34 *Food Vessel rim-sherd*: rectangular tooth comb-stamped horizontal line above zig-zag.

35 *Plain sherds*: five, including rim.   L6, 10

Flint utilised flakes

Wr	Btt	Ctx	Col.	L.	W.	Th.	L
36	L.	Pl.	x	Pat.	3.3	1.7	1.5	1
37	R.		X	Bt	2.6	2.1	0.3	2
38	LR.			M. Gr.	1.9	1.2	0.2	7
39	L.	Pl.		Pat.	3.1	1.1	0.4	9
40	R.	Pl.	x	M. Gr.	3.5	2.9	0.6	9
41	LR.	Pl.		Pat.	3.2	2.3	0.3	12

Flint flakes

	Btt	Ctx	Col.	L.	W.	Th.	L
42	Ct.	x	Pat.	1.8	1.4	0.3	1
43		x	Pat.	3.4	3.0	1.1	1
44		x	Pat.	2.0	2.9	0.4	3
45	Pl.	x	L. Gr.	1.5	1.3	0.2	3
46	Pl.	x	Pat.	2.2	0.8	0.3	4
47	Pl.		Pat.	2.0	2.0	0.6	4
48			Pat.	2.2	1.3	0.6	4
49	Pl.	x	M. Gr.	2.9	2.0	0.7	5
50	Pl.		Pat.	2.3	1.9	0.7	5
51	Pl.		Pat.	3.6	2.5	0.4	6
52	Pl.	x	M. Gr.	2.9	2.8	0.5	6
53	Dh.		M. Gr.	2.2	3.5	0.9	7
54		x	M. Gr.	3.4	3.8	0.6	8
55			Pat.	1.8	1.3	0.2	8
56	Pl.		Pat.	2.1	1.7	0.4	8
57			M. Gr.	1.5	1.2	0.4	9
58			Pat.	2.7	1.9	1.2	9
59	Pl.		Pat.	4.1	3.4	1.0	10
60			M. Gr.	3.5	2.2	0.5	10
61	Ct.	x	D. Gr.	2.2	1.4	0.3	10
62	Pl.		M. Gr.	3.7	2.2	1.1	11
63	Pl.		M. Gr.	2.6	3.2	0.6	12
64			Pat.	2.8	2.1	1.2	12
65			Pat.	2.8	2.3	0.5	12
66	Pl.		Pat.	3.2	3.2	0.7	12
67			Pat.	2.6	3.1	0.7	12
68		x	M. Gr.	1.8	1.4	0.4	12
69			M. Gr.	1.8	1.5	0.3	12
70			Pat.	3.0	2.7	0.8	12
71		x	M. Gr.	2.5	1.8	0.3	13
72		x	M. Gr.	4.5	1.7	0.6	13
73		x	Pat.	2.4	1.7	0.7	13
74	Pl.		Pat.	4.3	1.5	1.0	14

75 *Flint core*: two platforms with parallel flake scars; cortex remnant; patinated to dark grey.
L. 2.7 cm; W. 2.3 cm; Th. 1.3 cm.   L2

76 *Flint core*: one platform with multidirectional flake scars, traces of previous platforms; light grey.
L. 3.8 cm; W. 3.3 cm; Th. 2.7 cm.   L4

77 *Flint core*: one platform with multidirectional flake
scars, traces of previous platforms; cortex remnant;
patinated.
L. 3.9 cm; W. 3.3 cm; Th. 3.0 cm.   L8

78 *Flint core fragment*: multidirectional flake scars;
patinated.
L. 5.2 cm; W. 2.5 cm; Th. 1.3 cm.   L8

79 *Flint core*: one platform with parallel flake scars;
cortex remnant; light grey.
L. 6.7 cm; W. 5.2 cm; Th. 2.9 cm.   L10

67 RUDSTON (Cranswick I)   67:1-134

Yorkshire E.R.; North Humberside   TA 107 666

ROUND BARROW: Diam. 31 m, H. 2.7 m, reduced by ploughing;
basal layer of 'dark fatty earth' with much burnt earth
and charcoal, covered by chalk.
BB 257-62.

Burial 1: adult male inhumation, crouched on R. with
head WNW.; 1.8 m above old surface in inserted hollow
with earth fill, 4.2 m SW. of centre; chalk slabs on edge
behind back; Food Vessel at head and scraper behind
head.

1 *Food Vessel*: Yorkshire Vase; twisted cord: on internal rim bevel, external bevel and neck, herringbone; on body, short vertical and diagonal lines
forming herringbone in places; six imperforate lugs.
M. 13.9-15.3 cm; H. 13.5 cm; B. 7.4 cm.
BAP no. 108.   79 12-9 924

2 *'Flint scraper'*: not identified.   79 12-9 929

Burial 2: adult male inhumation, crouched on L. with
head NNW.; 1.4 m above old surface, 9 m W. by S. of
centre; knife at feet.

3 *Flint plano-convex knife*: bifacial invasive retouch
on distal, proximal and L.; unifacial invasive
retouch on R.; cortex remnant; patinated.
L. 5.1 cm; W. 2.5 cm; Th. 0.9 cm.   79 12-9 930
Clark 1932, no. 5.9.

Burial 3: adult female inhumation, crouched on R. with
head NW. by N.; 1.8 m above old surface in inserted
hollow with earth fill, 6.3 m WSW. of centre; chalk slab
over knees and adjacent Food Vessel.

4 *Food Vessel*: coarse twisted cord: on internal rim
bevel, one to two lines; externally, horizontal
lines.
M. 13.1-14.4 cm; H. 11.6 cm; B. 7.8 cm.
BAP no. 109.   79 12-9 923

Burial 4: 'disturbed' inhumation; near Burial 3.

5 *Beaker sherds*: tooth-comb stamped: zones of horizontal lines separated by reserved zones.   79 12-9 925

6 *Beaker sherd*: tooth-comb stamped multiple concentric
lozenges.   79 12-9 925a
Clarke no. 1378.

Burial 5: adult female inhumation, crouched on R. with
head N. by W.; 1.8 m above old surface, 6.3 m W. by S. of
centre, legs cut away by insertion of Burial 3; Beaker
behind head.

7 *Beaker*: twisted cord horizontal lines.
M. 10.8 cm; H. 10.7 cm; B. 6.6 cm.   79 12-9 926
BAP no. 143; *Clarke* no. 1376.

Burial 6: child inhumation, crouched on R. with head
SSW.; 1.9 m above old surface, 3.6 m SSE. of centre.

Burial 7: child inhumation, crouched on R. with head N.
by E.; 2.1 m above old surface, 2.2 m SSE. of centre.

Burial 8: child inhumation; 2.1 m above old surface, 1.8
m SE. by S. of centre.

Burial 9: child cranial fragment; 2.4 m above old
surface, W. of Burial 8.

Burial 10: double inhumation: two children crouched on
L. with heads NE. by E.; c. 2 m above old surface, 1.2 m
ESE. of centre; two flakes between heads.

8-9 *'Flint flakes'*: two; not identified.
79 12-9 1036-7

Burial 11: child inhumation; c. 2 m above old surface,
1.8 m E. of centre.

Burial 12: disturbed bones of child inhumation; c. 2 m
above old surface, 0.9 m E. of centre.

Burial 13: adult female inhumation, crouched on R. with
head SW. by S.; c. 2 m above old surface, 2.3 m NNE. of
centre; Food Vessel at chest.

10 *Food Vessel*: Yorkshire Vase; incised: on internal rim
bevel, lozenges enclosed by opposed diagonal lines;
externally, herringbone; three of four imperforate
lugs surviving.
M. 16.2 cm; H. 13.0 cm; B. c. 8.0 cm.   79 12-9 922
BAP no. 106.

Burial 14: double inhumation: infant crouched on L. with
head N. by E., near incomplete disarticulated adult
female; at E. end of wood-lined hollow L. 1.5 m, W. 0.9
m, 2.1 m NNE. of centre.

Burial 15: child inhumation; 2 m above old surface, 4.5 m
NE. of centre; Food Vessel at head.

11 *Food Vessel*: plain.
M. 9.5 cm; H. 8.6 cm; B. 6.2 cm.   79 12-9 928
BAP no. 107.

Burial 16: child inhumation; 0.4 m E. of Burial 15;
Beaker at face.

12 *Beaker*: incised: on neck, row of chevrons above zone
of four horizontal lines, separated from similar zone
by row of lattice or lozenge, itself separated from
zone of five horizontal lines with row of chevrons
above by row of lattice or lozenge; on body, zone of
five horizontal lines bordered above and below by row
of chevrons.
M. 9.8 cm; H. 12.5 cm; B. 6.4 cm.   79 12-9 927
BAP no. 142; *Clarke* no. 1377.

Burial 17: adult male inhumation, extended with head W.
by N.; 2 m above old surface, 6.4 m E. by N. of centre.

Burial 18: adult male inhumation, extended with head W.
by N.; 0.3 m N. of Burial 17.

Burial 19: adult male inhumation, extended with head W.
by N; 0.5 m N. of Burial 18.

Burial 20: adult male inhumation, crouched on R. with
head SW.; 0.6 m NW. of Burial 19.

Burial 21: adult inhumation; disturbed in ploughsoil, at
feet of Burials 17-19.

Mound material

13 *'Stone axe fragment'*: not identified. 79 12-9 1047
14 *Quartzite pebble fragment*   79 12-9 1045
15 *Gritstone pebble fragment*   79 12-9 1046
16 *Flint leaf arrowhead*: partial bifacial invasive
retouch; point broken; patinated.
L. 3.8 cm; W. 2.0 cm; Th. 0.5 cm.   79 12-9 1005
17 *Flint leaf arrowhead*: all over bifacial invasive
retouch; patinated.
L. 3.8 cm; W. 2.5 cm; Th. 0.4 cm.   79 12-9 1006
18 *Flint lozenge arrowhead*: all over bifacial invasive
retouch; broken; patinated.
L. 3.0 cm; W. 2.8 cm; Th. 0.4 cm.   79 12-9 1007
Green 1980, no. A170.

19 *Flint pointed implement*: on blade; converging edge retouch; punctiform butt; cortex remnant; patinated.
L. 5.5 cm; W. 1.6 cm. Th. 0.5 cm.   79 12-9 1008

20 *Flint pointed implement*: worn edge retouch on distal and partial on bilateral; platform butt; patinated.
L. 5.5 cm; W. 2.1 cm; Th. 0.7 cm.   79 12-9 1009

21 *Flint horseshoe scraper*: edge retouch on distal and partial bilateral at 75 degrees; punctiform butt; patinated.
L. 3.8 cm; W. 3.0 cm; Th. 0.7 cm.   79 12-9 989

22 *Flint horseshoe scraper*: edge retouch on distal and bilateral at 60 degrees; platform butt; patinated.
L. 3.5 cm; W. 3.0 cm; Th. 1.0 cm.   79 12-9 996

23 *Flint end- and side-scraper*: edge retouch on proximal and R. at 75 degrees; mottled grey.
L. 3.8 cm; W. 3.9 cm; Th. 1.0 cm.   79 12-9 994

24 *Flint end-scraper*: edge retouch on distal at 60 degrees; broken; cortex remnant; patinated.
L. 2.8 cm; W. 3.4 cm; Th. 0.7 cm.   79 12-9 990

25 *Flint end-scraper*: edge retouch on distal at 60 degrees; cortex remnant; broken; mottled grey.
L. 4.0 cm; W. 3.0 cm; Th. 0.6 cm.   79 12-9 992

26 *Flint end-scraper*: edge retouch on distal and partial R. at 60 degrees; dihedral butt; patinated.
L. 4.9 cm; W. 2.6 cm; Th. 0.6 cm.   79 12-9 993

27 *Flint end-scraper*: edge retouch on distal at 60 degrees; platform butt; patinated.
L. 5.3 cm; W. 3.0 cm. Th. 1.6 cm.   79 12-9 995

28 *Flint end-scraper*: edge retouch on distal at 80 degrees; corticated butt; patinated.
L. 4.0 cm; W. 3.0 cm; Th. 1.0 cm.   79 12-9 997

29 *Flint end-scraper*: edge retouch on distal at 75 degrees; punctiform butt; cortex remnant; grey.
L. 4.2 cm; W. 2.1 cm; Th. 1.3 cm.   79 12-9 998

30 *Flint end-scraper*: edge retouch on proximal at 60 degrees; cortex remnant; patinated.
L. 4.6 cm; W. 2.4 cm; Th. 1.0 cm.   79 12-9 1000

31 *Flint end-scraper*: edge retouch on distal and partial R. at 60 degrees, inverse invasive retouch on L.; platform butt; cortex remnant; patinated.
L. 3.4 cm; W. 4.3 cm; Th. 1.0 cm.   79 12-9 1004

32-5 *'Flint scrapers'*: four; not identified.
          79 12-9 991, 999, 1001 and 1003

36 *Flint plano-convex knife fragment*: all over invasive retouch; cortex remnant; broken; grey.
L. 3.9 cm; W. 2.4 cm; Th. 0.8 cm.   79 12-9 975

37 *Flint discoidal knife*: bifacial flaking; mottled grey.
L. 4.7 cm; W. 4.8 cm; Th. 0.9 cm.   79 12-9 1011

38 *Flint bifacial implement*: partial bifacial invasive retouch; punctiform butt; damaged; patinated.
L. 3.3 cm; W. 1.6 cm; Th. 0.3 cm.   79 12-9 976

39 *Flint serrated flake*: fine edge retouch on R., eight teeth per cm; punctiform butt; patinated.
L. 4.4 cm; W. 1.7 cm; Th. 0.6 cm.   79 12-9 933

40 *Flint serrated flake*: fine edge retouch on L., six teeth per cm; distal and R. worn; broken; patinated.
L. 4.3 cm; W. 2.2 cm; Th. 0.8 cm.   79 12-9 959

41 *Flint worked flake*: edge retouch on R.; platform butt; mottled grey.
L. 7.4 cm; W. 3.0 cm; Th. 1.1 cm.   79 12-9 942

42 *Flint worked blade*: inverse edge retouch on L; platform butt; cortex remnant; grey.
L. 4.9 cm; W. 1.5 cm; Th. 0.8 cm.   79 12-9 952

43 *Flint worked flake*: edge retouch on L., wear on R.; patinated.
L. 5.0 cm; W. 2.3 cm; Th. 0.5 cm.   79 12-9 955

44 *Flint worked flake*: partial edge retouch on R.; punctiform butt; cortex remnant; grey.
L. 4.1 cm; W. 2.2 cm; Th. 0.5 cm.   79 12-9 956

45 *Flint worked blade*: edge retouch on distal, bilateral wear; patinated.
L. 6.7 cm; W. 1.6 cm; Th. 0.6 cm.   79 12-9 957

46 *Flint worked flake*: edge retouch on L; punctiform butt; cortex remnant; patinated.
L. 4.6 cm; W. 2.3 cm; Th. 0.9 cm.   79 12-9 960

47 *Flint worked flake*: partial edge retouch on L., wear on R.; dihedral butt; patinated.
L. 4.0 cm; W. 3.1 cm; Th. 0.7 cm.   79 12-9 961

48 *Flint worked flake*: partial edge retouch on L.; punctiform butt; patinated.
L. 4.5 cm; W. 1.7 cm; Th. 0.3 cm.   79 12-9 962

49 *Flint worked flake*: bifacial invasive retouch on proximal, some invasive retouch on distal; patinated.
L. 4.3 cm; W. 1.9 cm; Th. 0.6 cm.   79 12-9 972

50 *Flint worked flake*: edge retouch on R.; platform butt; burnt.
L. 4.7 cm; W. 2.7 cm; Th. 0.9 cm.   79 12-9 987

51-2 *'Flint implements'*: two; not identified.
          97 12-9 988, 1010

Flint utilised flakes

	Wr	Btt	Ctx	Col.	L.	W.	Th.	79 12-9
53	LRD1.	Pnct.		Gr.	5.7	1.5	0.5	931
54	L.		x	Pat.	6.0	1.1	0.5	932
55	LR.	Pnct.		M. Gr.	5.0	1.3	0.5	934
56	L.	Dh.	x	Gr.	5.9	1.8	0.4	935
57	R.	Pnct.	x	Gr.	6.3	1.8	0.7	936
58	L.	Dh.	x	Pat.	4.8	1.6	0.6	937
59	L.		x	Pat.	4.5	2.6	0.7	938
60	LR.		x	Pat.	5.4	1.6	0.4	939
61	R.	Pnct.	x	M. Gr.	4.1	1.1	0.6	940
62	L.	Pnct.		M. Gr.	4.3	1.6	0.3	941
63	LR.	Pnct.		Pat.	5.6	1.9	0.8	943
64	R.	Pnct.	x	Gr.	4.4	1.8	0.9	944
65	LR.	Pl.	x	Pat.	6.4	3.7	1.4	945
66	LR.	Pnct.		Pat.	4.9	2.8	0.7	946
67	R.	Pnct.	x	Gr.	4.5	1.8	0.6	947
68	L.		x	Pat.	3.7	1.9	0.8	948
69	LR.			Pat.	4.3	1.9	0.6	951
70	R.	Pnct.		Gr.	4.0	2.2	0.3	954
71	LR.			Pat.	4.9	1.7	0.5	958
72	LR.	Pnct.		Pat.	4.4	1.5	0.4	963
73	R.	Pnct.		Bt	4.6	1.6	0.6	964
74	R.		x	Gr.	4.0	1.6	0.8	965
75	R.	Pl.	x	Gr.	4.0	2.5	0.7	967
76	R.	Dh.		Pat.	3.7	2.5	0.4	968
77	L.	Pnct.	x	Gr.	3.6	2.5	0.8	969
78	R.		x	Pat.	4.0	3.2	0.6	971
79	R.	Pl.		Pat.	4.5	2.0	0.5	973
80	R.		x	Gr.	4.0	1.5	0.6	977
81	L.	Pl.	x	Gr.	4.0	1.8	0.8	982
82	LR.		x	M. Gr.	4.3	1.5	0.7	983
83	R.			M. Gr.	2.7	1.9	0.4	984
								75 4-3
84	R.		x	Gr.	4.0	1.5	0.6	22
85	LR.	Pl.	x	Gr.	4.2	1.3	0.4	23
86	LR.		x	Gr.	3.6	1.7	0.6	24

Flint blades

	Btt	Ctx	Col.	L.	W.	Th.	79 12-9
87	Pnct.	x	M. Gr.	7.0	1.9	0.9	953
88	Pnct.		Pat.	4.1	1.2	0.3	981
89	Pl.	x	Pat.	7.3	2.4	0.9	1018
90	Pnct.	x	Gr.	7.2	1.7	0.7	1019
91	Pnct.		Pat.	4.1	1.3	0.4	1025
92	Pnct.		Pat.	4.0	1.3	0.2	1026
93	Pnct.		Gr.	5.5	1.3	0.3	1027
94	Pnct.		Pat.	4.0	0.7	0.2	1028

Flint blades

	Btt	Ctx	Col.	L.	W.	Th.	79 12–9
95	Pnct.	x	Gr.	4.8	1.4	0.5	1034
96	Pnct.		Gr.	4.2	1.3	0.3	1035
97	Pnct.		Pat.	3.4	0.9	0.3	1038
98	Pnct.		Bge	3.6	1.0	0.3	1040

Flint flakes

	Btt	Ctx	Col.	L.	W.	Th.	79 12–9
99	Pnct.	x	Gr.	5.7	2.9	0.8	978
100	Pl.	x	Gr.	5.2	3.0	0.9	979
101	Pl.	x	Gr.	4.5	5.0	1.2	980
102	Pl.		M. Gr.	6.2	5.2	1.3	1012
103	Pnct.	x	Pat.	3.1	1.1	0.4	1033
							75 4–3
104	Pnct.	x	Gr.	8.0	3.5	1.3	21

105–26 *'Flint flakes'*: twenty-two; not identified.
79 12–9 949–50, 966, 970, 974, 985–6, 1013–17, 1020–24, 1029–32, 1039

127 *Flint core*: two opposed platforms with parallel flake scars, traces of previous platforms; cortex remnant; patinated.
L. 4.5 cm; W. 4.7 cm; Th. 3.5 cm.   79 12–9 1042

128 *Flint core*: one platform with parallel flake scars, on reverse at right angles corticated platform with irregular flake scars; traces of previous platforms; cortex remnant; patinated.
L. 4.2 cm; W. 4.1 cm; Th. 4.3 cm.   79 12–9 1043

129 *Flint core*: cortex remnant; burnt.
L. 3.9 cm; W. 3.5 cm; Th. 2.7 cm.   79 12–9 1044

130 *Flint core-trimming flake*: struck to remove hinge from platform; punctiform butt; cortex remnant; mottled grey.
L. 5.0 cm; W. 1.8 cm; Th. 1.2 cm.   79 12–9 1002

131 *Flint core-rejuvenation flake*: struck at right angles to cortical platform; mottled grey.
L. 5.6 cm; W. 2.7 cm; Th. 2.1 cm.   79 12–9 1041

132 *Antler tine*: red deer; tip worn, butt broken.
L. 31.6 cm; max. Diam. 3.7 cm.   79 12–9 1050

133–4 *'Antler fragments'*: two; not identified.
79 12–9 1048–9

68   RUDSTON (Cranswick II)   68:1–17

Yorkshire E.R.; North Humberside   TA 08 65

ROUND BARROW: Diam 12 m, H. 1 m, extensively disturbed; earth core H. 0.5 m with chalk capping; opened November 1870.
BB 262–9.

Burial 1: adult inhumation, crouched on R. with head NNW; 0.5 m above old surface, 2.3 m SW. of centre.

Burial 2: child inhumation; 0.5 m above old surface, 2.1 m SW. by W. of centre.

Burial 3: adult male inhumation, crouched on R. with head SW.; on old surface, 0.6 m S. of centre.

Burial 4: child inhumation, crouched on L. with head SW.; at level of old surface at centre, above Burial 6.

Burial 5: disturbed bones of adult and child; in central area, with burnt earth and charcoal.

Burial 6: adult male inhumation, crouched on L. with head SE. by E.; at base of central oval grave L. 2.7 m, W. 2.5 m (basal L. 2.4 m, W. 1.4 m), D. 2 m, aligned NE.–SW., chalk fill with charcoal at base; at chest 'sponge-finger' over ring over buttons with backs together, 'strike-a-light' at upper chest, dagger with horn hilt pointing away from face, on ? moss.

1 *Bronze dagger*: Gerloff Type Butterwick; lingulate blade of lenticular section with edge bevels; trilobate butt with edge partly bevelled and omega hilt line; two rivets in damaged holes and three loose, all with irregular faceted shanks (Table 1:4).
L. 12.1 cm; W. 4.4 cm; Th. 0.2 cm.
Rivets L. 1.1–1.4 cm; shank Diam. 0.3–0.4 cm.
BB fig. 125; *Gerloff 1975, no. 38*.   79 12–9 1057

2 *Stone sponge-finger*: fine schist ground and polished to plano-convex section; slight traces of lateral abrasion on both tips.
L. 10.0 cm; W. 2.0 cm; Th. 0.7 cm.   79 12–9 1052
BB fig. 14; *Smith and Simpson 1966, fig. 6*.

3 *Jet ring*: cut and polished to square section; joined double drilled V-perforation on edge; hollowed on each face between inner and outer flanges to receive fine radial incisions; transverse incisions around edge between two incised lines and crossed by a third irregular line.
Diam. (outer) 2.6 cm; (inner) 1.6 cm; Th. 0.6 cm.
BB fig. 123; *ASI fig. 371*.   79 12–9 1053

4 *Jet button*: cut and polished to peaked dome bevelled to flat base with central drilled V- perforation; on dome outer register of incised alternate hatched and reserved zones between two concentric lines, around area with four pendant triangles made by hatched band around reserved centre defining reserved Maltese cross.
Diam. 3.5 cm; Th. 0.7 cm.   79 12–9 1054
BB fig. 124; *ASI fig. 372*.

5 *Jet button*: cut and polished to peaked dome bevelled to flat base with central drilled V-perforation.
Diam. 3.9 cm; Th. 0.7 cm.   79 12–9 1055

6 *Strike-a-light*
Flint fabricator: abraded edge retouch on distal and R.; sub-triangular section; cortex remnant; mottled grey.
L. 6.6 cm; W. 2.2 cm; Th. 1.1 cm.   79 12–9 1060
'Split iron pyrites nodule': not identified.
BB fig. 31; *ASI fig. 223*.   79 12–9 1060

Burial 7: adult male inhumation, crouched on L. with head SE.; at NE. end of grave L. 2.1 m, W. 1.4 m, D. 1.7 m, aligned NE.–SW., connected to SW. end of Burial 6 grave; objects at back.

7 *Jet button*: cut and polished to dome with flat base with central circular boss drilled for V-perforation.
Diam. 4.7 cm; Th. 1.0 cm.   79 12–9 1058

8 *Jet button*: cut and polished to peaked dome bevelled to flat base with central drilled V-perforation.
Diam. 4.8 cm; Th. 1.1 cm.   79 12–9 1059

9 *Strike-a-light*
Flint fabricator: abraded steep edge retouch on distal and R.; sub-rectangular section; platform butt; cortex remnant; dark grey.
L. 6.2 cm; W. 2.0 cm; Th. 1.4 cm.   79 12–9 1056
Split iron pyrites nodule: abraded.
L. 4.5 cm; W. 3.7 cm; Th. 2.0 cm.   79 12–9 1056

Burial 8: adult male inhumation, crouched on L. with head NE. by E.; in grave L. 1.5 m, W. 1.7 m, D. 1.4 m, aligned NE. by N.–SW. by S., connected to N. side of graves of Burials 6 and 7; knife with 'horn' hilt pointing away from face, battle-axe and flint behind shoulders.

10 *Bronze razor-knife*: Butler and Smith class 1A; parallel-sided blade with central thickening and traces of broad hollowed edge-bevels; sub-rectangular butt with straight hilt line, rectangular butt with straight hilt line, single rivet in hole and traces of wood with longitudinal grain; point lacking (Table 1:17).

L. 6.6 cm; W. 3.0 cm; Th. 0.2 cm.
Rivet L. 0.7 cm;· Th. 0.4 cm.   79 12-9 1061
Butler and Smith 1956, 50; *Jockenhovel* 1980, no. 17.

11 *Stone battle-axe*: Group XV greywacke, Y828, Roe IIc;
all over ground and polished, bilateral and bifacial
bevelling; drilled hourglass perforation; blade edge
bevelled.
L. 13.5 cm; W. 6.3 cm; Th. 4.8 cm; Diam. (perf.) 3.0
cm.   79 12-9 1062
BB fig. 126; *Roe* 1966, no. 274.

12 *Flint pointed implement*: bilateral edge retouch at 60
degrees converging on distal; platform butt; cortex
remnant; mottled grey.
L. 4.3 cm; W. 2.0 cm; Th. 1.7 cm.   79 12-9 1063

Mound material

13 *'Pottery fragment'*: not identified.   79 12-9 1051
14 *Flint horseshoe scraper*: edge retouch on distal and
bilateral at 70 degrees; punctiform butt; cortex
remnant; patinated.
L. 3.9 cm; W. 2.8 cm; Th. 0.9 cm.   79 12-9 1064
15 *Flint scraper*: partial bilateral edge retouch;
platform butt; cortex remnant; mottled grey.
L. 3.8 cm; W. 3.0 cm; Th. 1.1 cm.   79 12-9 1065
16 *Flint worked flake*: bilateral edge retouch; platform
butt; broken; mottled grey.
L. 2.7 cm; W. 2.9 cm; Th. 0.6 cm.   79 12-9 1066
17 *Flint worked flake*: all round edge retouch; wear on
R.; cortex remnant; mottled grey.
L. 4.7 cm; W. 2.3 cm; Th. 1.2 cm.   79 12-9 1587

69   RUDSTON (Jordan)   69:1-51

Yorkshire. E.R.; North Humberside   TA 11 65

ROUND BARROW: Diam. 18 m; H. 1 m; earth.
BB 269-71.

Burial 1: inhumation and cremation: adult male extended
with head W., adult male cremation against L. knee; in
central grave L. 2 m, W. 1m, D. 0.4 m at E. rising to
surface at W., aligned ENE.-WSW.; Food Vessel at R. hip,
knife at L. arm.

1 *Food Vessel*: Yorkshire Vase; on internal rim bevel,
three to four twisted cord lines; on external bevel
and upper neck, twisted cord herringbone; on lower
neck, row of diagonal stab-and-drag jabs made with
point; on shoulder groove and lugs, vertical rows of
similar jabs; on body, two horizontal twisted cord
lines above herringbone; four imperforate lugs.
M. 15.6 cm; H. 12.4 cm; B. 8.4 cm.   79 12-9 1067
BAP no. 151.

2 *Flint plano-convex knife*: all over invasive retouch;
platform butt; dark grey.
L. 7.0 cm. W. 3.0 cm; Th. 0.6 cm.   79 12-9 1094
Clarke 1932, no. 2.20.

Mound material

3 *Stone rubber or hammer*: fine-grained sandstone
pebble with one smoothed and polished face; abraded
band around edges, more pronounced at ends.
L. 7.8 cm; W. 4.8 cm; Th. 2.7 cm.   79 12-9 1113
4 *Stone cupped pebble*: fine grained sandstone pebble
with ground hollow on flat face.
L. 6.9 cm; W. 3.9 cm; Th. 2.0 cm. cup Diam. 2.5 cm; D.
0.8 cm.   79 12-9 1114
5 *Sandstone pebble*   79 12-9 1115
6-7 *Sandstone fragments*: two; tabular. 79 12-9 1116-7
8 *Flint axe roughout fragment*: irregular thinning
flake-scars; cortex remnant; patinated.
L. 4.5 cm; W. 4.6 cm; Th. 1.9 cm.   79 12-9 1112
9 *Flint leaf arrowhead*: all round bifacial invasive
retouch; patinated.
L. 5.2 cm; W. 1.9 cm; Th. 0.4 cm.   79 12-9 1092

10 *Flint hollow-based arrowhead*: converging invasive
retouch unifacial on L. and bifacial on R.; half
inverse and half obverse edge retouch on base; dark
grey.
L. 3.1 cm; W. 1.7 cm; Th. 0.3 cm.   79 12-9 1093
Green 1980, no. A171.
11 *Flint laurel-leaf point fragment*: bifacial invasive
flaking; cortex remnant; snapped; mottled grey.
L. 3.6 cm; W. 4.1 cm; Th. 0.8 cm.   79 12-9 1106
12 *Flint pointed implement*: on blade; converging edge
retouch on L. and invasive retouch on R.; inverse
invasive retouch on proximal; dark grey.
L. 6.5 cm; W. 2.2 cm; Th. 0.7 cm.   79 12-9 1095
13 *Flint double-ended piercer*: on single platform core
fragment; partial edge retouch on terminals; wear on
R.; cortex remnant; grey.
L. 6.8 cm; W. 1.9 cm; Th. 1.2 cm.   79 12-9 1101
14 *Flint horseshoe scraper*: edge retouch on distal and
bilateral at 80 degrees; cortex remnant; speckled
grey.
L. 4.9 cm; W. 3.6 cm; Th. 1.1 cm.   79 12-9 1069
15 *Flint horseshoe scraper*: edge retouch on distal and
bilateral at 70 degrees; cortex remnant; light grey.
L. 3.3 cm; W. 2.6 cm; Th. 0.8 cm.   79 12-9 1070
16 *Flint end- and side-scraper*: edge retouch on distal
and L. at 55 degrees; broken; grey.
L. 2.2 cm; W. 2.8 cm; Th. 0.9 cm.   79 12-9 1074
17 *Flint end- and side-scraper*: edge retouch on distal
and L. at 65 degrees; burnt.
L. 3.8 cm; W. 4.2 cm; Th. 1.0 cm.   79 12-9 1079
18 *Flint end-scraper*: distal edge retouch at 70 degrees;
partial bifacial invasive retouch; cortex remnant;
dark grey.
L. 5.4 cm; W. 4.2 cm; Th. 1.2 cm.   79 12-9 1068
19 *Flint end-scraper*: distal edge retouch at 50 degrees;
corticated butt; grey.
L. 4.2 cm; W. 2.8 cm; Th. 0.9 cm.   79 12-9 1071
20 *Flint end-scraper*: distal edge retouch at 55 degrees;
corticated butt; mottled grey.
L. 3.8 cm; W. 2.9 cm; Th. 1.2 cm.   79 12-9 1072
21 *Flint end-scraper*: distal edge retouch at 65 degrees;
wear on R.; platform butt; speckled grey.
L. 4.6 cm; W. 3.2 cm; Th. 1.0 cm.   79 12-9 1084
22 *Flint end-scraper*: distal edge retouch at 60 degrees;
platform butt; patinated.
L. 3.6 cm; W. 2.8 cm; Th. 0.8 cm.   79 12-9 1085
23 *Flint end-scraper*: distal edge retouch at 70 degrees;
punctiform butt; mottled grey.
L. 2.8 cm; W. 2.5 cm; Th. 0.5 cm.   79 12-9 1088
24-34 *'Flint scrapers'*: eleven; not identified.
79 12-9 1073, 1075-8, 1080-1, 1083, 1086-7, 1089
35 *Flint knife*: on blade; partial invasive retouch on
L., inverse invasive retouch on R.; both ends
snapped; cortex remnant; grey.
L. 5.0 cm; W. 1.8 cm; Th. 0.5 cm.   79 12-9 1097
36 *Flint knife*: invasive retouch on R., cortex on L.;
broken; grey.
L. 3.8 cm; W. 1.8 cm. Th. 0.8 cm.   79 12-9 1100
37 *Flint knife*: invasive retouch on L.; platform butt;
cortex remnant; mottled grey.
L. 6.0 cm; W. 2.5 cm; Th. 0.8 cm.   79 12-9 1102
38-42 *'Flint knives'*: five; not identified.
79 12-9 1096, 1098, 1103-5
43 *Flint notched flake*: partial notching edge retouch.on
R.; wear on L.; punctiform butt; snapped; grey.
L. 3.5 cm; W. 2.9 cm; Th. 0.8 cm.   79 12-9 1108
44 *Flint worked flake*: partial obverse retouch; some
inverse invasive retouch; platform butt; cortex
remnant; mottled grey.
L. 3.3 cm; W. 2.6 cm; Th. 0.7 cm.   79 12-9 1082

45 *Flint worked flake*: partial inverse edge retouch on
   L.; platform butt; mottled grey.
   L. 4.5 cm; W. 3.7 cm; Th. 1.1 cm.   79 12-9 1090
46 *Flint worked fragment*: bifacially flaked to sub-
   triangular section; cortex remnant; mottled grey.
   L. 5.1 cm; W. 3.8 cm; Th. 1.8 cm.   79 12-9 1091
47 *Flint worked flake*: partial edge retouch on R.;
   punctiform butt; cortex remnant; broken; grey.
   L. 4.0 cm; W. 3.9 cm; Th. 1.2 cm.   79 12-9 1107
48 *Flint utilised blade*: distal and bilateral wear;
   fluted butt; patinated.
   l. 7.6 cm; w. 2.0 cm; th. 0.5 cm.   79 12-9 1099
49 *Flint utilised flake*: bilateral wear; distal
   removed; platform butt; cortex remnant; mottled
   grey.
   L. 4.0 cm; W. 1.9 cm; Th. 0.9 cm.   79 12-9 1111
50 *Flint flake*: cortex remnant; grey.
   L. 6.0 cm; W. 2.5 cm; Th. 1.2 cm.   79 12-9 1109
51 *Flint blade*: distal removed; punctiform butt; cortex
   remnant; mottled grey.
   L. 4.4 cm; W. 1.7 cm; Th. 0.6 cm.   79 12-9 1110

70 FOLKTON (Flixton 2)   70:1-11

Yorkshire E.R.; North Yorkshire   TA 040 768

ROUND BARROW: Diam. 8.5 m, H. 1 m; chalk and earth;
previously opened.
BB 272-4.

Burial 1: child inhumation traces; on old surface 4 m S.
of centre.
1 *Food Vessel*: on internal rim bevel, transverse
   twisted cord and fingernail impressions.
   M. 12.3 cm; H. 10.2 cm; B. 6.0 cm.   79 12-9 1123
   BAP no. 122.

Burial 2: infant inhumation traces; on old surface 2.5 m
SSW. of centre.
2 *Collared Vessel sherds*: seven including rim and
   collar; twisted cord: on internal rim bevel, three
   horizontal lines; on collar, horizontal lines.
                                               79 12-9 1125
   Longworth no. 1137a.
3 *Collared Vessel rim sherd*: twisted cord: on internal
   moulding, rough zigzag; on collar and neck,
   horizontal lines.   79 12-9 1126
   Longworth no. 1138.
4 *Bronze Age sherds*: three.   79 12-9 1126a

Burial 3: infant inhumation traces; 0.5 m above old
surface, 2.7 m SSE. of centre.
5 *Food Vessel*: twisted cord: on internal rim bevel,
   lozenges; on neck, two rows of zigzag; on body,
   vertical and diagonal lines.
   M. 11.6-12.4 cm; H. 9.5 cm; B. 7.0 cm. 79 12-9 1121
   BAP no. 120.

Burial 4: child inhumation, head SE.; on old surface 2.7
m SE. by S. of centre.

Burial 5: adult female inhumation, crouched on L. with
head SSE.; on old surface, 1.5 m SW. by S. of centre.

Burial 6: double inhumation: child against chest of
adult male, both crouched on L. with heads N. by W.; 0.5
m above old surface, 2.1 m W. by S. of centre.

Burial 7: adolescent inhumation, crouched on R. with
head E.; on old surface, 2.7 m E. of centre.

Burial 8: adult ?female inhumation, crouched on L. with
head ESE.; on old surface, 2.1 m NE. by N. of centre;
vessel at face.

6 *Collared Vessel*: twisted cord: on internal rim bevel,
   three lines; at base of internal moulding, one
   intermittent line; on collar, horizontal lines; on
   neck, row of short diagonal lines separated from a
   second row of opposed diagonal lines by three
   horizontal lines with a further three beneath; on
   body, zone of horizontal lines above zone of short
   diagonal lines separated from a second zone of
   opposed short diagonal lines by three horizontal
   lines above zone of horseshoes with three lines
   beneath; at base, two rows of horseshoes above line
   of jabs.
   M. 13.0 cm; H. 21. 6 cm; B. 8.3 cm.   79 12-9 1124
   BB fig. 84; *BAP* no. 119; *Longworth* no. 1137.

Burial 9: child inhumation, crouched on L. with head W.
by S.; above old surface, 2.8 m N. by W. of centre; Food
Vessel at face.
7 *Food Vessel*: on internal rim bevel, row of jabbed
   impressions; beneath rim, three horizontal twisted
   cord lines; above and below shoulder, row of diagonal
   jabbed impressions.
   M. 15.0 cm; H. 11.5 cm; B. 7.3 cm.   79 12-9 1120
   BAP no. 121.

Burial 10: adult male inhumation, crouched on L.,
aligned W. by N.-E. by S.; 0.3 m above old surface, 2.1 m
NNW. of centre; head removed in previous opening.

Burial 11: redeposited bones of adult and adult female
(with bones of Burial 10); collected in pit cut near
pelvis of Burial 10 in previous opening.

Burials 12-13 were in a grave L. 1.7 m, W. 1.4 m, D. 1 m,
NW of centre.

Burial 12: child cremation deposit; at top of grave fill
at N. side; Food Vessel beneath.
8 *Food Vessel*: plain.
   M. 12.5 cm; H. 9.5 cm; B. 6.5 cm.   79 12-9 1122
   BAP no. 118.

Burial 13: adult male inhumation, crouched on R. with
head SSE.; at S. side on basal chalk slab paving; pin at
chest, blade 'below the head', right foreleg of pig at
face.
9 *Boar tusk pin*: cut and polished to round section;
   butt broken across two of four drilled perforations.
   L. 10.4 cm; Diam. 0.7 cm.   79 12-9 1127
   BB fig. 9.
10 *Boar tusk blade*: split and one side ground to sharp
   edge; both ends broken.
   L. 6.7 cm; W. 1.9 cm; Th. 0.4 cm.   79 12-9 1128

Grave fill
11 *'Bone implement'*: not identified.   79 12-9 1129
   BB fig. 36.

71 FOLKTON (Flixton III)   71:1-20

Yorkshire E.R.; North Yorkshire   TA 043 767

ROUND BARROW: Diam. 11 m, H. 1.5 m; SW. of chalk, NE. of
earth.
BB 274-9.

Burial 1: adolescent inhumation, crouched on L. with
head E. by S.; 0.3 m above old surface, 2.5 m S. by E. of
centre, beneath chalk slabs.

Burial 2: infant inhumation, head S.; 0.3 m above old
surface, 2.3 m SW. by S. of centre.

Burial 3: adult male inhumation, crouched on R. with
head W. by N. but lower part of body displaced with bones
redeposited near head of Burial 2; 2 m SW. by W. of
centre.

Burial 4: scattered cremated bones; 0.5 m above old surface, S. of centre.

Burial 5: adolescent inhumation, crouched on R. with head WNW.; 0.8 m above surface, N. of Burial 4.

Burial 6–8 were in an oval grave L. 2.9 m, W. 1.8 m, D. 1.5 m, aligned SE.–NW., 2.7 m SSW. of centre; chalk fill.

Burial 6: adult female inhumation, crouched on R. with head S.; at D. 1.2 m at centre, surrounded by chalk slabs; Food Vessel at face, scraper 'below head', decorated beads at R. elbow, plain bead and awl 'below hips', R. foreleg and ribs of pig at hips.

1   *Bronze awl*: Thomas Type 1B; round-sectioned with central swelling squared by lozenge facets; tips lacking (Table 1:36).
    L. 3.9 cm; W. 0.2 cm; Th. 0.2 cm.   79 12–9 1146
    BB fig. 39; *Thomas* 1968, 23.

2   *Food Vessel*: Yorkshire Vase; on internal rim bevel, knot impressions in one area and horizontal whipped cord elsewhere; on external rim bevel and over lugs, knot impressions; in neck between lugs, horizontal twisted cord lines; on shoulder for most of circumference, row of knot impressions; on body, horizontal twisted cord lines above vertical to diagonal lines; six horizontally-perforated lugs.
    M. 15.5 cm; H. 12.4 cm; B. 9.0 cm.   79 12–9 1130
    BAP no. 88; *Simpson* 1968, fig. 45.5.

3   *Flint end-scraper*: edge retouch on distal at 65 degrees; platform butt; cortex remnant; patinated.
    L. 3.4 cm; W. 3.0 cm; Th. 1.0 cm.   79 12–9 1136
    Bone beads: cut and polished from segment of caprovine-size radius shaft utilising natural perforations; decoration accomplished by slight charring of surface to create darker zones.
    BB fig. 50.

4   *Bone bead*: dark cruciform design on flatter face; traces of reserved cruciform on reverse.
    L. 1.5 cm; W. 1.3 cm; Th. 0.9 cm.   79 12–9 1141

5   *Bone bead*: reserved cruciform on flatter face, opposed reserved triangles bisected by dark band on reverse.
    L. 1.5 cm; W. 1.3 cm; Th. 0.9 cm.   79 12–9 1142

6   *Bone bead*: opposed reserved triangles on flatter face, with darker areas flaked by heat-treatment, opposed reserved triangles bisected by dark band on reverse.
    L. 1.5 cm; W. 1.3 cm; Th. 0.9 cm.   79 12–9 1143

7   *Bone bead*: all over heat treatment on reverse.
    L. 1.9 cm; W. 1.3 cm; Th. 0.9 cm.   79 12–9 1144

Burial 7: adult male inhumation, crouched on L. with head NE. by E.,; at NE. end at base of grave, surrounded by turf.

Burial 8: bones of adult and child inhumation; in grave fill.

8   *Flint end-scraper*: edge retouch on distal and some bilateral at 65 degrees; platform butt; cortex remnant; mottled grey.
    L. 2.0 cm; W. 2.2 cm; Th. 0.7 cm.   79 12–9 1589

9   *Flint plano-convex knife fragment*: converging bilateral invasive retouch; cortex remnant; snapped; mottled grey.
    L. 3.3 cm; W. 2.9 cm; Th. 0.7 cm.   79 12–9 1588

Burial 9: scattered cremated bones of adult; 0.9 m above old surface at centre, in deposit of dark earth and charcoal Diam. 1.5 m, Th. 0.2 m.

Burial 10: adult ?male inhumation, crouched on L. with head ENE.; 1.2 m above old surface, at centre; vessel at knees.

10 *Collared Vessel sherds*: bone epiphyseal impressions: on collar, two rows; on shoulder, one row.
    Longworth no. 1139.   79 12–9 1132

Burial 11: child inhumation, head S.; 0.3 m above old surface, 1.5 m N. of centre.

Burial 12: disturbed adult male inhumation, crouched on R., aligned N.–S.; 0.3 m above old surface, 2.4 m NNE. of centre; cranium displaced into fill of grave of Burials 13–15; scraper on knees.

11 *Flint end- and side-scraper*: edge retouch on distal and R. at 65 degrees; corticated butt; patinated.
    L. 2.2 cm; W. 2.3 cm; Th. 0.7 cm.   79 12–9 1140

Burials 13–15 were in an oval grave L. 1.8 m, W. 1.4 m, D. 1.2 m, aligned E. by S.–W. by N., 2.4 m NW. of centre.

Burial 13: adult male inhumation, crouched on L. with head ESE.; at D. 0.4 m at S. side of grave; cranium of Burial 12 near knees; scrapers nos 12–13 at face, no. 14 beneath head, wooden object L. 0.6 m at front.

12 *Flint horseshoe scraper*: edge retouch on distal and partial bilateral at 55 degrees; punctiform butt; cortex remnant; patinated.
    L. 3.3 cm; W. 3.0 cm; Th. 0.9 cm.   79 12–9 1138

13 *Flint end scraper*: edge retouch on distal and partial bilateral at 50 degrees; platform butt; cortex remnant; patinated.
    L. 5.3 cm; W. 3.8 cm; Th. 0.9 cm.   79 12–9 1137

14 *Flint end scraper*: edge retouch on distal at 50 degrees; punctiform butt; patinated.
    L. 4.5 cm; W. 2.6 cm; Th. 0.7 cm.   79 12–9 1139
    '*wooden object*': not preserved.

Burial 14: disturbed bones of adult and child; in mound above grave and in grave fill to depth of Burial 13.

Burial 15: adult male inhumation, crouched on R. with head NE. by E.; at base of grave at centre, head protected by three chalk slabs on edge with fourth as 'capstone'; button under neck, Food Vessel behind shoulders, pig 'trotters' at feet.

15 *Food Vessel*: twisted cord: on internal rim bevel, three lines; on upper body, short vertical lines above row of finger-pinches; on lower body, short vertical to diagonal lines; at base, row of ?finger-pinches.
    M. 16.5 cm; H. 16.4 cm; B. 7.7 cm.   79 12–9 1131
    BAP no. 87.

16 *Bone button*: cut and polished to dome returning to flat base with central drilled V-perforation; ovate.
    L. 1.4 cm; W. 1.2 cm; Th. 0.6 cm.   79 12–9 1145

Mound material

17 *Collared Vessel sherd*: plain.   79 12–9 1135
    Longworth no. 1139a.

18 *Food Vessel sherds*: five including base; ?plaited cord horizontal line above short diagonal lines.
            79 12–9 1133

19 *Bipartite Vessel sherds*: forty, including rim; twisted cord: on internal rim bevel, single horizontal line; between rim and cordon, two horizontal lines above, and intersecting with, vertical and diagonal lines with single horizontal line beneath.   79 12–9 1134

Not located

20 '*Flint implement*': not identified.   79 12–9 1147

72 CHERRY BURTON (Gardham I)

Yorkshire E.R.; North Humberside   SE 942 405

ROUND BARROW: Diam. 15 m, H. 1 m, reduced by ploughing;
earth and chalk, opened 22 March 1866.
BB 280; *GM* 1866, I: 493-4.

Burial 1: adult male inhumation, crouched on L. with
head SE.; in central oval hollow L. 1.4 m, W. 1 m, D. 0.3
m, aligned E.-W., burnt earth and charcoal in fill.

73 CHERRY BURTON (Gardham II)   73:1-6

Yorkshire E.R.; North Humberside   SE 942 405

ROUND BARROW: Diam. 14 m, H. 0.9 m, reduced by ploughing;
earth with some chalk; opened March 1866.
BB 280-1; *GM* 1866, I: 493-4.

Burial 1: infant cremation deposit; in inverted urn 0.8
m above old surface, 1 m ENE. of centre, flint blocks
around.
1   *Collared Urn*: collar and upper neck; on collar,
    twisted cord herringbone.
    M. 25.2-27.3 cm.   79 12-9 1148d
    Longworth no. 677.

Burial 2: adult cremation deposit; in inverted urn 0.8 m
above old surface, 1 m WSW. of centre, flint blocks
around.
2   *Collared Urn sherd*: whipped cord herringbone.
                                                79 12-9 1148
    Longworth no. 676a.
3   *Food Vessel rim sherd*: on internal rim bevel, incised
    diagonal lines.   79 12-9 1148a
4   *Bronze Age rim sherd*: plain; eroded.
                                                79 12-9 1148b
5   *Bronze Age sherds*: twenty-five, including base.
                                                79 12-9 1148c

Burial 3: adolescent cremation deposit; in inverted urn
in hollow Diam. 0.5 m, D. 0.5 m, ENE. of centre, fill of
burnt earth and charcoal.
6   *Collared Urn*: on internal moulding, row of twisted
    cord vertical loops with row of jabs and single line
    above, and single line below; on internal rim bevel,
    row of diagonal jabs; on collar, twisted cord lattice
    with row of diagonal jabs and single line above, and
    single line below; on neck, twisted cord horizontal
    lines; on shoulder, row of jabs.
    M. 23.5 cm; H. *c.* 28.5 cm; B. *c.* 9.5 cm.
    Longworth no. 676.   79 12-9 1149

74 CHERRY BURTON (Gardham IV)

Yorkshire E.R., North Humberside   SE 942 405

ROUND BARROW: Diam. 6 m, H. 0.4 m, reduced by ploughing;
earth.
BB 281; *GM* 1866, I:493-4.

Burial 1: adult cremation deposit, in heap Diam. 0.2 m;
in slight hollow, ?burnt *in situ*.

75 CHERRY BURTON (Gardham VII)

Yorkshire E.R.; North Humberside   SE 943 406
ROUND BARROW: Diam 14 m, H. 0.8 m, reduced by ploughing;
earth, layer of burnt chalk and flint, Th. 0.2 cm, above
old surface.
BB 281.

Burial 1: few cremated bones of adult; in slight hollow
at centre, ?burnt *in situ*.

Mound material
    '*portions of a cinerary urn*': not preserved.

76 ETTON (Paulinus IX)   76:1

Yorkshire E.R.; North Humberside   SE 99 44

ROUND BARROW: Diam. 15 m, H. 0.5 m; earth.
BB 282.

Burial 1: adult female cremation deposit; in central
hollow Diam 0.9 m, D. 0.2 m, with burnt fill; central
area Diam. 2.1 m burnt; cup at W. side of hollow, flake
with bones.
1   *Accessory Cup*: twisted cord: on internal rim bevel,
    two lines; on body, chevrons between two lines above
    and one below; no perforations.
    M. 6.3 cm; H. 5.4 cm; B. 5.5 cm.   79 12-9 1150
    BB fig. 128; *BAP* no. 313.
    '*burnt flint flake*': not preserved.

77 ETTON (Paulinus X)

Yorkshire E.R.; North Humberside   SE 99 44

ROUND BARROW: Diam. 14 m, H. 0.4 m; earth.
BB 283.

Burial 1: adult male inhumation, contracted on R. with
head N.; on old surface at centre.

78 ETTON (Paulinus XI)

Yorkshire E.R.; North Humberside   SE 99 44

ROUND BARROW: Diam. 13.5 m, H. 0.5 m; earth.
BB 283.

Burial 1: adult male inhumation, crouched on R. with
head N.; in shallow grave at centre.

79 ETTON (Etton Wold)   79:1-2

Yorkshire E.R.; North Humberside   SE 935 438

ROUND BARROW: Diam. 18 m, H. 0.5 m, reduced by ploughing
(16.5 m by 15.5 m, H. 0.3 m: Coombs); earth with some
chalk and flint, over bank of chalk and flint Diam. 3.3 m
(horizontally laid turves, over bank of chalk and flint
Diam. 7.5 m, W. 1.2 m, H. 0.2 m, enclosing central hollow
Diam. 4.5 m, D. 0.4 m: Coombs); opened *c.* 1865 by WG, re-
excavated 1969 by Coombs.
BB 283-4; *Coombs* 1974.

Burial 1: adult cremation deposit; on old surface 4.2 m
SW. by S. of centre.
Burial 2: adult ?male cremated *in situ*, crouched on R.
with head NE. by E.; in hollow Diam 0.8 m, D. 0.3 m, 2.6 m
W. by S. of centre (central hollow, surrounding surface
burnt: Coombs); vessel behind hips, ?awl at chest, burnt
pig scapula, radius and ulna associated.
    '*bronze drill or awl*': not preserved.
1   *Collared Vessel*: twisted cord: on internal rim bevel,
    two lines; on collar, filled triangles bordered above
    by single line.
    M. 13.0 cm; H. 17.3 cm; B. 7.5 cm.   79 12-9 1151
    Longworth no. 683.

Mound material
    '*food vessel sherd*': not preserved.
    '*cinerary urn sherd*: not preserved.

Backfill of WG trench (1969)
2 *Collared Vessel rim sherds*: two; on collar and neck, incised herringbone.　　　　　　P1975 4-1 1
  Coombs 1974, fig. 6, Longworth no. 684.

80　ETTON (Etton I)

Yorkshire E.R.; North Humberside　　　　SE 935 438

OVAL BARROW: L. 21 m, W. 18.5 m, H. 1.2 m, reduced by ploughing; earth with some chalk and flint.
BB 284.

Burial 1: adult ?male cremation deposit; in central grave Diam 0.5 m, D. 0.3 m with charcoal, ?burnt *in situ*.

81　ETTON (Etton II)

Yorkshire E.R.; North Humberside　　　　SE 935 438

ROUND BARROW: Diam 18 m, H. 1 m, reduced by ploughing (ditch Diam. 18.5 m, W. 0.6-1.2 m, D. 0.2-0.5 m: Coombs); earth with some chalk and flint, on natural knoll; opened c. 1865 by WG, excavated 1969 by Coombs.
BB 284-5; Coombs 1974.

Burial 1: child cremation deposit; in central pit Diam. 0.35 m, D. 0.5 m, sand and charcoal fill.

82　ETTON (Riley)　　　　　　　　　82:1-3

Yorkshire E.R.; North Humberside　　　　SE 93 45

ROUND BARROW: Diam. 15 m, H. 0.5 m, reduced by ploughing; earth and some chalk.
BB 285-6.

Burial 1: double cremation deposit, adult and child in heap Diam. 0.3 m; at base of grave L. 1.4 m, W. 0.8 m, D. 0.7 m, aligned E.-W., 1.2 m S. of centre; knife among bones.

1 *Flint plano-convex knife*: on blade; all over invasive retouch; all round fine serration, nine teeth per cm; damaged; dark grey.
  L. 6.6 cm; W. 2.0 cm; Th. 0.6 cm.　　79 12-9 1153
  BB fig. 129; AS1 fig. 240A; Clark 1932, no. 6.3.

Burial 2: child inhumation, crouched on L. with head NNW.; at N. end of grave L. 1.2 m, W. 0.8 m, D. 0.6 m, aligned SSE.-NNW., 1.2 m N. of centre, with cover of flint blocks; pin at neck, sherd in flints.
2 *'Pottery fragment'*: not identified.　　79 12-9 1152
3 *Bone pin*: caprovine longbone splinter, cut to point; broken and very eroded.
  L. 5.9 cm; W. 0.9 cm; Th. 0.3 cm.　　79 12-9 1154

83　GOODMANHAM (Enthorpe I)　　　83:1-3

Yorkshire E.R.; North Humberside　　　　SE 91 45

ROUND BARROW: Diam. 14.5 m, H. 1 m; earth and some flints.
BB 287-8.

Burial 1: adolescent cremation deposit; with charcoal and burnt earth around upright vessel, 0.2 m above old surface, 4 m E. of centre.
1 *Collared Vessel*: point-toothed comb-stamped: on internal rim bevel, short diagonal lines; on collar, filled triangles bordered by single horizontal lines.
  M. c. 12.0 cm; H. 16.3 cm; B. 8.5 cm.　79 12-9 1155
  BAP no. 115; Longworth no. 690.
  'piece of calcined flint': not preserved.

Burial 2: child cremation deposit; with charcoal and burnt earth around upright vessel, 0.4 m above old surface, 3.7 m E. of centre.
2 *Collared Vessel*: twisted cord: on collar, horizontal lines; on neck, chevron.
  M. 9.5 cm; H. 10.9 cm; B. 6.3 cm.　　79 12-9 1156
  BAP no. 115a; Longworth no. 689.

Mound material
3 *Flint end-scraper*: edge retouch on distal at 75 degrees; bilateral wear; platform butt; cortex remnant; mottled grey.
  L. 5.1 cm; W. 2.5 cm; Th. 0.9 cm.　　79 12-9 1157

84　GOODMANHAM (Enthorpe II)　　　84:1-5

Yorkshire E.R.; North Humberside　　　　SE 91 45

ROUND BARROW: Diam. 11 m, H. 0.6 m; earth.
BB 288-90.

Burial 1: cremation deposit, scatter Diam. 0.3 m; on old surface, 4.5 m ESE. of centre, ?burnt *in situ*.

Burial 2: cremation deposit; 0.3 m above old surface, 3.3 m S. of centre, ?burnt *in situ*.

Burial 3: cremation deposit; 0.3 m above old surface, 1.4 m E. of Burial 2, ?burnt *in situ*.

Burial 4: cremated bone fragment; with burnt earth and charcoal around vessel on side with mouth E. and overlying Accessory Cup, 0.3 m above old surface, 2.7 m SE. of centre.
1 *Collared Vessel*: on collar, three rows of short incised vertical lines with one diagonal section; on neck, two to three rows of jabbed impressions.
  M. 10.3-11.4 cm; H. 11.8 cm; B. 6.6 cm.
  　　　　　　　　　　　　　　79 12-9 1158
  BAP no. 105a; Longworth no. 693.
2 *Accessory Cup*: on top of rim, indistinct diagonal and transverse impressions; no perforations.
  M. 6.4 cm; H. 3.2 cm; B. 6.2 cm.　　79 12-9 1159
  BAP no. 105c.

Burial 5: adult cremation deposit, in heap Diam. 0.2 m; 0.4 m above old surface, 1.8 m E. of centre, ?burnt *in situ*.
3 *Flint knife*: converging invasive retouch on distal and bilateral; burnt.
  L. 4.8 cm; W. 2.1 cm; Th. 0.9 cm.　　79 12-9 1162

Burial 6: adolescent cremation deposit; around upright vessel, 0.4 m above old surface, 1.8 m WSW. of centre, ?burnt *in situ*.
4 *Collared Vessel*: plain.
  M. 9.8 cm; H. 9.2 cm; B. 7.2 cm.　　79 12-9 1160
  BAP no. 105b; Longworth no. 691.

Burial 7: adult cremation deposit, in heap Diam. 0.25 m; on old surface 1.8 m ENE. of centre.

Burial 8: cremation deposit, with burnt earth and charcoal around inverted vessel, 0.5 m above old surface, at centre, ?burnt *in situ*.
5 *Collared Vessel*: on collar and neck, incised herringbone.
  M. 9.6 cm; H. 11.5 cm; B. 6.2 cm.　　79 12-9 1161
  BB fig. 61; BAP no. 105; Longworth no. 692.

85 GOODMANHAM (Enthorpe III)   85:1-2

Yorkshire E.R.; North Humberside   SE 91 45

ROUND BARROW: Diam. 13m, H. 0.6 m; earth around natural rise.
BB 290.

Burial 1: double cremation deposit: two children; around upright vessel 1 standing on vessel 2 on side with mouth W., on old surface at centre, ?burnt *in situ*.
1 *Collared Vessel*: plain.
   M. 13.0 cm; H. 16.3 cm; B. 9.0 cm.   79 12-9 1163
   BAP no. 114a; *Longworth* no. 695.
2 *Collared Vessel*: plain.
   M. 14.1-15.0 cm; H. 20.8 cm; B. 7.8 cm.
   BAP no. 114; *Longworth* no. 694.   79 12-9 1164

86 GOODMANHAM (Enthorpe IV)   86:1-3

Yorkshire E.R.; North Humberside   SE 91 45

ROUND BARROW: Diam. 17 m, H. 1.4 m; earth with some chalk.
BB 290-3.

Burial 1: adult male, crouched on R. with head SW. and burnt *in situ*; in hollow Diam. 1 m, D. 0.2 m, 0.9 m above old surface at centre, burnt fill with charcoal; upright vessel at face.
1 *Collared Vessel*; twisted cord: on internal rim bevel, two lines; on collar, hurdle pattern separated and bordered beneath by single horizontal lines; on neck and shoulder, four rows of horseshoes.
   M. 14.1 cm; H. 18.5 cm; B. 9.3 cm.   79 12-9 1165
   BB fig. 130; *Longworth* no. 696.
2 'Quartz pebble': not identified.   79 12-9 1167
3 'Flint core': not identified.   79 12-9 1166

87 GOODMANHAM (Enthorpe VI)   87:1

Yorkshire E.R.; North Humberside   SE 91 45

ROUND BARROW: Diam 21 m, H. 0.5 m, reduced by ploughing; composition not recorded.
BB 293.

Burial 1: adult cremation deposit; in central hollow Diam. 0.7 m, D. 0.9 m with cover of flint blocks, ?burnt *in situ*; stone nearby.
1 *Stone grinding-slab*: tabular sandstone block; both faces ground.
   L. 11.9 cm; W. 10.3 cm; Th. 4.8 cm.   79 12-9 1591

88 GOODMANHAM (Enthorpe V)

Yorkshire E.R.; North Humberside   SE 91 45

ROUND BARROW: Diam 17 m, H. 0.6 m; earth.
BB 293-4.

Burial 1: adult ?male inhumation, crouched on L. with head SE.; in central oval grave L. 3 m, W. 2.4 m, D. 1.2 m, charcoal layer over body, cranial fragment in fill.

89 GOODMANHAM (Enthorpe IX)   89:1-12

Yorkshire E.R.; North Humberside   SE 91 45

ROUND BARROW: Diam. 24 m, H. 1.2 m, reduced by ploughing; earth with some chalk lenses, core H. 0.9 m sealed by burnt layer.
BB 294-300.

Burial 1: adult cremation deposit; in hollow Diam. 0.8 m, D. 0.3 m at centre of burnt area Diam. 1.2 m, cut into core, 5.5 m SE. by S. of centre; cup and flint among bones.
1 *Accessory Cup*: twisted cord: on rim, two lines; on body, filled triangles; no perforations.
   M. 6.3 cm; H. 3.8 cm; B. 4.6 cm.   79 12-9 1170
   BB fig. 131; *BAP* no. 106d.
   'piece of calcined flint': not preserved.

Burial 2: adult ?female cremation deposit; in hollow Diam. 0.5 m, D. 0.4 m, cut into core, 5.5 m SSW. of centre, ?burnt *in situ*; cup among bones.
2 *Accessory Cup*: on internal rim bevel, row of round impressions; on body, incised filled triangles enclosed by triple horizontal lines; no perforations.
   M. 6.9 cm; H. 6.2 cm; B. 6.0 cm.   79 12-9 1169
   BAP no. 106b.

Burial 3: adult cremation deposit; in hollow Diam. 0.5 m, D. 0.5 m, cut into core 5.2 m SW. of centre; cup among bones at W.
3 *Accessory Cup*: twisted cord: on internal rim bevel, three lines; on upper body, chevrons enclosed above by three and below by two horizontal lines; on lower body, chevrons enclosed above by two and below by three horizontal lines; two perforations through outer rim edge; squashed.
   M. 6.6-7.4 cm; H. 5.6 cm; B. 5.3 cm.   79 12-9 1171
   BB fig. 62; *BAP* no. 106c.

Burial 4: adult inhumation, crouched on L. with head N. by W.; 0.3 m above old surface, 3 m S. of centre.

Burial 5: adult inhumation, crouched on R. with head SSW.; on old surface, 3.4 m SE. of centre; wood remains beneath upper body, flint block at chest.

Burial 6: adult female inhumation, crouched on L. with head NE.; 0.2 m above old surface, 2.3 m E. of centre; inverted vessel at head, pendant behind head.
4 *Collared Vessel*: on collar and neck, incised herringbone.
   M. 13.3 cm; H. 14.2 cm; B. 7.5 cm.   79 12-9 1172
   BAP no. 106; *Longworth* no. 697.
5 *Jet pendant*: cut and polished to trapezoidal outline with bevelled ends and flat sides; drilled transverse perforation at narrow end.
   L. 1.9 cm; W. 0.5-1.3 cm; Th. 0.7 cm.   79 12-9 1174

Burial 7: child cranial fragment; 0.5 m above old surface, 0.9 m S. of centre.
6 *Collared Vessel*: on collar, incised herringbone; on neck, roughly executed incised linear lozenges replaced in one section by incised herringbone; on shoulder, row of fingertip impressions.
   M. 10.3 cm; H. 10.7 cm; B. 6.4 cm.   79 12-9 1173
   BAP no. 106a; *Longworth* no. 698.

Burial 8: adult ?female cremation deposit, in heap Diam. 0.3 m; on old surface, 2.1 m ESE. of centre.

Burial 9: disturbed double inhumation: adolescent crouched on R. with head ESE., at back of adult male crouched on L., aligned SSE.-NNW.; lower part of adolescent and upper part of male lacking; on old surface, 1.2 m ESE. of centre.

Burial 10: child inhumation, crouched on R. with head E. by S.; on old surface, 1.4 m SW. by S. of centre.

Burial 11: adolescent cremation deposit; in hollow Diam. 0.6 m, D. 0.3 m, SSW. of centre; ?burnt *in situ*; battle-axe and pin among bones.

7 *Stone battle-axe*: lithic sandstone, Y798; Roe IVD; all over ground and polished; drilled bevelled cylindrical perforation.
     L. 10.2 cm; W. 4.4 cm; Th. 3.8 cm.   79 12-9 1175
     BB fig. 12; *Roe 1966*, no. 263.
     '*pointed end of a bone pin*': not preserved.

Burial 12: double inhumation: extended adolescent with head WSW., to N. of and partly overlying extended child with head ENE.; in rectangular grave L. 2.4 m, W. 0.8 m, D. 0.2 m, aligned ENE.-WSW., N. of centre; sandstone at R. knee of adolescent, scraper and pin at head of child.
8 *Sandstone pebble fragment*: split; one end abraded.
     L. 5.2 cm; W. 2.9 cm; Th. 1.4 cm.   79 12-9 1178
9 *Flint end-scraper*: edge retouch on distal at 50 degrees; platform butt; mottled grey.
     L. 2.5 cm; W. 2.1 cm; Th. 0.5 cm.   79 12-9 1176
10 *Bone pin fragment*; split caprovine longbone; broken and very eroded.
     L. 5.3 cm; W. 1.0 cm; Th. 0.2 cm.   79 12-9 1177
Mound material
11 *Collared Vessel*: (in ploughsoil, 4.5 m S. by E. of centre) plain.
     M. *c.* 14.0 cm; H. 16.9 cm; B. 7.1 cm.   79 12-9 1168
     BAP no. 106e *Longworth* no. 699.
12 '*Flint scraper*': not identified.   79 12-9 1179

90   GOODMANHAM (Paulinus V)   90:1
Yorkshire E.R.; North Humberside   SE 915 455

ROUND BARROW: Diam. 30 m, H. 2.4 m, reduced by ploughing; 'clayey earth'.
BB 300-1.

Burial 1: adult male inhumation, crouched on R. with head SW. by W.; in central hollow, with wooden lining and cover of ?planks; vessel at knees, flint at shoulder.
1 *Food Vessel*: Yorkshire Vase; twisted cord; on internal rim bevel, four lines; on external rim bevel and neck groove, herringbone; on shoulder groove, filled pendant triangles; below shoulder, herringbone.
     M. 17.8 cm, H.. 13.2 cm; B. 6.8 cm.   79 12-9 1180
     BAP no. 172.
     '*flint flake*': not preserved.

91   GOODMANHAM (Goodmanham I)   91:1-3
Yorkshire E.R.; North Humberside   SE 91 46

ROUND BARROW: Diam. 30 m, H. 1.4 m, reduced by ploughing; 'clayey earth'.
BB 301.

Mound material
1 *Food Vessel*: (0.3 m above old surface, 3.3 m SE. by S. of centre) plain.
     M. 13.0 cm; H. 11.1 cm; B. 6.9 cm.   79 12-9 1181
2 *Flint leaf arrowhead*: partial bifacial invasive retouch; cortex remnant; damaged; grey.
     L. 3.6 cm; W. 2.2 cm; Th. 0.3 cm.   79 12-9 1182
     Green 1980, no. A42.
3 *Flint horseshoe scraper*: edge retouch on distal and bilateral at 65 degrees; platform butt; grey.
     L. 2.3 cm; W. 2.5 cm; Th. 0.7 cm.   79 12-9 1183

92   GOODMANHAM (Goodmanham XIII)   92:1-2
Yorkshire E.R.; North Humberside   SE 91 46

ROUND BARROW: Diam. 26 m, H. 1.5 cm; earth.
BB 301-2

Burial 1: adult male inhumation, crouched on R. with head W. by S.; in central oval hollow L. 1.2 m, W. 0.6 m, aligned E.-W., 0.5 m above old surface, wood-lined; scraper at chest.
1 *Flint horseshoe scraper*: edge retouch on distal and bilateral at 65 degrees, all over invasive retouch; corticated butt; grey.
     L. 2.0 cm; W. 2.7 cm; Th. 0.9 cm.   79 12-9 1184

Burial 2: adult ?female cremation deposit, in heap Diam. 0.3 m; on level of old surface at centre.

Burial 3: child inhumation, crouched on R. with head NW.; in central oval hollow L. 1.7 m, W. 0.4 m, aligned SE.-NW., wood-lined; knife at hips.
2 *Flint plano-convex knife*: all over invasive retouch; mottled grey.
     L. 4.5 cm; W. 1.6 cm; Th. 0.6 cm.   79 12-9 1185
     Clark 1932, no. 5.6.

93   GOODMANHAM (Goodmanham X)   93:1-4
Yorkshire E.R.; North Humberside   SE 91 46

ROUND BARROW: Diam. 20 m, H. 1 m, reduced by ploughing; earth.
BB 302.

Burial 1: adult cremation deposit; in inverted Collared Urn, in ploughsoil 0.9 m above old surface, 2.7 m NW. of centre.
1 *Collared Urn*: *c.* one-third surviving; twisted cord: on internal rim bevel, two to three lines; on collar, horizontal lines (incised in one sector); on neck, horizontal lines; below shoulder, horizontal line.
     Longworth no. 700.   79 12-9 1186

Burial 2: cremation deposit in upright Collared Urn, on old surface at centre.
2 *Collared Urn sherds*: forty-four; whipped cord: on collar, herringbone; at base of neck, short vertical lines.
     Longworth no. 701.   79 12-9 1187
Mound material
3 *Collared Vessel rim sherd*: on collar, plaited cord filled triangles.   79 12-9 1188
     Longworth no. 702.
     '*a small cinerary urn*': (in ploughsoil, 4.2 m W. by S. of centre) not preserved.
4 '*Flint scraper*': not identified.   79 12-9 1189

94   GOODMANHAM (Goodmanham XII)   94:1-4
Yorkshire E.R.; North Humberside   SE 91 46

ROUND BARROW: Diam. 20 m, H. 1.4 m; earth.
BB 302-3.

Burial 1: adult male inhumation, extended with head W.; in central hollow, wood-lined; Food Vessel on side at R. of head, over knives.
1 *Food Vessel*: Irish Vase; on internal rim bevel, twisted and plaited cord lines; on external rim bevel, short diagonal twisted cord lines; in neck, twisted and plaited cord horizontal lines, with short diagonal twisted cord lines above in one sector; beneath shoulder, twisted cord herringbone.
     M. 16.3 cm; H. 16.6 cm; B. 7.7 cm.   79 12-9 1191
     BAP no. 71.

2 *Flint knife*: invasive retouch on distal and bilateral
   at 30 degrees; platform butt; damaged; patinated.
   L. 3.9 cm; W. 3.0 cm; Th. 0.6 cm.   79 12-9 1192
3 *Flint knife*: invasive retouch on distal at 35
   degrees; grey.
   L. 2.5 cm; W. 2.6 cm; Th. 0.8 cm.   79 12-9 1193
Mound material
4 *Food Vessel*: twisted cord: on internal rim bevel, two
   lines; on neck, diagonal lines; below shoulder,
   diagonal lines; at base, short vertical lines.
   M. 14.0 cm; H. 14.2 cm; B. 6.2 cm.   79 12-9 1190
   BAP no. 72.

95 GOODMANHAM (Goodmanham IV)   95:1-2

Yorkshire E.R.; North Humberside   SE 91 46

ROUND BARROW: Diam. 16 m, H. 1.1 m; earth.
BB 304.

Burials 1-2 were in a central grave L. 2.2 m, W. 1.2 m,
D. 1.8 m, aligned SE. by S.-NW. by N. with extension at
S. to W. L. 1.2 m, W. 0.7 m, chalk fill.

Burial 1: adult inhumation traces; in upper fill.

Burial 2: adult male inhumation, crouched on R. with
head S. by E.; at base at S. end.

Not located
1-2 *'Flint flakes'*: two; not identified.
                                             79 12-9 1194-5

96 GOODMANHAM (Goodmanham III)

Yorkshire E.R.; North Humberside   SE 91 46

ROUND BARROW: Diam. 12 m, H. 0.5 m, reduced by ploughing;
earth.
BB 304.

Burial 1: adult female cremation deposit, in heap Diam.
0.3 m; at base of central oval grave L. 1.7 m, W. 1.1 m,
D. 1.5 m, aligned SE by S.-NW. by W., fill of chalk and
earth with heap of large flints over.

97 GOODMANHAM (Paulinus VII)   97:1-2

Yorkshire E.R.; North Humberside   SE 91 46

ROUND BARROW: Diam. 30m, H. 2.5 m, reduced by ploughing;
earth and flint rubble.
BB 304-5.

Burial 1: adult male inhumation, crouched on R. with
head WSW.; in central hollow, wood-lined; Food Vessel at
R. hand, flint at head.
1 *Food Vessel*: Yorkshire Vase; twisted cord: on
   internal and external rim bevels, horizontal lines;
   on neck and shoulder grooves, herringbone with
   vertical lines over lugs; on body, whipped cord
   herringbone above twisted cord horseshoes, upper two
   and basal rows set vertically, enclosed rows set
   horizontally to diagonally; four imperforate lugs.
   M. 16.8 cm; H. 14.7 cm; B. 6.4 cm.   79 12-9 1196
   BAP no. 157.
2 *'flint flake'*: not preserved.

98 GOODMANHAM (Goodmanham II)   98:1-2

Yorkshire E.R.; North Humberside   SE 91 46

ROUND BARROW: Diam. 14 m, H. 0.3 m; earth.
BB 305-8.

Burials 1-3 were in a central oval grave L 2.1 m, W. 1.4
m, D. 1 m.

Burial 1: adult female cremation deposit; on level of
old surface at W. edge of grave; cup at S. side of bones.
1 *Accessory Cup and lid*: on lid, circumferential row of
   deep triangular impressions above fine twisted cord
   line and chain-plaited line; on cup: at junction of
   rim and body, similar design set above and below; on
   lower body, double row of triangular impressions with
   points outwards above two rows of similar triple cord
   impressions; single perforation through peak of lid.
   Lid Diam. 5.5 cm; H. 2.0 cm.
   M. *c.* 5.8 cm; H. *c.* 5.9 cm; B. 8.8 cm. 79 12-9 1197
   BB fig. 132.

Burial 2: disturbed inhumation; bones in grave fill;
vessel on old surface at NW. side of grave ?originally
associated.
2 *Food Vessel*: on internal rim bevel, three plaited
   cord lines; on external rim bevel, row of triangular
   impressions made with sharp implement set horizontally; in neck, row of triangular impressions with
   implement set vertically, enclosed between single
   horizontal plaited cord lines; on body, vertical and
   diagonal plaited cord lines enclosed by single
   horizontal plaited cord lines.
   M. 14.0 cm; H. 9.2 cm; B. 5.7 cm.   79 12-9 1198
   BB fig. 73; *BAP* no. 230.

Burial 3: adult male inhumation, crouched on L. with
head ESE.; at base near W. end.

99 GOODMANHAM (Goodmanham VIII)   99:1-3

Yorkshire E.R; North Humberside   SE 91 46

ROUND BARROW: Diam. 18 m, H. 1.2 m; earth with some
chalk; previously opened.
BB 308-11.

Burial 1: two disturbed inhumations: bones of adult male
and child; in backfill of previous opening, in mound.

Burials 2-5 were in a central grave L. 3.1 m, W. 1.5 m,
D. 1.6 m, aligned SSE.-NNW., partly disturbed by
previous opening.

Burial 2: three disturbed inhumations: bones of
adolescent and two adult males; the legs of one of the
latter *in situ* at D. 0.8 m, remaining bones in backfill
of previous opening.

Burial 3: adult male inhumation crouched on L. with head
N.; at D. 1.2 m towards N. end.

Burial 4: adult female inhumation, on R. with head NW.,
post-cranial bones disturbed by insertion of Burial 5;
at base at S. end; Beaker no. 1 at face and no. 2 0.6 m to
N. of head.
1 *Beaker*: tooth-comb stamped: in neck grooves, lattice
   zones enclosed by single horizontal lines; on body,
   single horizontal line above pendant triangles
   partly filled with vertical chevrons; naked barley
   impression.
   M. 11.9 cm; H. 14.7 cm; B. 8.1 cm.   79 12-9 1199
   BB fig. 133; *BAP* no. 133; *Clarke* no. 1310; *Jessen and
   Helbaek* 1944, 18.
2 *Beaker*: internally, deep zone of horizontal twisted
   cord lines; externally tooth-comb stamped: in neck,

herringbone split and enclosed by single horizontal lines and bordered beneath by row of zigzag above two horizontal lines; below, four narrow zones of alternate short vertical and horizontal lines, each zone enclosed by single horizontal lines and separated from next by reserved zone; at base, row of short vertical lines enclosed by single horizontal lines above short horizontal lines with zone of horizontal lines beneath.

M. 14.4 cm; H. 17.5 cm; B. 10.0 cm.   79 12-9 1201
BB fig. 81; BAP no. 134; Clarke no. 1311.

Burial 5: child inhumation, crouched on R. with head NW.; displacing Burial 4; Beaker at face.

3 *Beaker*: tooth-comb stamped: on neck, vertical herringbone filling row of incised upright triangles enclosed by horizontal lines; on belly and upper body, horizontal and diagonal lines filling row of incised pendant triangles enclosed by narrow lattice zones bordered above and below by pairs of horizontal lines; at base, horizontal line above herringbone.

M. 15.2 cm; H. 20.5 cm; B. 9.3 cm.   79 12-9 1200
BB fig. 134; BAP no. 132; Clarke no. 1309.

100   GOODMANHAM (Goodmanham V)   100:1

Yorkshire E.R.; North Humberside   SE 91 46

ROUND BARROW: Diam. 13.5 m, H. 0.8 m; earth.
BB 311.

Feature A: slight hollow, 2.6 m NE. by N. of centre.

1 *Food Vessel*: twisted cord: on neck, three horizontal lines; on shoulder, row of impressions; on body, two horizontal lines above diagonal lines.

M. 11.5-12.2 cm; H. 10.2 cm; B. 10.1 cm.
79 12-9 1202

101   GOODMANHAM (Goodmanham XIV)

Yorkshire E.R.; North Humberside   SE 91 46

ROUND BARROW: Diam. 37 m, 'almost entirely removed'; composition not recorded; central area and surviving mound burnt over Diam. 9m.
BB 311-12.

Burial 1: 'some unburnt bodies'; discovered in levelling.

'two vessels of pottery': not preserved.

Burial 2: adult male inhumation, crouched on L. with head SE.; at base of central grave L. 3.1 m, W. 2 m, D. 2.4 m, aligned SE. by E.-NW. by W., surrounded by large flint blocks, fill of chalk with central funnel-shaped fill to D. 1.2 m of earth, burnt earth and charcoal.

102   GOODMANHAM (Jarrett VIII)   102:1-2

Yorkshire E.R.; North Humberside   SE 91 46

ROUND BARROW: Diam. 25 m, H. 1.8 m, reduced by ploughing; earth.
BB 312.

Burial 1: adult male inhumation, crouched on R. with head WNW.; in central hollow L. 1.5 m, W. 0.6 m, D. 0.2 m, aligned ESE.-WNW., wood-lined; Food Vessel on side at head, knife at face.

1 *Food Vessel*: Yorkshire Vase; on internal rim bevel, two rows of pinpricks separated and enclosed by single plaited cord lines; on external rim bevel, short vertical twisted cord lines enclosed by single plaited cord lines; in neck and shoulder grooves, horizontal plaited cord lines; on lugs, vertical

herringbone split by vertical plaited cord lines; on body, whipped cord herringbone split and enclosed by horizontal plaited cord lines; three horizontally perforated lugs.

M. 13.0 cm; H. 10.2 cm; B. 6.4 cm.   79 12-9 1203
BAP no. 130.

2 *Flint plano-convex knife*: on blade; all over invasive retouch; ?punctiform butt; dark grey.

L. 6.2 cm; W. 2.0 cm; Th. 0.7 cm.   79 12-9 1204
Clark 1932, no. 2.15.

103   GOODMANHAM (Jarrett II)   103:1-2

Yorkshire E.R.; North Humberside   SE 91 46

ROUND BARROW: Diam. 24 m, H. 1.2 m; earth with some chalk and flint.
BB 312-14.

Burial 1: adult female inhumation, crouched on R. with head NE. by N.; 0.3 m above old surface, 4.8 m SE. by E. of centre; shank on skull.

1 *Bronze shank fragment*: round-sectioned and tapered; ?facet traces at broad end; broken and corroded (Table 1:42)

L. 1.6 cm; Diam. 0.2 cm.   79 12-9 1206

Burial 2: adult male inhumation, crouched on L. with head W.; in central hollow L. 2.3 m, W. 0.6 m, D. 0.2 m, aligned E.-W., wood-lined and covered; Food Vessel at face.

2 *Food Vessel*: Yorkshire Vase; on internal rim bevel, two rows of pinpricks separated and enclosed by plaited cord lines; on external rim bevel, short vertical whipped cord lines enclosed by single twisted cord lines; on neck and shoulder grooves, horizontal plaited cord lines; on lugs, vertical whipped cord herringbone split by vertical whipped or plaited cord lines; on body, short vertical to diagonal whipped cord lines in part to form herringbone split by single horizontal plaited cord lines with row of whipped cord herringbone beneath; at base, row of whipped cord short diagonal lines; three imperforate lugs.

M. 13.8 cm; H. 10.8 cm; B. 6.0 cm.   79 12-9 1205
BAP no. 142.

104   GOODMANHAM (Jarrett I)

Yorkshire E.R.; North Humberside   SE 91 46

ROUND BARROW: Diam. 17 m, H. 0.6 m; earth with some chalk.
BB 315.

Burial 1: adult cremation deposit, in heap Diam. 0.3 m; 0.2 m above level of old surface at centre.

Burial 2: adult male inhumation, crouched on R. with head W. by S.; at base of central grave L. 1.7 m, W. 1.2 m, D. 0.7 m, aligned E.-W.

105   GOODMANHAM (Jarrett III)

Yorkshire E.R.; North Humberside   SE 91 46

ROUND BARROW: Diam. 14.5 m, H. 0.3 m; chalk rubble.
BB 315-16.

Burial 1: adult male inhumation, crouched on L. with head S. by W.; at base of pit 0.6 m N. of centre; pit Diam. 10.8 m decreasing in five steps to Diam. 4.2 m, D. 1.4 m, basal penannular trench W. 0.5 m, D. 0.5-0.6 m from SSW. to beyond NNE., chalk rubble fill (disturbed by badger sett) with some human and animal bones.

106 GOODMANHAM (Jarrett IV)   106:1

Yorkshire E.R.; North Humberside   SE 91 46

ROUND BARROW: Diam. 18.5 m, H. 0.8 m; earth and chalk;
previously opened at centre.
BB 316-17.

Burial 1: two disturbed inhumations, bones in backfill
of previous opening.

Burial 2: adult female inhumation, crouched on R. with
head E. by N.

Backfill of opening
1 *'Sherds'*: two; not identified.   79 12-9 1207

107 GOODMANHAM (Jarrett VI)   107:1

Yorkshire E.R.; North Humberside   SE 91 46

ROUND BARROW: Diam. 24 m, H. 1 m; earth.
BB 317.

Burial 1: adult male inhumation, crouched on L. with
head SE.; at base of central grave Diam. 1.8 m, D. 0.3 m.

Burial 2: infant bones; in mound.
Mound material: 0.4 m above old surface at centre.
1 *Accessory Cup*: plain; no perforations.
   M. 2.6 cm; H. 2.5 cm; B. 2.2 cm.   79 12-9 1208
   BB fig. 135.

108 GOODMANHAM (Jarrett VII)

Yorkshire E.R.; North Humberside   SE 91 46

ROUND BARROW: Diam. 14.5 m, H. 0.3 m; earth.
BB 317-18.

Burial 1: cremated bones of adult and adolescent;
scattered on old surface at centre.
   'two pieces of pottery': not preserved.

109 GOODMANHAM (Jarrett V)   109:1

Yorkshire E.R.; North Humberside   SE 91 46

ROUND BARROW: Diam. 17 m, H. 0.5 m; earth.
BB 318.

Burial 1: child cremation deposit, in heap Diam. 0.3; on
old surface at centre with charcoal, ?burnt *in situ*;
vessel on bones, pin and flint among bones.
   'a vessel of pottery': (Collared Vessel) not preserved.
   'a worked piece of burnt flint': not preserved.
1 *Bone pin*: cut and polished point on splinter of longbone ?of large bird; burnt, point damaged, butt
   broken.
   L. 6.8 cm; W. 0.7 cm; Th. 0.2 cm.   79 12-9 1209

110 GOODMANHAM (Paulinus I)

Yorkshire E.R; North Humberside   SE 91 46

ROUND BARROW: Diam. 17.5 m, H. 0.6 m; earth and chalk.
BB 318-19.

Burial 1: adult male inhumation, crouched on R. with
head N. by E.; 0.3 m above old surface, 4 m E. by S. of
centre.

Burial 2: adult male inhumation, crouched on L. with
head E. by S.; 0.4 m above old surface, E. of centre;
scraper at face.
   'a small round flint scraper': not preserved.

Burial 3: adult male inhumation, crouched on R. with
head SW. by W.; in shallow grave at centre; knife behind
head.
   'a well-made flint knife': not preserved.

Mound material
   'an axe of hone-stone': not preserved.
   (According to Greenwell Ms. 5, these finds were
   retained in the possession of Lord Northesk.)

111 GOODMANHAM (Paulinus II)   111:1-10

Yorkshire E.R.; North Humberside   SE 91 46

ROUND BARROW: Diam. 15 m, H. 0.4 m; earth with some
chalk.
BB 319-21.

Burial 1: adult male inhumation, crouched on R. with
head WSW.; on old surface, 4.5 m S. of centre.

Burial 2: adult female inhumation, crouched on L. with
head NE. by N.; in grave L. 1.6 m, W. 1 m, D. 0.4 m,
aligned N. by E.-S by W., 3.3 m E. of centre.

Burial 3: child inhumation, crouched on L. with head E.;
on old surface, 2.4 m SSE. of centre; cup behind head.
1 *Accessory Cup*: on rim and externally, herringbone
   made with fine point, on upper body running over
   horizontal grooves; no perforations.
   M. 9.4 cm; H. 5.3 cm; B. 5.0 cm.   79 12-9 1210
   BAP no. 55.

Burial 4: child inhumation, crouched on L. with head S.
by E.; on old surface, 1.5 m SSE. of centre; pin behind
shoulders.
2 *Bone pin*: cut and all-over polished on splinter of
   ?roe-deer metacarpal; eroded, point broken.
   L. 19.5 cm; W. 1.4 cm; Th. 1.1 cm.   79 12-9 1214

Burial 5: adult female inhumation, crouched on L. with
NE. by E.; in slight hollow, 0.9 m SSE. of centre; Food
Vessel at face, scraper near neck.
3 *Food Vessel*: Yorkshire Vase; on internal rim bevel
   and externally to below shoulder and over lugs,
   incised herringbone; on lower body, short diagonal
   incised lines; four imperforate lugs.
   M. 14.6 cm; H. 13.2 cm; B. 6.9 cm.   79 12-9 1211
   BAP no. 54.
   'flint scraper': not preserved.

Burial 6: adult female inhumation, crouched on L. with
head NE.; on old surface, 1 m SW. by W. of centre; flint
block at face over sherds.
4 *Beaker sherds*: two including rim; tooth-comb stamp:
   below rim, zone of ill-defined impressions above
   reserved band above horizontal line over herringbone; on body, lattice zone enclosed by bands of
   horizontal lines with zone of indefinite impressions
   below.   79 12-9 1213a
   Clarke no. 1312.
5 *Collared Vessel sherds*: seven, from lower collar and
   neck; on collar and neck, incised herringbone.
   Longworth no. 702a.   79 12-9 1592
6 *Collared Vessel sherd*: lower collar, whipped cord
   herringbone.   79 12-9 1592a
   Longworth no. 702b.
7 *Collared Vessel sherds*: fourteen, including rim and
   base; plain.   79 12-9 1592b
   Longworth: no. 702c.
8 *Food Vessel sherds*: forty-three; whipped cord: on
   internal rim bevel, short transverse lines; on body,
   herringbone.   79 12-9 1213 and 1213b

Burial 7: adolescent inhumation, crouched on R. with
head E.; on old surface, 3.4 m SW. by S. of centre.

Burial 8: child inhumation traces; on old surface, 3.6 m SW. of centre; beneath flint block.

Burial 9: adult ? male inhumation traces; on old surface, 4.8 m SSW. of centre; scraper near head.

    'a round flint scraper': not preserved.

Feature A: pit L. 3.3 m, W. 0.9 m, D. 1 m sloping up to surface at SW., aligned NE.-SW.; burnt deposit at D. 0.3 m; sherds and animal bones.

    'potsherds': possibly among nos 9-10.

Mound material or Feature A

9 *Peterborough Ware sherds*: four; remains of impressions, some by flint flake.   79 12-9 1212

10 *Peterborough Ware sherds*: five, including two rim; on rim, blurred impressions; externally, rows of short vertical to diagonal twisted cord lines.

    NPY no. 29; Manby 1956.   79 12-9 1211a and 1212a

112 GOODMANHAM (Paulinus III)

Yorkshire E.R.; North Humberside   SE 91 46

ROUND BARROW: Diam. 12 m, H. 0.2 m, reduced by ploughing; composition not recorded.
BB 321.

Burials 1-3 were in a central rectangular grave L. 2 m, W. 1.1 m, D. 0.5 m, aligned NE.-SW.

Burial 1: adult female inhumation, crouched on L. with head NNE.; on top of grave, with child mandible fragment; knife at face and sherds nearby.

    'flint knife': not preserved.

    'a few potsherds': not preserved.

Burial 2: adult female inhumation, crouched on R. with head SW. by S.; at base of grave near S.; awl behind head.

    'bronze awl': not preserved.

Burial 3: bones of adolescent, legs apparently in position above Burial 2; scattered in grave fill; scraper perhaps originally associated.

    'round flint scraper': not preserved.

Feature A: pit Diam. 0.8 m, D. 0.8 m, 3 m SW. by S. of centre; burnt sides and fill, with burnt flint fragments.

113 GOODMANHAM (Paulinus IV)   113:1-4

Yorkshire E.R.; North Humberside   SE 91 46

ROUND BARROW: Diam. 12.5 m, H. 0.5 m; earth and chalk around natural rise.
BB 321-3.

Burial 1: adult male inhumation, crouched on L. with head NE.; on old surface, 1.5 m SE. of centre; Beaker behind shoulders over flint.

1 *Handled Beaker*: point-tooth comb stamped: beneath rim, zone of horizontal lines; on neck, zone of bar chevron filled with lattice; on body, similar zone enclosed by zones of horizontal lines; on handle, vertical lines.

    M. 13.3 cm; H. 18.1 cm; B. 7.8 cm.   79 12-9 1215

    BB fig. 86; BAP no. 293; Clarke no. 1314.

2 *Flint utilised blade*: bilateral wear; cortex remnant; platform butt; mottled grey.

    L. 6.0 cm; W. 2.9 cm; Th. 0.9 cm.   79 12-9 1218

Burial 2: adult ?female inhumation, crouched on R. with head ENE.; above old surface, at centre; Food Vessel behind head.

3 *Food Vessel*: on rim, in neck groove and below, single lines of jabbed impressions; six imperforate lugs.

    M. 17.2 cm; H. 16.7 cm; B. 9.8 cm.   79 12-9 1216

    BB fig. 136.

Burial 3: disturbed inhumation and cremation; bones above Burial 2; sherds nearby.

4 *Beaker sherds*: two, including rim; alternate zones of finger-pinching and rectangular tooth-comb lattice separated by reserved zones outlined by single horizontal tooth-comb lines.   79 12-9 1217

    Clarke no. 1313.

Burials 4-7 were in a grave L. 2.4 m, W. 1.5 m, D. 1.1 m, aligned E.-W., SW. of centre; covered by flint blocks, ?wood-lined base at S.

Burial 4: adult male inhumation, crouched on L. with head NE. by N.; on E. edge of grave on wood remains, displaced by shrinkage of fill.

Burial 5: disturbed adult female inhumation; skull near Burial 4, some post-cranial bones in bundle at S. side in upper fill.

Burial 6: adult male inhumation, crouched on L. with head SE. by S.; on W. edge of grave on wood remains, displaced by shrinkage of fill.

Burial 7: adult male inhumation, crouched on L. with head E. by S.; at base, near centre.

114 GOODMANHAM (Paulinus VI)   114:1

Yorkshire E.R.; North Humberside   SE 91 46

ROUND BARROW: Diam. 17.5 m, H. 0.8 m, reduced by ploughing; earth and chalk.
BB 323-4.

Burial 1: adult cremation deposit; in inverted urn in ploughsoil at centre.

1 *'Collared Urn sherds'*: not identified. 79 12-9 1600

Burial 2: double inhumation: remains of adult female and child; on old surface, 1.2 m S. of centre.

Burial 3: child inhumation, crouched on R. with head NW. by W.; in central rectangular grave L. 1.5 m, W. 0.8 m, D. 0.8 m; vessel at face.

    'food vessel': not preserved.

115 GOODMANHAM (Paulinus VIII)   115:1-8

Yorkshire E.R.; North Humberside   SE 91 46

ROUND BARROW: Diam. 15 m, H. 0.3 m, reduced by ploughing; composition not recorded.
BB 324-5.

Burial 1: adult female inhumation, crouched on L. with head E. by S.; on old surface, 3.6 m SSE. of centre; Food Vessel at face, awl behind head, earrings in place.

1 *Bronze awl*: Thomas Type 1; tang with square section and point with round section with central expansion with transverse bevels and rhomboid section; tips lacking (Table 1: 38).

    L. 3.4 cm; W. 2.4 cm; Th. 2.3 cm.   79 12-9 1221

    Thomas 1968, 23.

    Bronze earrings: narrow strips of curved cross-section; four ribs and upturned rims on outer faces, each rib flanked by chevrons formed by punch-marks L. 0.5 mm at 15 per cm; indented edges.

2 *Bronze earring*: one narrowed tongue terminal, other end broken (Table 1: 48).

    Diam. 3.2 cm; W. 0.8 cm; Th. 0.1 cm.   79 12-9 1222

3 *Bronze earring*: both ends broken (Table 1:49).
   Diam 3.0 cm; W. 0.8 cm; Th. 0.1 cm.   79 12-9 1223
   BB fig. 48; *ABI* fig. 491.
4 *Food Vessel*: fine twisted cord: on internal rim
   bevel, herringbone; on external rim bevel, short
   vertical lines; in grooves and over body, herringbone; over lugs, vertical lines; three imperforate
   lugs of four surviving.
   M. 16.6 cm; H. *c.* 14.0 cm.   79 12-9 1219
   Simpson 1968, fig. 45.1.

Burial 2: adult male inhumation, crouched on L. with
head SE.; on old surface, 1.8 m S. of centre; Beaker
fragment at feet.
5 *Beaker*: lower body only; all over finger-pinched
   rustication.
   B. 10.5 cm.   79 12-9 1593

Burial 3: bones of child; in ploughsoil at centre.
6 *Collared Vessel sherds*: ninety-eight, including rim,
   neck and shoulder; on rim, vertical to diagonal
   incised lines; on collar and neck, incised herringbone.
   Longworth no. 704.   79 12-9 1594
7 *Collared Vessel sherds*: nineteen, including rim of
   collar; on rim and collar, incised herringbone.
   Longworth no. 704a.   79 12-9 1594a

Burial 4: adult ?male inhumation, crouched on L. and
aligned NE.-SW.; headless, 2 cranial fragments nearby;
on old surface at centre, beneath flints.

Not located.
8 *Bronze awl*: Thomas Type 2D; short wedge-shaped tang
   with rectangular section and round-sectioned point
   (Table 1:37).
   L. 4.1 cm; W. 0.2 cm; Th. 0.2 cm.   79 12-9 1220
   Thomas 1968, 23.

116 GOODMANHAM (Goodmanham IX)   116:1

Yorkshire E.R.; North Humberside   SE 90 46

ROUND BARROW: Diam. 7 m, H. 0.3 m; capped by flint
blocks.
BB 325-6.

Burial 1: adult ?female inhumation; on level of old
surface, at centre; Beaker at head.
1 *Beaker*: incised: on neck, rectangular panels filled
   with horizontal lines alternating with reserved
   panels enclosed above and below by four horizontal
   lines; on body, reserved zone containing horizontally arranged hexagons filled with lattice, above
   band of three to four horizontal lines, above zone of
   reserved bar chevrons with pendant triangles filled
   with diagonal lines and upright triangles filled with
   diagonal lines or lattice; on base, reserved cross
   with enclosed spaces filled with lattice.
   M. 10.7-11.2 cm; H. 13.4 cm; B. 6.4 cm.
                                         79 12-9 1224
   BB figs 89-90; *BAP* no. 111; *Clarke* no. 1316.

Burial 2: bones of adult male, incomplete; at base of
central grave L. 1.8 m, W. 0.8 m, D. 0.8 m, aligned SE.
by S.-NW. by N.

117 GOODMANHAM (Goodmanham VII)   117:1

Yorkshire E.R.; North Humberside   SE 90 46

ROUND BARROW: D. 6 m, H. 0.5 m; chalk with some flint and
earth, capped by flint blocks, set in slight hollow.
BB 326-7.

Burials 1-2 were in a central grave L. 2.1 m, W. 0.8 m,
D. 0.8 m, aligned SSE.-NNW.

Burial 1: adult female inhumation, crouched on R. with
head NW. by W.; in rough cist of chalk and flint blocks
L. 0.9 m, W. 0.5 m, aligned SE.-NW., in upper fill of
grave; pendant at neck.
1 *Boar tusk pendant*: tusk rubbed down and perforated at
   root; broken and eroded.
   L. 5.1 cm; W. 1.8 cm; Th. 1.3 cm; D. perf. 0.5 cm.
                                         79 12-9 1225

Burial 2: adult male inhumation, crouched on L. with
head SSE.; at base of grave.

118 GOODMANHAM (Jarrett IX)   118:1

Yorkshire E.R.; North Humberside   SE 90 46

ROUND BARROW: Diam. 14.5 m, H. 0.8 m; earth.
BB 327-8.

Burial 1: adolescent inhumation, crouched on R. with
head SE. by E.; on wood remains at base of central grave
L. 2.1 m, W. 0.8 m, D. 0.7 m, aligned SE. by S.-NW. by N.;
Food Vessel and ochre at head.
1 *Food Vessel*: whipped cord: on internal and external
   rim bevels, short diagonal lines; on top and bottom
   of neck and shoulder grooves and below shoulder,
   short vertical to diagonal lines.
   M. 15.0 cm; H. 17.7 cm; B. 8.4 cm.   79 12-9 1226
   BAP no. 189.
   'yellowish-red ochre': not preserved.

119 GOODMANHAM (Jarrett X)   119:1

Yorkshire E.R.; North Humberside   SE 90 46

ROUND BARROW: Diam. *c.* 15 m, H. 0.1 m; composition not
recorded.
BB 328-9.

Burial 1: adolescent inhumation, crouched on R. with
head NNW.; at N. end of central rectangular grave L. 2 m,
W. 1 m, D. 1.2 m, aligned S. by E.-N. by W., fill of earth
with wood traces around body; vessel at feet.
1 *Food Vessel*: on internal rim bevel, two rows of bone
   or twig impressions; on neck, twisted cord zigzag
   between single horizontal lines; below shoulder,
   twisted cord zigzag.
   M. 15.3 cm; H. 12.9 cm; B. 8.5 cm.   79 12-9 1227
   BAP no. 210.

120 GOODMANHAM (Enthorpe X)

Yorkshire E.R.; North Humberside   SE 90 46

ROUND BARROW: dimensions uncertain, reduced by ploughing; scattered flint blocks.
BB 329.

Burials 1-2 were in a grave L. 2.2 m, W. 1.5 m, D. 1.8 m,
aligned NE.-SW., upper fill of flint blocks over chalk
rubble with some earth.

Burial 1: adult ?male cranial fragment; among flints.

Burial 2: inhumation and cremation: adult male crouched on L. with head ENE. with adult male cremation deposit at arms; at base near centre, with partial surround of flint blocks.

121 GOODMANHAM (Money Hill; Goodmanham XI)
121:1-3

Yorkshire E.R.; North Humberside   SE 921 455

OVAL BARROW: L. 13 m, W. 9.5 m, H. 1.8 m, aligned E. by S.-W. by N.; earth and chalk.
BB 329-31.

Burial 1: several disturbed inhumations; near surface of mound, disturbed by tree-planting.

Burial 2: adult female inhumation, head E.; 0.9 m above old surface, 3.7 m S. by E. of centre, with child cranial fragments at back; Food Vessel inverted below hips.
1 *Food Vessel*: plain.
   M. 14.4 cm; H. 12.0 cm; B. 8.5 cm.   79 12-9 1228

Burial 3: adult ?female cremation deposit; on old surface, 3.7 m SE. by S. of centre.

Burial 4: child inhumation, head E.; 0.8 m above old surface, 3.3 m SE. by E. of centre; vessel below head.
2 *Collared Vessel sherds*: twenty-nine, mainly rim and collar; on internal rim bevel, twisted cord horizontal and short diagonal lines and horseshoes; on collar and neck, incised herringbone.
   Longworth no. 703.   79 12-9 1229

Burial 5: disturbed bones of adult male and adult; in mound in central area.

Burial 6: adolescent inhumation, crouched on R. with head WNW.; at base of central grave L. 1.8 m, W. 0.9 m, D. 0.9 m, aligned SSE.-NNW., chalk fill with basal wood-lining; necklace in place, ochre near body.
3 *Jet necklace*: one hundred and twenty-four cut and polished disc beads and one mitriform pendant with central drilled hourglass perforation.
   Bead Diam. 0.4-0.6 cm; Th. 0.2 cm.
   Pendant L. 1.7 cm; W. 1.4 cm; Th. 0.7 cm; Diam. perf. 0.3 cm.   79 12-9 1230
   'some lumps of a yellowish substance ... ochre': not preserved.

122 LONDESBOROUGH
122:1

Yorkshire E.R.; North Humberside   SE 89 49

ROUND BARROW: Diam. 13.5 m, H. 0.8 m; earth with some chalk.
BB 331.

Burial 1: disturbed bones of adolescent; 0.2 m above old surface, 1.8 m S. of centre.

Burial 2: child inhumation, crouched on L. with head SE.; at base of central grave L. 1.7 m, W. 1.1 m, D. 0.8 m, aligned SE.-NW.; vessel at face.
1 *Food Vessel*: twisted cord: on internal rim bevel, two lines; below rim and above and below shoulder, short vertical to diagonal lines; at base, row of short vertical lines.
   M. 13.6-14.3 cm; H. 16.2 cm; B. 8.7 cm.
    79 12-9 1596

123 LONDESBOROUGH (Benjamin I)
123:1

Yorkshire E.R.; North Humberside   SE 89 49

ROUND BARROW: dimensions uncertain, mound removed.
BB 331-2.

Burial 1: adult male inhumation, crouched on R. with head SW. by S.; at centre of base of grave L. 3.7 m, W. 1.4 m, D. 1 m, aligned S. by E.-N. by W., with central offset towards W. L.1 m, W. 0.8 m, base wood-lined.

Mound material: at S. side.
1 *Food Vessel sherds*: thirteen; on internal rim bevel and externally, whipped cord herringbone.
    79 12-9 1231

124 EGTON (William Howe)
124:1-3

Yorkshire N.R.; North Yorkshire   NZ 776 034

ROUND CAIRN: Diam. 24 m, H. 1.8 m, reduced by stone-robbing; stones; opened April and/or August 1864.
BB 334-5; *Greenwell* 1865, 112-13.

Burial 1: adult cremation deposit; on old surface in area Diam. 0.9 m, 4 m SE. of centre; beads scattered among bones.
1 *Jet necklace*: fourteen fusiform and one square-sectioned cut and polished beads.
   Fusiform L. 2.6-4.4 cm; central Th. 0.5-0.7 cm; terminal Th. 0.4-0.5 cm; square-sectioned L. 2.8 cm; Th. 0.5 cm.   79 12-9 1234
   Greenwell 1865, fig. 2; *BB* fig. 137; *ASI* fig. 379.

Burial 2: adult cremation deposit; 0.9 m above old surface, E. of centre; vessel among bones.
2 *Food Vessel*: impressions made by blunt instrument: on internal rim bevel, single row; above and below neck cordon and above and below shoulder cordon, opposed impressions.
   M. 14.2 cm; H. 13.2 cm; B. 7.1 cm.   79 12-9 1233

Cairn material
3 'Flint flake': not identified.   79 12-9 1235

125 EGTON (Three Howes North)

Yorkshire N.R.; North Yorkshire   NZ 795 012

ROUND BARROW: Diam. 20.5 m, H. 2.2 m; alternate layers of sand and ?turf, with few stones; opened 21-2 April 1864.
BB 335-6; *Greenwell* 1865, 113-14.

Burial 1: cremation deposit, in heap Diam. 0.3 m; 0.3 m below mound surface, 7.5 m S. of centre.

Burial 2: cremation deposit, in heap Diam. 0.3 m; 1.2 m above old surface, 2.7 m E. of centre.

126 OVER SILTON
126:1-6

Yorkshire N.R.; North Yorkshire   SE 48 91

ROUND BARROW: Diam. 19 m, H. 1.7 m; clayey sand, birch branches over old surface at centre.
BB 336-7.

Burial 1: adult cremation deposit; in central hollow Diam. 0.2 m, D. 0.15 m, 1.3 m above old surface.

Burial 2: adult cremation deposit; in and below upright urn, 1 m above old surface, 1.5 m SE. by E. of centre; flint among bones.
1 *Urn*: lower body and base; plain.
   B. 12.0 cm.   79 12-9 1236
2 *Flint utilised flake*: bilateral wear; burnt and broken.
   L. 4.4 cm; W. 1.4 cm; Th. 0.5 cm.   79 12-9 1237

Mound material

3 *Flint transverse arrowhead*: bilateral edge retouch;
   grey.
   L. 2.8 cm, W. 1.6 cm, Th. 0.5 cm.   79 12-9 1238
   Clarke 1934, no. B7; *Green* 1980, no. A12.

4-5 '*Flint scrapers*': two; not identified.
                                             79 12-9 1240-1

6 '*Flint flake*': not identified.   79 12-9 1239

127 COLD KIRBY

Yorkshire N.R.; North Yorkshire   SE 513 832

ROUND BARROW: Diam. 9 m, H. 1.2 m; limestone flags laid
flat around central pitched core Diam. 3.6 m; opened 26
April 1864.
BB 337-8; *Greenwell* 1865, 115; *Varley* 1982.

128 COLD KIRBY   128:1-3

Yorkshire N.R.; North Yorkshire   SE 516 827

ROUND BARROW: Diam. 13 m, H. 1.5 m; earth and clay with
some stones; opened 28 April 1864.
BB 338-9; *Greenwell* 1865, 115-16; Varley 1982.

Burial 1: adult cremation deposit; in upright Collared
Urn, 0.9 m above old surface, 0.9 m ESE. of centre.
1 *Collared Urn*: twisted cord: on internal rim bevel,
   single line; on collar, filled triangles enclosed
   above by one and below by two lines; on neck, double
   zigzag; on shoulder, row of short horizontal whipped
   cord impressions.
   M. *c.* 24.0 cm; H. 30.5 cm; B. 10.3 cm. 79 12-9 1242
   BB fig. 138; *BAP* no. 111a; *Varley* 1982, fig. 3.2;
   Longworth no. 1107.

Burial 2: adolescent cremation deposit; in upright
Collared Urn packed round with charcoal and covered by
stones, 0.3 m above old surface at centre.
2 *Collared Urn*: twisted cord: on internal rim bevel,
   two lines; on collar, hurdle pattern between pairs of
   lines; on neck, vertical to diagonal rows of jabbed
   impressions.
   M. 31.2 cm; H. 40.9 cm; B. 11.7 cm.   79 12-9 1243
   BB fig. 54; *BAP* no. 111; *Varley* 1982, fig. 3.1;
   Longworth no. 1106.

Mound material

3 *Flint horseshoe scraper*: edge retouch on distal and
   bilateral at 60 degrees; platform butt; cortex
   remnant; patinated.
   L. 2.5 cm; W. 2.5 cm; Th. 1.1 cm.   79 12-9 1243a
   Varley 1982, fig. 2.

129 KILBURN (Wass Moor I)   129:1-7

Yorkshire N.R.; North Yorkshire   SE 543 806

ROUND BARROW: Diam. 17 m, H. 1.5 m; core of alternate
layers of yellow and white sand with charcoal D. 9 m H.
1.2 m, capped by small stones.
BB 340-1.

Mound material

1 *Stone rubber*: broken quartzitic pebble, one face
   polished smooth.
   L. 14.8 cm; W. 8.8 cm; Th. 3.6 cm.   79 12-9 1250
2 *Stone cup-marked block*: sandstone; opposing cup-
   marks roughly pecked from two faces.
   L. 18.2 cm; W. 13.0 cm; Th. 7.9 cm; cups Diam. 4.7 cm,
   D. 2.6 cm; and Diam. 4.6 cm, D. 2.7 cm.   76 4-2 7
3 '*Flint scraper*': not identified.   79 12-9 1244
4-7 '*Flint flakes*': four; not identified.
                                             79 12-9 1245-8

130 KILBURN (Wass Moor II)   130:1

Yorkshire N.R.; North Yorkshire   SE 543 806

ROUND BARROW: Diam 13 m, H. 1.2 m; sand.
BB 341.

Burial 1: adult ?male cremation deposit; in central
hollow Diam. 0.8 m, D. 0.4 m; old surface in area burnt
and mass of oak charcoal, including logs, Diam. 1.2 m,
1.2 m W. of centre.

Not located

1 '*Flint scraper*': not identified.   79 12-9 1249

131 KILBURN (Wass Moor III)   131:1-4

Yorkshire N.R.; North Yorkshire   SE 543 806

ROUND CAIRN: Diam. 12.5 m, extensively robbed; stones.
BB 341-3.

Cairn material

1 *Stone decorated block*: ferruginous sandstone; deep
   cruciform incision on flat face extending to adjacent
   faces; eroded.
   L. 19.7 cm; W. 14.6 cm; Th. 11.2 cm.   76 4-2 8
2 *Stone cup-marked block*: ferruginous sandstone; two
   pecked cup-marks and remains of third in row on one
   face; broken and eroded.
   L. 27.3 cm; W. 14.8 cm; Th. 8.0 cm; cups Diam. 5.7 cm,
   D. 2.7 cm and Diam. 4.4 cm, D. 1.4 cm.   79 12-9 1939
3 *Stone cup-marked block*: ferruginous sandstone;
   pecked cup-mark on one face; eroded.
   L. 15.4 cm; W. 12.8 cm; Th. 9.5 cm; cup Diam. 6.3 cm,
   D. 2.8 cm.   79 12-9 1940
4 '*Flint implement*': not identified.   79 12-9 1251

132 GILLING   132:1-6

Yorkshire N.R.; North Yorkshire   SE 61 74

ROUND BARROW: Diam. 14 m, H. 1.2 m; sand, internal circle
of stones Diam. 11 m.
BB 344.

Burial 1: cremation deposit; in upright urn (one of nos
3-6 below), near mound surface, 1.8 m S. of centre; flint
among bones.
1 *Flint flake*: burnt and broken.
   L. 3.8 cm; W. 1.5 cm; Th. 0.4 cm.   79 12-9 1253

Burial 2: cremation deposit; in urn (one of nos 3-6
below) near mound surface, 2.1 m SE. of centre; scraper
among bones.
2 *Flint scraper*: partial edge retouch on distal at 60
   degrees; platform butt; burnt and broken.
   L. 3.3 cm; W. 3.2 cm; Th. 0.9 cm.   79 12-9 1254

Burials 1-2

3 *Collared Urn*: upper half; on collar, linear incised
   filled triangles; on neck, linear incised lattice.
   M. 27.0-28.0 cm.   79 12-9 1252
   Longworth no. 1149.
4 *?Biconical Urn sherds*: three including rim; beneath
   rim, row of indefinite impressions.   79 12-9 1252a
5 *Bronze Age sherd*: twisted cord lines. 79 12-9 1252b
6 *Bronze Age sherd*: irregularly slashed lattice.
                                            79 129 1252c

133 GILLING (Grimston Moor II)   133:1-3

Yorkshire N.R.; North Yorkshire   SE 61 74

ROUND BARROW: Diam. 21 m, H. 1.4 m; sand.
BB 344-5.

Burial 1: cremation deposit, in heap Diam. 0.25 m; 1 m
above old surface, 4.5 m SE. of centre; knife among
bones.
1 *Flint knife:* converging bilateral invasive retouch;
   mottled grey.
   L. 5.3 cm; W. 2.6 cm; Th. 0.7 cm.   79 12-9 1255
   Clark 1932, no. 6.5.

Burial 2: cremation deposit, in heap Diam. 0.25 m; near
Burial 1.

Burial 3: cremation deposit, in heap Diam. 0.3 m; 0.9 m
above old surface, 3.6 m S. of centre.

Burial 4: adult cremation deposit; in urn, near surface
of mound 3.6 m SW. of centre.
   'cinerary urn of the usual shape': not preserved.

Burial 5: adult cremation deposit; in central oval
hollow L. 1 m, W. 0.6 m, D. 0.3 m, aligned E.-W.

Mound material
   'vessel of pottery': (0.9 m above old surface, 5.4 m
   SE. of centre) not preserved.
2 *Flint leaf arrowhead:* all over bifacial invasive
   retouch; beige; snapped at base and point.
   L. 3.0 cm; W. 2.8 cm; Th. 0.3 cm.   79 12-9 1256
   Green 1980, no. A15.
3 *'Flint flake':* not identified.   79 12-9 1257

134 GILLING

Yorkshire N.R.; North Yorkshire   SE 61 74

ROUND BARROW: Diam. 15.5 m, H. 1.1 m; sand.
BB 345.

Burial 1: adolescent cremation deposit, in heap Diam.
0.3 m; 0.3 m above old surface, 5.1 m E. of centre,
beneath heap of stones Diam. 0.8 m, H. 0.6 m.

135 GILLING

Yorkshire N.R.; North Yorkshire   SE 61 74

ROUND BARROW: Diam. 5.5 m, H. 0.5 m; sand.
BB 345-6.

Burial 1: probable inhumation; in central oval cist L.
0.9 m, W. 0.8 m, of six stones with single capstone.

136 GILLING

Yorkshire N.R.; North Yorkshire   SE 61 74

ROUND BARROW: Diam. 12.5 m, H. 0.6 m; sand, with stones
at E. side.
BB 346.

Burial 1: adult cremation deposit; in central hollow
Diam. 0.8 m, D. 0.3 m, with burnt clay lining; cup
inverted on bones.
   'incense cup': not preserved.

137 GILLING (Grimston Moor VI)   137:1

Yorkshire N.R.; North Yorkshire   SE 61 74

ROUND BARROW: Diam. 17 m, H. 0.9 m; sand.
BB 346-7.

Burial 1: cremation deposit; in central oval hollow
L. 1.4 m, W. 1.2 m, D. 0.3 m; vessel on bones.
1 *Food Vessel:* Yorkshire Vase; on internal rim bevel,
   whipped cord herringbone; on external rim bevel,
   short diagonal whipped cord lines; on neck, short
   whipped cord lines above diagonally set horseshoes
   with single, double in one sector, horizontal twisted
   cord line above row of short vertical to diagonal
   whipped cord lines; in shoulder groove, two rows of
   short diagonal whipped cord lines; on body, twisted
   cord herringbone above rows of diagonally set
   horseshoes; at base, row of twisted cord vertically
   set horseshoes; three, originally four, imperforate
   lugs.
   M. 15.2 cm; H. 11.6 cm; B. 6.2 cm.   79 12-9 1258
   BAP no. 166.

138 SLINGSBY (Hall Moor)   138:1-17

Yorkshire N.R.; North Yorkshire   SE 69 73

ROUND BARROW: Diam. 17 m, H. 1.5 m; sand and clay;
previously opened at centre, opened 7-8 September 1864.
BB 347-9; Greenwell 1865, 250-1.

Burial 1: disturbed cremated bones; in backfill of
previous opening, but originally in central hollow Diam.
0.6 m, D. 0.3 m.
1 *Collared Vessel sherds:* seven including rim, collar
   and neck; on rim, collar and neck, vertical spatulate
   impressions.
   M. *c.* 11.0 cm.   79 12-9 1259
   Longworth no. 1258.
2 *Collared Vessel sherds:* two from rim, collar and
   neck; fine twisted cord: on rim, two lines; on
   collar, herringbone split by single and enclosed
   above by two and below by three horizontal lines; on
   neck, lattice enclosed by horizontal lines.
   Longworth no. 1259.   79 12-9 1259a
3 *Collared Vessel sherd:* base of collar; coarse twisted
   cord horizontal lines.   79 12-9 1259b
   Longworth no. 1260.
4 *Collared Vessel rim sherd:* on internal moulding and
   externally, horizontal twisted cord lines.
   Longworth no. 1261.   79 12-9 1259c
5 *Collared Vessel neck sherd:* blurred twisted cord
   herringbone.   79 12-9 1259d
   Longworth no. 1262.
6 *Collared Vessel sherds:* twenty-one including collar
   and base; eroded surfaces.   79 12-9 1259e
   Longworth no. 1262a.
7 *Collared Vessel sherds:* five; plain.   79 12-9 1259f
   Longworth no. 1262b.
8 *Collared Vessel sherds:* five including neck,
   shoulder and base; on neck, twisted cord lattice; on
   shoulder, row of jabbed impressions.
                              79 12-9 1260a
   Longworth no. 1263.
9 *Flint disc-scraper:* all-round edge and invasive
   retouch at 65 degrees; platform butt; mottled grey.
   L. 3.5 cm; W. 3.4 cm; Th. 1.4 cm.   79 12-9 1261
   BB fig. 139; *Greenwell* 1865, fig. 16.
10 *'Flint knife':* not identified.   79 12-9 1268
11-12 *'Flint flakes':* two; not identified.
                              79 12-9 1262-3

Burial 2: adult ?female cremation deposit; in upright urn 0.9 m above old surface, 4.5 m SE. by S. of centre; knife among bones.

13 *Collared Urn*: on rim, discontinuous twisted cord line; on collar, carelessly applied discontinuous horizontal and diagonal lines.
   M. 29.0-30.3 cm; H. 33.0 cm; B. 10.2 cm.
   BAP no. 147; *Longworth* no. 1257.   79 12-9 1260
14 *Flint knife*: converging bilateral invasive retouch; punctiform butt; burnt and fragmented.
   L. 8.2 cm; W. 3.2 cm; Th. 0.8 cm.   79 12-9 1264

Mound material

15 '*Flint scraper*': not identified.   79 12-9 1267
16-17 '*Flint flakes*': two; not identified.
                                              79 12-9 1265-6

139 SLINGSBY

Yorkshire N.R.; North Yorkshire   SE 69 73

ROUND BARROW: Diam. 4.5 m, H. 0.4 m; sand, with basal ?burnt layer; opened 7-8 September 1864.
BB 349: *Greenwell* 1865, 251-2.

Burial 1: cremation deposit; in central hollow Diam. 0.3 m, D. 0.1 m, below charcoal layer.

140 SLINGSBY (Hall Moor)   140:1-2

Yorkshire N.R.; North Yorkshire   SE 69 73

ROUND BARROW: Diam. 18 m, H. 2.2 m; layer of burnt sand, clay and gravel H. 0.5 m, above and capped by sand; opened 9 September 1864.
BB 349-50; *Greenwell* 1865, 252-3.

Burial 1: cremation deposit; 1.4 m above old surface on burnt layer, at centre.

1 *Food Vessel*: on internal rim bevel, impressed herringbone; on external rim bevel, lower edge of neck groove and above and below shoulder, single rows of vertically placed impressions.
   M. 13.8-15.5 cm; H. 13.4 cm; B. 8.7 cm.
   Greenwell 1865, fig. 17; *BAP* no. 192.   79 12-9 1269
2 *Flint knife*: bilateral edge retouch at 50 degrees; punctiform butt; damage at distal; mottled grey.
   L. 5.2 cm; W. 3.0 cm; Th. 0.9 cm.   79 12-9 1270

141 SLINGSBY

Yorkshire N.R.; North Yorkshire   SE 69 73

ROUND BARROW: Diam. 17 m, H. 1.7 m; sand.
BB 350.

Burial 1: adult cremation deposit, in heap Diam. 0.3 m; on old surface at centre.

142 SLINGSBY

Yorkshire N.R.; North Yorkshire   SE 69 73

ROUND BARROW: Diam. 4.8 m, H. 0.3 m; sand.
BB 350-1.

Burial 1: adult cremation deposit, with charcoal on old surface at centre.

143 SLINGSBY   143:1

Yorkshire N.R.; North Yorkshire   SE 69 73

ROUND BARROW: Diam. 5.4 m, H. 0.5 m; sand.
BB 351.

Burial 1: adult cremation deposit; among burnt earth and charcoal in central hollow Diam. 0.9 m, D. 0.5 m; flint among bones.
   '*single piece of unburnt flint*': not preserved.

Mound material

1 *Vase*: plain.
   M. 9.5 cm; H. 9.6 cm; B. 6.2 cm.   79 12-9 1271
   Manby 1980, 354.

144 SLINGSBY   144:1

Yorkshire N.R.; North Yorkshire   SE 69 73

ROUND BARROW: Diam. 9.5 m, H. 1 m; sand.
BB 351.

Burial 1: adolescent cremation deposit; in central hollow Diam. 0.6 m, D. 0.3 m with fill of burnt earth and charcoal, ?burnt *in situ*; cup on bones.
1 *Accessory Cup*: on upper body, four horizontal twisted cord lines; no perforations.
   M. 5.3 cm; H. 3.5 cm; B. 5.1 cm.   79 12-9 1272
   BB fig. 64; *BAP* no. 315.

145 SLINGSBY (Hall Moor)   145:1-7

Yorkshire N.R.; North Yorkshire   SE 72 70

ROUND BARROW: Diam. 14 m, H. 0.6 m, reduced by ploughing; sand on natural rise.
BB 352-3.

Burial 1: adolescent cremation deposit; in upright Collared Urn on old surface, 4.5 m S. of centre, damaged by ploughing; objects among bones.
1 *Collared Urn sherds*: forty including rim, collar, shoulder and base; on rim, transverse impressions; on collar and base of neck, rows of vertical impressions.   79 12-9 1275
   Longworth no. 1265a.
2 *Flint barbed-and-tanged arrowhead*: all over bifacial invasive retouch; burnt, point snapped.
   L. 3.8 cm; W. 2.2 cm. Th. 0.5 cm.   79 12-9 1276
   BB fig. 140; *Green* 1980, no. 72.
3 *Flint utilised flake*: bilateral wear; mottled grey.
   L. 3.8 cm; W. 2.2 cm; Th. 0.4 cm.   79 12-9 1277
4 *Bone 'belt-hook'*: cut and polished from bos-size long-bone fragment; incised grooves on hook; burnt and distorted.
   L. 2.6 cm; W. 1.4 cm; hook Th. 0.4 cm. 79 12-9 1279
   BB fig. 7.
5 *Bone perforated pin*: cut and polished long-bone sliver; cut perforation in expanded head; burnt and point snapped.
   L. 4.1 cm; head W. 1.0 cm; shank Th. 0.2 cm.
   BB fig. 141.   79 12-9 1278

Burial 2: double cremation deposit: two adults; in inverted Collared Urn 0.3 m above old surface, 0.9 m NW. of centre, damaged by ploughing.
6 *Collared Urn*: upper half; twisted cord: on internal moulding, hurdle pattern; on collar and neck, carelessly applied horizontal and diagonal lines.
   M. 32.1 cm.   79 12-9 1273
   BAP no. 121; *Longworth* no. 1264.

Mound material: on old surface between two stones, 3.3 m SE. of centre.

7 *Collared Vessel*: on collar, neck and shoulder, irregularly placed impressions; distorted.

    M. 13.5-16.6 cm; H. 17.4 cm; B. 8.0 cm.

    Longworth no. 1265.   79 12-9 1274

146 SLINGSBY

Yorkshire N.R.; North Yorkshire   SE 72 70

ROUND BARROW: Diam. 4.8 m, H. 0.3 m, reduced by ploughing; composition not recorded, on natural rise.
BB 353.

Burial 1: child cremation deposit; beneath charcoal in central hollow Diam. 0.3 m, D. 0.3 m, ?burnt *in situ*.

147 SLINGSBY   147:1

Yorkshire N.R.; North Yorkshire   SE 72 70

ROUND BARROW: removed by ploughing; on natural rise.
BB 353-4.

Burials 1-2 were in a hollow Diam. 0.6 m, D. 0.5 m.

Burial 1: adult cremation deposit; on flat stone at D. 0.25 m.

Burial 2: adolescent cremation deposit; at base; cup among bones.

1 *Accessory Cup*: plain; no perforations.

    M. 7.4 cm; H. 3.7 cm; B. 8.1 cm.   79 12-9 1280

    BAP no. 316.

148 SLINGSBY   148:1-2

Yorkshire N.R.; North Yorkshire   SE 72 70

ROUND BARROW: removed by ploughing; on natural rise.
BB 354.

Burial 1: adult female cremation deposit; in hollow Diam. 0.6 m, D. 0.3 m, fill of burnt earth; cup no. 1 above bones, no. 2 among bones.

1 *Accessory Cup*: twisted cord: on internal rim bevel, two lines; on upper body, filled triangles between pairs of lines; no perforations.

    M. 6.6 cm; H. 4.8 cm.   79 12-9 1281

    BAP no. 288.

2 *Accessory Cup*: twisted cord: on internal rim bevel, two lines; on body, horizontal lines; wall pierced by nine vertical rows of triple perforations.

    M. 6.8 cm; H. 4.3 cm; B. 8.9 cm.   79 12-9 1282

    BB fig. 63; *BAP* no. 288a.

149 SLINGSBY   149:1

Yorkshire N.R.; North Yorkshire   SE 72 70

ROUND BARROW: removed by ploughing; on natural rise.
BB 354-5.

Burial 1: child cremation deposit; in hollow Diam. 0.6 m, D. 0.2 m, below much charcoal; cup above bones.

1 *Accessory Cup*: point-tooth comb stamped: on internal rim bevel, two lines; on body, horizontal lines in fingertip rilling; on base, irregular impressions; no perforations.

    M. 5.1-6.1 cm; H. 4.6 cm; B. 5.2 cm. 79 12-9 1283

    BB fig. 142; *BAP* no. 317.

150 SLINGSBY (Hall Moor)   150:1

Yorkshire N.R.; North Yorkshire   SE 72 70

ROUND BARROW: Diam. 7 m, H. 0.5 m, reduced by ploughing; sand; opened 6 July 1865.
BB 355-6.

Burial 1: adult cremation deposit; in central hollow Diam. 0.6 m, D. 0.5 m, ?burnt *in situ*; scraper among bones.

1 *Flint end-scraper*: edge retouch on distal at 60 degrees; broken; cortex remnant; brown.

    L. 2.5 cm; W. 2.3 cm; Th. 0.6 cm.   79 12-9 1284

151 WELBURN (Carmire Gate)   151:1-16

Yorkshire N.R.; North Yorkshire   SE 736 674

ROUND BARROW: Diam. 18.5 m, H. 2.1 m; core of sand and clay H. 0.9 with capping of earth; opened 5 January 1866 (apparently not by Greenwell who acquired the finds from the Rev. Ishmael Fish).
BB 356-7.

Burial 1: cremation deposit; in Collared Urn, 1.7 m above old surface at centre.

1 *Collared Urn sherds*: nineteen of rim, collar and neck; twisted cord: on internal rim bevel, short diagonal lines between single horizontal lines; on internal surface below bevel, rows of hollow reed impressions; on collar, complex panelled scheme including, in part, vertical zigzag lines with spaces filled with vertical lines, and elsewhere panels of diagonal lines with some crossed by vertical zigzag leaving triangular spaces either reserved or filled with opposed diagonal lines, all enclosed between single horizontal lines; on neck, rows of hollow reed impressions.   79 12-9 1285

    Longworth no. 1297.

Mound material

2 *Flint point roughout*: bifacially flaked; brown.

    L. 3.9 cm; W. 3.1 cm; Th. 1.0 cm.   79 12-9 1288

3 *Flint end- and side-scraper*: edge retouch on distal at 55 degrees and on L. at 70 degrees; platform butt; cortex remnant; grey.

    L. 3.6 cm; W. 2.0 cm; Th. 0.9 cm.   79 12-9 1299

4 *Flint end-scraper*: edge retouch on distal at 60 degrees; bulbar end removed; cortex remnant; patinated.

    L. 3.3 cm; W. 3.0 cm; Th. 0.9 cm.   79 12-9 1289

5 *Flint end-scraper*: on fragment; edge retouch on distal and on to R. and L. at 70 degrees; cortex remnant; patinated.

    L. 3.9 cm; W. 2.5 cm; Th. 1.2 cm.   79 12-9 1290

6 *Flint end-scraper*: edge retouch on distal at 65 degrees; platform butt; cortex remnant; patinated.

    L. 2.9 cm; W. 2.7 cm; Th. 1.2 cm.   79 12-9 1291

7 *Flint end-scraper*: edge retouch on distal at 60 degrees; platform butt; cortex remnant; grey.

    L. 2.6 cm; W. 2.2 cm; Th. 0.6 cm.   79 12-9 1292

8 *Flint end-scraper*: edge retouch on distal at 65 degrees; platform butt; cortex remnant; mottled grey.

    L. 3.4 cm; W. 2.5 cm; Th. 1.0 cm.   79 12-9 1293

9 *Flint end-scraper*: edge retouch on distal at 55 degrees; platform butt; cortex remnant; mottled beige.

    L. 3.8 cm; W. 3.5 cm; Th. 1.2 cm.   79 12-9 1294

10 *Flint end-scraper*: edge retouch on distal at 55 degrees; dihedral butt; cortex remnant; grey.

    L. 2.5 cm; W. 1.9 cm; Th. 0.5 cm.   79 12-9 1295

11 *Flint end-scraper*: edge retouch on distal at 60
    degrees; corticated butt; broken; mottled grey.
       L. 2.4 cm; W. 2.6 cm; Th. 1.3 cm.   79 12-9 1298
12 *Flint scraper fragment*: edge retouch on distal at 70
    degrees; cortex remnant; broken; grey.
       L. 6.1 cm; W. 2.8 cm; th. 0.7 cm.   79 12-9 1296
13 *Flint scraper fragment*: partial edge retouch on L.;
    broken; grey.
       L. 1.8 cm; W. 1.5 cm; Th. 0.6 cm.   79 12-9 1297
14 *Flint worked flake*: edge retouch on L.; cortex
    remnant; burnt.
       L. 4.1 cm; W. 2.5 cm; Th. 0.8 cm.   79 12-9 1286
15 *Flint worked fragment*: edge retouch on L.; grey.
       L. 3.9 cm; W. 1.9 cm; Th. 0.9 cm.   79 12-9 1287

Not located
16 *'Sandstone pounder'*: not identified.   79 12-9 1300

152 HUTTON BUSCEL (Three Tremblers I)
                                                        152:1-5

Yorkshire N.R.; North Yorkshire   SE 936 879

ROUND BARROW: Diam. 30 m, H. 3.3 m; sand with some
stones, internal stone circle Diam. 20 m; opened 31 May
to 2 June 1864.
BB 357-61; *Greenwell* 1865, 241-5.

Burial 1: ?decayed inhumation; in cist L. 0.6 m, W. 0.3
m, D. 0.3 m with floor-slab, two side-slabs and
capstone, 0.9 m above old surface, 7.2 m SE. of centre,
sand fill; Food Vessel on side.
1   *Food Vessel*: twisted cord: on internal rim bevel,
    three to four horizontal lines; on outer lip, single
    horizontal line; on neck, two horizontal lines.
       M. 12.5 cm; H. 10.6 cm; B. 5.1 cm.   79 12-9 1301
    BB fig. 143; *Greenwell* 1865, fig. 5; *BAP* no. 123.

Burial 2: ?decayed inhumation; 2.1 m above old surface,
0.6 m SE. of centre; dagger and knife together.
2   *Bronze dagger*: Gerloff Type ?Armorico-British B;
    broad flat midrib tapering towards tip and ?butt;
    surviving edge bevel or internal furrow flanked by
    double groove; heavily corroded (Table 1:5).
       L. 12.8 cm; W. 4.8 cm; Th. 0.6 cm.   79 12-9 1302
    Greenwell 1865, fig. 6; *BB* fig. 144; *Gerloff* 1975,
    no. 128.
3   *Flint plano-convex knife*: all round invasive
    retouch; platform butt; grey.
       L. 10.2 cm; W. 6.4 cm; Th. 1.2 cm.   79 12-9 1303
    BB fig. 145; *Greenwell* 1865, fig. 7; *ASI* fig. 242.

Burial 3: inhumation traces; on old surface, 0.6 m SE. of
centre.
4   *'Bronze fragment'*: not identified.   79 12-9 1304

Mound material
5   *Flint leaf arrowhead*: partial bifacial invasive
    retouch; light grey.
       L. 2.7 cm; W. 1.9 cm; Th. 0.4 cm.   79 12-9 1305
    Green 1980, no. A52.

153 HUTTON BUSCEL (Three Tremblers II)
                                                        153:1-5

Yorkshire N.R.; North Yorkshire   SE 935 879

ROUND BARROW: Diam. 18.5 m, H. 1.8 m; sand, internal
stone circle Diam 10 m; previously opened at centre,
opened 25 April 1866.
BB 361-2.

Burial 1: adult cremation deposit; in inverted Urn 0.3 m
below mound surface, 5.7 m S. of centre.

1   *Food Vessel Urn*: on internal rim bevel, two rows of
    deep rectangular impressions enclosing row of short
    diagonal incised lines; on top of rim, row of
    diagonal incised lines; on outer rim bevel and in
    neck and shoulder groove, rows of round-based pits.
       M. 40.9 cm.   79 12-9 1306
    BAP no. 487; *Cowie* 1978, no. YOR 13.

?Burial 2: ?decayed inhumation; on old surface, 5 m SE.
of centre; jet beneath flat stone, flints together
nearby.
2   *Jet pendant*: cut and polished to irregular triangular
    outline; plano-convex faceted section; drilled
    perforation.
       L. 3.4 cm; W. 2.4 cm; Th. 1.1 cm; perf. Diam. 0.2 cm.
                                                       79 12-9 1307
3   *Flint knife*: invasive retouch on distal; platform
    butt; mottled grey.
       L. 3.1 cm; W. 4.7 cm; Th. 0.7 cm.   79 12-9 1308
4   *Flint knife*: converging invasive retouch on L. and
    partially on R.; platform butt; cortex remnant; grey.
       L. 5.3 cm; W. 3.1 cm; Th. 0.7 cm.   79 12-9 1310
5   *Flint worked flake*: partial invasive retouch on L.,
    some edge retouch on R.; platform butt; cortex
    remnant; mottled grey.
       L. 5.7 cm; W. 4.6 cm; Th. 1.3 cm.   79 12-9 1309

154 HUTTON BUSCEL
                                                        154:1-6

Yorkshire N.R.; North Yorkshire   SE 937 891

ROUND CAIRN: Diam. 9 m, H. 1.2 m; small stones, kerb of
larger stones; opened 5-6 June 1864.
BB 362-5; *Greenwell* 1865, 245-6.

Burial 1: adult cremation deposit, area Diam. 0.4 m; on
old surface, 2.7 m NW. of centre.

Burial 2: adult cremation deposit, over area Diam. 0.9
m; on old surface, 1.8 m N. by E. of centre; Food Vessel
and knife among bones.
1   *Food Vessel*: twisted cord: on internal rim bevel,
    four horizontal lines; on neck and over shoulder,
    herringbone beneath single horizontal line.
       M. 14.7 cm; H. 13.2 cm; B. 7.7 cm.   79 12-9 1311
    BB fig. 146; *Greenwell* 1865, fig. 8; *BAP* no.496.
2   *Flint plano-convex knife*: all over invasive retouch;
    patinated.
       L. 3.9 cm; W. 1.9 cm; Th. 0.6 m.   79 12-9 1314
    Clark 1932, no. 2.17.

Burial 3: tibia and ulna fragments; 0.6 m above old
surface, 2.4 m W. of centre.

Burials 4-5 were at W. and E. within a circle of stones
set on edge Diam. 1.2 m on old surface at centre, fill of
burnt stones and earth.

Burial 4: cremation deposit; in upright Collared Urn
covered by inverted Bipartite Vessel.
3   *Collared Urn sherds*: thirteen lacking lower collar;
    twisted cord: on rim, two lines; on upper collar,
    horizontal lines; on lower neck, row of zigzag
    enclosed above by single and below by three
    horizontal lines.   79 12-9 1313
    BB fig. 148; *Greenwell* 1865, fig. 11; *Longworth* no.
    1093.
4   *Bipartite vessel*: plain; two vertically perforated
    lugs.
       M. 9.0 cm; H. 8.9 cm; B. 6.1 cm.   79 12-9 1312
    BB fig. 147; *Greenwell* 1865, fig. 10; *BAP* no. 486.
5   *Bronze Age sherds*: four; plain.   79 12-9 1313a

Burial 5: cremation deposit; in upright urn.
    'cinerary urn': not preserved.

Old surface
6   *'Quartz pebble hammerstone'*: not identified.
                                                       79 12-9 1315

155 HUTTON BUSCEL

Yorkshire N.R.; North Yorkshire   SE 937 891

ROUND CAIRN: Diam. 4.8 m; stones added to natural rise; opened 5-6 June 1864.
BB 365; *Greenwell* 1865, 246.

Burial 1: adult cremation deposit; in central hollow Diam. 0.6 m, D. 0.4 m.
   'piece of calcined flint': not preserved.

156 HUTTON BUSCEL

Yorkshire N.R.; North Yorkshire   SE 937 891

RECTANGULAR CAIRN: L. 4.8 m, W. 3.6 m; stones added to natural rise; opened 5-6 June 1864.
BB 365; *Greenwell* 1865, 246.

Burial 1: adult cremation deposit; in central hollow Diam. 0.5 m, D. 0.6 m.
   'four flint chippings': not preserved.

157 HUTTON BUSCEL   157:1-29

Yorkshire N.R.; North Yorkshire   SE 95 88

ROUND BARROW: Diam. 8 m, H. 1.2 m with addition at S. projecting 1.5 m; sand; linear charcoal deposit W. 1.5 m, D. 0.3 m across mound; opened 7-8 June 1864.
BB 365-9; *Greenwell* 1865, 247-9.

Burial 1: adult cremation deposit; over area Diam. 0.5 m; on original mound surface beneath addition, 2.4 m SW. of centre; objects among bones.

1 *Bronze shank fragments*: two; one with ?square section, ?awl; heavily corroded.
   L. 1.8 and 1.1 cm; W. 0.1 cm; Th. 0.1 cm.
                                             79 12-9 1323
2 *Accessory Cup*: on external rim bevel, incised filled triangles; on upper body, two rows of incised chevrons; no perforations.
   M. 5.1 cm; H. 5.4 cm; B. 6.1 cm.   79 12-9 1316
   BB fig. 149; *Greenwell* 1865, fig. 12; *BAP* no. 107d.
3 *Jet pendant*: cut and polished to sub conical dome stepped to flat base; drilled V-perforation from one edge to base; on dome, central incised ring surrounded by circle of spaced incised triangles.
   Diam. 1.7 cm; Th. 0.8 cm.   79 12-9 1327
4 *Jet bead*: cut and polished to square section and longitudinal convexity; drilled perforation.
   L. 2.9 cm; central Th. 0.9 cm; terminal Th. 0.7 cm.
                                             79 12-9 1324
5 *Jet bead*: cut and polished to barrel form; drilled perforation.
   L. 1.9 cm; central Diam. 0.9 cm; terminal Diam. 0.7 cm.   79 12-9 1325
6 *Jet bead*: cut and polished to barrel form; drilled perforation.
   L. 1.1 cm; central Diam. 0.9 cm; terminal Diam. 0.7 cm.   79 12-9 1326
   BB fig. 150; *Greenwell* 1865, fig. 13; *ASI* fig. 380.
7 *'Flint flake'*: not identified.   79 12-9 1322

Burial 2: cremation deposit; 0.3 m below mound surface, 2.4 m, NE. of centre; objects among bones.
   'urn': not preserved.
8 *'Flint scraper'*: not identified.   79 12-9 1332
9 *Flint blade*: platform butt; burnt and broken.
   L. 5.9 cm; W. 2.5 cm; Th. 0.9 cm.   79 12-9 1328
10-12 *'Flint flakes'*: three; not identified.
                                             79 12-9 1329-31

Burial 3: disturbed cremation deposits; 0.9 m above old surface, at centre.
13 *Collared Vessel sherds*: three, including collar; on collar and upper neck, rows of diagonal impressions. *Longworth* no. 1321.   79 12-9 1321
14 *?Food Vessel sherds*: three, including rim; beneath rim, opposed twisted cord loops; on body, diagonal twisted cord lines.   79 12-9 1321a
15 *?Food Vessel base sherd*: plain.   79 12-9 1321b
16 *Bronze Age rim sherd*: plain bowl.   79 12-9 1321c
17 *Bronze Age sherds*: two, including rim; plain.
                                             79 12-9 1321d
18 *Bronze Age shoulder sherd*: plain.   79 12-9 1321e
19 *Bronze Age sherds*: two; one with diagonal fine twisted cord lines above horizontal line.
                                             79 12-9 1321f
20 *Bronze age sherds*: twenty-three; plain.
                                             79 12-9 1321g

Burial 4: adolescent cremation deposit; in upright Collared Urn on old surface, 0.6 m SE. of centre; urn with stone slab cover and charcoal surround, smaller vessel inverted inside, point with bones in larger.
21 *Collared Urn*: on internal rim bevel, two twisted cord lines; on collar, rows of impressions in rough herringbone; on neck, rows of knot impressions.
   M. 27.2 cm; H. 32.5 cm; B. 9.0 cm.   79 12-9 1318
   BB fig. 56; *Greenwell* 1865, fig. 15; *BAP* no. 107; *Longworth* no. 1318.
22 *Collared Vessel*: on internal rim bevel, two twisted cord lines; on collar, twisted cord hurdle pattern between single rows of impressions; on neck, four rows of impressions.
   M. 15.0 cm; H. 17.7 cm; B. 8.4 cm.   79 12-9 1317
   BB fig. 152; *Greenwell* 1865, fig. 15*; *BAP* no. 107a; *Longworth* no. 1319.
23 *Flint point*: converging bilateral edge retouch; burnt and damaged.
   L. 5.0 cm; W. 2.2 cm; Th. 0.6 cm.   79 12-9 1333
   BB fig. 151; *Greenwell* 1865, fig. 14.

Burial 5: adolescent cremation deposit; in and around upright Collared Urn on old surface, SE. of Burial 4.
24 *Collared Urn*: on collar, carelessly executed twisted cord herringbone; surface eroded.
   M. 13.5 cm; H. 17.3 cm; B. 7.6 cm.   79 12-9 1320
   BAP no. 107b; *Longworth* no. 1322.

Burial 6: adult cremation deposit; below mound surface, 1.8 m SW. of centre; objects among bones.
25 *Collared Vessel*: on collar, twisted cord hurdle pattern beneath single horizontal line.
   M. 14.5 cm; H. 19.3 cm; B. 7.9 cm.   79 12-9 1319
   BAP no. 107c; *Longworth* no. 1320.
26 *Flint barbed-and-tanged arrowhead fragment*: bifacial invasive retouch; burnt and damaged.
   L. 3.3 cm; W. 2.6 cm; Th. 0.4 cm.   79 12-9 1334
   Green 1980, no. 95.
27 *Flint worked flake*: burnt and broken.
   L. 3.2 cm; W. 3.6 cm; Th. 0.9 cm.   79 12-9 1335
28-9 *'Flint flakes'*: two; not identified.
                                             79 12-9 1336-37

158 HUTTON BUSCEL   158:1-3

Yorkshire N.R.; North Yorkshire   SE 95 88

ROUND BARROW: Diam. 8.5 m, H. 1.4 m; sand, stone kerb;
opened 8 June 1864.
BB 369; *Greenwell* 1865, 250.

Burial 1: adult cremation deposit; in upright Collared
Urn on old surface, 0.6 m S. of centre; flints among
bones.
1 *Collared Urn*: on collar, rows of deeply-impressed
   bone or stick-end impressions.
   M. 27.2 cm; H. 32.8 cm; B. 14.0 cm.   79 12-9 1338
   BAP no. 138; *Longworth* no. 1323.
2-3 *'Flint flakes: calcined'*: two; not identified.
                                          79 12-9 1730-1

159 HUTTON BUSCEL (Porter I)   159:1-3

Yorkshire N.R.; North Yorkshire   SE 95 88

ROUND BARROW: Diam. 5.5 m, H. 0.6 m; earth with some
stones; opened May 1866.
BB 369.

Burial 1: cremation deposit; in and around Collared Urn
on side on old surface at centre; flints among bones.
1 *Collared Urn*: distorted; incised: on internal rim
   bevel, zigzag; on collar, linear filled triangles
   between single horizontal lines; on neck, linear
   lattice.
   M. 9.2-11.7 cm; H. 12.5 cm; B. 6.6 cm. 79 12-9 1339
   Longworth no. 1324.
2 *Flint scraper fragment*: edge retouch on R.; burnt and
   broken.
   L. 2.8 cm; W. 2.4 cm; Th. 0.7 cm.   79 12-9 1341
3 *Flint worked fragment*: all over invasive retouch
   surviving on one side; cortex remnant; burnt and
   damaged.
   L. 4.2 cm; W. 2.5 cm; Th. 0.6 cm.   79 12-9 1340
   Green 1980, no. 94.

160 HUTTON BUSCEL (Porter II)   160:1-2

Yorkshire N.R.; North Yorkshire   SE 95 87

ROUND BARROW: Diam. 8 m, H. 0.8 m; sand with some stones,
surrounding ditch W. 1 m, D. 0.8 m; opened 26 June 1866.
BB 369-70.

Burial 1: cremation deposit; in inverted vessel 0.4 m
above old surface, at centre.
1 *Food Vessel*: plain.
   M. 11.8 cm; H. 10.9 cm; B. *c*. 8.0 cm. 79 12-9 1343
   Manby 1980, 352
   'calcined flint chipping': not preserved.

Burial 2: cremation deposit; in hollow Diam. 0.5 m, D.
0.6 m with stone surround, 0.5 m S of centre; vessel on
side over bones.
2 *Collared Vessel*: point tooth-comb stamped: on
   internal rim bevel, zigzag; on collar, lattice; on
   neck, zigzag above two horizontal lines.
   M. 10.9-12.0 cm; H. 16.4 cm; B. 7.5 cm.
   BAP no. 154; *Longworth* no. 1325.   79 12-9 1342

161 FERRY FRYSTON   161:1-5

Yorkshire W.R.; West Yorkshire   SE 474 245

ROUND BARROW: Diam. 16 m, H. 2.1 m, reduced by ploughing
(two concentric ditches Diam. 16.5 m, D. 0.8 m and Diam.
22.5 m, D. 0.2 m: Pacitto); composition not recorded, on
natural limestone knoll; opened 1811 and 1863, re-opened
c. 1865 by WG, excavated 1962 by Pacitto.
BB 371-4; *Pacitto* 1969.

Burial 1 (1811): several inhumations recorded in upper
mound.

Burial 2 (1863): three extended inhumations in mound.

Burial 3 (1863): adult male inhumation, crouched with
head S.; in central cist L. 1 m, W. 0.6 m, D. 0.4 m, four
side-slabs with capstone and small stone paving, fill of
fine gravel, 0.9 m above old surface; vessel and knife at
chest.
   'food vessel': not preserved.
   'flint knife': not preserved.

Burial 4 (1863): many bone fragments; below and around
Burial 3 cist.
   'potsherds': not preserved.

Burial 5 (1863): cremation deposit; in urn on N. side of
mound.
1 *Collared Urn*: distorted; on internal rim bevel,
   incised linear lattice; on collar, rows of bone
   impressions; on neck, incised linear lattice; on
   shoulder, row of bone impressions.
   M. 13.6-15.6 cm; H. 17.2 cm; B. 9.4 cm.
   BAP no. 168; *Longworth* no. 1595; *Pacitto* 1969, fig.
   6.4.   79 12-9 1344

Burial 6 (1863): cremation deposit; in urn on N. side of
mound.
2 *Collared Urn*: on neck, alternate rows of bone
   impressions and plaited cord lines; below shoulder,
   row of twisted cord short vertical lines.
   B. 9.0 cm.   79 12-9 1345
   Longworth no. 1594; *Pacitto* 1969, fig. 6.3.

Burial 7: child cremation deposit; on slab on old
surface, 3.6 m SE. of centre.

Burial 8: inhumation and cremation: adult male crouched
on R. with head S., partly overlying adult male
cremation; vessel behind back and overlying cremation.
3 *Food Vessel*: Yorkshire Vase; on internal rim bevel
   and over exterior including lugs, finely impressed
   herringbone made with pointed implement; one surviving of four horizontally perforated lugs.
   M. *c*. 13.0 cm; H. 11.0 cm; B. 5.8 cm. 79 12-9 1346
   BAP no. 104; *Manby* 1969, fig. 1.5; *Pacitto* 1969, fig.
   6.2.

Burial 9: adult inhumation, crouched on R. with head W.;
in central grave Diam. 1.8 m, D. 0.8 m; Beaker at feet,
awl behind knees.
4 *Bronze awl*: rounded section with at least one
   flattened face; traces of two lozenge facets at
   centre; corroded and tips lacking (Table 1:39).
   L. 2.7 cm; W. 0.1 cm; Th. 0.1 cm.   79 12-9 1348
   Pacitto 1969, fig. 6.1.
5 *Beaker*: tooth-comb stamped: on neck, three narrow
   zones of short vertical lines above narrow zone of
   double zigzag with upright triangles filled with
   short diagonal lines and, in one place, two pendant
   triangles filled with fingernail impressions, separated and enclosed by pairs of horizontal lines; on
   body, two to three similar narrow zones of short
   vertical lines separated, and the upper two enclosed
   and separated, by pairs of horizontal lines with

fingernail impressions between lowest pair, with two further zones of vertical lines in part separated by a single horizontal line.

M. 12.2 cm; H. 17.3 cm; B. 7.4 cm.   79 12-9 1347
BAP no. 109; Clarke no. 1275; Pacitto 1969, fig. 6.1.

Burial 10: many bone fragments; over and around Burial 9 grave.

162 RYLSTON   162:1
Yorkshire W.R.; North Yorkshire   SD 971 569

ROUND BARROW: Diam. 9 m, H. 1.5 m; clay, enclosing ditch; previously opened at centre, opened 25 Oct. 1864.
BB 375-7; Greenwell 1865, 253-4.

Burial 1: decayed inhumation; in oak-trunk coffin L. 2.2 m, W. 0.6 m, cavity L. 1.9 m, W. 0.3 m, in slight hollow aligned S.-N., at centre; damaged by previous opening but remains of textile wrapping of body.
1 *Woollen textile fragments*: plain tabby weave with variable thread counts: 7/8, 8/8, 9/9, 10/8 and 11/6 threads per cm in different areas; irregular and uneven weave; warp and weft of same quality wool, spun on worsted principle; spinning Z in both systems; no selvedges or borders preserved; stained dark brown (*identified* E. Crowfoot).
L. 13.0 cm; W. 6.0 cm.   79 12-9 2065
L. 11.0 cm; W. 8.5 cm.   79 12-9 2064
L. 8.0 cm; W. 6.0 cm.   79 12-9 2067
Small fragments 79 12-9 1595 and 2066; 73 12-19 219
Henshall 1950, 133.

163 CASTLE CARROCK   163:1
Cumberland; Cumbria   NY 539 559

CIST: four upright slabs and capstone, dimensions not recorded, aligned NE.-SW.; in natural rise; opened by farmers 1865, material recovered by Greenwell.
BB 379.

Burial 1: adult male inhumation, crouched on L. with head NE.; Beaker behind head.
1 *Beaker*: from rim to base, horizontal grooved lines with intervening ridges with diagonal impressions set in alternate directions.
M. 16.0 cm; H. 19.0 cm; B. 8.7 cm.   79 12-9 1349
BAP no. 161; Clarke no. 110.

164 CASTLE CARROCK   164:1
Cumberland; Cumbria   NY 539 559

ROUND BARROW: Diam. 2.4 m, H. 0.5; earth and stones on natural rise; opened 10 April 1866.
BB 379-80.

Burial 1: adult cremation deposit; in central oval hollow L. 0.9 m, W. 0.8 m, D. 0.4 m, aligned NE.-SW., fill of dark earth and stones; knife below bones.
1 *Flint plano-convex knife*: on blade; all-over unifacial invasive flaking; proximal damaged; grey.
L. 8.5 cm; W. 2.2 cm; Th. 0.5 cm.   79 12-9 1350
BB fig. 153; ASI fig. 239; Clark 1932, no. 6.2.

165 KIRBY STEPHEN
Westmorland; Cumbria   NY 74 05

ROUND BARROW: Diam. 16.5 m, H. 1.5 m; clayey earth.
BB 382.

Burial 1: adult cremation deposit, in heap Diam. 0.3 m; 0.6 m above old surface, 5 m ESE. of centre.

166 KIRBY STEPHEN
Westmorland; Cumbria   NY 74 05

ROUND BARROW: Diam. 9.5 m, H. 1.2 m; limestone rubble and earth.
BB 382.

Burial 1: ?decayed inhumation; in rough central cist of limestone slabs on old surface at centre.

167 KIRBY STEPHEN
Westmorland; Cumbria   NY 74 05

ROUND BARROW: Diam 9 m, H. 1.2 m; stones and earth.
BB 382-3.

Burial 1: adult male inhumation, crouched on R. with head S.; in central grave L. 1 m, W. 0.6 m, D. 0.8 m, aligned N.-S., fill of earth and stones with animal bone fragments.

168 KIRBY STEPHEN
Westmorland; Cumbria   NY 74 05

ROUND BARROW: Diam. 5.5 m, H. 0.8 m; stones and earth, kerb of small stones; extensively disturbed.
BB 383.

Burial 1: disturbed cremated and unburnt bones; in backfill.

169 KIRBY STEPHEN   169:1
Westmorland; Cumbria   NY 776 044

ROUND CAIRN: Diam. 4.5 m, H. 0.5 m; stones, remains of kerb.
BB 383-4.

Burial 1: child cremation deposit; in earth fill of central hollow Diam. 0.5 m, D. 0.4 m with flat stone cover; ?pin among bones, cup above.
1 *Accessory Cup*: on neck, short diagonal point toothcomb stamped lines; on body, point tooth-comb stamped chevrons above horizontal line; on base, fine twisted cord lattice; one surviving perforation.
H. (surviving) 4.3 cm; B. 4.5 cm.   79 12-9 1351
'piece of calcined bone, pierced with two holes': not preserved.

170 KIRBY STEPHEN   170:1
Westmorland; Cumbria   NY 761 071

ROUND BARROW: Diam. 8.5 m, H. 0.5 m, reduced by robbing; stones and earth.
BB 384-5.

Burial 1: disturbed cremation deposit.

Mound material or Burial 1
1 *Flint point*: converging edge retouch on distal and R.; platform butt; patinated.
L. 1.7 cm; W. 1.1 cm; Th. 0.5 cm.   79 12-9 1352
Green 1980, no. 52.

171   WARCOP

Westmorland; Cumbria   NY 73 16

ROUND BARROW: Diam. 22 m, H. 1.5 m, reduced by ploughing; sand.
BB 385-6.

Burial 1: inhumation traces; on old surface at centre with much charcoal.

172   ASBY

Westmorland; Cumbria   NY 66 01

ROUND CAIRN: Diam. 10 m, H. 0.9 m; stones, stone kerb.
BB 386.

Burial 1: disturbed bones of two adults; in mound, 1.5 m ESE. of centre.

Burial 2: adult cremation deposit; in central oval hollow L. 0.5 m, W. 0.4 m, D. 0.15 m, aligned NE.-SW.

173   CROSBY GARRETT

Westmorland; Cumbria   NY 707 068

ROUND CAIRN: Diam. 11 m, H. 1.2 m; pitched limestone and sandstone slabs.
BB 387-9; *Kinnes* 1979, no. ACd 3.

Burial 1: disarticulated and fragmentary bones of adult and adult male; 0.3 m below mound surface, 3.2 m SW. by W. of centre.

Burial 2: disarticulated and fragmentary bones of adult and adult male; 0.5 m below mound surface, 0.3 m SW. of Burial 1.

Burial 3: fragmentary bones; 0.8 m below mound surface 1.4 m SE. of centre.

Burial 4: fragmentary bones of adult female; 0.8 m below mound surface, 1.8 m W. of centre.

Burial 5: fragmentary bones; 0.3 above old surface, S. of centre.

Burial 6: cranial fragments of adult, child and infant with some post-cranial bones; 0.2 m above old surface at centre.

174   CROSBY GARRETT   174:1-9

Westmorland; Cumbria   NY 65 07

OVAL CAIRN: L. 20 m, W. 12 m, H. 0.5 m, aligned N.-S., reduced by robbing; stones, on limestone outcrop.
BB 389-91; *Kinnes* 1979, no. Eb2; *Manby* 1974, 120.

Burial 1: disturbed adult male inhumation, crouched on L. with head SSW.; on old surface, 7 m SSE. of centre; objects near face.

1   *Worked boar tusk:* sliced facets on ventral and point; point broken; fragmentary.
      Chord L. 11.6 cm; W. 2.2 cm; Th. 1.9 cm.
                                                          79 12-9 1361

2   *Worked boar tusk:* sliced facet on ventral at point; fragmentary.
      Chord L. 8.9 cm; W. 1.8 cm; Th. 1.6 cm.
                                                          79 12-9 1362

3   *Bone side-looped pin:* cut and polished to round section with terminal side-loop of sub-rectangular section; cut conical perforation; broken and eroded.
      L. 9.9 cm; Diam. 0.7 cm; loop W. 1.6 cm; perf. Diam. 0.7 cm.
                                                          79 12-9 1359

Burial 2: scattered bones of two adults and child; near Burial 1.

Burial 3: disturbed adult male inhumation, crouched on R. with head NE.; on old surface, 4.2 m S. of centre.

Burial 4: adult male inhumation, crouched on R. with head N.; on old surface, 1.5 m S. of centre; macehead at knees, strike-a-light at R. arm, knife at face.
      'piece of iron ore': not preserved.

4   *Flint knife:* bilateral invasive retouch; platform butt; patinated.
      L. 6.5 cm; W. 2.5 cm; Th. 0.6 cm.   79 12-9 1365

5   *Flint fabricator:* on blade; edge retouch on distal and bilateral; abraded; punctiform butt; cortex remnant; patinated.
      L. 9.5 cm; W. 2.4 cm; Th. 1.6 cm.   79 12-9 1364

6   *Antler macehead:* cut from base of red-deer shed antler beam; surviving ends cut and smoothed; central cut cylindrical perforation; broken.
      L. 8.9 cm; w. 6.0 cm; Th. 4.2 cm; perf. Diam. 3.0 cm.
      BB fig. 154.   79 12-9 1363

Burial 5: scattered burnt and unburnt bones; in cairn.

Cairn material

7   *Bone pin:* cut and polished to circular section; broken and eroded.
      L. 13.1 cm; Diam. 0.7 cm.   79 12-9 1360

Not located

8   *Stone polished axe fragment:* flake struck from polished greenstone axe.
      L. 2.9 cm; W. 1.7 cm. Th. 0.4 cm.   79 12-9 1366

9   *Quartz pebble*   79 12-9 1367

175   CROSBY GARRETT

Westmorland; Cumbria   NY 65 07

ROUND CAIRN: Diam. 8 m, H. 0.5 m, reduced by robbing; stones, on limestone outcrop.
BB 391.

Burial 1: disturbed adult male inhumation; on old surface at centre.
      'a piece of a drinking-cup': not preserved.

176   CROSBY GARRETT   176:1-4

Westmorland; Cumbria   NY 65 07

ROUND CAIRN: Diam. 7 m, H. 0.3 m, reduced by robbing; stones, on limestone outcrop.
BB 391-3.

Burial 1: many broken bones; scattered throughout cairn S. of centre.

Burial 2: cremation and double inhumation: adult female cremation overlain by two infants; on old surface at centre; objects in nearby disturbed contexts probably associated.

1   *Jet spacer-plate:* cut and polished to sub-rectangular outline and section with bevelled ends; four drilled perforations.
      L. 3.6 cm; W. 2.1 cm; Th. 0.5 cm.   79 12-9 1368

2   *Bone chisel fragment:* on bovid metapodial shaft; cut facet for blade with abrasion; broken.
      L. 6.2 cm; W. 0.7 cm; Th. 0.7 cm.   79 12-9 1371

3   *Bone pin fragment:* cut and polished to circular section; both ends broken.
      L. 13.5 cm; Diam. 0.7 cm.   79 12-9 1369

4   *Bone bead fragment:* longbone shaft cut and polished to barrel form; two zones of incised decoration,

separated by reserved zone, each infilled with chevrons in part replaced by parallel lines and bordered externally by two and internally by one line; in reserved band three coterminous drilled perforations; broken.
L. 3.9 cm; Diam. 2.3 cm.   79 12-9 1370
BB fig. 53.

177 RAVENSTONEDALE (Hardrig)   177:1-2

Westmorland; Cumbria   NY 685 059

ROUND BARROW: Diam. 8 m, H. 0.8 m; earth with some stones.
BB 393-4.

Burial 1: adult female cremation; in inverted Collared Urn on stone slab 0.3 m above old surface, ?at centre; bead among bones.
1 *Collared Urn*: plain.
   M. 21.5 cm; H. 26.7 cm; B. 9.0 cm.   79 12-9 1372
   Longworth no. 219.
2 *Fired clay bead*: bobbin-shaped varying from straight to concave-sided; either end with one to two irregular circles of round and arcuate jabs; on sides nine irregular vertical rows of round and arcuate jabs; cylindrical perforation.
   L. 2.1 cm; Diam. 2.1 cm; perf. Diam. 0.4 cm.
   BB fig. 52.   79 12-9 1373

178 ORTON (Orton I)   178:1

Westmorland; Cumbria   NY 653 090

ROUND CAIRN: Diam. 15 m, reduced by previous opening; stones.
BB 394-5.

Burial 1: bones of three adults; in backfill of previous opening.

Burial 2: adolescent inhumation, crouched on L. with head S.; in central grave L. 2.4 m, W. 1.5 m, D. 0.6 m, aligned N.-S.; point at head.
1 *Flint pointed implement*: converging bilateral edge retouch; patinated.
   L. 6.0 cm; W. 2.3 cm; Th. 0.8 cm.   79 12-9 1374

179 ORTON (Little Kinman)   179:1

Westmorland; Cumbria   NY 665 090

ROUND CAIRN: Diam. 9.5 m, H. 0.8 m; stones; previously opened.
BB 395-6.

Burial 1: disturbed bones of two inhumations; in backfill of previous opening.

Burial 2: disturbed adult male inhumation, originally crouched on L. with head NE; in central cist L. 1.1 m, W. 0.7 m, D. 0.6 m aligned NE.-SW., four side-slabs but capstone(s) removed, on old surface.

Burial 3: disturbed bones of adult and adult female; around central cist.

Burial 2 or 3
1 *Stone double-ended chisel*: ground and polished to rectangular section with lateral bevels on lower face; ends slightly-splayed and bevelled to blades; one end abraded, the other chipped by use.
   L. 12.4 cm; W. 1.6 cm; Th. 0.8 cm.   79 12-9 1375

180 CROSBY RAVENSWORTH

Westmorland; Cumbria   NY 648 120

ROUND CAIRN: Diam. 7.5 m, H. 0.6 m; stones, stone kerb remnant; previously opened.
BB 397.

Burial 1: disturbed adult inhumation; on old surface at centre.

181 CROSBY RAVENSWORTH   181:1

Westmorland; Cumbria   NY 648 120

ROUND CAIRN: Diam. 10 m, H. 0.9 m; stones, stone kerb remnant; previously opened.
BB 397-8.

Burial 1: adult ?female cremation, in upright urn 0.5 m above old surface, 2.5 m SE of centre.
1 *'Fragments of urn'*: not identified.   79 12-9 1376

Burial 2: fragmentary bones of two adult males; in backfill of previous opening at centre.

182 CROSBY RAVENSWORTH (Seal Howe)

Westmorland; Cumbria   NY 595 127

ROUND CAIRN: Diam. 10.5 m, H. 0.6 m; stones; previously opened.
BB 398-400.

Burial 1: double cremation deposit; adult female and infant; in upright urn on old surface, 2.8 m S. of centre.
   'urn': not preserved.

Burial 2: disturbed adult male inhumation; on old surface at centre.

183 ASKHAM (Standing Stones)   183:1-2

Westmorland; Cumbria   NY 494 220

ROUND CAIRN: Diam. 5.4 m; layer of stones within circle Diam. 5.4 m of ten upright stones H. 0.9 m.
BB 400-1.

Burial 1: adult cremation deposit; in central hollow Diam. 0.6 m, D. 0.6 m; covered by fine sand with Food Vessel on side above; sherds in hollow.
1 *Food Vessel*: Yorkshire Vase; on internal rim bevel and over external surface except lugs, fine twisted cord herringbone; four imperforate lugs.
   M. 14.5 cm; H. 14.2 cm; B. 6.7 cm.   79 12-9 1377
   BAP no. 164.
2 *'Sherds'*: two; not identified.   79 12-9 1378

184 FORD   184:1-11

Northumberland   NT 93 39

ROUND BARROW: Diam. 5 m, H. 0.8 m; earth with some stones; crest of mound disturbed, opened 17 October 1863.
BB 403-6; *Greenwell 1868a, 197-9.*

Burial 1: ?decayed inhumation; in disturbed material 0.3 m below mound surface, W. of centre.
1 *Beaker sherds*: joining; circular bone end impressions in zones of vertical to diagonal lines separated by single and double horizontal lines.
                                          79 12-9 1379
   Greenwell 1868a, pl. XIII; Clarke no. 672; Tait 1965, no. 79.

Burial 2: cremation deposit; in and around upright
Collared Urn above old surface at centre.
2 *Collared Urn*: distorted; plain.
    M. 13.5-16.5 cm; H. 19.5 cm; B. 9.3 cm.
                        79 12-9 1380
    BAP no. 116d; *Gibson* 1978, no. 134; *Longworth* no.
    1049.

Burials 3 and 4 were separated by an upright slab in a
central rectangular hollow L. 0.8 m, W. 0.6 m, D. 0.4 m,
aligned E.-W., covered by stones.

Burial 3: adult cremation deposit; in upright Collared
Urn at W. end; awl and pin among bones, upright empty
Collared Vessel to W.
3 *Bronze shank fragment*: heavily corroded.
    L. 1.1 cm; W. 0.3 cm; Th. 0.3 cm.   79 12-9 1385
4 *Collared Urn*: twisted cord: on internal rim bevel,
    short diagonal lines; on collar, filled triangles
    between single horizontal lines.
    M. 27.2 cm; H. 37.2 cm; B. 11.3 cm.   79 12-9 1381
    Greenwell 1868a, pl. XIII; *BAP* no. 116; *Gibson* 1978,
    no. 139; *Longworth* no. 1046.
5 *Collared Vessel*: distorted; twisted cord: on rim,
    single line; on collar, filled triangles; on neck,
    vertical lines.
    M. 10.0-13.8 cm; H. 18.5 cm; B. 7.7 cm.
                        79 12-9 1382
    Greenwell 1868a, pl. XIII; *BAP* no. 116a; *Gibson* 1978,
    no. 120; *Longworth* no. 1048.
6 *Bone pin fragment*: cut and polished to fine point;
    burnt and broken.
    L. 3.3 cm; Diam. 0.5 cm.   79 12-9 1386

Burial 4: cremation deposit; in upright Collared Urn at
E. end; cup among bones, empty vessel to N.
7 *Collared Urn*: on collar, twisted cord hurdle pattern.
    M. 19.0 cm; H. 23.4 cm; B. 9.8 cm.   79 12-9 1383
    BAP no. 116b; *Gibson* 1978, no. 135; *Longworth* no.
    1047.
8 *Collared Vessel sherds*: twenty-four from upper half
    of tripartite vessel; on rim, two twisted cord lines;
    on collar, twisted cord lattice; on neck, two rows of
    vertically-placed bone impressions.   79 12-9 1389
    Longworth no. 1050.
9 *Accessory Cup*: plain; heat pitting over much of
    surface; no perforations.
    M. 6.6 cm; H. 4.6 cm; B. 5.1 cm.   79 12-9 1384
    BB fig. 155; *Greenwell* 1868a, pl. XIII; *BAP* no. 116c.

Burial 5: adult cremation deposit; in sand fill of cist
L. 0.5 m, W. 0.5 m, four side slabs and capstone, aligned
E.-W. on old surface E. of centre.

Mound Material:
10 *Stone pebble*: gritstone.
    L. 16.0 cm; W. 6.8 cm; Th. 4.1 cm.   79 12-9 1388
11 *Flint fragment*: both ends snapped; grey.
    L. 2.0 cm; W. 1.5 cm; Th. 0.5 cm.   79 12-9 1387

185 FORD   185:1-2
Northumberland   NT 958 384

ROUND BARROW: slight traces, reduced by ploughing; on
natural knoll; opened 16 June 1863.
BB 406-7; *Greenwell* 1868a, 196-7.

Burial 1: cremation deposit; in 'gravelly sand' fill of
cist L. 0.6 m, W. 0.5 m, four sandstone side slabs and
capstone, aligned NE.-SW.
1 *Neolithic Bowl sherd*   79 12-9 1390
2 *Flint plano-convex knife*: all over unifacial in-
    vasive retouch; punctiform butt; grey.
    L. 6.4 cm; W. 2.5 cm; Th. 0.6 cm.   79 12-9 1391
    BB fig. 156; *Greenwell* 1868a, pl. XIII; *AS1* fig. 240;
    Clark 1932, no. 6.4.

186 FORD   186:1-6
Northumberland   NT 95 38

ROUND BARROW: Diam. 4.2 m, H. 0.5 m, earth and stones on
natural knoll; according to Greenwell MS. 12 p. 40
opened in 1860 by John Smith the gamekeeper and finds
given to WG, according to *BB* p. 406 one of 'two small
barrows which had been left until then undisturbed' and
opened WG [circumstantial detail suggests that Burial 3
may have been that found by Smith].
BB 407.

Burial 1: cremation deposit; on old surface, 1.5 m SE. of
centre.

Burial 2: cremation deposit; on old surface, 0.6 m from
Burial 1.

Burial 3: adult female cremation deposit; in upright
Collared Urn on old surface at centre; objects among and
above bones.
1 *Collared Urn*: twisted cord: on internal rim bevel,
    two lines; on collar, hurdle pattern.
    M. *c*. 19.0 cm; H. 21.2 cm; B. 11.0 cm. 79 12-9 1392
    Gibson 1978, no. 136; *Longworth* no. 1051.
2 *Jet button fragment*: cut and polished to ovate dome
    bevelled to flat base with remains of drilled V-
    perforation; broken.
    Diam. 1.3 cm; Th. 0.8 cm.   79 12-9 1397
3 *Jet bead*: cut and polished to barrel form; drilled
    perforation; one end broken.
    L. 1.8 cm; central Diam. 0.7 cm; terminal Diam. 0.6
    cm.   79 12-9 1394
4 *Jet bead*: cut and polished to barrel form; drilled
    perforation; one end broken.
    L. 1.5 cm; central Diam. 0.6 cm; terminal Diam. 0.5
    cm.   79 12-9 1395
5 *Jet bead fragment*: cut and polished to barrel form;
    drilled perforation; split and broken.
    L. 1.4 cm; central Diam. 0.8 cm, terminal Diam. 0.6
    cm.   79 12-9 1396
6 *Flint worked fragment*: bifacial invasive retouch;
    burnt and broken.
    L. 3.1 cm; W. 1.7 cm; Th. 0.8 cm.   79 12-9 1393

187 FORD   187:1-5
Northumberland   NT 965 370

ROUND BARROW: Diam. 4.8 m, H. 0.9 m; core of earth and
stones, capping of stones, circle of projecting stones
'set on edge' Diam. 3.6 m; opened 22 June 1858.
BB 408-9; *Greenwell* 1862.

Burial 1: child inhumation vestiges, head N.; in cist L.
0.9 m, W. 0.6 m, D. 0.5 m, four sandstone side-slabs with
capstone, clay-luted, aligned N.-S., on old surface at
centre; Food Vessel at head.
1 *Food Vessel*: Yorkshire Vase; incised: on internal rim
    bevel, herringbone; on external rim bevel, short
    diagonal lines; on neck and body, herringbone; on
    shoulder, grooved line.
    M. 10.7 cm; H. 10.1 cm; B. 4.9 cm.   79 12-9 1401
    Greenwell 1862, pl. 12.1; *BAP* no. 98; *Gibson* 1978,
    no. 50.

Burials 2-7 were around the central cist within the
stone circle.

Burial 2: adolescent cremation deposit; in inverted
clay-sealed Collared Urn; objects with bones.
2 *Collared Urn*: incised: on rim, short vertical to
    diagonal lines; on collar and neck, haphazardly
    executed herringbone giving way on one sector of
    collar to light vertical lines.

M. 21.5 cm; H. 26.6 cm; B. 9.4 cm.   79 12-9 1402
Greenwell 1862, pl. 12.2; *BAP* no. 119; *Gibson* 1978,
no. 113; *Longworth* no. 1052.

3 *Flint knife*: on blade; invasive retouch on L.; edge
   retouch on R.; punctiform butt; burnt.
   L. 5.2 cm; W. 1.6 cm; Th. 0.4 cm.   79 12-9 1404
   Greenwell 1862, pl. 12.3.

4 *Bone pin fragment*: on caprovine-size ulna fragment;
   cut and polished to fine point; burnt and broken.
   L. 3.9 cm; Diam. 0.5 cm.   79 12-9 1403

Burials 3-7: five cremation deposits; each in upright
urn, three with stone slab cover; knife in one.
   '*five cinerary urns*': not preserved.

5 *Flint knife*: edge-retouch on R.; burnt and broken.
   L. 2.7 cm; W. 1.4 cm; Th. 0.4 cm.   79 12-9 1405

Burial 8: cremation deposit; in urn at E. outside stone
circle.
   '*cinerary urn*'; not preserved.

188 FORD (Broomridge)   188:1-47

Northumberland   NT 965 371

ROUND BARROW: Diam. 4.8 m, H. 0.9 m; earth and stones;
opened 1 July 1858.
BB 410; *Greenwell* 1862; *Newbigin* 1935; *Kinnes* 1979, Abl.

Burial 1: multiple cremation deposit; in discontinuous
layer of burnt earth and charcoal Th. 5 cm on old
surface.

1 *Neolithic Bowl sherds*: one hundred and fifty;
   predominantly quartz temper.   79 12-9 1406
2 *Neolithic Bowl rim sherd*: fine quartz temper.
                                          79 12-9 1406a
3-5 *Neolithic Bowl rim sherds*: three, quartz temper.
                                          79 12-9 1406b-d
6-7 *Neolithic Bowl rim sherds*: two; fine quartz temper.
                                          79 12-9 1406e-f
8 *Neolithic Bowl rim sherd*: sand and quartz temper.
                                          79 12-9 1406g
9-12 *Neolithic Bowl rim sherds*: four; quartz temper.
                                          79 12-9 1406h-k
13 *Neolithic Bowl rim sherd*: sand and quartz temper.
                                          79 12-9 1406l
14 *Neolithic Bowl sherd*: carinated; fine quartz temper.
                                          79 12-9 1406m
15 *Neolithic Bowl sherd*: vertical rilling.
                                          79 12-9 1406n
16 *Neolithic Bowl sherds*: ten; porous fabric.
                                          79 12-9 1406o
17 *Neolithic Bowl sherds*: seventeen; sandy fabric.
                                          79 12-9 1406p
18 *Neolithic Bowl*: five joining sherds; sandy fabric.
   M. *c.* 16.0 cm.   79 12-9 1418a
   Newbigin 1935.
19 *Bronze Age base sherd*   79 12-9 1406q
20 *Fired clay*: two fragments.   79 12-9 1406r
21 *Flint polished axe fragment and core*: ground and
   polished with narrow side bevel; broken and re-used
   on one face as blade core with single platform; grey.
   L. 4.5 cm; W. 2.6 cm; Th. 1.7 cm.   79 12-9 1408
22 *Flint polished axe fragment*; grey, as no. 21.
   L. 2.7 cm; W. 1.7 cm; Th. 0.3 cm.   79 12-9 1414e
23 *Flint laurel-leaf point*: all over bifacial invasive
   retouch; cortex remnant; dark grey.
   L. 7.0 cm; W. 4.2 cm; Th. 1.0 cm.   79 12-9 1407
   BB fig. 157; *ASI* fig. 245; *Green* 1980, no. 47.
24 *Flint point*: bilateral edge retouch converging on
   proximal; patinated.
   L. 3.2 cm; W. 3.2 cm; Th. 0.9 cm.   79 12-9 1412

25 *Flint horseshoe scraper*: edge retouch on distal and
   partial bilateral at 55 degrees; cortex remnant;
   mottled grey.
   L. 3.6 cm; W. 3.5 cm; Th. 0.9 cm.   79 12-9 1413
26 *Flint end- and side-scraper*: very worn edge retouch
   on distal and R., wear on L.; platform butt; mottled
   grey.
   L. 6.2 cm; W. 3.8 cm; Th. 0.9 cm.   79 12-9 1409
27 *Flint end-scraper*; on core fragment; edge retouch on
   distal at 70 degrees; cortex remnant; mottled grey.
   L. 5.0 cm; W. 2.8 cm; Th. 1.8 cm.   79 12-9 1414
28 *Flint scraper fragment*: edge retouch on distal at 50
   degrees; cortex remnant; broken; mottled grey.
   L. 2.7 cm; W. 0.9 cm; Th. 0.6 cm.   79 12-9 1414k
29 *Flint worked fragment*: all over invasive retouch,
   some invasive retouch on inverse; cortex remnant;
   broken; mottled grey.
   L. 4.9 cm; W. 2.2 cm; Th. 1.4 cm.   79 12-9 1410
30 *Flint worked fragment*: all over invasive retouch,
   some invasive retouch on inverse; broken; mottled
   grey.
   L. 1.5 cm; W. 2.8 cm; Th. 0.8 cm.   79 12-9 1411
31 *Flint worked fragment*: edge retouch on R. on inverse;
   cortex remnant; broken; dark grey.
   L. 2.1 cm; W. 1.6 cm; Th. 0.5 cm.   79 12-9 1414a
32 *Flint utilised flake*: wear on R.; platform butt;
   cortex remnant; broken; mottled grey.
   L. 4.3 cm; W. 3.2 cm; Th. 1.0 cm.   79 12-9 1415

Flint flakes

	Btt	Ctx	Col.	L.	W.	Th.	79 12-9
33	Pl.		M. Gr.	3.1	2.1	0.2	1414b
34	Pl.		M. Gr.	3.6	1.5	0.8	1414f
35			M. Gr.	2.4	2.0	0.6	1414g
36	Pl.		M. Gr.	3.4	1.8	0.5	1414h
37	Pl.	x	M. Gr.	2.3	1.0	0.2	1414j
38			M. Gr.	1.6	1.9	0.3	1414m
39	Pl.		M. Gr.	2.1	1.4	0.9	1414o
40	Pl.		Pat.	2.6	2.2	0.7	1414p
41	Dh.	x	Bge	2.7	2.0	0.9	1414q
42	Pl.		M. Gr.	5.5	3.0	1.0	1416
43	Pl.		M. Gr.	4.2	1.6	0.9	1417

Flint blades

	Btt	Ctx	Col.	L.	W.	Th.	79 12-9
44	Pl.		D. Gr.	2.9	1.2	0.3	1414l
45	Pl.		M. Gr.	3.7	1.2	0.2	1414n
46	Pl.	x	M. Gr.	2.1	0.5	0.2	1414s

47 *Flint fragments*: five; mottled grey.
                    79 12-9 1414 c-d, i and r, 1418

189 DODDINGTON   189:1-4

Northumberland   NT 99 32

CIST: L. 1 m, W. 0.9 m, five side-slabs and single
capstone, aligned E.-W.; opened by Rev. William Proctor
21 June 1867.
BB 411.

Burial 1: adult ?male inhumation, crouched on R. with
head W.; remains of leather garment, vessel at head,
flints in cist.

1 *Food Vessel*: incised: on rim for three-quarters of
   circumference, single line; on body for three-
   quarters of circumference, zone of herringbone
   enclosed between three horizontal lines; on one of
   four vertical handles, vertical herringbone.
   M. 17.9 cm; H. 17.3 cm; B. *c.* 9.0 cm. 79 12-9 1420
   BB fig. 78; *BAP* no. 226; *Gibson* 1978, no. 61.

2 *Flint knife*: invasive retouch on R.; punctiform butt; cortex remnant; mottled grey.
   L. 7.1 cm; W. 2.9 cm; Th. 1.1 cm.   79 12-9 1421
3 *Flint flake*: snapped; beige.
   L. 2.7 cm; W. 2.5 cm; Th. 0.6 cm.   79 12-9 1422
4 *Leather or hide fragment*: scalloped edges of ?overstitched seams on longer sides; torn; species unknown.
   L. 3.1 cm; W. 3.0 cm.   79 12-9 2069

190 CHATTON

Northumberland   NU 02 28

ROUND BARROW: Diam. 4.5 m, H. 0.8 m; sandy earth; previously opened; opened 21-23 November 1863.
BB 412; *Greenwell* 1868a, 201.

Burial 1: ?decayed inhumation; in central cist L. 0.9 m, W. 0.8 m, D. 0.5 m, five side-slabs and two capstones, aligned NE.-SW., on old surface at centre, fill of fine white sand.

191 CHATTON

Northumberland   NU 02 28

ROUND BARROW: Diam. 4.8 m, H. 0.9 m; earth and stones, stone kerb; previously opened; opened 21-23 November 1863.
BB 412; *Greenwell* 1868a, 201.

Burial 1: disturbed cremation deposit, in and around central cist, aligned E.-W. (dimensions not recorded), five side-slabs and single capstone, on old surface at centre.

192 CHATTON   192:1

Northumberland   NU 02 28

ROUND BARROW: Diam. 2.4 m, H. 0.3 m; earth with some stones over; opened 21-23 November 1863.
BB 412; *Greenwell* 1868a, 201.

Burial 1: adult cremation deposit; in central cist 0.35 m square D. 0.25 m, four side-slabs with double capstone at level of old surface at centre, basal fill of sand and upper fill (with cremation) of earth and pebbles.
1 *Flint worked flake*: converging edge retouch; broken; burnt.
   L. 4.4 cm; W. 3.0 cm; Th. 0.6 cm.   79 12-9 1423

193 BAMBOROUGH (Lucker Moor)   193:1-4

Northumberland   NU 116 268

ROUND CAIRN: Diam. 19 m, H. 3 m; pitched stones with kerb remnant; opened by Major Luard-Selby 1862, re-opened by WG.
BB 413-14.

Burial 1: adult inhumation, crouched on L. with head E.; in central cist L. 1.2 m, W. 0.8 m, D. 0.7 m, four side-slabs with two paving slabs and single capstone; vessel behind shoulders.
   'beaker': not preserved [note that *Clarke* no. 658 (Maidstone Museum) is not this vessel. but from Cocklaw Dean, Northumberland].

Cairn material
1 *Stone quern fragment*: sandstone; one face ground smooth to concave surface; broken.
   L. 16.3 cm; W. 9.0 cm; Th. 5.2 cm.   79 12-9 1425

2 *Stone quern fragment*: sandstone; one face ground smooth to flat surface; broken.
   L. 29.3 cm; W. 16.2 cm; Th. 8.2 cm.   79 12-9 2004
3 *Stone quern fragment*: sandstone; one face ground smooth to uneven concave surface; broken.
   L. 35.5 cm; W. 17.5 cm; Th. 15.0 cm.   79 12-9 2003
4 'Quartzite pebble': not identified.   79 12-9 1424

194 BAMBOROUGH

Northumberland   NU 117 267

ROUND CAIRN: Diam. 19 m, H. 3 m; stones; opened 1862 by Major Luard-Selby, re-opened by W.G.
BB 414.

Burial 1: ?decayed inhumation; central rectangular grave L. 1.4 m, W. 1 m, D. 0.7 m, aligned E. by S.-W. by N., stone fill; in SE. corner hole, L. 0.5 m, W. 0.3 m, D. 0.5 m, clay and stone fill.

Cairn material
   'whetstone': not preserved.

195 BAMBOROUGH

Northumberland   NU 118 267

ROUND CAIRN: Diam. 16.5 m, H. 3 m; stones; opened 1863 by Dennis (farm tenant).
BB 414-5.

Burial 1: ?decayed inhumation; in central 'rudely-formed' cist.

196 BAMBOROUGH

Northumberland   NU 118 264

ROUND CAIRN: Diam. 18 m, H. 3 m; stones; opened 1863 by Dennis (farm tenant).
BB 415; *Dennis letter* 22 September 1863 (BM).

Burial 1: ?decayed inhumation, central cist L. 1.2 m, W. 0.8 m, D. 0.7 m, aligned SE.-NW., with capstone L. 2 m, W. 1.6 m, clay-luted.

197 BAMBOROUGH (Rosbrough I)   197:1-2

Northumberland   NU 118 258

ROUND CAIRN: Diam. 7.5 m, H. 0.9 m; stones.
BB 415-17.

Burial 1: double cremation deposit; adult ?female and adult; in inverted Food Vessel at centre on cover of cist (Burial 2).
1 *Food Vessel Urn*: on internal and external rim bevels, incised herringbone split by horizontal row of reed-end impressions; on applied knobs, diagonal incised lines; in neck, confused design of incised horizontal and vertical herringbone; on body, roughly executed incised filled triangle pattern.
   M. 31.8 cm; H. 38.0 cm; B. 10.3 cm.   79 12-9 1426
   BB fig. 60; *BAP* no. 120; *Gibson* 1978, no. 90; *Cowie* 1978, NOR 12.
   'flint knife': not preserved.

Burial 2: inhumation traces, crouched on R. with head E.; in central cist L. 1 m, W. 0.7 m, D. 0.6 m, aligned E.-W., four sandstone side-slabs and capstone L. 1.3 m, W. 1 m, Th. 0.2 m, flooring of gravel and fill of sand with charcoal; Beaker at face.

2 *Beaker*: tooth-comb stamped: beneath rim, seven horizontal lines above row of short diagonal lines; in neck and on upper body, zones of horizontal lines bordered above and below by short diagonal lines; on lower body, single horizontal line bordered above and below by short diagonal lines.
  M. 11.7 cm; H. 14.1 cm; B. 7.5 cm.   79 12-9 1427
  BB fig. 158; *BAP* no. 181; *Tait* 1965, no. 58; *Clarke* no. 659.

198 BAMBOROUGH (Rosbrough II)   198:1-7

Northumberland   NU 13 26

ROUND CAIRN: Diam. 5.5 m, H. 0.9 m; stones.
BB 417.

Burial 1: adult cremation deposit; in upright urn at centre on old surface with sandstone slab cover.
1 *Collared Urn*: twisted cord: on internal rim bevel, two lines; on collar, hurdle pattern between pairs of horizontal lines; on neck, two horizontal lines.
  M. *c.* 14.0 cm; H. 16.6 cm; B. 10.2 cm. 79 12-9 1428
  Gibson 1978, no. 123; *Longworth* no. 1036.
2 *Bone pin fragment*: on caprovine-size longbone fragment; polished to ovate section with fine point; burnt and broken.
  L. 6.6 cm; W. 0.9 cm; Th. 0.7 cm.   79 12-9 1430
3 *Bone pin fragment*: on longbone splinter; polished to ovate section with fine point; burnt and broken.
  L. 3.7 cm; W. 0.4 cm; Th. 0.2 cm.   79 12-9 1431
4 *Bone pin fragment*: on longbone splinter; polished; burnt and broken, point lacking.
  L. 4.0 cm; W. 0.7 cm; Th. 0.3 cm.   79 12-9 1432
5 *Bone pin fragment*: on longbone splinter; fine point; burnt and broken.
  L. 3.0 cm; Diam. 0.3 cm.   79 12-9 1433

Old surface: 0.6 m SSW. of centre.
6 '*Sherd*': not identified.   79 12-9 1429

Not located
7 *Stone quern fragment*: sandstone; one face ground smooth to flat surface; broken.
  L. 7.8 cm; W. 6.4 cm; Th. 5.1 cm.   79 12-9 1434

199 BAMBOROUGH

Northumberland   NU 13 26

ROUND CAIRN: Diam. 4 m, H. 0.8 m; stones; opened 1865.
BB 417.

Burial 1: ?decayed inhumation; in central oval hollow L. 0.7 m, W. 0.6 m, charcoal-lined.

200 EGLINGHAM (Blawearie)   200:1-3

Northumberland   NU 082 223

ROUND CAIRN: Diam. 11 m, reduced by stone-robbing; surviving layer of stones within slab kerb; previously opened; opened 30 May 1866.
BB 418-21; *Greenwell* 1868a, 203-4.

Burial 1: (previously discovered): ?decayed inhumation; in central cist.
  '*vessel of pottery*': not preserved.

Burial 2: ?decayed inhumation: in cist L. 1 m, W. 0.6 m, D. 0.6 m aligned SE.-NW., 2.8 m SW. of centre; four side slabs with capstone at level of old surface; basal sand fill with vessel on side in N. corner.

1 *Food Vessel*: incised: on internal rim bevel, herringbone; on external rim bevel, short diagonal lines; on neck and body, herringbone.
  M. 15.4 cm; H. 16.4 cm; B. 8.2 cm.   79 12-9 1435
  BAP no. 124; *Gibson* 1978, no. 1.

Burial 3: ?decayed inhumation, in disturbed cist L. 0.8 m, W. 0.7 m, D. 0.4 m, aligned SE.-NW., 0.9 m W. of Burial 2; three surviving side slabs; basal sand fill with necklace in N. corner and knife near centre.
2 *Jet necklace*: four barrel-shaped, four flattened barrel-shaped and ninety-two disc beads surviving; cut and polished.
  Barrels L. 1.9-2.4 cm; central Diam. 0.7-0.8 cm; terminal Diam. 0.5-0.6 cm.
  Flattened barrels L. 1.7-2.4 cm; W. 0.7-0.8 cm; Th. 0.5-0.6 cm.
  Discs Diam. 0.4-0.9 cm; Th. 0.1-0.2 cm.
  BB fig. 159.   79 12-9 1436
3 *Flint knife*: bilateral invasive retouch; platform butt; distal snapped; grey.
  L. 4.2 cm; W. 2.5 cm; Th. 0.7 cm.   79 12-9 1437

Burial 4: ?decayed inhumation; in cist L. 0.7 m, W. 0.4 m, D. 0.4 m, aligned NE.-SW., 3.8 m NW. of centre; four side slabs and capstone.

201 EGLINGHAM (Harehope Moor)   201:1-2

Northumberland   NU 09 21

ROUND CAIRN: Diam. 6 m, reduced by stone-robbing; kerb; opened 27 November 1863.
BB 421-2; *Greenwell* 1868a, 201-2.

Burial 1: ?decayed inhumation; in central cist, L. 1.4 m, W. 0.8 m, D. 0.8 m, aligned NE.-SW., four side-slabs, paving slab and capstone at level of old surface; knife at NE.
1 *Bronze Age sherd*: plain.   79 12-9 1438a
  Gibson 1978, no. 116.
2 *Flint knife*: invasive retouch bifacially on distal and bilateral; platform butt; speckled grey.
  L. 6.8 cm; W. 3.1 cm; Th. 1.0 cm.   79 12-9 1438
  Greenwell 1868a, pl. XIII.

202 ALWINTON (Harbottle Peels)   202:1-6

Northumberland   NT 94 05

ROUND CAIRN: removed by stone-robbers.
BB 422-5.

Burial 1: ?decayed inhumation; in cist L. 0.8 m, W. 0.7 m, D. 0.3 m, aligned NE.-SW., four side-slabs, paving slab and capstone at level of old surface; vessel in W. corner.
  '*food vessel*': not preserved.

Burial 2: ?decayed inhumation; in cist L. 1 m, W. 0.7 m, D. 0.5 m, aligned N.-S., four side-slabs, paving slab and capstone at level of old surface, 1.4 m N. of Burial 1; vessel in SW. corner, S. slab decorated.
1 *Food Vessel*: Yorkshire Vase; on internal and external rim bevels, neck, shoulder groove and upper half of body: incised herringbone; two surviving imperforate lugs of probably four.
  M. 16.2 cm; H. 12.8 cm; B. 7.2 cm.   79 12-9 1439
  Gibson 1978, no. 37.
2 *Stone decorated slab*: sandstone; pecked sub-ovate outline ('footmark') at centre.
  L. 56.0 cm; W. 39.0 cm; Th. 14.3 cm.   76 4-2 1

Burial 3: adult cremation deposit; in inverted urn in pit D. 0.5 m, N. of Burial 2.
  '*cinerary urn*': not preserved.

Burial 4: child cremation deposit, in heap Diam. 0.2 m; on old surface 0.9 m SE. of Burial 3.

Burial 5: ?decayed inhumation; on old surface 2 m NW. of Burial 2.

3 *Food Vessel*: Yorkshire Vase; incised lines and pin pricks or impressions: on internal rim bevel, alternate horizontal lines and rows of pricks; on external rim bevel, two rows of pricks; on neck and in shoulder groove, alternate horizontal lines and rows of pricks with one zone left blank in the neck; on three lugs, one to two rows of pricks, fourth lug abraded; on body, pendant triangles filled with lines, the upright triangles being outlined by pricks, separated from a reciprocal scheme by zone of alternate horizontal lines and pricks; on base, cross outlined by pricks; four imperforate lugs.
M. 14.2 cm; H. 12.8 cm; B. 6.0 cm.   79 12-9 1440
BB fig. 71; *BAP* no. 145; *Gibson* 1978, no. 43.

Burial 6: ?decayed inhumation; in cist L. 1.0 m, W. 0.4 m, D. 0.4 m, aligned ESE.-WNW., four side-slabs, paving slab and capstone at level of old surface, 3 m NNE. of Burial 2; vessel in N. corner.

4 *Food Vessel*: Yorkshire Vase; on internal rim bevel and over external surface, incised herringbone; three surviving imperforate lugs.
M. 10.8-12.0 cm, H. 12.9 cm, B. 5.8 cm.
BAP no. 146; *Gibson* 1978, no. 36.   79 12-9 1441

Burial 7: ?decayed inhumation; in cist L. 0.9 m, W. 0.6 m, D. 0.7 m, 5.4 m N. of Burial 6.

Burial 8: ?decayed inhumation; on old surface 2 m NW. of Burial 1.

5 *Food Vessel*: on external rim bevel, short diagonal incised lines; on neck and over shoulder, incised herringbone.
M. 15.8 cm.   79 12-9 1442
BAP no. 200; *Gibson* 1978, no. 6.

Burial 9: adult ?male cremation deposit; on old surface 2.7 m NW. by W. of burial 8.

Cairn material

6 *'Stone disc'*: not identified.   79 12-9 1443

203 ALWINTON

Northumberland   NT 93 05

ROUND CAIRN: Diam. 10 m H. 0.8 m, reduced by stone-robbing; pitched stones; kerb.
BB 425-6.

Burial 1: adult cremation deposit, in heap Diam 0.3 m; on old surface, 2.2 m E. of centre.

Burial 2: adult cremation deposit, in heap Diam 0.3 m; 0.2 m above old surface, 0.9 m SE. by S. of centre.

Burial 3: few burnt bones; on old surface, below Burial 2.

204 ALWINTON   204:1

Northumberland   NT 950 020

ROUND CAIRN: Diam 7.2 m, H. 1 m; stones with some earth.
BB 426-7.

Burial 1: adult cremation deposit; in pit Diam. 0.4 m, D. 0.3 m, 1.7 m SSE. of centre.

Burial 2: adult cremation deposit, in heap Diam. 0.25 m; 0.2 m above old surface, 1.2 m SSE. of centre.

Burial 3: ?decayed inhumation and few burnt bones; in central cist L. 0.6 m, W.. 0.4 m, D. 0.5 m, aligned SE.-NW., four side-slabs and capstone at level of old surface, fill of fine sand; vessel at E. corner.

1 *Food Vessel*: Yorkshire Vase; on internal rim bevel, row of pricks above incised herringbone; on external rim bevel, incised herringbone; in neck, incised herringbone above row of jabs extending over lugs; in shoulder groove for three-quarters of circumference, diagonal jabs; below shoulder groove, incised jabs with, in one segment, row of jabs above; on body, incised vertical split herringbone; three imperforate lugs surviving of original four.
M. 11.8 cm, H.. 10.6 cm, B. 6.6 cm.   79 12-9 1444
BAP no. 163; *Gibson* 1978, no. 45.

205 ALWINTON (Holystone Common II)   205:1-8

Northumberland   NT 961 004

ROUND CAIRN: Diam. 7.2 m, H. 0.5 m, reduced by stone-robbing; stones and some earth; opened 1870.
BB 427-8.

Burial 1: multiple cremation deposit: two adult ?females and child; in pit Diam. 0.4 m, D. 0.6 m, lined and covered by small slab, 2.4 m SE. of centre.
'four pieces of flint': ?nos 6-8 below.

1 *Bone perforated pin*: on split caprovine metatarsal; burnt, damaged and point lacking; cut hourglass perforation.
L. 7.4 cm; W. 2.2 cm; Th. 1.2 cm; perf. Diam. 0.3 cm.
79 12-9 1453

Burial 2: multiple cremation deposit: two or three adults, in heap Diam. 0.3 m; on old surface 2.4 m SSE. of centre.
'three pieces of flint': ?nos 6-8 below.

Burial 3: adolescent cremation deposit, in heap Diam 0.3 m; on old surface 1.2 m S. of centre; vessel, containing charcoal and smaller vessel, on side at SE.

2 *Collared Vessel*: on collar, plaited cord diagonal lines between single horizontal lines; on neck, twisted cord lattice between single horizontal plaited cord lines.
M. *c.* 10.5 cm; H. *c.* 16.0 cm; B. 7.5 cm.
79 12-9 1446
Gibson 1978, no. 124; *Longworth* no. 1035.

3 *Miniature Collared Vessel*: twisted cord: on rim, possible remains of transverse lines; on collar, diagonal lines; on upper body, short vertical to diagonal lines bordered beneath by single horizontal line; distorted by heat.
M. 6.4-7.4 cm; H. 8.4 cm; B. 5.4 cm.   79 12-9 1445
Longworth no. 1035a; *Gibson* 1978, no. 124a.
'two pieces of flint': ?nos 7-8 below.

4 *Bone pin fragments*: two; on caprovine-size ulna; burnt and broken.
L. 2.2 and 3.6 cm; W. 1.0 cm.   79 12-9 1451-52

Burial 4: adult cremation deposit; on old surface at centre, vessel on bones.

5 *Food Vessel*: plain; eroded.
M. 10.5 cm; H. 11.2 cm; B. 7.0 cm.   79 12-9 1447

Burials 1, 2 or 3

6 *Flint end-scraper*: edge retouch on proximal at 65 degrees; burnt.
L. 3.9 cm; W. 2.0 cm; Th. 0.6 cm.   79 12-9 1449

7 *Flint flake*; burnt.
L. 4.0 cm; W. 2.3 cm; Th. 1.0 cm.   79 12-9 1448

8 *Flint fragment*: burnt.
L. 2.8 cm; W. 1.9 cm; Th. 0.8 cm.   79 12-9 1450

Old surface, 1.5 m E. of centre
'small vessel of pottery': not preserved.

206 ROTHBURY

Northumberland   NU 04 05

ROUND CAIRN: Diam. 10 m, H. 0.9 m; stones.
BB 429.

Burial 1: adult inhumation traces; in central cist
L. 1 m, W. 0.7 m, D. 0.6 m, aligned N.-S., three side-
slabs (N. absent) and capstone 0.2 m below old surface.

Burial 2: adult cremation deposit, on level of old
surface in charcoal matrix above pit Diam. 0.3 m,
D. 0.4 m, fill of burnt earth.

207 ROTHBURY

Northumberland   NU 04 05

ROUND CAIRN: Diam 4.5 m, reduced by stone-robbing;
stones, within circle of eight stones.
BB 429-30.

Burial 1: adult cremation deposit; in central pit Diam.
0.5 m, D. 0.8 m.

208 ROTHBURY

Northumberland   NU 023 005

ROUND CAIRN: Diam. 10 m, H. 1.5 m; stones.
BB 430.

Burial 1: ?decayed inhumation; in central cist L. 1.1 m,
W. 0.5 m, D. 0.7 m, aligned N.-S., four side-slabs and
capstone, on old surface.

209 ROTHBURY

Northumberland   NT 023 005

ROUND CAIRN: Diam. 8 m, H. 1.2 m; stones.
BB 430.
Burial 1: ?decayed inhumation; in central cist L. 0.8 m,
W. 0.5 m, D. 0.5 m, aligned ENE. WSW., four side-slabs
and capstone, on old surface, fill of fine sand.
   '*two small pieces of pottery*': not preserved.

210 KIRK WHELPINGTON (The Fawns)   210:1-3

Northumberland   NZ 007 853

ROUND BARROW: Diam. 12 m, H. 0.9 m; stones and earth,
central disturbance.
BB 433.

Burial 1: adult cremation deposit; in pit Diam. 0.4 m,
D. 0.5 m, 3 m SSW. of centre.
   '*piece of calcined flint*': not preserved.

Burial 2: infant cremation deposit; in inverted vessel
on slab on old surface, 0.5 m W. of Burial 1.
1 *Food Vessel*: forty-six sherds representing half of
   vessel; in neck groove, short diagonal whipped cord
   lines.   79 12-9 1461
2 *Stone cup-marked slab*: sandstone; pecked cup-mark on
   one face.
      L. 25.4 cm; W. 22.4 cm; Th. 6.7 cm; cup Diam. 3.7 cm,
      D. 1.1 cm.   76 4-2 6

Burial 3: cremation deposit; in backfill of central
disturbance with sherds of urn.
3 '*Cinerary urn*': not identified.   79 12-9 1462

211 KIRK WHELPINGTON (Catcherside)   211:1-2

Northumberland   NY 992 877

ROUND CAIRN: Diam. 9 m, H. 0.5 m, reduced by stone-
robbing; stones and some earth, stone kerb remnant.
BB 433-4.
Burial 1: cremation deposit; in inverted urn in hollow
D. 0.3 m with slab cover, 2.7 m E. of centre.
1 *Food Vessel Urn*: on internal and external rim bevels,
   respectively three and one twisted cord lines; in
   neck and on upper body, rows of pits.
      M. 32.7 cm; H. 36.8 cm; B. *c.* 9.0 cm.   79 12-9 1463
      BAP no. 494; *Gibson* 1978, no. 86; *Cowie* 1978, NOR 4.

Burial 2: cremation deposit; in inverted urn over slab
on old surface with surround of three slabs, 1.5 m NE. of
centre.
2 '*Urn sherds*': not identified.   79 12-9 1464
   Longworth no. 1058; *Gibson* 1978, no. 93.

212 HARTBURN (Green Leighton)   212:1

Northumberland   NZ 09 86

ROUND BARROW: Diam. 6 m, H. 0.6 m; stones and earth;
previously disturbed at centre.
BB 434-5.

Burial 1: ?decayed inhumation; on old surface, 3 m E. by
S. of centre.
1 *Food Vessel Urn*: on internal and external rim bevels,
   in neck and shoulder grooves and over shoulder, rows
   of various jabbed impressions.
      M. 22.0 cm; H. 25.5 cm; B. 8.6 cm.   79 12-9 1465
      Gibson 1978, no. 94; *Cowie* 1978, NOR 10.

Burial 2: ?decayed inhumation; in previously opened
central hollow L. 0.9 m, W. 0.6 m D. 0.2 m.

213 CHOLLERTON

Northumberland   NY 95 72

ROUND BARROW: Diam. 12 m, H. 1 m; with stone capping;
opened 6 December 1847.
BB 436-7.

Burial 1: adult cremation deposit; on old surface
beneath slab, 3.6 m S. of centre.

Burial 2: adolescent cremation deposit; in upright urn
on old surface, 2.7 m SSE. of centre.
   '*cinerary urn*': not preserved.

Burial 3: adult inhumation traces, head NW.; in central
cist on old surface L. 1.1 m, W. 0.7 m, H. 0.7 m aligned
SE.-NW., seven upright slabs and two capstones.

Mound material
   '*flint flake*': not preserved.

214 OVINGHAM (Prudhoe)   214:1-3

Northumberland   NZ 099 655

ROUND BARROW: slight remnant, destroyed by ploughing.
BB 437-9.

Burial 1: ?decayed inhumation; in cist L. 1 m, W. 0.7 m,
D. 0.5 m aligned ENE.-WSW., six upright slabs and three
capstones.

Burial 2: adult cremation deposit; in inverted urn in
pit D. 1.2 m with upper stone packing, 2.7 m W. of Burial
1; knife among bones.

1 *Food Vessel Urn*: twisted cord: on internal rim bevel, hurdle pattern; on external rim bevel, diagonal lines; on neck, hurdle pattern; in shoulder groove and below shoulder, herringbone; on body, irregular triangles and vertical panels filled with horizontal and vertical herringbone and short diagonal lines.
M. 20.0-21.7 cm; H. 24.1 cm; B. 11.0 cm.
79 12-9 1466
BB fig. 57; *BAP* no. 485; *Gibson* 1978, no. 99; *Cowie* 1978, NOR 3A.

2 *Flint knife*: invasive retouch on L.; platform butt; cortex remnant; mottled grey.
L. 4.6 m; W. 5.2 cm; Th. 1.0 cm.   79 12-9 1468

Burial 3: adult cremation deposit; in inverted urn in pit with capstone, 3 m NW. of Burial 1.

3 *Food Vessel Urn*: on internal rim bevel, whipped cord herringbone; on external rim bevel, short diagonal whipped cord lines; in neck, applied chevron cordon with, in one place, applied vertical bar; on shoulder and upper body, incised herringbone in part breaking down into short vertical, horizontal or diagonal lines; on body, rough incised linear lattice.
M. 34.6 cm; H. 39.0 cm; B. 11.5 cm.   79 12-9 1467
BB fig. 59; *BAP* no. 497; *Gibson* 1978, no. 109; *Cowie* 1978, NOR 3B.

Burial 4: ?decayed inhumation; in cist L. 1.1 m, W. 0.8 m, D. 0.4 m aligned ESE.-WNW., six side-slabs and single capstone at D. 0.3 m, pebble paving, 4.2 m from Burial 1.

Burial 5: adolescent cremation deposit; on basal sand fill of cist aligned E.-W., six side-slabs and two capstones, floor at D. 1.2 m, 1.8 m SSW. of Burial 1.

Burial 6: adult cremation deposit; on pebble paving of cist L. 0.7 m, W. 0.4 m, D. 0.3 m, four side-slabs and single capstone, floor at D. 1.2 m.

215 SOUTH SHIELDS (Trow Rocks)   215:1

Durham; Tyne and Wear   NZ 36 66

ROUND BARROW: Diam. 9 m, H. 0.9 m; earth and some stones. *BB* 442.

Burial 1: adult ?male inhumation, crouched on R. with head SE.; in central cist L. 1.2 m, W. 0.6 m, D. 0.6 m, aligned SSE.-NNW., six upright slabs and two capstones at level of old surface; knife at face.

1 *Flint plano-convex knife*: bilateral invasive retouch; platform butt; cortex remnant; mottled grey.
L. 6.0 cm; W. 3.4 cm; Th. 1.0 cm.   79 12-9 1469

216 NETHER SWELL (Swell II)   216:1-8

Gloucestershire   SP 132 263

ROUND CAIRN: Diam. 13.5 m, H. 1.7 m; central inner cairn of pitched stones Diam. 1.9 m, H. 0.8 m, covered by earth layer Th. 0.2 m, capped by pitched slabs; opened *c.* 1874.
BB 446-7; *LBC* 91; *GB* 131.

Burials 1 and 2 were in a pit cut into the cairn, Diam. 0.8 m, D. 0.6 m, 1.7 m S. by W. of centre, fill of earth with some stones.

Burial 1: adult cremation deposit; in inverted urn on flat stone at D. 0.4 m; razor among bones.

1 *Bronze razor*: Butler and Smith Class 1B; trapezoidal tang with broken end; ovate blade with flattened midrib defined by one or two shallow bevels (Table 1:18).
L. 7.4 cm, W. 3.1 cm, Th. 0.3 cm.   79 12-9 1472
Butler and Smith 1956, 33, *Jockenhövel* 1980, no. 84.

2 *Biconical Urn*: on shoulder, row of vertical fingertip impressions.
M. 23.0 cm; H. *c.* 31.5 cm; B. *c.* 14.0 cm.
BAP no. 376a.   79 12-9 1470

Burial 2: adult cremation deposit; in crushed inverted urn on flat stone below Burial 1.

3 *Wessex Biconical Urn*: twisted cord: between rim and shoulder, four applied horseshoes, each enclosing lattice with areas between partly filled with triangles between lines; between shoulder cordon and body cordon, four applied horseshoes and one applied bar.
M. 38.0 cm; H. 47.0 cm; B. 19.0 cm.   79 12-9 1471
BAP no. 376.

Burial 3: adult male inhumation, crouched on L. with head NNE.; in central grave L. 1.2 m, W. 0.9 m, D. 0.6 m, aligned NNE.-SSW., with slab lining and paving, earth fill with charcoal.

Mound material (earth layer)

'*decorated rim-sherd*': not preserved.

4 '*Quartzite pebble*': not identified.   79 12-9 1475

5 *Flint end-scraper*: edge retouch on distal and partial L at 55 degrees; faceted butt; cortex remnant; patinated; broken.
L. 5.5 cm; W. 3.3 cm; Th. 1.0 cm.   79 12-9 1473

6 *Flint core-trimming flake*: struck from platform to remove hinge; dihedral butt; patinated.
L. 6.1 cm; W. 1.8 cm; Th. 1.5 cm.   79 12-9 1477

7 *Flint flake*: burnt.
L. 3.5 cm; W. 4.2 cm; Th. 0.9 cm.   79 12-9 1474

8 *Flint flake*: patinated.
L. 4.7 cm; W. 2.0 cm; Th. 0.7 cm.   79 12-9 1476

217 NETHER SWELL (Swell V)   217:1

Gloucestershire   SP 132 263

CHAMBERED ROUND CAIRN: Diam 11 m, H. 0.6 m, reduced by stone-robbing; pitched slabs, larger over smaller, much charcoal on old surface; opened *c.* 1874.
BB 447-52; *LBC* 91; *GB* 131.

Feature A: central drystone-walled chamber of heptagonal plan Diam. 1.7 m, with floor rock-cut to D. 0.8 m and partly slab-paved, walls corbelled at H. 1.1 m, some burning at N. side; passage at NW. L. 5.9 m, W. 0.8 m, sloping upward from chamber floor, N. drystone-walled and S. rock-cut.

'*two iron shoe fragments*': not preserved.
'*four iron nails*': not preserved.
'*clay pipe stem*': not preserved.
'*single piece of coarse pottery*': not preserved.

Unlocated

1 *Flint utilised flake*: wear on R.; punctiform butt; cortex remnant; grey.
L. 4.2 cm; W. 2.2 cm; Th. 0.5 cm.   79 12-9 1478

218 NETHER SWELL (Swell III)   218:1-2

Gloucestershire   SP 132 263

ROUND BARROW: Diam. 11m, H. 1.2 m; earth core Diam. 4 m, H. 1 m with stone capping; opened *c.* 1874.
BB 452; *LBC* 91; *GB* 132.

Burial 1: adult ?female cremation deposit; in setting of small slabs 3 m WNW. of centre and 0.1 m above old surface.

Burial 2: adolescent cremation deposit, ?burnt *in situ*; in central pit Diam. 0.3 m, D. 0.4 m in burnt area Diam. 2.4 m; pins among bones.

1 *Bone pin*: split caprovine metatarsal shaft; cut edges
   polished to converge on fine point; burnt and
   distorted.
   L. 7.9 cm; W. 1.2 cm; Th. 0.4 cm.   79 12-9 1479a
2 *Bone pin*: caprovine radius shaft splinter; cut and
   polished to fine point; butt lacking; burnt, broken
   and distorted.
   L. 7.7 cm; W. 1.3 cm; Th. 0.6 cm.   79 12-9 1479b

219 NETHER SWELL

Gloucestershire   SP 132 263

ROUND CAIRN: Diam. 10 m, H. 0.6 m; pitched stones; opened
c. 1874.
BB 452-3 *LBC* 91; *GB* 132.

Burial 1: adult cremation deposit; in central area Diam.
0.6 m on old surface.

220 NETHER SWELL   220:1

Gloucestershire   SP 132 264

ROUND CAIRN: Diam. 11 m, reduced by stone-robbing;
opened *c.* 1874.
BB 453; *LBC* 91; *GB* 132.

Burial 1: adult ?male cremation deposit; in central
hollow Diam. 0.6 m, D. 0.1 m in burnt area Diam. 1.8 m;
pin above bones.
1 *Bone pin or point*: split roe deer metatarsal shaft;
   cut and polished to fine point.
   L. 11.6 cm; W. 1.9 cm; Th. 0.9 cm.   79 12-9 1480

221 EBBERSTON (Howe Hill)

Yorkshire N.R.; North Yorkshire   SE 892 861

LONG BARROW: L. 50 m, W. 16 m, H. 2.7 m, aligned E.-W.;
oolite rubble with some clay and earth; ?internal kerb
located at NW., limestone slabs W. 2.4 m; opened 22-23
March 1864.
BB 484-7; *Greenwell* 1865, 102-5: *Times* 11 May 1866.

Burial 1: adult inhumation, ?crouched; 0.6 m below mound
surface, 6 m from E. and 4 m S. of axial line.

Burial 2: minimum fourteen fragmentary and disarticulated individuals, burnt *in situ*; in axial crematorium
structure L. 12 m, W. 1 m, H. 0.9 m from E. end, oolitic
rubble with earth and small stones around, burning
decreasing westward; W. terminal in cairn of pitched
stones Diam. 5.4 m.

222 WILLERBY (Willerby Wold)   222:1-7

Yorkshire N.R.; North Yorkshire   TA 029 761

LONG BARROW: L. 40 m, W. 15 m, H. 2.1 m, aligned E.-W.;
chalk rubble, flints and earth; opened 1865.
Re-excavated 1958-60 by Manby: mound filling trapezoid
enclosure L. 35 m, W. 8.2 m formed by narrow ditches with
concave post-facade at E.; earth and turf core capped by
chalk rubble from flanking ditches.
BB 487-90; *Times* 11 May 1866; *Manby* 1963.

Burial 1: adult inhumation, crouched on L. with head E.;
0.6 m below mound surface, on axial line 11.5 m from E.

Burial 2: multiple fragmentary and disarticulated
individuals, burnt *in situ*; in axial crematorium
structure L. 9 m, W. 1 m, H. 1.2 m from E. end, burnt
chalk and flint. Defined by Manby as embanked chamber L.
6.3 m, W. 1 m, banks of earth, chalk rubble and turf,

with terminal pit at centre of facade and internal pit
2.1 m from E.; subsequently infilled, facade burnt down,
then mound erected and crematorium fired to 1200 degrees
C; charcoal from facade dated at 3010 ± 150 bc (BM-189)
and from crematorium at 2950 ± 150 bc (BM-188).
1 *Neolithic Bowl sherds*: two, including rim; shell
   tempered.   79 12-9 1481-2
   'bone pin': not preserved.

Burial 3: disarticulated bones; 0.6 m above old surface,
below Burial 1.
   'sherd': not preserved.
2 *'Antler fragment'*: not identified.   79 12-9 1597

Mound material: (limited area at E).
3 *Neolithic Bowl rim sherd*: porous fabric.
                                               1963 5-3 1
4 *Neolithic Bowl rim sherd*: porous fabric.
                                               1963 5-3 2
5 *Neolithic Bowl rim sherd*: porous fabric.
                                               1963 5-3 11
6 *Neolithic Bowl sherds*: seven; porous fabric.
                                    1963 5-3, 3-4 and 6-10
7 *Neolithic Bowl sherd*: flint and shell temper.
                                               1963 5-3 5

(The remaining material recorded by Manby was not
available: Sewerby Hall Museum, Bridlington.)

223 WESTOW   223:1-2

Yorkshire E.R.; North Yorkshire   SE 759 652

LONG BARROW: L. 19 m, W. 11 m, aligned ESE.-WNW., with
addition at S. to create final mound L. 22.5 m, W. 12 m,
aligned SE.-NW., reduced by ploughing; earth and rubble,
with earth addition; opened *c.* 1865.
BB 491-7.

Burials 1-4 were beneath the added part of the mound.

Burial 1: child inhumation, crouched on R. with head W.
by N., with few adult bones; in oval cist L. 1.1 m, W.
0.9 m, H. 0.5 m, aligned ESE.-WNW., ten side-slabs with
two capstones and three paving slabs; on old surface 4.3
m SSW. of centre.

Burial 2: adult female inhumation, crouched on L. with
head WSW.; in oval cist L. 0.9 m, W. 0.6 m, H. 0.3 m,
aligned NE. by E.-SW. by W., eight side-slabs with three
capstones and small slab paving; 0.3 m above old surface
4.3 m SSE. of centre.

Burial 3: disturbed bones; above and to E. of Burial 2
cist.

Burial 4: adult female inhumation, crouched on R. with
head SW. by W.; in plough-damaged cist L. 0.8 m,
W. 0.7 m, H. 0.3 m, 0.9 m above old surface 5 m SE. of
centre.

Burial 5: two adult females, two adults and two
children, with some bones of one adult male, burnt *in
situ*; in axial crematorium structure L. 9 m, W. 1.4 m,
slab paving W. 0.6 m covered by burnt earth and capped by
pitched slabs; terminal pit L. 3.6 m, W. 1.4 m, D. 0.9 m,
beyond paving at ESE., burnt fill.
1 *'Plain sherd'*: not identified.   79 12-9 1483
   NPY pl. xiv.3.

Feature A: ?post facade trench: L-shaped with N. arm
L. 2.4 m, W. 0.8 m, D. 0.6 m adjacent to crematorium, E.
arm L. 3 m, W. 2 m, D. 0.6 m, fill of burnt earth and
stones.

Mound material
2 *'Plain sherd'*: not identified.   79 12-9 1484
   NPY pl. xiv. 4.

224   RUDSTON   224:1

Yorkshire E.R.; North Humberside   TA 076 678

LONG BARROW: L. 64 m, W. 22.5 m, H. 1.2 m, aligned ESE.-WNW., at ESE. meeting second mound L. 78 m, W. 13.5 m, H. 1 m, aligned SW.-NE. (since established as part of linear earthwork); both of earth and chalk, finds confined to first mound; opened December 1868.
BB 497-501; *Times* 19 December 1868; *YAJ* 43 (1971) 193.

Burial 1: multiple fragmentary and disarticulated individuals, burnt *in situ*; in axial crematorium structure L. 11.6 m, W. 1.8 m, H. 0.8 m from ESE., chalk rubble (final 2.6 m at WNW. unburnt); terminal pit beneath ESE. end L. 3.6 m, W. 1.8 m, D. 1.5 m, with burnt earth and chalk fill.

Burial 2: cremation deposit, in heap Diam. 0.3 m; 0.3 m above old surface c. 11 m from ESE. end.

Features A-E were recorded from a 'centre-point' 11 m from ESE., on axial line.

Feature A: oval pit L. 0.9 m, W. 0.6 m, D. 0.6 m; chalk, earth and charcoal fill; 6.3 m SW. of 'centre'.

Feature B: pit Diam. 0.8 m, D. 0.6 m; chalk, earth and charcoal fill; 0.3 m E. of Feature A.

Feature C: pit Diam. 0.8 m, D. 0.6 m; chalk, earth and charcoal fill; 6.3 m WSW. of 'centre'.

Feature D: oval pit L. 1.2 m, W. 0.8 m, D. 0.3 m, aligned NNE.-SSW.; burnt earth and charcoal fill; 2.7 m SE. of 'centre'.
1   *'Flint flake'*: not identified.   79 12-9 1486

Feature E: oval pit L. 1.2 m, W. 0.9 m, D. 0.5 m; fill of earth and chalk; 4.5 m NW. of 'centre'.

225   KILBURN   225:1

Yorkshire N.R.; North Yorkshire   SE 563 802

OVAL BARROW: L. 18 m, W. 13.5 m, H. 1.4 m, aligned N.-S., reduced by stone-robbing; oolite rubble and clayey sand; opened 1869.
BB 501-5.

Burial 1 (found previously): inhumation, crouched with head N.; in cist of four side-slabs with capstone and small slab paving, 0.8 m above old surface c. 4.2 m 'from the highest part of the mound'.

Burial 2: multiple fragmentary and disarticulated individuals, burnt *in situ*; in axial crematorium structure L. 6 m, W. 1 m from S., limestone rubble; overlying three pits: terminal at S. L. 1.8 m, W. 0.8 m, D. 0.8 m with extension to W. L. 1.1 m, W. 1.1 m, D. 0.8 m, at 3 m L. 1.1 m, W. 0.8 m, D. 0.6 m, at 3.6 m L. 1.1 m, W. 0.9 m, D. 1.4, all with fills of burnt earth and stones.
1   *'Plain sherds'*: two; not identified.
   NPY pl. xiv, 1-2.   79 12-9 1487, 1598

Feature A: ?mortuary house: two parallel drystone walls with external facing slabs w. 0.9 m, H. 1.4 m, aligned N.-S., 3.6 m square.

226   MARKET WEIGHTON   226:1-4

Yorkshire E.R.; North Humberside   SE 906 410

LONG BARROW: L. 34 m, W. 23 m, H. 0.6 m, aligned E.-W., reduced by ploughing; sandy earth with chalk rubble capping; opened 23-29 September 1866 by Professor Rolleston.
BB 505-9.

Burial 1: two adults and fragmentary and disarticulated bones of one adult male, three adult females, thirteen adults and five children, burnt *in situ*; in axial crematorium structure L. 20 m, W. 0.8-1.7 m, H. 0.6 m from E., chalk rubble with sand capping; overlying pits at E. L. 2 m, W. 2.9 m, D. 1.7 m, at 5 m L. 1.4 m, W. 0.8 m, D. 0.4 m, at 9 m L. 1.1 m, W. 0.5 m, D. 0.4 m, at 9.6 m L. 1 m, W. 0.6 m, D. 1.1 m, and at 17.5 m L. 0.8 m, W. 0.7 m, D. 0.3 m, all with fills of burnt earth, rubble and charcoal.

Burial 1 or mound material
1   *Neolithic Bowl sherds*: six, including rim; flint temper.   Ashm. 1936.26-27
2   *Neolithic Bowl sherds*: six, including two rim, two horizontal rows of ovate impressions on inside of rim; calcareous temper.   Ashm. 1936.26-27
3   *Neolithic Bowl sherds*: fifteen; grit-tempered.
                                              Ashm. 1936.26-27

Mound material
4   *'Bone pin'*: not identified.   79 12-9 1488

227   OVER SILTON (Kepwick Moor)   227:1

Yorkshire N.R.; North Yorkshire   SE 492 904

LONG BARROW: L. 31 m, W. 9 m, H. 1.2 m, aligned SE.-NW.; earth; opened 1868.
BB 509-10.

Burial 1: fragmentary and disarticulated bones of minimum two adults and three adolescents; along axial line for 17 m from SE., beneath 'some stones'.

Mound material
1   *'Flint flake'*: not identified.   79 12-9 1489

228   CROSBY GARRETT (Raiset Pike)

Westmorland; Cumbria   NY 684 072

LONG CAIRN: L. 54 m, W. 19 m, H. 3 m, aligned SE.-NW.; limestone and sandstone blocks; opened 1864.
BB 510-13; *Clare* 1979.

Burial 1: fragmentary and disarticulated bones of minimum three adult males and three adolescents; in axial crematorium structure L. 8.6 m, W. 1.05-2 m from SE., charcoal capped by limestone slabs; terminal pit at SE. L. 2.4 m, W. 0.9 m, D. 1.1 m, second pit at 4.7 m, L. 0.9 m, W. 0.7 m, D. 0.7 m, both with burnt earth and charcoal fills; terminal transverse standing stone at NW. H. 1.8 m.

Burial 2: few burnt bones; 2.1 m above old surface, W. of standing stone.

Burial 3: many disarticulated bones, mainly of children; at various levels from old surface upward in cairn to NW. of Feature A.

Feature A: standing stone L. 1.5 m, W. 0.9 m, H. 1 m, on axial line 32.5 m from SE.

229   NETHER SWELL (Swell I; Cow Common)
                                              229:1-15

Gloucestershire   SP 135 263

CHAMBERED LONG CAIRN: L. 45 m, W. 23 m, H. 1.5 m, aligned SSE.-NNW., reduced by stone-robbing; limestone slabs and rubble with drystone kerb and internal walling; cuspate forecourt at SSE.; opened 1867-8 by Rev. Royce, September 1874 by W.G. and Professor Rolleston.
BB 513-14; *Rolleston* 1876, 139-53; *LBC* 90, 92; *GB* 90.

Burial 1: disarticulated and fragmentary bones of two adults and one child; in ruined orthostatic chamber, L. 0.9 m, W. 0.9 m, with drystone-walled passage, at N. side 16.5 m from E. end.

Burial 2: bones, mainly disarticulated, of three adults and two children; in cairn, outside and to SW. of Burial 1.

Burial 3: disarticulated and fragmentary bones of two adults and one child; in oval drystone-walled ?chamber at base of forecourt and E. of axial line.

Mound material

1 *Pottery 'spoon' fragments*: two; butt and section of cylindrical handle; shell tempered; broken.
   L. 3.3 cm; D. 1.3 cm.   73 12-19 195
   L. 3.2 cm; D. 1.3 cm.   73 12-19 196
2 *Pottery 'spoon' fragment*: cylindrical handle recurved to ?bowl; shell tempered; broken.
   L. 10.0 cm; D. 1.1 cm.   Ashm. 1886.1487
   Leeds 1927, pl. XVI, 4.
3 *Pottery 'spoon' fragments*: two, butt and section of cylindrical handle; shell tempered; broken.
   L. 2.5 cm; D. 1.2 cm.
   L. 2.9 cm. D. 1.5 cm.   Ashm. 1886.1489
   Leeds 1927, pl. XVI. 6-7.
4 *Pottery 'spoon' fragments*: two; butt of handle of ovate section and base of handle with part of bowl; shell tempered; broken.
   L. 2.7 cm; W. 2.2 cm; Th. 1.7 cm.
   L. 3.6 cm; W. 1.4 cm; Th. 2.3 cm.   Ashm. 1886.1487
   Leeds 1927, pl. XVI. 2.3.
5 *Flint serrated flake*: partial serration on R. at 11 teeth per cm; platform butt; patinated.
   L. 4.5 cm; W. 1.8 cm; Th. 1.1 cm.   Ashm. 1886.1487

Not located

6 *Neolithic Bowl sherds*: fourteen, including six rim; oolite tempered.   Ashm. 1936.21
7 *Neolithic Bowl sherds*: six; flint temper.
                      Ashm. 1936.21

Flint flakes

Btt	Ctx	Col	L.	W.	Th.	Ashm.
8 Pl.		Pat.	2.8	2.1	0.5	1936.10
9 Pl.	x	Pat.	2.8	2.5	0.6	1936.10
10 Pl.		Pat.	2.3	1.4	0.4	1936.10
11 Bkn		Pat.	2.1	1.4	0.3	1936.10
12 Bkn		Bt	2.6	2.4	0.9	1936.10
13 Ct.	x	Pat.	4.3	2.2	0.7	1886.1487
14 Ct.	x	M. Gr.	5.8	2.3	1.1	1886.1487

15 *Flint core*: single platform with multi-directional flake scars; cortex remnant; mottled grey.
   L. 3.6 cm; W. 2.4 cm; Th. 2.0 cm.   Ashm. 1936.10

230 EYFORD (Swell VI; Upper Slaughter 1)
230:1-3

Gloucestershire   SP 143 258

CHAMBERED LONG CAIRN: L. 33 m, W. 13.5 m, H. 1 m, (L. 51 m, W. 15 m, H. 1.5 m: GB), aligned ENE.-WSW. (NE.-SW.:GB), **reduced** by ploughing and stone-robbing; oolitic slabs and rubble with drystone kerb; U-shaped forecourt at ENE.; opened September 1874 by Professor Rolleston, Rev. Royce and W.G.
BB 514-20; *Rolleston* 1876, 153-65; *LBC* 94-7; *GB* 93.

Burial 1: disarticulated bones of adult and child; in disturbed cairn material on axial line 5.4 m from E. end.

Burial 2: disarticulated bones of adult and child; on paving of ruined orthostatic chamber (C) L. *c.* 2.4 m,

W. *c.* 0.8 m, H. *c.* 0.7 m with drystone-walled passage W. 1.2 m, opening from N. side at 8.1 m from E. end.

Burial 3: child inhumation, crouched on R.; outside S. kerb, 13.8 m from E. end.

Burial 4: disarticulated bones of adult male and female and four children; on slab paving of ruined orthostatic chamber (D) L. 1.7 m, W. 1.2 m, aligned NNW.-SSE., on axial line 24 m from E. end.

Burial 5: disarticulated bones of five adult males, three adult females, two adults and one child, on and below slab paving of ruined bottle-shaped orthostatic chamger (E) L. 2.3 m, W. 0.9 m-1.4 m, H. 0.5 m, aligned NNW.-SSE. and ending 0.6 m from N. kerb, NE. of Burial 4.
1 *Jet or shale bead*: cut and polished to ovate with flattened oval section; drilled cylindrical perforation.
   L. 2.5 cm; W. 2.4 cm; th. 1.2 cm; perf. Diam. 0.6 cm.
   BB fig. 162.   79 12-9 1599

Burial 6: adolescent inhumation, crouched on R. with head E.; in orthostatic chamber L. 0.9 m, W. 0.9 m, H. 0.3 m, S. of Burial 4; vessel at knees.
2 *Neolithic Bowl*: one perforation with second uncompleted made after firing, adjacent to old crack; shell-tempered.
   M. *c.* 26.0 cm.   79 12-9 1910
   LBC 96.

Cairn material

3 *'Beaker sherds'*: not identified.   Ashm. 1936. 11
   Clarke no. 289; *Clifford* 1937, fig. 2.

231 UPPER SWELL (Swell VII; Pole's Wood South)
231:1-6

Gloucestershire   SP 167 264

CHAMBERED LONG CAIRN: L. 53 m, W. 17 m, H. 2.5 m, aligned E.-W. (L. 54 m, W. 21 m, H. 3 m:GB); oolitic slabs and rubble with drystone kerb, internal axial and transverse walls; cuspate forecourt at E.; opened October-November 1874 by Professor Rolleston and W.G.
BB 521-4; *Rolleston* 1876; *LBC* 125-8; *GB* 90.

Burial 1: disturbed bones of nine adults (in chamber) and bones of adult female and child beneath adult male, crouched on L. with head SW. by S. (at inner end of passage); in orthostatic and drystone-built chamber L. 2.1 m, W. 1.2 m, H. 1.1 m with paved orthostatic passage L. 2.1 m, W. 0.8 m to sill and jamb entrance, aligned N.-S., opening from N. kerb 7.2 m from W. end.

Burial 1 or mound material

1 *Neolithic Bowl rim sherd*: shell- and limestone-tempered.   79 12-9 1490
2 *Neolithic Bowl rim sherd*: shell-tempered.
                      79 12-9 1491
3 *Neolithic Bowl sherds*: two; shell-tempered.
                      79 12-9 1491a

Mound material

4 *Peterborough Ware bowl*: internally, comb-impressed herringbone; on inner edge of rim, vertical fingernail impressions; on outer rim bevel, comb-impressed diagonal lines; in neck, irregular diagonal slashes; on body, groups of diagonal comb-impressed lines.
   M. *c.* 10.5 cm; H. 10.5 cm; B. 5.4 cm. 79 12-9 1493
   BAP no. 16; *LBC* 128.
5 *Antler fragment*: red deer; beam and base of bez tine with incised groove around base of tine; broken.
   L. 11.2 cm, W. 6.2 cm.   79 12-9 1493a

Not located

6 *Quartz pebble fragment*   79 12-9 1492

232 UPPER SWELL (Pole's Wood East)   232:1-24

Gloucestershire   SP 172 265

CHAMBERED LONG CAIRN: L. 36 m, w. 12 m, H. 1.5 m, aligned NNE.-SSW., reduced by stone-robbing; oolitic slabs and rubble with drystone kerb; U-shaped forecourt at NNE.; opened 1875-6 by Professor Rolleston and Rev. Royce. *BB* 524-41; *LBC* 124-5; *GB* 91.

Burial 1: 'nearly-perfect' adult female inhumation, crouched on R. with head E., and disarticulated and fragmentary bones of minimum four adult males, five adult females, five adults and five children; in transverse chamber formed by rock-cut trench L. 8.5 m, W. 1.9 m, D. 0.6 m, aligned SE.-NW. with remains of narrow slab-walled passages at each end with access blocked by kerb walls, 18.3 m from N. end.
1 *Neolithic Bowl*: plain.
    M. 11.7 cm, H. 6.3 cm.   Corinium Museum
2 *Bone 'chisel'*: on bos-size longbone fragment; cut and one end polished to worn bevel; butt and one edge broken.
    L. 7.5 cm; W. 3.9 cm; Th. 1.4 cm.   Ashm. 1886.1483
3 *Bone 'chisel'*: on bos-size longbone fragment; cut and both ends polished to bevels; ends and one side damaged.
    L. 13.7 cm; W. 3.3 cm; Th. 1.0 cm.   Ashm. 1886.1483

Burial 1 or not located
4 *Flint horseshoe scraper*: edge retouch on L., R. and distal; burnt and broken.
    L. 3.3 cm; W. 0.4 cm; Th. 0.9 cm.   Ashm. 1886.1483
5 *Flint end-scraper*: edge retouch on distal at 80 degrees; platform butt; cortex remnant; mottled grey to patinated.
    L. 4.9 cm; W. 2.7 cm; Th. 0.7 cm.   Ashm. 1886.1484

Flint flakes (Ashm. 1886.1484)

	Btt	Ctx	Col.	L.	W.	Th.
6	Pl.	x	M. Gr./Pat.	6.8	2.8	0.8
7	Pl.		M. Gr./Pat.	4.8	4.9	0.7
8	Pl.	x	M. Gr./Pat.	5.6	5.2	1.1
9	Pl.	x	M. Gr./Pat.	6.0	4.8	0.8
10	Pl.	x	M. Gr./Pat.	4.4	3.2	0.7
11	Pl.	x	M. Gr./Pat	4.0	2.9	0.7
12	Pl.	x	M. Gr./Pat.	4.3	2.1	0.7
13	Pl.		M. Gr./Pat.	4.1	2.4	0.6
14	Pl.		M. Gr./Pat	3.7	2.7	0.5
15	Fc.	x	M. Gr./Pat	5.8	3.3	0.8
16	Ct.	x	M. Gr./Pat.	6.2	2.4	0.7
17	Ct.	x	M. Gr./Pat.	4.8	2.2	0.9
18	Bkn	x	M. Gr./Pat.	6.1	2.8	0.8
19	Bkn	x	M. Gr./Pat.	4.6	2.4	0.8
20	Bkn	x	M. Gr./Pat.	4.5	3.0	0.8
21	Bkn		M. Gr./Pat.	3.4	3.1	1.0
22		x	M. Gr./Pat.	4.9	2.3	1.1
23			M. Gr./Pat.	3.7	3.8	0.7

24 *Flint core*: single platform with multi-directional flake scars; cortex remnant; mottled grey to patinated.
    L. 4.9 cm; W. 3.1 cm; Th. 2.5 cm.   Ashm. 1886.1484

233 GILLING (Black Hill)   233:1-5

Yorkshire N.R.; North Yorkshire   SE 602 741

LONG BARROW: L. 43 m, W. 18 m, H. 2.4 m, aligned S.-N.; sand; internal stone kerb along each side, 12 m, apart at S. and 8 m, at N.; opened 1867.
BB 550-3.

Burial 1: ?decayed inhumation; in disturbed cist L. 1.2 m, in top of mound 18 m from S.
1 *Food Vessel*: Yorkshire Vase; twisted cord: on internal rim bevel, horizontal lines above short diagonal lines; on external rim bevel, short diagonal lines; in neck, hurdle pattern with vertical lines carried over shoulder lugs; in shoulder groove, horizontal lines; four perforated lugs spanning shoulder groove.
    M. 17.5 cm; H. 13.8 cm; B. 8.0 cm.   79 12-9 1494
    BAP no. 139.
2 *Flint plano-convex knife*: all over invasive retouch; punctiform butt; cortex remnant; grey.
    L. 7.5 cm; W. 2.0 cm; Th. 1.0 cm.   79 12-9 1495
    BB fig. 163; *Clarke* 1932, no. 2.14.
3 *Chert plano-convex knife*: invasive retouch on distal and bilateral; platform butt; mottled grey.
    L. 6.3 cm; W. 2.6 cm; Th. 0.8 cm.   79 12-9 1496
    BB fig. 164.
4 *Flint flake*: platform butt; cortex remnant; white.
    L. 5.2 cm; W. 3.4 cm; Th. 1.0 cm.   79 12-9 1497

Feature A: line of flat stones L. 3 m, above old surface 6 m from S. and 1.8 m within line of W. kerb.

Mound material
5 *'Flint flake'*: not identified.   79 12-9 1498

234 KILHAM (Rudston II))   234:1-11

Yorkshire E.R.; North Humberside   TA 056 673

LONG BARROW: L. 51 m, W. 18 m, H. 1.2 m, aligned NE. by E.-SW. by W., reduced by ploughing; chalk rubble and earth; opened 1868, excavated 1965-9 by T.G. Manby: basic sequence established as:
a) ?mortuary enclosure defined by parallel ditches 7 m apart, L. 36 m (N.) and 42 m (S.) W. 1-1.2 m, D. 1.1-1.3 m; embanked chamber; avenue of posts to E., excavated L. 22 m, W. 7 m.
b) Trapezoid mortuary enclosure defined by post-bedding trench L. 58 m, W. 8.5-10.7 m, causeways at NE. and centrally at W.; internal ?mortuary house with four corner postholes and two postholes and two pits inside, 6 m square; chamber in use.
c) Primary mound of chalk rubble infilling W. end of enclosure; first flanking quarry ditches L. 40 m, W. 7 m, D. 2 m.
d) Mortuary enclosure burnt, charcoal dated at 2880 ± 125bc (BM-293); chamber filled with chalk rubble.
e) Final mound infilling enclosure; quarry ditches extended by 21.5 m to E.
    BB 553-6; *Times* 19 December 1868; *Manby* 1976.
At least five of the burials seem to have been in the chamber (Feature A), but available information prevents certainty.

Burial 1: adult male inhumation, crouched on L. with head W.; 0.3 m above old surface, 17.5 m ENE. of centre and 3.6 m S. of axial line, on earth layer on chalk slabs over Burial 2.

Burial 2: adult ?male inhumation, crouched on R. with head WSW.; on old surface below Burial 1.

Burial 3: disturbed inhumation with some burnt bones; on old surface and in mound 16 m NE. by E. of centre on axial line; sherds nearby.
1 *Neolithic Bowl*: plain, shell-tempered.
    M. 28.5 cm.   79 12-9 1499
    Manby 1976, fig. 16.

Burial 4: cremation deposit; 0.2 m above old surface 0.5 m N. of Burial 3.

Burial 5: adult female inhumation, crouched on R. with head W.; 0.2 m above old surface 16 m E. by N. of centre and 4.8 m S. of axial line; scraper at face.
2 *'Flint scraper'*: not identified.   79 12-9 1503

Burial 6: disturbed adolescent inhumation, head E.; 0.1 m above old surface 10.5 m NE. by E. of centre on axial line.

Burial 7: disturbed adult female inhumation with bones of two children; 0.1 m above old surface, 9.5 m NE. by E. of centre and 0.3 m S. of axial line.

Burial 8: adult ?female inhumation, crouched on L. with head N. by W.; 0.3 m above old surface 4.8 m ENE. of centre and 1.5 m S. of axial line.

Burial 9: disturbed adult female inhumation; 1.8 m SW. of centre on axial line.
3 *Food Vessel sherds*: Yorkshire Vase; four, including rim: on internal and external rim bevels, three and two twisted cord lines; in neck, whipped cord or tooth-comb stamped herringbone; in and below shoulder groove, whipped cord impressions; one horizontally-perforated lug surviving.   79 12-9 1500

Burial 10: adolescent inhumation, crouched on R. with head W. by S.; above old surface, at W. end of mound; vessel at face.
4 *Food Vessel*: on ridges, vertical to diagonal impressions.
   M. 18.8-19.8 cm; H. 18.2 cm; B. 7.9 cm.
                                                    79 12-9 1501

Burial 11 (1966): adult female inhumation overlying adolescent inhumation, both crouched and facing N.; in hollow D. 0.07 m adjacent to W. end of N. ditch of first phase.

Feature A: chamber L. 13 m, W. 1.3 m, with flanking earthen banks W. 1.8 m H. 1.3 m; three transverse pits within and fourth externally at E., earth fills; within E. end of enclosure, S. of and oblique to main axis.

Mound material
5 *'Stone pebble fragment'*: not identified.
                                                    79 12-9 1508
6 *'Flint scraper'*: not identified.   79 12-9 1504
7 *'Flint knife'*: not identified.   79 12-9 1502
8-10 *'Flint flakes'*: three; not identified.
                                                    79 12-9 1505-7
11 *Antler fragment*: red-deer beam with bez tine; beam cut and broken from transverse incisions.
   L. 36.4 cm; W. 9.6 cm; Th. 3.0 cm.   79 12-9 1711
   (**The remaining material recorded by Manby was not available: Sewerby Hall Museum, Bridlington.**)

235   WILLERBY (Folkton VI)   235:1-9
Yorkshire E.R.; North Yorkshire   TA 01 76

ROUND BARROW: Diam. 14 m, H. 0.6 m; earth, flint and chalk; internal ditch Diam. 6 m, W. 0.3-0.5 m, D. 0.4-0.5 m, central burnt area on old surface Diam. 3.6 m; opened 23 October 1889.
RR 2-4; *WG Ms* 1.

Burials 1-2 were in a central grave Diam. 2 m, D. 1 m with burnt sides and fill of earth, clay and flints, cut into fill of Burial 3 grave.

Burial 1: adult inhumation, crouched on L. with head N.; at N. side 0.5 m above base; vessel and scraper no. 2 at face, scrapers nos 3 and 4 behind head.

1 *Beaker/Food Vessel*: twisted cord: internally, diagonal lines; externally, horizontal to diagonal lines.
   M. 11.0 cm; H. 10.8 cm; B. 7.3 cm.   93 12-28 1
   BAP no. 151; *Clarke* no. 1408.
2 *Flint horseshoe scraper*: invasive retouch on distal and bilateral at 50 degrees; corticated butt; mottled grey.
   L. 3.0 cm; W. 3.0 cm; Th. 1.1 cm.   93 12-28 2
3 *Flint scraper fragment*: edge retouch on distal and R. at 65 degrees; cortex remnant; broken; mottled grey.
   L. 3.0 cm; W. 2.2 cm; Th. 1.0 cm.   93 12-28 3
4 *Flint flake*: corticated butt; broken; mottled grey.
   L. 1.5 cm; W.. 1.9 cm; Th. 0.6 m   93 12-28 4

Burial 2: adult inhumation, crouched on L. with head NNE.; at base of grave; knife at face.
5 *Flint knife*: invasive retouch on L.; platform butt; cortex remnant; mottled grey.
   L. 6.0 cm; W. 3.5 cm; Th. 1.0 cm.   93 12-28 5

Burial 3: double inhumation: adult male crouched on L. with head ENE. and adult crouched on R. with head WSW.; at base of central grave Diam. 2.7 m (basal Diam. 1.2 m), D. 2.4 m, basal fill of earth with much charcoal, beneath large flints with some charcoal.

Mound material
Axes 6-9 were 'close together on their edges', 2.4 m E. of centre and 0.15 m above old surface.
6 *Bronze flat axe*: Schmidt and Burgess Type Scrabo Hill; well-expanded cutting edge with edge bevels, weak gently curved stop bevels, thin butt with slight arcuate outline; dished faces emphasising corners; surviving hammermarks on both faces; sides roughly double-faceted and partly rippled by hammermarks (Table 1:25).
   L. 16.6 cm; blade W. 11.6 cm; Th. 1.2 cm.   WG 1805
   Schmidt and Burgess 1981, no. 337.
7 *Bronze low-flanged axe*: Schmidt and Burgess Type Falkland; moderately expanded cutting edge with edge bevels, asymmetrically curved stop bevels with adjacent side swellings, damaged thin butt; slightly convex faces with triple-faceted sides; faces largely occupied by punched closely set rain-pattern ornament, on one face underlined by single weak arc-furrow above edge bevel; parts of flange crests lined with small indentations (Table 1:26).
   L. 18.6 cm; blade W. 9.9 cm; Th. 1.2 cm; flange H. 0.05 cm.   WG 1806
   Schmidt and Burgess 1981, no. 327.
8 *Bronze low-flanged axe*: Schmidt and Burgess Type Falkland; moderately expanded cutting edge with straight edge bevels, pronounced stop bevels, thin arched butt; slightly convex faces with rounded sides; punched rain-pattern ornament on both faces (Table 1:27).
   L. 14.8 cm; blade W. 6.9 cm; Th. 1.5 cm; flange H. 0.05 cm.   WG 1807
   Schmidt and Burgess 1981, no. 328.
9 *Bronze low-flanged axe*: Schmidt and Burgess Type Falkland; well-expanded cutting edge with curved edge bevels below broad furrow, pronounced stop bevels, low-arched butt with sharp profile; slightly convex faces with rounded sides; punched chevron bordered by double lines above blade furrow, below rain-pattern continuing on butt and divided by herringbone on stop bevel; blade damaged (Table 1:28).
   L. 14.8 cm; blade W. 8.1 cm; Th. 1.2 cm; flange H. 0.07 cm.   WG 1808
   RR fig. 1; *Schmidt and Burgess* 1981, no. 326.

236 WILLERBY (Folkton VII)   236:1
Yorkshire E.R.; North Yorkshire   TA 01 76

ROUND BARROW: Diam. 22 m, 'almost entirely removed'; opened October 1889.
RR 4–5; *WG Ms* 1.

Burial 1: adult male inhumation, crouched on R. with head NW.; in central wood-lined grave L. 1.8 m; W. 0.9 m; D. 0.5 m.

Old surface near centre
1 *Flint fragment*: thermal flake; cortical.
   L. 7.3 cm; W. 4.0 cm; Th. 1.7 cm.   93 12–28 6

237 FOLKTON (Sharp Howe I)   237:1-5
Yorkshire E.R.; North Yorkshire   TA 050 777

ROUND BARROW: Diam. 24 m, H. 2.4 m, crest lowered and disturbed; basal platform of chalk blocks faced by chalk slab wall Diam. 13 m, H. 0.5 m, with central mound of large chalk blocks Diam. 11 m, capped by layers of earth and chalk, chalk rubble and earth.
RR 5–6.

Burial 1: mandible fragment and clavicle; in disturbed central area.

Burial 2: adult ?female inhumation, crouched on R. with head W.; in central grave L. 2.3 m, W. 1.5 m, D. 1.5 m, aligned E.-W., with fill of large chalk slabs on edge; vessel at feet.
1 *Food Vessel*: deeply impressed whipped cord: on internal rim bevel, chevrons; in neck and shoulder groove, two and three horizontal lines respectively; on body, roughly executed lozenge/lattice.
   M. 21.0 cm; H. 20.0 cm; B. 9.0 cm.   89 2–2 1
   RR fig. 2; *BAP* no. 190; *Cowie* 1978, YOR 12.

Mound material
2 *Stone polished axe fragment*: greenstone; ground and polished; broken.
   L. 3.4 cm; W. 4.0 cm; Th. 0.5 cm.   89 2–2 2
3-5 '*Flint scrapers*': three; not identified.
                                                  89 2–2 3–5

238 FOLKTON (Sharpe Howes III)   238:1-8
Yorkshire E.R.; North Yorkshire   TA 049 778

ROUND BARROW: Diam. 13.4 m, H. 0.8 m, reduced by ploughing; inner mound Diam. 6.4 m of chalk, flints and earth with kerb of flint blocks, capped by earth with some chalk and flints; previously opened, opened by W.G., excavated by T.C.M. Brewster, 1967.
RR 6–7; *Exc AR* 1967, 12.

Burial 1: adult male inhumation, crouched on R. with head W.; 0.3 m above old surface, 3 m WSW. of centre; vessel behind head.
1 *Food Vessel*: twisted cord: on internal and external rim bevels, two rows of vertical impressions; at base of neck and neck ridge, one row; in shoulder groove, three rows; beneath shoulder, one row.
   M. 18.3-19.0 cm; H. 16.6 cm; B. 7.7 cm.   89 2–2 6

Burial 2: disturbed bones; in vicinity of Burial 1.

Burial 3: ?inhumation; in robbed central grave L. 2.5 m, W. 1.8 m, D. 1 m.

Burial 3 grave-fill (1967)
2 *Food Vessel sherd*: short vertical impressions. TCMB

Burial 4 (1967): disturbed inhumation; in mound NE. of centre.

Mound material (1967)
3 *Plain sherds*: four.   TCMB
4 *Stone rubber*: sandstone pebble; one face ground and hollowed by abrasion.
   L. 11.0 cm; W. 9.3 cm; Th. 3.8 cm.   TCMB
5 *Hammerstone*: sandstone pebble; both ends abraded.
   L. 5.4 cm; W. 4.0 cm; Th. 2.6 cm.   TCMB
6 *Flint awl or piercer*: bilateral edge retouch converging on distal; mottled grey.
   L. 3.2 cm; W. 1.8 cm; Th. 0.4 cm.   TCMB
7 *Flint worked flake*: partial invasive retouch on L., edge retouch on R.; cortex remnant; mottled grey.
   L. 4.2 cm; W. 4.0 cm; Th. 0.7 cm.   TCMB
8 *Flint flake*: mottled grey.
   L. 3.5 cm; W. 1.3 cm; Th. 0.6 cm.   TCMB

239 FOLKTON (Sharp III)   239:1-13
Yorkshire E.R.; North Yorkshire   TA 048 776

ROUND BARROW: Diam. 14.5 m, H. 0.5 m; earth and some chalk.
RR 7–8.

Burial 1: adult male inhumation, crouched on R. with head WSW.; at base of oval grave L. 2.3 m, W. 1.5 m, D. 1 m aligned ENE.-WSW., 3.2 m SSE. of centre, knife at face.
1 *Flint plano-convex knife*: all over invasive retouch on dorsal; platform butt; mottled grey.
   L. 5.5 cm; W. 2.3 cm; Th. 0.8 cm.   89 2–2 7
   Clark 1932, no. 5.5.

Burial 2: inhumation and cremation: adult crouched on R. with head SW., with cremation over hands and knees; at NW. of oval grave L. 1.9 m W. 1.5 m, D. 0.6 m, aligned ENE.-WSW., 3.7 m E. by S. of centre, fill of earth with some chalk; knife with cremation.
2 *Flint plano-convex knife*: invasive retouch on distal and bilateral; corticated butt; mottled beige.
   L. 5.9 cm; W. 3.6 cm; Th. 0.7 cm.   89 2–2 8

Burial 3: adult inhumation, crouched on R. with head WNW.; in oval grave L. 2 m, W. 1.5 m, D. 0.8 m, aligned ESE.-WNW., 2.4 m SW. of centre.

Burial 4: adult inhumation, crouched on R. with head WNW.; at base of oval grave L. 1.7 m, W. 1.2 m, D. 0.9 m, aligned ESE.-WNW., 2.7 m NNE. of centre, fill of chalk with some earth; vessel at face, other objects behind head.
3 *Food Vessel sherds*: seventy-eight; on internal and external rim bevels and at base of neck groove, vertical whipped cord lines; in shoulder groove, vertical twisted cord lines; below shoulder, twisted cord horseshoes.
   M. *c.* 15.5 cm.   89 2–2 9
4 *Jet fragment*: unworked; broken.
   L. 3.7 cm; W. 2.8 cm; Th. 0.9 cm.   89 2–2 10
5 *Flint end-scraper*: edge retouch on distal at 65 degrees; platform butt; patinated.
   L. 3.5 cm; W. 2.3 cm; Th. 0.9 cm.   89 2–2 11
6 *Flint end-scraper*: edge retouch on distal at 65 degrees; corticated butt; mottled grey.
   L. 2.5 cm; W. 2.5 cm; Th. 0.8 cm.   89 2–2 12
7 *Flint scraper fragment*: edge retouch at 65 degrees; broken ; patinated.
   L. 3.0 cm; W. 3.1 cm; Th. 0.6 cm   89 2–2 13

Mound material
8-12 '*Flint scrapers*': five; not identified.
                                                89 2–2 14–18
13 '*Flint flake*': not identified.   89 2–2 19

240 FOLKTON (Sharpe Howes II)   240:1-14

Yorkshire E.R.; North Yorkshire   TA 049 778

ROUND BARROW: Diam. 18.3 m, H. 0.9 m, reduced by ploughing; inner mound of earth with some chalk (grey clay with chalk revetment Diam. 3.6 m: Brewster) covered by earth and chalk with chalk block revetment (Diam. 13.2 m with SE. gap: Brewster), capped by earth; opened by W.G., excavated by T.C.M. Brewster, 1967.
RR 9; *Exc AR* 1967, 12-13.

Burial 1: adult inhumation, crouched on R. with head S.; on old surface 7.5 m E. of centre.
1   '*Food Vessel sherds*': not identified.   89 2-2 20

Feature A: central pit L. 2.4 m, W. 1.5 m, D. 1.2 m, aligned ESE.-WNW.; basal fill of earth, upper fill of chalk.

Features B-E: four oval quarry-pits around mound, average dimensions L. 10.5 m, W. 6 m, D.. 1.8 m; finds from bases.
2   *Antler pick*: shed red-deer antler; tines and beam broken.
    L. 29.0 cm; W. 4.9 cm; Th. 3.4 cm.   TCMB
3   *Antler pick*: shed red-deer antler; brow tine and beam broken.
    L. 15.8 cm; W. 4.0 cm; Th. 3.4 cm; tine L. 26.0 cm.
                                                  TCMB
4   *Antler pick fragment*: shed red-deer antler; crown and brow tine broken.
    Tine L. 25.4 cm; tine W.. 3.6 cm; tine th. 2.7 cm.
                                                  TCMB
5   *Antler fragments*: ?red deer.   TCMB

Mound material
6   *Plain sherds*: six.   TCMB
7   *Romano-British rim sherd*: Crambeck ware.   TCMB
8   *Perforated chalk block*: central cut hourglass perforation; edges unworked.
    L. 6.4 cm; W. 5.2 cm; Th. 2.1 cm; Perf. Diam. 0.8-1.1 cm.   TCMB
9   *Flint triangular arrowhead*: all over bifacial invasive retouch; mottled grey.
    L. 2.7 cm; W. 1.9 cm; Th. 0.5 cm.   TCMB
10 *Flint scraper*: partial edge retouch on distal and bilateral; mottled grey.
    L. 2.3 cm; W. 1.7 cm; Th. 0.4 cm.   TCMB
11 *Flint utilised blade*: wear on R.; mottled grey.
    L. 3.0 cm; W. 0.9 cm; Th. 0.4 cm.   TCMB
12 *Flint flake*: mottled grey.
    L. 4.1 cm; W. 3.4 cm; Th. 0.9 cm.   TCMB
13 *Flint core rejuvenation flake*: cortex remnant; mottled grey.
    L. 3.5 cm; W. 4.5 cm; Th. 1.0 cm.   TCMB
14 *Antler point*; cut and polished bifacially to lentoid section; eroded.
    L. 7.1 cm; W. 1.3 cm; Th. 0.7 cm.   TCMB

241 FOLKTON (Sharp V; Sharpe Howes 1)
                                                 241:1-63

Yorkshire E.R; North Yorkshire   TA 049 778

ROUND BARROW: Diam. 18.3 m, H. 1.5 m (Diam. 33 m, H. 1.4 m: Brewster); earth with some chalk (core of grey clay Diam. 12 m, H. 0.9 m with earth and chalk capping: Brewster) previously opened, excavated by T.C.M. Brewster, 1967.
RR 9-10; *Exc AR* 1967, 12-13.

Burial 1: disturbed burnt and unburnt bones; 0.6 m above old surface 6 m ESE. of centre.

Burial 2: adolescent cremation deposit; in hollow Diam. 0.4 m, D. 0.3 m, lined and covered by chalk slabs, 0.9 m above old surface, 5.4 m E. of centre; knife and pin among cremation, Food Vessel adjacent to hollow at N.
1   *Food Vessel*: Yorkshire Vase; on internal rim bevel, blurred impressions partly in herringbone; on neck, impressed herringbone above one to two rows of diagonal fingernail impressions; on upper margin of shoulder groove, vertical impressions; in and below shoulder groove, impressed herringbone; on body, two to three rows of impressions above rows of diagonal fingernail impressions; four imperforate lugs spanning shoulder groove.
    M. 14.5 cm; H. 10.3 cm; B. 7.4 cm.   89 2-2 21
    BAP no. 162.
2   *Flint knife*: bilateral invasive retouch converging on distal; platform butt; patinated.
    L. 4.8 cm; W. 2.9 cm; Th. 0.7 cm.   89 2-2 22
    Clark 1932, no. 2.8.
3   *Bone pin*: cut and polished from caprovine metapodial splinter; perforation at butt drilled from interior; broken and point lacking.
    L. 7.3 cm: W. 1.4 cm; Th. 0.4 cm; perf. Diam. 0.2 cm.
                                                 89 2-2 23

Burial 3: adult cremation deposit; in hollow Diam. 0.4 m, D. 0.3 m, covered by chalk slabs, 1.4 m above old surface, 2.2 m of centre.

Burial 4: disturbed inhumation; in previously opened central oval grave L. 2.2 m, W. 1.4 m, D. 0.6 m.

Feature A (1967): rectangular pit L. 2.1 m, W. 0.4 m, NW. of centre.

Mound material (1967)
4   *Grooved Ware sherds*: five; grooved herringbone.
                                                  TCMB
5   *Beaker sherd*: twisted cord horizontal lines. TCMB
6   *Plain sherds*: two.   TCMB
7   *Stone whetstone*: lozenge section; variable abrasion on all faces and one end.
    L. 9.5 cm; W. 2.5 cm; Th. 1.9 cm.   TCMB
8   *Stone rubber*: one face partially smoothed by abrasion.
    L. 9.3 cm; W. 7.5 cm; Th. 3.1 cm.   TCMB
9   *Stone rubber*: one face ground smooth by abrasion.
    L. 11.0 cm; W. 6.1 cm; Th. 8.4 cm.   TCMB
10 *Stone rubber*: one face ground smooth by abrasion.
    L.8.6 cm; W. 6.0 cm; Th. 5.6 cm.   TCMB
11 *Stone rubber*: one face ground smooth by abrasion.
    L. 13.0 cm; W. 8.6 cm; Th. 3.8 cm.   TCMB
12 *Hammerstone*: one edge abraded.
    L. 4.3 cm; W. 4.0 cm; Th. 2.1 cm.   TCMB
13 *Flint barbed-and-tanged arrowhead*: all over bifacial invasive retouch; one barb broken; mottled grey.
    L. 2.6 cm; W. 2.0 cm; Th. 0.4 cm.   TCMB
14 *Flint awl or piercer*: bilateral edge retouch on distal; proximal removed; cortex remnant; mottled grey.
    L. 4.2 cm; W. 2.1 cm; Th. 0.7 cm.   TCMB
15 *Flint end- and side-scraper*: edge retouch on distal and R.; broken; cortex remnant; mottled grey.
    L. 3.8 cm; W. 3.6 cm; Th. 1.1 cm.   TCMB
16 *Flint end- and side-scraper*: edge retouch on distal and L.; mottled grey.
    L. 3.5 cm; W. 2.4 cm; Th. 0.7 cm.   TCMB
17 *Flint end-scraper*: edge retouch on distal; cortex remnant; mottled grey.
    L. 2.2 cm; W. 2.0 cm; Th. 0.9 cm.   TCMB
18 *Flint end-scraper*: edge retouch on distal; mottled grey.
    L. 3.1 cm; W. 2.6 cm; Th. 0.7 cm.   TCMB

19 *Flint side-scraper*: edge retouch on R.; cortex remnant on L.; mottled grey.
L. 4.0 cm; W. 3.4 cm; Th. 1.1 cm.   TCMB

20 *Flint scraper*: partial edge retouch on distal and bilateral; cortex remnant; mottled grey.
L. 3.0 cm; W. 3.0 cm; Th. 1.0 cm.   TCMB

21 *Flint scraper*: partial edge retouch on distal and bilateral; cortex remnant; mottled grey.
L. 3.4 cm; W. 3.9 cm; Th. 1.2 cm.   TCMB

22 *Flint scraper*: partial edge retouch on distal and bilateral; mottled grey.
L. 4.5 cm; W. 3.6 cm; Th. 1.1 cm.   TCMB

23 *Flint scraper*: partial edge retouch on distal and bilateral; cortex remnant; mottled grey.
L. 2.5 cm; W. 2.5 cm; Th. 0.9 cm.   TCMB

24 *Flint scraper*: partial edge retouch on distal and R.; L. broken; mottled grey.
L. 2.5 cm; W. 2.5 cm; Th. 0.6 cm.   TCMB

25 *Flint knife*: edge retouch on distal and bilateral; mottled grey.
L. 4.0 cm; W. 1.6 cm; Th. 0.5 cm.   TCMB

26 *Flint knife fragment*: invasive retouch on distal and bilateral; snapped; mottled grey.
L. 2.6 cm; W. 2.7 cm; Th. 0.6 cm.   TCMB

27 *Flint worked flake*: partial edge retouch on R., flakes removed from proximal; mottled grey.
L. 3.2 cm; W. 2.7 cm; Th. 0.9 cm.   TCMB

Flint blades   TCMB

	Btt	Ctx	Col.	L.	W.	Th.
28			M. Gr.	3.6	1.2	0.5
29		x	M. Gr.	4.9	1.7	0.6

Flint flakes   TCMB

	Btt	Ctx	Col.	L.	W.	Th.
30	Pl.		M. Gr.	4.4	1.9	0.5
31	Pl.		M. Gr.	2.2	1.2	0.3
32	Pl.		M. Gr.	2.7	1.3	0.3
33	Hinge		M. Gr.	5.8	3.5	1.0
34			M. Gr.	3.0	1.7	0.6
35			M. Gr.	4.6	3.0	1.4
36			M. Gr.	2.9	2.1	0.8
37			M. Gr.	2.9	1.2	0.2
38	Hinge		M. Gr.	2.8	2.1	0.6
39	Sn.		M. Gr.	2.9	1.6	0.4
40			M. Gr.	3.9	2.0	0.5
41			M. Gr.	4.1	3.9	1.5
42			M. Gr.	3.9	2.4	0.7
43		x	M. Gr.	3.3	5.0	0.8
44		x	M. Gr.	3.2	3.7	0.9
45			M. Gr.	3.5	3.7	1.5
46			M. Gr.	4.3	2.3	0.7
47			M. Gr.	3.5	3.2	0.8
48			M. Gr.	3.8	2.0	0.6
49			M. Gr.	5.1	1.8	0.6
50			M. Gr.	3.7	3.0	0.8
51		x	M. Gr.	2.3	4.5	0.8
52			M. Gr.	3.1	2.5	0.5
53			M. Gr.	3.3	1.5	0.6
54			M. Gr.	2.4	2.6	0.4
55	Hinge		M. Gr.	4.2	2.7	0.4

56 *Flint core*: one platform with flake scars; cortex remnant; mottled grey.
L. 3.7 cm; W. 3.2 cm; Th. 2.3 cm.   TCMB

57 *Flint core*: two platforms at 90 degrees with flake scars; cortex remnant; mottled gey.
L. 3.2 cm; W. 4.3 cm; Th. 3.4 cm.   TCMB

58 *Flint core remnant*: flake scars; mottled grey.
L. 6.3 cm; W. 3.6 cm; Th. 1.9 cm.   TCMB

59 *Flint core remnant*: flake scars; cortex remnant; burnt.
L. 3.8 cm; W. 5.0 cm; Th. 1.5 cm.   TCMB

60 *Flint core remnant*: flake scars; mottled grey.
L. 5.2 cm; W. 4.2 cm; Th. 1.6 cm.   TCMB

61 *Flint core rejuvenation flake*: mottled grey.
L. 3.8 cm; W. 1.3 cm; Th. 0.7 cm.   TCMB

62 *Flint core rejuvenation flake*: mottled grey.
L. 6.4 cm; W. 1.5 cm; Th. 1.3 cm.   TCMB

63 *Flint core rejuvenation flake*: cortex remnant; mottled grey.
L. 4.3 cm; W. 4.8 cm; Th. 1.7 cm.   TCMB

242 FOLKTON (Sharp VI)   242:1-17

Yorkshire E.R.; North Yorkshire   TA 051 770

ROUND BARROW: Diam. 18 m, H. 0.9 m, reduced by ploughing; earth, chalk and flints.
RR 10–12.

Burial 1: child inhumation, crouched on L. with head ESE.; in oval grave L. 1.2 m, W. 0.9 m, D. 0.5 m, aligned ESE.–WNW., 3.9 m E. by S. of centre, fill of earth and chalk; Beaker at feet.

1 *Beaker*: rectangular tooth-comb stamped: all over reserved hexagon pattern with internal hexagons and pendant triangles filled with lattice, upright triangles filled with horizontal and diagonal lines; the scheme bordered above and below by single lines.
M. 14.7 cm; H. 18.6 cm; B. 8.4 cm.   89 2-2 24
RR fig. 3; *BAP* no. 108; *Clarke* no. 1280.

Burial 2: disturbed inhumation; in ploughsoil 3.9 m of centre.

2 *Food Vessel*: whipped cord: on internal rim bevel, four discontinuous horizontal lines; on top of rim and on external bevel, herringbone; on neck, irregular diagonal lines; on shoulder for part of circumference, blurred impressions.
M. c. 18.5 cm; H. 16.0 cm; B. 8.2 cm.   89 2-2 25
BAP no. 196.

Burial 3: adult male inhumation, crouched on R. with head WNW.; in grave L. 2.3 m, W. 0.8 m, D. 0.7 m, aligned ESE.–WNW., 3.9 m SE. of centre; 'the hind quarter of a pig' at knees.

Burial 4: double inhumation: adult crouched on R. with head WNW., facing infant; in hollow D. 0.2 m, 4.5 m N. of centre, fill of flint blocks.

Burial 5: adult inhumation, crouched on L. with head ESE.; in wood-lined hollow D. 0.3 m, aligned ESE.–WNW., 2.7 m NNW. of centre, covered by flint blocks; vessel behind head.

3 *'Food Vessel sherds'*: not identified.   89 2-2 26

Burial 6: adult inhumation, crouched on R. with head N. by W.; at centre on wood on old surface; flints nos 5, 6, 9 behind head, no. 7 beneath head, nos 4 and 8 at chest.

4 *Flint plano-convex knife*: incomplete all over invasive retouch; inverse invasive retouch on proximal; cortex remnant; dark grey.
L. 4.7 cm; W. 2.1 cm; Th. 0.9 cm.   89 2-2 31

5 *Flint horseshoe scraper*: edge retouch on distal and bilateral at 55 degrees; platform butt; cortex remnant; grey.
L. 3.7 cm; W. 3.5 cm; Th. 1.0 cm.   89 2-2 27

6 *Flint side-scraper fragment*: edge retouch on L. at 50 degrees; cortex remnant; grey; broken.
L. 2.6 cm; W. 3.4 cm; Th. 0.6 cm.   89 2-2 30

7 *Flint utilised flake*: bilateral wear; platform butt; cortex remnant; mottled grey.
L. 3.1 cm; W. 2.4 cm; Th. 0.6 cm.   89 2-2 29

8 *Flint flake*: platform butt; grey.
  L. 3.1 cm; W. 3.0 cm; Th. 0.6 cm.   89 2-2 28
9 *Flint flake*: platform butt; cortex remnant; mottled
  grey.
  L. 4.5 cm; W. 2.3 cm; Th. 0.7 cm.   89 2-2 32

Mound material

10 *'Quartzite hammerstone'*: not identified.   89 2-2 33
11-12 *'Flint knives'*: two; not identified.
                                              89 2-2 34-35
13 *'Flint scraper'*: not identified.   89 2-2 36
14-16 *'Flint flakes'*: three; not identified.
                                              89 2-2 37-39
17 *Flint core*: one platform with blade scar; second
   platform at right angles with flake scar; traces of
   previous platforms; mottled grey.
   L. 4.8 cm; W. 4.6 cm; Th. 2.8 cm.   89 2-2 40

243 FOLKTON (Sharp VII)   243:1-6

Yorkshire E.R.; North Yorkshire   TA 049 771

ROUND BARROW: Diam. 18 m, H. 0.5 m; composition not
recorded.
RR 12-13.

Burial 1: adult inhumation, crouched on L. with head
NE.; in central wood-lined hollow L. 1 m, W. 0.7 m,
aligned NE.-SW.; objects at face.

1 *Food Vessel*: Yorkshire Vase; on internal rim bevel,
  incised herringbone between single rows of impressions; on external rim bevel, triangular impressions
  ?made with corner of broken blade set alternately to
  produce raised chevrons; in neck, incised herringbone above rows of triangular impressions to give
  herringbone effect with similar impressions over
  lugs, shoulder groove and upper half of body; on
  lower body, incised herringbone bordered above by
  three and below by four incised lines; one perforated
  of ?two in neck and four of ?five imperforate lugs
  surviving on shoulder.
  M. 13.2 cm; H. 12.1 cm; B. 5.6 cm.   89 2-2 41
  RR fig. 4; *BAP* no. 152.
2 *Flint end- and side-scraper*: edge retouch on distal
  and L. at 50 degrees; corticated butt; dark grey.
  L. 3.4 cm; W. 3.2 cm; Th. 1.2 cm.   89 2-2 43
3 *Flint end-scraper*: edge retouch on proximal at 50
  degrees; cortex remnant; grey.
  L. 4.6 cm; W. 2.3 cm; Th. 1.0 cm.   89 2-2 44
4 *Flint plano-convex knife*: on blade; all over invasive
  retouch; punctiform butt; distal broken; beige.
  L. 7.0 cm; W. 1.8 cm; Th. 0.5 cm.   89 2-2 42
  Clark 1932, no. 2.9.

Mound material

5 *Flint side scraper*: edge retouch on R. at 35 degrees;
  invasive flaking on L.; platform butt; cortex
  remnant; mottled grey.
  L. 3.7 cm; W. 4.0 cm; Th. 1.0 cm.   89 2-2 45
6 *Flint blade*: patinated.
  L. 6.6 cm; W. 1.6 cm; Th. 0.5 cm.   89 2-2 46

244 FOLKTON (Folkton I)   244:1-8

Yorkshire E.R.; North Yorkshire   TA 050 736

ROUND BARROW: Diam. 15 m, H. 0.6 m, reduced by ploughing;
earth, flint and some chalk; opened 14 October 1889.
RR 13-14; *WG Ms* 1.

Burial 1: adult cremation deposit, in oval heap; on old
surface 3.6 m S. of centre.

Burial 2: infant cremation deposit; on old surface 1 m
SW. of centre.
1 *Accessory Cup*: plain.
  M. 6.7 cm; H. 6.4 cm; B. 4.2 cm.   93 12-28 7

Burial 3: adult cremation deposit; in urn in central pit
Diam. 0.3 m, D. 0.5 m; sandstone slab cover for urn, pit
filled with flint blocks and charcoal.
  'cinerary urn': not preserved.
2-5 *'Flint scrapers'*: four; not identified.
                                              93 12-28 11-14
6 *'Flint knife'*: not identified.   93 12-28 10
7-8 *Flint flakes*: two; not identified.   93 12-28 8-9

245 FOLKTON (Folkton II; 'Bording Dale')   245:1-128

Yorkshire E.R.; North Yorkshire   TA 059 778

ROUND BARROW: Diam. 16 m, H. 0.8 m, reduced by ploughing;
alternate layers of earth with chalk and flint and chalk
rubble over central cairn of chalk and flint; inner
ditch Diam. 7.2 m, W. 0.8 m, D. 0.5 m with earth fill;
outer ditch Diam. 12 m, W. 0.6 m, D. 0.9 m; previously
opened, opened October 1889.
?Site re-excavated by T.C.M. Brewster 1969: mound
destroyed; inner ditch not located; outer ditch Diam. 17
m.
RR 14-16; *WG Ms* 1; *Exc AR* 1969; *Manby* 1974, 122.

Burial 1: adolescent inhumation, crouched on R. with
head N.; in basal fill of oval grave L. 0.9 m, W. 0.5 m,
D. 0.4 m (L. 1.6 m *Ms* 1; L. 1.5 m, W. 0.9 m, D. 0.2 m:
1969), aligned N.-S., near inner edge of outer ditch E.
by S. of centre; drum 1 behind head, 2 and 3 and pin
behind hips.

Chalk drums: each with cylindrical body decorated with
four panels separated by vertical lines, plain convex
base and decorated top with raised roundel (Plate 4).
RR plates 1-2.

1 *Chalk drum*
  Top: on roundel, 'eyes' motif formed by two reserved
  circles surrounded by two concentric incised circles
  and then by concentric incised arcs; at base of
  roundel, single encircling incised line.
  Body: at top and at base, three and two incised
  encircling lines respectively; on surface, two broad
  and two narrow panels separated by triple vertical
  incised lines with inner enclosed moulding nicked
  from left or both sides.
    Panel A: incised triple cross; upper field: incised
    'eyes and eyebrow' motif; lower field: alternate
    rows of incised filled and reserved lozenges, with
    uppermost lozenge triple with central incision and
    lowest row double and filled with vertical incised
    lines, the intervening mouldings nicked from left;
    left field: reserved chevron with double incised
    triangle filled with repeated incised chevrons;
    right field: reserved chevron with double incised
    triangle occupied by traces of filled and reserved
    triangles (surface eroded).
    Panel B: double incised vertical bar chevron filled
    with vertical lines, with intervening mouldings
    nicked from left, with reserved bar chevron above
    and below; upper and basal triangles plain; top
    eroded.
    Panel C: opposed incised double to triple bar
    chevrons filled with vertical incised lines with
    intervening mouldings from left; upper field:
    plain; lower field: incised triangular, lozenge
    and sub-rectangular spaces filled with incised
    lattice; left field: incised triangle filled with

triangles alternately reserved and filled with vertical lines, with intervening mouldings nicked from left; right field: incised triangle filled with lozenges and triangles, reserved or filled with vertical lines, with intervening mouldings nicked from right.
Panel D: opposed quadruple chevrons with central moulding nicked from both sides; lower lateral and basal triangular spaces filled with incised lattice; upper lateral triangles filled; uppermost triangle plain, enclosed lozenge with filled hourglass pattern.
Max. Diam. 10.4 cm; H. 8.7 cm; Wt. 1214.7 g.
                                                93 12-28 17

2   *Chalk drum*
Top: on roundel, four triple circles; between circles and roundel, three spaced incised triangles; at edge and base of roundel, eroded traces of two incised circumferential lines.
Body: at top, three encircling incised lines; on surface, two broad and two narrow panels separated by triple vertical incised lines; ferruginous inclusions erupting in Panels A and B.
Panel A: opposed double incised triangles with central vertical double incised lozenge, with internal reserved lozenges surmounted by double opposed 'hook' motif; left triangle filled with reserved opposed bar chevrons with intervening spaces carved away; right triangle with irregular reserved triangular shapes with intervening spaces carved away; at base, one to two incised horizontal lines.
Panel B: two pairs of incised opposed reserved triangles enclosing central incised double lozenge; basal incised chevron ?lattice-filled; upper incised chevron subdivided vertically with right half carved away; lateral chevrons plain.
Panel C: opposed double incised bar chevrons; upper field: filled with groups of incised vertical lines, with intervening mouldings nicked from left; left field: reserved triangles in relief, with intervening spaces carved away, traces of vertical filling in lower border; right field: reserved lozenges and triangles, with hint of vertical filling in places, in similar technique; lower field: rectangles and triangles in relief, the former filled with vertical incised lines.
Panel D: split into three sub-panels by pairs of horizontal incised lines; upper panel: single incised chevron; middle panel: triple incised chevron; lower panel: double incised chevron.
Max. Diam. 12.5 cm; H. 10.7 cm; Wt. 2041.8 g.
                                                93 12-28 16

3   *Chalk drum*
Top: on roundel, five concentric incised circles at centre of four-rayed star pattern; fields between rays with incised triangles, three lattice-filled and one filled with vertical lines; at base of roundel, one incised circumferential line.
Body: at top and base, three and two encircling grooved lines respectively; on surface, two broad and two narrow panels separated by triple vertical incised lines.
Panel A: 'eyebrow, nose and eyes' motif in relief; below, central triple incised lozenge, flanked by triple incised triangles divided by single incised lines with left lower and right upper half lattice-filled; beneath, triple incised vertical chevron.
Panel C: opposed reserved bar chevron outlined by triple incised lines; centre: triple incised lozenge; left and right fields: quadruple tri-

angles divided by double incised lines, the upper halves filled with incised lattice; upper field: vertical bar chevron with incised double lozenge and triangles filled with incised lattice; lower field: eroded but ?similar with bar chevron inverted and one triangle filled with vertical lines.
Panels B and D: 'flag' pattern formed by triple incised opposed chevrons; each field divided with one half scraped and left plain, the other filled with incised lattice; in lateral triangles, divisions formed by double incised lines.
Max. Diam. 14.6 cm; H. 10.7 cm; Wt. 2978.5 g.
                                                93 12-28 15

4   *Bone pin*: cut and polished from longbone sliver to circular section with rounded butt; broken and point lacking; eroded.
L. 7.8 cm; Diam. 0.5 cm.   93 12-28 18

Burial 2: adult male inhumation, crouched on R. with head NE.; 3.3 m ESE. of centre, 0.3 m above old surface.

Burial 3: disturbed adult inhumation; in ploughsoil 2.7 m ESE. of centre, 0.6 m above old surface.

Burial 4: adult inhumation, crouched on L. with head W.; 2.9 m SE. of centre in hollow D. 0.2 m (L. 2.1 m, W. 0.6 m, D. 0.1 m: 1969).

Burial 5: adult male inhumation, crouched on R. with head WSW.; 4.2 m N. of centre, on old surface at edge of inner ditch.

Burial 6: child inhumation, crouched on L. with head S.; 4.2 m NW. by N. of centre, above old surface at edge of inner ditch.

Burial 7: disturbed bones of adult male and female; in disturbed central cairn.

5   *Beaker*: rectangular tooth-comb stamped: above neck cordon, two rows of opposed multiple chevron; below cordon, multiple chevron above five horizontal lines; on body, broad zone of multiple lozenges; on lower body, row of incised lozenges above three horizontal lines with multiple chevron beneath.
H. *c.* 20.5 cm; M. *c.* 15.0 cm; B. *c.* 8.0 cm.
RR fig. 5; *Clarke* no. 1281.   93 12-28 19

Burial 8 (1969): child inhumation crouched on R. with head W., and separate infant skull and post-cranial fragments; in grave L. 0.9 m, W. 0.7 m, D. 0.4 m, aligned E.-W., SW. of centre; Beakers at shoulder of adolescent and necklace *in situ*, toggle and flints in lower grave fill.

6   *Beaker*: twisted cord: all over horizontal lines.
H. 9.0 cm; M. 9.5 cm; B. 5.5 cm.   P1982 1-1 86
7   *Beaker*: twisted cord: all over horizontal lines.
H. 8.0 cm; M. 8.5 cm; B. 5.6 cm.   P1982 1-1 87
8   *Jet necklace*; 160 disc beads; cut and polished with drilled perforations.
Diam. 0.6-0.7 cm; Th. 0.1-0.5 cm.   P1982 1-1 88

Burial 8 grave fill
9   *Flint scraper fragment*: edge retouch at 80 degrees; broken; mottled grey.
L. 2.7 cm; W. 4.9 cm; Th. 1.2 cm.   P1982 1-1 89
10 *Flint flake*: burnt and broken.
L. 4.7 cm; W. 2.4 cm; Th. 1.1 cm.   P1982 1-1 90a
11 *Flint flake*; mottled grey.
L. 2.3 cm; W. 1.0 cm; Th. 0.3 cm.   P1982 1-1 90b
12 *Bone toggle or belt ring*: cut and polished from longbone segment; ring of oval section; tang of oval section with opposed cut notches at butt; broken.
L. 5.8 cm (restored); tang W. 1.4 cm; Th. 0.5 cm; ring Diam. (ext.) 2.9 cm, (int.) 1.8 cm.   P1982 1-1 91

Feature A: pit Diam. 1.5 m, D. 1.2 m (Diam. 0.8 m, D. 0.2 m: 1969), fill of earth with capping of flint blocks; 4.5 m SSE. of centre.

Feature B: (1969): hearth of burnt stones with burnt earth and charcoal near outer edge of outer ditch near Burial 1.

Feature C: (1969): pit L. 1.2 m, W. 1 m, aligned E.–W., fill of dark earth and charcoal with capping of flint blocks; 2.1 m SE. of Burial 1.

Feature D: (1969): pit L. 1 m, D. 0.4 m, aligned N.–S.; fill of earth.

Feature E: (1969): pit L. 1 m, D. 0.3 m, aligned N.–S.; fill of earth.

Feature F: (1969): pit or posthole Diam. 0.3 m, D. 0.3 m, fill of dark earth with flint packing capped by burnt stones.

13 *Neolithic Bowl sherds*: two, one with applied ovate lug; vesicular fabric.   P1982 1-1 92a-b

Flint blades

	Btt	Ctx	Col.	L.	W.	Th.	P1982 1-1
14		x	M. Gr.	4.6	1.5	0.4	93a
15			M. Gr.	4.7	1.6	0.7	93b
16			M. Gr.	3.5	0.8	0.3	93c

Flint flakes

	Btt	Ctx	Col.	L.	W.	Th.	P1983 1-1
17			M. Gr.	4.9	5.0	1.0	94a
18			M. Gr.	2.5	1.5	0.3	94b

Mound material

19 *Peterborough Ware rim sherd*: on internal edge of rim and externally: rows of impressions set diagonally.   P1982 1-1 95

20 *Peterborough Ware rim sherd*: plain.   P1982 1-1 96

21 *Peterborough Ware sherds*: three; plain.   P1982 1-1 97a-c

22 *?Peterborough Ware neck sherd*: ?fingernail impressions.   P1982 1-1 98

23 *?Peterborough Ware sherd*: incised line.   P1982 1-1 99

24 *?Peterborough Ware sherds*: two; plain.   P1982 1-1 100a-b

25 *Urn sherds*: four plain.   P1982 1-1 101a-d

26 *Bronze Age sherd*: plain.   P1982 1-1 102

27 *Plain rim sherd*.   P1982 1-1 103

28 *Plain sherds*: four, including rim.   P1982 1-1 104

29 *Plain sherd*: ?remains of strap handle.   P1982 1-1 105

30 *Plain sherds*: five.   P1982 1-1 106a-e

31 *Flint horseshoe scraper*: edge retouch on bilateral and distal at 80 degrees; platform butt; cortex remnant; mottled grey.
   L. 3.2 cm; W. 3.5 cm; Th. 0.9 cm.   P1982 1-1 107

32 *Flint horseshoe scraper*: edge retouch on bilateral and distal at 80 degrees; corticated butt; mottled grey.
   L. 2.7 cm; W. 2.5 cm; Th. 0.7 cm.   P1982 1-1 108

33 *Flint horseshoe scraper*: edge retouch on bilateral and distal at 70 degrees; corticated butt; mottled grey.
   L. 2.2 cm; W. 3.2 cm; Th. 0.9 cm.   P1982 1-1 109

34 *Flint scraper*: on thermal flake; irregular edge retouch; patinated.
   L. 2.5 cm; W. 2.2 cm; Th. 0.6 cm.   P1982 1-1 110

35 *Flint scraper fragment*: edge retouch at 80 degrees; broken; patinated.
   L. 2.6 cm; W. 2.9 cm; Th. 0.9 cm.   P1982 1-1 111

36 *Flint scraper fragment*: edge retouch at 60 degrees; cortex remnant; broken; mottled grey.
   L. 3.1 cm; W. 2.4 cm; Th. 0.3 cm.   P1982 1-1 112

37 *Flint plano-convex knife*: all over invasive retouch on dorsal; broken; mottled grey.
   L. 4.7 cm; W. 2.3 cm; Th. 0.6 cm.   P1982 1-1 113

38 *Flint knife*: bilateral edge retouch converging on distal; mottled grey.
   L. 4.6 cm; W. 2.4 cm; Th. 0.6 cm.   P1982 1-1 114

39 *Flint biface*: irregular bifacial invasive retouch; cortex remnant; mottled grey.
   L. 5.6 cm; W. 4.2 cm; Th. 1.1 cm.   P1982 1-1 115

40 *Flint notched flake*: semi-circular notch on L.; bilateral wear; mottled grey.
   L. 4.0 cm; W. 1.8 cm; Th. 0.5 cm.   P1982 1-1 116

41 *Flint serrated blade*: bilateral serration at 11 teeth per cm; mottled grey.
   L. 3.8 cm; W. 1.2 cm; Th. 0.2 cm.   P1982 1-1 117

42 *Flint worked flake*: edge retouch on L. at 60 degrees; wear on R.; corticated butt; broken; mottled grey.
   L. 2.4 cm; W. 1.7 cm; Th. 0.6 cm.   P1982 1-1 118

43 *Flint worked flake*: irregular bilateral edge retouch; broken; mottled grey.
   L. 3.8 cm; W. 2.6 cm; Th. 0.8 cm.   P1982 1-1 119

44 *Flint worked flake*: edge retouch on R.; corticated butt; broken; mottled grey.
   L. 3.7 cm; W. 1.6 cm; Th. 0.5 cm.   P1982 1-1 120

Flint utilised blades

	Wr	Btt	Ctx	Col.	L.	W.	Th.	P1982 1-1
45	L.	Pl.	x	M. Gr.	5.9	2.4	0.7	121a
46	R	Sn.	x	M. Gr.	3.5	2.0	0.7	121b
47	R	Ct.	x	M. Gr.	5.8	1.3	0.6	121c
48	LR	Sn.	x	M. Gr.	3.8	1.5	0.6	121d
49	R	Sn.	x	M. Gr.	7.0	2.0	1.5	121e
50	LR	Sn.	x	M. Gr.	3.4	1.4	0.6	121f
51	LR	Pl.		M. Gr.	2.5	1.5	0.5	121g
52	R		x	M. Gr.	5.3	1.8	0.5	121h
53	R	Sn.		M. Gr.	6.2	1.5	0.7	121i
54	R	Pl.		M. Gr.	3.7	1.4	0.3	121j

55 *Flint utilised flake*: wear on R.; cortex remnant; broken; mottled grey.
   L. 4.6 cm; W. 2.8 cm; Th. 1.0 cm.   P1982 1-1 122

Flint blades

	Btt	Ctx	Col.	L.	W.	Th.	P1982 1-1
56		x	M. Gr.	3.6	1.4	0.3	123a
57		x	M. Gr.	4.2	1.4	0.3	123b
58	Pl.		M. Gr.	4.0	1.6	0.7	123c
59	Pl.	x	M. Gr.	6.5	1.7	1.4	123d
60	Sn.	x	M. Gr.	4.5	1.6	1.0	123e
61	Pl.	x	M. Gr.	3.6	1.8	0.5	123f
62	Pl.		M. Gr.	4.2	1.5	0.6	123g
63		x	M. Gr.	4.2	1.6	0.6	123h
64		x	M. Gr.	3.1	1.2	0.4	123i
65		x	M. Gr.	3.1	0.8	0.3	123j
66	Pl.		M. Gr.	4.4	1.7	0.5	123k
67			M. Gr.	2.9	1.0	0.3	123l
68			M. Gr.	4.0	1.4	0.7	123m

Flint flakes

	Btt	Ctx	Col.	L.	W.	Th.	P1982 1-1
69		x	M. Gr.	3.9	2.7	0.8	124a
70	Sn.	x	M. Gr.	3.2	2.3	0.3	124b
71			M. Gr.	3.9	1.6	1.1	124c
72			M. Gr.	2.1	2.5	0.3	124d
73	Bkn	x	M. Gr.	3.4	3.1	1.2	124e
74	Pl.		M. Gr.	3.6	3.2	0.6	124f
75	Ct.	x	M. Gr.	3.6	2.9	0.8	124g

	Btt	Ctx	Col.	L.	W.	Th.	P1982 1-1
76	Pl.	x	M. Gr.	4.3	1.8	0.7	124h
77		x	M. Gr.	4.5	2.1	0.5	124i
78		x	M. Gr.	3.0	2.4	0.9	124j
79			M. Gr.	2.8	1.7	0.3	124k
80	Sn.	x	M. Gr.	3.7	2.1	0.8	124l
81	Ct.	x	M. Gr.	4.8	2.2	1.0	124m
82	Pl.	x	M. Gr.	3.0	1.6	0.8	124n
83		x	M. Gr.	3.7	3.0	0.8	124o
84	Bkn	x	M. Gr.	3.2	2.7	0.7	124p
85		x	M. Gr.	3.2	2.5	0.3	124q
86	Bkn	x	M. Gr.	2.0	2.4	0.5	124r
87	Bkn	x	M. Gr.	1.5	2.2	0.3	124s
88			M. Gr.	1.9	1.9	0.3	124t
89	Pl.	x	M. Gr.	2.9	1.5	0.3	124u
90	Pl.	x	M. Gr.	3.1	2.5	0.5	124v
91	Pl.		M. Gr.	2.7	1.5	0.5	124w
92	Ct.	x	M. Gr.	3.5	1.6	0.5	124x
93		x	M. Gr.	2.0	2.7	0.8	124y
94			M. Gr.	2.6	1.4	0.2	124z
95			M. Gr.	3.5	1.8	0.4	124aa
96			M. Gr.	2.1	2.1	0.2	124ab
97			M. Gr.	1.4	1.1	0.2	124ac
98			M. Gr.	2.9	2.8	0.8	124ad
99	Ct.	x	M. Gr.	3.0	3.4	0.5	124ae
100	Pl.		M. Gr.	3.4	2.4	0.5	124af
101	Pl.	x	M. Gr.	4.4	2.4	0.7	124ag
102	Ct.	x	M. Gr.	1.7	2.1	0.5	124ah
103	Pl.	x	M. Gr.	3.1	2.2	0.8	124ai
104		x	M. Gr.	3.0	2.2	0.5	124aj
105			M. Gr.	1.7	1.6	0.4	124ak
106		x	M. Gr.	2.4	1.2	0.4	124al
107		x	M. Gr.	2.9	3.0	0.8	124am
108	Pl.		M. Gr.	4.0	3.8	1.3	124an
109	Pl.		M. Gr.	2.2	2.3	0.4	124ao
110	Pl.		M. Gr.	2.5	2.3	0.4	124ap
111	Pl.		M. Gr.	2.7	2.7	0.4	124aq
112		x	M. Gr.	4.6	2.8	1.3	124ar
113			M. Gr.	2.0	2.2	0.3	124as
114			M. Gr.	2.2	1.0	0.2	124at
115	Pl.		Pat.	4.2	1.9	0.7	124au

Flint cores

	Pl.	Sc.	Ctx	Col.	L.	W.	Th.	P1982 1-1
116	Single	Fl.	x	M. Gr.	4.0	3.3	2.8	125a
117	Single	Fl.	x	M. Gr.	3.7	3.4	1.7	125b
118	Single	Fl.		M. Gr.	4.3	3.6	3.0	125c
119	Double	Fl.	x	M. Gr.	2.7	3.0	2.2	125d
120	Double	Fl.	x	M. Gr.	3.5	3.4	2.6	125e
121	Double	Bl.		M. Gr.	3.2	2.4	2.5	125f
122	Single	Bl.	x	M. Gr.	2.7	3.1	2.1	125g

Core rejuvenation flakes

	Btt	Sc.	Ctx	Col.	L.	W.	Th.	P1982 1-1
123	Ct.	Fl.	x	M. Gr.	4.4	5.1	1.5	126a
124	Ct.	Fl.	x	M. Gr.	3.1	3.4	1.0	126b
125		Fl.	x	M. Gr.	3.3	3.4	1.4	126c
126		Fl.	x	M. Gr.	3.1	2.3	1.4	126d
127	Pl.	Bl.		M. Gr.	2.9	2.4	0.9	126e

128 *Stone cupped pebble*: sandstone; two opposed pecked cups; broken.
L. 3.3 cm; W. 3.9 cm; Th. 2.9 cm.
Cup Diam. 2.0-2.1 cm; D. 0.6-0.8 cm. P1982 1-1 127

246 FOLKTON (Folkton III)   246:1-2

Yorkshire E.R.; North Yorkshire   TA 055 777

ROUND BARROW: Diam. 15 m, H. 0.6 m; earth and flint; opened October 1889.
RR 16; *WG Ms* 1.

Mound material

1 '*Lignite fragment*': not identified.   93 12-28 20
2 '*Flint scraper*': not identified.   93 12-28 21
  '*two flint scrapers*': not preserved.
  '*many flint chippings*': not preserved.

247 FOLKTON (Flotmanby)   247:1-11

Yorkshire E.R.; North Yorkshire   TA 065 785

ROUND BARROW: Diam. 21 m, H. 1.2 m; earth with some flint; previously opened at centre.
RR 16-17.

Burial 1: ?inhumation; secondary hollow 3.3 m from centre and 0.8 m above old surface.

1 *Collared Vessel*: twisted cord: on top of rim and internal surface, single lines; on collar, confused pattern of lozenges filled, as with lower triangular spaces, with diagonal lines, between single lines; on neck, confused lattice and filled triangle pattern between single lines, with line beneath shoulder.
M. 17.0-18.0 cm; H. 23.8 cm; B. 9.0 cm.   89 2-2 47
Longworth no. 1140.

Mound material

2 *Peterborough Ware rim sherd*: on top of rim, ?twisted cord diagonal lines; externally, rows of twisted cord diagonal lines.   89 2-2 57
Manby 1956, fig. 4.2.
3 *Hammerstone*: quartzite; limited abrasion at each end.
L. 11.4 cm; W. 9.5 cm; Th. 7.5 cm.   89 2-2 48
4 *Hammerstone*: quartzite; abrasion at each end.
L. 7.8 cm; W. 7.0 cm; Th. 5.8 cm.   89 2-2 49
5 *Flint end-scraper*: edge retouch on distal at 60 degrees; broken; cortex remnant; grey.
L. 3.0 cm; W. 3.6 cm; Th. 0.9 cm.   89 2-2 53
6 *Flint end-scraper*: edge retouch on distal at 70 degrees; dihedral butt; cortex remnant; mottled grey.
L. 3.0 cm; W. 3.1 cm; Th. 0.7 cm.   89 2-2 54
7 *Flint end-scraper*: edge retouch on distal at 70 degrees; dihedral butt; cortex remnant; mottled grey.
L. 4.2 cm; W. 3.0 cm; Th. 1.5 cm.   89 2-2 55
8 *Flint core*: one platform with irregular flake scars; lateral platform at right angles with irregular flake scars; traces of previous platforms; mottled grey.
L. 3.1 cm; W. 3.7 cm; Th. 3.6 cm.   89 2-2 50
9 *Flint core*: one platform with parallel flake scars; second platform at right angles with parallel flake scars; traces of previous platforms; mottled grey.
L. 4.5 cm; W. 5.0 cm; Th. 4.7 cm.   89 2-2 51
10 *Flint core*: one platform with irregular flake scars; opposed platform with flake scar; traces of previous platforms; cortex remnant; mottled grey.
L. 3.8 cm; W. 3.8 cm; Th. 2.9 cm.   89 2-2 52
11 *Flint core*: one platform with parallel flake scars; opposed platform with flake scar; traces of previous platform; cortex remnant; mottled grey.
L. 4.1 cm; W. 3.0 cm; Th. 1.5 cm.   89 2-2 56

248 FOLKTON (Folkton IV)   248:1-7

Yorkshire E.R.; North Yorkshire   TA 065 785

ROUND BARROW: on natural knoll, dimensions unknown, reduced by ploughing; opened October 1889.
RR 17; WG Ms 1.

Burial 1: adult inhumation, crouched on L. with head E.; at base of central oval grave L. 2.1 m, W. 1.8 m, D. 1.5 m, aligned E.-W.; basal fill of earth and clay succeeded by flints and cobbles, earth and clay, and earth, with upper fill and pile of flints.

Mound material

1   'Flint knife': not identified.   93 12-28 22
2-7 'Flint flakes': six; not identified.
                                                      93 12-28 23-28

249 FOLKTON (Folkton V)   249:1-21

Yorkshire E.R.; North Yorkshire   TA 065 785

ROUND BARROW: Diam. 15 m, H. 0.5 m; earth; opened October 1889.
RR 17; WG Ms 1.

Feature A: central pit Diam. 1.8 m, basal Diam. 1 m, D. 2.1 m, ?stakehole at D. 1.5 m; vessel at D. 1.1 m.
    'the bottom of a vessel': not preserved.
    'flint flake': not preserved.

Mound material

    'several potsherds': not preserved.
1-5 'Flint scrapers': five; not identified.
                                                      93 12-28 30-34
6   'Flint knife': not identified.   93 12-28 35
7   Flint flake: punctiform butt; cortex remnant; mottled grey.
    L. 8.1 cm; W. 4.7 cm; Th. 1.9 cm.   93 12-28 29
8-21 'Flint flakes': fourteen; not identified.
                                                      93 12-28 36-49

250 HUNMANBY (Folkton VIII)   250:1-11

Yorkshire E.R.; North Yorkshire   TA 075 742

ROUND BARROW: Diam. 31 m, H. 0.9 m, reduced by ploughing; turf with some flint and chalk gravel; internal chalk wall Diam. 23 m, W. 0.9 m, H. 0.2 m; opened October 1889.
RR 18-21; WG Ms 1.

Burial 1: child inhumation, crouched on R. with head W.; in oval grave L. 1.2 m, W. 0.9 m, D. 0.2 m, aligned E.-W., 8 m SE. by S. of centre; vessel, pin and flint no. 3 at face, flint no. 4 beneath hips.
1   Food Vessel: Yorkshire Vase; whipped cord: on internal rim bevel, short vertical to diagonal lines; on external surface and over lugs, herringbone, in places breaking down into confused pattern of short diagonal lines; three of four perforated lugs surviving.
    M. 12.3 cm; H. 12.1 cm; B. 5.4 cm.   93 12-28 54
    BAP no. 136.
2   Bone ring-headed pin: on caprovine humerus splinter, cut to oval section; head broken, eroded.
    L. 7.7 cm; W. 0.8 cm; Th. 0.4 cm.   93 12-28 55
3   Flint end- and side-scraper: edge retouch on distal and R. at 75 degrees; some edge retouch on L.; platform butt; cortex remnant; mottled grey.
    L. 3.3 cm. W. 3.5 cm; Th. 0.7 cm.   93 12-28 56
4   Flint flake: platform butt; beige.
    L. 1.9 cm; W. 1.8 cm; Th. 0.4 cm.   93 12-28 57

Burial 2: adult male inhumation, crouched on L. with head SW. by W.; in oval grave L. 1.5 m, W. 0.9 m, D. 0.2 m, aligned NE. by E.-SW. by W., 8 m SE. of centre.

Burial 3: adult inhumation, crouched on R. with head W.; in oval grave L. 2.4 m, W. 1.7 m, D. 0.3 m, aligned E.-W., 7.2 m E. by N. of centre; fill of earth with few flints and covered by two large flint blocks; buttons in row from neck to waist, ring at hips, sherd near feet, 'seven ribs of a small ox' behind hips.
5   Bronze ring: overlapping terminals; oval section swelling towards terminals with rounded ends (Table 1:45).
    Diam. 3.9-4.2 cm; W. 0.3 cm; Th. 0.3 cm.
    RR fig. 7.   93 12-28 52
6   Jet or shale buttons: twenty; cut and polished to conical face bevelled to flat base with central drilled V-perforation; one damaged.
    Diam. 1.5-1.6 cm; Th. 0.7-1.0 cm.   93 12-28 53
    RR fig. 6.

Burial 4: adult male inhumation, crouched on R. with head W. by N.; 0.3 m above old surface, 4.5 m NE. by N. of centre; knife at knee.
7   Flint knife: bilateral invasive retouch; damaged; grey.
    L. 4.5 cm; W. 1.9 cm; Th. 0.3 cm.   93 12-28 58

Burial 5: disturbed adult inhumation, crouched on R. with head SSE.; 0.3 m above old surface, 3.9 m ENE. of centre, above Burial 6.

Burial 6: adult male inhumation, crouched on L. with head N.; below Burial 5; scraper at face.
8   Flint horseshoe scraper: edge retouch on distal and bilateral at 65 degrees; platform butt; cortex remnant; mottled grey.
    L. 2.6 cm; W. 2.7 cm; Th. 0.7 cm.   93 12-28 59

Burial 7: adult female inhumation, crouched on L. with head E. by N.; 0.3 m above old surface, 3.9 m SE. by S. of centre; flakes at knee, feet and under hips.
9   Flint flake: corticated butt; mottled grey.
    L. 3.9 cm; W. 2.5 cm; Th. 0.4 cm.   93 12-28 60
10 Flint blade fragment: snapped; mottled grey.
    L. 4.8 cm; W. 1.6 cm; Th. 0.5 cm.   93 12-28 61
11 Flint flake fragment: platform butt; broken; cortex remnant; mottled grey.
    L. 2.7 cm; W. 2.5 cm; Th. 0.8 cm.   93 12-28 62

Burial 8: adolescent inhumation, crouched on L. with head S. by W.; 0.6 m above old surface, 4.4 m NE. of centre.

Burial 9: disturbed inhumation remnants; near mound surface, 0.4 m NW. of Burial 8.

Burial 10: infant inhumation; 0 5 m above old surface, 3.3 m S. by W. of centre.

Burial 11: adolescent inhumation, crouched on L. with head S. by W.; 0.3 m above old surface, 2.7 m E. by S. of centre.

Burial 12: adult inhumation, crouched on R. with head SE.; on old surface, 4.2 m NNW. of centre.

Burial 13: disarticulated adult inhumation; scattered in fill at SE. of central grave L. 2.7 m, W. 1.4 m, D. 1 m aligned SE.-NW.; fill of chalk gravel mainly at NW. and earth mainly at SE.

Burial 14: adult male inhumation, crouched on R. with head NNE.; in grave L. 1.8 m, W. 1.5 m, D. 0.6 m, aligned N. by E.-S. by W., cutting SE. end of Burial 13 grave; flake under head, sherds on base of grave.
    'sherds': not preserved.
    'flint flake': not identified.   93 12-28 63

Burial 15: adult female inhumation, skull lacking, crouched on R. and aligned E. by N.–W. by S.; on old surface and partly over fill of Burial 14 grave.

Burial 16: disturbed infant inhumation; humerus in fill of Burial 14 grave, ribs near Burial 15.

Mound material

    'flint flake': not preserved.
    'antler fragment': not preserved.

251 HUNMANBY (Folkton IX)   251:1-2

Yorkshire E.R.; North Yorkshire   TA 08 75

ROUND BARROW: Diam. uncertain, H. 0.2 m, reduced by ploughing; internal ditch Diam. 7.2 m, W. 0.5 m, D. 0.5 m with basal pit at NW. Diam. 0.5 m, D. 0.3 m, fill of chalk rubble; opened October 1889.
RR 21-2; WG Ms 1.

Burial 1: adult inhumation, crouched on L. with head SE.; on old surface 4 m W. of centre; Beaker behind knees, antler near head.
1 *'Beaker'*: not identified.   93 12-28 50
    Clarke no. 1339.
    'antler implement': not preserved.

Burial 2: two disarticulated and incomplete inhumations; in fill of grave L. 1.7 m, W. 0.8 m, D. 0.6 m, aligned SSE.–NNW., 3 m WSW. of centre.
    'sherds of two roughly made vessels': not preserved.
2 *'Flint flake'*: not identified.   93 12-28 51
    'antler fragment': not preserved.

Burial 3: disturbed child inhumation; on old surface at centre.
    'pieces of a drinking cup': not preserved.
    'antler fragment': not preserved.

Burial 4: disturbed inhumation; on old surface 1.8 m W. of centre.
    'pieces of a drinking cup': not preserved.
    'sherds of roughly made pottery': not preserved.
    'antler fragment': not preserved.

Feature A: pit L. 1.8 m, W. 0.8 m, D. 0.6 m, aligned NNE.–SSW., 1.2 m NE. of centre, fill of chalk and earth.

252 WOLD NEWTON (Willie Howe)

Yorkshire E.R.; North Humberside   TA 062 724

ROUND BARROW: Diam. 37 m, H. 7.5 m; chalk with some earth; opened by Lord Londesborough 13 October 1857, re-opened 1887.
RR 22-4.

Feature A: central pit L. 1.2 m, W. 0.8 m, D. 3.7 m; fill of successively chalk and earth to D. 1.5 m, chalk to D. 2.4 m, chalk with some earth to D. 3 m, chalk grit to D. 3.6 m, chalk with some earth to base; animal bone fragments in fill.
    'five chippings and a flake of flint': not preserved.

253 BEMPTON (Metlow Hill)   253:1-41

Yorkshire E.R.; North Humberside   TA 219 720

ROUND BARROW: Diam. 27 m, H. 0.6 m, reduced by ploughing; earth and some stones on natural knoll, traces of stone kerb Diam. 23m at S. and E.
RR 28-9.

Burial 1: ?decayed inhumation; on old surface 7.5 m S. by W. of centre; vessel on side.

1 *Food Vessel*: Yorkshire Vase; on internal rim bevel, incised herringbone between twisted cord lines; on external rim bevel, incised herringbone; in neck, twisted cord lines; in shoulder groove, incised herringbone; beneath shoulder, incised herringbone between twisted cord lines; at base, row of incised diagonal lines; four imperforate lugs.
    M. 13.5 cm; H. 11.3 cm; B. 5.9 cm.   79 12-9 2013
    BAP no. 36.

Burial 2: child inhumation, crouched on R. with head W.; in central grave L. 1.5 m, w. 0.6 m, D. 0.8 m, aligned E.–W., wood-lined and covered, with stakehole Diam. 0.15 m, D. 0.1 m at W. end visible also as cavity in mound above; Food Vessel at face.
2 *Food Vessel*: on internal rim bevel, four rows of toothed-stamp impressions; on external rim bevel, vertical jabbed impressions; in neck, over shoulder groove and on upper body, deeply incised herringbone.
    M. 11.1 cm; H. 9.5 cm; B. 6.0 cm.   79 12-9 2014
    BAP no. 35.

Mound material

3 *Food Vessel sherds*: five, including base; plain.
    B. c. 7.5 cm.   79 12-9 2052
4 *Food Vessel Urn sherds*: two; irregular jabbed herringbone above irregular bone impressions.
                                           79 12-9 2052a
5 *'Quartzite hammerstone'*: not identified.
                                           79 12-9 2051
6 *Flint ?point or knife*: invasive retouch on distal converging with some inverse edge retouch on R.; cortex remnant; brown.
    L. 2.7 cm; W. 5.6 cm; Th. 0.9 cm.   79 12-9 2032
    Green 1980, no. A172.
7 *Flint disc scraper*: all around invasive flaking at 60 degrees; platform butt; dark grey.
    L. 4.0 cm; W. 3.8 cm; Th. 2.2 cm.   79 12-9 2027
8 *Flint horseshoe scraper*: on fragment; edge retouch on distal and bilateral at 60 degrees; cortex remnant; patinated.
    L. 4.9 cm; W. 4.9 cm; Th. 1.5 cm.   79 12-9 2024
9 *Flint horseshoe scraper*: edge retouch on distal and bilateral at 65 degrees; faceted butt; damaged; mottled grey.
    L. 4.0 cm; W. 2.0 cm; Th. 0.7 cm.   79 12-9 2038
10 *Flint end- and side-scraper*: edge retouch on distal and R. at 70 degrees; platform butt; cortex remnant; mottled brown.
    L. 5.8 cm; W. 5.9 cm; Th. 1.9 cm.   79 12-9 2016
11 *Flint end- and side-scraper*: edge retouch on distal and R. at 70 degrees; ?faceted butt; mottled grey.
    L. 4.4 cm; W. 3.6 cm; Th. 0.7 cm.   79 12-9 2018
12 *Flint end- and side-scraper*: edge retouch on distal and L. at 65 degrees, some edge retouch on R.; platform butt; mottled pink to grey.
    L. 5.6 cm; W. 5.1 cm. Th. 1.4 cm.   79 12-9 2019
13 *Flint end- and side-scraper*: partial edge retouch on distal and L. at 75 degrees; platform butt; cortex remnant; light grey.
    L. 5.2 cm; W. 4.1 cm; Th. 1.0 cm.   79 12-9 2023
14 *Flint end- and side-scraper*: on fragment; edge retouch on distal and L. at 60 degrees; grey.
    L. 3.6 cm; W. 4.2 cm; Th. 1.6 cm.   79 12-9 2026
15 *Flint nosed end- and side-scraper*: edge retouch on distal and R. at 65 degrees; platform butt; mottled grey.
    L. 4.7 cm; W. 3.7 cm; Th. 1.1 cm.   79 12-9 2031
16 *Flint end-scraper and serrated flake*: edge retouch on distal at 75 degrees; fine retouch on L. with seven teeth per cm; punctiform butt; mottled pink.
    L. 6.0 cm; W. 3.5 cm; Th. 0.9 cm.   79 12-9 2037

17 *Flint end-scraper*: edge retouch on distal at 70 degrees; platform butt; cortex remnant; mottled brown.
L. 6.7 cm; W. 5.4 cm; Th. 1.4 cm.   79 12-9 2015

18 *Flint end-scraper*: edge retouch on distal at 70 degrees; edge wear on R.; faceted butt; cortex remnant; mottled grey.
L. 5.9 cm; W. 3.4 cm; Th. 1.2 cm.   79 12-9 2017

19 *Flint end-scraper*; edge retouch on distal at 60 degrees; platform butt; mottled grey.
L. 3.2 cm; W. 2.2 cm; Th. 0.5 cm.   79 12-9 2020

20 *Flint end-scraper*: edge retouch on distal at 75 degrees; platform butt; cortex remnant; mottled grey.
L. 4.2 cm; W. 3.3 cm; Th. 1.2 cm.   79 12-9 2021

21 *Flint end-scraper*: edge retouch on distal at 65 degrees; platform butt; mottled grey.
L. 4.8 cm; W. 3.4 cm; Th. 0.9 cm.   79 12-9 2025

22 *Flint double side-scraper*: edge retouch on R. at 55 degrees; inverse edge retouch on L. at 50 degrees; corticated butt; dark grey.
L. 3.9 cm; W. 4.0 cm; Th. 1.0 cm.   79 12-9 2029

23 *Flint side-scraper*: edge retouch on R. at 75 degrees; dihedral butt; cortex remnant; mottled grey.
L. 3.7 cm; W. 3.1 cm; Th. 1.0 cm.   79 12-9 2022

24 *Flint side-scraper*: edge retouch on R. at 65 degrees; corticated butt; mottled grey.
L. 6.7 cm; W. 3.0 cm; Th. 1.6 cm.   79 12-9 2033

25 *Flint worked flake*: partial bilateral edge retouch; platform butt; mottled grey.
L. 3.7 cm; W. 3.9 cm; Th. 1.0 cm.   79 12-9 2028

26 *Flint worked flake*: edge retouch on distal; cortex remnant; damaged; burnt.
L. 2.1 cm; W. 3.0 cm; Th. 0.5 cm.   79 12-9 2030

27 *Flint worked core-rejuvenation flake*: struck from one platform to remove part of opposed platform; edge retouch on L., inverse edge retouch on R.; platform butt; cortex remnant; mottled grey.
L. 6.1 cm; W. 5.9 cm; Th. 1.8 cm.   79 12-9 2034

28 *Flint worked flake*: invasive retouch on L.; dark grey.
L. 6.0 cm; W. 3.6 cm; Th. 1.5 cm.   79 12-9 2035

29 *Flint worked flake*: edge retouch on distal; punctiform butt; cortex remnant; mottled grey.
L. 5.4 cm; W. 2.0 cm; Th. 0.9 cm.   79 12-9 2042

30 *Flint worked flake*: edge retouch on L.; platform butt; mottled grey.
L. 4.0 cm; W. 2.3 cm; Th. 0.9 cm.   79 12-9 2047

31 *Flint utilised blade*: bilateral wear; cortex remnant; mottled grey.
L. 5.8 cm; W. 2.0 cm; Th. 0.7 cm.   79 12-9 2036

32 *Flint utilised flake*: edge wear on R.; platform butt; cortex remnant; pink.
L. 7.0 cm; W. 5.2 cm; Th. 2.0 cm.   79 12-9 2050

Flint blades

	Btt	Ctx	Col.	L.	W.	Th.	79 12-9
33	Sn.		M. Gr.	8.2	2.6	1.0	2039
34			Gr.	5.4	0.9	0.5	2045

Flint flakes

	Btt	Ctx	Col.	L.	W.	Th.	79 12-9
35	Pnct.		Gr.	4.3	2.3	0.8	2041
36	Pl.	x	Pat.	5.5	3.7	0.8	2046
37		x	M. Gr.	4.3	3.0	1.0	2048

38 *Flint core*: opposed parallel blade scars; cortex remnant; mottled grey.
L. 7.5 cm; W. 3.8 cm; Th. 2.1 cm.   79 12-9 2040

39 *Flint core rejuvenation flake*: struck at right angles to cortical platform; mottled beige.
L. 8.2 cm; W. 2.1 cm; Th. 1.5 cm.   79 12-9 2043

40 *Flint core trimming flake*: struck from platform to remove projection; corticated butt; beige.
L. 8.4 cm; W. 2.0 cm; Th. 1.3 cm.   79 12-0 2044

41 *Flint core trimming flake*: struck from platform to remove hinge; cortex remnant; mottled grey.
L. 4.4 cm; W. 2.2 cm; Th. 1.3 cm.   79 12-9 2049

254 HARPHAM (Little Kelk)   254:1-6

Yorkshire E.R.; North Humberside   TA 112 612

ROUND BARROW: Diam. 17 m, H. 0.6 m, reduced by ploughing; earth.
RR 29-30.

Burial 1: adult cremation deposit; in central pit Diam. 0.5 m, D. 0.2 m, earth fill.
1 *Flint flake*: burnt and broken.
L. 1.7 cm; W. 1.5 cm; Th. 0.7 cm.   79 12-9 2010

Mound material
2 *Stone polished axe fragment*: greenstone; ground and polished to ovate section; broken.
L. 4.7 cm; W. 6.2 cm; Th. 3.1 cm.   79 12-9 2007

3 *Flint end-scraper*: edge retouch on distal at 70 degrees; corticated butt; burnt.
L. 3.7 cm; W. 3.2 m; Th. 1.0 cm.   79 12-9 2008

4 *Flint double side-scraper*: bilateral edge retouch at 65 degrees; cortex remnant; burnt.
L. 2.9 cm; W. 2.0 cm; Th. 0.8 cm.   79 12-9 2009

5 *Flint knife*: invasive retouch on R.; cortex remnant on L.; platform butt; beige.
L. 3.7 cm; W. 2.6 cm; Th. 1.0 cm.   79 12-9 2011

6 *Flint worked blade*: some bilateral edge and invasive retouch; cortex remnant; brown.
L. 4.8 cm; W. 1.6 cm; Th. 0.5 cm.   79 12-9 2012

255 BISHOP BURTON (Littlewood I)   255:1-7

Yorkshire E.R.; North Humberside   SE 955 377

ROUND BARROW: Diam. 30 m, H. 2.7 m, reduced by ploughing; earth and clay with some chalk; previously opened ?by Dr Hull.
RR 30-2.

Burial 1: adult cremation deposit, in heap Diam. 0.2 m; 0.8 m beneath mound surface, 3.1 m SW. by W. of centre; knife among bones.
1 *Flint plano-convex knife*: all over invasive retouch; burnt.
L. 3.0 cm; W. 2.0 cm; Th. 0.5 cm.   79 12-9 1603

Burial 2: ?decayed inhumation; 1.8 m above old surface, 0.6 m N. of centre.
2 *Food Vessel*; Yorkshire Vase; incised; on internal rim bevel, herringbone; on external rim bevel, diagonal lines; in neck, shoulder groove and on upper body, herringbone above row of jabbed impressions; three of original five imperforate lugs surviving.
M. 13.8-14.5 cm; H. 10.6 cm; B. 8.0 cm.
BAP no. 49.   79 12-9 1600a

Burial 3: adult inhumation, crouched on L. with head ESE.; on central chalk mound H. 0.5 m, within wooden setting; vessel behind head, knife at face.
3 *Food Vessel*: Yorkshire Vase; twisted cord: internal rim bevel eroded; on neck, vertical lines between two to three horizontal lines; in shoulder groove and on upper body, horizontal lines; on lower body, roughly-executed lattice; seven imperforate lugs.
M. 14.9 cm; H. 12.6 cm; B. 5.7 cm.   79 12-9 1605a
RR fig. 9; *BAP* no. 48.

4 *Flint plano-convex knife*: on blade; all over invasive
retouch, all round fine serration with twelve teeth
per cm; punctiform butt; beige.
  L. 6.4 cm; W. 1.8 cm. Th. 0.6 cm.   79 12-9 1602
  RR fig. 8; *Clark* 1932, no. 2.5.

Feature A: pit L. 0.9 m, w. 0.6 m, D. 0.3 m, S. of upcast
Burial 3 mound; human vertebra on fill.

Backfill of previous opening
5 *Handled Beaker sherds*: three, including rim and
handle; plain.
  M. *c.* 8.5 cm.   79 12-9 1601
  Clarke no. 1241.

Mound material
  'the bottom of a vessel': not preserved.
6-7 *'Flint flakes'*: two, not identified.
                                         79 12-9 1604-5

256 BISHOP BURTON (Littlewood II)   256:1-13
Yorkshire E.R.; North Humberside   SE 954 377

ROUND BARROW: Diam. 15 m, H. 0.9 m, reduced by ploughing;
on natural rise, composition not recorded.
RR 32.

Burial 1: adult cremation deposit, in round heap; on old
surface, 3.9 m SSW. of centre.

Burial 2: child inhumation, crouched on R. with head
WSW.; on old surface, 3.3 m SSE. of centre.

Burial 3: disturbed cremation deposit; in ploughsoil,
1.5 m ESE. of centre.
1 *Collared Vessel sherds*: twenty-eight, including base
of collar, grooved shoulder, body and base; on
collar, incised herringbone; above and below
shoulder groove, opposed incised short diagonal
lines.   79 12-9 1606
  Longworth no. 665.

Burial 4: inhumation traces; in slight natural hollow,
W. of centre.
2 *Flint plano-convex knife*: bilateral invasive
retouch; corticated butt; mottled grey.
  L. 6.7 cm; W. 4.7 cm; Th. 0.8 cm.   79 12-9 1609

Mound material
3 *Peterborough Ware sherd*: plain.   79 12-9 1607d
4 *Grooved Ware sherds*: two; plain vertical applied
cordons.   79 12-9 1607b
5 *Beaker rim sherd*: diagonal lines of bone impressions.
                                         79 12-9 1607
6 *Beaker sherd*: vertical fingertip impressions.
                                         79 12-9 1607a
7 *'Beaker sherd'*: not identified.   79 12-9 1608
8 *Collared Vessel rim sherd*: on collar, blurred
diagonal twisted cord lines.   79 12-9 1607c
  Longworth no. 666.
9 *'Quartzite pebble'*: not identified. 79 12-9 1614
10 *Flint end- and side-scraper*: edge retouch on distal
and R. at 65 degrees; platform butt; patinated.
  L. 4.5 cm; w. 2.8 cm; Th. 0.8 cm.   79 12-9 1610
11 *Flint end- and side-scraper*: edge retouch on distal
and R. at 65 degrees; platform butt; cortex remnant;
mottled grey.
  L. 4.3 cm; W. 4.0 cm; Th. 1.3 cm.   79 12-9 1611
12 *'Flint scraper*: not identified.   79 12-9 1612
13 *Flint blade*: proximal snapped; mottled grey.
  L. 5.5 cm; W. 1.5 cm; Th. 0.8 cm.   79 12-9 1613

257 BISHOP BURTON (Littlewood III)   257:1-8
Yorkshire E.R.; North Humberside   SE 95 37

ROUND BARROW: Diam. 21 m, H. 1.7 m, reduced by ploughing;
sandy earth capped by clayey earth.
RR 33-4.

Burial 1: adult cremation deposit, in heap Diam. 0.25 m;
0.9 m above old surface, 0.9 m SSW. of centre; point on
bones.
1 *Flint point*: converging bilateral edge retouch;
corticated butt; beige.
  L. 4.8 cm; W. 2.8 cm; Th. 0.7 cm.   79 12-9 1619

Burial 2: adult cremation deposit, in round heap; 0.9 m
above old surface, 1.2 m SSE. of centre.

Burial 3: ?decayed inhumation; 1.1 m above old surface,
2.3 m W. by S. of centre; vessel on side.
2 *Food Vessel*: Yorkshire Vase; on internal rim bevel,
incised herringbone; on external rim bevel, incised
short vertical lines; in neck, short horizontal
impressions above impressed herringbone; on margins
of shoulder groove and on lugs, incised short
vertical lines; in groove, rows of horizontal
impressions; on body, incised vertical strokes; four
horizontally perforated lugs.
  M. 12.5 cm; H. 10.8 cm; B. 5.2 cm.   79 12-9 1615
  RR fig. 10; *BAP* no. 79.

Burial 4: adult inhumation traces, crouched on R. with
head W.; in wood-lined grave L. 1.8 m, W. 0.6 m, D. 0.6
m, aligned E. by S.-W. by N., 1.2 m W. of centre; vessel
and knife at face.
3 *Food Vessel*: half of surface eroded; twisted cord: on
rim, chevron; on body, row of lozenges separated by
horizontal line from part-row of zigzag becoming
confused with discontinuous short horizontal and
diagonal lines over rest of body.
  M. 14.8 cm; H. 13.2 cm; B. 8.2 cm.   79 12-9 1673
  BAP no. 78.
4 *Flint plano-convex knife*: all over invasive retouch;
platform butt; broken; mottled grey.
  L. 5.4 cm; W. 3.9 cm; Th. 1.0 cm.   79 12-9 1617
  Clark 1932, no. 2.6.

Mound material
5 *Beaker sherd*: comb-stamped herringbone band between
horizontal lines.   79 12-9 1674
  Clarke no. 1239.
6 *Food Vessel sherds*: five, including rim; in and
beneath grooves, coarse twisted cord horizontal
lines.   79 12-9 1620
7 *Flint end- and side-scraper*: edge retouch on distal
and R. at 55 degrees; broken; patinated.
  L. 3.7 cm; W. 3.4 cm; Th. 0.8 cm.   79 12-9 1618
8 *Flint biface*: bifacial invasive flaking; cortex
remnant; yellow-brown.
  I. 9.8 cm; W. 5.3 cm; Th. 1.9 cm.   79 12-9 1616

258 BISHOP BURTON (Littlewood IV)   258:1-6
Yorkshire E.R.; North Humberside   SE 95 37

ROUND BARROW: Diam. 19 m, H. 1.4 m, reduced by ploughing;
composition not recorded; previously opened ?by Dr Hull.
RR 34-5.

Burial 1: disturbed cremation deposit; in backfill of
previous opening and 0.2 m above old surface, 2.1 m SE.
of centre.
1 *Collared Urn*: on internal rim bevel, collar, neck and
body, incised herringbone.
  M. 8.8 cm; H. 10.7 cm; B. *c.* 4.3 cm. 79 12-9 1621
  Longworth no. 666a.

Burial 2: adult inhumation, crouched on R. with head W. by N.; in central oval grave L. 1.4 m, W. 0.6 m, D. 0.3 m, aligned E. by S.-W. by N., pit Diam. 0.2 m, D. 0.2 m at each end, plank-lined and covered; vessel at face.

2   *Food Vessel*: Yorkshire Vase; on internal rim bevel, twisted cord lines; on external rim bevel, incised short vertical lines between single twisted cord lines; in neck, incised herringbone, replaced by twisted cord over two lugs, above single twisted cord line; across lugs, incised horizontal to diagonal lines; in shoulder groove, incised herringbone split by pair of twisted cord lines; on body, incised herringbone; four of five horizontally perforated lugs surviving.
M. 15.0 cm; H. 12.4 cm; B. 7.0 cm.   79 12-9 1620a
BAP no. 131.

Mound material

3   *Flint horseshoe scraper*: edge retouch at 50 degrees; cortex remnant; mottled grey.
L. 3.1 cm; W. 3.8 cm; Th. 0.9 cm.   79 12-9 1624
4   *Flint worked flake*: edge retouch on R.; dihedral butt; mottled grey.
L. 6.0 cm; W. 2.9 cm; Th. 0.9 cm.   79 12-9 1623
5   *Flint flake*: corticated butt; grey.
L. 4.6 cm; W. 4.2 cm; Th. 1.4 cm;   79 12-9 1622
6   *Flint flake*: platform butt; patinated.
L. 5.2 cm; W. 3.7 cm; Th. 0.6 cm.   79 12-9 1625

259 BISHOP BURTON (Littlewood V)   259:1-3

Yorkshire E.R.; North Humberside   SE 95 37

ROUND BARROW: Diam. 20 m, H. 1 m, reduced by ploughing; composition not recorded.
RR 35.

Mound material

1   *Flint horseshoe scraper*: edge retouch on distal and bilateral at 75 degrees; platform butt; grey.
L. 2.5 cm; W. 2.7 cm; Th. 0.7 cm.   79 12-9 1628
2   *Flint end-scraper*: edge retouch on distal at 55 degrees; punctiform butt; mottled grey.
L. 3.7 cm; W. 3.0 cm; Th. 0.9 cm.   79 12-9 1627
3   *Flint utilised flake*: wear with gloss on L.; cortex remnant; mottled grey.
L. 5.0 cm; W. 1.7 cm; Th. 1.0 cm.   79 12-9 1626

260 BISHOP BURTON (Littlewood VIII)

Yorkshire E.R.; North Humberside   SE 95 37

ROUND BARROW: Diam. 26 m, H. 1.7 m, reduced by ploughing; composition not recorded.
RR 35.

Mound material

'portions of a food vessel': not preserved.
'many potsherds': not preserved.
'numerous flakes and cores': not preserved.

261 BISHOP BURTON (Littlewood VI)   261:1

Yorkshire E.R.; North Humberside   SE 95 37

ROUND BARROW: Diam. 13.5 m, H. 0.6 m, reduced by ploughing; composition not recorded except for central area of burnt earth Diam. 1.2 m, 0.3 m above old surface.
RR 36.

Burial 1: few burnt bones; in burnt earth upper fill of central pit Diam. 0.6 m D. 0.7 m, basal fill of earth.

Burnt earth layer

1   *Food Vessel sherds*: twenty-seven, including rim; beneath rim, in neck groove and on body, incised lozenge or lattice; on one ridge, row of oblique impressions on upper surface; on body, remains of incised chevron.   79 12-9 1629

262 BISHOP BURTON (Littlewood VII)   262:1-8

Yorkshire E.R.; North Humberside   SE 95 37

ROUND BARROW: Diam. 13.5 m, H. 0.6 m, reduced by ploughing; composition not recorded.
RR 36.

Burial 1: cremation deposit, in area Diam. 0.6 m; on old surface at centre; cup on bones at E.

1   *Accessory Cup*: on internal rim bevel, single fine twisted cord line; beneath rim and at greatest diameter, two zones of incised herringbone, upper bordered above by twisted cord line and split and bordered below by single incised lines, lower enclosed by single twisted cord lines and split by incised line; at base, two horizontal twisted cord lines; six perforations; heat-damaged.
M. 5.5 cm; H. 4.5 cm; B. 5.1 cm.   79 12-9 1630
RR fig. 11; *BAP* no. 308.

Mound material

2   *Neolithic Bowl rim sherd*: plain.   79 12-9 1632
NPY no. 27.
3   *Food Vessel sherds*: seven, including base; above shoulder, twisted cord short diagonal lines above two comb-impressed horizontal lines; below shoulder, band of twisted cord short vertical lines separated from row of short diagonal lines by plaited cord horizontal line with another beneath.
B. 7.4 cm.   79 12-9 1631
4   *Bronze Age sherds*: three joining including part of base angle; plain.   79 12-9 1631a
5   *Bronze Age sherds*: four; one with two twisted cord lines.   79 12-9 1631b
6   *Flint blade*: punctiform butt; cortex remnant; broken; mottled grey.
L. 6.8 cm; W. 2.3 cm; Th. 0.7 cm.   79 12-9 1635
7   *Flint flake*: corticated butt; broken; grey.
L. 4.9 cm; W. 3.0 cm; Th. 1.5 cm.   79 12-9 1634
8   *Flint core*: one platform with parallel blade scars, one opposed blade scar; traces of previous bipolar flaking; cortex remnant; mottled grey.
L. 3.2 cm; W. 2.3 cm; Th. 3.3 cm.   79 12-9 1633

263 BISHOP BURTON (Littlewood IX)

Yorkshire E.R.; North Humberside   SE 95 37

ROUND BARROW: Diam. 12.5 m, H. 0.8 m, reduced by ploughing; composition not recorded.
RR 36-7.

Burial 1: adult cremation deposit; in central hollow L. 0.6 m, W. 0.4 m, D. 0.2 m, aligned SE.-NW., in burnt area Diam. 1.2 m.

264 BISHOP BURTON (Littlewood X)   264:1

Yorkshire E.R.; North Humberside   SE 95 37

ROUND BARROW: Diam. ?, H. 0.3 m, reduced by ploughing; composition not recorded.
RR 37.

Burial 1: cremation deposit, in hollow L. 0.8 m, W. 0.4 m, D. 0.5 m, aligned N.-S., at E. end of burnt area L. 1.4 m, W. 0.6 m, aligned E.-W.

Mound material

1 *Flint utilised flake*: wear on distal and R.; cortex
   remnant; mottled grey.
   L. 5.1 cm; W. 2.4 cm; Th. 1.4 cm.   79 12-9 1636

265 BISHOP BURTON (Littlewood XI)   265:1-5

Yorkshire E.R.; North Humberside   SE 95 37

ROUND BARROW: Diam. 13.5 m, H. 0.7 m, reduced by
ploughing; composition not recorded.
RR 37.

Burial 1: adult cremation deposit; in inverted urn 0.2 m
above old surface 3.3 m S. by W. of centre.
1 *Collared Urn*: on internal moulding, collar and neck,
   rows of twisted cord short diagonal lines.
   M. 25.4 cm; H. 31.5 cm; B. 11.2 cm.   79 12-9 1637
   Longworth no. 667.

Burial 2: adult inhumation, crouched on R. with head
WSW.; in central grave L. 2.1 m, W. 1.5 m, D. 0.7 m,
aligned SE. by S.-NW. by N., wood lining at NW.; knife at
face.
2 *Flint plano-convex knife*: all over invasive retouch;
   partially patinated.
   L. 3.8 cm; W. 1.7 cm; Th. 0.5 cm.   79 12-9 1640

Mound material

3 *Flint ?discoidal knife roughout*: bifacial marginal
   flaking; cortex remnant; mottled grey.
   L. 5.4 cm; W. 4.6 cm; Th. 1.3 cm.   79 12-9 1638
4 *'Flint core'*: not identified.   79 12-9 1639

Not located

5 *'Pebble fragment'*: not identified.   79 12-9 1641

266 GRISTHORPE

Yorkshire N.R.; North Yorkshire   TA 09 83

ROUND BARROW: Diam. 24 m, H. 1.4 m, reduced by ploughing;
earth; opened early C19, re-opened 1887.
RR 38.

Burial 1: adult cremation deposit; in earth fill of cist
L. 0.4 m, W. 0.3 m, D. 0.25 m, aligned SE.-NW., four
side-slabs with single capstone and paving slab, 0.3 m
above old surface 7.2 m SSE. of centre.
   'three pieces of burnt and one of unburnt flint': not
   preserved.

Burial 2: disturbed adult male inhumation; in central
cist L. 1.4 m, W. 0.7 m, D. 0.5 m, aligned SE.-NW., side-
slabs with capstone at level of old surface; previously
opened.

Mound material

   'four round scrapers of flint': not preserved.
   'quartzite pebble hammerstone': not preserved.

267 FYLINGDALES

Yorkshire N.R.; North Yorkshire   NZ 95 01

ROUND BARROW: Diam 18 m, H. 0.5 m, with surrounding ditch
W. 1.2 m, D. 0.6 m; composition not recorded; platform
profile; previously opened.
RR 39.

Burial 1: cremation deposit; in central grave L. 1.5 m,
W. 1.2 m, D. 1 m, aligned NE.-SW., stone fill; previously
opened.

268 FYLINGDALES (Robin Hood II)   268:1

Yorkshire N.R.; North Yorkshire   NZ 962 018

ROUND BARROW: Diam. 5.4 m, H. 0.6 m; sandy earth.
RR 39-40.

Burial 1: adult cremation deposit; scattered at base of
central grave 1.1 m square, D. 0.5 m, below thick layer
of large charcoal capped by clay.
1 *Flint flake*: cortex remnant; burnt.
   L. 5.4 cm; W. 3.5 cm; Th. 0.7 cm.   79 12-9 1655

269 FYLINGDALES (Robin Hood IV; Old Wife
Houes)   269:1-4

Yorkshire N.R.; North Yorkshire   NZ 963 020

ROUND BARROW: Diam. 13 m, H. 0.9 m; sand with stone kerb;
inner stone kerb Diam. 10.6 m, extensive burning at 0.4 m
above old surface.
RR 40.

Burial 1: adult cremation deposit; on charcoal layer 0.4
m above old surface 3.6 m S. by E. of centre.

Burial 2: adult cremation deposit; in hollow Diam. 0.3
m, D. 0.2 m, 0.4 m above old surface 3.8 m S. of centre.
1-4 *'Flint flakes'*: four; not identified. 79 12-9 1656

Burial 3: adult cremation deposit; in central hollow L.
0.5 m, W. 0.4 m, D. 0.3 m, charcoal fill and cover slab
L. 0.7 m, W. 0.5 m.

270 FYLINGDALES (Robin Hood V)   270:1-3

Yorkshire N.R.; North Yorkshire   NZ 96 02

?RING CAIRN: area Diam. 12 m, enclosed by bank of earth
and stones W. 2.1 m, H. 0.8 m, possible entrance at W.
RR 41.

Feature A: circular area Diam. 1.4 m defined by small
stones on edge with slab paving over burnt earth layer,
1.2 m, SE. by S. of centre.

Feature B: similar circle Diam. 0.9 m, 0.9 m NE. of
Feature A.

Feature A or B

1-3 *'Flint flakes'*: three; not identified.
                                   79 12-9 1657-1659

271 FYLINGDALES (Robin Hood VI)   271:1-8

Yorkshire N.R.; North Yorkshire   NZ 95 01

ROUND BARROW: Diam. 18 m, H. 1 m; clayey earth with some
stones.
RR 41-2.

Burial 1: adult ?female cremation deposit; in inverted
urn 0.4 m above old surface 4.9 m SW. by S. of centre;
beads among bones.
1 *Collared Urn*: plain.
   M. 20.2 cm; surviving H. 21.5 cm.   79 12-9 1672
   BAP no. 112; *Longworth* no. 1142.
2 *Jet beads*: twelve: nine sub-globular and three
   fusiform; cut and polished; one globular broken.
   Fusiform L. 1.7-2.6 cm; Diam. (end) 0.5 cm, (central)
   0.7 cm; globular L. 0.5-0.8 cm; Diam. (central) 0.7-
   0.8 cm.   79 12-9 1661
   RR fig. 12.

Burial 2: adult cremation deposit; in inverted urn
adjacent to Burial 1.

3 *Collared Urn*: plain; distorted.
  M. 12.0-14.0 cm; H. 17.9 cm; B. 8.5 cm.
  BAP no. 112a; *Longworth* no. 1143.   79 12-9 1660

Burial 3: cremation deposit; in hollow Diam. 0.2 m, D. 0.2 m in burnt area Diam. 1.4 m, 0.5 m SW. of Burials 1 and 2 and ? at same level.

Burial 4: adult cremation deposit; in central oval grave L. 0.5 m, W. 0.4 m, D. 0.3 m, aligned SE.-NW., charcoal fill; cup inverted on bones at N.
4 *Accessory Cup*: twisted cord: on internal rim bevel, three lines; on upper body, filled triangles between pairs of horizontal lines; no perforations.
  M. 7.0 cm; H. 5.4 cm; B. 2.3 cm.   79 12-9 1671
  RR fig. 13; *BAP* no. 112b.

Burial 5: inhumation traces; on old surface 0.8 m S. of centre.

Mound material
5-6 *'Flint scrapers'*: two; not identified.
                                             79 12-9 1662-3
7 *'Flint flake'*: not identified.   79 12-9 1664

Not located
8 *Quartzite pebble*.   79 12-9 1665

272 FYLINGDALES (Robin Hood VII)   272:1-3

Yorkshire N.R.; North Yorkshire   NZ 953 013

ROUND CAIRN: Diam. 6.3 m, reduced by stone-robbing; stones with stone kerb.
RR 42-3.

Burial 1: adult cremation deposit; scattered on old surface 1.4 m SW. of centre.
1 *'Sherds'*: three; not identified.   79 12-9 1666
2 *'Flint flake, calcined'*: not identified.
                                             79 12-9 1667

Burial 2: adult cremation deposit; in earth fill of central hollow L. 0.6 m, W. 0.5 m, D. 0.2 m, aligned SE.-NW.
3 *'Flint flake fragment'*: not identified.
                                             79 12-9 1668

273 FYLINGDALES

Yorkshire N.R.; North Yorkshire   NZ 96 02

ROUND BARROW: Diam. 12 m, H. 0.6 m; stones and earth, extensive burning traces.
RR 43.

Burial 1: adult cremation deposit; in charcoal fill of central oval grave L. 0.7 m, W. 0.5 m, D. 0.3 m, aligned ESE.-WNW., in burnt area Diam. 1.5 m.

274 LYTHE (Lythe I: Whinny Hill)   274:1-7

Yorkshire N.R.; North Yorkshire   NZ 833 145

ROUND BARROW: Diam. 19 m, H. 0.4 m, reduced by ploughing and stone robbing; earth and stones.
RR 43-5.

Burial 1: ?decayed inhumation; in central cist L. 1.1 m, D. 0.4 m, aligned ESE.-WNW., part-destroyed; vessel at W. end.
1 *Food Vessel*: on internal rim bevel, row of triangular impressions; on external rim bevel, incised herringbone split by single incised line; on neck, discontinuous scored horizontal lines above row of raised chevrons created by alternate upright and

pendant triangular impressions with two further discontinuous scored lines beneath; on body, groups of scored horizontal lines separated and enclosed by single rows of triangular impressions.
  M. 16.2 cm; H. 15.7 cm; B. 7.8 cm.   79 12-9 1643
  RR fig. 14; *BAP* no. 188.
'pieces of jet': not preserved.
'calcined flint': not preserved.

Burial 2: ?decayed inhumation; in slab-lined pit L. 1.3 m, W. 0.6 m, D. 0.6 m, aligned NNE.-SSW., earth fill, 3.6 m ENE. of centre.
'calcined flint': not preserved.

Mound material
2 *Stone cup-marked block*: ferruginous sandstone; one irregular pecked cup-mark on each of three faces.
  L. 24.0 cm; W. 23.0 cm; Th. 14.5 cm.
  cup-marks Diam. 7.3 cm, D. 2.5 cm; Diam. 6.4 cm, D. 3.3 cm; Diam. 6.0 cm, D. 2.6 cm.   79 12-9 1941
3 *Jet ring*: cut and polished to square section.
  Diam. 4.6 cm; W. 0.5 cm; Th. 0.5 cm.   79 12-9 1664
4 *Jet bead*: cut and polished to faceted fusiform.
  L. 2.8 cm; Diam. (end) 0.5 cm, (central) 0.8 cm.
                                             79 12-9 1665
5 *Flint horseshoe scraper*: edge retouch on distal and bilateral at 65 degrees; platform butt; cortex remnant; mottled grey.
  L. 2.5 cm; W. 2.3 cm; Th. 1.1 cm.   79 12-9 1648
6 *Flint scraper fragment*: edge retouch at 60 degrees; burnt and broken.
  L. 2.5 cm; W. 2.4 cm; Th. 0.5 cm.   79 12-9 1646
7 *'Flint flake'*: not identified.   79 12-9 1647

275 LYTHE (Lythe II)   275:1-3

Yorkshire N.R.; North Yorkshire   NZ 83 14

ROUND BARROW: Diam. 16 m, H. 0.6 m; earth.
RR 45.

Burial 1: ?decayed inhumation; on wood layer L. 1.4 m, W. 0.6 m on old surface at centre.

Mound material
1 *'Flint knife'*: not identified.   79 12-9 1649
2-3 *'Flint flakes'*: two; not identified.
                                             79 12-9 1650-1

276 ALDBOURNE (Aldbourne I)   276:1-12

Wiltshire   SU 249 773

BELL BARROW: Diam. 18 m, H. 3.3 m, berm W. 4.8 m, ditch W. 3.6 m (22 m, 3 m, 4.2 m, 3.6 m *per VCH*); earth core H. 1 m, covered by successive layers of dark earth Th. 0.2 m, chalk Th. 0.2 m, earth and chalk, clayey sand, chalk rubble capping Th. 0.9 m; at centre at H. 1.8 m three successive circular sarsen layers separated by charcoal deposits, the lower two Diam. 1.2 m, upper Diam. 3.6 m with central burnt area.
RR 46-8; *Piggott* 1938, no. 31; *VCH Wilts.* 206.

Burial 1: adult cremation deposit, in heap Diam. 0.4 m; 0.6 m above old surface, 1.2 m E. of centre.

Burial 2: cremation deposit; scattered over central area Diam. 0.9 m on old surface level, surrounded by charcoal.

Burial 3: adult cremation deposit; in central grave L. 0.5 m, W. 0.5 m, D. 0.6 m.
1 *Accessory Cup*: plain; no perforations.
  M. 4.1 cm; H. 4.3 cm; B. 4.5 cm.   79 12-9 1806
  BAP no. 240.

2   *Amber beads*: six: two cylindrical, two sub—conical, two fragmentary; cut and polished.
    cylindrical L. 0.9 cm, Diam. 1.1 cm; sub—conical L. 0.8 cm, Diam. 0.9 cm.   79 12—9 1808
    'amber beads': two, one 'flat'; not preserved.
3   *Bone perforated pin*: on longbone sliver; cut and polished; cut hour—glass perforation; point broken.
    L. 6.0 cm; W. 1.0 cm; Th. 0.2 cm; Diam. perf. 0.4 cm.
                                                 79 12—9 1889
    'flint flake': perhaps one of nos 7—12 below.

Mound material

4   *Beaker base sherd*: tooth—comb stamped band of horizontal lines.   79 12—9 1807
    Clarke no. 1024.
5   *Beaker sherd*: fingertip rustication.   79 12—9 1807a
6   *Flint end- and side-scraper*: edge retouch on distal and R. at 65 degrees; punctiform butt; patinated.
    L. 5.1 cm; W. 3.9 cm; Th. 1.0 cm.   79 12—9 1809
7   *Flint blade*: platform butt; patinated.
    L. 7.0 cm; W. 1.2 cm; Th. 0.6 cm.   79 12—9 1813

Flint flakes

	Btt	Ctx	Col.	L.	W.	Th.	79 12—9
8	Pl.	x	Pat.	7.3	4.7	1.5	1810
9	Pl.	x	Pat.	5.0	4.2	1.3	1811
10	Pl.	x	Pat.	4.4	4.6	1.4	1812
11	Pl.	x	M. Gr.	4.3	2.0	0.9	1814
12	Fc.		Br.	4.8	3.9	0.6	1815

277 ALDBOURNE (Albourne VI)   277:1-4

Wiltshire   SU 249 773

BELL BARROW: Diam. 20 m, H. 2.1 m, berm W. 7 m, ditch W. 2.4 m (20 m, 2.4 m, 4.8 m, 4 m *per VCH*); earth and chalk with some sarsens; previously opened by central shaft; opened October 1878.
RR 48; *Times* 8 October 1878; *Piggott* 1938, no. 32; *VCH Wilts*. 206.

Burial 1: inhumation traces; in central grave L. 1.8 m, W. 0.9 m, D. 0.6 m (W. 1.2 m, D. 0.9 m *per Times*), aligned SE. by E.—NW. by W.
1   *Flint tanged arrowhead*: bifacial invasive retouch; cortex remnant; patinated.
    L. 2.9 cm; W. 2.2 cm; Th. 0.4 cm.   79 12—9 1853
    Green 1980, no. 257.

Burial 2: disturbed inhumation; in fill of Burial 1 grave.
2   *Bronze knife-dagger*: triangular blade with lozenge-section midrib bordered by groove, rib and broad furrow inside edge bevel; curved hilt line; three rivet holes damaged and butt broken (Table 1.12).
    L. 9.0 cm, W. 3.5 cm; Th. 0.4 cm.   79 12—9 1852
    RR fig. 15; *Gerloff* 1975, no. 330.

Mound material

3   *Bronze Age sherd*: indefinite impressions.
                                               79 12—9 1850
4   *Stone polished axe fragment*: greenstone; ground and polished; broken and eroded.
    L. 7.0 cm; W. 4.8 cm; Th. 3.2 cm.   79 12—9 1851

278 ALDBOURNE (Aldbourne V)   278:1-12

Wiltshire   SU 249 773

BELL BARROW: Diam. 21 m, H. 3.6 m, berm W. 3 m, ditch W. 3 m (24 m, 3 m, 3.6 m, 3.9 m *per VCH*), earth and chalk with much charcoal on old surface, opened October 1878.
RR 48-9; *Times* 8 October 1878; *VCH Wilts*. 206.

Burial 1: adult cremation deposit; in central oval grave L. 1 m, W. 0.5 m, D. 0.4 m, with upcast mound to WSW. L. 1 m, W. 0.8 m, H. 0.5 m.
1   *Bone perforated pin*: ?bird longbone splinter; cut and polished to rectangular to round section; cut hourglass perforation in sub—rectangular flat head; burnt and broken, point lacking.
    L. 8.5 cm; Diam. 0.4 cm; Diam. (perf.) 0.3 cm.
                                               79 12—9 1842

Mound material

2   *Beaker sherd*: tooth—comb stamped: triangular space outlined and filled with lines.   79 12—9 1841a
    Clarke no. 1025.
3   *Collared Vessel sherd*: lower collar: remains of twisted cord diagonal lines.   79 12—9 1841
    Longworth no. 1621a.
4   *Bronze Age sherds*: two including base; plain.
                                               79 12—9 1841b
5   *Bronze Age sherds*: four; plain.   79 12—9 1841c
6   *Flint end- and side-scraper*: bifacial invasive retouch on distal and L.; platform butt; mottled grey.
    L. 4.7 cm; W. 3.6 cm; Th. 1.0 cm.   79 12—9 1843
7   *Flint end-scraper*: edge retouch on distal at 65 degrees; punctiform butt; mottled grey.
    L. 6.6 cm; W. 4.0 cm; Th. 1.6 cm.   79 12—9 1845
8   *Flint blade*: cortex remnant; patinated.
    L. 7.2 cm; W. 1.8 cm; Th. 1.3 cm.   79 12—9 1847

Flint flakes

	Btt	Ctx	Col.	L.	W.	Th.	79 12—9
9	Pl.	x	Pat.	7.0	4.7	1.5	1844
10	Pl.		Pat.	4.3	2.4	0.7	1846
11	Pl.	x	Pat.	5.2	4.5	1.2	1848
12	Pl.	x	Pat.	4.4	2.8	1.0	1849

279 ALDBOURNE (Aldbourne II)   279:1

Wiltshire   SU 250 773

ROUND BARROW: Diam. 25 m, H. 3.6 m, ditch W. 2.4 m (27m, 3 m *per VCH*); earth with some chalk and sarsens; previously opened at centre; opened October 1878.
RR 49; *Times* 8 October 1878; *VCH Wilts*. 147.

Burial 1: disturbed inhumation fragments in backfill of previous opening at centre.

Burial 2: cranial fragment; 0.6 m below mound surface, 7.2 m S. of centre.

Burial 3: adult cremation deposit; in central hourglass-shaped pit L. 1.2 m, W. 0.6 m, D. 0.4 m, aligned SE.—NW., four sarsens over.
1   *Beaker sherd*: fingernail vertical impressions.
                                               79 12—9 1816

280 ALDBOURNE (Aldbourne IV)   280:1-29

Wiltshire   SU 247 771

ROUND BARROW: Diam. 27 m, H. 1.8 m, reduced by ploughing; core of sarsens Diam. 8.5 m, H. 1.5 m capped by earth with some chalk and sarsens; opened October 1878.
RR 50-3; *Greenwell* 1881; *Times* 8 October 1878; *Piggott* 1938, no. 33; *VCH Wilts*. 147.

Burial 1: cremation deposit; at centre on wood remains in deturfed area L. 1.4 m, W. 1 m, aligned N.—S., covered by 'ashes', vessel 4 at S. and 5 outside at N., other objects among bones.

1 *Bronze blade fragments*: seven; one with remains of rivet hole (Table 1:22).
   L. 2.2 cm; W. 1.6 cm; Th. 0.1 cm.
   L. 1.8 cm; W. 1.6 cm; Th. 0.1 cm.
   L. 1.4 cm; W. 1.2 cm; Th. 0.1 cm.   79 12-9 1820
   Gerloff 1975, no. 278.
2 *Bronze awl fragments*: wedge-shaped tang with rhomboidal section; broken and point lacking, corroded (Table 1:40).
   L. 1.4 cm; W. 0.2 cm; Th. 0.3 cm.   79 12-9 1821
3 *Bronze shank fragment*: oval section; both ends broken (Table 1:43).
   L. 2.4 cm; W. 0.2 cm; Th. 0.2 cm.   79 12-9 1822
4 *Aldbourne Cup and Lid*: incised.
   Cup: internally, row of reserved lozenges split and enclosed by single lines, the upright and pendant triangles filled with *pointillé* (some pricks piercing wall); on lower body, similar scheme below row of incised chevrons alternately filled with *pointillé* and reserved, enclosed above by line; on base, concentric band of upright triangles filled with *pointillé* alternating with pendant reserved triangles between single lines; one pair of perforations in lower body.
   M. 10.1 cm; H. 5.1 cm; B. 7.2 cm.
   Lid: on top, three concentric bands outlined by single lines, the lower two forming split reserved lozenge with upright and pendant triangles filled with *pointillé*, the uppermost with upright triangles filled with *pointillé* alternating with pendant reserved triangles; on side, band of reserved lozenges split and enclosed by single lines with upright and pendant triangles filled with *pointillé*; on lip, row of upright triangles, with similar band internally; remains of horizontal perforation through knob.
   Diam. 10.3 cm; H. 6.0 cm.   79 12-9 1818
   RR fig. 16; *BAP* no. 213.
5 *Aldbourne Cup*; incised: internally, two rows of short diagonal strokes between single horizontal lines above zone of upright triangles filled with *pointillé*, bordered beneath by horizontal line; externally, zone of herringbone with spaces alternately filled with *pointillé* and reserved, enclosed between single horizontal lines; on lower body, zone of jabbed impressions above single horizontal line; on base, two concentric rows of impressions; one pair of perforations.
   M. 9.9 cm; H. 4.8 cm; B. 7.7 cm.   79 12-9 1819
   RR fig. 19.
6 *Stone pebble*: haematite; polished.
   L. 0.9 cm; W. 0.8 cm; Th. 0.5 cm.   79 12-9 1831
7 *Fossil*: bivalve; polished.   79 12-9 1830
8 *Fossil 'bead'*: encrinoid.   79 12-9 1825
9 *Jet or shale ring*: cut and polished to sub-rectangular section.
   Diam. 4.3 cm; W. 1.1 cm; Th. 0.7 cm.   79 12-9 1827
   RR fig. 17.
10 *Jet or shale pendant*: cut and polished to sub-circular section ring with rectangular projection with drilled perforation.
   L. 3.2 cm; W. 2.6 cm; Th. 0.6 cm; Diam. (perf.) 1.5 cm.   79 12-9 1828
   RR fig. 18.
11 *Shale button*: cut and polished to sub-conical dome with flat base with central drilled V-perforation.
   Diam. 2.2 cm; Th. 1.0 cm.   79 12-9 1829
12 *Shale bead fragment*; cut and polished to barrel form; drilled perforation; broken.
   L. 1.2 cm; Diam. (end) 0.5 cm, (central) 0.7 cm.   79 12-9 1826

13 *Faience beads*: one of three surviving; five segments; broken.
   L. 1.1 cm; Diam. 0.4 cm.   79 12-9 1823
14 *Amber beads*: one of two surviving; drilled perforation; broken.
   L. 0.8 cm; Diam. 0.8 cm.   79 12-9 1824
   'flint flake': perhaps one of nos 15-17 below.

Fill above Burial 1
15 *Flint utilised flake*: bilateral wear; platform butt; cortex remnant; patinated.
   L. 5.3 cm; W. 3.3 cm; Th. 1.4 cm.   79 12-9 1834
16 *Flint flake*: platform butt; cortex remnant; grey.
   L. 6.9 cm; W. 2.7 cm; Th. 0.9 cm.   79 12-9 1832
17 *Flint flake*: corticated butt; grey.
   L. 5.8 cm; W. 3.5 cm; Th. 1.0 cm.   79 12-9 1833
   'flint flakes': three; not preserved.

Sarsen core
18 *Peterborough Ware shoulder sherd*: whipped cord short diagonal lines opposed above and below shoulder.
   79 12-9 1840f
19 *Beaker rim sherd*: fine tooth comb impressions: two horizontal lines.   79 12-9 1840
   Clarke no. 1026.
20 *Beaker neck sherd*: rectangular tooth-comb stamped: two bands of horizontal lines separated by reserved zone.   79 12-9 1840a
21 *Beaker sherd*: rectangular tooth-comb stamped horizontal lines.   79 12-9 1840b
22 *Beaker sherd*: diagonal spatula impressions.
   79 12-9 1840c
23 *Beaker sherd*: rectangular tooth-comb stamped horizontal lines.   79 12-9 1840d
24 *Beaker sherds*: seven; plain.   79 12-9 1840e
25 *Flint triangular arrowhead*: all over bifacial invasive retouch; damaged; burnt.
   L. 2.0 cm; W. 1.9 cm; Th. 0.4 cm.   79 12-9 1836
   Green 1980, no. A133.
26 *Flint barbed-and-tanged arrowhead*: all over bifacial invasive retouch; broken; patinated.
   L. 2.3 cm; W. 2.2 cm; Th. 0.5 cm.   79 12-9 1835
   Green 1980, no. A133.
27 *Boar tusk point*: sliced facet on ventral at point; broken.
   L. 6.0 cm; W. 1.5 cm; Th. 1.9 cm.   79 12-9 1837
28 *Boar tusk fragment*: broken.
   L. 4.2 cm; W. 1.0 cm; Th. 0.2 cm.   79 12-9 1838

Not located
29 *Stone pebble*   79 12-9 1839

281 ALDBOURNE (Aldbourne III)   281:1

Wiltshire   SU 245 782

ROUND BARROW: Diam. 18 m, H. 2.2 m, ditch W. 1.8 m; earth and chalk with much burnt material at base.
RR 53-4; *VCH Wilts.* 148.

Burial 1: adult cremation deposit; in central oval grave L. 0.6 m, W. 0.5 m, D. 0.4 m, aligned ESE.-WNW.
1 *Flint flake*: platform butt; patinated.
   L. 3.7 cm; W. 2.6 cm; Th. 0.7 cm.   79 12-9 1817

282 ALDBOURNE (Aldbourne VIII)   282:1-4

Wiltshire   SU 242 784

ROUND BARROW: Diam. 18 m, H. 2.4 m; core of sarsens Diam.
3.6 m, H. 1.8 m covered by earth and chalk with chalk
capping; burnt deposit below capping at SE., and old
surface covered with charcoal outside cairn area; opened
November 1879.
RR 54-5; *Times* 6 November 1879; *VCH Wilts.* 148.

Burial 1: adult cremation deposit; in central oval grave
L. 0.9 m, W. 0.6 m, D. 0.5 m, aligned S. by E.-N. by W.,
objects on bones.

1 *Bronze knife*: flattened triangular midrib flanked by
   shallow furrows and broad edge bevels; curved hilt
   line with bifacial traces of wood grain on butt; one
   surviving rivet hole (Table 1:13).
   L. 6.2 cm; W. 2.7 cm; Th. 0.2 cm.   79 12-9 1864
   Gerloff 1975, no. 277.
2 *Bone pin*: longbone splinter; cut and polished to fine
   point; point and butt broken.
   L. 8.2 cm; W. 0.7 cm; Th. 0.3 cm.   79 12-9 1865

Mound material

3 *Collared Vessel sherd*: lower collar; twisted cord
   lattice bordered beneath by three horizontal lines.
   Longworth no. 1621b.   79 12-9 1863
4 *Collared Vessel sherd*: collar or neck; twisted cord
   diagonal lines.   79 12-9 1863a
   Longworth no. 1621c.
   'numerous flakes and chippings of flint': not
   preserved.

283 ALDBOURNE (Aldbourne IX)   283:1-12

Wiltshire   SU 246 764

BELL BARROW: Diam. 19 m, H. 2.4 m, berm W. 4.8 m, ditch
W. 3.6 m (19 m, 2 m, 4.5 m, 3.6 m *per VCH*); earth and some
chalk; opened November 1879.
RR 55; *Times* 6 November 1879; *VCH Wilts.* 206.

Burial 1: adult cremation deposit; in central oval grave
L 1 m, W. 0.6 m, D. 0.3 m, aligned E. by N.-W. by S.;
upper sarsen stone packing.

1 *Flint arrowhead fragment*: all-over unifacial invasive retouch; limited inverse edge retouch; broken
   and point snapped; mottled grey.
   L. 2.9 cm, W. 2.6 cm, Th. 0.4 cm.   79 12-9 1873
2 *Bone trefoil-headed pin*: longbone splinter; cut and
   polished to fine point and oval section; two cut
   holes in head and at either side in shaped lobes; one
   lobe broken off; burnt.
   L. 11.9 cm; W. 0.6 cm; Th. 0.3 cm.   79 12-9 1888
   RR fig. 20.
3 *Bone pin fragment*: cut and polished to fine point;
   snapped.
   L. 2.0 cm; W. 0.5 cm; Th. 0.3 cm.   79 12-9 1890

Mound material

4 *'Sherds'*: three; not identified.   79 12-9 1866
5 *Flint end- and side-scraper*: edge retouch on distal
   and L. at 65 degrees; platform butt; grey.
   L. 3.8 cm; W. 3.5 cm; th. 1.0 cm.   79 12-9 1871
6 *Flint end- and side-scraper*: edge retouch on distal
   and L. at 70 degrees; platform butt; cortex remnant;
   grey.
   L. 4.3 cm; W. 3.7 cm; Th. 1.3 cm.   79 12-9 1872
7 *Flint end-scraper*: edge retouch on distal at 55
   degrees; dihedral butt; burnt.
   L. 3.9 cm; W. 2.6 cm; Th. 0.8 cm.   79 12-9 1867
8 *Flint end-scraper or knife*: edge retouch on distal at
   50 degrees, invasive retouch on R.; platform butt;
   cortex remnant; patinated.
   L. 4.8 cm; W. 3.3 cm; Th. 0.6 cm.   79 12-9 1868

9   *Flint side-scraper*: on hinge-fractured flake; edge
    retouch on R. at 55 degrees; platform butt; cortex
    remnant; patinated.
    L. 3.7 cm; W. 3.9 cm; Th. 0.9 cm.   79 12-9 1869
10 *Flint knife*: invasive retouch on R; platform butt;
    cortex remnant; grey.
    L. 4.3 cm; W. 2.7 cm; Th. 0.8 cm.   79 12-9 1870
11 *Flint flake*: platform butt; patinated.
    L. 4.4 cm; W. 3.7 cm; Th. 0.9 cm.   79 12-9 1874
12 *Flint flake*: platform butt; patinated.
    L. 4.3 cm; W. 3.4 cm; Th. 0.9 cm.   79 12-9 1875

284 ALDBOURNE (Aldbourne X)   284:1-4

Wiltshire   SU 243 764

ROUND BARROW: Diam. 21 m, H. 2.4 m; earth and chalk
(earth only; *Times*); old surface burnt W of centre;
opened November 1879.
RR 55-6; *Times* 6 November 1879; *VCH Wilts.* 148.

Burial 1: adult male cremation deposit; in central grave
Diam. 0.5 m, D. 0.5 m; objects among bones.

1 *Stone bracer*: ground and polished to rectangular form
   and plano-convex section with bevelled edges; two
   drilled hourglass perforations at one end; snapped
   with one incomplete perforation at new end.
   L. 5.9 cm; W. 3.3 cm; Th. 0.6 cm.   79 12-9 1877
   RR fig. 22.
2 *Stone pendant*: ?slate; cut and polished to ovate
   outline and rectangular section; drilled hourglass
   perforation; damaged.
   L. 6.2 cm; W. 2.9 cm; Th. 0.7 cm; perf. Diam. 0.5 cm.
   RR fig. 23.   79 12-9 1876
3 *Bone tweezers*: cut and polished from longbone shaft
   with cancellous tissue surviving on inner faces of
   prongs; prongs of rectangular section with inturned
   rounded and bevelled tips; expanded flat head above
   hollow neck with central drilled vertical perforation.
   L. 4.8 cm; Diam. (head) 1.9 cm, (perf.) 0.2 cm; prong
   W. 0.6 cm, Th. 0.2 cm.   79 12-9 1878
   RR fig. 21.
4 *Bone perforated pin*: long-bone splinter, cut and
   polished to oval section; cut hourglass perforation;
   broken.
   L. 4.4 cm; W. 1.0 cm; Th. 0.4 cm; Diam. (perf.) 0.4
   cm.   79 12-9 1879

285 ALDBOURNE (Aldbourne XI)   285:1-6

Wiltshire   SU 243 765

ROUND BARROW: Diam. 15 m, H. 0.6 m; earth; opened
November 1879.
RR 56-7; Times 6 November 1879; *Piggott* 1938, no. 34; *VCH
Wilts.* 148.

Burial 1: adult cremation deposit; in central grave
Diam. 0.8 m, D. 0.4 m; pottery on bones, beads among
bones.

1 *Accessory Cup*: twisted cord; on neck, chevrons
   enclosing short vertical lines; on body, herringbone; no perforations.
   M. 6.4 cm; H. 5.8 cm; B. 4.7 cm.   79 12-9 1880
   BAP no. 255.
2 *Accessory Cup sherds*: nine including rim and
   shoulder; on rim, two incised lines; incised diagonal
   lines opposed above and below shoulder.
   79 12-9 1881

3 *Jet or shale bead*: cut and polished to barrel form; drilled perforation; damaged.
L. 1.2 cm; Diam. (end) 0.4 cm, (central) 0.7 cm.
79 12-9 1885

4 *Shale bead*: cut and polished to sub-globular form; drilled hourglass perforation.
L. 0.6 cm; Diam 1.1 cm. 79 12-9 1884

5 *Bone beads*: ten; cut and polished to sub-globular form; drilled perforations.
L. 0.8-1.2 cm; Diam. 1.0-1.3 cm. 79 12-9 1882

6 *Shell bead*: cut and polished to globular form; drilled perforation.
L. 0.9 cm; Diam. 1.0 cm. 79 12-9 1883
RR fig. 24.

286 ALDBOURNE (Aldbourne VII) 286:1-8

Wiltshire SU 235 779

ROUND BARROW: Diam. 24 m, H. 2.1 m, reduced by ploughing; earth and some chalk with remnants of chalk capping; opened October 1878.
RR 57; *Times* 8 October 1878; *VCH Wilts.* 148.

Burial 1: adult cremation deposit; in central grave L. 1 m, W. 0.8 m, D. 0.4 m, aligned ESE.-WNW.; in remains of wooden box packed around with charcoal; knife on bones.
1 *Bronze knife*: triangular blade with slight constriction to sub-rectangular butt; thick flattened midrib flanked by furrows and edge bevels; two cast rivetholes; straight hilt line (Table 1:14).
L. 7.4 cm; W. 2.4 cm; Th. 0.2 cm. 79 12-9 1855
Gerloff 1975, no. 258.

Mound material
2 *Flint end- and side-scraper*: edge retouch on distal and L. at 65 degrees; platform butt; grey.
L. 2.4 cm; W. 2.3 cm; Th. 1.0 cm. 79 12-9 1857
3 *Flint end-scraper*: edge retouch on distal at 60 degrees; platform butt; patinated.
L. 4.7 cm; W. 2.6 cm; Th. 0.7 cm. 79 12-9 1858
4 *Flint side-scraper*: edge retouch on R. at 50 degrees; punctitorm butt; cortex remnant; grey.
L. 3.6 cm; W. 3.0 cm; Th. 1.1 cm. 79 12-9 1856

Flint flakes

	Btt	Ctx	Col.	L.	W.	Th.	79 12-9
5	Pl.		Pat.	4.3	2.2	0.7	1859
6	Ct.	x	Gr.	3.6	3.0	0.9	1860
7	Pl.	x	Gr.	5.9	3.2	0.7	1862

8 *Flint core trimming flake*: struck from platform to remove projection; cortex remnant; patinated.
L. 5.0 cm; W. 3.0 cm; Th. 1.1 cm. 79 12-9 1861

287 HINTON 287:1-2

Wiltshire SU 235 800

ROUND BARROW: Diam. 20 m, H. 2.6 m; earth and chalk with chalk capping; much charcoal on old surface; opened November 1879.
RR 57-8; *Times* 6 November 1879; *VCH Wilts.* 159.

Burial 1: adult cremation deposit; in central oval grave L. 1 m, W. 0.6 m, D. 0.3 m, aligned SE.-NW.; dagger on bones.
1 *Bronze dagger*: Gerloff Group Ridgeway; flat blade with pronounced midrib and edge bevels; convex butt with central rivet-notch and two rivets in holes; loose third rivet; bifacial traces of wooden ?sheath with longitudinal grain on blade, ending at omega hilt-line defined by narrow flange of ?organic

material; rivets with round-sectioned shanks and expanded heads (Table 1:6).
L. 10.6 cm; W. 4.7 cm; Th. 0.5 cm.
Rivets L. 1.2-1.5 cm; shank Diam. 0.5 cm.
RR fig. 25; *Gerloff* 1975, no. 99. 79 12-9 1891

Not located
2 *Flint utilised flake*: wear on R.; platform butt; mottled brown.
L. 4.1 cm; W. 3.8 cm; Th. 1.0 cm. 79 12-9 1892

288 LAMBOURN

Berkshire SU 356 825

ROUND BARROW: Diam. 15 m, H. 1.4 m, reduced by ploughing; chalk and earth, ditched.
RR 59-60.

Feature A: central pit Diam. 1.2 m, D. 1.1 m, fill of chalk with some earth.

289 LAMBOURN (Stancomb II) 289:1-8

Berkshire SU 356 825

ROUND BARROW: Diam. 19 m, H. 1.5 m, reduced by ploughing; earth with some chalk, ditched.
RR 60-1.

Burial 1: adult male cremation deposit; in central oval grave L. 1 m, W. 0.8 m, D. 0.2 m, aligned NE.-SW., surrounded by charcoal; objects on bones.
1 *Bronze razor or razor knife*: Butler and Smith Class 1; thick rectangular tang of rectangular section thinning to willow leaf blade with flat midrib and traces of hollowed edge bevels (Table 1:19).
L. 8.0 cm; W. 1.7 cm; Th. 0.4 cm. 79 12-9 1799
Butler and Smith 1956, 51; *Jöckenhovel* 1980, no. 47.
2 *Accessory Cup*: on top of rim, two rows of impressed chevrons; at base of neck, row of impressed chevrons; three pairs of perforations through neck.
M. 6.2 cm; H. 3.9 cm. 79 12-9 1795
BAP no. 229.
3 *Stone battle-axe*: Roe VE(S); Group XII, SW. 1329; all-over ground and polished; rounded butt, blunt blade edge; central drilled cylindrical perforation.
L. 12.8 cm; W. 5.4 cm; Th. 3.0 cm; blade W. 6.2 cm; perf. Diam. 2.3 cm. 79 12-9 1798
RR fig. 26; *Roe* 1966, no. 3.
4 *Antler 'hammer'*: shed red-deer antler ?fossil; crown and brow tines cut and polished smooth; beam cut and polished to bevel; cut and polished cylindrical perforation; no trace of use or abrasion.
L. 16.8 cm; W. 7.2 cm; Th. 5.1 cm; perf. Diam. 2.5 cm.
79 12-9 1797
RR fig. 27.

Feature A: pit Diam. 0.25 m, D. 0.2 m, charcoal fill, 1.8 m E. by S. of centre and 0.3 m above old surface.

Old surface 1.2 m S. of centre
5 *Accessory Cup*: point-tooth comb stamped; on rim, impressions; on body, irregular rows of short vertical lines; no perforations.
M. c. 5.8 cm; H. 4.7 cm; B. 3.0 cm. 79 12-9 1796
BAP no. 229a.

Mound material
6 *Collared Vessel sherd*: lower collar; irregular incised herringbone. 79 12-9 1802
Longworth no. 56a.
7 *Collared Vessel neck sherd*: plain. 79 12-9 1802a
Longworth no. 56b.
8 *Bone pin*: split caprovine metacarpal; cut and polished to fine point.
L. 8.7 cm; W. 1.1 cm; Th. 0.9 cm. 79 12-9 1800

290   LETCOMB BASSETT   290:1

Berkshire; Oxfordshire   SU 360 825

ROUND BARROW: Diam. 31 m, H. 1.5 m, reduced by ploughing; earth and some chalk, extensive animal disturbance.
RR 61-2.

Burial 1: disturbed cremation deposit; on old surface near centre.
1 *Flint barbed-and-tanged arrowhead:* all over bifacial invasive retouch; patinated.
   L. 2.8 cm; W. 2.6 cm; Th. 0.4 cm.   79 12-9 1804

Burial 2: adult cremation deposit; in central grave Diam. 0.3 m, D. 0.7 m, earth and chalk over basal chalk fill.

291   LETCOMB BASSETT   291:1-3

Berkshire; Oxfordshire   SU 360 825

ROUND BARROW: Diam. 14 m, H. 0.2 m, reduced by ploughing; composition not recorded; ?previously opened.
RR 62.

Burial 1: disturbed burnt and unburnt bones; near centre.

Mound material
1 *Beaker sherd:* tooth-comb stamped irregularly placed short lines.   79 12-9 1805
2 *Collared Vessel sherds:* two, including lower collar, neck and shoulder; twisted cord: on collar, horizontal lines; on neck, two horizontal lines. *Longworth* no. 1374a.   79 12-9 1805a
3 *Bronze Age sherds:* nine; plain.   79 12-9 1805b

292   CHILDREY (Childrey I)   292:1-5

Berkshire; Oxfordshire   SU 344 852

ROUND BARROW: Diam. 28 m, H. 1.7 m, reduced by ploughing; earth and chalk, two large sarsens 0.2 m above old surface 1.8 m SE. by E. of centre.
RR 63-4.

Burial 1: cremation deposit; in and on central oval grave L. 0.8 m, W. 0.7 m D. 0.4 m, aligned NNE.-SSW., charcoal fill capped by chalk.

Mound material
1 *Flint hollow-based arrowhead:* all over bifacial invasive retouch; patinated.
   L. 2.6 cm; W. 2.5 cm; Th. 0.4 cm.   79 12-9 1791
   Green 1980, no. A137.
2 *Flint end- and side-scraper:* edge retouch on distal and L. at 55 degrees; platform butt; patinated.
   L. 1.9 cm; W. 2.5 cm; Th. 0.6 cm.   79 12-9 1792

Not located
3 *Beaker sherds:* four; tooth-comb stamped; horizontal and diagonal reserved bands, one enclosed triangular space filled with jabbed impressions. 79 12-9 1793
4 *Beaker sherd:* plain.   79 12-9 1793a
5 *Flint flake:* dihedral butt; patinated.
   L. 5.4 cm; W. 2.2 cm; Th. 1.1 cm.   79 12-9 1794

293   CHILDREY (Childrey III)   293:1-2

Berkshire; Oxfordshire   SU 331 842

ROUND BARROW: Diam. 15 m, H. 0.2 m, reduced by ploughing; earth and chalk, ditched; previously opened at centre.
RR 64-5.

Burial 1: disturbed cremation deposit; with fragments of urn in and around previously opened central grave L. 0.8 m, W. 0.5 m, D. 0.5 m, aligned NE.-SW., with circular pit Diam. 0.5 m, D. 0.3 m at base at SW.
1 *Collared Urn:* twisted cord: on internal rim bevel, horizontal lines; on collar, two zones of filled triangles, split by two lines and enclosed above and below by three lines; on shoulder, row of horseshoes.
   M. 30.2 cm; H. 41.9 cm; B. 16.5 cm.   79 12-9 1790
   RR fig. 28; *Longworth* no. 1380.
2 *'Lignite bead':* not identified.   79 12-9 1801

294   BRIMPTON

Berkshire   SU 578 626

ROUND BARROW: Diam. 27 m, H. 2.1 m; gravelly sand.
RR 65-6.

295   BRIMPTON

Berkshire   SU 578 626

ROUND BARROW: dimensions not recorded; gravelly sand.
RR 65-6.

296   WARKWORTH   296:1-3

Northumberland   NU 277 043

ROUND CAIRN: Diam. 12 m, H. 1.5 m; beach pebbles, beneath dune; part recorded in destruction by quarrying by G. H. Thompson, remainder opened 1883.
RR 66-70.

Burial 1: inhumation traces, head E.; in central cist L. 1.1 m, W. 0.6 m, D. 0.6 m, aligned E. by N.-W. by S., four side-slabs and cover at level of old surface.
1 *Bronze knife:* flat triangular blade with arched butt and traces of diffuse edge bevels; rivets with faceted shanks and slightly expanded heads (Table 1:15).
   L. 3.5 cm; W. 2.9 cm; Th. 0.1 cm.
   rivet L. 0.8 cm; shank Diam. 0.3 cm.   84 12-23 3
   RR fig. 29; *Gerloff* 1975, no. 260.
   'food-vessel': not preserved.
   'worked flint': not preserved.

Burial 2: cremation deposit; on capstone of Burial 1 cist, slab cover.

Burial 3: child inhumation traces; in irregular cist L. 0.4 m, E. of Burial 1 cist.

Burial 4: adult cremation deposit, in heap Diam. 0.25 m; 0.4 m above old surface, 0.9 m SW. of Burial 1 cist.

Burial 5: disturbed cremation deposit; ?in urn, in cist L. 0.6 m, W. 0.3 m, D. 0.3 m, four side-slabs and capstone, 1.8 m SSW. of Burial 1 cist.
2 *Bipartite Vessel:* incised: on internal rim bevel, short diagonal lines; on neck and on to upper body, herringbone.
   M. 11.0 cm; H. 13.5 cm; B. *c.* 8.0 cm.   84 12-23 1
   RR fig. 30; *BAP* no. 206; *Gibson* 1978, no. 27.

Burial 6: unknown; in cist E. of Burial 5.
   'food-vessel': present location unknown.

Burial 7: unknown; in cist E. of Burial 5.
   'food-vessel': present location unknown.

Burial 8: unknown; in cist L. 0.8 m, W. 0.4 m, D. 0.4 m, aligned E. by S.-W. by N., on old surface 4 m SSW. of Burial 1 cist.
   'pot': not preserved.

Burial 9: inhumation traces; 0.6 m above old surface, 1.8 m N. of Burial 1 cist.

3 *Food Vessel:* incised;; on internal rim bevel, herringbone; on external rim bevel, single horizontal line; on neck, row of diagonal lines above four horizontal lines; on body, herringbone above three horizontal lines partly made by conjoining impressions.

M. 12.0 cm; H. 13.8 cm; B. 6.0 cm.   84 12-23 2
BAP no. 212; *Gibson* 1978, no. 85.

Burial 10: inhumation traces, crouched on L. with head E.; in cist L. 1.2 m, W. 0.5 m, D. 0.6 m, aligned NE.-SW., four side-slabs and capstone with clay-luting, on old surface adjacent to Burial 9.

Burial 11: adult male inhumation, crouched on L.; in cist L. 1.8 m, W. 0.6 m, D. 0.6 m, four side-slabs and capstone; location unknown.

Burial 12: inhumation traces, in cist L. 1.2 m, W. 0.7 m, D. 0.6 m, aligned N.-S., paved; location unknown.

'cinerary urn': present location unknown.

Burials or cairn material

'bronze blade': present location unknown.
'cinerary urn': present location unknown.

297 SNOWSHILL   297:1-4

Gloucestershire   SP 092 332

ROUND BARROW: Diam. 20 m, H. 1.7 m, reduced by ploughing; opened by ? in January 1881: information obtained *via* G. B. Witts.
RR 70-2; *AHG* no. 18; *GB* 130.

Burial 1: inhumation traces; in central cist L. 1.2 m, W. 0.9 m, D. 0.8 m, four side-slabs and capstone, partly sunk into old surface.

1 *Bronze tanged-and-collared spearhead:* ogival blade with stout lozenge-sectioned midrib flanked by band of four grooves, low step and hollowed edge bevel; midrib continuing on tang to produce hexagonal section; tang with bevelled end and two loops in contact with collar; separate collar with groove to seat base of blade and bands of four grooves at top and base; thick rivets, that in tang square-sectioned with faceted corners (Table 1:1).
Blade L. 23.8 cm; W. 5.9 cm; Th. 1.2 cm.
Collar W. 5.9 cm; Th. 2.7 cm.
Tang rivet L. 2.9 cm; shank Diam. 0.7 cm.   WG 2126
RR fig. 31; *Needham* 1979, no. 23; *Gerloff* 1975, no. 40.

2 *Bronze dagger:* Gerloff Type Snowshill; ogival blade with lozenge-sectioned midrib flanked by triple groove, low step and hollowed edge bevel; arched butt with omega hilt line; one surviving thick rivet of square section with faceted corners (Table 1:7).
L. 21.5 cm; W. 6.5 cm; Th. 0.7 cm.
Rivet L. 2.2 cm; shank Diam. 0.8 cm.   WG 2127
RR fig. 32; *Gerloff* 1975, no. 153.

3 *Bronze crutch-headed pin:* head with slightly trapezoidal section and rounded ends, convex underside; round-sectioned shank; tip lacking (Table 1:44).
L. 16.6 cm; W. 1.6 cm; shank Diam. 0.5 cm. WG 2128
RR fig. 33; *Piggott* 1973, 359.

4 *Stone battle-axe:* Roe VE(S); Group XII picrite, SW. 1502; ground and polished with blunt blade and bevelled angular butt; drilled central perforation of modified hourglass profile.
L. 15.9 cm; W. 5.6 cm; Th. 2.3 cm; blade H. 6.4 cm;
perf. Diam. 2.1 cm.   WG 2129
RR fig. 34; *Roe* 1966, no. 75.

UNNUMBERED BARROWS 1–146

ROWCROFT (Yattenden: England's Battle) UN 1:1

Berkshire   SU 55 75

ROUND BARROW: Diam. 11 m, H.?; core of 'large rough flints' with earth capping; opened by W. Dewe, *c.* 1861. [This dagger previously recorded as Burrow Hill, Stanmore].
Dewe 1861; Palmer 1873; Peake 1931, 51.

Burial 1: 'bone dust'; on old surface at centre.

1 *Bronze dagger:* Gerloff Type Camerton: arched butt with central indent partly formed by forging and traces of omega hilt line; two rivet holes, one retaining thick rivet with irregularly formed heads; thick rounded midrib tending to lozengic section towards tip, flanked by four close-set grooves, one furrow and narrow edge bevel at either side; edges damaged by corrosion (Table 1:8).
L. 18.5 cm; W. 5.2 cm; Th. 8.1 cm.
rivet L. 1.7 cm; Diam. (shank) 0.8 cm, (head) 0.9–1.0 cm.   WG 2068
Gerloff 1975, nos 180 and 187.

WYTHAM   UN 2:1-2

Berkshire; Oxfordshire   SP 47 08

UNKNOWN CONTEXT: no information.
Unpublished.

Burial 1: cremation deposit.

1 *Flint knife:* edge retouch on bilateral converging on distal; burnt and broken.
L. 3.9 cm; W. 1.8 cm; Th. 0.3 cm.   79 12-9 1786

2 *Bone belt-hook:* cut and polished from longbone segment; sub-rectangular plate curved to lingulate hook; two parallel lines incised along each side of hook; burnt and distorted.
L. 2.5 cm; W. 2.5 cm; Th. 0.4 cm.   79 12-9 1785

COPT HILL   UN 3:1-14

Durham; Tyne and Wear   NZ 353 492

ROUND CAIRN: Diam. 20 m, H. 2.4 m; limestone and sandstone boulders and slabs; opened by W. G. and T. W. U. Robinson, 20 September 1877.
WG Ms 3; Trechmann 1914, 123-30; Kinnes 1979, Aa 8.

Burial 1: crematorium deposit; multiple disarticulated inhumations burnt *in situ*; in burnt limestone matrix in rectangular boulder setting L. 10 m, W. 1.8 m, aligned E.–W., 1.5 m S. of centre; terminal pits L. 0.9 m, W. 0.5 m, D. 0.6 m, with boulder lining and fill of burnt earth and charcoal.

Burial 2: scattered cremation deposit, Diam. 0.8 m; 0.6 m above old surface, 7 m SE. by S. of centre.
'*piece of calcined flint*': not preserved.

Burial 3: child inhumation traces, crouched on R. with head NNW.; in cist L. 0.6 m, W. 0.3 m, D. 0.3 m, aligned SE. by S.–NW. by N., four side-slabs with capstone and paving slab; 5 m SSW. of centre.

Burial 4: double inhumation traces; 0.5 m below mound surface, 1 m SE. of centre.
'*flint scraper*': perhaps no. 4 or 5 below.

Burial 5: inhumation traces, crouched on L. with head WSW.; 1.5 m above old surface, 5.1 m ESE. of centre.

Burial 6: inhumation traces; 0.3 m above old surface, 4.8 m ENE. of centre; vessel at head.
'*food vessel*': not preserved.

Burial 7: cremation deposit; 0.3 m above Burial 6.

Burial 8: cremation deposit; 0.3 m above Burial 6, 0.3 m from Burial 7.

Burial 9: cremation deposit; in inverted urn within stone setting, 0.6 m above old surface, 4.8 m NE. by E. of centre.

1 *Food Vessel Urn:* impressed end of snapped flint blade: on internal rim bevel and neck, herringbone; on external rim bevel and shoulder groove, single rows of diagonal impressions.
M. 27.2 cm; H. 33.8 cm; B. 11.7 cm   90 11-11 1
Trechmann 1914, fig. 4; BAP no. 484; Cowie 1978, DUR 1; Gibson 1978, no. 92.

Not located

2 *Shale pebble*   90 11-11 14
3 *Flint plano-convex knife:* all over invasive retouch; limited inverse retouch on obverse; burnt.
L. 6.0 cm; W. 2.5 cm; Th. 0.8 cm.   90 11-11 3
4 *Flint horseshoe scraper:* edge retouch at 50 degrees; mottled grey.
L. 2.0 cm; W. 1.8 cm; Th. 0.4 cm.   90 11-11 4
5 *Flint end- and side-scraper:* edge retouch on R. and distal at 40 degrees; mottled grey.
L. 5.9 cm; W. 4.2 cm; Th. 1.2 cm.   90 11-11 2

Flint flakes

	Btt	Ctx	Col.	L.	W.	Th.	90 11-11
6	Pl.	x	M. Gr.	3.4	1.4	0.2	5
7		x	Bge	3.2	0.9	0.3	6
8	Pl.	x	M. Gr.	2.6	2.4	0.5	7
9	Pl.	x	Pat.	2.8	2.3	0.5	8
10	Pl.		Bt	2.2	1.7	0.3	9
11			Bt	1.7	2.1	0.7	10
12	Pl.	x	Pat.	2.3	2.2	0.9	11
13			Pat.	2.4	1.4	0.4	12

14 *Flint fragment*   90 11-11 13

SACRISTON   UN 4:1

Durham   NZ 240 470

CIST: found 1888.
Greenwell 1889; Trechmann 1914, 134-5.

Burial 1: adult ?male inhumation; in cist L. 1.1 m, W.
0.6 m, D. 0.6 m, aligned E.-W., four side-slabs with
capstone at level of 'natural surface'.

1   *Beaker:* beneath rim, zone of eight grooved horizontal
    lines; below, three zones in rectangular toothed comb
    stamp: upper, opposed herringbone separated and
    bordered beneath by pairs of horizontal lines;
    central, lattice separated and bordered by pairs of
    horizontal lines; basal, five horizontal lines.
    M. *c.* 14.8 cm; H. *c.* 18.2 cm; B. 9.1 cm.   WG 2285
    BAP no. 177; *Clarke* no. 223; *Tait* 1965, no. 68;
    Trechmann 1914, 176.

STEEPLE HILL   UN 5

Durham; Tyne and Wear   NZ 40 53

ROUND BARROW: 'small'; earth and stones on natural
mound; recorded in destruction by W.G. February 1876.
BB 441.

Burial 1: inhumation and cremation: adult male crouched
with head W. and child cremation deposit; in cist L. 1.2
m, W. 0.8 m, D. 0.7 m, aligned E.-W., six side-slabs and
capstone; vessels at chest, one containing cremation.
    'two food vessels': not preserved.

Burial 2: adult female inhumation, crouched with head
W.; in rough stone setting; 0.9 m W. of Burial 1.

STONEBRIDGE   UN 6:1-3

Durham   NZ 258 414

UNKNOWN CONTEXT: no information; found 1899.
Trechmann 1914, 170-2.

Burial 1: cremation deposit; in urn 1 with vessel 2
inverted over.

1   *Collared Urn:* on internal rim bevel, two plaited cord
    lines; on collar, plaited cord lattice; on neck,
    roughly executed incised linear lattice.
    M. 27.5 cm; H. 36.0 cm; B. *c.* 11.5 cm.   WG 2411
    Trechmann 1914, fig. 23; *Gibson* 1978, no. 140;
    Longworth no. 532.
2   *Collared Vessel:* on collar, twisted cord horizontal
    lines.
    M. 16.5-17.4 cm; H. 23.0 cm; B. 7.4 cm.   WG 2412
    Trechmann 1914, fig. 25; *Gibson* 1978, no. 99;
    Longworth no. 533.

Burial 2: cremation deposit; 0.6 m from Burial 1.
3   *Accessory Cup:* plain, no perforations.
    M. 6.8 cm; H. 5.8 cm; B. 5.9 cm.   WG 2413
    Trechmann 1914, fig. 24.

TRIMDON GRANGE   UN 7:1-2

Durham   NZ 372 358

ROUND BARROW: no information.
BB 442; *VCH Durham* I, 207.

Not located
1   *Food Vessel Urn rim sherd:* whipped cord: on internal
    rim bevel, herringbone; on neck, row of short
    diagonal lines above herringbone; below shoulder,
    row of short diagonal lines.   79 12-9 1733
    Cowie 1978, DUR 5; *Gibson* 1978, no. 88.
2   *?Food Vessel Urn sherd:* very coarse whipped cord
    short vertical lines.   79 12-9 1733a

ULVERSTON (Urswick)   UN 8:1-4

Lancashire; Cumbria   SD 242 724

?CEMETERY: in natural sand knoll; accidentally discovered *c.* 1861-64.
Fell 1957.

Burial 1: cremation deposit; in urn.
1   *Bronze razor-knife:* Butler and Smith Class 1B; narrow
    tang expanding towards broken terminal; drooping and
    blunted shoulders for bowed triangular blade with
    broken tip; broad edge-bevels (Table 1:20).
    L. 8.0 cm; w. 2.4 cm; Th. 0.3 cm.   79 12-9 1783
    Butler and Smith 1956, 51, no. 5; *Jöckenhovel* 1980,
    no. 48.
2   *Collared Urn:* jabbed impressions, obliterated in
    places by later smoothing; on collar, rows in rough
    herringbone; on neck, irregular.
    M. *c.* 27.0 cm; H. 31.3 cm; B. 12.3 cm. 79 12-9 1781
    Longworth no. 242.

Burial 2: cremation deposit; in urn 3 with vessel 4.
3   *Collared Urn:* incised: on collar, linear filled
    triangles enclosed between groups of three
    horizontal lines; on neck, linear lattice enclosed
    between groups of three to four horizontal lines.
    M. 34.0 cm; H. 41.4 cm; B. 11.6 cm.   79 12-9 1780
    Longworth no. 241.
4   *Bipartite Vessel:* twisted cord: on top of rim, single
    line; on upper body, diagonal lines enclosed between
    single horizontal lines; on lower body, short
    diagonal lines.
    M. *c.* 10.0-11.4 cm; H. 11.5 cm; B. 8.2 cm.
                                            79 12-9 1782

DENTON   UN 9:1

Lincolnshire   SK 86 32

CONTEXT UNKNOWN: no information.
Unpublished.

Burial 1: inhumation traces.
1   *Beaker:* tooth-comb stamped: on neck, deep zone of
    alternate reserved and filled bar chevrons, chevrons
    and triangular spaces above and below filled with
    vertical to diagonal spatula impressions, enclosed
    above by four and below by three horizontal lines; on
    body, narrow zone of vertical to diagonal spatula
    impressions enclosed above by four and below by three
    horizontal lines, separated by reserved zone from
    basal zone of two narrow bands of diagonal lines,
    upper made with spatula, bordered above by three and
    separated by four horizontal lines.
    M. 12.0 cm; H. 14.9 cm; B. 7.4 cm.   WG 2282
    BAP no. 58; *Clarke* no. 445.

ALWINTON (Farnham)   UN 10:1-3

Northumberland   NT 92 06

?CEMETERY: no information.
Unpublished.

Burial 1: inhumation; in cist.
1   *Beaker:* tooth-comb stamped: below rim, band of
    lattice above three horizontal lines with row of
    short diagonal lines beneath, and second zone of
    horizontal lines bordered above and below by short
    diagonal lines; on belly, zone of horizontal lines
    bordered above by short diagonal lines and below by
    chevrons; on lower body, zone of horizontal lines
    bordered above by chevrons and below by lozenges; at
    base, zone of horizontal lines bordered above by
    lozenges.
    M. *c.* 14.0 cm; H. 18.5 cm; B. 8.3 cm. 79 12-9 1764
    BAP no. 162; *Clarke* no. 650; *Tait* 1965, no. 36.

Burial 2: cremation deposit; in urn with stone lid.

2 *Food Vessel Urn*: twisted cord: on internal rim bevel, two discontinuous horizontal lines; on external rim bevel, neck and upper body, rows of short vertical lines.

M. 21.6 cm; H. 24.7 cm; B. *c.* 9.5 cm.   79 12-9 1762
Cowie 1978, NOR 6; *Gibson* 1978, 87.

3 *Stone 'lid'*: tufa fragment, roughly chipped and broken along one edge.

L. 19.4 cm; W. 17.6 cm; Th. 2.7 cm.   79 12-9 1763

ANCROFT (The Cursed Field)   UN 11:1

Northumberland   NU 041 456

CIST: opened 1890 by unknown.
WG Ms 6.

Burial 1: adult? male inhumation, crouched on L. with head W.; in cist L. 1 m, W. 0.7 m, D. 0.6 m, four side-slabs and capstone; Beaker at face.

1 *Beaker*: tooth-comb stamped; on neck, narrow zone of lattice enclosed between horizontal lines above zone of pendant triangles filled with horizontal lines; on shoulder, zone of lattice enclosed between single horizontal lines, above zone of pendant triangles filled with horizontal lines, above zone of lattice enclosed by single horizontal lines.

M. 16.0 cm; H. 17.8 cm; B. 8.6 cm.   WG 2286
BAP no. 180; *Clarke* no. 656; *Tait* 1965, no. 73.

BEWICK MOOR   UN 12:1-2

Northumberland   NU 09 22

ROUND CAIRN: no details; opened by shepherd 28 April 1865.
BB 418.

Burial 1: no information; in cist.

1 *'Sherds of drinking-cup'*: not identified.
Tait 1965, no. 95.   79 12-9 1750

Burial 2: no information; in cist.

Not located

2 *Food Vessel Urn rim sherd*: on internal rim bevel, incised herringbone; on outer edge of rim, short diagonal impressions; beneath rim, incised lattice.
79 12-9 1751

BLUEBELL INN (North Sunderland)   UN 13:1-2

Northumberland   NU 215 315

CIST: opened 30 May 1862.
Simpson 1862.

Burial 1: child inhumation, with head SE.; in cist L. 1 m, W. 0.8 m, D. 0.8 m, aligned E.-W.; Beakers in NE. corner.

1 *Beaker*: beneath rim, zone of short diagonal tooth-comb stamped lines above four horizontal grooved lines with fringe of diagonal spatula impressions below; on belly, three horizontal tooth-comb stamped lines between opposed fringes of diagonal spatula impressions; on body, similar zone but with spatula impressions in same plane.

M. 11.0 cm; H. 12.6 cm; B. 6.8 cm.   WG 2283
BAP no. 179; *Clarke* no. 695; *Tait* 1965, no. 51.

2 *Beaker*: tooth-comb stamped: in neck, zone of three narrow bands of short diagonal lines enclosed by chevrons, bordered above by single horizontal grooved line and separated by narrow reserved band

enclosed by single grooved lines; on body, three similar bands separated by horizontal lines, the uppermost bordered by three horizontal lines and fringe of chevrons.

M. 14.3 cm; H. 20.7 cm; B. 6.8 cm.   WG 2284
BAP no. 178; *Clarke* no. 696; *Tait* 1965, no. 52.
'beaker': not preserved.

BROOMRIDGE 1   UN 14:1

Northumberland   NT 94 37

ROUND BARROW: no information.
Unpublished.

Burial 1: cremation deposit.

1 *'Fragments of urn'*: not identified.   79 12-9 1748

BROOMRIDGE 2   UN 15:1-3

Northumberland   NT 94 37

ROUND BARROW: Diam.?, H. 0.3 m; opened by Capt. Carpenter 28 March 1852.
BB 408 fn. 1.

Burial 1: cremation deposit; in urn 1 with vessel 2 inverted over, in circular clay-lined hollow.

1 *Collared Urn*: twisted cord: on internal moulding, lozenges between single lines; on collar and neck to below shoulder, herringbone.

M. *c.* 16.7-18.5 cm; H. 24.0 cm; B. *c.* 8.3-9.7 cm.
Longworth no. 1044.   79 12-9 1398

2 *Collared Vessel*: twisted cord: on collar and neck, horizontal lines; beneath shoulder, short diagonal lines.

M. 11.9 cm; H. 13.1 cm; B. 6.0 cm.   79 12-9 1399
Longworth no. 1045.

Burial 2: cremation deposit; near Burial 1.
'incense cup': not preserved.

Not located

3 *Urn sherds*: two; horizontal twisted cord lines.
79 12-9 1400

CHESWICK   UN 16:1

Northumberland   NU 03 46

CIST: in natural knoll; opened by Donaldson.
Donaldson 1838.

Burial 1: inhumation traces; in cist L. 0.8 m, W. 0.8 m, D. 0.6 m, four side-slabs and capstone; dagger at head.

1 *Bronze dagger*: Gerloff Type Ridgeway: blade of sinuous profile with narrow edge-bevels; low midrib of rounded section changing to lozenge section towards tip and defined by slight grooves; one damaged rivet hole with thick rivet; W-shaped hilt line defined by variation in patina (Table 1:9).

L. 16.9 cm; W. 5.2 cm; Th. 3.7 cm.
rivet L. 1.1 cm; Diam. (shank) 0.9 cm, (head) 0.9 cm.
Gerloff 1975, no. 96.   79 12-9 1755

CROOKHAM   UN 17:1

Northumberland   NT 91 38

UNKNOWN CONTEXT: no information.
Unpublished.

1 *Food Vessel*: on internal rim bevel, incised short diagonal lines; on external rim bevel, vertical impressions; on neck, scored discontinuous horizon-

tal lines; on shoulder, row of jabbed impressions; on body, zone of scored herringbone bordered above by two and separated by three scored discontinuous horizontal lines from zone of diagonal lines, separated by three similar lines from zone of scored herringbone bordered beneath by row of jabbed impressions above scored horizontal lines.
M. 15.1 cm; H. 14.3 cm; B. *c.* 9.8 cm.
BB fig. 80; *Gibson* 1978, no. 13.   79 12-9 1419

CROOKHAVEN   UN 18:1-6

Northumberland   NT 94 37

UNKNOWN CONTEXT: 'found at different times near Ford.' *Longworth* 1969.
1 *Neolithic Bowl rim sherds*: two; on rim, twisted cord curved lines; on body discontinuous diagonal strokes.
M. *c.* 35.0 cm.   79 12-9 1743
Longworth 1969, fig. 1.2.
2 *Neolithic Bowl sherds*: two; scored short irregular lines, some crossing.   79 12-9 1743a
3 *Neolithic Bowl sherd*: twisted cord short diagonal lines; on interior, traces of whipped cord impressions.   79 12-9 1743b
4 *Neolithic Bowl rim sherd*: on rim, twisted cord concentric semi-circles beneath two horizontal lines; on external rim bevel, incised herringbone; on shoulder, two twisted cord horizontal lines; on body, twisted cord diagonal lines.
M. *c.* 24.0 cm.   79 12-9 1744
Longworth 1969, fig. 1.3.
5 *Neolithic Bowl rim sherd*: on rim, twisted cord concentric semi-circles beneath two twisted cord lines; on external rim bevel, incised herringbone; on body, twisted cord diagonal lines.
M. *c.* 20.0 cm.   79 12-9 1745
Longworth 1969, fig. 1.4.
6 *Neolithic Bowl rim sherd*: on rim, incised herringbone.
M. *c.* 31.0 cm.   79 12-9 1746
Longworth 1969, fig. 1.1.

DODDINGTON MOOR   UN 19:1-5

Northumberland   NU 00 32

ROUND BARROW: no information; previously disturbed, opened by W.G. 1858.
Unpublished.

Not located
1 *Collared Vessel sherd*: twisted cord: on collar, filled triangles; on neck, lattice.   79 12-9 1778
Longworth no. 1042.
2 *Collared Vessel sherds*: seven including rim; twisted cord: on internal rim bevel, four horizontal lines; on collar, filled triangles enclosed by triple horizontal lines.
M. *c.* 16.0 cm.   79 12-9 1778a
Longworth no. 1043.
3 *?Collared Vessel sherds*: three, including base; plain.   79 12-9 1778b
4 *?Collared Vessel sherds*: four, including base; plain.   79 12-9 1778c
5 *Bronze Age sherds*: two; traces of coarse twisted cord impressions.   79 12-9 1778d

FORD   UN 20:1-4

Northumberland   NT 94 37

ROUND BARROW(S): no information.
Unpublished.

Not located
1 *Beaker*: rectangular tooth-comb stamped: beneath rim, zone of five grooved horizontal lines above two deep zones of lattice separated by narrow zone of horizontal lines, bordered below by further zone of lines.
M. *c.* 13.4 cm; H. 15.4 cm; B. *c.* 8.0 cm.
                              79 12-9 1740
BAP no. 164; *Clarke* no. 671; *Tait* 1965, no. 46.
2 *Food Vessel Urn*: twisted cord: on internal and external rim bevels, horizontal lines; on neck, applied vertical chevrons with single lines, the spaces between filled with vertical and diagonal twisted cord lines; on body, irregularly placed vertical to diagonal lines.
M. *c.* 27.0 cm; surviving H. 15.0 cm.   79 12-9 1739
Gibson 1978, no. 112; *Cowie* 1977, NOR7.
3 *Accessory Cup*: twisted cord: above shoulder, five to six horizontal lines crossed at intervals by groups of vertical to diagonal lines; one pair of perforations set vertically surviving.
M. 6.6 cm; H. 5.3 cm; B. 5.4 cm.   79 12-9 1741
BAP no. 327.
4 *Accessory Cup*: plain; one pair of perforations.
M. 5.4 cm; H. 4.3 cm; B. 4.6 cm.   79 12-9 1742
BAP no. 306.

FOWBERRY (Chatton)   UN 21:1-4

Northumberland   NU 038 276

CIST: no information.
Unpublished.

Burial 1: inhumation.
1 *Bronze awl*: Thomas Type 1A or 1B; central swelling with remains of lozenge facet on each of four faces; corroded and tips lacking (Table 1:41).
L. 2.7 cm; W. 0.3 cm; Th. 0.2 cm.   79 12-9 1758
Thomas 1968, 23.
2 *Food Vessel*: Yorkshire Vase; on internal and external rim bevels, on neck, in shoulder groove and over body and lugs, incised herringbone; three surviving of four lugs spanning shoulder groove.
M. 15.5 cm; H. 15.0 cm; B. 6.7 cm.   79 12-9 1757
3 *Beaker sherds*: eight joining of body and base; tooth-comb stamped: on lower neck, zone of horizontal lines above fringe of two rows of spatulate-end impressions; on body, zone of split herringbone separated from zone of double to triple zigzag by pair of horizontal lines, the whole enclosed above and below by a zone of spatulate-end impressions bordered by two to three horizontal lines with further two rows of spatulate-end impressions at base of neck.
B. 7.0 cm.   POA 170
4 *Beaker sherds*: five including rim and base; tooth-comb stamped: on top of rim, lozenge or lattice; externally, zone of short diagonal lines above zone of lattice bordered above and below by pairs of grooved horizontal lines; beneath, zone of zigzag separated from zone of diagonal lines by pair of grooved horizontal lines; at base, zone of horizontal lines.   POA 171
Tait 1965, no. 98; *Clarke* nos 673-4.

GREAT TOSSON   UN 22:1-5

Northumberland   NU 030 005

ROUND BARROW: 'low', reduced by ploughing; found in quarrying 1858.
BB 431–2; *Tate* 1861; *Davis & Thurnam* 1865, pl. 54.

Burial 1: adult? female inhumation, crouched with head S.; in grave.
1 *Food Vessel*: on internal and external rim bevels and over neck and body, incised herringbone.
   M. 14.9 cm; H. 13.7 cm; B. 7.6 cm.   79 12–9 1457
   BB fig. 161; *Gibson* 1978, no. 2.
2 *Jet button*: cut and polished to concave dome bevelled to flat base with off-centre drilled V-perforation.
   Diam. 3.8 cm; Th. 1.0 cm.   79 12–9 1455
   BB fig. 160.

Burial 2: adult inhumation, crouched with head S.; in grave.
3 *Food Vessel Urn*: twisted cord: on internal rim bevel, four lines; on external rim bevel, short vertical lines; on neck and shoulder groove and over shoulder, herringbone; beneath shoulder, row of short vertical lines.
   M. *c.* 19.3 cm; H. 21.2 cm; B. *c.* 8.7 cm.
                                               79 12–9 1458
   Gibson 1978, no. 98; *Cowie* 1978, NOR 9.
4 *Jet button*: cut and polished to dome slightly bevelled to convex base with drilled V-perforation.
   Diam. 5.1 cm; Th. 1.2 cm.   79 12–9 1456
5 *Antler ?pick*: shed red-deer antler; beam and brow and bez tines broken.
   L. 41.8 cm; Diam. 5.0 cm.   79 12–9 1737

Burial 3: inhumation; in grave.

Burial 4: inhumation; in grave.

GREENHILL (Ilderton)   UN 23:1

Northumberland   NU 02 22

CIST: no information; discovered 27 July 1872.
Greenwell 1872, 419–20.

Burial 1: ?decayed inhumation; in cist.
1 *Food Vessel*: on internal rim bevel, rows of jabbed impressions; on external rim bevel, short diagonal whipped cord lines; on neck, whipped cord herringbone split by one to two rows of jabbed impressions and three discontinuous horizontal whipped cord lines and bordered beneath by single similar line; over shoulder groove, irregular rows of jabbed impressions; on body, discontinuous whipped cord horizontal lines.
   M. 14.5 cm; H. 11.6 cm; B. 7.0 cm.   79 12–9 1752
   BAP no. 171; *Gibson* 1978, no. 53.

GRUNDSTONE LAW   UN 24

Northumberland   NZ 004 734

ROUND BARROW: Diam. 12 m, H. 1.2 m; earth and stones with remains of boulder kerb; opened by Coulson and re-opened by W.G. and Embleton 14 June 1862.
Greenwell & Embleton 1862.

Burial 1: (excavated Coulson) inhumation traces; on slab in mound at centre.

Burial 2: double inhumation: adult male on L. with head E. and few scattered bones of adult male; in central pit L. 1.8 m, W. 0.8 m, Diam. 0.7 m, aligned E.-W., partly slab-lined with four capstones.

GUNNERTON   UN 25:1

Northumberland   NY 905 750

CIST: no information.
Unpublished.

Burial 1: inhumation; in cist.
1 *Bone pin or point*: cut and polished from bovid size radius shaft to oval section; drilled perforation at butt; transverse line above double chevron incised on edge at butt; point broken.
   L. 17.1 cm; W. 2.5 cm; Th. 1.4 cm; Diam. perf. 0.4 cm.
                                               79 12–9 1773

HARTBURN   UN 26

Northumberland   NZ 08 86

FLAT GRAVE: opened by W.G.
BB 435; *Kinnes* 1979, 127.

Burial 1: adult inhumation traces, extended with head W.; in grave L. 1.7 m, W. 0.8 m, D. 0.5 m, aligned E.-W.; at E. and along each side surface setting of ten stones; 0.8 m to W., oval pit L. 1.3 m, W. 0.7 m, D. 0.5 m with basal circular pit at N. D. 0.3 m, aligned N.-S., fill of earth and stones with some charcoal; two stones at W. side of pit, L. 1.4 m.

HEDLEY WOOD   UN 27:1-2

Northumberland   NT 985 006

CIST: no information.
Unpublished.

Burial 1: no information; in cist.
1 *Collared Vessel*: on internal moulding, collar, neck and body, incised herringbone.
   M. 16.6 cm; H. *c.* 23.0 cm.   79 12–9 1766
   Longworth no. 1060.
2 *Flint side-scraper*: edge retouch on R. at 50 degrees; edge damage and limited retouch on L.; cortex remnant; mottled grey.
   L. 6.8 cm; W. 4.6 cm; Th. 0.8 cm.   79 12–9 1767

HEPPLE 1 (Rothbury) or FENTON (Doddington)

                                                 UN 28:1

Northumberland   NU 06 01 or NT 97 33

UNKNOWN CONTEXT: no information.
BB 424 fn.
1 *Miniature Food Vessel*: Yorkshire Vase; on internal rim bevel, whipped cord herringbone; on external rim bevel, twisted cord horizontal line; on neck and body, twisted cord herringbone; on base, twisted cord rough cross; two surviving of four horizontally perforated lugs.
   M. 6.8 cm; H. 4.4 cm; B. 4.2 cm.   79 12–9 1454/1509
   BB fig. 79.
(According to *WG Ms* 12, 51: found with an inhumation in a cist at Fenton.)

HEPPLE 2 (Rothbury)   UN 29:1

Northumberland   NU 06 01

ROUND CAIRN: no information.
Unpublished.

Burial 1: cremation deposit.
1 *Jet bead*: cut and polished to barrel form; drilled perforation.
   L. 2.5 cm; Diam. terminal 0.7 cm, central 1.3 cm.
                                               79 12–9 1735

HOWBURN (Carham)   UN 30:1

Northumberland   NT 821 357

CIST: no information.
Unpublished.

Burial 1: ?decayed inhumation; in cist.
1 *Food Vessel*: coarse whipped cord: on internal rim
   bevel, short diagonal lines; on neck and body, short
   vertical lines.
   M. *c.* 14.0 cm; H. 11.7 cm; B. 9.6 cm. 79 12-9 1754
   Gibson 1978, no. 29.

LONG FRAMLINGTON   UN 31:1

Northumberland   NU 13 01

CIST: no information.
Unpublished.

Burial 1: no information; in cist.
1 '*Sherds of urn*': not identified.   79 12-9 1776

NORHAM   UN 32:1

Northumberland   NT 905 475

ROUND BARROW: no information.
Unpublished.

Not located
1 *Beaker*: tooth-comb stamped: on neck, zone of multiple
   vertical chevrons bordered above by three and below
   by two horizontal lines, each with a fringe of
   spatula impressions; on belly, two similar zones
   separated by three horizontal lines and bordered
   above by two and below by three horizontal lines,
   each with a fringe of spatula impressions; at base,
   zone of multiple vertical chevrons bordered above by
   three horizontal lines with fringe of spatula
   impressions and below by three horizontal lines.
   M. *c.* 13.0 cm; H. 18.0 cm; B. 9.0 cm. 79 12-9 1738
   BAP no. 183; *Clarke* no. 692; *Tait* 1965, no. 60.

NORTH CHARLTON   UN 33:1

Northumberland   NU 16 22

ROUND CAIRN: 'large'; recorded in destruction January
1824.
Tate 1891, 271-2.

Burial 1: inhumation traces; in cist L. 1.2 m, W. 0.6 m,
four side-slabs and capstone.

Burial 2: inhumation, head W.; in cist L. 1.8 m, W. 0.6
m, D. 0.8 m, side-stones and capstone with clay-luting;
dagger on chest.
1 *Bronze dagger*: Gerloff Type Masterton: blade of flat
   section with narrow hollowed edge-bevels; remains of
   one rivet hole and W-shaped hilt line on broken butt;
   point broken (Table 1:10).
   L. 12.9 cm; w. 5.2 cm; Th. 0.2 cm. 79 12-9 1756
   ABI 237; *Gerloff* 1975, no. 82.

OLD BEWICK   UN 34:1

Northumberland   NU 06 21

UNCERTAIN CONTEXT: found beneath a projecting stone,
April 1865.
Unpublished.
1 *Accessory Cup*: plain; no perforations.
   M. 9.8 cm; H. 7.3 cm. 79 12-9 1749
   Piggott 1931, fig. 7.6.

OLD ROTHBURY   UN 35:1

Northumberland   NU 06 01

CIST: no information.
BB 433.

Burial 1: no information; in cist.
1 *Beaker*: tooth-comb stamped: on rim, short diagonal
   lines; on neck, zone of upright triangles outlined by
   double lines of short impressions and filled with
   similar horizontal impressions, enclosed by irregular horizontal lines; on belly and at base, two
   similar zones with pendant triangles, enclosed by
   horizontal lines.
   M. *c.* 13.4 cm; H. 17.0 cm; B. 7.9 cm. 79 12-9 1736
   BAP no. 158; *Clarke* no. 703; *Tait* 1965, no. 81.

PLESSY MILL   UN 36:1-8

Northumberland   NZ 241 793

CEMETERY: no information.
Unpublished.

Burial 1: cremation deposit; in inverted vessel at D.
0.6 m.
1 *Food Vessel*: twisted cord: on internal rim bevel,
   vertical lines; on body, panels of diagonal lines
   split by paired vertical lines and enclosed above by
   one and below by three horizontal lines; on lower
   body, zone of three horizontal lines.
   M. *c.* 14.0 cm; surviving H. 15.0 cm. WG 2415
   BAP no. 493a.

Burial 2: cremation deposit; in inverted vessel at D.
0.6 m, 4.5 m from Burial 1.
2 *Food Vessel*: Yorkshire Vase; incised: on internal and
   external rim bevels, herringbone; on neck and in
   shoulder groove, herringbone split by horizontal
   lines; on lugs, vertical herringbone; on body,
   herringbone above herringbone split by horizontal
   lines; at base, two horizontal lines; four imperforate lugs, one damaged, spanning shoulder groove.
   M. 14.8 cm; H. 15.8 cm; B. 7.7 cm. WG 2414
   BAP no. 493b.

Burial 3: cremation deposit; in inverted vessel at D.
0.6 m, 4.5 m from Burials 1 and 2.
3 *Food Vessel*: on internal rim bevel, short diagonal
   lines/herringbone in cardial impression replaced in
   one sector by incision; on neck, irregular cardial-
   impressed herringbone; on shoulder, short diagonal
   incised lines; on body, confused incised herringbone.
   M. 11.2 cm; H. 11.1 cm; B. 6.4 cm. WG 2416
   BAP no. 493; *Gibson* 1978, no. 3.

Burials 1, 2 and 3
4 *Flint plano-convex knife*: all over invasive retouch;
   burnt and broken.
   L. 3.7 cm; W. 2.0 cm; Th. 0.8 cm. WG 2418
5 *Flint knife*: bilateral edge retouch converging on
   distal; burnt.
   L. 5.5 cm; W. 2.8 cm; Th. 0.7 cm. WG 2417
6 *Flint knife*: bilateral edge retouch converging on
   distal; burnt.
   L. 4.9 cm; W. 1.7 cm; Th. 0.6 cm. WG 2419
7 *Flint knife fragment*: edge retouch on L.; broken;
   mottled beige.
   L. 4.2 cm; W. 1.2 cm; Th. 0.4 cm. WG 2420
8 *Flint fragment*: burnt. WG 2421

Burials 4-23: cremation deposits, in group; unlocated.

RATCHEUGH   UN 37:1-3

Northumberland   NU 231 152

ROUND BARROW: no information.
Unpublished.

Not located

1   *Beaker sherds*: four including rim and base; grooved:
    on internal rim bevel, two horizontal lines;
    externally, deep zone formed by reserved extended
    chevron pattern outlined by single lines with
    triangular and pentagonal spaces filled with
    vertical lines, and, above and below this, narrow
    zones formed by double chevrons bordered above by
    short lines enclosed between triple horizontal
    lines.
    M. *c.* 17.0 cm; H. 14.3 cm; B. *c.* 11.7 cm.
                                                    79 12-9 1779
2   *Food Vessel Urn rim sherds*: three; twisted cord: on
    top of rim, short transverse to diagonal lines;
    externally, short vertical lines becoming longer on
    body.
    Gibson 1978, no. 89.   79 12-9 1768
3   *Food Vessel Urn rim sherd*: on internal and external
    rim bevels, jabbed impressions; in first groove,
    short diagonal incised lines above row of jabbed
    impressions; in second groove, imperforate applied
    knob with remains of incised chevron on each side and
    bordered above and below by single rows of jabbed
    impressions; in third groove, remains of jabbed
    impression.   79 12-9 1769
    Gibson 1978, no. 101.

RED SCAR BRIDGE   UN 38:1

Northumberland   NT 950 337

UNKNOWN CONTEXT: beneath slab at D. 0.5 m, found 21 April
1865.
Longworth 1969, 260-1.
1   *Bronze Age sherd*: triangles outlined by three grooved
    lines, alternately plain and decorated with short
    vertical jabbed impressions through which runs a line
    of pits, one perforating the wall.
    Longworth 1969, fig. 1.5.   79 12-9 1747

ROSEDEAN (Roseden Edge)   UN 39:1-2

Northumberland   NU 02 21

UNKNOWN CONTEXT: no information; found *c.* 1835.
Hardy 1886, 277-8.

Burial 1: inhumation.
1   *Food Vessel*: whipped cord: on top of rim and on
    ridges, short diagonal lines; in grooves, discon-
    tinuous horizontal lines; on body, filled triangles
    above zone of discontinuous horizontal lines.
    M. 16.6 cm; H. 14.0 cm; B. 7.8 cm.   WG 2287
    Hardy 1886, pl. 5.2; *Gibson* 1978, no. 64.

Burial 2: cremation.
2   *Accessory Cup*: incised: on rim, triple chevrons; on
    upper body, upright quadruple chevrons with some of
    pendant fields filled with light incised lattice,
    enclosed above by two and below by one horizontal
    lines; beneath shoulder, pendant quadruple chevrons
    between single horizontal lines; on base, opposed
    chevrons; two perforations.
    M. 9.7 cm; H. 7.2 cm; B. 3.9 cm.   WG 2287a
    BAP no. 286; *Hardy* 1886, pl. 5.1; *Gibson* 1978, no. 71.

SEGHILL   UN 40:1

Northumberland   NZ 28 74

CIST: accidental find, 1866.
WG Ms 12, 38; *Greenwell* 1868b.

Burial 1: inhumation; in cist of four side-slabs with
capstone.
1   *Stone battle-axe*: quartzite; Roe II B; ground and
    polished to blunt blade and angular butt; drilled
    hourglass perforation.
    L. 16.2 cm; W. blade 6.4 cm, central 5.0 cm, butt 7.6
    cm; Th. 5.9 cm; Diam. perf. 2.4 cm.   Sturge
    ASI fig. 136; *Roe* 1966, no. 148; *Smith* 1931, fig. 470.

SMALESMOUTH   UN 41:1

Northumberland   NY 731 858

CIST: no information; opened J. Beatty December 1863.
BB 436; *WG Ms* 12, 51.

Burial 1: inhumation; in cist.
1   *Beaker*: tooth-comb stamped: on neck, zone of diagonal
    lines bordered above and below by impressions in
    chevron, above horizontal grooved lines bordered
    below by double row of impressions; on body, three
    zones of horizontal lines, the upper two bordered
    above and below and the lowest only above by double
    rows of impressions.
    M. 14.2 cm; H. 17.5 cm; B. 7.2 cm.   79 12-9 1770
    BAP no. 174; *Clarke* no. 664; *Tait* 1965, no. 55.

SPINDLESTON   UN 42:1-2

Northumberland   NU 15 33

ROUND BARROW: no information.
Unpublished.

Not located

1   *Food Vessel base sherd*: haphazard jabbed impressions
    between converging twisted cord lines.
                                                    79 12-9 1775
2   *Food Vessel Urn rim sherd*: on internal and external
    rim bevels, neck and shoulder grooves, incised
    herringbone; scar of former lug.
    Gibson 1978, no. 95.   79 12-9 1774

TANTALLON'S GRAVE (Tom Tallon's Grave)   UN 43:1

Northumberland   NT 932 280

ROUND CAIRN: Diam. *c.* 23 m, H. ?m, reduced by stone-
robbing; opened by Tate 1857.
Tate 1862, 445-6.

Burial 1: inhumation traces; in cist at E., L. 1 m, W.
0.5 m, aligned SE.-NW., four side-slabs with paved floor
and capstone.

Not located

1   *Collared Vessel sherds*: twenty-nine; on internal rim
    bevel, two whipped cord lines; on collar, twisted
    cord filled triangles between pairs of whipped cord
    lines; on neck, whipped cord vertical lines; on
    shoulder, row of jabs.   79 12-9 1777
    Longworth no. 1057; *Gibson* 1978, no. 118.

WARKSHAUGH   UN 44:1-3

Northumberland   NY 867 765

ROUND BARROW: Diam. *c.* 15 m, H. ?m, reduced by ploughing;
earth and stone layers, boulder kerb; opened by G. Rome
Hall 1865.
Rome Hall 1867.

Burial 1: cremation deposit; in inverted urn in upper
part of mound at SW.
1 *Collared Urn*: on collar and neck, incised herringbone.
   M. *c.* 35.0 cm; surviving H. 37.0 cm.   79 12-9 1759
   Rome Hall 1867, fig. 3; *Longworth* no. 1041.

Burial 2: ?decayed inhumation; in sand fill of cist L. 1
m, W. 0.8 m, D. 0.6 m, aligned E.-W., four side slabs and
capstone; at SSE. side of mound.
2 *Food Vessel*: on internal rim bevel, two rows of
   jabbed impressions; on external rim bevel, neck,
   shoulder groove and body, similar impressions mainly
   in roughly horizontal rows becoming diagonal on lower
   body.
   M. *c.* 15.5 cm; H. 14.8 cm; B. 9.0 cm.   79 12-9 1760
   Rome Hall 1867, fig. 4.
3 *Flint knife*: bilateral edge retouch converging on
   distal; corticated butt; mottled grey.
   L. 3.9 cm; W. 2.1 cm; Th. 0.4 cm.   79 12-9 1761

Burial 3: inhumation traces; in sand fill of cist L. 1 m,
W. 0.6 m, D. 0.7 cm, aligned E.-W., four side-slabs and
capstone; at S. edge of mound.

Burial 4: ?decayed inhumation; in sand fill of cist L.
0.7 m, W. 0.4 m. D. 0.6 m, aligned E.-W., seven side-
slabs and capstone; at SE side of mound.

Burial 5: ?decayed inhumation; in sand fill of central
cist L. 1 m, W. 0.5 m, D. 0.5 m, aligned E.-W., four
side-slabs and capstone.

WHITTINGHAM   UN 45:1

Northumberland   NU 06 11

ROUND BARROW: no information.
Unpublished.

Not located
1 *Food Vessel*: on internal rim bevel, two rows of
   diagonal incised strokes separated by row of bone
   impressions; on external rim bevel, row of diagonal
   incised strokes above row of vertical to diagonal
   strokes; in grooves, on ridges, and on upper part of
   body, rows of bone impressions.
   M. 11.7 cm; H. 12.1 cm; B. 6.4 cm.   79 12-9 1765

WOODHORN   UN 46:1

Northumberland   NZ 29 88

CIST: no information.
Unpublished.

Burial 1: inhumation; in cist.
1 *Beaker*: tooth-comb stamped: on neck, three zones
   separated and bordered by plain cordons, the
   upppermost with two rows of impressions bordering a
   reserved zone, the second with lattice, the lowest
   with multiple vertical chevrons; on body, zones of
   multiple vertical chevrons and lattice separated and
   bordered above by zones of horizontal lines with deep
   zone of similar lines beneath.
   M. 13.3 cm; H. 17.5 cm; B. 8.2 cm.   79 12-9 1753
   BAP no. 160; *Clarke* no. 711; *Tait* 1965, no. 70.

WOOLER   UN 47:1-2

Northumberland   NT 99 28

CIST: opened by Wightman, June 1872.
Greenwell 1872, 416-19.

Burial 1: adult male inhumation, crouched on L. with
head E.; in cist L. 1.4 m, W. 0.8-1 m, D. 0.6 m, aligned
E.-W., four side-slabs and capstone at D. 0.9 m.
1 *Food Vessel*: whipped cord: on internal and external
   rim bevels, filled triangles; on neck and upper body,
   zones of double zigzag above and below two zones of
   lozenges split and enclosed by pairs of horizontal
   lines.
   M. *c.* 20.0 cm; H. *c.* 17.0 cm; B. *c.* 9.0 cm.
                                               79 12-9 1772
2 *Jet button*: cut and polished to conical profile
   bevelled to flat base with central drilled V-
   perforation; broken.
   Diam. 5.3 cm; Th. 1.3 cm.   79 12-9 1771

SUMMERTOWN   UN 48:1-3

Oxfordshire   SP 51 09

GRAVE: no information, found 1875.
Unpublished.

Burial 1: inhumation.
1 *Beaker*: over neck and body, tooth-comb stamped
   horizontal lines; emmer and naked barley impressions.
   M. 13.7 cm; H. 20.1 cm; B. 7.5 cm.   79 12-9 1788
   BAP no. 75; *Clarke* no. 761; *Jessen & Helbaek* 1944, 18.
2 *Beaker*: over neck and body, shallow incised vertical
   to diagonal strokes.
   M. 10.2 cm; H. 12.3 cm; B. 5.8 cm.   79 12-9 1789
   Clarke no. 762.
3 *Flint barbed-and-tanged arrowhead*: all over invasive
   retouch; patinated.
   L. 2.8 cm; W. 2.0 cm; Th. 0.3 cm.   79 12-9 1787
   Green 1980, no. 180.

YARNTON   UN 49:1

Oxfordshire   SP 473 115

GRAVE: no information.
Unpublished.

Burial 1: crouched inhumation.
1 *Beaker*: three incised zones; upper, short diagonal
   lines; lower two, carelessly executed lozenges.
   M. *c.* 8.4 cm; H. 12.2 cm; B. 4.9 cm.   79 12-9 1784
   BAP no. 79; *Clarke* no. 777.

AMPTON (Seven Hills)   UN 50:1-2

Suffolk   TL 863 737

ROUND BARROW: Diam. 25 m, H. 2.6 cm (Diam. 24 m, H. 1.2
m: 1977); sand; opened by W.G. 26 May 1868.
Anon 1869; *Martin* 1981.

Burial 1: cremation deposit; in hollow Diam. 0.4 m at D.
0.5 m, 9 m S. by E. of centre.

Burial 2: cremation deposit; in hollow Diam. 0.3 m, D.
0.3 m, 9 m E. by N. of centre.

Burial 3: cremation deposit; 0.5 m above old surface, 5 m
ENE. of centre.

Burial 4: cremation deposit; in inverted urn 0.9 m above old surface, 3.7 m E. by S. of centre.

1 *Collared Urn*: on collar, twisted cord hurdle pattern.
   M. 24.1-25.6 cm; H. 35.2 cm; B. 12.1 cm.
   Longworth no. 1426.   79 12-9 1901
2 *Accessory Cup*: plain; no perforations.
   M. *c.* 5.0 cm; H. 5.2 cm; B. *c.* 5.0 cm. 79 12-9 1902

Burial 5: cremation deposit; 2.1 m above old surface, 3.6 m SW. by S. of centre.

Burial 6: child cremation deposit; near mound surface, 4.5 m NW. by W. of centre.

Mound material
   'many flints': not preserved.

BARTON HILLS   UN 51:1-2

Suffolk   TL 710 722

OVAL BARROW: L. 29 m, W. 23 m, H. 1.1 m, reduced by ploughing; sand with internal kerb of 'clunch' Diam. 11.5 m, W. 2.1 m, H. 0.7 m; opened by W.G. 2 June 1869.
Anon 1869; *Martin* 1981.

Burial 1: adolescent inhumation remains; in top of kerb, 5.4 m E. by S. of centre.

Burial 2: adult inhumation, crouched on L. with head NE.; in top of kerb, 6 m SE. by S. of centre.

Burial 3: cremation deposit; on kerb, 6.3 m S. by E. of centre.

Burial 4: inhumation traces; on old surface at centre.

Feature A: hollow Diam. 0.3 m, D. 0.2 m, 3.9 m NNE. of centre; fill of charcoal and burnt flints.

Mound material
   'plain sherds': not preserved.
1 *Flint double side-scraper*: bilateral edge retouch at 60 degrees; corticated butt; brown.
   L. 3.7 cm; W. 3.9 cm; Th. 1.0 cm.   79 12-9 1909
2 *'Flint core'*: not identified.   79 12-9 1908

LONG HEATH FIELD 1 (Risby 5)   UN 52

Suffolk   TL 783 681

ROUND BARROW: Diam. 17 m, H. ?m, (Diam. 28 m, H. 0.4 m: 1977); composition not recorded; opened by W.G. 26 February 1869.
Greenwell 1869; *Martin* 1981.

LONG HEATH FIELD 2 (Risby 6)   UN 53

Suffolk   TL 785 680

ROUND BARROW: Diam. 20 m, H. 0.9 m; composition not recorded; opened by W.G. 26 February 1869.
Greenwell 1869; *Martin* 1981.

Burial 1: cremation deposit; in pit L. 0.6 m, W. 0.3 m, D. 0.3 m, aligned SE.-NW., in burnt area Diam. 1.2 m; 5.7 m WSW. of centre.
   'burnt flints': not preserved.

Burial 2: cremation deposit; in pit L. 0.6 m, W. 0.5 m, D. 0.3 m, in burnt area Diam. 1.2 m; 1.7 m NW. of centre.

Mound material: 0.3 m above old surface, 5.4 m WSW. of centre.
   'fragments of urn': not preserved.

RISBY 1   UN 54:1-2

Suffolk   TL 776 679

ROUND BARROW: Diam 18 m, H. 1.5 m, reduced by ploughing; sand with chalk capping; opened by W.G. 25-6 February 1869, excavated by A.R. Edwardson 1959.
Greenwell 1869; *Edwardson* 1959; *Martin* 1981.

Burial 1: disturbed adolescent inhumation; on circular paving of chalk and flints Diam. 0.3 m, on old surface 7.2 m SSE. of centre.

Burial 2: adult female inhumation, crouched on R. with head NW. by N.; 0.6 m above old surface, 6.6 m SW. by S. of centre.

Burial 3: adolescent cremation deposit; in urn, 0.6 m above old surface, 7.8 m SW. by S. of centre.
   'urn': not preserved.

Burial 4: inhumation traces, crouched; 0.6 m above old surface, 0.9 m S. of centre.

Burial 5: adult male inhumation, crouched on R. with head W. by N.; on old surface at base of intrusive grave, 6.6 m W. by S. of centre.

Burial 6: adult male inhumation, crouched on L. with head NW.; in shallow grave, N. of centre.

Mound material (1869)
   'flint scraper': not preserved.

Mound material (1959)
1 *Flint pick*: made on patinated nodular fragment; sliced butt; bifacial invasive retouch around distal and in limited area on L.
   L. 11.1 cm; W. 3.5 cm; Th. 2.8 cm.   MHM 1980-106
2 *'Flint blade'*: not identified.   MHM

RISBY 2   UN 55:1-3

Suffolk   TL 776 678

ROUND BARROW: Diam. 23 m, H. 1.1 m, reduced by ploughing; sand with chalk capping from enclosing ditch; opened by W.G. 26 February 1869, excavated by Edwardson 1959.
Greenwell 1869; *Edwardson* 1959; *Martin* 1981.

Burial 1: cremation deposit; in urn, 0.6 m above old surface, 2.1 m SW. by W. of centre.
   'urn': not preserved.

Burial 2 (1959): adult cremation deposit; in hollow 5.1 m NW. by W. of centre.

Mound material (1869)
   'flint scraper': not preserved.

Mound material (1959)
1 *Collared Vessel sherds*: ten including collar and upper neck; on collar, rows of twisted cord zig-zag.
   Longworth no. 1515.   MHM 1977-854
2-3 *'Flint scrapers'*: two; not identified.   MHM

TUDDENHAM   UN 56:1

Suffolk   TL 74 71

ROUND BARROW: no information.
Fox 1923, 328.

Not located
1 *Handled Beaker*: tooth-comb stamped: on external rim bevel, short diagonal lines above horizontal line; on neck, deep zone of vertical panels consisting of short horizontal lines, vertical reserved bar chevrons with some triangular spaces filled with

short diagonal lines and vertical reserved lozenges
with some triangular spaces filled with short
vertical to diagonal lines, all separated by groups
of two or three vertical lines, and zone enclosed by
pairs of horizontal lines; on body, three narrow
zones, the uppermost of bar chevron filled with
vertical lines, the lower pair of lattice, separated
by reserved zones and enclosed between triple
horizontal lines; handle missing.
M. 11.5 cm; H. 14.9 cm; B. 7.6 cm.   79 12-9 1900
BAP no. 46; *Clarke* no. 952.

UNDLEY BARROW (Lakenheath)   UN 57:1-2

Suffolk   TL 698 619

ROUND BARROW: no information; opened *c.* 1895.
Fox 1923, 326.

Not located

1 *Beaker*: on rim, row of impressed jabs; tooth-comb
   stamped: on neck, deep zone of opposed bar chevrons
   with lozenge and triangular sections filled with
   vertical lines, enclosed by pairs of horizontal lines
   with further pair below rim; on body, four narrow
   zones of lattice enclosed by single horizontal lines
   and separated by reserved zones; at base, row of
   vertical triangles filled with horizontal lines.
   M. 14.8 cm; H. 18.5 cm; B. 7.5 cm.   79 12-9 1895
   BAP no. 61; *Clarke* no. 953.
2 *Beaker*: all over vertical to diagonal light finger-
   pinching.
   M. 12.0 cm; H. 14.4 cm; B. 6.6 cm.   79 12-9 1896
   Clarke no. 954.

WARREN HILL (Three Hills)   UN 58:1

Suffolk   TL 742 742

ROUND BARROW: no information; perhaps opened by Sir H.
E. Bunbury 1820.
Fox 1923, 327.

Not located

1 *Handled Food Vessel*: plain.
   M. 12.8 cm; H. 8.6 cm; B. 8.3 cm.   79 12-9 1899

CISSBURY   UN 59:1

Sussex   TQ 14 08

ROUND BARROW: no information.
Unpublished.

Burial 1: inhumation.
1 *Beaker*: tooth-comb stamped horizontal lines.
   M. 8.5 cm; H. 15.6 cm; B. 6.5 cm.   79 12-9 2099
   Clarke no. 989.

CROSBY MOOR   UN 60

Westmorland; Cumbria   NY 60 15

ROUND BARROW: Diam. 7.2 m, H. 1.2 m; earth; opened by
W.G.
BB 398.

ALDBOURNE (Aldbourne XII)   UN 61:1-10

Wiltshire   SU 24 76

ROUND BARROW: no information; opened by W.G.
Unpublished.

Not located

1 *Beaker rim sherds*: two; tooth-comb stamped horizontal above diagonal lines.   79 12-9 1886
2 *Beaker rim sherd*: horizontal rows of elongated
   impressions.   79 12-9 1886a
3 *Beaker rim sherd*: twisted cord: two horizontal lines
   above vertical chevron.   79 12-9 1886b
4 *Beaker sherd*: oval tooth-comb stamped lines.
                                           79 12-9 1886c
5 *Beaker sherd*: heavy finger-pinched rustication.
                                           79 12-9 1886d
6 *Beaker sherd*: finger-nail horizontal rustication.
                                           79 12-9 1886e
7 *Beaker base sherds*: two.   79 12-9 1886f
8 *Plain sherds*: two; porous fabric.   79 12-9 1886g
9 *Plain sherds*: four, varying fabrics; weathered.
                                           79 12-9 1886h
10 *'Antler fragment'*: not identified.   79 12-9 1887

WEST KENNET (Avebury 22)   UN 62:1

Wiltshire   SU 105 677

CHAMBERED LONG BARROW: opened by J. Thurnam 1859;
excavated by S. Piggott and R.J.C. Atkinson 1955-6.
Thurnam 1861: *Piggott* 1960.

West Chamber (1859)

1 *'Four sherds with unusual ornament'*: not identified.
   (Inventory published in Piggott 1960.) 79 12-9 1894

WINTERBOURNE STOKE 1   UN 63:1-5

Wiltshire   SU 100 415

LONG BARROW: L. 72 m, W. 22 m, H. 3 m, aligned NE.-SW.;
chalk rubble, flanking ditches; opened by J. Thurnam 6
August 1863.
Thurnam 1864, 140-5; 1869, 180; 1872, 379; *VCH Wilts*
1.1, 146.

Burial 1: adult male inhumation, crouched on R. with
head SW.; on old surface at E.; flint at R. arm; three
pits, one Diam. 0.5 m, D. 0.5 m, at back.
1 *Flint blade core*: cortical nodule with single
   platform with multiple blade scars; mottled grey.
   L. 20.5 cm; W. 3.8 cm; Th. 3.9 cm.   73 12-19 12
   Thurnam 1869, fig. 2.

Burial 2: multiple inhumations: adult male, adult female
and four children, all crouched; in mound at E. at D. 0.6
m.
2 *Food Vessel*: plain.
   M. 14.8 cm; H. 14.5 cm; B. 9.4 cm.   73 12-19 2
   Thurnam 1872, fig. 67.
3 *Flint knife*: edge retouch on R. at 65 degrees;
   platform butt; cortical flake; patinated.
   L. 6.4 cm; W. 3.4 cm; Th. 0.8 cm.   73 12-19 13
   Thurnam 1872, fig. 112.

Not located

4 *Flint end- and side-scraper*: edge retouch on distal
   and R. at 65 degrees; platform butt; patinated.
   L. 6.0 cm; W. 5.0 cm; Th. 1.7 cm.   79 12-9 1893
5 *Flint blade*: patinated.
   L. 4.3 cm; W. 1.1 cm; Th. 0.3 cm.   73 12-19 14

ARRAS (Lady's Barrow)   UN 64:1-10

Yorkshire E.R.; North Humberside   SE 930 413

ROUND BARROW: Diam. 4.2 m, H. 0.5 m; composition not recorded; opened by workmen, re-opened by W.G. 1877. *BB* 454-6; *EIABY* 284-5; *Stead* 1979, 20-1.

Burial 1: adult ?female inhumation, crouched on L. with head N. or W.; in grave Diam. 3.6 m, D. 0.9 m; bones of two pigs behind head, mirror below head, wheels behind body, bits at chest, terret and mount unlocated.

   '*bronze mount*': not preserved.

1-2 *Iron tyre fragments*: two represented; broken and distorted.
   Diam. *c.* 78.0-90.0 cm; W. 3.6-3.8 cm. 77 10-16 1-2
3-6 *Bronze and iron nave-hoops*: four; iron ring of oval section with wide bronze cover whose ends overlap and are pierced by two bronze nails; the two best-preserved nail heads with concentric ring decoration; two nail shafts bent near point.
   Diam. (int.) 12.4-13.0 cm; W. iron ring 0.7 m, bronze cover 4.0-4.6 cm; nails L. 2.5-3.1 cm.
   EIABY fig. 28; *Stead* 1979, fig. 11.1. 77 10-16 3-6
7-8 *Bronze and iron horse-bits*: two; rings of iron encased in bronze with external ridge expanding into lobe near side-link; stops at either side of side-links formed by globular-headed bronze pins; side-links of solid bronze fixed at angle of 145 degrees to rings; perforations of side- and central-links worn.
   side-links L. 5.5 cm, perf. 0.9 x 1.2 cm; central links L. 4.9 cm.
   L. 23.6 cm, rings 6.5 x 7.1 cm and 6.4 x 6.8 cm.
                                          77 10-16 10
   L. 24.4 cm, rings 7.0 x 7.5 cm and 7.1 x 7.2 cm.
   EIABY fig. 29; *Stead* 1979, fig. 16. 77 10-16 11
9   *Bronze and iron terret*: curved iron bar with bronze penannular section cast on and enclosing bar terminals; ten lip-mouldings, those near the terminals abbreviated.
   W. 5.8 cm.   77 10-16 9
   EIABY fig. 30; *Stead* 1979, fig. 17.2.
10 *Bronze and iron mirror*: iron plate attached by bronze fitting to square-sectioned iron handle with ring terminal; bronze fitting above ring with mouldings encircling either end of ring and uniting to leave triangular space adjoining handle at either side with traces of infilling punched decoration in this space on one side; upper fitting with similar moulding over handle and triangular spaces infilled with punched decoration on both sides beneath lunate shape with two fastening bronze rivets; this fitting repaired by inserted piece attached by two small bronze rivets.
   Diam. plate 17.0-17.5 cm, ring 2.5 cm; handle L. 15.7 cm.   77 10-16 8
   EIABY fig. 31; *Stead* 1979, fig. 32.

BEVERLEY 1   UN 65:1-6

Yorkshire E.R.; North Humberside   TA 020 390

ROUND BARROW: Diam. 6.3 m, H. 0.6 m; composition not recorded; opened by W.G. 1875.
BB 456; *EIABY* 278; *Stead* 1979, 20.

Burial 1: ?decayed inhumation; in central oval grave L. 1.9 m, W. 1.4 m, D. 0.8 m; aligned N.-S., earth fill; wheels laid flat at E., bits at W.

1   *Iron tyre fragments*: two tyres represented, obscured by conglomerate.
   Diam. *c.* 72 cm (after W.G.); W. 3.6-4.0 cm.
                                          75 10-5 1

2   *Iron nave-hoop*: rectangular section.
   Diam. *c.* 13.2 cm; W. 1.0 cm; Th. 0.7 cm. 75 10-5 2
   Stead 1979, fig. 11.4.
3   *Iron nave-hoop fragments*: two represented; corroded; one of ovate section.   75 10-5 2
4-5 *Iron horse-bits*: two; obscured by conglomerate.
   Ring Diam. *c.* 8.5-9 cm.   75 10-5 3
6   *Iron harness ring*: obscured by conglomerate.
   Stead 1979, 51.   75 10-5 3

BEVERLEY 2   UN 66

Yorkshire E.R.; North Humberside   TA 020 390

ROUND BARROW: 'small'; composition not recorded; opened by W.G. 1875.
EIABY 278.

Burial 1: ?decayed inhumation; in grave.

BISHOP BURTON (Littlewood)   UN 67:1

Yorkshire E.R.; North Humberside   SE 95 38

ROUND BARROW: no information; 'rifled', re-opened by W.G.
Unpublished.

Not located

1   *Flint horseshoe scraper*: edge retouch at 70 degrees; faceted butt;; patinated.
   L. 3.6 cm; W. 3.4 cm; Th. 1.5 cm.   79 12-9 1642

BLANCH FARM   UN 68:1-5

Yorkshire E.R.; North Humberside   SE 89 53

ROUND BARROW(S): no information; opened by J. Silburn 24 February 1852.
Unpublished.

Not located

1   *Collared Vessel*: twisted cord: on top of rim, single line; on collar, hurdle pattern enclosed between single horizontal lines; on neck, vertical lines; on shoulder, row of jabs.
   M. 13.7 cm; H. 18.1 cm; B. 8.6 cm.   79 12-9 1989
   Longworth no. 759.
2   *Food Vessel*: Yorkshire Vase; on internal rim bevel, two zones of three fine twisted cord lines; on external rim bevel, two twisted cord lines; on neck and shoulder groove to below shoulder, incised herringbone, in part replaced by whipped cord herringbone, above three horizontal twisted cord lines; on body, striations; five horizontally perforated lugs spanning shoulder groove.
   M. 15.0 cm; H. 12.3 cm; B. *c.* 6.5 cm. 79 12-9 1990
3   *Food Vessel*: Yorkshire Vase; on internal rim bevel, pin pricks enclosed between three fine twisted cord lines; on external rim bevel, vertical fine twisted cord lines; on neck groove, four horizontal twisted cord lines above row of short diagonal lines; on lugs and in shoulder groove, fine horizontal twisted cord lines above row of short vertical to diagonal incised lines; on body, horizontal twisted cord lines above herringbone mainly in twisted cord but some incised, above zone of horizontal twisted cord lines, above zone of twisted cord herringbone split by single line and bordered beneath by two lines; four horizontally perforated lugs spanning shoulder groove.
   M. 14.9 cm; H. 10.8 cm; B. 7.2 cm.   79 12-9 1990a
4   *Food Vessel*: Yorkshire Vase; on internal rim bevel, whipped cord herringbone; on external rim bevel,

short diagonal whipped cord impressions; on neck, row of jabbed impressions above incised herringbone above row of whipped cord herringbone; on upper and lower borders of shoulder groove, whipped cord impressions; in shoulder groove and over body, impressed herringbone; on lugs, vertical whipped cord herringbone; two surviving of four horizontally perforated lugs spanning shoulder groove.

M. 16.1 cm; H. 11.8 cm; B. 6.3-7.1 cm. 79 12-9 1991

5 *Handled Food Vessel*: whipped cord: on top of rim, three lines; externally, two discontinuous horizontal lines above hurdle pattern (in one part of twisted cord) with irregular rows of short vertical and diagonal lines beneath to base; remains of horizontal strap handle at rim.

M. 14.8 cm; H. 13.7 cm; B. 10.0 cm.   79 12-9 1998

BROUGH   UN 69:1-2

Yorkshire E.R., North Humberside   SE 933 282

GRAVE: discovered in quarrying 1891.
Sheppard 1902.

Burial 1: adult male inhumation; in grave D. 1.2 m; dagger at side and pin at shoulder.

1 *Bronze dagger*: Gerloff Type Armorico - British B: narrow flat midrib stepped to blade wings with triple grooves and traces of edge bevels; three rivets surviving, of original four or six, with round section shanks and expanded heads; hilt line marked by slight ridge; traces of vertically aligned wood-grain on hilt plate; small patch of fibrous organic material on one blade face (Table 1:11).

L. 16.9 cm; W. 7.5 cm; Th. 0.6 cm.
Rivets L. 1.25-1.35 cm; Diam. shank 0.4-0.45 cm, head 0.5-0.6 cm.   WG 2019
Gerloff 1975, no. 125.

2 *Bone quatrefoil-headed pin*: cut and polished from longbone segment; circular-sectioned shaft with blunt tip expanding to triangular head with central perforation; below head, pair of circular perforated loops decorated on external faces by transverse incisions; above head, pair of circular perforated loops each with two incised lines around rim.

L. 6.0 cm; W. (upper loops) 2.5 cm; W. head 1.2 cm, lower loops 2.1 cm; Th. head 0.4 cm; Diam. shaft 0.6 cm.   WG 2069

DANES GRAVES 15-28   UN 70 to 83; 74:1

Yorkshire E.R.; North Humberside   TA 018 633

ROUND BARROWS: Diam. 5-7.2 m, H. 0.6-1.2 m, chalk rubble; opened by W.G. 27-28 March 1864.
Greenwell 1865, 108-12; *Stead* 1979, 100.

UN 70: 15 Burial 1: child inhumation; in mound.

UN 71-73: 16-18 Burials 1: inhumation in each; each with vessel.

'three pots': not preserved.

UN 74: 19 Burial 1: adult male inhumation, crouched on R. with head W.; in grave; brooch at face, caprovine skeleton at each side.

1 *Iron brooch*: three coil mock-spring; fragmentary and corroded.

L. 9.0 cm.   79 12-9 2073
Greenwell 1865, fig. 1; *Stead* 1965, fig. 26.1

UN 75-83: 20-28 Burials 1: inhumation in each; in graves.

DANES GRAVES 48, 53-4, 65, 70, 79   UN 84:1
                                                  to 89:1

Yorkshire E.R.; North Humberside   TA 018 633

ROUND BARROWS: Diam. 3-9 m; H. 0.3-0.8 m (individual barrows not specified); opened by W.G., J. R. Mortimer and T. Boynton July 1898.
Mortimer 1911; *EIABY* 258-9; *Stead* 1979, 100-1.

UN 84:48 Burial 1: adult inhumation, crouched on R. with head SW.; in grave; brooch behind head.

1 *Bronze involuted brooch*: short bow with 'stop' at head and mouldings at end, on underside of catch-plate and adjoining foot-disc; foot-disc perforated and cross-hatched on upper surface to secure missing ornament; three coil mock-spring mechanism with ribbed central coil and linked by cylinder-rivet.

L. 3.6 cm.   1918 7-10 1
EIABY fig. 14; *Stead* 1979, fig. 26.4.

UN 85:53 Burial 1: adult inhumation, crouched on L. with head WSW.; in grave; vessel containing pig humerus behind shoulders.

1 *Early Iron Age vessel*: rock-tempered.
M. 12.8 cm; H. 13.8 cm; B. 8.5 cm.   1918 12-11 1
EIABY fig. 9; *Stead* 1979, 83.

UN 86:54 Burial 1: adult inhumation, crouched on L. with head NE.; in grave; vessel and pig humerus behind shoulders.

1 *Early Iron Age vessel*: rock-tempered.
M. 11.7 cm; H. 14.0 cm; B. 9.0 cm.   1918 12-11 2
EIABY fig. 9; *Stead* 1979, 83.

UN 87:65 Burial 1: adult inhumation, crouched on R. with head N.; in grave; iron object behind head, part of vessel and pig humerus at knees, part of vessel at feet.

'corroded article of iron': not preserved.

1 *Early Iron Age vessel*: calcareous temper.
B. 9.5 cm.   1918 12-11 5
EIABY fig. 9; *Stead* 1979, 83.

UN 88:70 Burial 1: adolescent inhumation, crouched on L. with head S.; in grave; vessel containing pig humerus behind head.

1 *Early Iron Age vessel*: calcite and rock-tempered.
M. 12.8 cm; H. 13.0 cm; B. 8.1 cm.   1918 12-11 3
EIABY, Fig. 9; *Stead* 1979, 83

UN 89:79 Burial 1: adult inhumation, crouched on L. with head NE.; in grave; vessel in fill above body.

1 *Early Iron Age vessel*: vesicular fabric.
M. 13.7 cm; H. 13.0 cm; B. 8.5 cm.   1918 12-11 4
EIABY fig. 9; *Stead* 1979, 83.

ELF HOWE   UN 90:1-2

Yorkshire E.R.; North Yorkshire   TA 042 772

ROUND BARROW: Diam. 18 m, H. 1.8 m; earth and chalk, recorded in destruction by W.G.
BB 271-2.

Burial 1: cremation deposit; 0.6 m above old surface near centre, in burnt earth beneath large flints.

Burial 2: adult male inhumation, crouched on R.. with head S.; 0.2 m above old surface, 5.1 m SSE. of centre.

Burial 3: infant inhumation traces; below Burial 2.

Burial 4: disturbed bones; on old surface below Burial 3.

Burial 5: adult male inhumation, crouched with head S.; in central grave L. 2.1 m, W. 2 m, D. 0.8 m, aligned SE.-NW.; vessel at head.

1 *Collared Vessel sherd*: twisted cord: on collar, diagonal lines above two horizontal lines.
Manby 1956, fig. 3.6; *Longworth* no. 1141.
79 12-9 1118

Not located
2 *Stone perforated implement fragment*: greywacke, Y794; ground and polished; drilled hourglass perforation; broken.
L. 5.1 cm; W. 6.0 cm; Th. 4.6 cm.   79 12-9 1119
Roe 1966, no. 257.

GANTON WOLD   UN 91:1-7
Yorkshire E.R.; North Yorkshire   TA 00 76

ROUND BARROW: no information; opened by W.G.
Unpublished.

Not located
1-7 *'Flint flakes'*: seven; not identified.
79 12-9 1679-85

GOODMANHAM   UN 92:1
Yorkshire E.R.; North Humberside   SE 91 45

ROUND BARROW: Diam. 21 m, H. ? m; previously opened, and re-opened by W.G.
BB 311.

Burial 1: ?inhumation; robbed central grave.

Not located
1 *'Flint flake'*: not identified.   79 12-9 1697

GOODMANHAM WOLD 1   UN 93:1
Yorkshire E.R.; North Humberside   SE 91 45

ROUND BARROW: Diam. 11 m, H. 0.8 m; composition not recorded; opened by Lord Londesborough 23 October 1851.
Londesborough 1851, 256-7.

Burial 1: cremation deposit, in pit at NW., Diam 0.5 m, D. 0.5 m.
1 *Accessory Cup*: plain; no perforations.
M. 4.7 cm; H. 4.9 cm; B. 5.4 cm.   79 12-9 1987
'accessory cup': not preserved.

GOODMANHAM WOLD 2   UN 94:1
Yorkshire E.R.; North Humberside   SE 91 45

ROUND BARROW: Diam. 18 m, H. 1.8 m; clay core with charcoal lenses capped by earth; opened by Lord Londesborough 23 October 1851.
Londesborough 1851, 257-8.

Burial 1: cremation deposit; near centre at D. 1.8 m.
1 *Food Vessel*: Yorkshire Vase: on internal rim bevel, incised herringbone split by discontinuous horizontal line of impressions; on external rim bevel, incised herringbone; in neck, two rows of vertical impressions above herringbone which continues over lugs; in shoulder groove, two rows of vertical impressions above incised herringbone extending on to upper body above rows of short vertical to diagonal incised lines; on base, cross formed by pairs of pin-prick lines; four imperforate lugs.
M. 15.5 cm; H. 11.0 cm; B. 6.5 cm.   79 12-9 1988
Londesborough 1851, pl. XX.10.

Burial 2: cremation deposit; 1.8 m E. of Burial 1.

Feature A: oval setting of large flint blocks, 3.6 m NW. of centre.

HELPERTHORPE (Esh I; Cross Thorns)   UN 95:1-5
Yorkshire E.R.; North Yorkshire   SE 963 679

LONG BARROW: L. 29 m, W. 12.5 m, H. 0.3 m, aligned E.-W., reduced by ploughing; chalk rubble, flanking quarry-ditches W. 3.6 m, D. 1.8 m; possible superimposed *round barrow* on W. end; opened by W.G. November 1866 and re-opened by Mortimer February 1868.
BB 53, 489 fn.; *Mortimer* 1905, 333-5.

Burial 1: crematorium deposit: broken and disarticulated bones in burnt chalk matrix; at E., perhaps between axial pits.

Burial 2: adolescent cremation deposit and charred bones of adult; in oval pit L. 1.8 m, W. 1.4 m, D. 0.8 m, aligned N.-S., on axial line 7.5 m E. of Feature A (perhaps part of Burial 1).

Feature A: pit; 'large', on axial line at W.
1 *Jet spacer-plate bead*: cut and polished to rectangular outline and lentoid section; drilled transverse perforation at each end and, between, two pairs of angled perforations opening to plain face; traces of ?thread abrasion on face between perforations; one face with double saltire of triple rows of drilled or punched *pointillé*.
L. 4.0 cm; W. 2.9 cm; Th. 0.6 cm.   79 12-9 1686
BB fig. 51.
2 *Jet spacer-plate bead fragment*: form and decoration as 1; one transverse and parts of two angled perforations survive.
L. 1.4 cm; W. 2.7 cm; Th. 0.6 cm.   79 12-9 1687
3 *Jet button*: cut and polished to domed profile bevelled to flat base with central drilled V-perforation; broken.
Diam. 2.0 cm; Th. 0.7 cm.   79 12-9 1688

Feature B: pit, Diam. 3.3 m, D. 3.6 m; fill of chalk rubble; coterminous with, and to W. of, Feature A.

Feature C: pit, L. 2.3 m, W. 2 m, D. 1.8 m, aligned NNE.-SSW.; fill of chalk rubble and earth; coterminous with, and to N. of, Feature A.
'small fragments of a British vase': not preserved.

Feature D: ditch, L. 4.8 m, W. 0.9 m, D. 0.8 m; fill of chalk rubble and earth; arcuate in plan, connecting Features B and C.

Not located
4-5 *'Stone rubbers'*: two; not identified.
79 12-9 1689-90

HELPERTHORPE CROSS   UN 96:1-3
Yorkshire E.R.; North Yorkshire   SE 96 68

WINDMILL MOUND: opened by W.G. and Lovel 1868.
Mortimer 1868.

Mound material
1 *'Glass bead'*: not identified.   79 12-9 1691
2 *'Flint flake'*: not identified.   79 12-9 1692
3 *'Bone or coral bead'*: not identified.   79 12-9 2053

HESLERTON WOLD (Abram)   UN 97:1-3
Yorkshire E.R.; North Yorkshire   SE 95 75

ROUND BARROW: no details; opened by W.G.
Unpublished.

Not located
1 *'Flint scraper'*: not identified.   79 12-9 1677
2 *Flint core*: single platform with parallel blade scars, traces of previous platform; cortex remnant; mottled grey.
L. 2.9 cm; W. 2.2 cm; Th. 1.4 cm.   79 12-9 1675
3 *'Flint core'*: not identified.   79 12-9 1676

HUGGATE WOLD 1   UN 98:1

Yorkshire E.R.; North Humberside   SE 85 54

UNKNOWN CONTEXT: ?barrow opened by J. Silburn.
Unpublished.

Not located

1 *Food Vessel*: Yorkshire Vase; on internal rim bevel,
   fine incised herringbone above and below circumferential groove; on external rim bevel, two rows of
   jabbed impressions; on neck, three rows of jabbed
   impressions in herringbone enclosed above by three
   and below by six fine twisted cord horizontal lines;
   beneath shoulder groove and extending onto lugs,
   three twisted cord lines above two rows of jabbed
   impressions; three surviving of four imperforate
   lugs spanning shoulder groove.
   M. 14.4 cm; H. 11.7 cm; B. 6.6 cm.   79 12-9 1999

HUGGATE WOLD 2   UN 99:1

Yorkshire E.R.; North Humberside   SE 85 54

ROUND BARROW: no information; opened by J. Silburn 27
October 1851.
Unpublished.

Not located

1 *Food Vessel*: Yorkshire Vase; incised: on internal rim
   bevel and over external surface, herringbone; on
   upper and lower edges of shoulder groove, short
   vertical lines; four horizontally perforated lugs
   spanning shoulder groove.
   M. 12.4 cm; H. 9.9 cm; B. 5.6 cm.   79 12-9 1992

KELLEYTHORPE 1 (M.C50; Driffield)   UN 100:1-9

Yorkshire E.R.; North Humberside   TA 015 573

ROUND BARROW: Diam. 20 m, H. ?m, reduced by ploughing; on
natural grave knoll, clay core with earth and gravel
capping; opened by Lord Londesborough 17-18 October
1851, re-opened by Mortimer 29 July 1872.
Londesborough 1851, 251-2; *Mortimer* 1905, 283-4.

Burial 1: adult inhumation, crouched on L. with head E.;
in central grave, knife at head.

1 *Flint knife*: bilateral edge retouch converging on
   distal; cortex remnant; mottled grey.
   L. 5.0 cm; W. 2.1 cm; Th. 0.6 cm.   79 12-9 1979
   Londesborough 1851, pl. XX. 1; *Mortimer* 1905, fig.
   830.

Mound material (Mortimer)

2 'Sherds of food-vase': not identified.   H.M.
3 'Flint barbed and tanged arrowhead': not identified.
                                                   H.M.
   Mortimer 1905, fig. 831; *Green* 1980, no. A160.
4 'Flint chisel arrowhead': not identified.   H.M.
   Green 1980, no. A161.
5-6 'Flint knives': two; not identified.   H.M.
7-9 'Flint flakes': three, not identified.   H.M.

KELLEYTHORPE 2 (M.C38; Driffield)   UN 101:1-8

Yorkshire E.R.; North Humberside   TA 017 567

ROUND BARROW: Diam. 18 m, H. 1.2 m, reduced by ploughing;
on natural gravel knoll; composition not recorded;
opened by Lord Londesborough October 1851, re-opened by
Mortimer 1-10 October 1870.
Londesborough 1851, 252-6; *Mortimer* 1905, 271-83.

Burial 1: double inhumation: two adults 'laid one upon
the other', heads SW.; N. of centre; Food Vessel and
knife at head, toggle in one hand.

1 *Food Vessel*; on internal rim bevel, row of pin pricks
   and row of bone impressions; on neck and shoulder
   grooves and upper body, rows of impressions.
   M. 16.3 cm; H. 14.4 cm; B. 8.0 cm.   79 12-9 1977
   Londesborough 1851, pl. XX. 9; *Mortimer* 1905, fig.
   737.
2 *Flint plano-convex knife*: all over invasive retouch;
   cortex remnant; mottled grey.
   L. 5.3 cm; W. 2.8 cm; Th. 0.5 cm.   79 12-9 1978
   Londesborough 1851, pl. XX. 3; *Mortimer* 1905, fig.
   738.
3 *Bone side-looped toggle*: cut and polished from
   longbone segment; round-ended bar of oval section
   with central lateral expansion with drilled perforation.
   L 5.3 cm; W. 1.0 cm, (loop) 1.4 cm; Th. 0.8 cm.
                                             79 12-9 1980
   Londesborough 1851, pl. XX. 2; *Mortimer* 1905, fig.
   739.

Burial 2: adult inhumation, crouched on L. with head E.;
on paved floor of central cist L. 1.2 m, W. 0.9 m, D. 0.8
m, aligned E.-W., four side slabs and capstone at level
of old surface; dagger behind back, Beaker at feet,
bracer on R. forearm, beads at neck, 'hawk's head' in
front of body.

4 *Copper knife-dagger*: high heeled butt with one
   surviving rivet and four rivet-notches; flat-
   sectioned blade with narrow edge bevels and internal
   furrows following concave edges; hilt line marked by
   curved ridge delimiting organic hilt remains with
   grain on slight diagonal to both faces; rivet with
   faceted shank and irregular closed heads (Table
   1:16).
   L. 8.7 cm; W. 3.8 cm; Th. 0.2 cm.
   rivet L. 1.1 cm; Diam. (shank) 0.3 cm, (head) 0.5 cm.
                                             79 12-9 1981
   Londesborough 1851, pl. XX. 8; *Mortimer* 1905, fig.
   742; *Gerloff* 1975, no. 237.
5 *Beaker*: tooth-comb stamped: on neck, herringbone
   separated by plain cordon from herringbone split by
   plain cordons with zone of three horizontal lines
   fringed by short diagonal lines beneath; on belly and
   lower body, zones of horizontal lines fringed by
   short diagonal lines with basal zone opposed.
   M. 14.0 cm; H. 18.3 cm; B. 8.2 cm.   79 12-9 1984
   BAP no. 149; *Clarke* no. 1265; *Londesborough* 1851, pl.
   XX. 6; *Mortimer* 1905, fig. 745.
6 *Stone bracer*: greenstone; ground and polished to sub-
   rectangular outline with concave sides and cres-
   centic section with bevelled edges; at each end pair
   of funnel-profile circular perforations drilled from
   back; in each perforation corroded traces of copper
   or bronze rivet with domed sheet-gold caps.
   L. 12.7 cm; W. (terminal) 3.3 cm, (central) 2.8 cm;
   Th. 0.6 cm.   84 5-20 1
   Mortimer 1905, fig. 741.
7 *Amber bead or button*: cut and polished to ovoid with
   drilled V-perforation on one face; broken and eroded.
   L. 2.9 cm; W. 2.2 cm; Th. 2.0 cm.   79 12-9 1982
   Londesborough 1851, pl. XX. 4; *Mortimer* 1905, fig.
   743.
8 *Amber bead or button fragment*: cut and polished to
   hemisphere; traces of drilled perforation from flat
   face; broken and eroded.
   L. 2.2 cm; W.. 1.2 cm; Th. 1.5 cm.   79 12-9 1983
   Londesborough 1851, pl. XX. 5; *Mortimer* 1905, fig.
   744.

Burial 3: multiple cremation deposit; in heap of burnt
gravel and charcoal Diam. 1.5 m, ENE. of centre.

LUND WARREN   UN 102:1-2

Yorkshire E.R.; North Humberside   SE 91 46

ROUND BARROW: no information; opened by W.G.
Unpublished.

Not located

1 *Food Vessel*: on internal surface, external rim bevel,
   neck and body below shoulder, twisted cord horizontal
   lines.
   M. 11.4 cm; H. 12.5 cm; B. 5.5 cm.   79 12-9 1698
2 *'Flint scraper'*: not identified.   79 12-9 1699

MAIDEN'S GRAVE   UN 103:1

Yorkshire E.R.; North Humberside   TA 09 71

?ROUND OR LONG BARROW: Diam. 11.5 m, H. 0.8 m (in text) or
L. 75 m, W. 24 m, H. 0.9 m, aligned ESE.-WNW. (on
separate sketch plan); site not now locatable; opened by
W.G. and T. Boynton 1 October 1901.
WG Ms 4.

Feature A: rectangular pit L. 3.3 m, W. 1.2 m, D. 0.3-0.9
m, aligned E.-W., W. end 5.4 m SE. by E. of centre; fill
of burnt earth and charcoal.

Feature B: square pit L. 1.5 m, W. 1.5 m, D. 0.6 m, with
deeper circular pit in SW. corner Diam. 0.6 m, D. 0.3 m,
3 m SSE. of centre; fill of dark earth.

Feature C: oval pit L. 1.5 m, W. 1.2 m, D. 0.5 m, 4.8 m
NNW. of centre; fill of dark earth.

Old surface (3 m SSE. of centre)

1 *Jet bead*: cut and polished to ovoid profile and
   flattened oval section with collared terminals and
   drilled longitudinal perforation; broken and
   abraded.
   L. 9.1 cm; W. (central) 4.0 cm, (terminal) 1.3 cm; Th.
   2.0 cm.   1902 2-14 1

RUDSTON/BURTON AGNES   UN 104:1

Yorkshire E.R.; North Humberside   TA 01 65

ROUND BARROW: no information.
Unpublished.

Not located

1 *Jet bead*: both faces cut and polished and edges
   roughly trimmed to discoidal form with central
   drilled hourglass perforation.
   Diam. 1.5 cm; Th. 0.5 cm.   79 12-9 1734

SHERBURN (Prodham II)   UN 105:1-8

Yorkshire E.R.; North Yorkshire   SE 96 74

ROUND BARROW: 'disturbed'; opened by W.G.
Unpublished.

Not located

1 *Flint end- and side-scraper*: on fragment; edge
   retouch on distal and L. at 60 degrees; cortex
   remnant; mottled grey.
   L. 3.5 cm; W. 2.7 cm; Th. 1.4 cm.   79 12-9 67
2 *Flint end- and side-scraper*: on core fragment; edge
   retouch on distal and R. at 60 degrees; platform
   butt; cortex remnant; dark grey.
   L. 2.9 cm; W. 2.2 cm; Th. 1.1 cm.   79 12-9 68
3 *Flint end- and side-scraper*: edge retouch on distal
   and L. at 75 degrees; cortex remnant; mottled grey.
   L. 2.8 cm; W. 2.1 cm; Th. 1.0 cm.   79 12-9 69
4 *Flint end-scraper*: edge retouch on distal at 80
   degrees; damaged; mottled grey.
   L. 2.9 cm; W. 3.5 cm; Th. 0.8 cm.   79 12-9 70

5 *Flint end-scraper*: edge retouch on distal at 65
   degrees; cortex remnant; damaged; mottled grey.
   L. 2.2 cm; W. 3.0 cm; Th. 0.6 cm.   79 12-9 71
6 *Flint utilised flake*: wear on L.; cortex remnant;
   mottled grey.
   L. 5.3 cm; W. 2.6 cm; Th. 1.2 cm.   79 12-9 70a
7 *Flint flake*: cortex remnant; mottled grey.
   L. 4.0 cm; W. 1.5 cm; Th. 0.6 cm.   79 12-9 70b
8 *Flint flake*: mottled grey.
   L. 2.9 cm; W. 2.5 cm; Th. 0.7 cm.   79 12-9 70c

SHERBURN/HESLERTON   UN 106

Yorkshire E.R.; North Yorkshire   SE 95 75

ROUND BARROW: Diam. 24 m, H. ?m (Diam. *c.* 17 m, H. 1.8 m:
1851); earth and chalk; internal circle of chalk blocks
Diam. 9 m with gap W. 2.7 m at E.; opened 28 December
1851 by Ruddock, re-opened *c.* 1865 by W.G.
BB 145-6; *TYD* 230-1; *Kinnes* 1979, Ba 4.

Burial 1 (1851): 'fifteen human skeletons ... without
much arrangement'; at centre; arrowhead inside skull,
bone point and bead nearby.
   'flint arrowhead': not preserved.
   'clay bead': not preserved.
   'bone point': not preserved.

Burial 2: adult inhumation, crouched on R. with head W.;
0.5 m above old surface, 5.4 m SE. of centre.

Burial 3: separate skull; on old surface, 6 m SSE. of
centre.

Feature A: oval pit L. 1.5 m, W. 1 m, D. 0.8 m, aligned
N.-S., fill of earth and chalk, below Burial 3.

Features B-C: two pits L. 1.5 m, W. 1 m and L. 1.4 m, W.
0.9 m, both D. 0.8 m, aligned NE.-SW., fill of earth and
chalk; at centre 0.5 m apart.

SHERBURN WOLD (Anderson)   UN 107:1

Yorkshire E.R.; North Yorkshire   SE 96 75

ROUND BARROW: no information; opened by W.G. 22 April
1867.
Unpublished.

Not located

1 *Flint leaf arrowhead*: all over invasive retouch;
   patinated.
   L. 3.5 cm; W. 2.6 cm; Th. 0.4 cm.   79 12-9 1678
   Green 1980, no. A49.

WARTER WOLD I (M259)   UN 108:1-2

Yorkshire E.R.; North Humberside   SE 899 532

ROUND BARROW: Diam. *c.* 20 m, H. *c.* 0.4 m, reduced by
ploughing; opened by J. Silburn 1851, re-opened by
Mortimer August 1883.
Mortimer 1905, 329.

Burial 1: adult male inhumation; in central shallow
grave.
1 *Food Vessel*: plain.
   M. 8.4 cm; H. 7.6 cm; B. 3.3 cm.   79 12-9 1994

Not located
2 *Food Vessel Urn*: on internal rim bevel, two rows of
   jabbed impressions alternating with two twisted cord
   horizontal lines; on external rim bevel, in neck and
   shoulder groove and on either side of shoulder,
   single rows of jabbed impressions; on ridge between
   neck and shoulder groove, short twisted cord
   impressions.
   M. 20.5 cm; H. 20.8 cm; B. 10.0 cm.   79 12-9 1993
   Cowie 1978, YOR 14.

WARTER WOLD 2   UN 109:1-3

Yorkshire E.R.; North Humberside   SE 899 532

ROUND BARROW: no information; opened by J. Silburn 13
November 1851.
Unpublished.

Burial 1: inhumation.
1 *Collared Vessel*: on collar, twisted cord hurdle
   pattern.
   M. 11.9-13.0 cm; H. 16.4 cm; B. 6.9-9.4 cm.
   Longworth no. 762.   79 12-9 1995

Not located
2 *Beaker*: tooth-comb stamped: beneath rim, zone of
   lattice bordered above and below by single horizontal
   lines above plain cordon; in neck, three zones, the
   upper and lower of lattice enclosed between single
   horizontal lines and separated by plain bands from a
   middle zone of reserved bar lozenges with pendant
   triangles filled with diagonal lines and upright
   triangles with lattice, the whole bordered above and
   below by single horizontal lines, above plain cordon;
   on body, three zones of lattice bordered above and
   below by single horizontal lines and separated by
   plain bands; near base, zone of vertical finger-
   pinching.
   M. 15.6 cm; H. 22.8 cm; B. 7.5 cm.   79 12-9 1996
   BAP no. 107; *Clarke* no. 1331.
3 *Food Vessel*: fine twisted cord in paired lines; on
   internal rim bevel, hurdle pattern; on external rim
   bevel, short vertical lines; on neck, hurdle pattern;
   on upper body, irregularly placed horizontal lines.
   M. 14.3 cm; H. 12.0 cm; B. 7.8 cm.   79 12-9 1997

WESTOW (Westow II)   UN 110: 1-10

Yorkshire E.R.; North Yorkshire   SE 77 65

ROUND BARROW: no information; opened by W.G.
Unpublished.

Burial 1: 'primary interment', no details.
1-2 *Flint knives*: two; not identified.
                                             79 12-9 1701-2

Not located
3 'Bronze fragment, edge of vessel or bell': not
   identified.   79 12-9 1710
4-7 *Flint scrapers*: four; not identified.
                                             79 12-9 1703-6
8-9 *Flint implements*: two; not identified.
                                             79 12-9 1707-8
10 *Flint flake*: not identified.   79 12-9 1709

WINTRINGHAM   UN 111:1

Yorkshire E.R.; North Yorkshire   SE 89 72

ROUND BARROW: no information.
Unpublished.

Not located
1 'Rim sherds': two; not identified.   79 12-9 2006

AMOTHERBY   UN 112:1

Yorkshire N.R.; North Yorkshire   SE 75 73

ROUND BARROW: no information; opened by W.G.
Unpublished.

Not located
1 *Polypod Bowl*: twisted cord herringbone above whipped
   cord herringbone, in part irregularly executed,
   extending over feet; remains of four feet.
   M. *c.* 12.5 cm; H. *c.* 6.5 cm.   79 12-9 1712
   Manby 1958, 398; 1969, 282.

AYTON EAST FIELD   UN 113:1-19

Yorkshire N.R.; North Yorkshire   TA 000 864

OVAL CAIRN: L. 26 m, W. 15 m; limestone rubble; opened by
A.D Conyngham 1848, excavated by F. Vatcher 1960
(information not available).
Conynham 1849, 104-5; *Kinnes* 1979, Dc 6.

Burial 1: crematorium deposit: multiple cremation
deposits in burnt rubble; E. of centre.

Burial 2: decayed inhumation; in mound, N. of centre.
1 'Flint flake': not identified.   79 12-9 1964

Burial 3: decayed inhumation; in mound, N. of centre.
2 'Flint flake': not identified.   79 12-9 1965

Burial 4: 'a very small portion of human bones'; below
slab at 0.2 m below mound surface, W. of centre.
3 'Stone rubber': not identified.   79 12-9 1963
4 *Flint polished-edge axe*: all over bifacial intrusive
   retouch on butt and body to concave sides and lentoid
   section; ground and polished blade; cortex remnant;
   patinated.
   L. 10.7 cm; W. 5.1 cm; Th. 1.5 cm.   79 12-9 1952
5 *Flint polished-edge axe*: all over bifacial intrusive
   retouch on butt to concave sides and lentoid section;
   ground and polished blade and part-body; cortex
   remnant; patinated.
   L. 13.4 cm; W. 4.5 cm; Th. 2.1 cm.   79 12-9 1953
6 *Flint polished-edge axe*: all over bifacial intrusive
   retouch on butt to concave sides and lentoid section;
   ground and polished blade and part-body; patinated.
   L. 9.7 cm; W. 2.7 cm; Th. 1.2 cm.   79 12-9 1955
7 *Flint polished-edge adze*: all over bifacial intrusive retouch on butt to concave sides and lentoid
   section; ground and polished blade and part-body;
   cortex remnant; patinated.
   L. 13.4 cm; W. 3.3 cm; Th. 1.7 cm.   79 12-9 1954
8 *Flint lozenge arrowhead*; all over bifacial invasive
   retouch; point snapped; patinated.
   L. 6.3 cm; W. 2.4 cm; Th. 0.2 cm.   79 12-9 1947
9 *Flint lozenge arrowhead*: all over bifacial invasive
   retouch; butt snapped,? recent damage on one edge;
   cortex remnant; patinated.
   L. 6.4 cm; 2.4 cm; Th. 0.3 cm.   79 12-9 1948
10 *Flint lozenge arrowhead*: all over bifacial invasive
   retouch; point snapped; patinated.
   L. 4.8 cm; W. 2.5 cm; Th. 0.3 cm.   79 12-9 1949
11 *Flint lozenge arrowhead*: all over bifacial invasive
   retouch; broken; patinated.
   L. 6.8 cm; W. 2.2 cm; Th. 0.3 cm.   79 12-9 1950
12 *Flint lozenge arrowhead*: all over bifacial intrusive
   retouch; point snapped; patinated.
   L. 5.6 cm; W. 2.1 cm; Th. 0.3 cm.   79 12-9 1951
   Green 1980, no. 327.
13 *Flint polished knife*: on blade; all over ground and
   polished to sharp edge on R. with bevelled ends;
   cortex remnant on L.; patinated.
   L. 10.8 cm; W. 2.5 cm; Th. 0.4 cm.   79 12-9 1958
14 'Flint plano-convex knife': not identified.
                                             79 12-9 1959
15 *Flint worked flake*: edge retouch on L., wear on R.;
   platform butt; mottled grey.
   L. 4.5 cm; W. 2.8 cm; Th. 1.0 cm.   79 12-9 1956
16 *Flint flake*: cortex remnant; mottled grey to
   patinated.
   L. 6.3 cm; W. 4.2 cm; Th. 0.6 cm.   79 12-9 1957
17 *Boar-tusk blade*: split tusk; eroded.
   L. chord 11.5 cm; W. 1.9 cm; Th. 0.3 cm.
                                             79 12-9 1960
18 *Boar-tusk blade*: split tusk; point snapped; eroded.
   L. chord 11.4 cm; W. 2.3 cm; Th. 0.4 cm.
                                             79 12-9 1961

19 *Antler 'macehead'*: on crown end of shed red-deer
   antler; beam and brow and bez tines cut and bevelled;
   cut circular perforation in beam.
   L. 11.2 cm; W. 5.2 cm; Th. 4.1 cm; Diam. perf. 2.7 cm.
                                                    79 12-9 1962

COLD KIRBY 1   UN 114:1-3

Yorkshire N.R.; North Yorkshire   SE 51 83

ROUND BARROW: no information; 'disturbed'; opened by
W.G. 23 March 1863.
Unpublished.

Burial 1: cremation deposit.
1-2 *'Flint flakes'*: two; not identified.
                                                    79 12-9 1717-18
3 *'Bone pin fragment'*: not identified.   79 12-9 1719

COLD KIRBY 2   UN 115

Yorkshire N.R.; North Yorkshire   SE 51 83

ROUND BARROW Diam. 20 m, H. 1 m; sand; opened by W.G. 25
April 1864.
Greenwell 1865, 114.

Feature A: burnt earth and charcoal Diam. 0.9 m, SE. of
centre.

Mound material
   'potsherds': not preserved.
   'flint chips': not preserved.

CROSSCLIFFE (Allerston)   UN 116:1-3

Yorkshire N.R.; North Yorkshire   SE 89 92

ROUND BARROW: no information.
WG Ms 12, 29.

Burial 1: cremation deposit; in urn.
   'urn': not preserved.
1 *Flint disc scraper*: edge retouch at 70 degrees with
   some invasive retouch; cortex remnant; burnt and
   damaged.
   L. 1.9 cm; W. 2.3 cm; Th. 0.7 cm.   79 12-9 1715
2 *Flint scraper fragment*: edge retouch at 70 degrees;
   burnt and broken.
   L. 2.5 cm; W. 2.4 cm; Th. 0.7 cm.   79 12-9 1714
3 *Flint knife*; bilateral edge retouch; cortex remnant;
   burnt and broken.
   L. 5.4 cm; W. 2.0 cm;Th. 0.8 cm.   79 12-9 1716

EGTON (Three Howes Central)   UN 117

Yorkshire N.R.; North Yorkshire   NZ 794 011

ROUND BARROW: Diam. 12 m, H. 1.5 m; alternate layers of
sand and turf; opened by W.G. 1864.
Greenwell 1865, 114.

EGTON MOOR   UN 118:1-4

Yorkshire N.R.; North Yorkshire   NZ 776 039

ROUND CAIRN: no information; previously disturbed,
opened by W.G. 1863.
Greenwell 1865, 113.

Cairn material
1 *Stone rubber*: sandstone; one face smoothed by
   abrasion.
   L. 15.5 cm; W. 3.9 cm; Th. 4.9 cm.   79 12-9 1724
2-4 *'Flint flakes'*: three; not identified.
                                                    79 12-9 1725-27

FYLINGDALES   UN 119:1-2

Yorkshire N.R.; North Yorkshire   NZ 90 00

ROUND BARROW: no information; 'disturbed'; opened by
W.G.
Unpublished.

Not located
1 *Collared Vessel*: on collar, twisted cord hurdle
   pattern.
   B. *c.* 7.0 cm.   79 12-9 1670
   Longworth no. 1146.
2 *Bronze Age sherds*: twelve; plain.   79 12-9 1669

HAGWORM HILL   UN 120:1-26

Yorkshire N.R.; North Yorkshire   TA 005 876

ROUND CAIRN: Diam. 18 m (Conyngham), Diam. 13.5 m
(Coombs); outer kerb and inner kerb Diam. 10.8 m; opened
by A.D. Conyngham 1849, excavated by Coombs 1973.
Conyngham 1849, 102-3; *inf. D.G. Coombs*.

Burial 1: cremation deposit; in vessel at E. end of pit
L. 1.7 m, W. 1.6 m, D. 0.7 m (Diam. 1.5 m, 1973), slab-
lined with single capstone, N. of centre.
1 *Food Vessel*: Yorkshire Vase; on internal rim bevel,
   five twisted cord lines; in neck and two shoulder
   grooves to below shoulder, herringbone made by
   pointed impressions; four imperforate lugs spanning
   each of shoulder grooves.
   M. 14.9 cm; H. 10.8 cm; B. 6.0 cm.   79 12-9 1942
   Conyngham 1849, fig. 1.
2 *'Flint flake'*: not identified.   79 12-9 1945

Burial 2: cremation deposit; near pit L. 2.3 m, W. 1.8 m,
D. 1.3 m with upright slab H. 1.3 m and adjacent vessel,
2.7 m S. of centre (E of B1: Coombs).
3 *Food Vessel*: on internal rim bevel, two rows of bone
   impressions; on outer edge of rim and neck and
   shoulder ridges, single rows of incised short
   diagonal lines set opposed.
   M. 14.6 cm; H. 13.5 cm; B. 8.9 cm.   79 12-9 1946

Feature A: pit L. 1.7 m, W. 1.4 m, D. 0.8 m; disturbed
fill; objects nearby.
4 *Food Vessel*: plain.
   M. 15.5 cm; H. 14.0 cm; B. 5.7 cm.   P1983 11-1 1
5 *Flint barbed-and-tanged arrowhead*: all over bifacial
   invasive retouch; tang snapped; mottled grey.
   L. 1.9 cm; W. 1.8 cm; Th. 0.3 cm.   P1983 11-1 2

Feature B: pit L. 7.3 m, W. 4.5 m, D. 1.2 m, below N. edge
of cairn; sherds 6-7 in lower fill, sherds 8-9 in upper
fill.
6 *Collared Vessel sherds*: two, including base of
   collar; on collar, remains of two twisted cord
   horizontal lines; beneath collar, one twisted cord
   horizontal line.   P1983 11-1 3
7 *Food Vessel Urn sherds*: two, including rim; on
   internal rim bevel, two rows of bone or stick
   impressions enclosed and separated by single twisted
   cord lines; on external rim bevel and neck,
   horizontal twisted cord lines.   P1983 11-1 4
8 *Early Iron Age jar sherds*: one hundred and twenty-
   one including five rim, representing minimum two
   vessels; vesicular fabric.   P1983 11-1 5
9 *Early Iron Age jar sherds*: twenty-one; rock-
   tempered.   P1983 11-1 6

Mound material
10 *Beaker sherds*: two, including base; vertical rows of
   triangular-shaped impressions.   P1983 11-1 7
11 *Jet fragments*: six; unworked.   P1983 11-1 8a-f
   'flint leaf arrowhead': not preserved.
   'flint barbed-and-tanged arrowhead': not preserved.

12 *Flint point fragment*: bifacial invasive retouch
converging on distal; snapped; mottled grey.
L. 3.9 cm; W. 2.1 cm; Th. 0.4 cm.   P1983 11-1 9
13 *Flint horseshoe scraper*: edge retouch on distal, L.
and R. at 60 degrees; mottled grey.
L. 2.8 cm; W. 2.4 cm; Th. 0.9 cm.   P1983 11-1 10
14 *Flint horseshoe scraper*: irregular edge retouch on
distal, L. and R.; distal damaged; platform butt;
mottled grey.
L. 5.0 cm; W. 3.5 cm; Th. 1.0 cm.   P1983 11-1 11
15 *Flint scraper fragment*: edge and invasive retouch on
distal and R.; cortex remnant; broken; mottled grey.
L. 3.0 cm; W. 3.3 cm; Th. 0.7 cm.   P1983 11-1 12
16 *Flint scraper fragment*: edge retouch on distal;
broken; beige.
L. 2.0 cm; W. 2.8 cm; Th. 0.9 cm.   P1983 11-1 13
17 *Flint knife*: edge retouch on L. and partially on R.;
mottled grey.
L. 5.3 cm; W. 2.4 cm; Th. 0.8 cm.   P1983 11-1 14
18 *Flint awl or piercer*: edge retouch on L. and R.
converging on distal; mottled grey.
L. 4.0 cm; W. 1.3 cm; Th. 0.4 cm.   P1983 11-1 15
19 *Flint worked blade*: limited inverse edge retouch on
L.; mottled grey.
L. 11.1 cm; W. 3.1 cm; Th. 1.3 cm.   P1983 11-1 16
20 *Flint worked flake*: irregular edge retouch on L.;
mottled grey.
L. 5.5 cm; W. 4.0 cm; Th. 0.9 cm.   P1983 11-1 17
21 *Flint worked flake*: limited edge retouch on distal
and L.; broken; mottled grey.
L. 3.6 cm; W. 3.5 cm; Th. 0.8 cm.   P1983 11-1 18
22 *Flint worked fragment*: invasive retouch on one end;
cortex remnant; mottled grey.
L. 2.8 cm; W. 2.5 cm; Th. 1.4 cm.   P1983 11-1 19

Flint blades

	Btt	Ctx	Col.	L.	W.	Th.	P1983 11-1
23			M. Gr.	4.2	1.4	0.8	20
24			M. Gr.	4.3	1.4	0.8	21
25			M. Gr.	3.3	1.0	0.4	22
26	Sn.	X	M. Gr.	1.1	1.1	0.3	23

HAWNBY   UN 121:1

Yorkshire N.R.; North Yorkshire   SE 55 90

ROUND BARROW: no information.
Unpublished.

Not located
1 *Flint horseshoe scraper*: edge retouch at 70 degrees
on bilateral and distal; cortex remnant; patinated.
L. 5.9 cm; W. 3.9 cm; Th. 1.6 cm.   79 12-9 1713

HELMSLEY   UN 122:1

Yorkshire N.R.; North Yorkshire   SE 60 85

ROUND BARROW: no information.
Unpublished.

Burial 1: inhumation; no information.
1 *Food Vessel*: bone impressions: on rim, transverse; at
base of neck, vertical.
M. *c.* 9.5 cm; H. 6.8 cm; B. 5.4 cm.   79 12-9 1723

HOLWICK IN TEESDALE   UN 123:1-2

Yorkshire N.R.; Durham   NY 90 26

ROUND BARROW: no information; opened 1867.
Unpublished.

Not located
1 *Jet spacer-plate*: cut and polished to trapezoid
outline and lenticular section; three drilled
transverse perforations; on one face opposed chevron
design infilled with drilled or punched *pointillé*;
damaged.
L. 3.6 cm; W. 2.2 cm; Th. 0.8 cm.   79 12-9 1720
2 *Jet spacer-plate fragment*: cut and polished to
trapezoid outline and lenticular section; two
surviving drilled transverse perforations; on one
face opposed chevron design infilled with drilled or
punched *pointillé*; broken.
L. 2.7 cm; W. 2.8 cm; Th. 0.8 cm.   79 12-9 1721

LEVISHAM MOOR   UN 124:1-34

Yorkshire N.R.; North Yorkshire   SE 833 936

ROUND CAIRN: no information; opened by Rev. R. Skelton
August 1851 (see note below).
Skelton 1852; Pierpoint and Phillips 1978.

Burial 1: cremation deposit; in urn near surface of
mound.
'*large urn*': not preserved.

Burial 2: cremation deposit; in central pit beneath
inverted urn with objects.
'*urn*': not preserved.
1 *Stone battle-axe*: Group XVIII, Y803; Roe IID; ground
and polished to blunt blade and angular butt; central
drilled hourglass perforation.
L. 13.2 cm; W. 5.8 cm; Th. 3.1 cm; Diam. perf. 2.9 cm.
1964 12 6 467
2 *Flint barbed-and-tanged arrowhead*: all over invasive
retouch; burnt and broken.
L. 2.8 cm; W. 1.8 cm; Th. 0.8 cm.   POA 172.29
Green 1980, no. 504.
3-4 *Flint fragments*: two; burnt.   POA 172.30-31

The following material derives from this site or from
any or all of six other barrows in the vicinity excavated
in 1851 by the Rev. Skelton.

Not located
5 *Flint leaf arrowhead*: all over bifacial invasive
retouch; light grey.
L. 3.0 cm; W. 1.7 cm; Th. 0.4 cm.   POA 172.1
6 *Flint leaf arrowhead*: bifacial edge retouch; point
snapped; mottled grey.
L. 3.3 cm; W. 2.1 cm; Th. 0.4 cm.   POA 172.2
7 *Flint barbed-and-tanged arrowhead*: all over bifacial
invasive retouch; mottled grey.
L. 2.8 cm; W. 1.9 cm; Th. 0.5 cm.   1965 2-9 88
Pierpoint and Phillips 1978, fig. 1b.
8 *Flint plano-convex knife*: all over invasive retouch;
some inverse invasive retouch; cortex remnant;
mottled grey/patinated.
L. 2.9 cm; W. 2.6 cm; Th. 0.5 cm.   POA 172.3
9 *Flint plano-convex knife*: all over invasive retouch;
some inverse invasive retouch; patinated.
L. 4.9 cm; W. 1.9 cm; Th. 0.8 cm.   1965 2-9 87
Pierpoint and Phillips 1978, fig. 1c.
10 *Flint plano-convex knife*: all over invasive retouch;
mottled grey.
L. 4.3 cm; W. 2.2 cm; Th. 1.0 cm.   POA 172.6
11 *Flint knife*: bilateral edge and invasive retouch
converging on distal; mottled grey.
L. 5.3 cm; W. 1.8 cm; Th. 0.9 cm.   POA 172.4

12 *Flint knife*: all round edge retouch; mottled grey.
   L. 5.1 cm; W. 2.1 cm; Th. 0.6 cm.   POA 172.5
13 *Flint knife*: bilateral edge and invasive retouch
   converging on distal; platform butt; mottled grey.
   L. 3.1 cm; W. 2.3 cm; Th. 0.7 cm.   POA 172.7
14 *Flint worked flake*: bilateral edge retouch; both ends
   snapped; patinated.
   L. 4.1 cm; W. 2.6 cm; Th. 0.8 cm.   POA 172.8
15 *Flint worked blade*: bilateral edge retouch; patinated.
   L. 3.9 cm; W. 1.2 cm; Th. 0.5 cm.   POA 172.9
16 *Flint worked blade*: bilateral edge retouch; mottled
   grey.
   L. 4.3 cm; W. 1.1 cm; Th. 0.4 cm.   POA 172.10
17 *Flint worked flake*: edge retouch on L.; burnt and
   broken.
   L. 2.5 cm; W. 1.9 cm; Th. 0.5 cm.   POA 172.11
18 *Flint worked flake*: edge retouch on R.; mottled grey.
   L. 5.3 cm; W. 2.0 cm; Th. 0.5 cm.   POA 172.12

Flint Utilised flakes

	Wr	Btt	Ctx	Col.	L.	W.	Th.	POA 172
19	LR	Fc.	x	M. Gr.	3.8	1.4	0.3	13
20	R			Bt	5.3	1.7	0.8	14
21	LR	Fc.		M. Gr.	4.0	1.4	0.3	15
22	LR	Pl.		M. Gr.	3.1	2.1	0.4	16
23	L	Sn.		M. Gr.	2.9	1.5	0.9	17
24	R	Pl.		Pat.	3.1	1.5	0.5	18
25	R	Pl.		M. Gr.	2.2	1.2	0.2	19

Flint flakes

	Btt	Ctx	Col.	L.	W.	Th.	POA 172
26	Pl.		M. Gr.	5.6	1.9	0.9	20
27			M. Gr.	3.2	1.1	0.4	21
28			M. Gr.	2.2	1.1	0.3	22
29			M. Gr.	3.2	2.3	0.4	23
30			M. Gr.	3.4	2.3	1.5	24
31			Pat.	2.1	1.9	0.6	25
32			Pat.	3.0	1.7	0.5	26
33			M. Gr.	4.9	1.3	0.8	27
34			Bt	3.2	2.1	0.7	28

LYTHE (Lythe IV)   UN 125:1-2

Yorkshire N.R.; North Yorkshire   NZ 83 14

ROUND BARROW: no information; opened by W.G.
Unpublished.

Not located
1-2 '*Flint scrapers*': two; not identified.
                                        79 12-9 1652-3

ORCHARD HILLS (Egton Bridge)   UN 126:1

Yorkshire N.R.; North Yorkshire   NZ 803 041

CIST: found 1861.
BB 333-4; *Greenwell* 1865, 261.

Burial 1: ?decayed inhumation; in cist of four side-
slabs and capstone.
   '*three bronze fragments*': not preserved.
1 *Beaker sherd*: incised: narrow bands of short diagonal
   lines bordered by roughly scored horizontal lines,
   with uppermost band underlined only, alternating
   with narrow reserved bands.
   M. *c*. 16.0 cm; H. 15.0 cm.   79 12-9 1232
   Greenwell 1865, fig. 18; *Clarke* no. 1269.

SCALBY   UN 127:1

Yorkshire N.R.; North Yorkshire   TA 02 90

ROUND BARROW: no information; opened 1864.
BB 69.

Burial 1: cremation deposit; in inverted urn.
1 *Collared Urn*: deeply impressed coarse whipped cord:
   on collar and neck, two rows of short diagonal lines;
   beneath shoulder, one row of short diagonal lines;
   one pair of perforations drilled through neck after
   firing.
   M. 33.3 cm; surviving H. 30.0 cm.   79 12-9 1722
   BAP no. 131; *Longworth* no. 1247.

SEAMER   UN 128:1

Yorkshire N.R.; North Yorkshire   TA 00 86

ROUND BARROW: no information; opened ?by WG 1866.
Unpublished.

Not located
1 *Flint utilised flake*: bilateral wear; faceted butt;
   cortex remnant; mottled grey to patinated.
   L. 9.7 cm; W. 4.1 cm; Th. 1.1 cm.   79 12-9 1700

SEAMER MANOR HOUSE   UN 129:1

Yorkshire N.R.; North Yorkshire   TA 024 860

ROUND BARROW: Diam. 20 m, H. ? m; internal boulder kerb;
opened by A.D. Conyngham 1849.
Conyngham 1849, 106.

Burial 1: ?decayed inhumation; in central triangular
stone setting W. 1.2 m; urn in N. corner.
   '*urn*': not preserved.

Burial 2: ?decayed inhumation; 1.8 m W. of centre.
1 *Food Vessel*: jabbed impressions: on internal rim
   bevel, two rows; in neck, three rows.
   M. 10.9 cm; H. 10.7 cm; B. 6.0 cm.   79 12-9 1968
   Conyngham 1849, fig. 5.

SEAMER MOOR 1   UN 130:1-2

Yorkshire N.R.; North Yorkshire   TA 02 86

ROUND BARROW: dimensions unknown; sandstone rubble;
opened Conyngham 1849.
Conyngham 1849, 105.

Burial 1: cremation deposit; on large stones near
centre.

Mound material
1-2 '*Flint flakes*': two; not identified.
                                        79 12-9 1966-67

SEAMER MOOR 2   UN 131:1-2

Yorkshire N.R.; North Yorkshire   TA 00 86

ROUND BARROW(S): no information; probably opened by W.G.
WGMs 12, 33; *ASI* 148.
(The existing records may refer to one or two barrows,
and one or two cremation deposits.)

Burial 1: cremation deposit(s).
1 *Stone polished axe*: Group VI tuff, Y831; all over
   ground and polished to lentoid section; broken and
   pitted.
   L. 11.8 cm; W. 5.7 cm; Th. 2.8 cm.   POA 168

Burial 1 or 2

2 *Stone polished axe fragment*: Group VI tuff, Y832; ground and polished; broken and extensively reworked.

L. 6.6 cm; W. 5.2 cm; Th. 1.9 cm.   POA 169

WHITBY   UN 132:1

Yorkshre N.R.; North Yorkshire   NZ 90 01

ROUND BARROW: no information.
Unpublished.

Not located

1 *Accessory Cup*: horizontal fingertip rilling; no perforations; eroded.

M. 5.9 cm; H. 6.1 cm; B. 5.7 cm.   WG 2422

WYKEHAM MOOR   UN 133:1-2

Yorkshire N.R.; North Yorkshire   SE 95 85

ROUND BARROW: no information; opened by W.G. 1869.
Unpublished.

Not located

1 *'Stone pebble'*: not identified.   79 12-9 1729
2 *'Flint scraper'*: not identified.   79 12-9 1728

BALLYMEANOCH   UN 134:1

Argyll; Strathclyde   NR 883 963

HENGE: central area Diam. 21.5 m surrounded by ditch W. 2.1-3.6 m with outer bank W. 7.2-8.5 m; cists opened by W.G. 15 October 1864.
Greenwell 1866, 348-9; *Campbell and Sandeman* 1962, no. 64.

Burial 1: triple inhumation traces; in cist L. 0.9 m, W. 0.4 m, D. 0.6 m, aligned NE.-SW., four side-slabs and capstone, SE. of centre.

1 *Beaker*: rectangular tooth comb-stamped: on neck, deep zone of upright triangles outlined by double lines and filled with short horizontal lines bordered above by three lines and below by three lines and fringe of short diagonal lines; on body, deep zone of similar but pendant triangles bordered above by two lines and fringe of short diagonal lines.

M. 17.6 cm; surviving H. 16.0 cm.   79 12-9 1913
Greenwell 1866, pl. XX.2; *BAP* no. 185; *Clarke* no. 1530.

Burial 2: ?decayed inhumation; cist L. 1.8 m, W. 0.8 m, D. 0.7 m, aligned NE-SW., four side-slabs and two capstones, pebble-paved, near centre.

DUNCRAGAIG   UN 135:1-2

Argyll; Strathclyde   NR 834 968

ROUND CAIRN: Diam. 30 m, reduced by stone-robbing; opened by W.G. 14 October 1864.
Greenwell 1866, 347-8; *Campbell and Sandeman* 1962, no. 95.

Burial 1: cremation deposit; on flagstone paving of central cist, L. 1.4 m, W. 0.8 m, D. 0.8 m, aligned ENE-WSW, four side-slabs with capstone.

1 *Food Vessel*: Irish Bowl; tooth-comb stamped with grooves or smoothed comb impressions: on internal rim bevel, short diagonal lines; on upper and lower body, zones of short vertical grooves, the upper bordered above by zone of short diagonal to horizontal lines

set between single horizontal grooves and below by multiple chevrons between single horizontal grooves, the lower bordered above and below by single horizontal lines; at base, zone of short diagonal lines bordered above by single horizontal line and below by single horizontal incised line; on base, three sets of chevrons or arcs.

M. 12.5 cm; H. 9.8 cm; B. 7.5 cm.   NMAS. HPO12
'flint chippings': not preserved.

Burial 2: inhumation traces, head E.; on capstone of central cist.

Burial 3: inhumation, crouched with head NE.; in clay fill below paving of central cist.

Burial 4: cremation deposit; in gravel fill of cist L. 0.5 m, W. 0.4 m, D. 0.4 m, aligned NE.-SW., 6.6 m E. of centre.

2 *Food Vessel*: Irish Bowl: tooth-comb stamped: on upper and lower body, zones of short vertical lines bordered above and below by single rows of triangular impressions and groups of horizontal lines; beneath rim and in constricted waist, respectively three and one rows of triangular impressions; at base, double zigzag with triangular impressions set in triangular spaces above and below; on base, cross formed by triangular impressions with chevrons between arms, the whole encircled by triangular impressions.

M. 12.3 cm; H. 9.7 cm; B. 8.6 cm.   NMAS. HPO11

Burial 5: multiple cremation deposits; above and below slab paving at W. end of boulder-walled cist L. 2.2 m, W. 0.9 m, D. 1.0 m, aligned ENE.-WSW., 8 m from S. side of cairn.

Cairn material

'greenstone axe': not preserved.
'whetstone': not preserved.
'flint knife': not preserved.

GLEBE   UN 136:1-2

Argyll; Strathclyde   NR 833 989

ROUND CAIRN: Diam. 33 m, H. 4 m; two internal circles Diam. 8 m and 11 m of stones W. 0.6 m, H. 0.9 m spaced *c.* 0.9-1.5 m apart; opened by W.G. 3-6 October 1864.
Greenwell 1866, 339-41; *Campbell and Sandeman* 1962, no. 105.

Burial 1: ?decayed inhumation; cist L. 1 m, W. 0.7 m, D. 0.5 m, aligned NE.-SW., four side-slabs and capstone, near centre.

1 *Food Vessel*: Irish Bowl: on internal rim bevel, single horizontal groove; on upper body, zone of tooth-comb stamped horizontal lines above deeper zone of hurdle pattern enclosed above by row of triangular impressions and single horizontal groove and below by row of triangular impressions and two horizontal grooves; in shoulder groove and over lugs, tooth-comb stamped herringbone; on lower body, zone of tooth-comb stamped herringbone enclosed above and below by single rows of triangular impressions, two horizontal grooves and single horizontal tooth-comb stamped line; at base, narrow zone of alternate triangular impressions forming raised bar chevron between single horizontal grooves.

M. 16.5 cm; H. 12.2 cm; B. 5.6 cm.   NMAS. HP09
'jet necklace': two spacer-plates, three cylindrical and twenty-three disc beads; not preserved.

Burial 2: ?decayed inhumation; in central grave L. 2.3 m, W. 0.9 m, D. 0.9 m, aligned NE.-SW., boulder-lined with capstone.

2 *Food Vessel*: tooth—comb stamped and triangular impressions: on internal rim bevel, short diagonal lines enclosed between rows of impressions; on upper two divisions, zone of short diagonal lines bordered above and below by single lines of impressions and narrow zones of horizontal lines; on external rim edge and body ridges, short vertical lines; on body, zone of irregularly placed horizontal lines above zone of lattice bordered by single rows of impressions and separated by zone of horizontal lines from basal zone of diagonal lines bordered by single rows of impressions.
M. 17.5 cm; H. 13.6 cm; B. 8.2 cm.   79 12—9 1924
Greenwell 1866, pl. XX.3.

NETHER LARGIE   UN 137:1-20

Argyll: Strathclyde   NR 828 979

Chambered Cairn: Diam. 41 m, (Diam. 36 m: Henshall), reduced by stone-robbing; opened by W.G. 7-10 October 1864.
Greenwell 1866, 341-7; *Henshall* 1972, 335-40.

Burial 1: ?decayed inhumation; in cist L. 1.1 m, W. 0.8 m, D. 0.9 m, aligned NE.-SW., four side-slabs and capstone; 12 m SW. of centre.

Burial 2: ?decayed inhumation; in cist L. 1.6 m, W. 0.9 m, D. 1.2 m, four side-slabs and capstone, 7.2 m N. of centre.
   decorated urn': not preserved.

Burials 3-7 were in central megalithic chamber L. 6 m, W. 1-1.8 m, H. 2 m, aligned NE-SW.; walls of orthostatic and drystone build with slab roofing; three sub-dividing septal slabs.

Burial 3: inhumation fragments; around disturbed cist L. 0.8 m, W. 0.6 m, four side-slabs and capstone; SE corner of innermost section.
   Beaker sherds: probably among nos 2-6 below.

Burial 4: scattered ?multiple cremation deposit; in dark earth layer on pebble paving; innermost section.

Burial 5: scattered? multiple cremation deposit; in dark earth layer on pebble paving; third section.
1 *Neolithic Bowl sherd*: lines of ?bone impressions.
                                          79 12—9 1914
2 *Beaker*: inside rim, row of incised lozenges enclosed between pairs of twisted cord lines; externally, five zones of which upper, middle and lower formed by single rows of incised lozenges separated by pairs of lines and enclosed by three tooth—comb stamped lines, the intervening zones formed by rows of horizontal lentoid impressions similarly separated and enclosed.
M. *c.* 16.5 cm; surviving H. 21.0 cm.   79 12—9 1925
BAP no. 198; *Clarke* no. 1551; *Henshall* 1972, 302 no. 3.
3 *Beaker sherds*: twenty-five, tooth—comb stamped: on lower neck and belly, zone bordered by horizontal lines separated by broad reserved band from zone of two bands of lattice separated by pair of horizontal lines and bordered above and below by bands of four horizontal lines.
                                          79 12—9 1914a
Henshall 1972, 302 no. 4.
4 *Beaker sherds*: two, including rim; on interior below rim, two to three twisted cord horizontal lines.
                                          79 12—9 1914b
Henshall 1972, 302 no. 6.
5 *Beaker rim sherd*: beneath rim, plain cordon above two to three tooth—comb stamped discontinuous horizontal lines above short diagonal lines in uncertain technique.   79 12—9 1914c
Henshall 1972, 302 no. 5.

6 *Beaker sherd*: tooth—comb stamped horizontal lines.
                                          79 12—9 1914d
7 *Food Vessel sherds*: eight, including rim; tooth—comb stamped: on internal rim bevel, herringbone; on external rim bevel, horizontal line; on neck and body, zones of horizontal lines occasionally interrupted by lines of opposed triangular impressions to give relief bar—chevron.   79 12—9 1914e
Henshall 1972, 302 no. 8.
8 *Food Vessel sherd*: lines of deep bone impressions.
                                          79 12—9 1914f

Burial 6: inhumation fragments; in disturbed fill of second section.
9 *Neolithic Bowl sherds*: eleven, including rim and imperforate horizontal lug; plain; grit-tempered.
Henshall 1972, 302 no. 2.   79 12—9 1914g
10 *Neolithic Bowl rim sherds*: three joining; on top of rim, shallow round-based impressions.
                                          79 12—9 1914h
11 *Neolithic Bowl sherd*: incised cross-hatched lines.
                                          79 12—9 1914i
12 *Neolithic Bowl*: over rim, on neck and body, shallow diagonal furrows.
M. 22.0-23.0 cm; H. 15.5 cm.   79 12—9 1912
Greenwell 1866, pl. XX.1; *Henshall* 1972, 302 no. 1.
13 *Flint barbed-and tanged-arrowhead*: all over bifacial invasive retouch; patinated.
L. 2.4 cm; W.. 2.1 cm; Th. 0.3 cm.   79 12—9 1916
Henshall 1972, 302 no. 10; *Green* 1980, no. 36.
   flint barbed-and tanged-arrowheads': four; not preserved.
14 *Flint knife fragment*: bilateral edge retouch at 45 degrees; cortex remnant; snapped; mottled grey.
L. 1.7 cm; W. 1.7 cm; Th. 0.3 cm.   79 12—9 1915
Henshall 1972, 302 no. 15.
15 *Flint worked fragment*: edge retouch on L.; snapped; mottled grey.
L. 2.9 cm; W.. 3.3 cm; Th. 0.5 cm.   79 12—9 1922
Henshall 1972, 302 no. 16.
16 *Flint utilised flake*: wear on R.; cortex remnant; mottled grey.
L. 6.7 cm; W. 3.4 cm; Th. 0.8 cm.   79 12—9 1919
17 *Flint flake*: cortex remnant; mottled grey.
L. 4.5 cm; W.. 2.8 cm; Th. 0.8 cm.   79 12—9 1920
Henshall 1972, 302 no. 17.
18 *Flint flake*: cortex remnant; mottled brown.
L. 3.5 cm; W. 2.3 cm; Th. 0.6 cm.   79 12—9 1921

Burial 7: inhumation fragments in disturbed fill of first section.
19 *Flint flake*: cortex remnant; mottled grey.
L. 7.5 cm; W. 4.4 cm; Th. 1.2 cm.   79 12—9 1917
20 *Flint flake*: mottled beige.
L. 3.7 cm; W. 3.3 cm; Th. 0.8 cm.   79 12—9 1918

RUDLE (Anaskeog 61)   UN 138:1-3

Argyll; Strathclyde   NR 841 953

ROUND CAIRN: Diam. 18 m, denuded by stone-robbing; opened by W.G. 16 October 1864.
Greenwell 1866, 349-50; *Campbell and Sandeman* 1962, no. 61.

Burial 1: ?decayed inhumation; in small cist at SE.
1 *Food Vessel*: whipped cord: on neck, vertical lines enclosed by single horizontal lines; on shoulder, short vertical lines; on body, vertical lines enclosed above by single line and below by three discontinuous horizontal lines.
M. 16.7 cm; H. 15.4 cm; B. 9.2 cm.   NMAS.HP07

Burial 2: inhumation traces; in small cist at SE.

2 *Food Vessel sherds*: twenty-two, including rim; incised: on top of rim, diagonal lines; on body, groups of diagonal lines.   79 12-9 1927

3 *Flint plano-convex knife*: converging bilateral edge retouch; some inverse edge retouch; corticated butt; white.
L. 5.1 cm; W. 2.5 cm; Th. 1.0 cm.   79 12-9 1926
Greenwell 1866, pl. XX.4.

Burial 3: ?decayed inhumation; in small cist at SE., previously opened.

TEALING HILL   UN 139:1-2

Forfar; Tayside   NO 40 40

CEMETERY: discovered in quarrying 1870.
Neish 1870.

Burial 1: cremation deposit; in inverted urn in 'disturbed soil' at D. 0.9 m.

1 *Collared Urn*: on collar, indistinct twisted cord paired lines forming lozenge pattern enclosed above by two and below by one horizontal line.
M. *c*. 22.5 cm; H. 27.6 cm; B. 8.8 cm.   79 12-9 1932
BAP no. 200; *Longworth* no. 1999.

Burial 2: cremation deposit; in inverted urn in 'disturbed soil' with some form of stone surround at D. 0.9 m, W. of Burial 1.

2 *Food Vessel Urn*: triangular jabs: on internal rim bevel, two to three horizontal rows; on external rim bevel and shoulder groove, single horizontal rows; in neck, diagonal rows; on body, diagonal incised lines.
M. 28.0 cm; H. 27.2 cm; B. 10.5 cm.   79 12-9 1933
BAP no. 516; *Cowie* 1978, AGS 6.

Burial 3: adult male inhumation, crouched on L. with head E.; in cist L. 1.2 m W. 0.6 m D 0.6m, aligned E.-W., four side-slabs and capstone at D. 1.8 m below Burials 1 and 2.

KIRKMABRECK (Creetown)   UN 140:1

Kirkcudbrightshire; Dumfries and Galloway   NX 48 56

CIST: no information.
Unpublished.

Burial 1: inhumation; in cist.

1 *Food Vessel*: whipped cord: on internal rim bevel, herringbone; on external surface from rim to upper body, herringbone with upper and lower rows split by single horizontal grooved lines except for uppermost and lowest.
M. 15.0 cm; H. 13.0 cm.   79 12-9 1938
BAP no. 422; *Simpson* 1965, no. 24.

KENNY'S HILLOCK (Urquhart)   UN 141:1-2

Moray; Grampian   NJ 302 607

ROUND CAIRN: Diam. 7.2 m, reduced by stone-robbing and ploughing; boulders with massive kerb; opened by Rev. J. Morrison 4 May 1870 and recorded in destruction 1879.
Morrison 1872, 260; 1880, 109-10; *Walker* 1966a, 117.

Burial 1: ?decayed inhumation; in grave D. 1.5 m, 1.8 m E. of centre; basal fill of 'ashes' covered by slab and boulders.

1 *Food Vessel*: on internal rim bevel, two twisted cord lines; on neck, whipped cord zigzag; on shoulder, row of whipped cord short vertical lines; on body, whipped cord herringbone.
M. 15.4 cm; H. 12.8 cm; B. 8.5 cm.   79 12-9 1928
Walker 1966a, no. 10.

Burial 2; ?decayed inhumation; in cist L. 1.2 m, W. 0.6 m, D. ?m, aligned N.-S., at base of oval pit D. 1.5 m, fill of boulders with much charcoal; location unknown; vessel in SE. corner.

2 *Food Vessel*: whipped twisted cord: beneath rim; two rows of opposed short impressions separated by single horizontal incised line; on upper body, deep zone of open lozenges, the lozenges and lower triangular spaces filled with short impressions, the whole enclosed between pairs of horizontal incised lines; on lower body, deep zone of zigzag and open lozenges, lozenges and upper and lower triangular spaces filled with short impressions, the whole bordered above by row of short impressions and single horizontal incised line and below by pair of horizontal incised lines; at base, two rows of short impressions separated by pair of horizontal incised lines.
M. 13.5 cm; H. 12.5 cm; B. 9.0 cm.   NMAS.EE6
BAP no. 415; *Walker* 1966a, no. 11 and fig. 6e.

URQUHART   UN 142:1-5

Moray; Grampian   NJ 30 60

CONTEXT UNCERTAIN: recorded as 'from barrow' [cf. Kenny's Hillock, Urquhart: UN141].
Walker 1966b.

Not located

1 *Beaker sherd*: irregularly executed incised horizontal lines.   79 12-9 1931a

2 *Food Vessel Urn sherds*: thirteen, including shoulder and base; on neck and shoulder, three rows of finger tip impressions; on body, row of finger tip impression between two pairs of incised horizontal lines above incised double to triple chevron pattern.   79 12-9 1930

3 *Bucket Urn rim sherd*: row of finger tip impressions beneath neck groove.   79 12-9 1931

4 *Bronze Age sherds*: three; plain.   79 12-9 1931b

5 *Stone vessel rim fragment*: steatite; ground and ?polished; thickened rim and shoulder cordon.
Diam. *c*. 17.0 cm.   79 12-9 1929

BLAIRGOWRIE   UN 143:1

Perthshire, Tayside   NO 17 45

CIST: no information.
Unpublished.

Burial 1: no information; in cist.

1 *Food Vessel*: on internal rim bevel, short vertical tooth-comb stamped lines; on neck, indistinct short vertical lines in ?tooth-comb stamp above irregular horizontal whipped cord lines; on shoulder, deep short tooth-comb stamped lines in herringbone; on body, irregular horizontal whipped cord lines; at base, row of short diagonal tooth-comb stamped lines.
M. 14.1 cm; H. 13.1 cm; B. 7.3 cm.   79 12-9 1934

HARRIETFIELD (Glenalmond)   UN 144:1

Perthshire, Tayside   NN 98 30

UNKNOWN CONTEXT: no information.
Unpublished.

Not located

1 *Food Vessel*: twisted cord: on top of rim, three lines; on external surface, roughly executed herringbone, in some areas becoming short diagonal lines.
M. 12.6 cm; H. 10.6 cm; B. 7.3 cm.   79 12-9 1935
BAP no. 344.

BLACKBURN   UN 145:1

Roxburghshire; Borders   NY 48 89

UNKNOWN CONTEXT
Unpublished.

1 *Jet ring fragments*: two; cut and polished to sub-
   triangular section; broken, and ends of both
   fragments polished smooth.
   Diam. ext. 4.0 cm, int. 2.0 cm; Th. 0.8 cm.
                                       79 12-9 1937

LANTON MAINS (Duddo House)   UN 146:1

Roxburghshire; Borders   NT 62 22

CIST: opened October 1870.
Hilson 1872

Burial 1: inhumation; in cist L. 1.1 m, W. 0.6 m, D. 0.5
m, aligned E.-W.
   'urn': not preserved.
1 *Flint flake*: platform butt; cortex remnant; mottled
   grey.
   L. 7.0 cm; W. 2.8 cm; Th. 0.9 cm.   79 12-9 1936
   'seventeen flint flakes': not preserved.

THE PLATES

NUMBERED BARROWS
DISTRIBUTION MAP

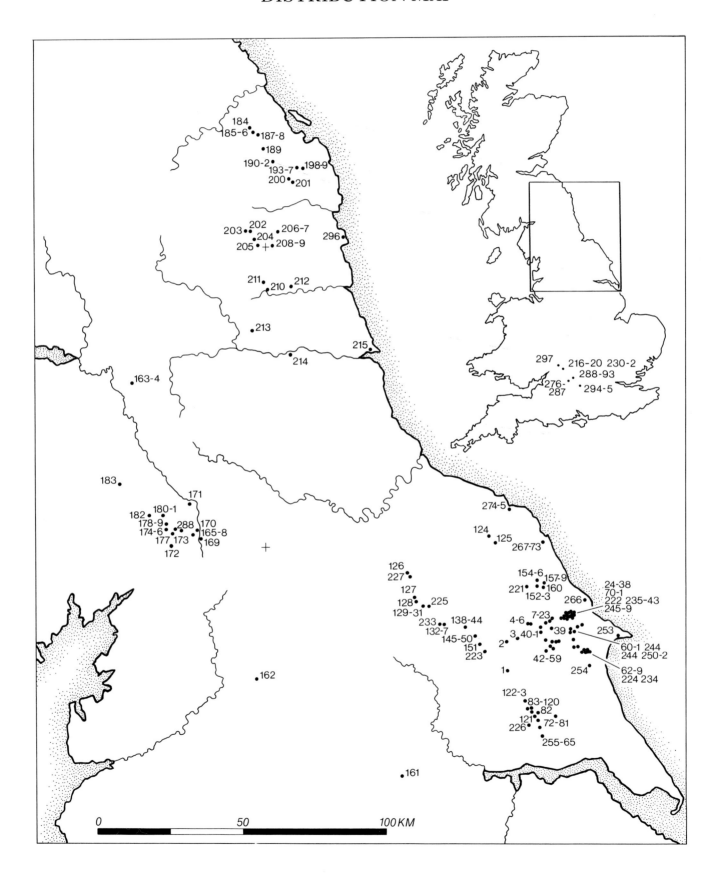

184
185-6 187-8
189
190-2 198-9
193-7
200 201

203 202 206-7
204 296
205 208-9

211 212
210

213

214 215

163-4

297 216-20 230-2
288-93
276-
287 294-5

183

171

182 180-1
178-9 288 170
174-6 165-8
177 173 169
172

274-5

124
125
267-73

126
227

127

128 225
129-31

233 138-44
132-7
145-50
151
223

162

1

161

154-6 157-9
221 160
152-3

266

4-6 7-23
3 40-1 39
2
42-59
254

24-38
70-1
222 235-43
245-9

253

60-1 244
244 250-2

62-9
224 234

122-3
83-120
82
121 72-81
226
255-65

0   50   100 KM

1 KIRBY UNDERDALE

Burial 1

Old surface

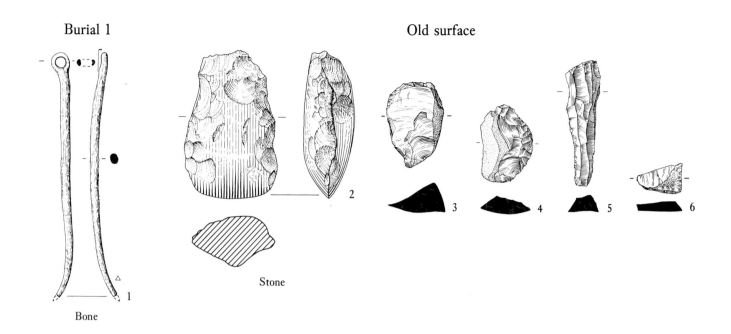

Bone

1

Stone

2

3

4

5

6

2 LANGTON

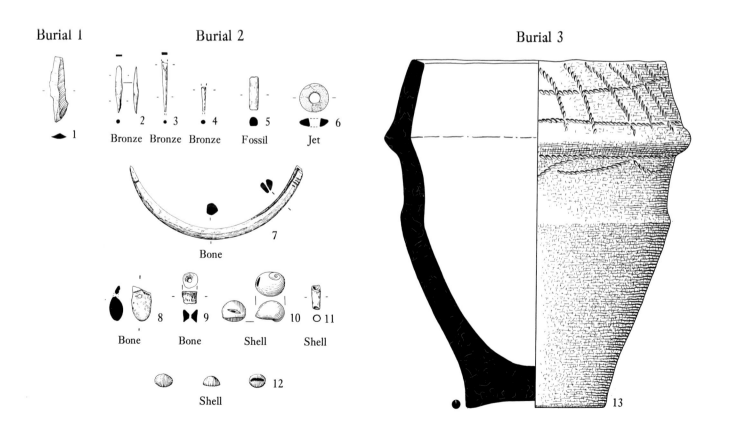

Burial 1

Burial 2

Burial 3

1

Bronze 2   Bronze 3   Bronze 4   Fossil 5   Jet 6

Bone 7

Bone 8   Bone 9   Shell 10   Shell 11

Shell 12

13

3 KIRBY GRINDALYTH

Mound 1867   Mound 1895

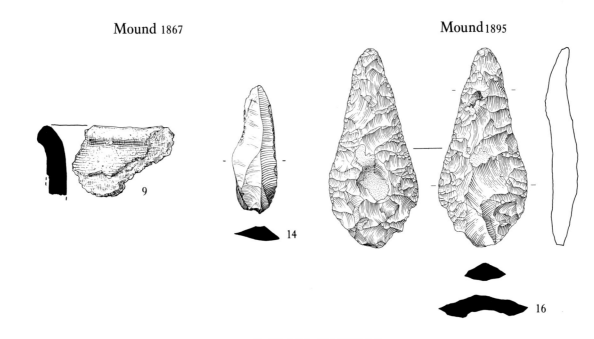

5 HESLERTON

Burial 1   Mound

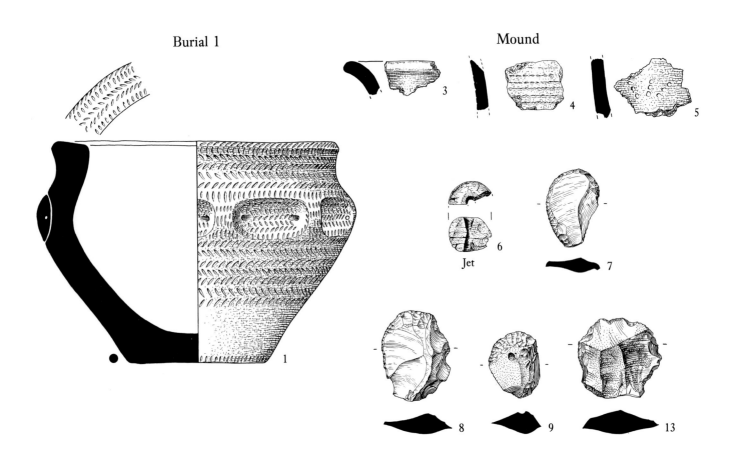

6 HESLERTON

Feature A

Feature A or Mound

Mound

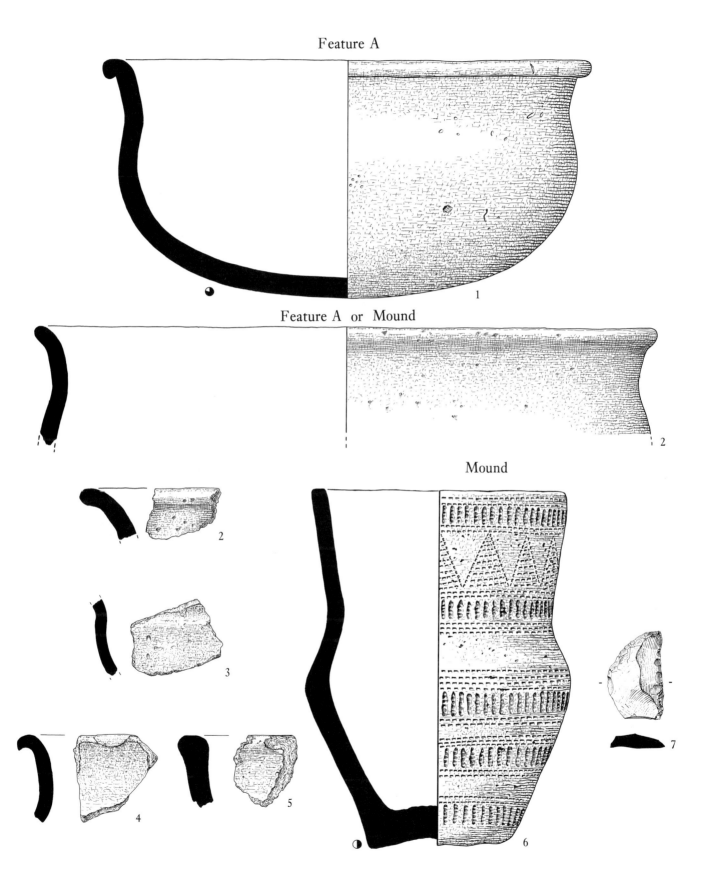

7 SHERBURN

Burial 2

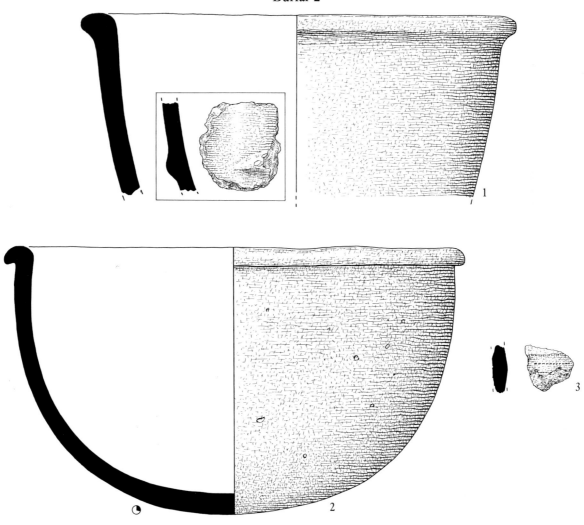

Burial 3

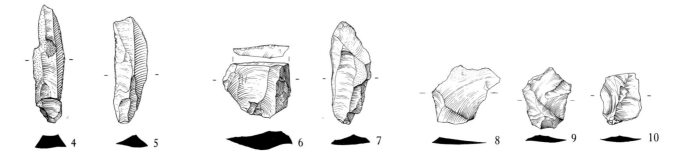

Burial 4

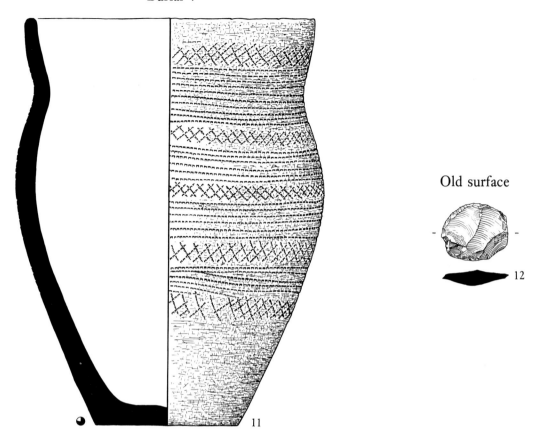

Old surface

12

11 SHERBURN

9 SHERBURN

Burial 1

Burial 2

Burial 3

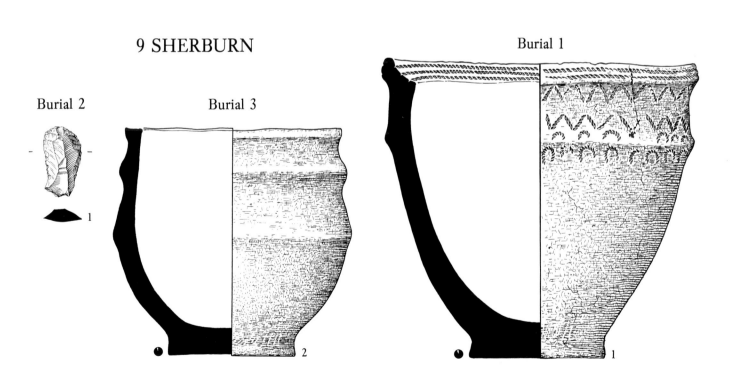

1

2

1

12 SHERBURN

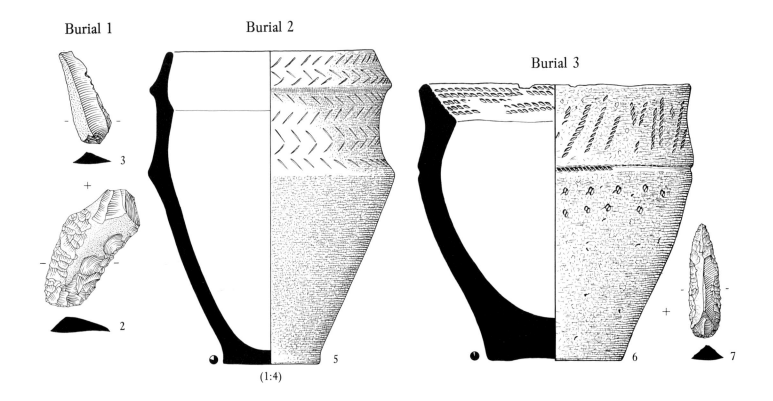

Burial 1

Burial 2

Burial 3

3

2

5

(1:4)

6

7

13 SHERBURN

Burial 1

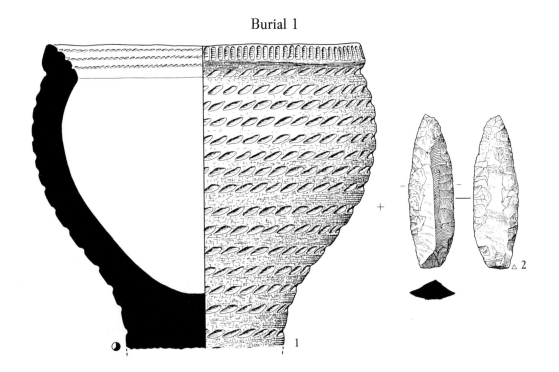

1

2

Burial 2

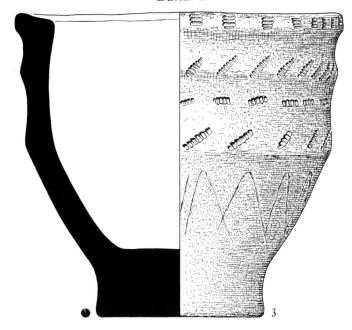

3

Mound

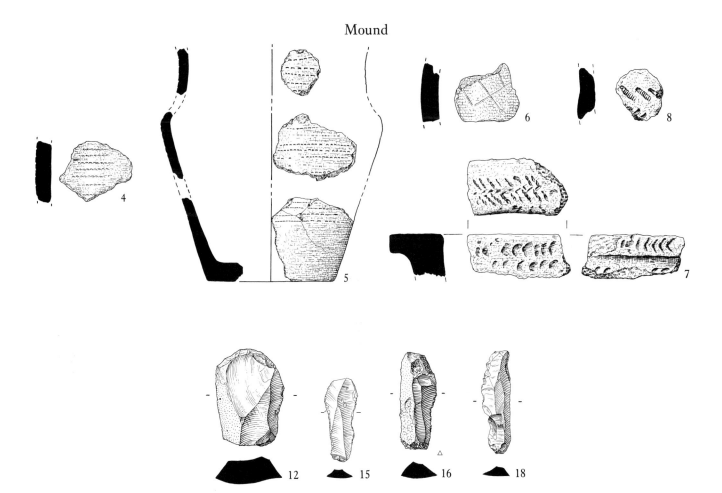

4

5

6

8

7

12   15   16   18

14 SHERBURN

16 GANTON

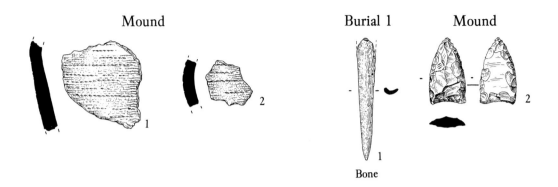

Mound

Burial 1

Mound

1

2

1

Bone

2

17 GANTON

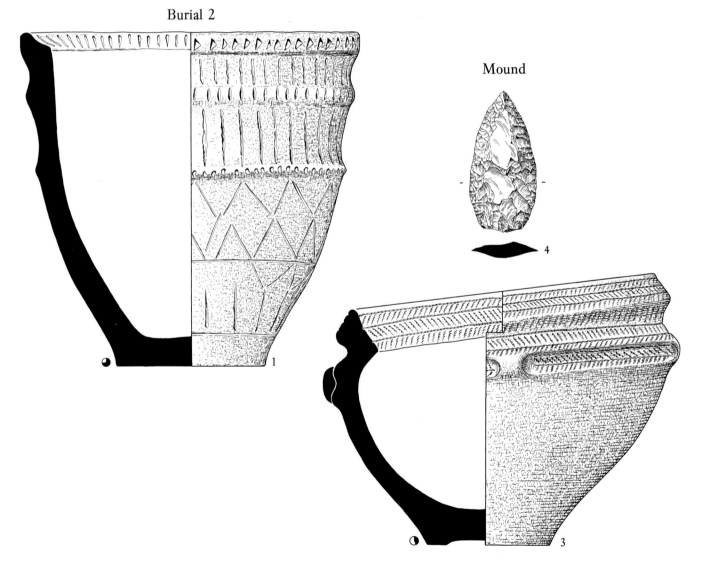

Burial 2

Mound

1

4

3

18 GANTON

Burial 1

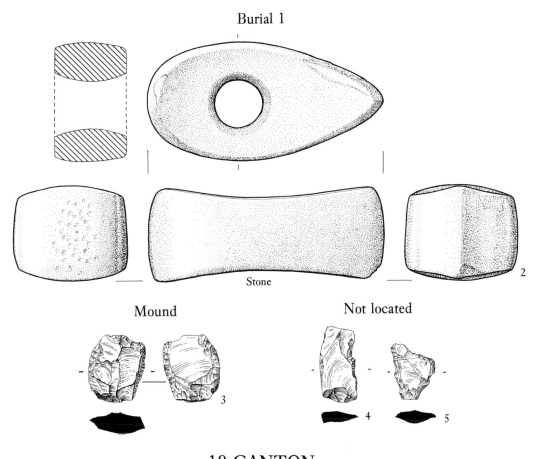

Stone

Mound

Not located

3

4   5

19 GANTON

Burial 1

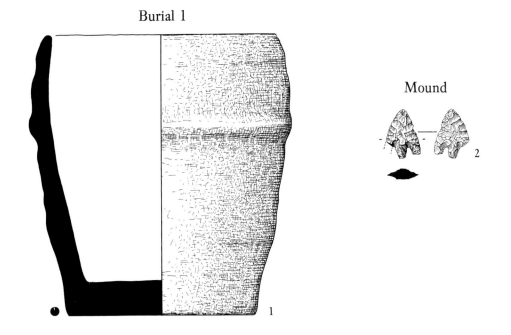

Mound

1

2

21 GANTON

Burial 1

Burial 4

Burial 5

Burial 7

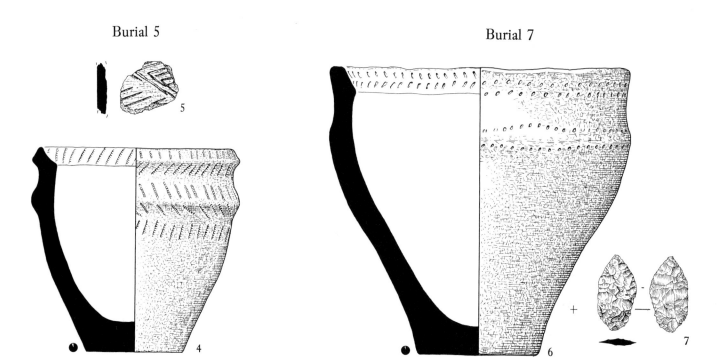

Burial 8

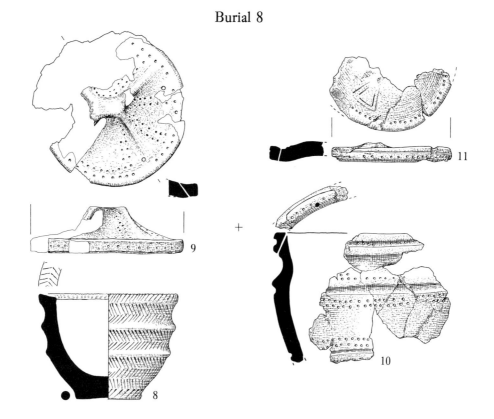

Burial 10

Mound

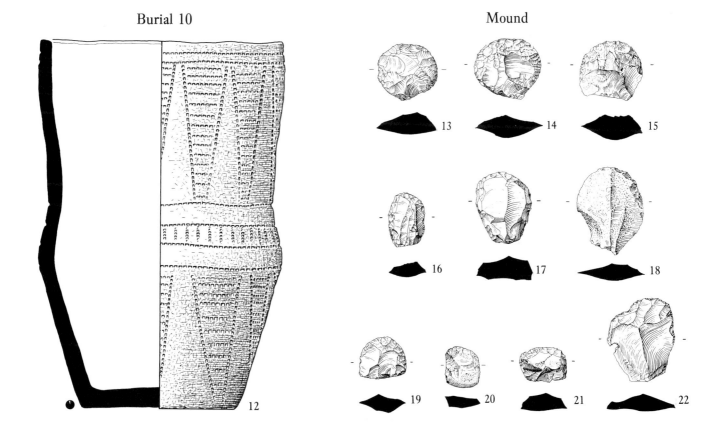

Mound

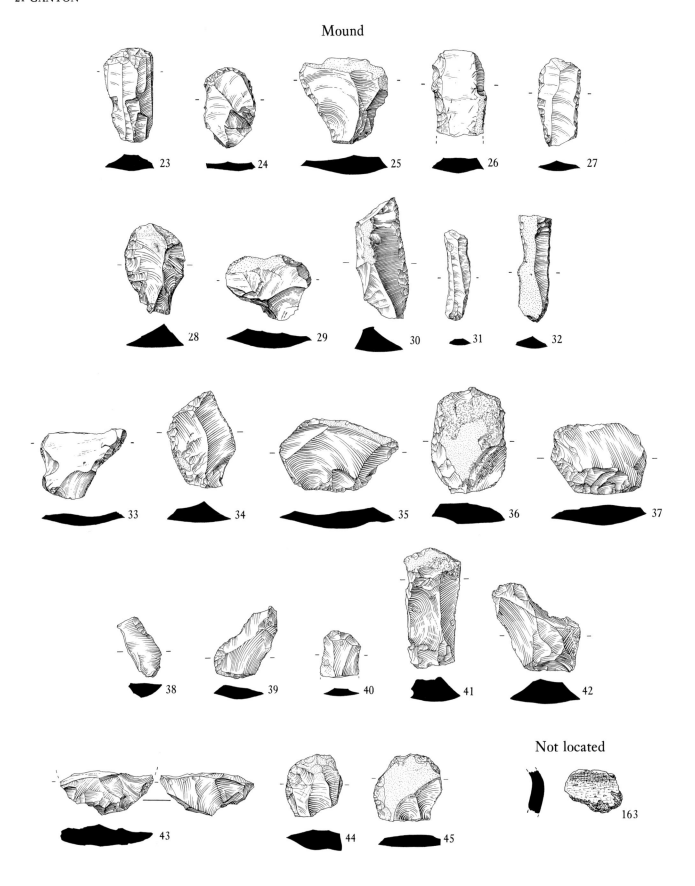

Not located

22 GANTON

Burial 4

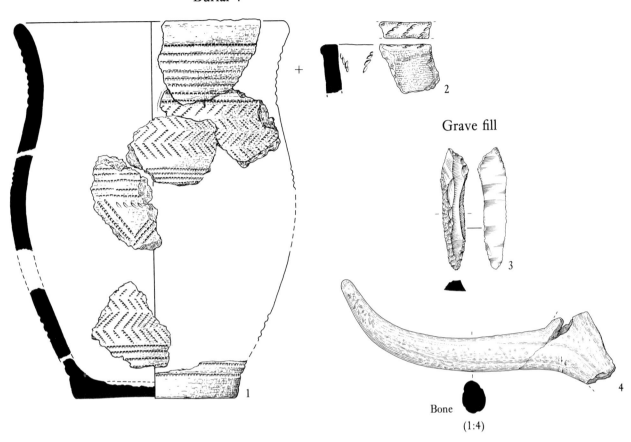

Grave fill

+

Bone

(1:4)

23 GANTON

Burial 2

Feature A or Mound

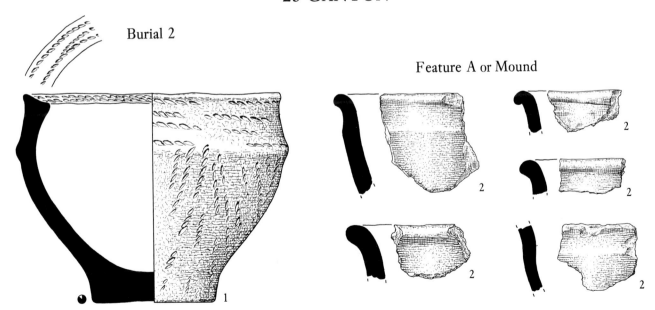

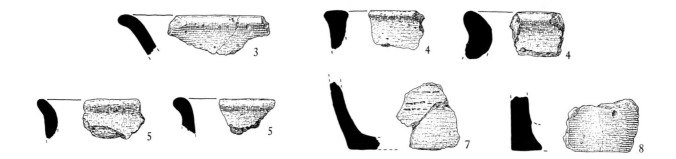

24 GANTON

Burial 1

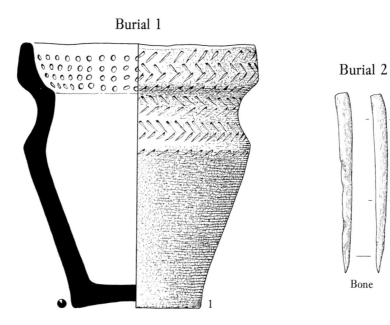

Burial 2

2

Bone

25 GANTON

Burial 2

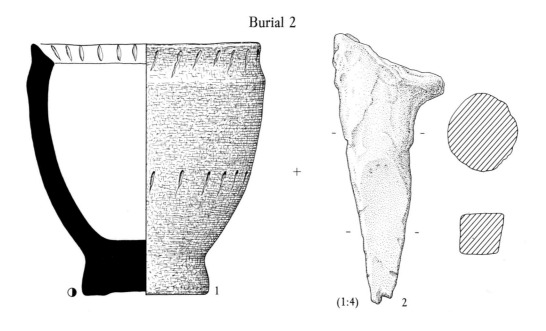

(1:4)

Mound

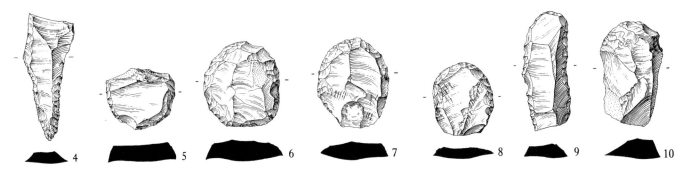

4 5 6 7 8 9 10

26 GANTON

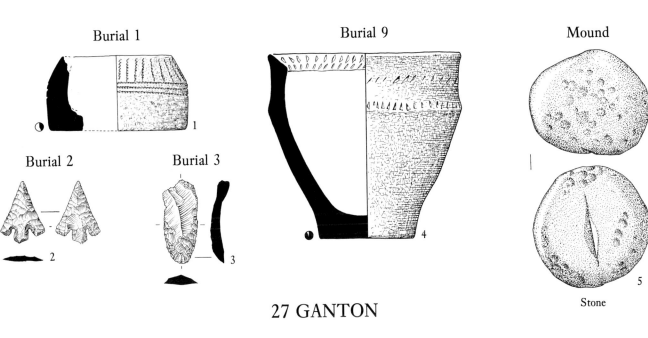

Burial 1

1

Burial 9

4

Mound

5

Stone

Burial 2

2

Burial 3

3

27 GANTON

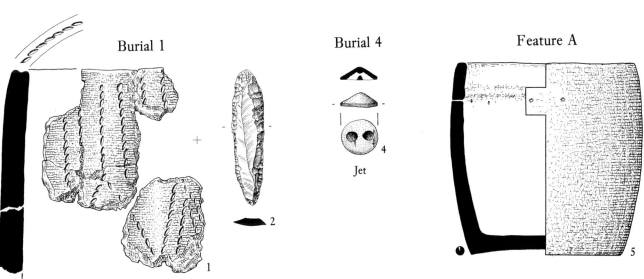

Burial 1

1 2

Burial 4

4

Jet

Feature A

5

28 GANTON

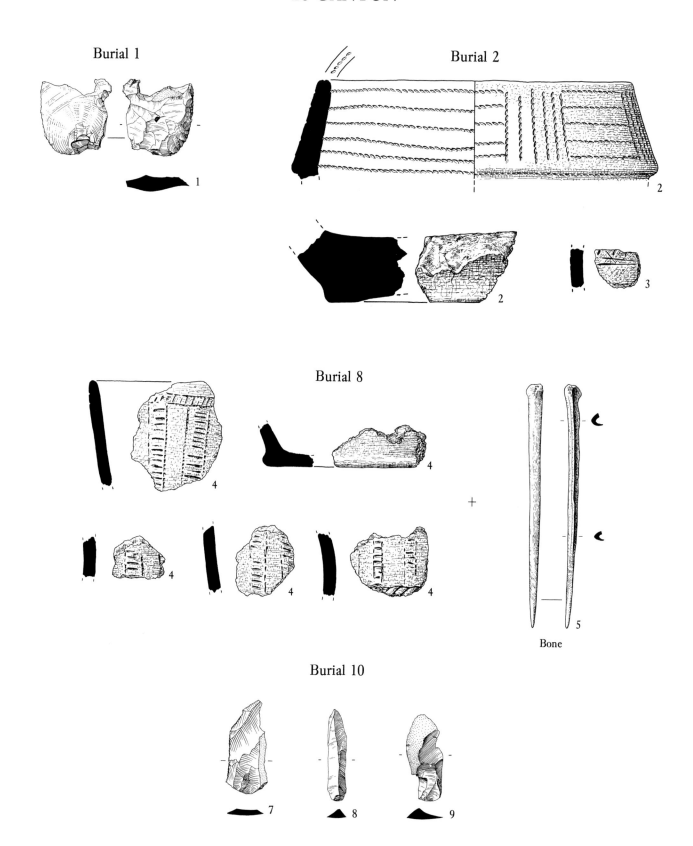

Burial 1

Burial 2

Burial 8

Bone

Burial 10

29 GANTON

30 GANTON

Burial 1

Not located

Burial 1

Mound

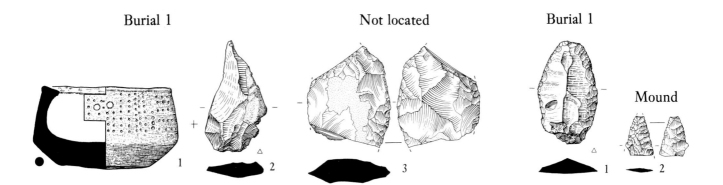

31 BINNINGTON

? Burial 2

Mound

? Burial 3

Stone

Not located

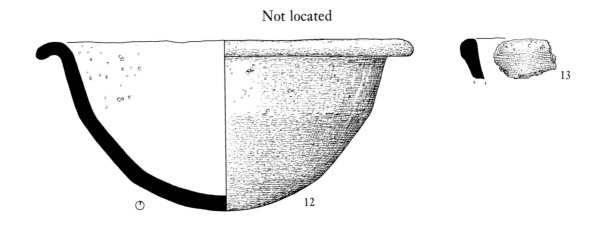

32 WILLERBY

Mound

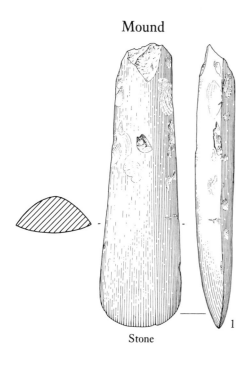

Stone

33 WILLERBY

Grave fill

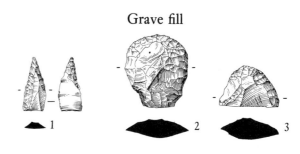

34 WILLERBY

Burial 1

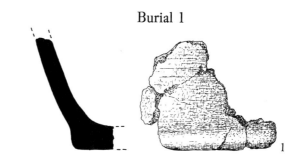

35 WILLERBY

Burial 1

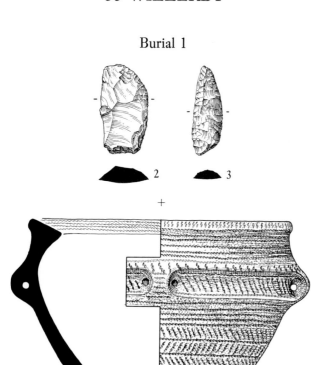

38 WILLERBY

Burial 2

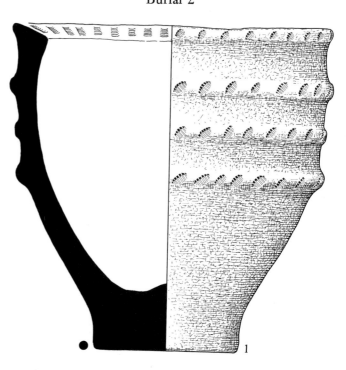

39 BUTTERWICK

Burial 1

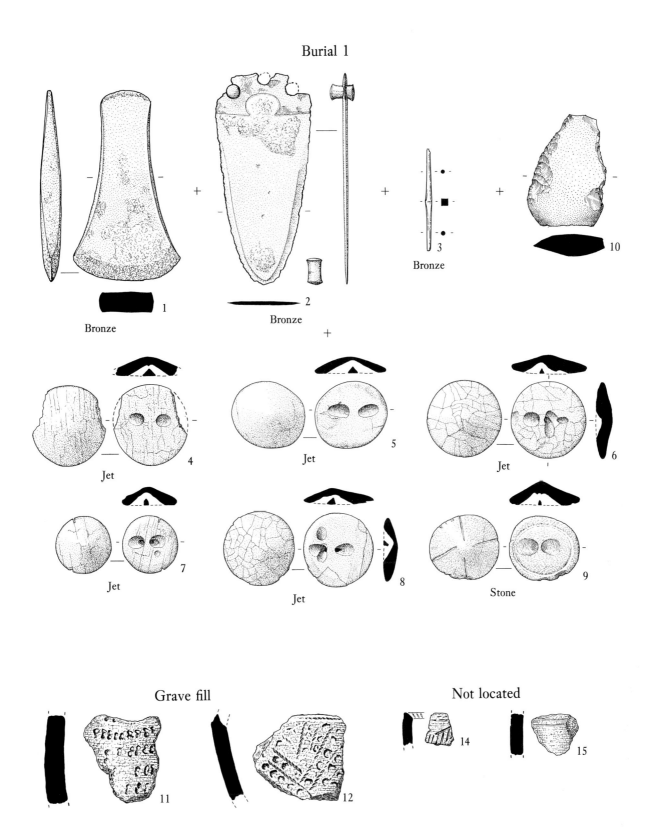

1 Bronze

2 Bronze

3 Bronze

4 Jet

5 Jet

6 Jet

7 Jet

8 Jet

9 Stone

10

Grave fill

11

12

Not located

14

15

40 HELPERTHORPE

Mound

1

2

41 HELPERTHORPE

Burial 1

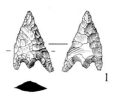

1

2

Burial 2

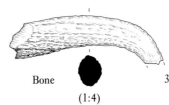

Bone (1:4) 3

Bone (1:4) 4

42 WEAVERTHORPE

Burial 2

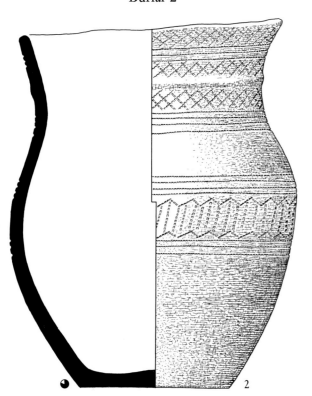

2

Feature A or Mound

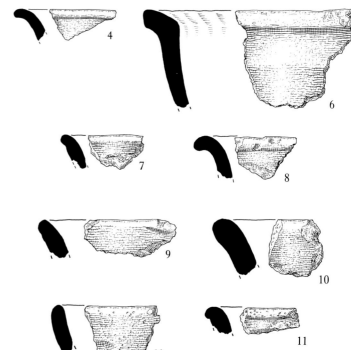

4

6

7

8

9

10

11

11

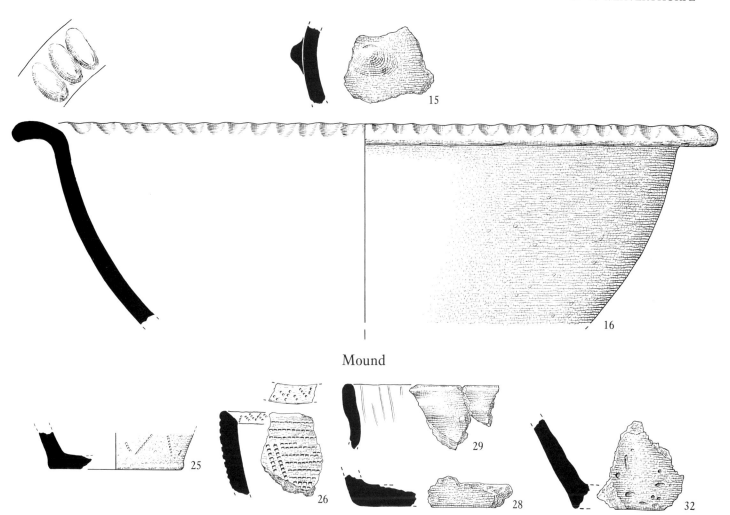

Mound

43 WEAVERTHORPE

Burial 1

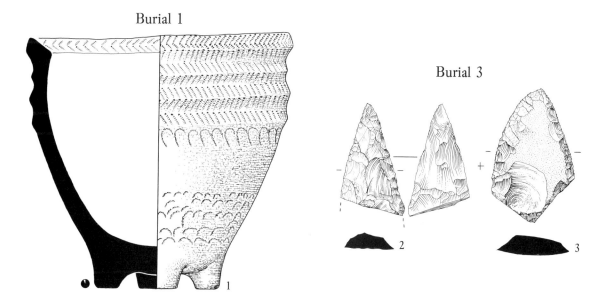

Burial 3

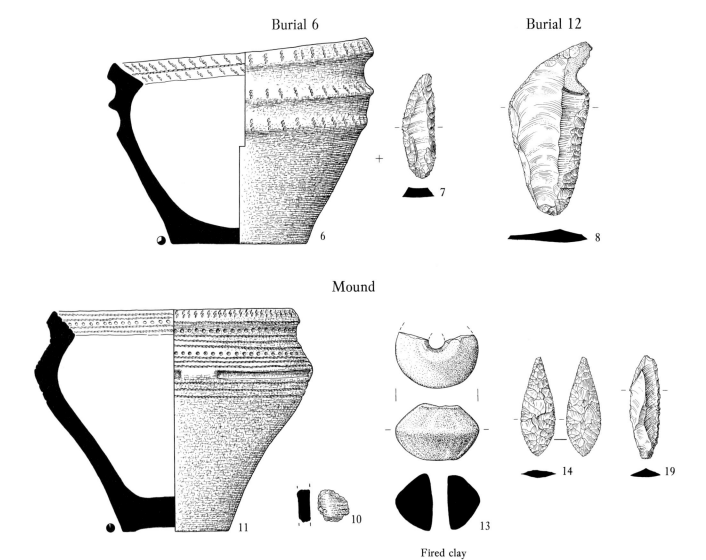

Burial 6

Burial 12

Mound

Fired clay

44 WEAVERTHORPE

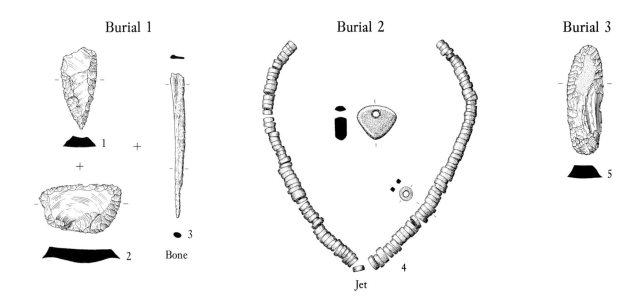

Burial 1

Burial 2

Burial 3

Bone

Jet

45 WEAVERTHORPE

Burial 3

Burial 2

1

2

Mound

Bone (1:4)

4

46 WEAVERTHORPE

Burial 5

Burial 7

Mound

1

Stone

2

3

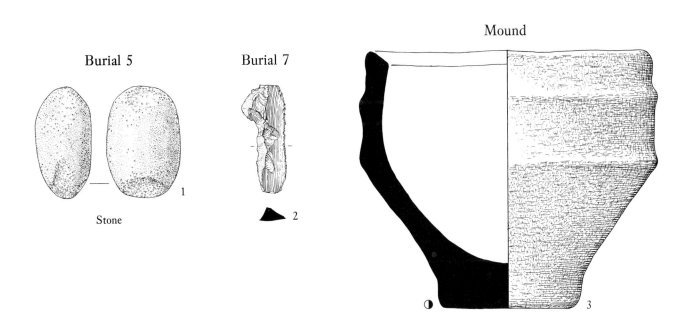

47 WEAVERTHORPE

Feature A

Burial 4

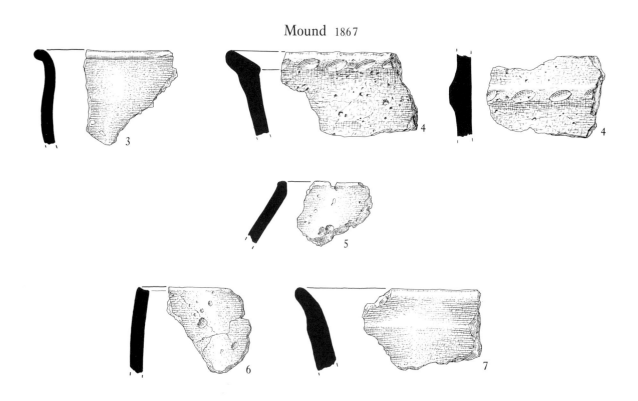

Mound 1867

1

2

3

4

4

5

6

7

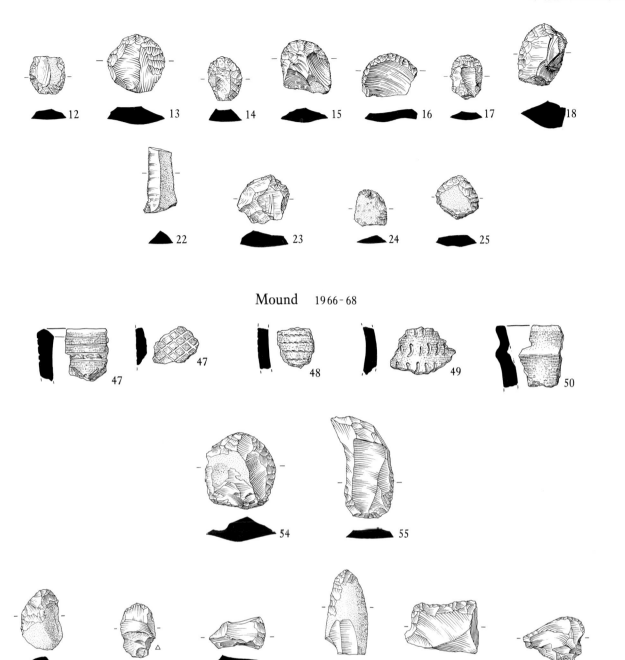

12   13   14   15   16   17   18

22   23   24   25

Mound   1966-68

47   47   48   49   50

54   55

56   57   58   59   60   61

Old surface   1966-68

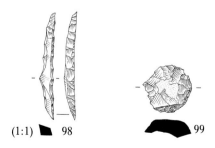

(1:1)   98   99

Ditch-fill 1867

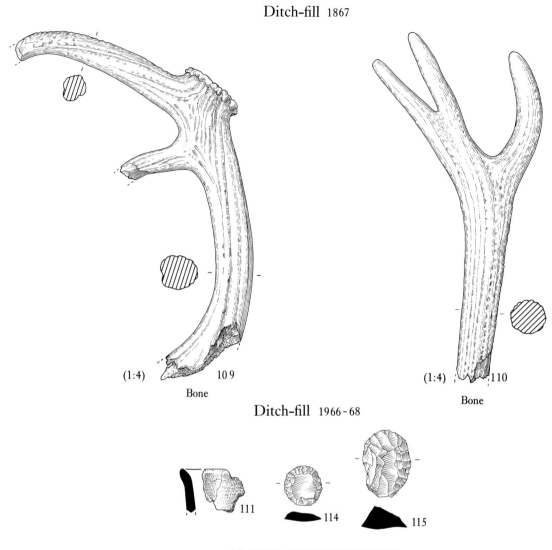

(1:4)   10 9

Bone

(1:4)   110

Bone

Ditch-fill 1966-68

111

114

115

49 HELPERTHORPE

Burial 6

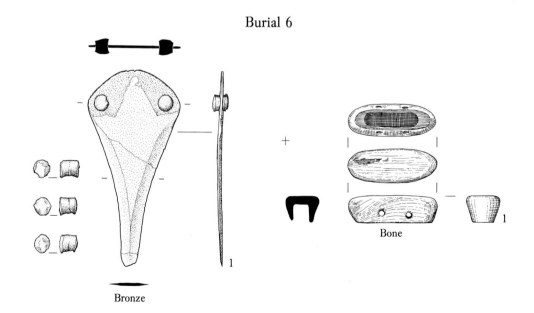

Bronze

Bone

1

1

Feature A

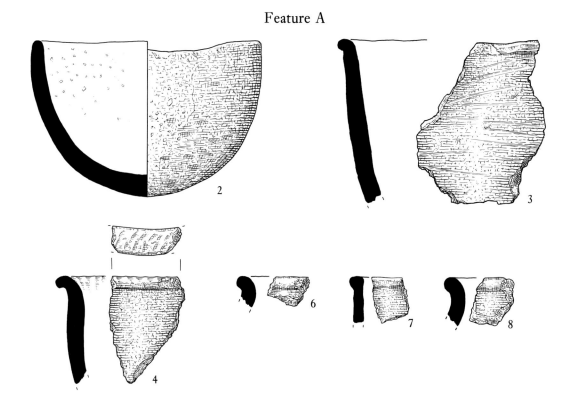

50 COWLAM

Burial 1

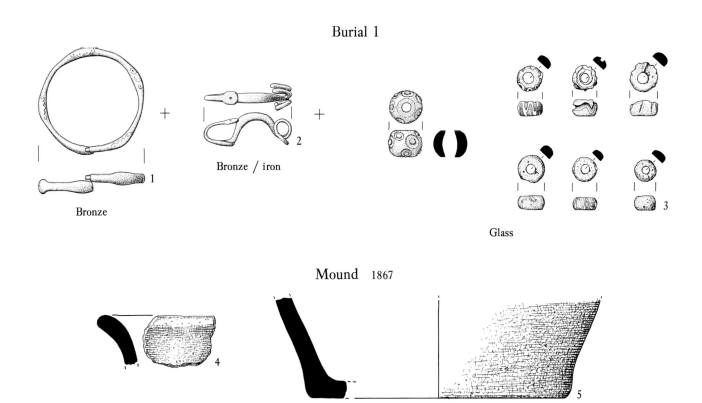

Bronze

Bronze / iron

Glass

Mound   1867

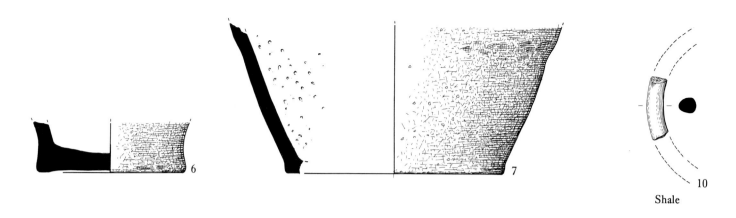

6   7   10

Shale

Mound 1969

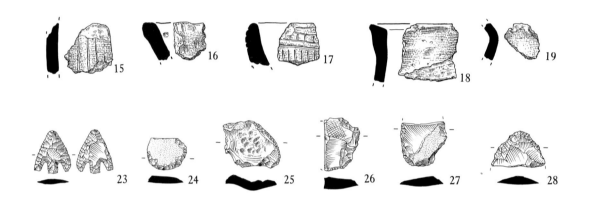

15   16   17   18   19

23   24   25   26   27   28

Ditch-fill 1969

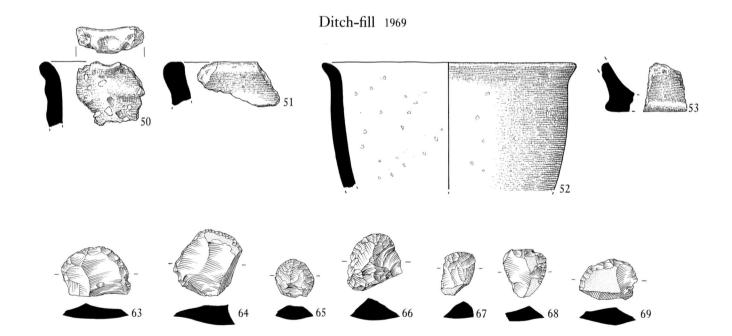

50   51   52   53

63   64   65   66   67   68   69

51 COWLAM

Burial 1

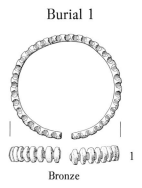

1

Bronze

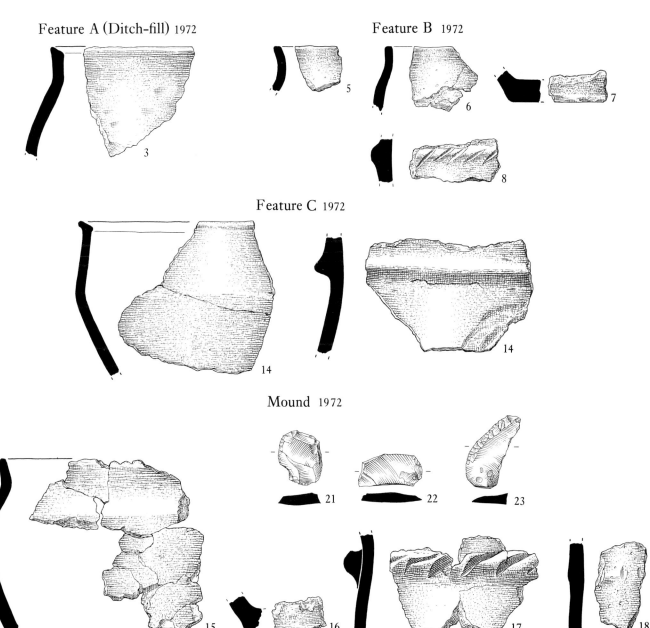

Feature A (Ditch-fill) 1972

3

Feature B 1972

5

6

7

8

Feature C 1972

14

14

Mound 1972

21

22

23

15

16

17

18

Ditch-fill 1972

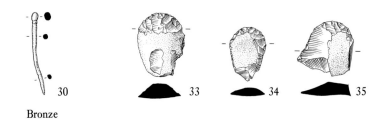

30

Bronze

33   34   35

Not located

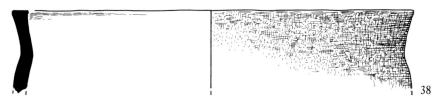

38

52 COWLAM

Feature A

1   2   3   4

5   5   6

Mound

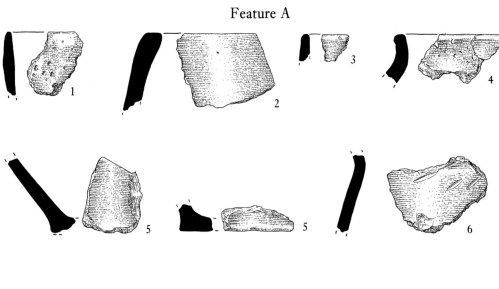

12   19   20

Ditch-fill 1969

Not located

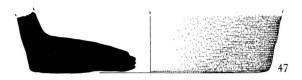

52 or 53 COWLAM

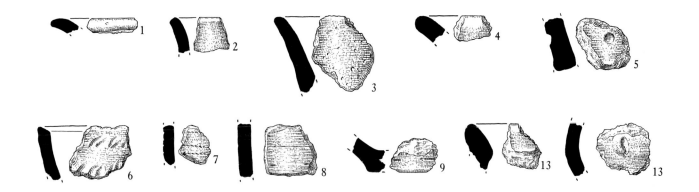

53 COWLAM

Mound 1867

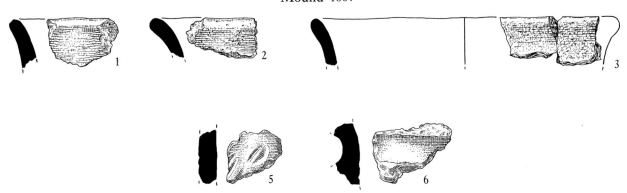

Mound 1972

Ditch-fill 1972

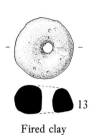

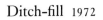

16   16   16   16

13

Fired clay

17

18

54 COWLAM

Mound 1969

1   2   3

4

Jet

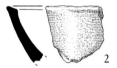

5   6

Ditch-fill 1969

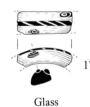

14

17

Glass

18   19   20   21   22   23   24

55 COWLAM

Grave fill 1968

Mound 1968

Stone

56 COWLAM

Burial 1

Burial 4

Burial 5

Mound 1968

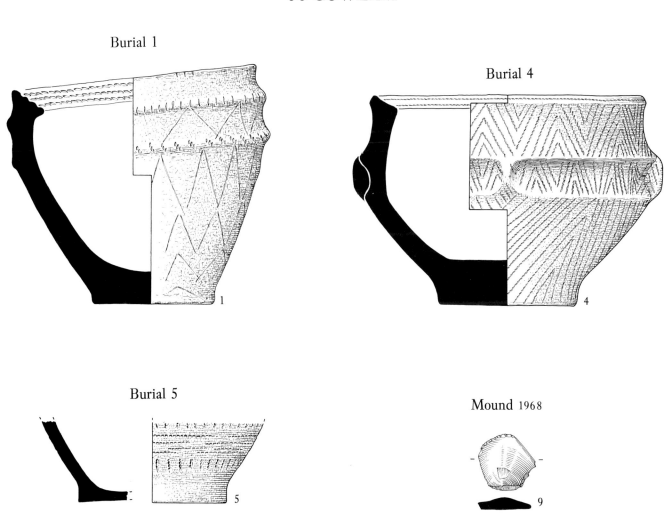

57 COWLAM

Burial 1

Burial 4

Burial 6

Burial 7

Mound

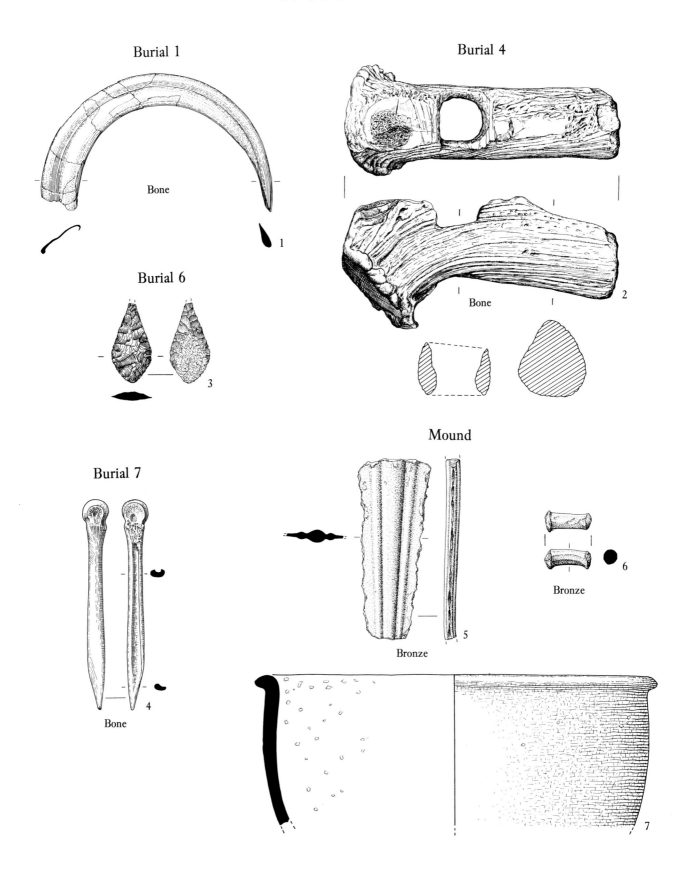

Bone

Bone

Bone

Bone

Bronze

Bronze

1

2

3

4

5

6

7

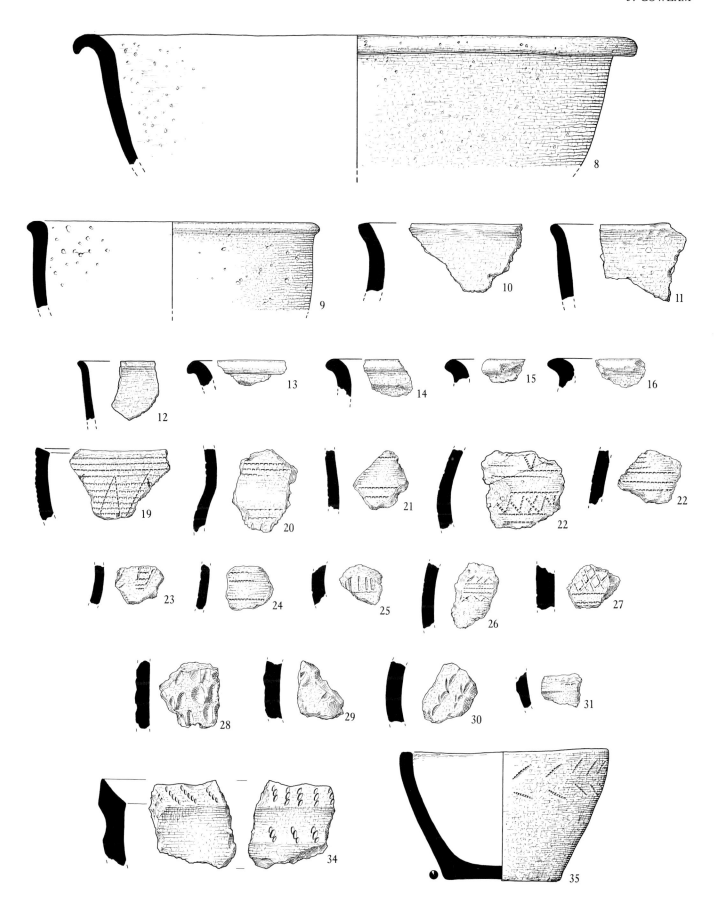

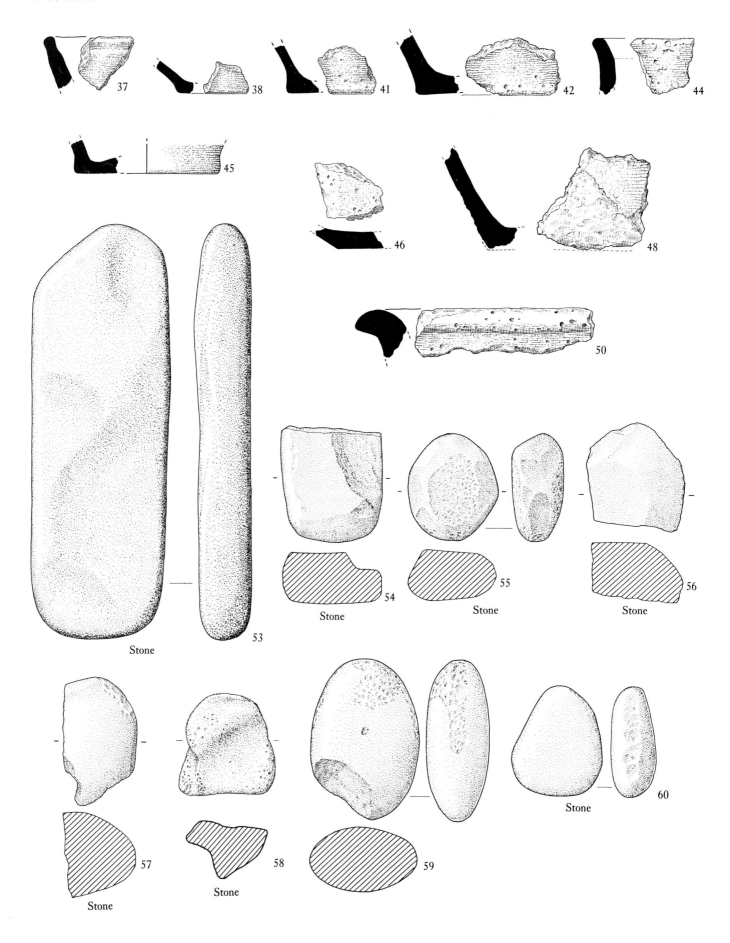

37

38

41

42

44

45

46

48

50

53

Stone

54

Stone

55

Stone

56

Stone

57

Stone

58

Stone

59

60

Stone

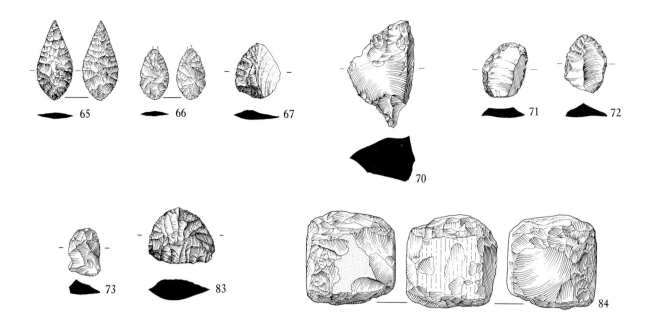

65   66   67   70   71   72

73   83   84

58 COWLAM

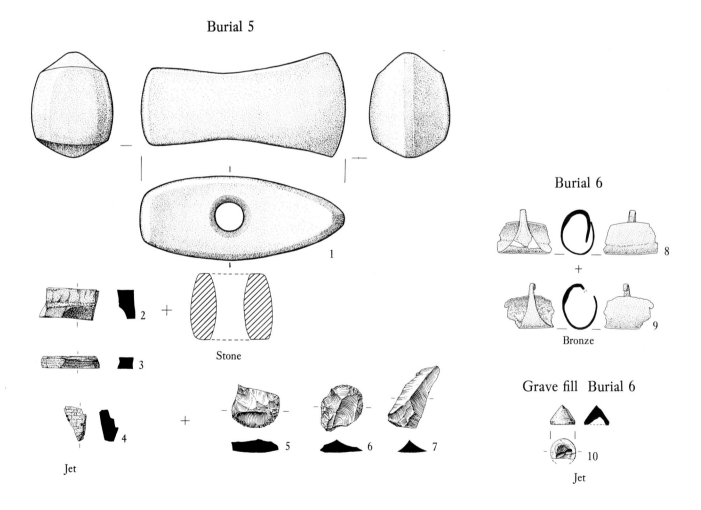

Burial 5

1

2

3

Jet

4

Stone

5   6   7

Burial 6

8

9

Bronze

Grave fill   Burial 6

10

Jet

Mound

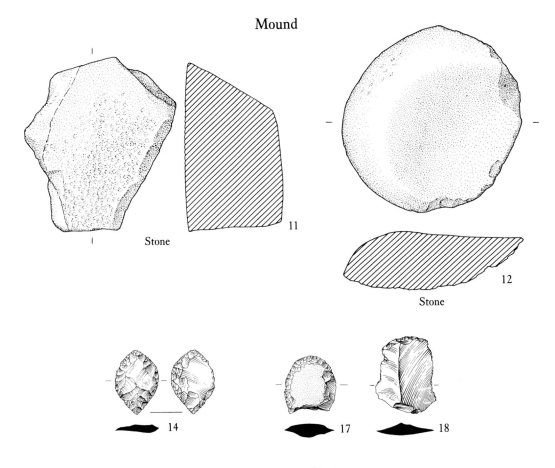

Stone

11

12

Stone

14

17

18

59 COWLAM

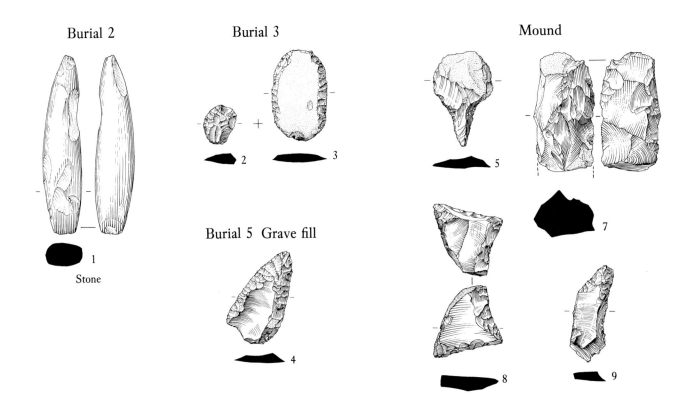

Burial 2

1

Stone

Burial 3

2

3

Burial 5 Grave fill

4

Mound

5

7

8

9

60 THWING

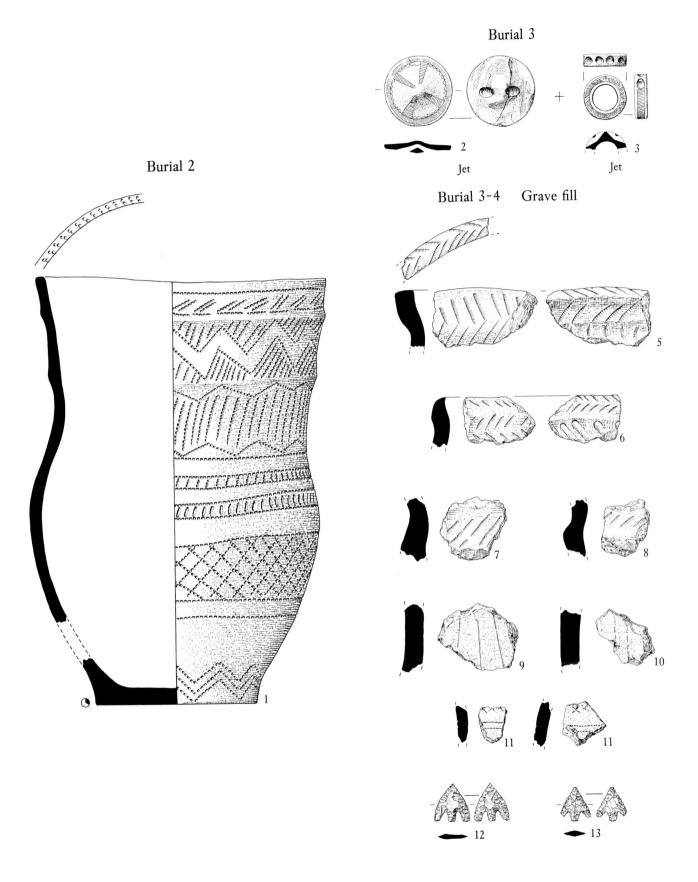

Burial 3

Burial 2

2 Jet

3 Jet

Burial 3-4   Grave fill

5

6

7

8

9

10

11

11

12

13

1

61 RUDSTON

Burial 2

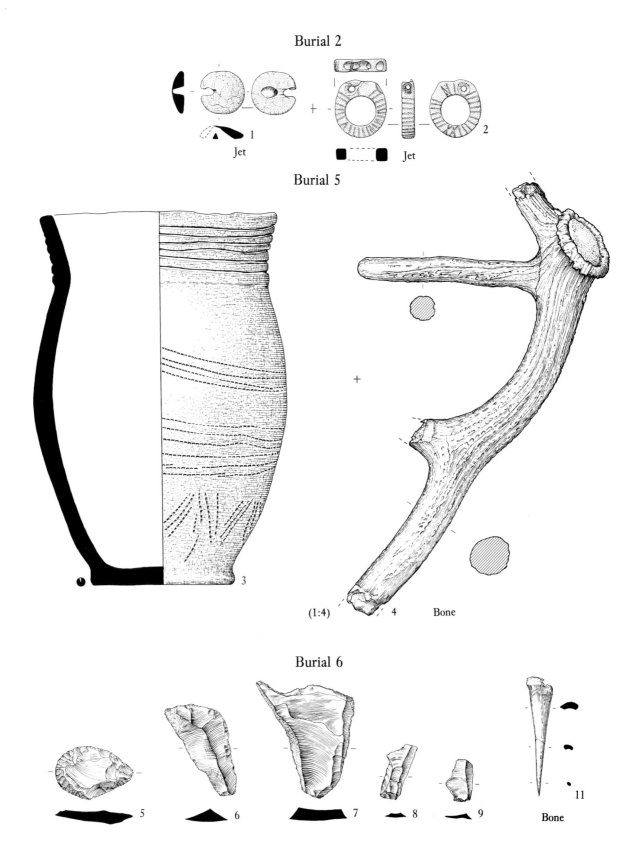

1 Jet

2 Jet

Burial 5

3

(1:4) 4 Bone

Burial 6

5

6

7

8

9

11

Bone

Burial 7

Feature A

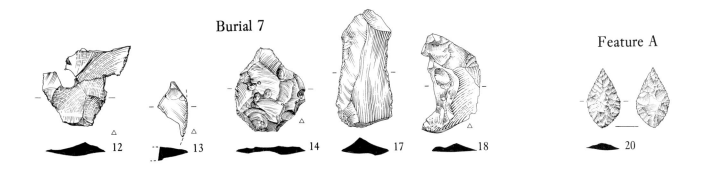

12   13   14   17   18   20

Feature A or B or Mound

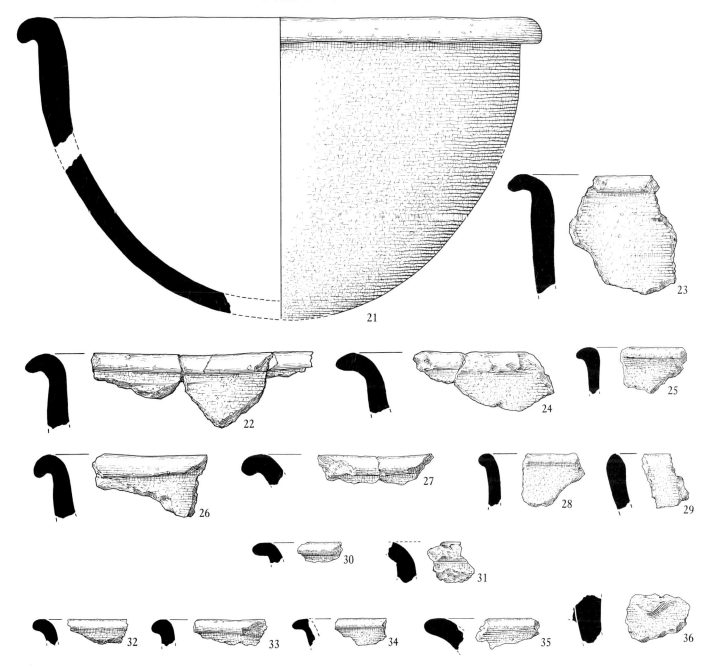

21   23   22   24   25   26   27   28   29   30   31   32   33   34   35   36

Mound

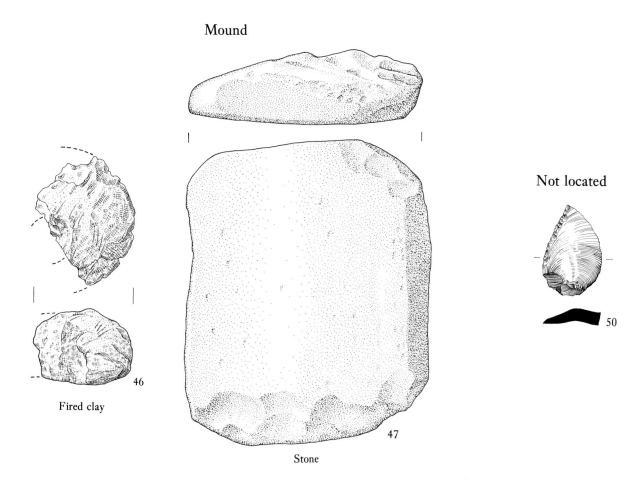

Not located

Fired clay

46

47

Stone

50

62 RUDSTON

Burial 1

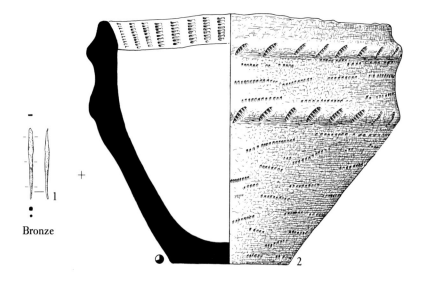

Bronze

1

2

Burial 4

Burial 6

Bronze

Burial 8

Stone

Stone

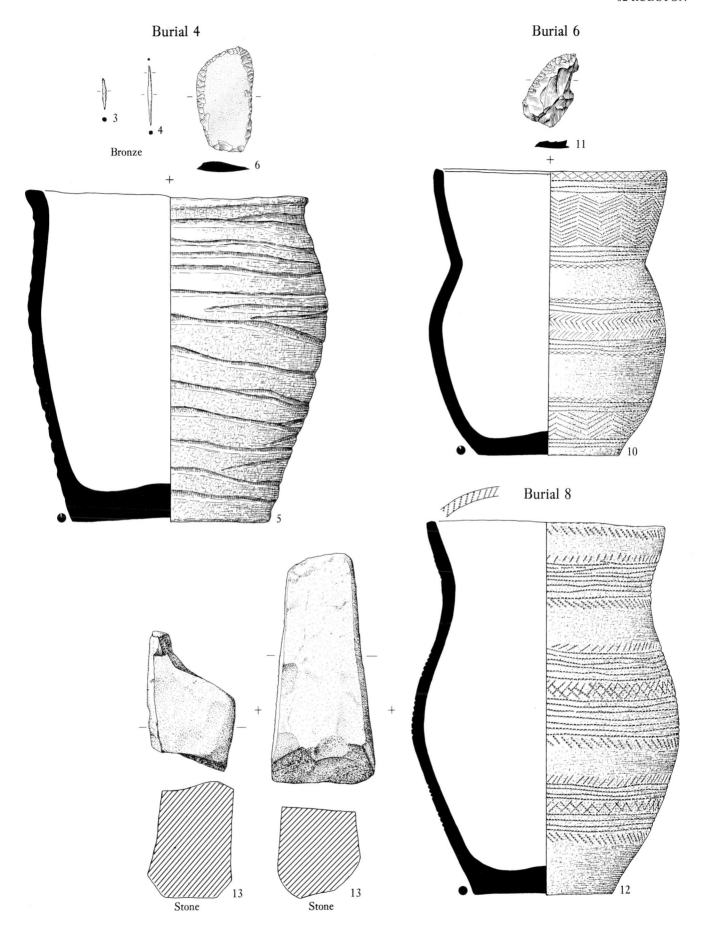

Burial 9

Burial 10

Grave fill

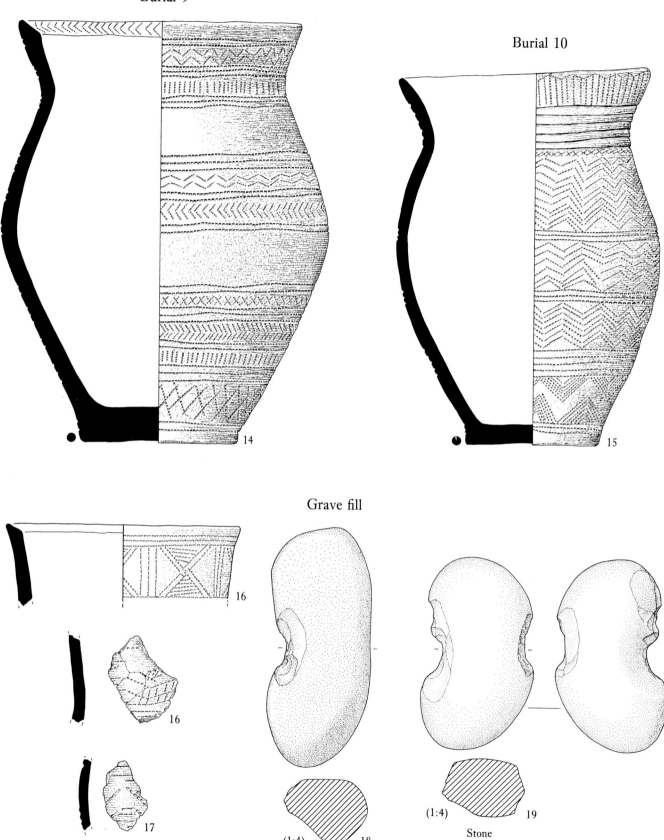

14

15

16

16

17

18

(1:4)

Stone

19

(1:4)

Stone

Mound 1869

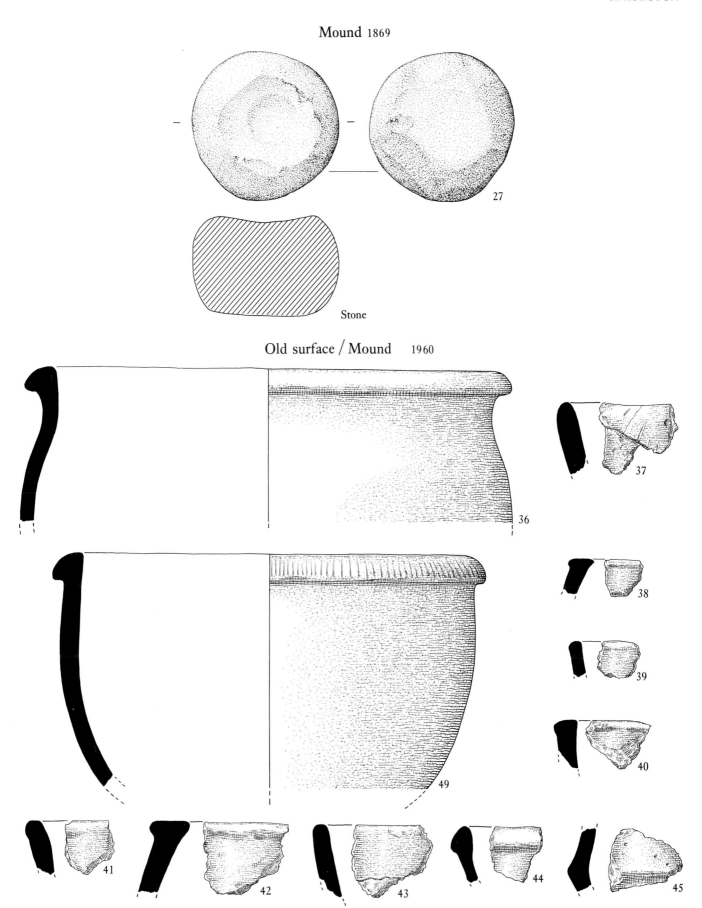

27

Stone

Old surface / Mound 1960

36

37

49

38

39

40

41

42

43

44

45

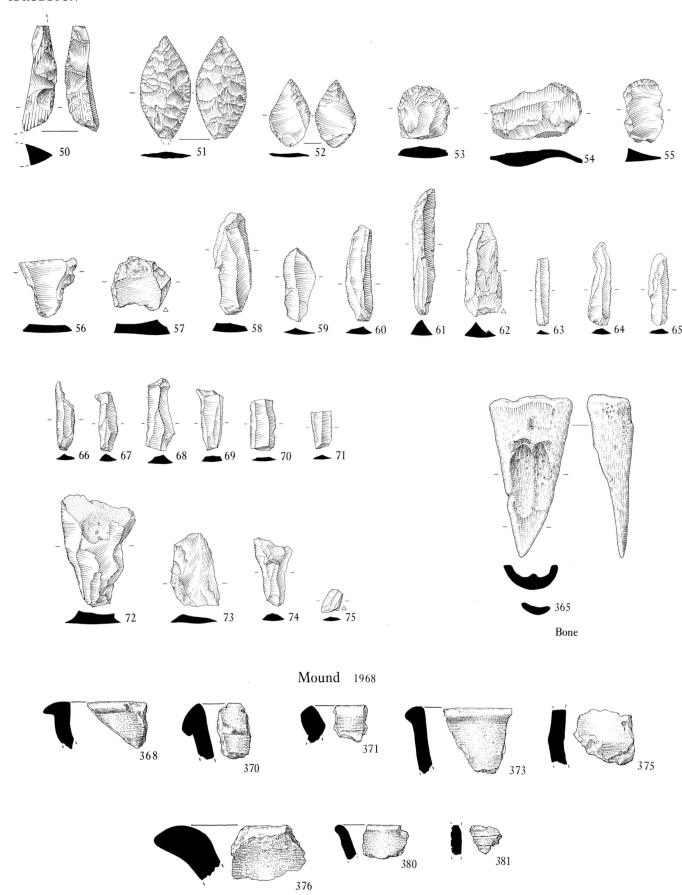

50   51   52   53   54   55

56   57   58   59   60   61   62   63   64   65

66   67   68   69   70   71

72   73   74   75

365

Bone

Mound   1968

368   370   371   373   375

376   380   381

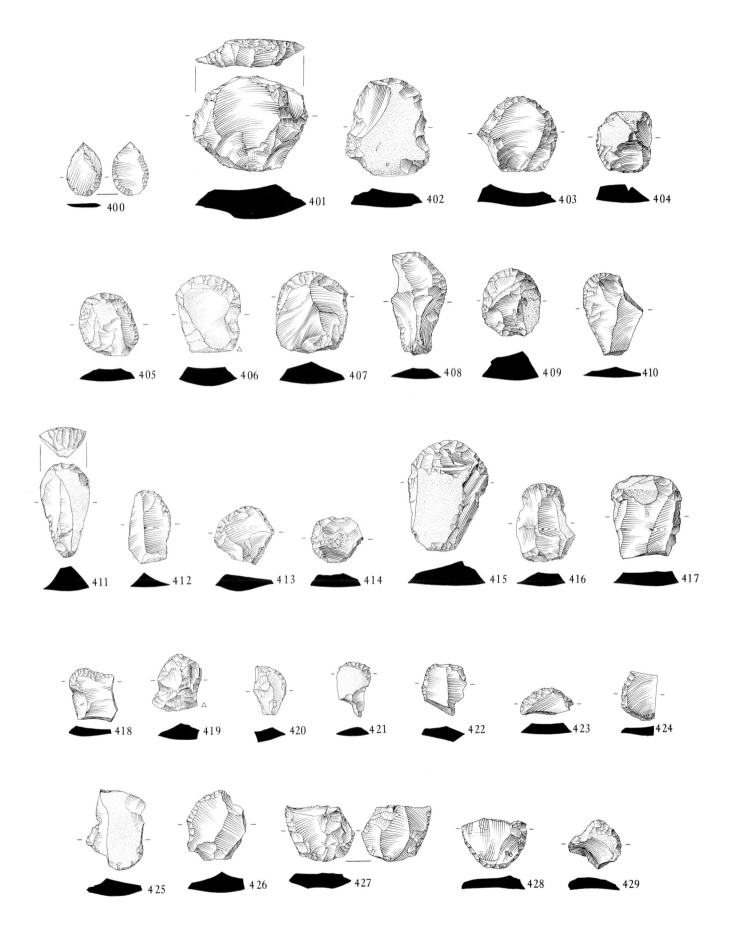

400 401 402 403 404

405 406 407 408 409 410

411 412 413 414 415 416 417

418 419 420 421 422 423 424

425 426 427 428 429

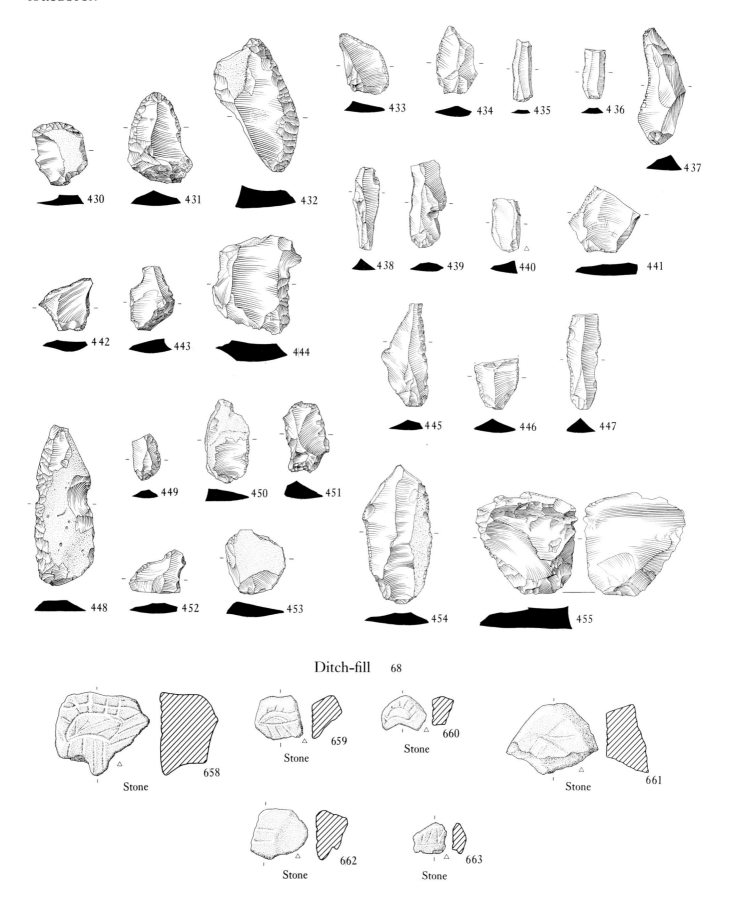

Ditch-fill 68

63 RUDSTON

Burial 2

1

Burial 3

2

Bone

Burial 10

4

Fossil

5

3

Burial 13

7

Mound

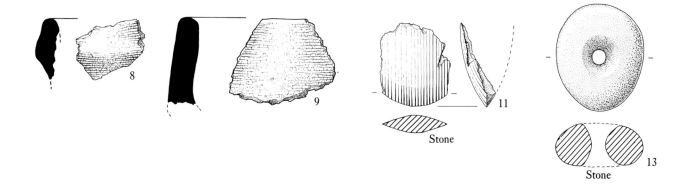

8

9

11

Stone

13

Stone

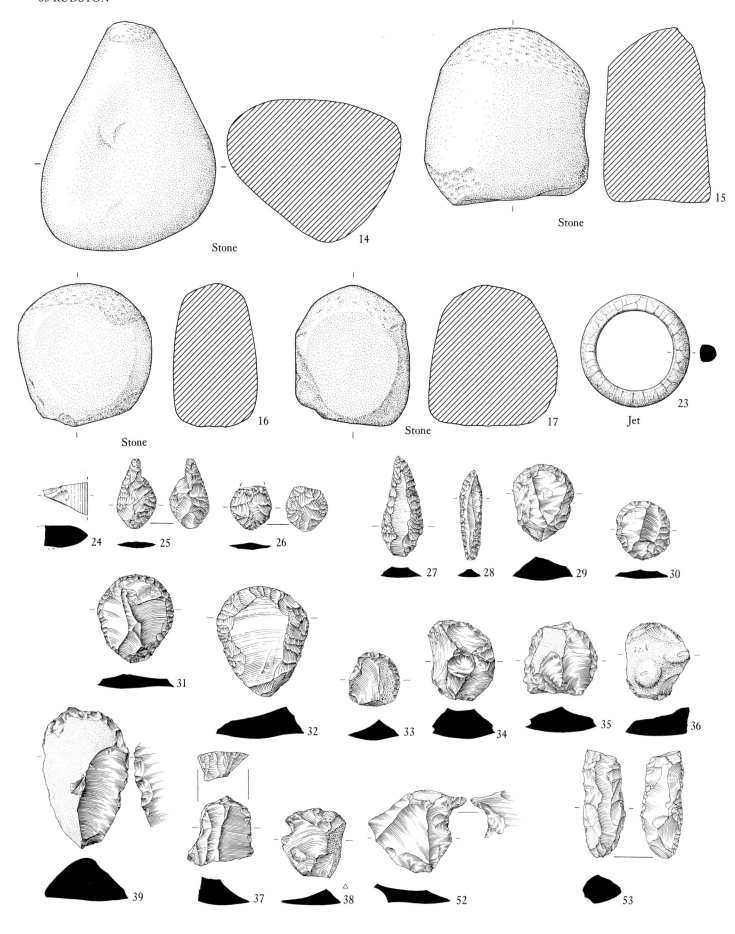

Stone

14

Stone

15

Stone

16

Stone

17

Jet

23

24 25 26 27 28 29 30

31 32 33 34 35 36

39 37 38 52 53

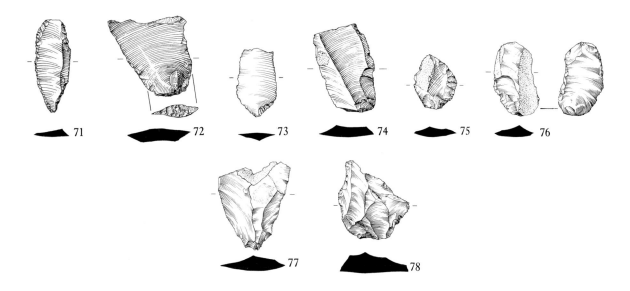

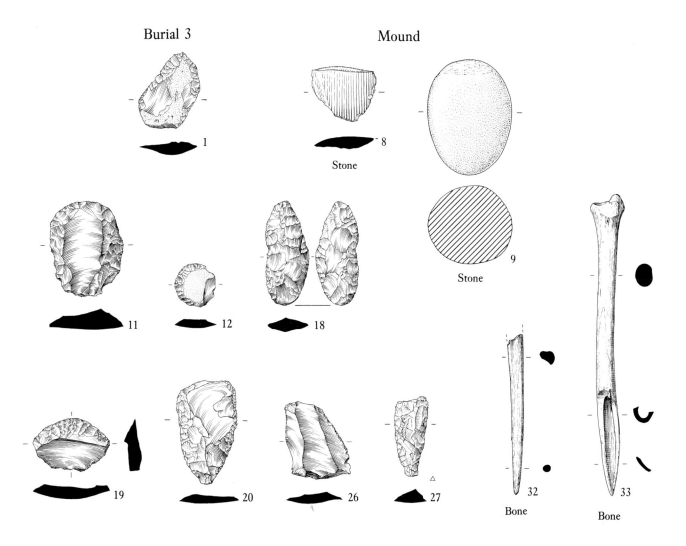

64 RUDSTON

Burial 3

Mound

Stone

Stone

Bone

Bone

65 RUDSTON

Mound

Burial 1

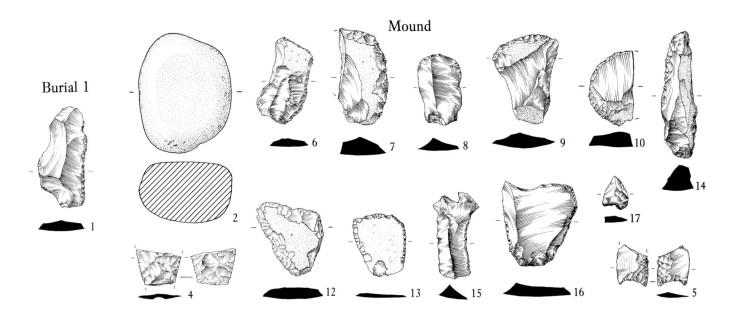

66 RUDSTON

Burial 1

Burial 2

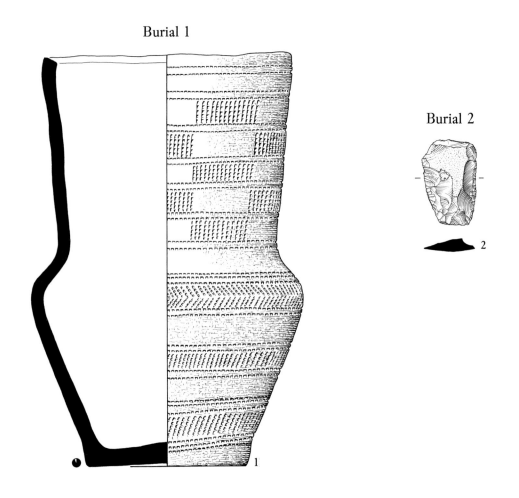

Burial 3

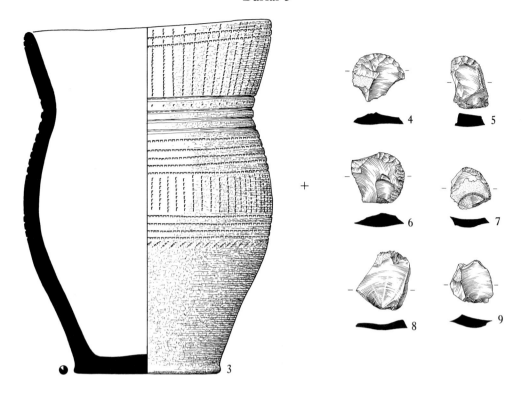

3

4

5

6

7

8

9

Mound (terminal)

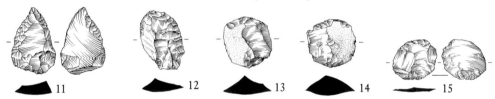

11

12

13

14

15

Mound (east)

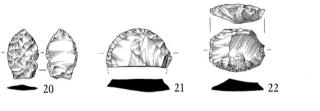

20

21

22

Ditch-fill

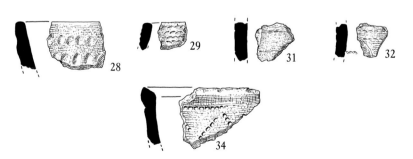

28

29

31

32

34

Mound (West)

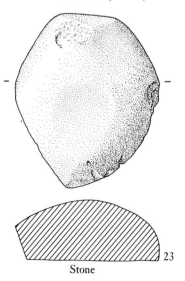

23

Stone

67 RUDSTON

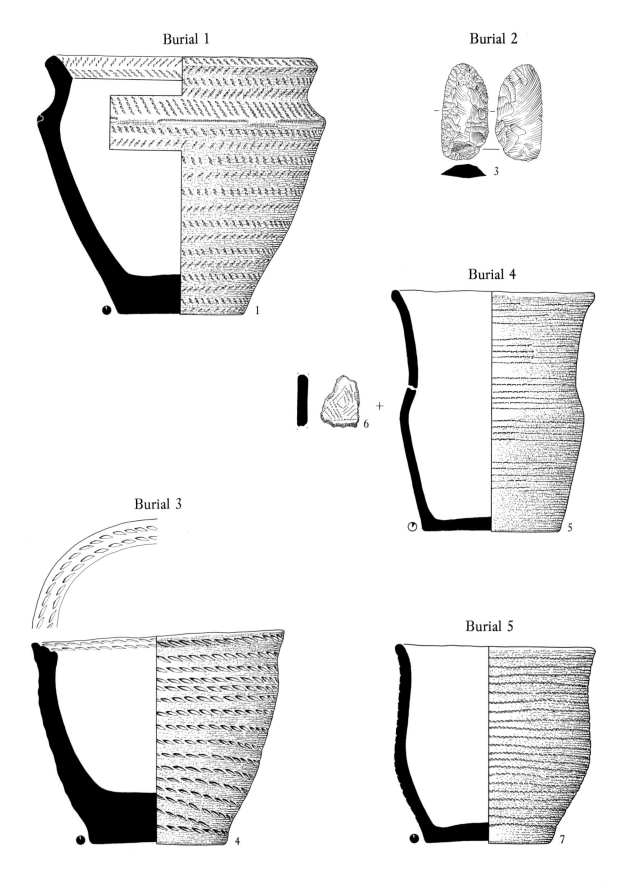

Burial 1

Burial 2

Burial 4

Burial 3

Burial 5

Burial 13

Burial 15

Burial 16

Mound

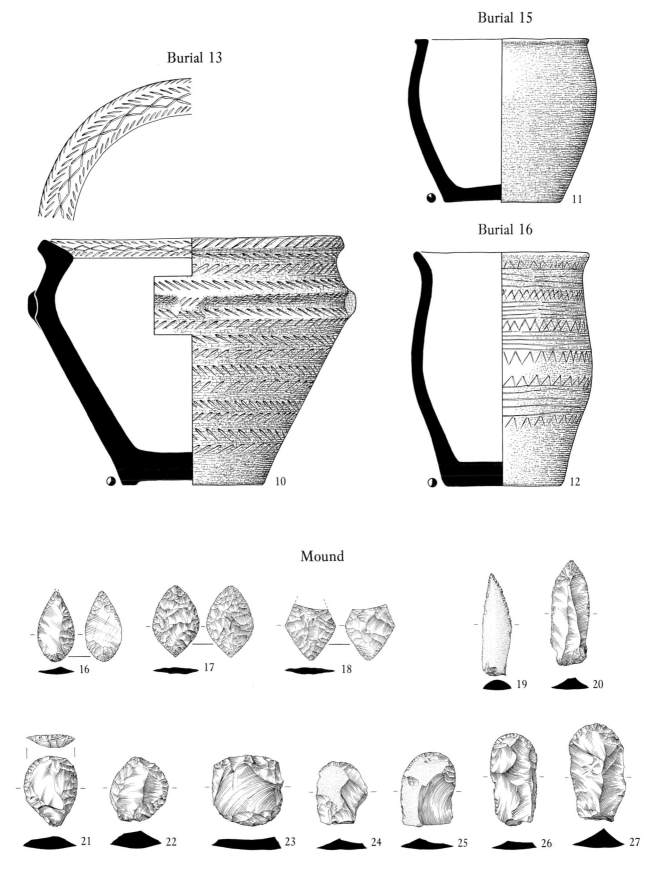

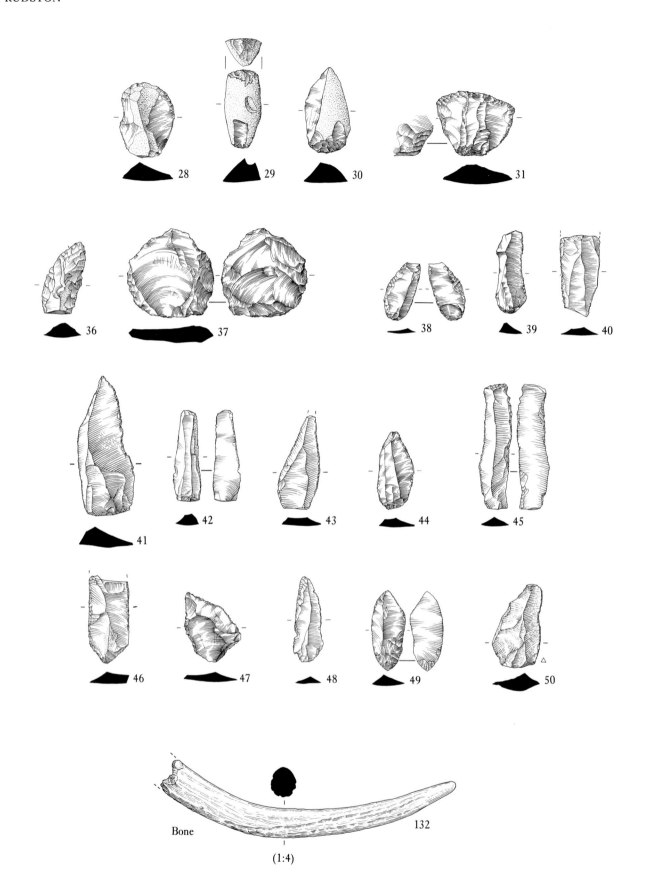

Bone   132

(1:4)

68 RUDSTON

Burial 6

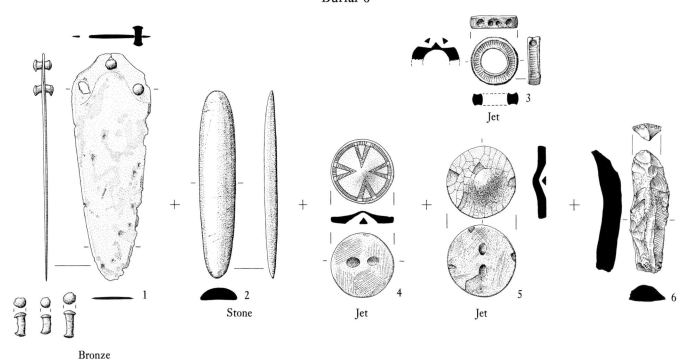

1 Bronze

2 Stone

3 Jet

4 Jet

5 Jet

6

Burial 7

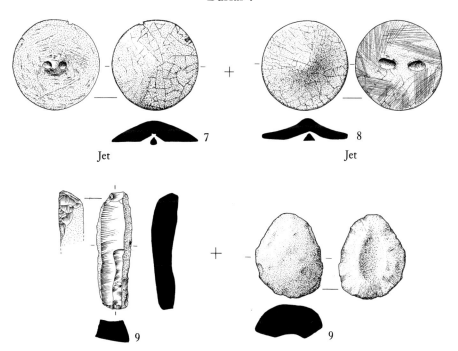

7 Jet

8 Jet

9

9

Burial 8

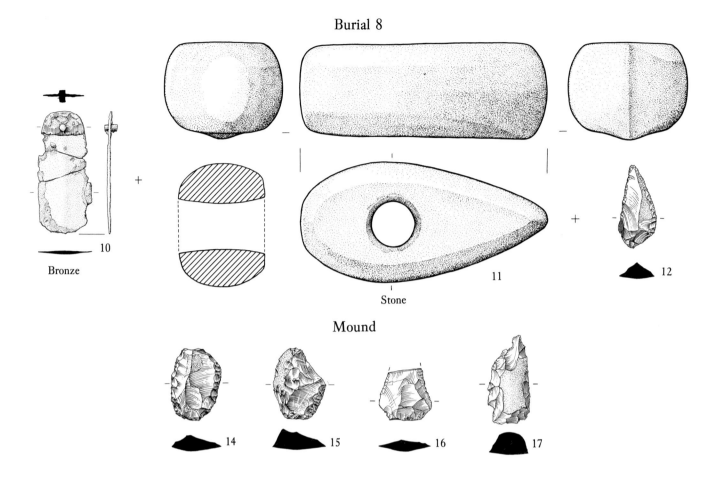

Bronze

10

Stone

11

12

Mound

14   15   16   17

69 RUDSTON

Burial 1

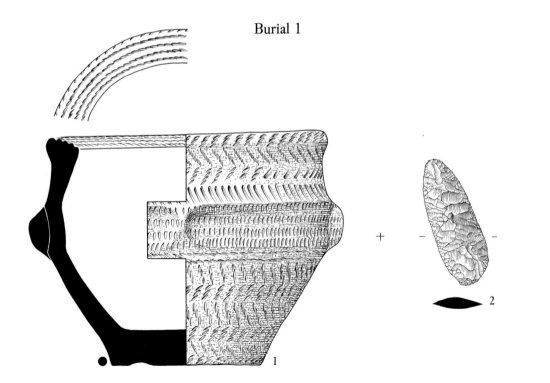

1

2

Mound

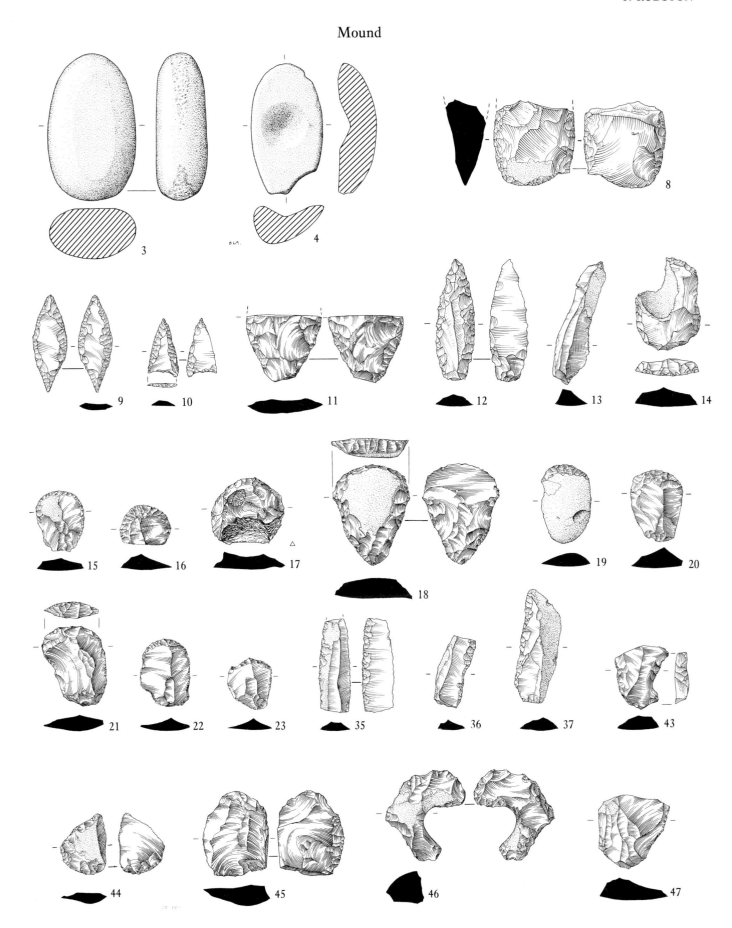

70 FOLKTON

Burial 1

Burial 2

Burial 8

Burial 3

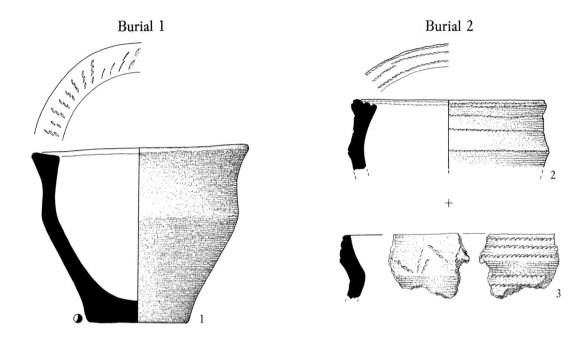

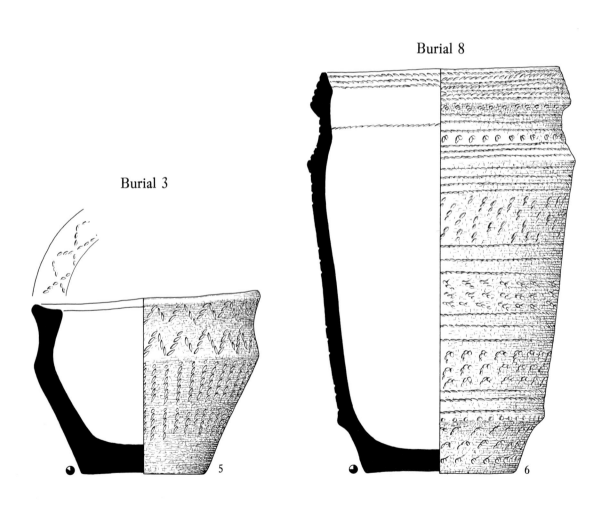

Burial 9

Burial 12

7

8

Burial 13

Bone

9

+

Bone

10

71 FOLKTON

Burial 6

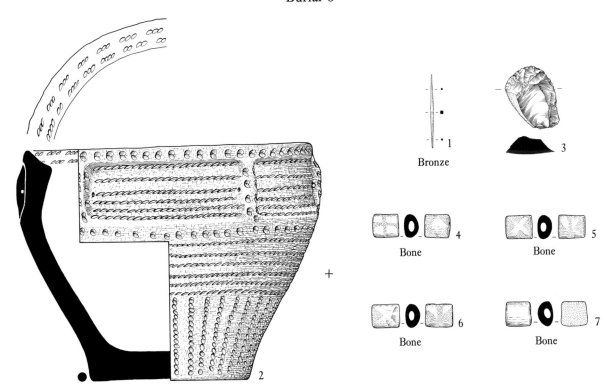

2

Bronze

1

3

Bone

4

Bone

5

Bone

6

Bone

7

+

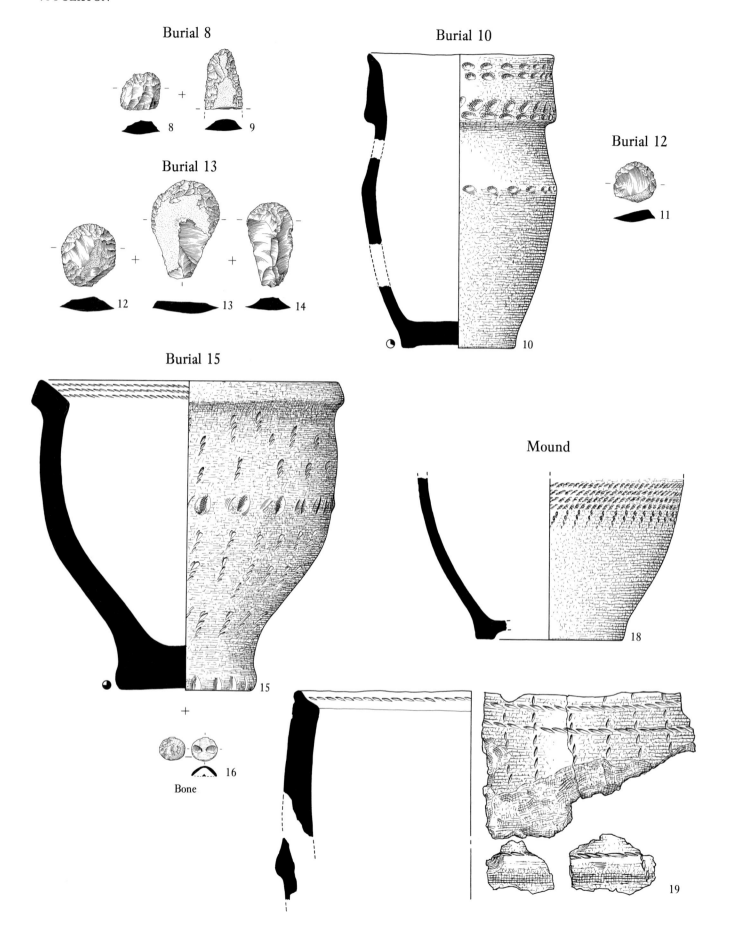

Burial 8

8 9

Burial 13

12 13 14

Burial 10

10

Burial 12

11

Burial 15

15

16

Bone

Mound

18

19

73 CHERRY BURTON

Burial 1

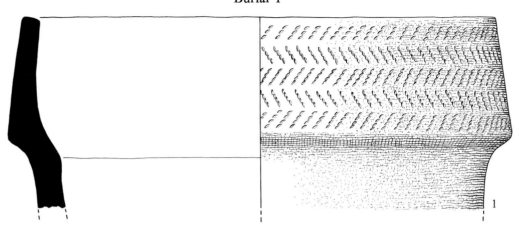

Burial 3

Burial 2

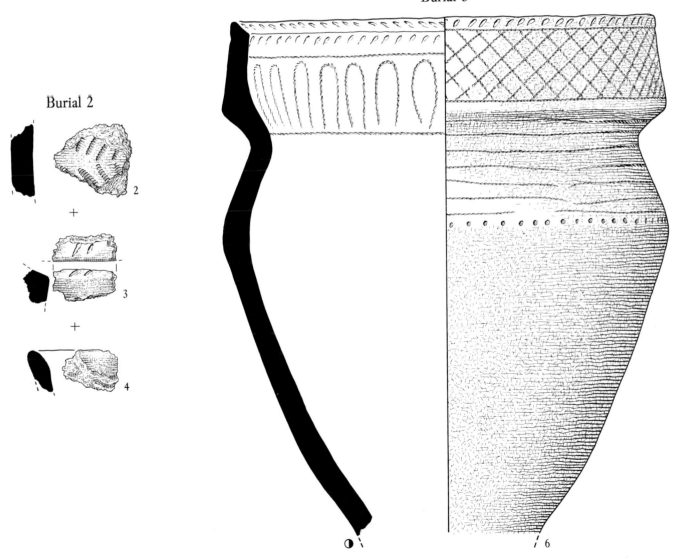

76 ETTON

79 ETTON

82 ETTON

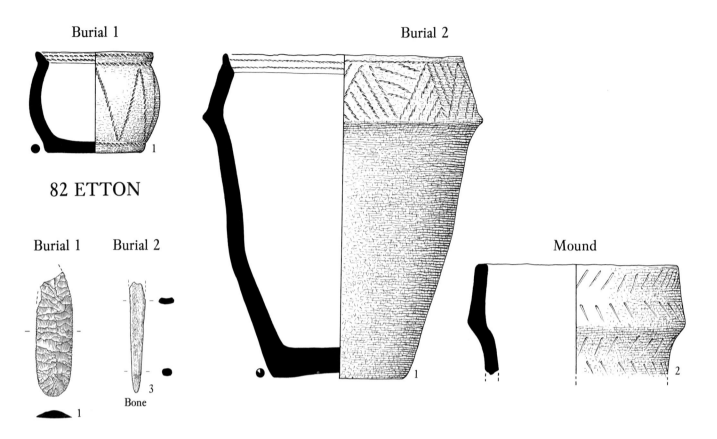

83 GOODMANHAM

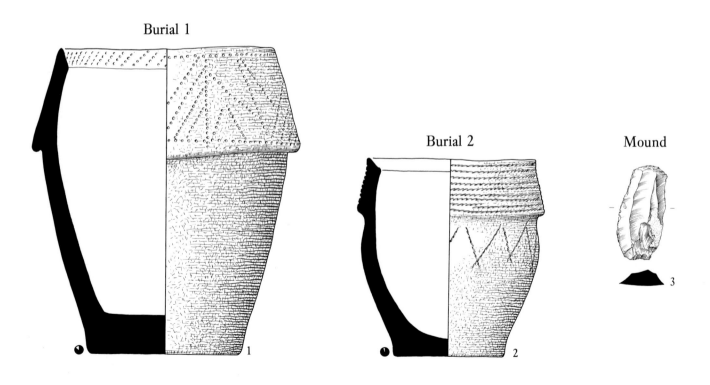

84 GOODMANHAM

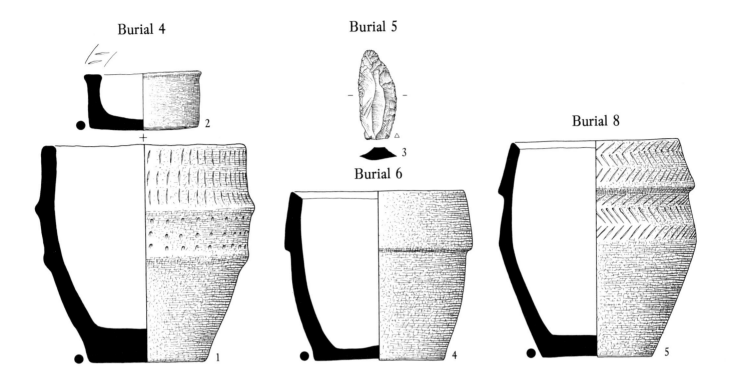

Burial 4

Burial 5

Burial 6

Burial 8

85 GOODMANHAM

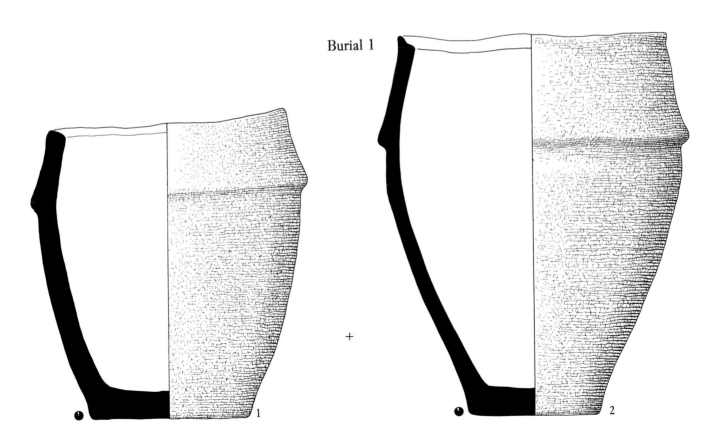

Burial 1

86 GOODMANHAM

87 GOODMANHAM

Burial 1

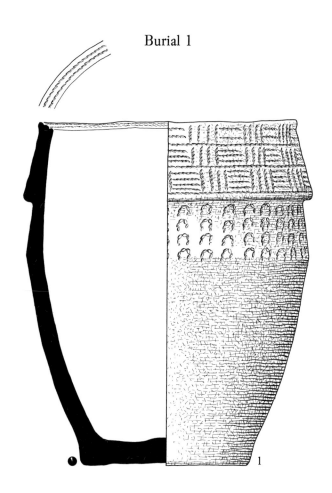

Burial 1

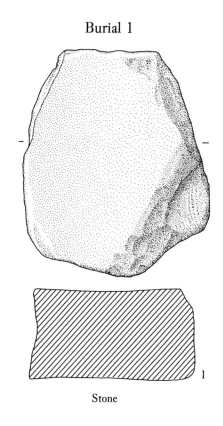

Stone

89 GOODMANHAM

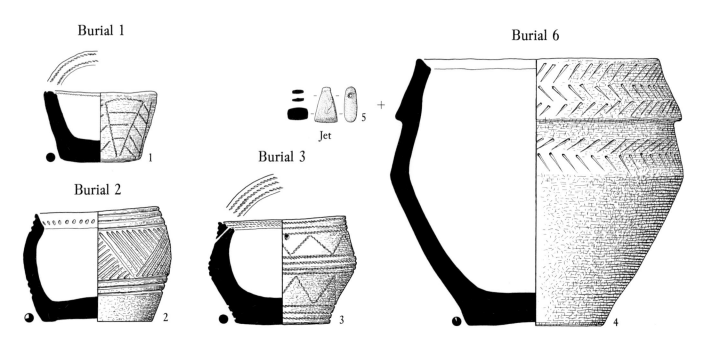

Burial 1

Burial 2

Burial 3

Jet

Burial 6

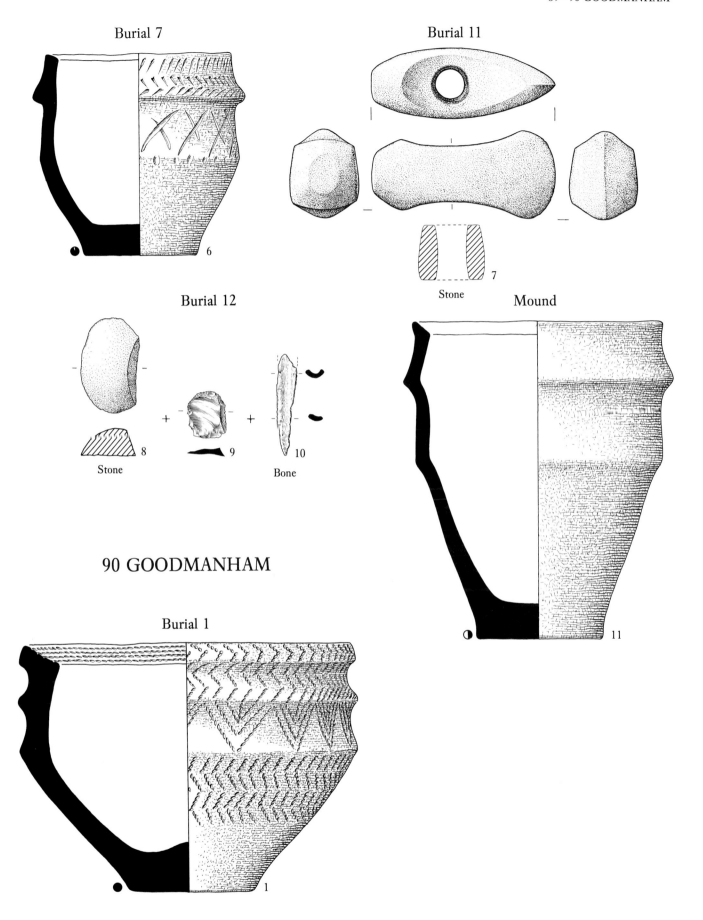

Burial 7

6

Burial 11

Stone

7

Burial 12

Stone

8

9

Bone

10

Mound

11

90 GOODMANHAM

Burial 1

1

91 GOODMANHAM

92 GOODMANHAM

Mound

Burial 1   Burial 3

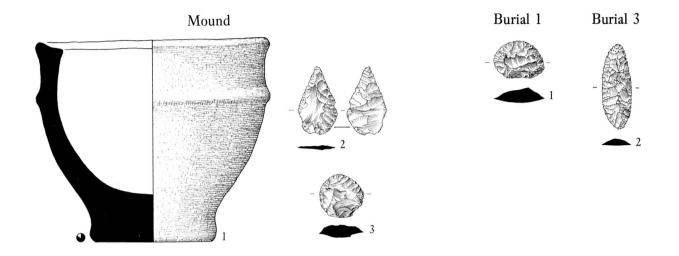

93 GOODMANHAM

Burial 1   Burial 2

Mound

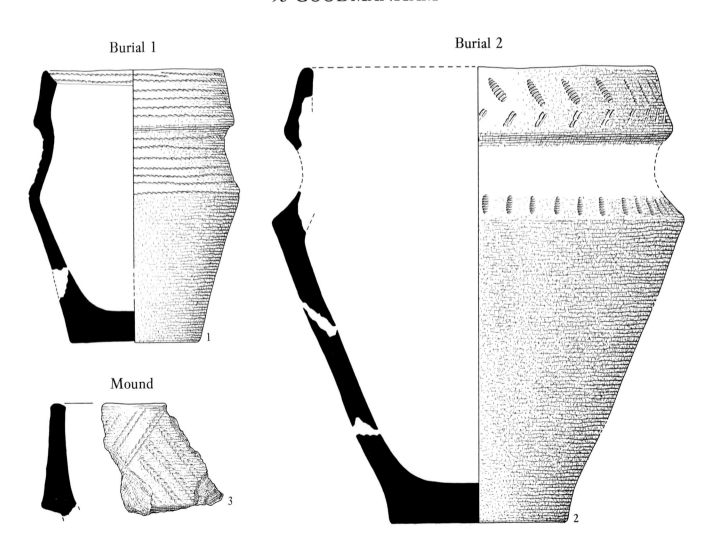

94 GOODMANHAM

Burial 1

Mound

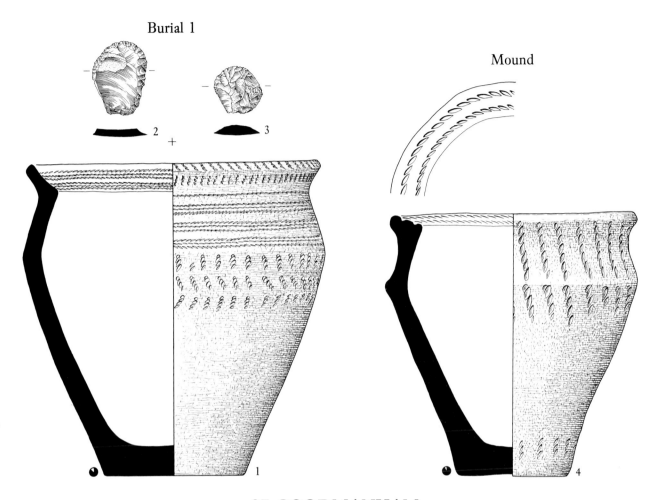

97 GOODMANHAM

Burial 1

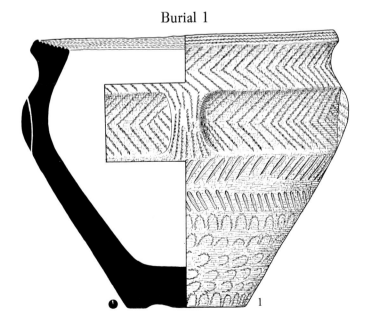

98 GOODMANHAM

Burial 1

Burial 2

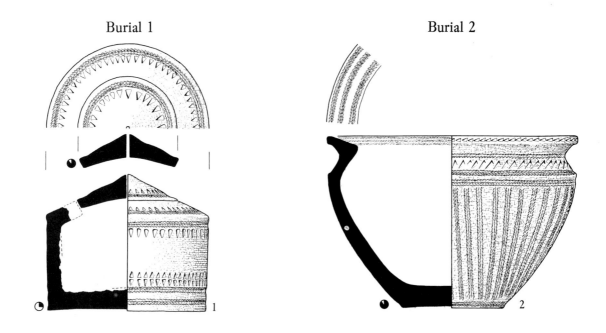

99 GOODMANHAM

Burial 4

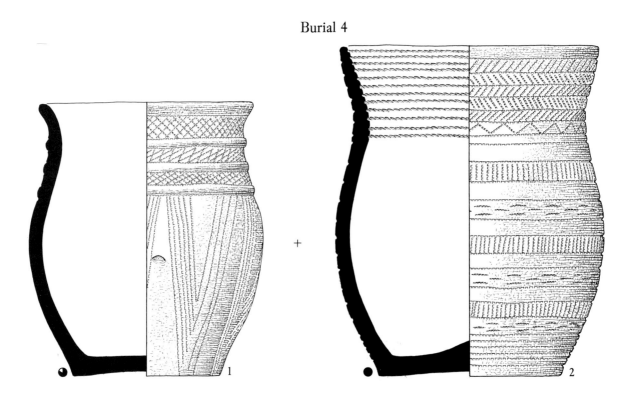

Burial 5

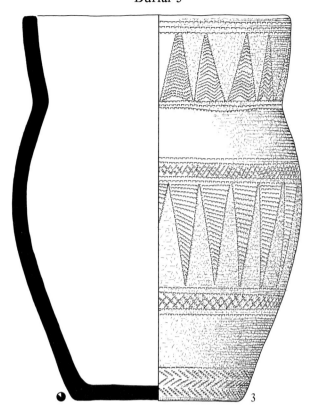

3

102 GOODMANHAM

100 GOODMANHAM

Burial 1

Feature A

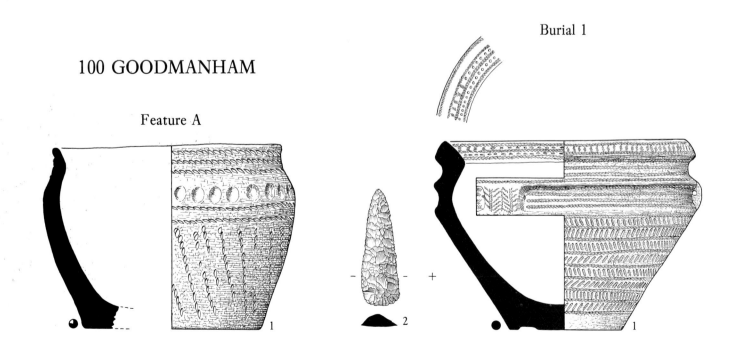

1

2

1

103 GOODMANHAM

107 GOODMANHAM

Burial 1

Burial 2

Mound

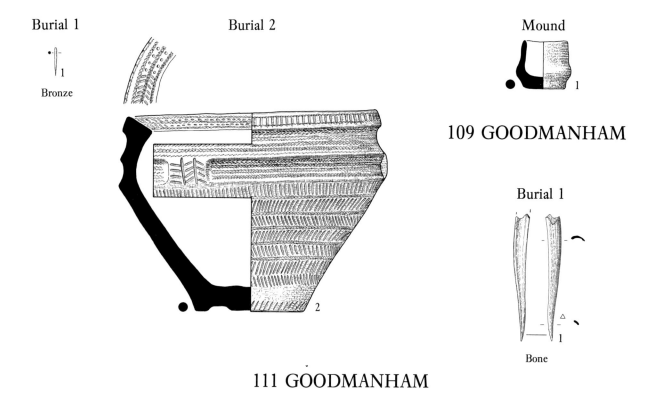

1

Bronze

109 GOODMANHAM

Burial 1

Bone

111 GOODMANHAM

Burial 4

Burial 5

Burial 3

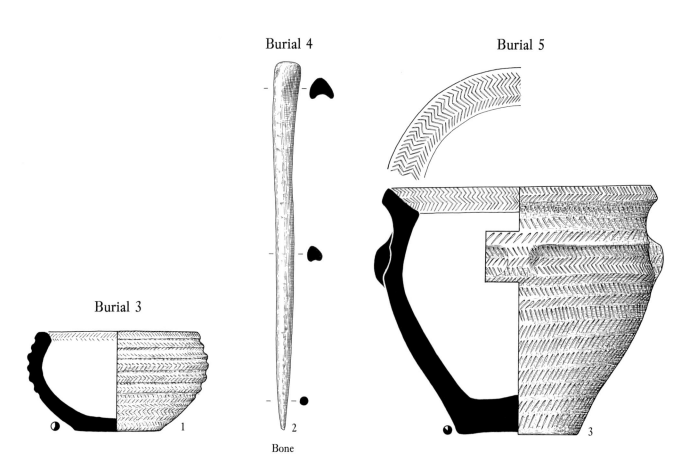

Bone

Burial 6

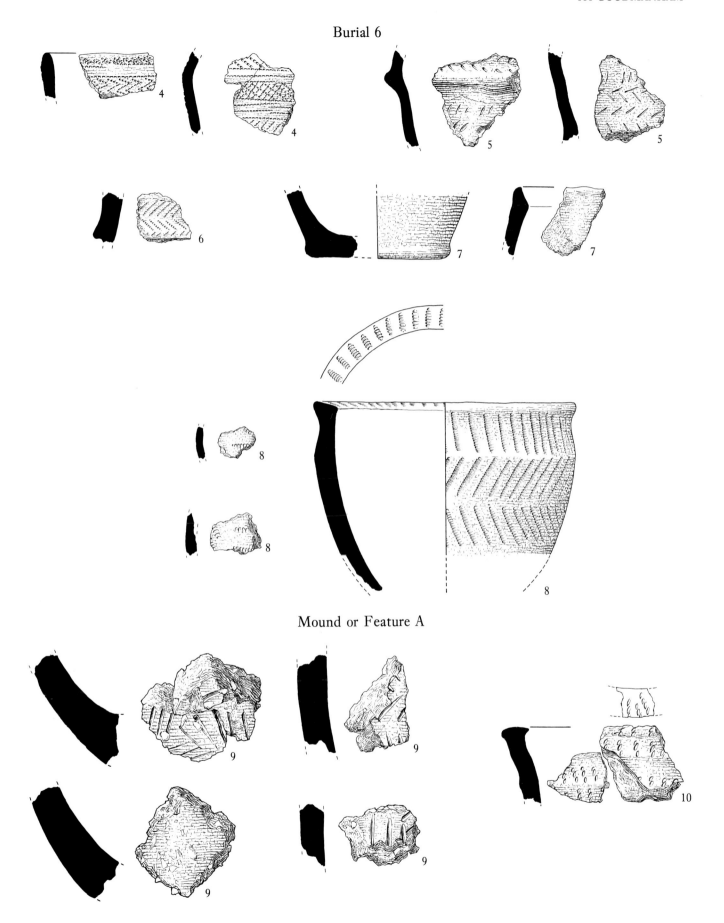

Mound or Feature A

113 GOODMANHAM

Burial 1

Burial 2

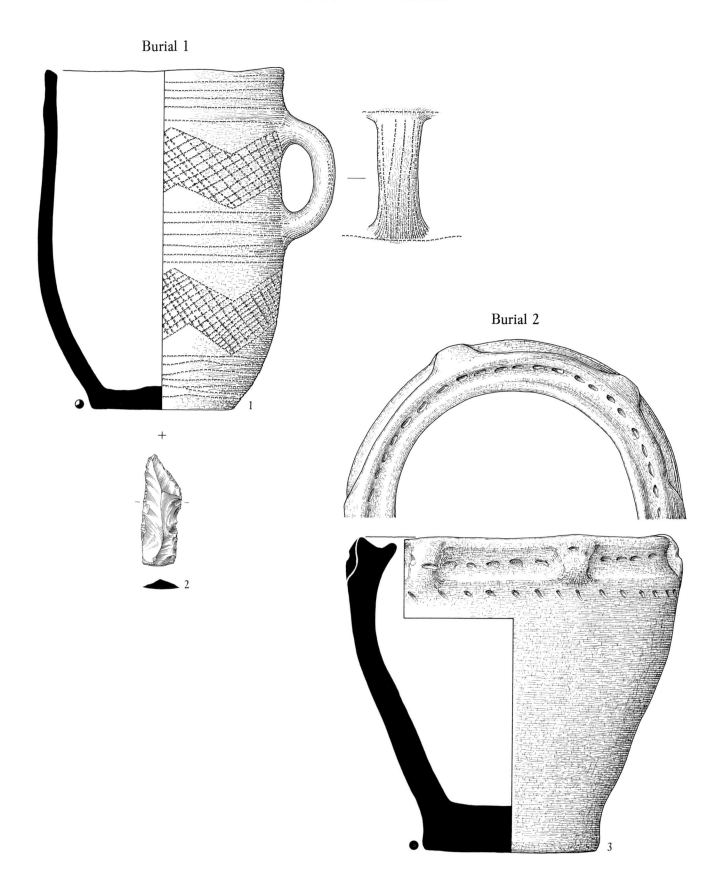

Burial 3

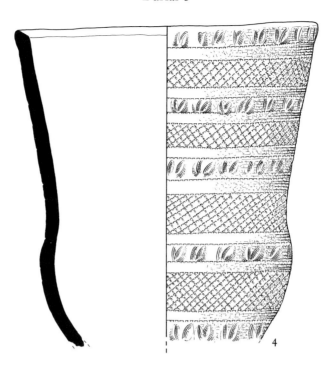

4

115 GOODMANHAM

Burial 1

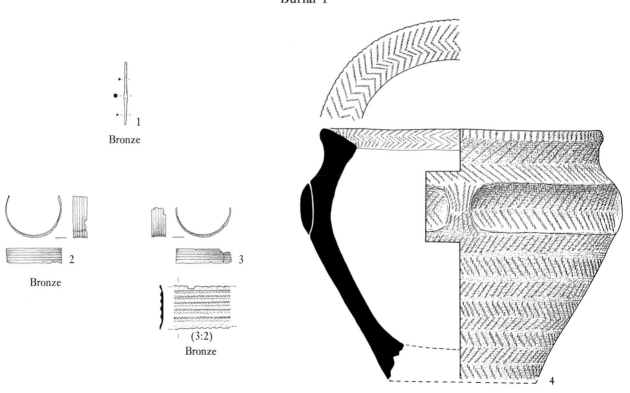

1

Bronze

2

Bronze

3

(3:2)

Bronze

4

Burial 2

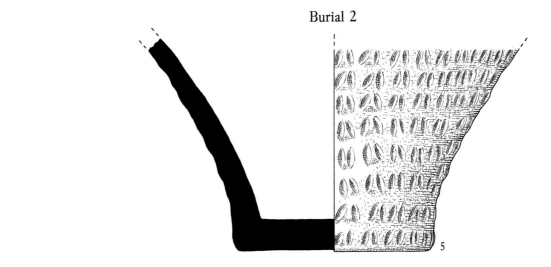

5

Burial 3

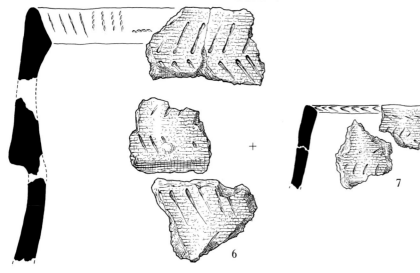

6

7

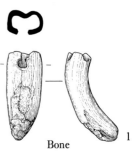

Not located

8

Bronze

116 GOODMANHAM

117 GOODMANHAM

Burial 1

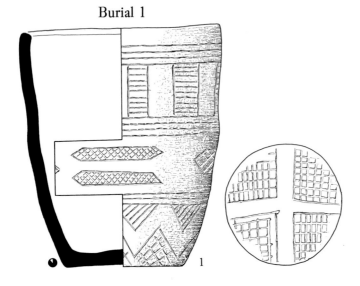

1

Burial 1

Bone

1

118 GOODMANHAM

Burial 1

119 GOODMANHAM

Burial 1

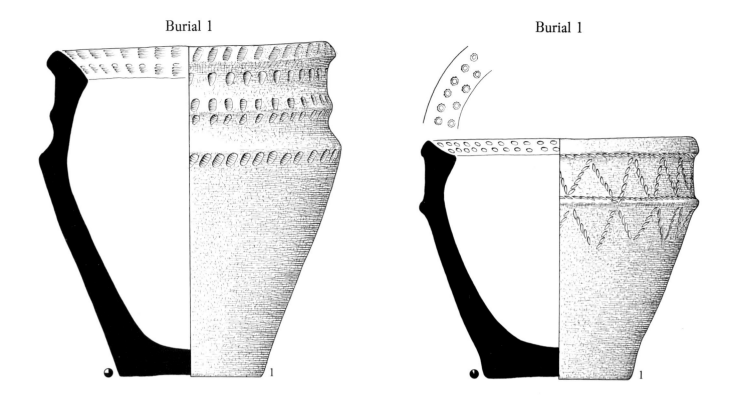

121 GOODMANHAM

Burial 2

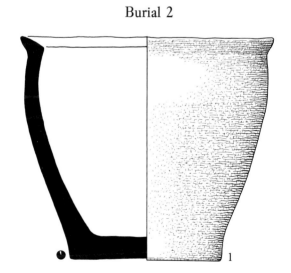

Burial 4

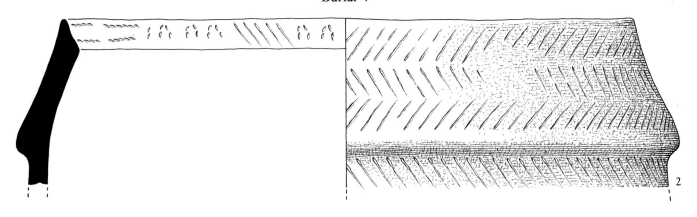

Burial 6

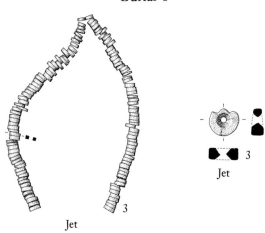

Jet

3

Jet

3

122 LONDESBOROUGH

123 LONDESBOROUGH

Burial 2

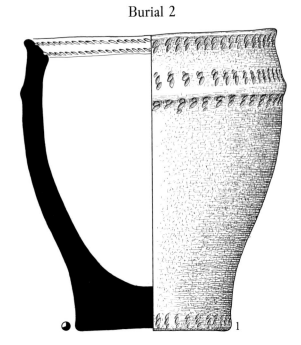

1

Mound

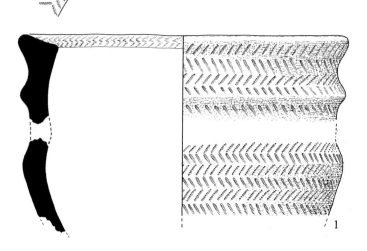

1

124 EGTON

Burial 1

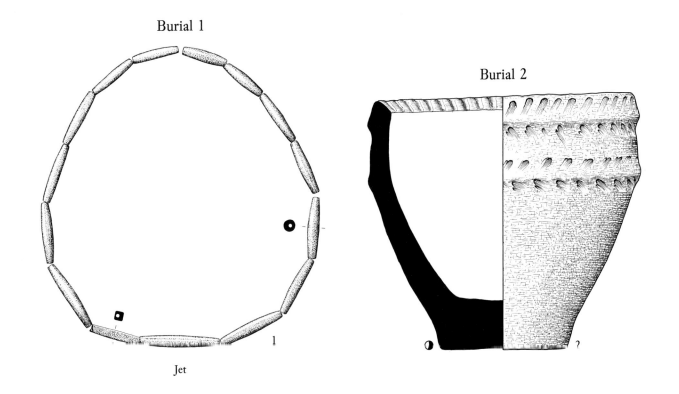

Jet

Burial 2

1

126 OVER SILTON

Burial 2

Mound

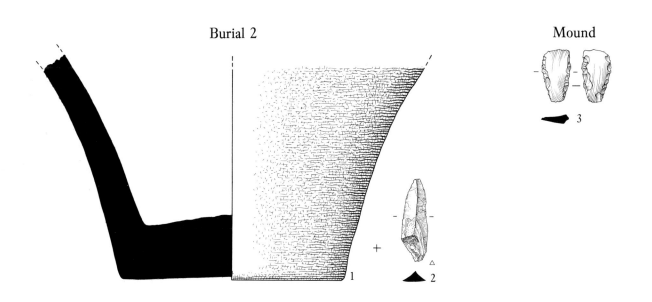

1

2

3

128 COLD KIRBY

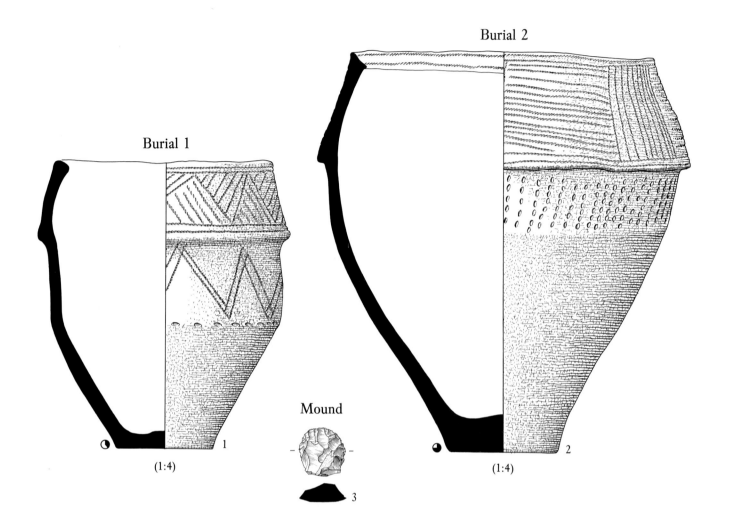

Burial 2

Burial 1

Mound

(1:4)   3   (1:4)

1   2

129 KILBURN

Mound

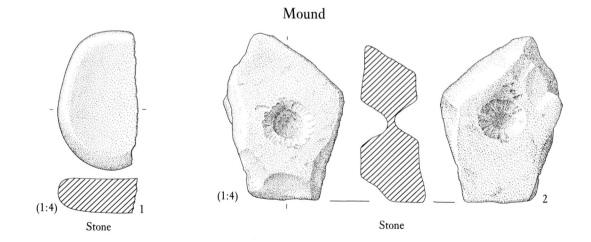

(1:4)   1   (1:4)   2

Stone   Stone

131 KILBURN

Cairn material

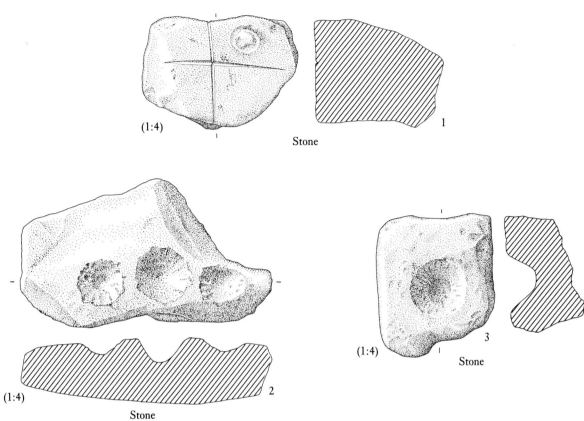

(1:4)

Stone

1

(1:4)

Stone

2

(1:4)

Stone

3

132 GILLING

Burial 1

1

Burial 2

2

Burial 1 - 2

4

5

6

Burial 1 – 2

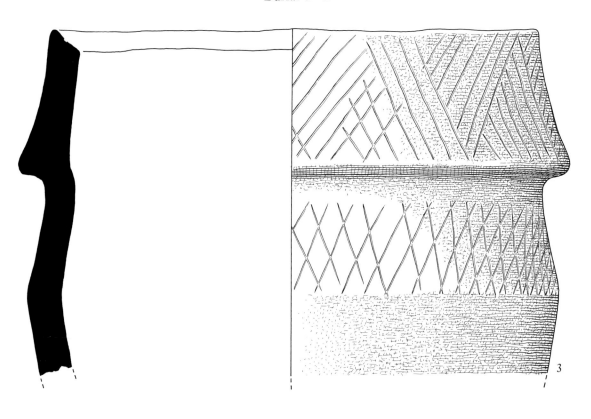

133 GILLING

Burial 1

137 GILLING

Burial 1

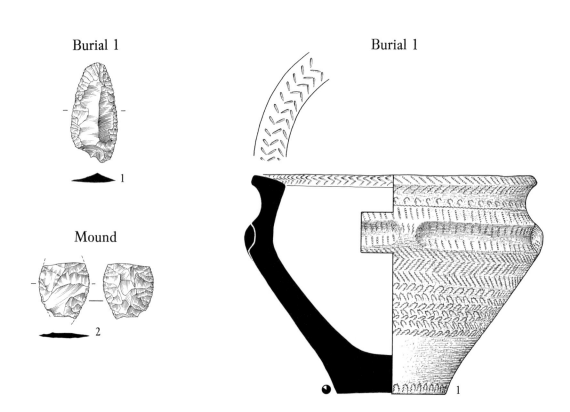

Mound

138 SLINGSBY

Burial 1

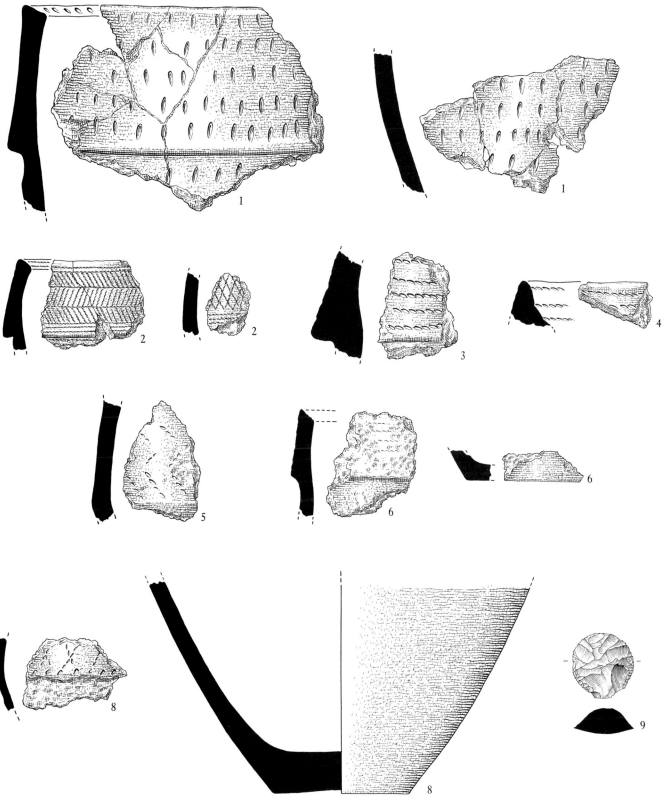

Burial 2

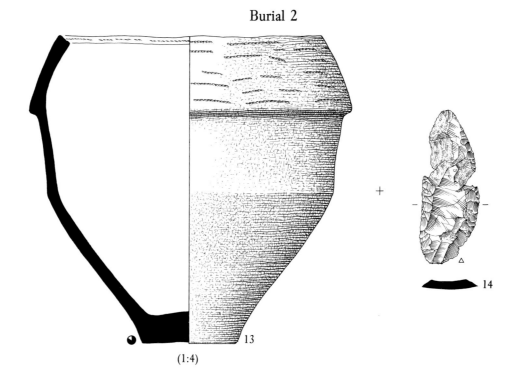

13

(1:4)

14

140 SLINGSBY

Burial 1

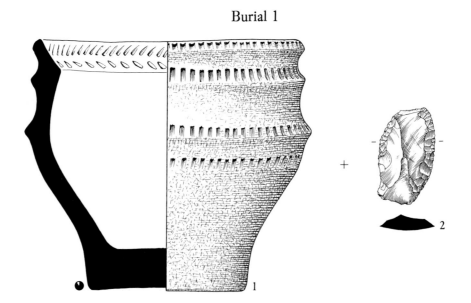

1

2

143 SLINGSBY

Mound

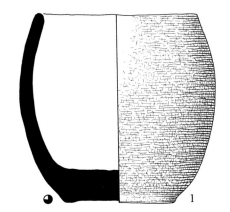

1

144 SLINGSBY

Burial 1

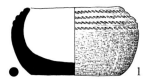

1

145 SLINGSBY

Burial 1

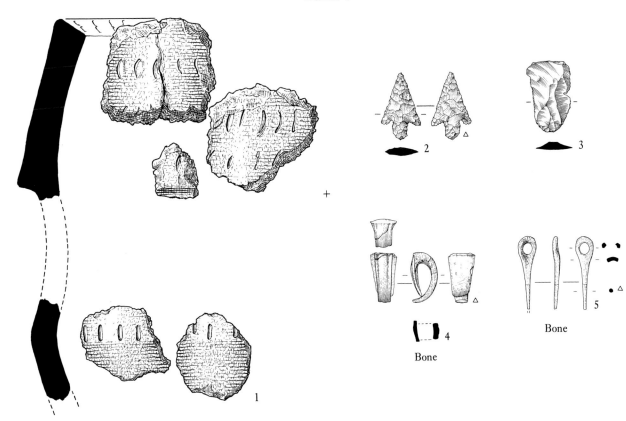

1

2

3

4

Bone

5

Bone

Burial 2

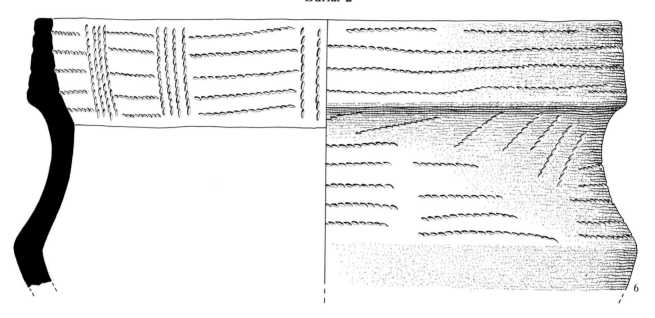

6

Mound

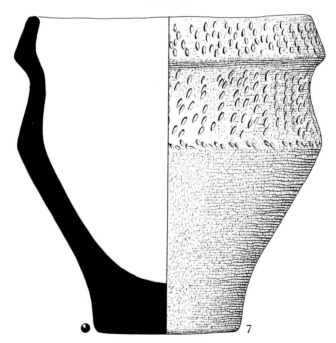

7

147 SLINGSBY

Burial 2

148 SLINGSBY

Burial 1

149 SLINGSBY

Burial 1

150 SLINGSBY

Burial 1

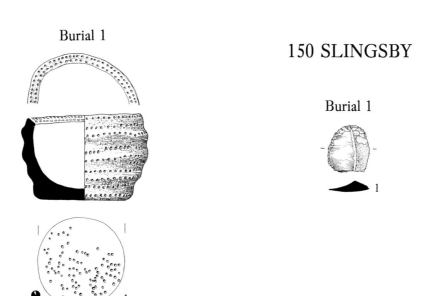

151 WELBURN

Burial 1

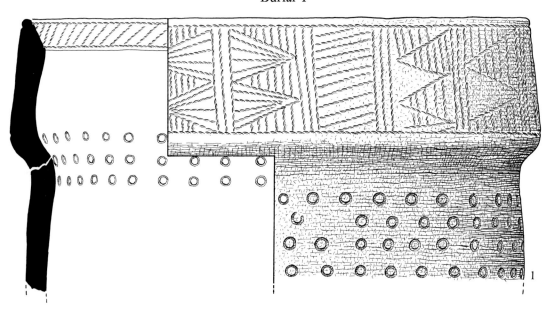

Mound

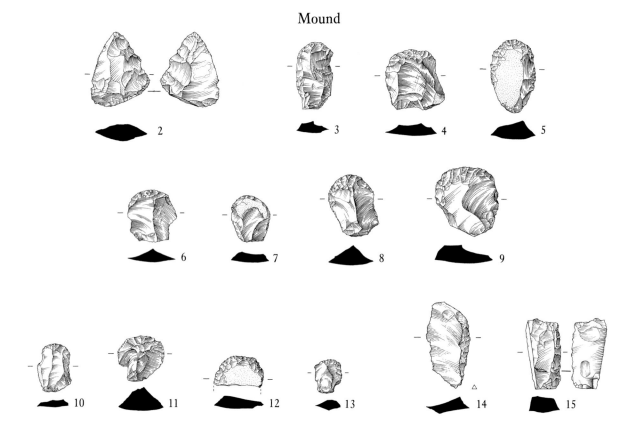

152 HUTTON BUSCEL

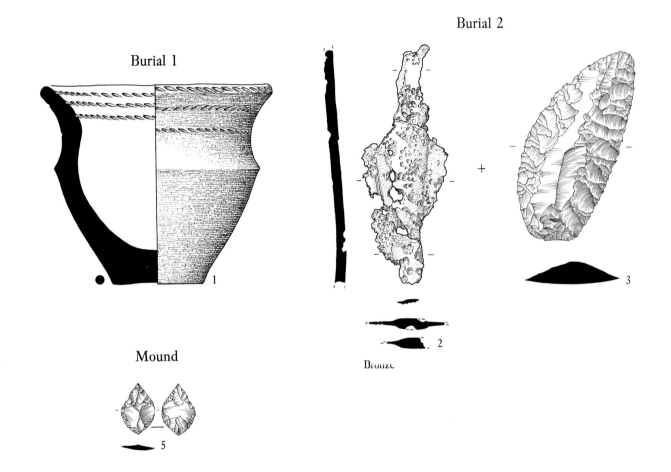

Burial 1

Burial 2

1

Mound

5

Bronze

2

3

153 HUTTON BUSCEL

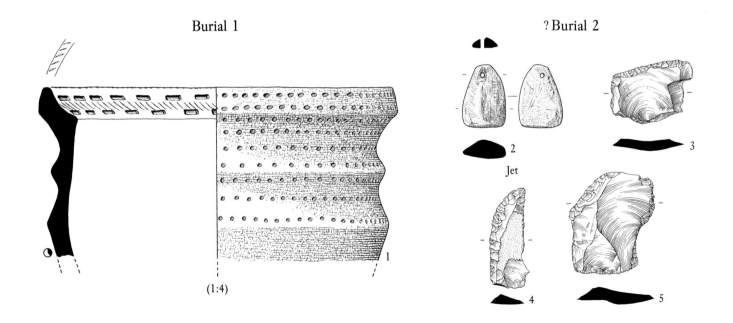

Burial 1

?Burial 2

1

(1:4)

Jet

2

3

4

5

154 HUTTON BUSCEL

Burial 2

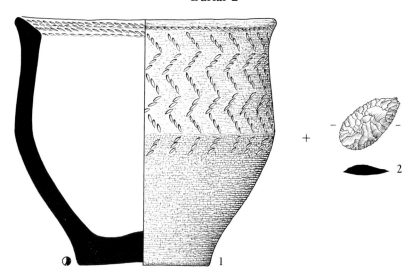

Burial 4

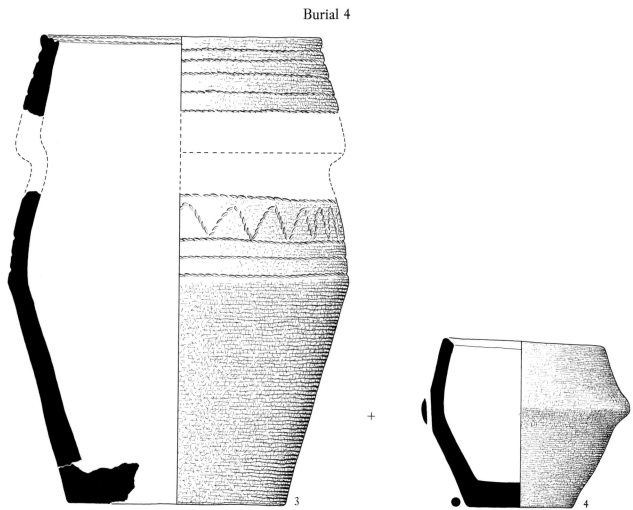

157 HUTTON BUSCEL

Burial 1

Burial 2

Awl
(bronze) 1

Jet 4

Jet 5

Jet 6

3

2

9

Burial 3

13

14

14

14

15

16

17

19

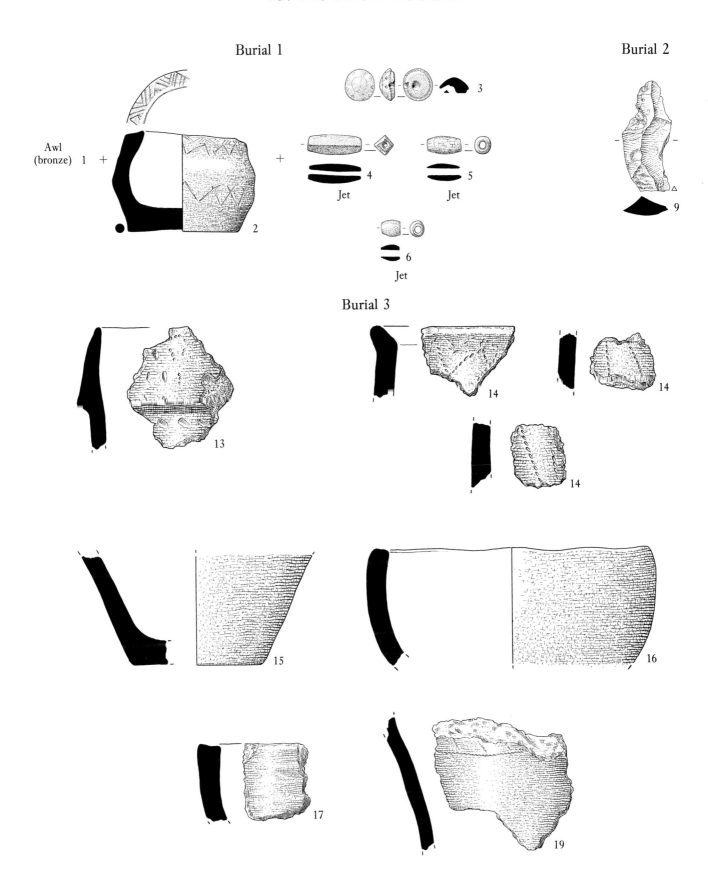

Burial 4

Burial 6

Burial 5

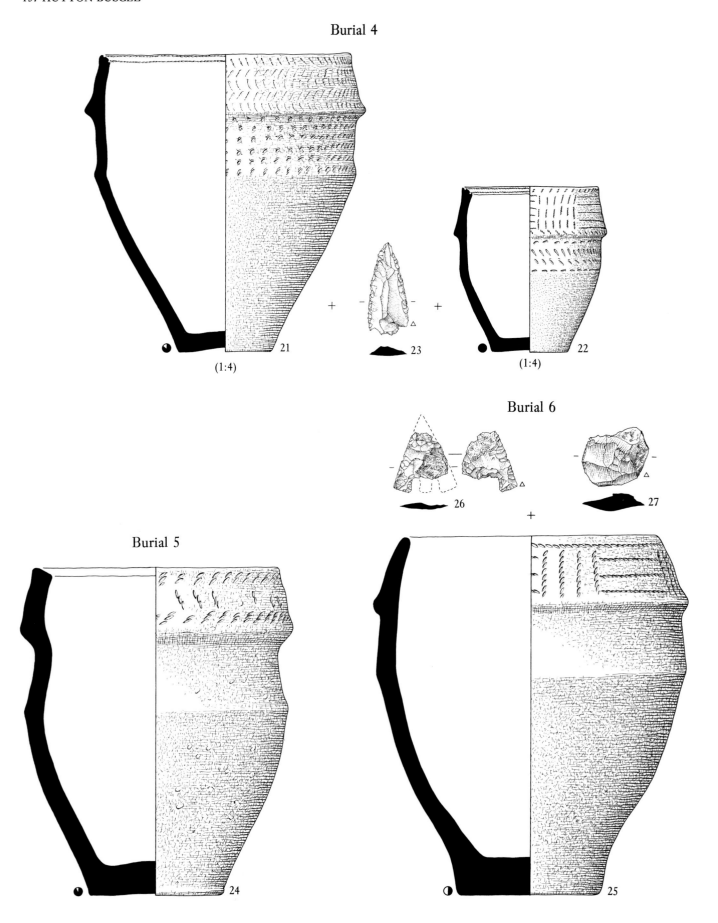

21
(1:4)

23

22
(1:4)

26

27

24

25

158 HUTTON BUSCEL

Burial 1

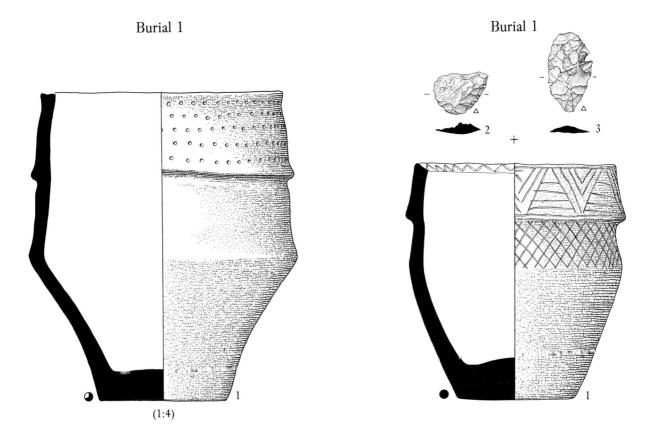

(1:4)

159 HUTTON BUSCEL

Burial 1

160 HUTTON BUSCEL

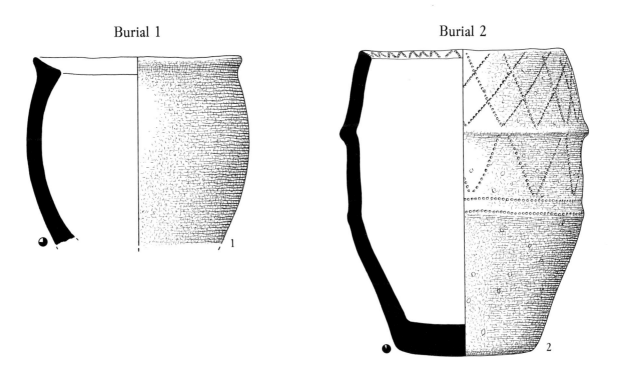

Burial 1

Burial 2

161 FERRY FRYSTON

Burial 5

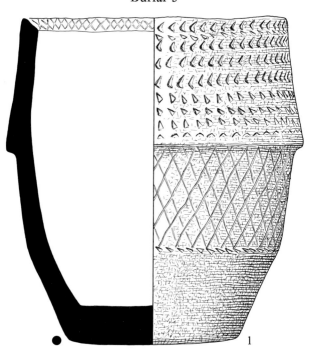

Burial 6

Burial 8

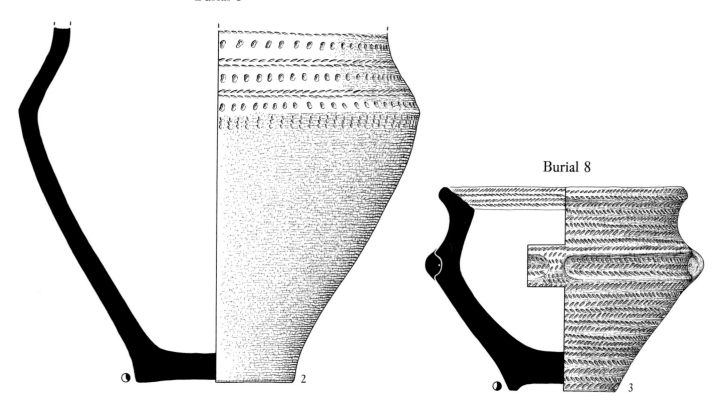

Burial 9

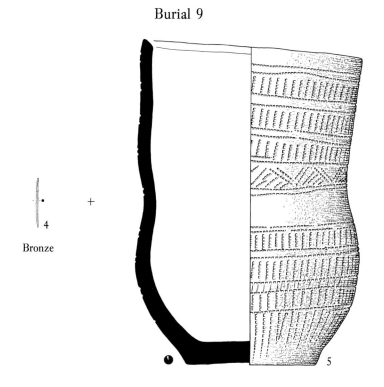

Bronze

162 RYLSTON

Burial 1

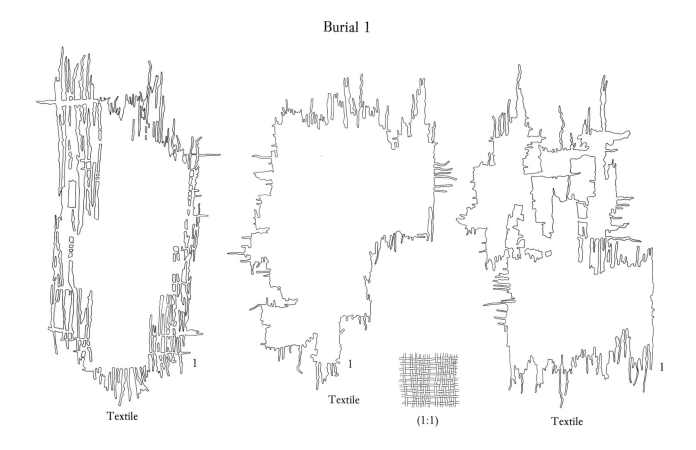

Textile

Textile

(1:1)

Textile

163 CASTLE CARROCK

Burial 1

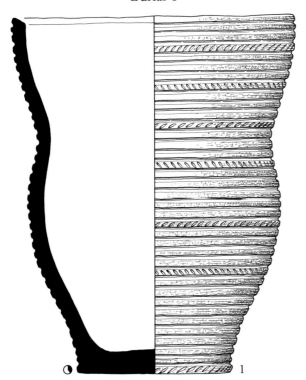

1

164 CASTLE CARROCK

Burial 1

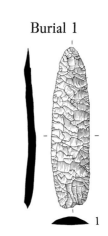

1

169 KIRBY STEPHEN

Burial 1

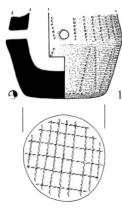

1

170 KIRBY STEPHEN

Mound or Burial 1

1

174 CROSBY GARRETT

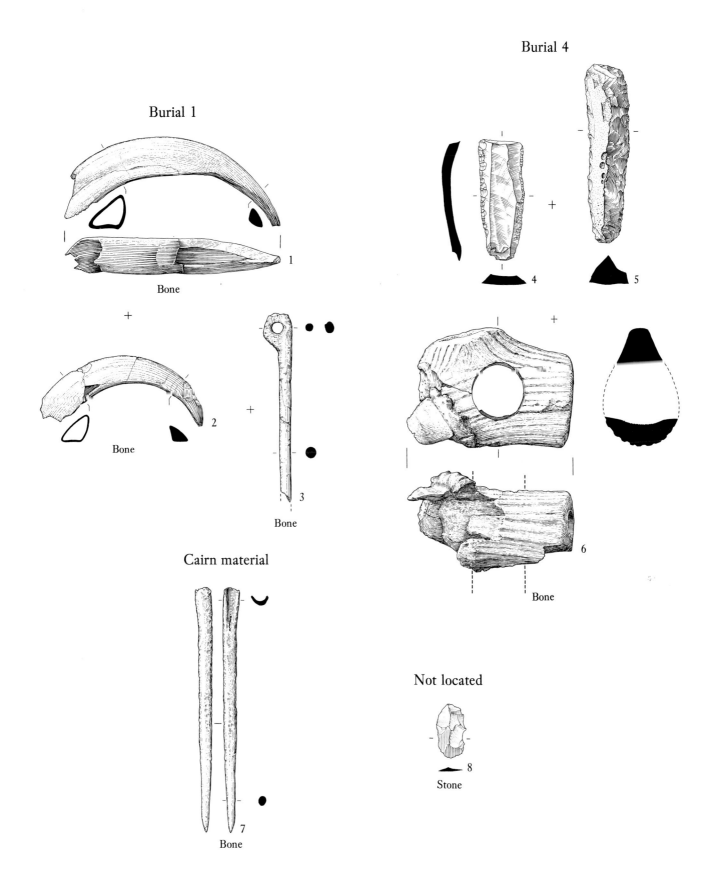

Burial 1

1

Bone

2

Bone

3

Bone

Burial 4

4

5

6

Bone

Cairn material

7

Bone

Not located

8

Stone

176 CROSBY GARRETT

Burial 2

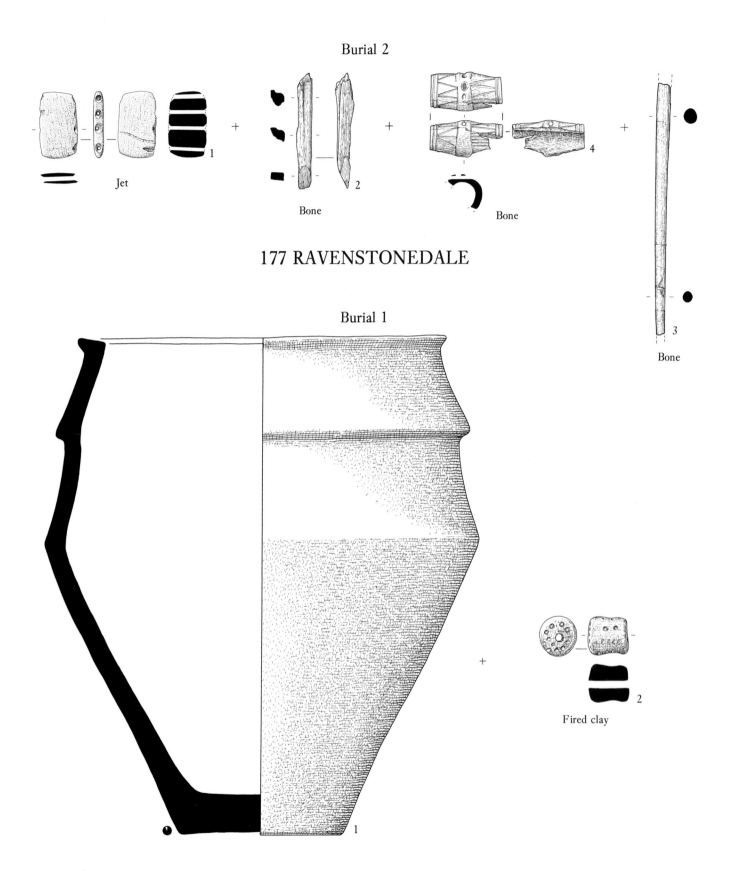

Jet

1

Bone

2

Bone

4

Bone

3

177 RAVENSTONEDALE

Burial 1

1

Fired clay

2

178 ORTON

Burial 2

1

179 ORTON

Burial 2 or Burial 3

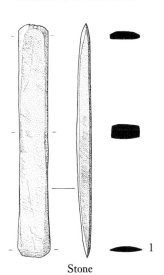

Stone

1

183 ASKHAM

Burial 1

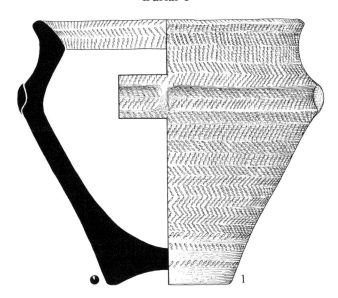

1

184 FORD

Burial 1

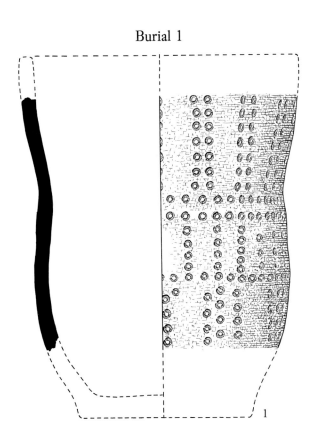

1

Burial 2

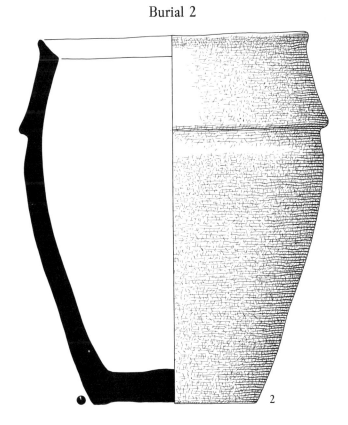

2

Burial 3

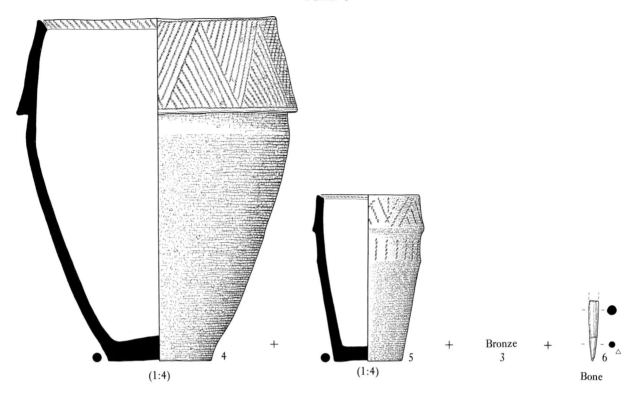

(1:4)   4   +   (1:4)   5   +   Bronze 3   +   6   Bone

Burial 4

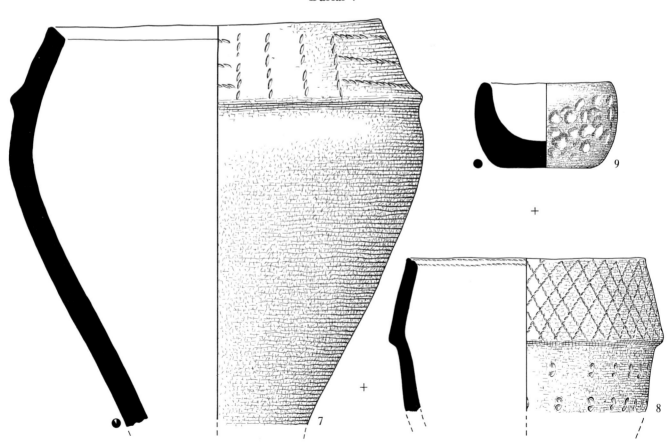

185 FORD

Burial 1

2

186 FORD

Burial 3

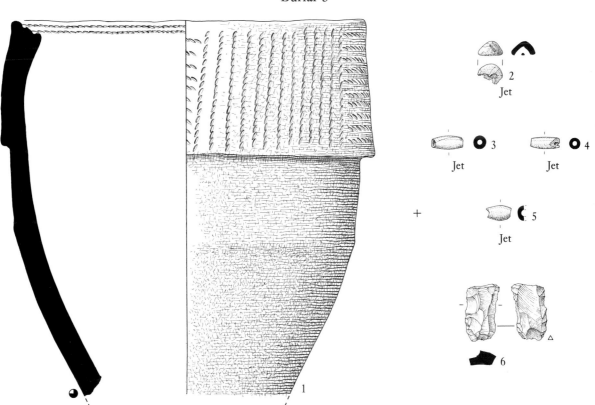

1

2
Jet

3
Jet

4
Jet

+

5
Jet

6

187 FORD

Burial 1

Burial 2

Bone

3

+

+

4

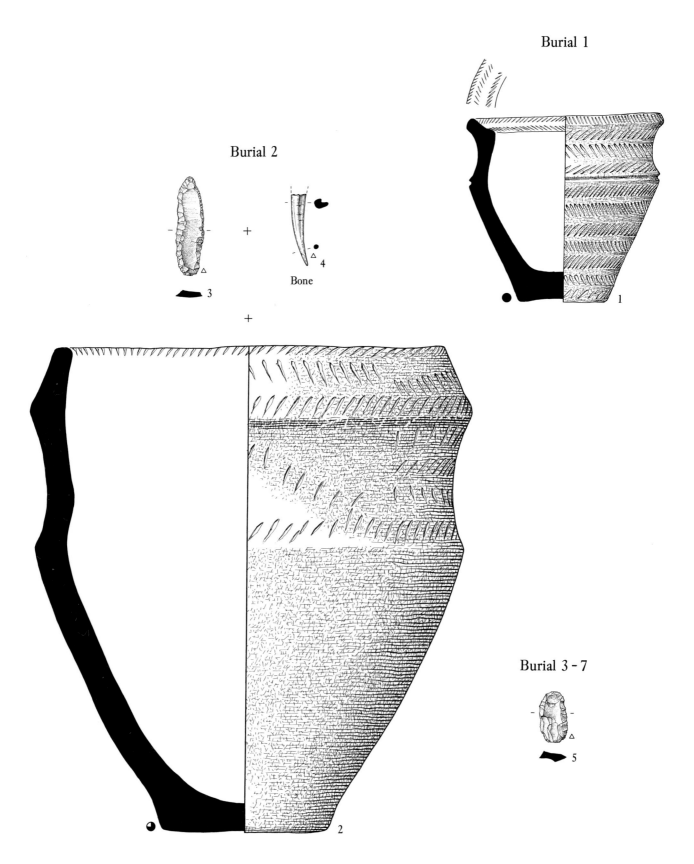

1

2

Burial 3 - 7

5

188 FORD

Burial 1

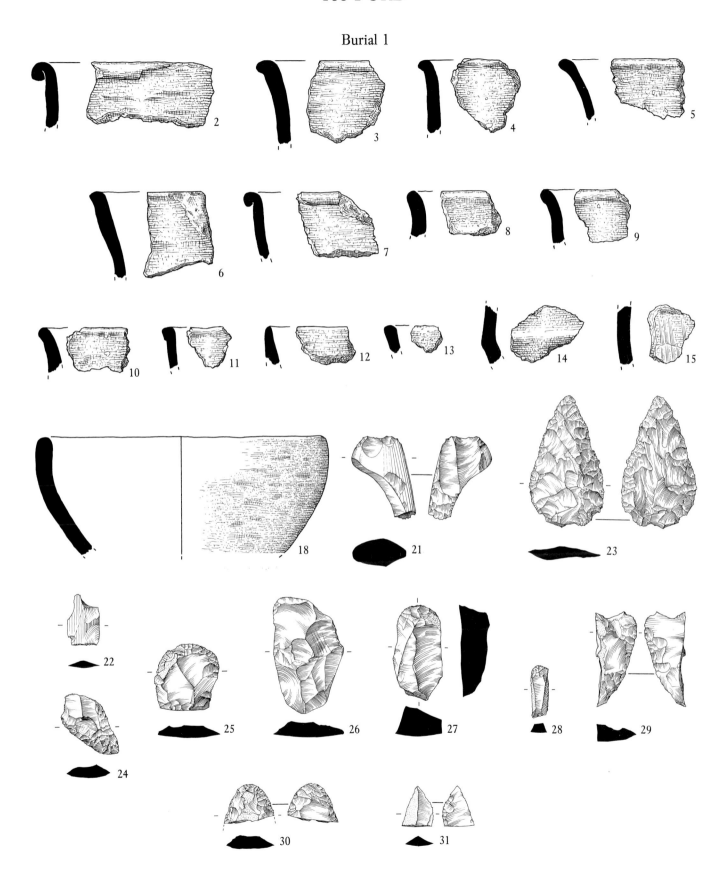

189 DODDINGTON

Burial 1

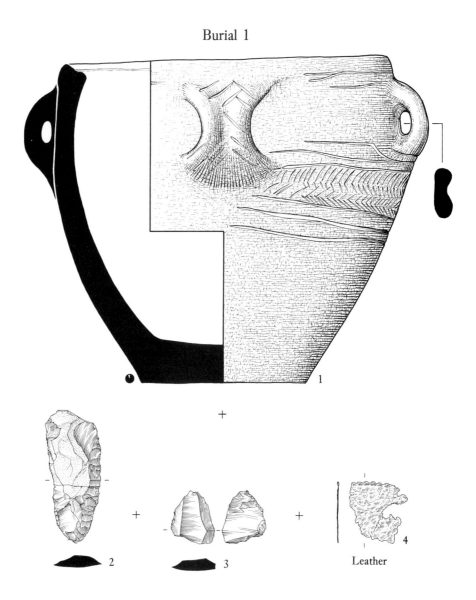

Leather

192 CHATTON

Burial 1

193 BAMBOROUGH

Cairn material

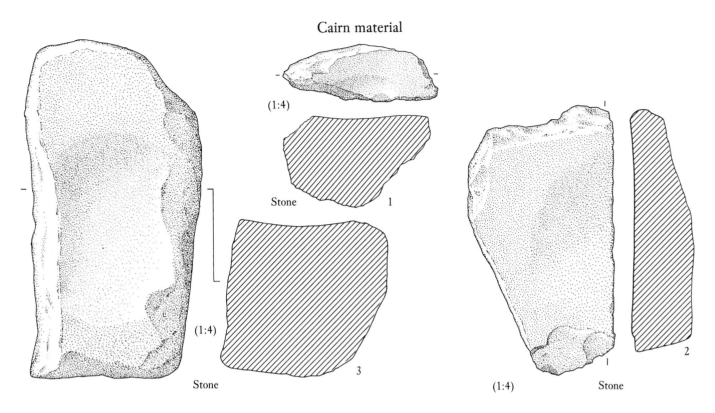

(1:4)

Stone 1

(1:4)

Stone 3

Stone

(1:4)

Stone 2

197 BAMBOROUGH

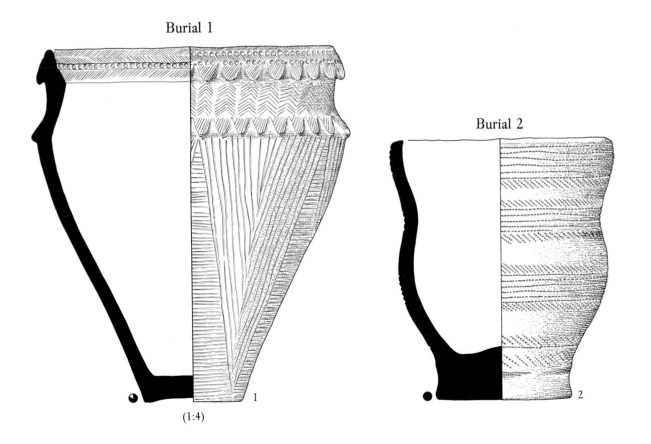

Burial 1

Burial 2

(1:4) 1

2

198 BAMBOROUGH

Burial 1

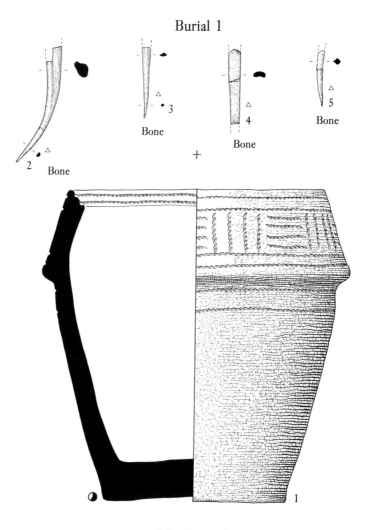

2 Bone

3 Bone

4 Bone

5 Bone

+

1

Not located

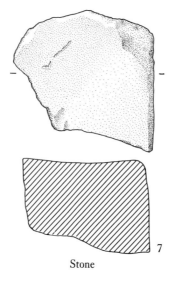

7

Stone

200 EGLINGHAM

Burial 2

1

Burial 3

Jet

2

3

201 EGLINGHAM

Burial 1

2

202 ALWINTON

Burial 2

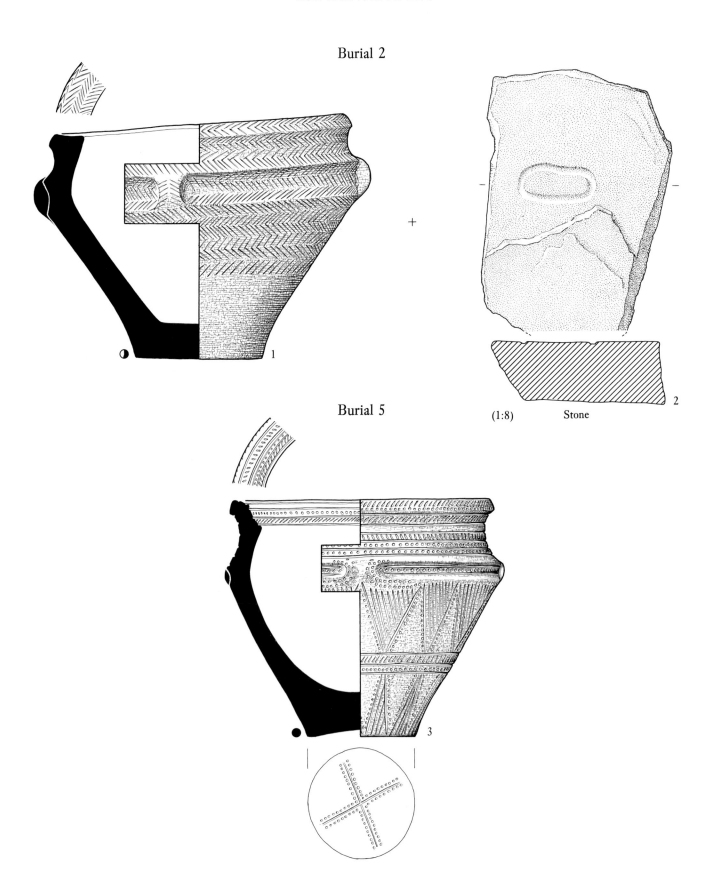

Burial 5

(1:8)   Stone

Burial 6

Burial 8

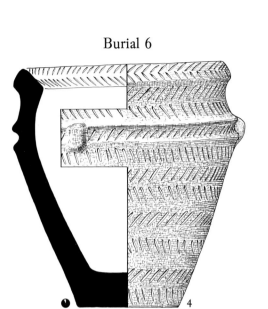

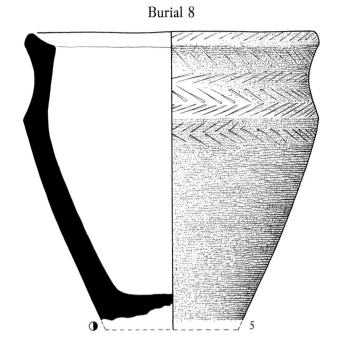

4

5

204 ALWINTON

Burial 3

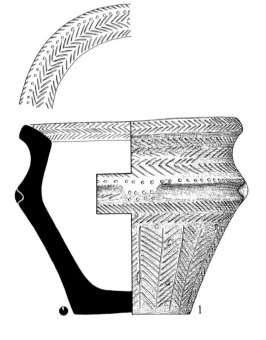

1

205 ALWINTON

Burial 1

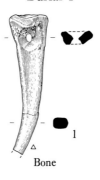

1

Bone

Burial 3

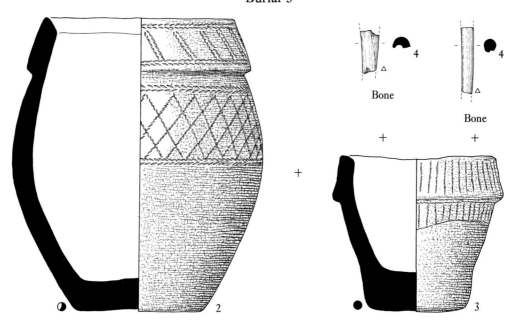

2

Bone
+

+
+

Bone
+

4

4

3

Burial 4

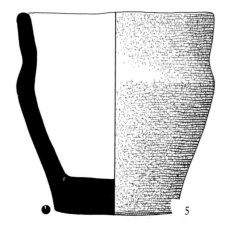

5

Burial 1 – 3

6
7
8

210 KIRK WHELPINGTON

Burial 2

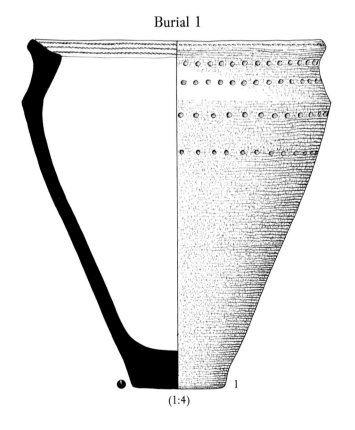

(1:4)   Stone

211 KIRK WHELPINGTON

Burial 1

(1:4)

212 HARTBURN

Burial 1

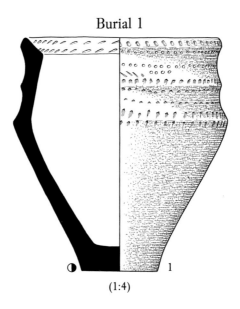

(1:4)

214 OVINGHAM

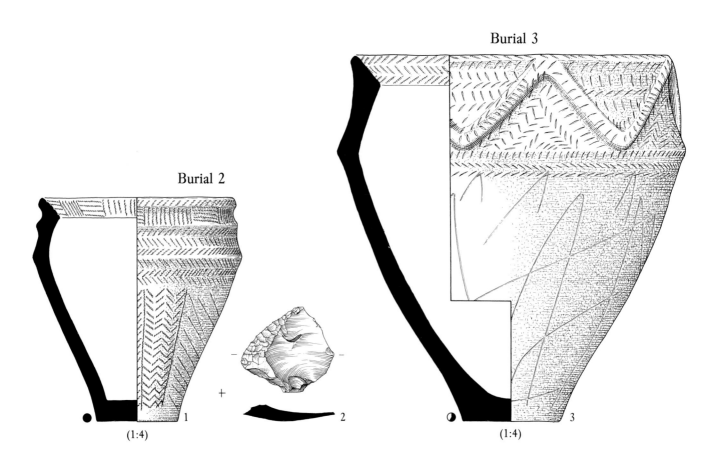

Burial 3

Burial 2

(1:4)

(1:4)

215 SOUTH SHIELDS

Burial 1

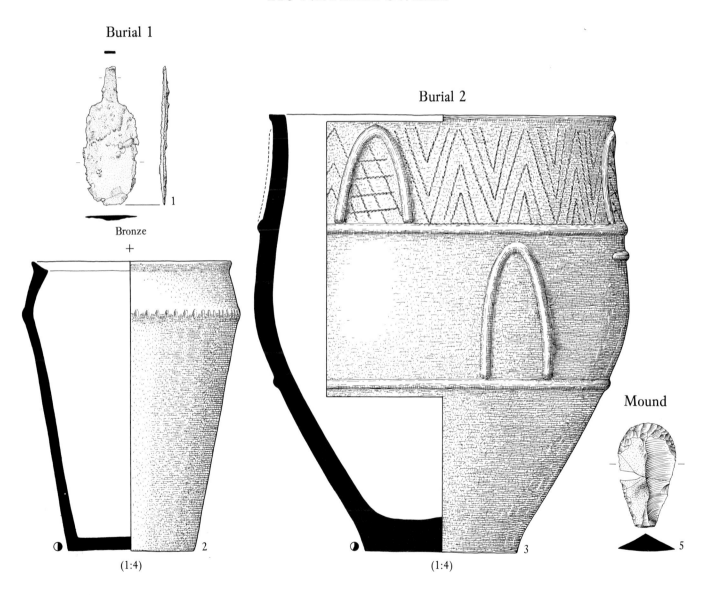

216 NETHER SWELL

Burial 1

Bronze

Burial 2

Mound

(1:4)   (1:4)

218 NETHER SWELL   220 NETHER SWELL   222 WILLERBY

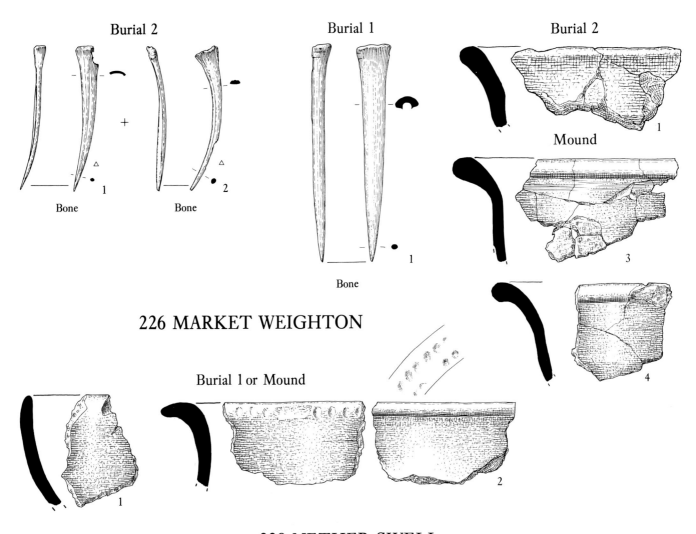

Burial 2

1

Bone

2

Bone

Burial 1

1

Bone

Burial 2

1

Mound

3

4

226 MARKET WEIGHTON

Burial 1 or Mound

1

2

229 NETHER SWELL

Mound

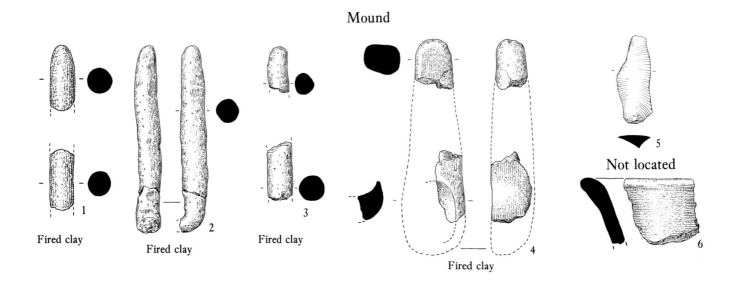

1

Fired clay

2

Fired clay

3

Fired clay

4

Fired clay

5

Not located

6

230 EYFORD

Burial 6

Burial 5

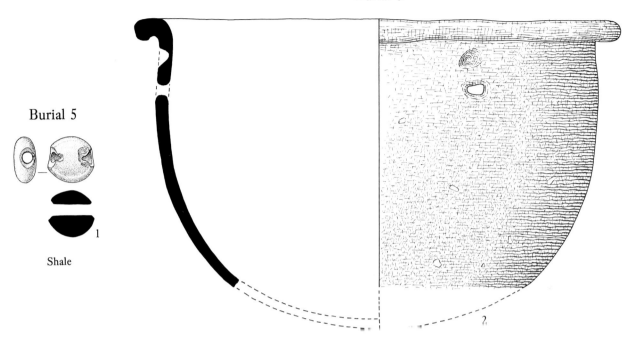

1

Shale

231 UPPER SWELL

Burial 1 or Mound

Mound

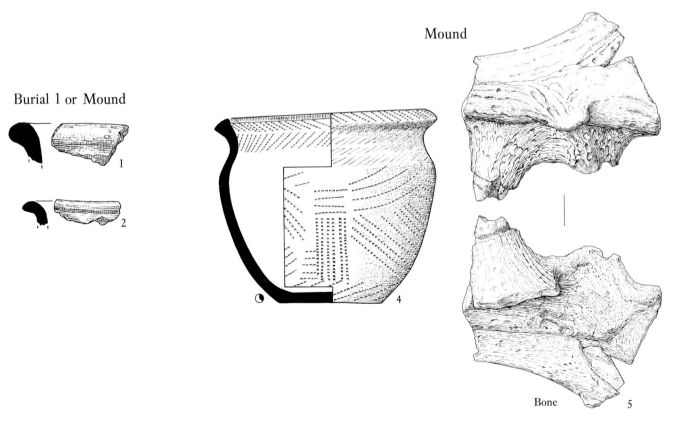

1

2

4

Bone 5

232 UPPER SWELL

Burial 1

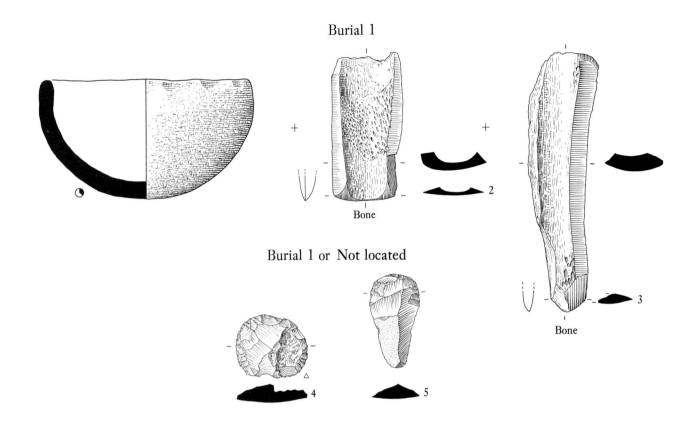

Bone

Burial 1 or Not located

Bone

233 GILLING

Burial 1

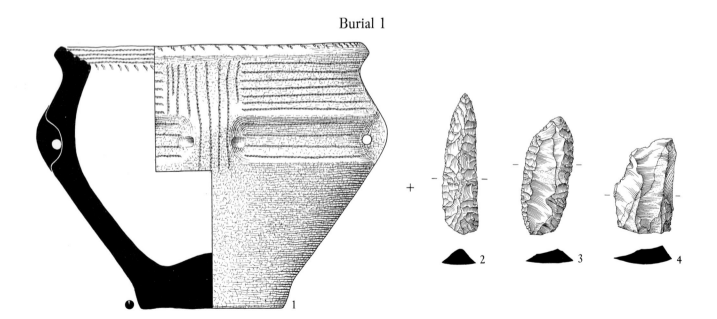

234 KILHAM

Burial 3

Mound

Burial 10

(1:4)   11
Bone

Burial 9

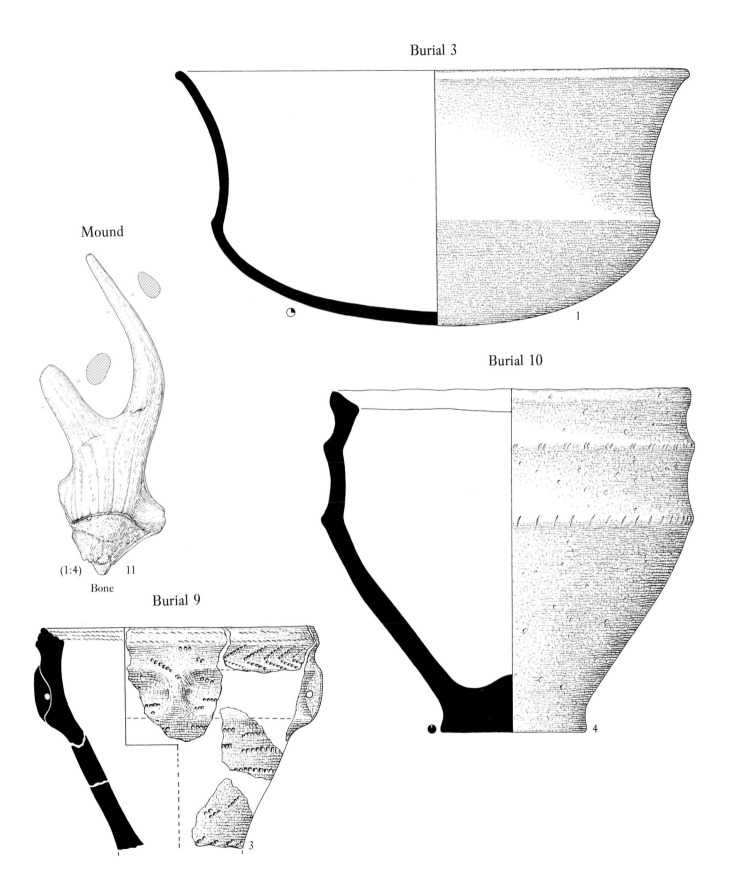

1

4

3

235 WILLERBY

Burial 1

Burial 2

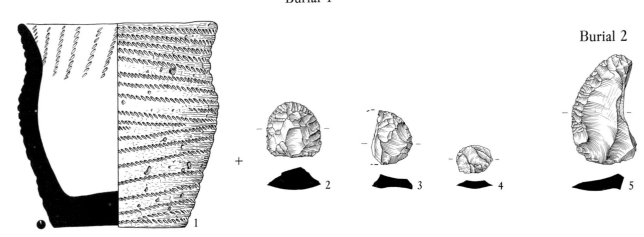

Mound

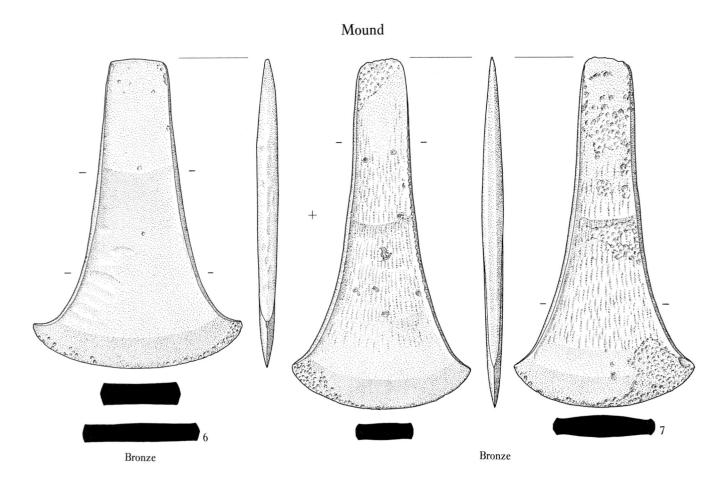

Bronze

Bronze

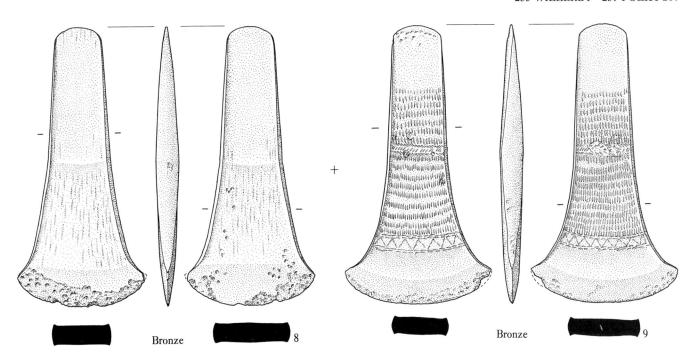

Bronze   8

Bronze   9

237 FOLKTON

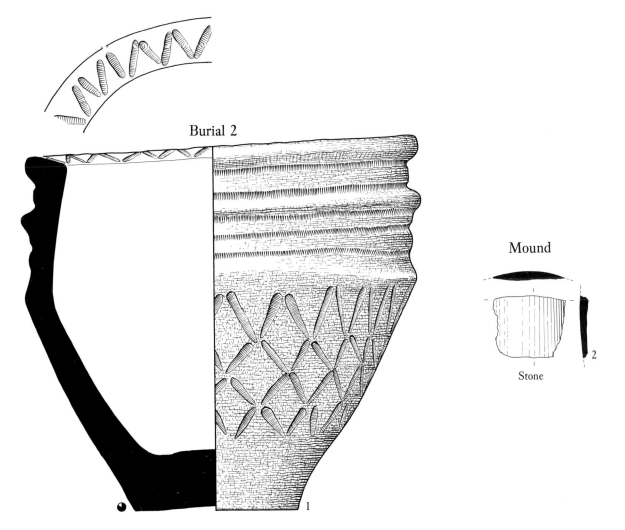

Burial 2

Mound

Stone

1

2

238 FOLKTON

Burial 1

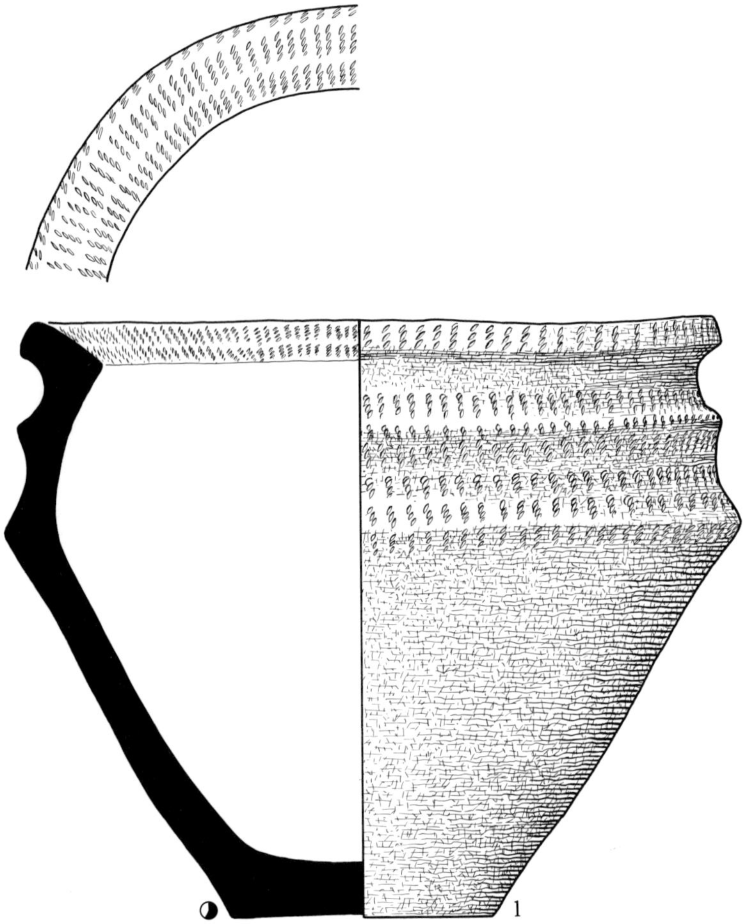

Burial 3   Grave fill

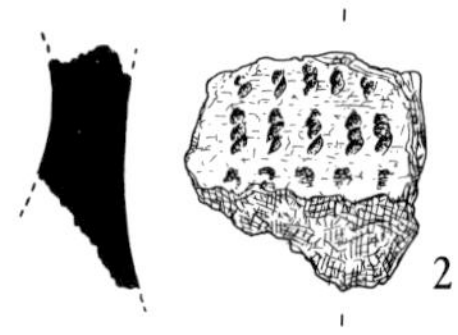

Mound 1967

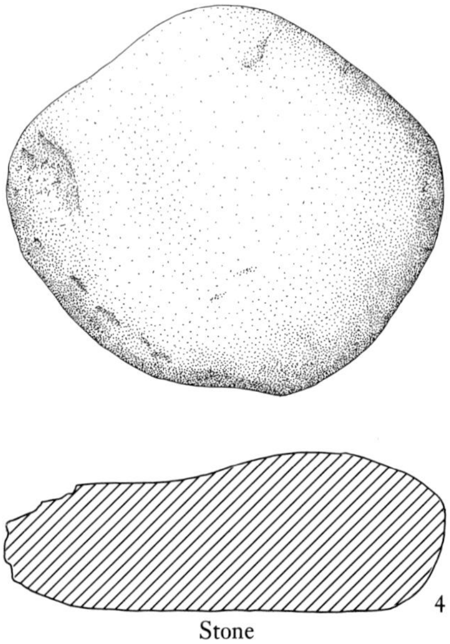

Stone

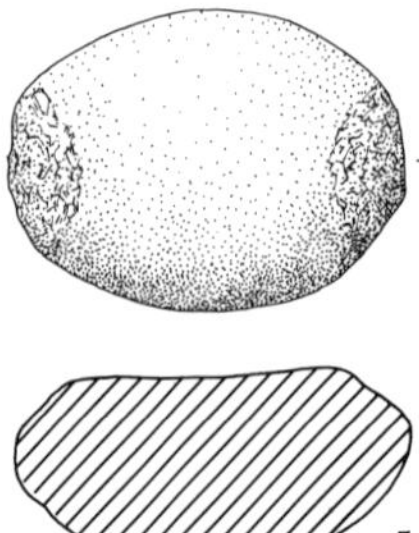

1

2

Stone

4

5

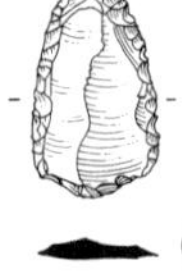

6

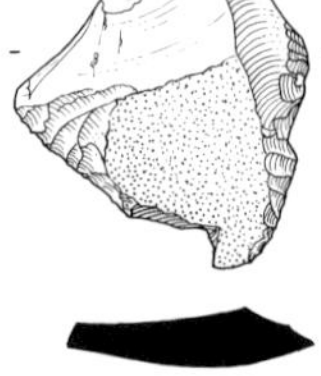

7

239 FOLKTON

Burial 1

Burial 4

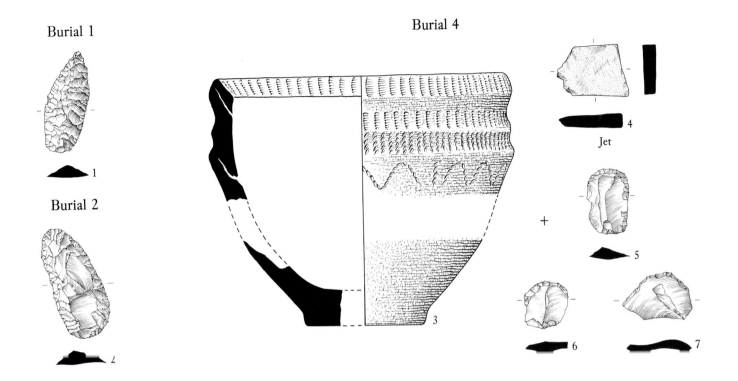

1

Burial 2

2

Jet

4

5

6

7

240 FOLKTON

Feature B-E

Mound

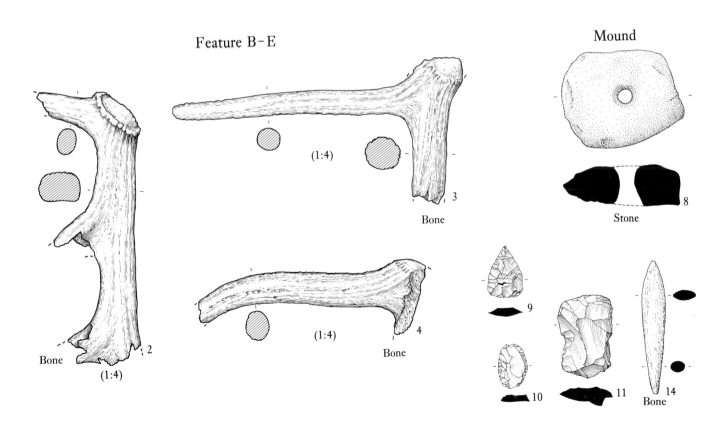

(1:4)

3

Bone

Bone

2

(1:4)

(1:4)

Bone

4

Bone

Stone

8

9

10

11

14

Bone

241 FOLKTON

Burial 2

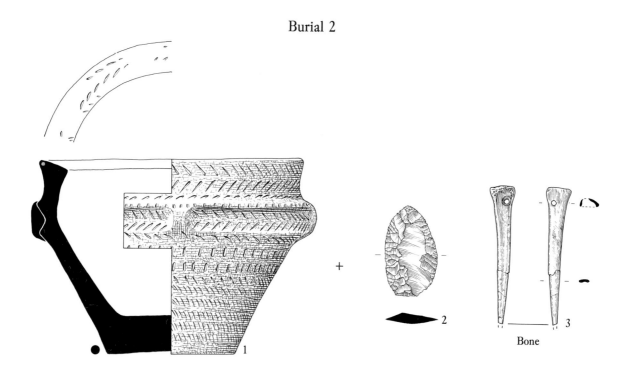

1

2

3

Bone

Mound 1967

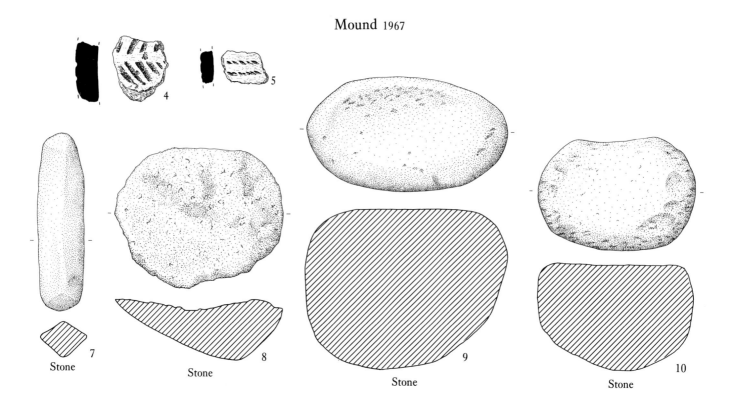

4

5

7

Stone

8

Stone

9

Stone

10

Stone

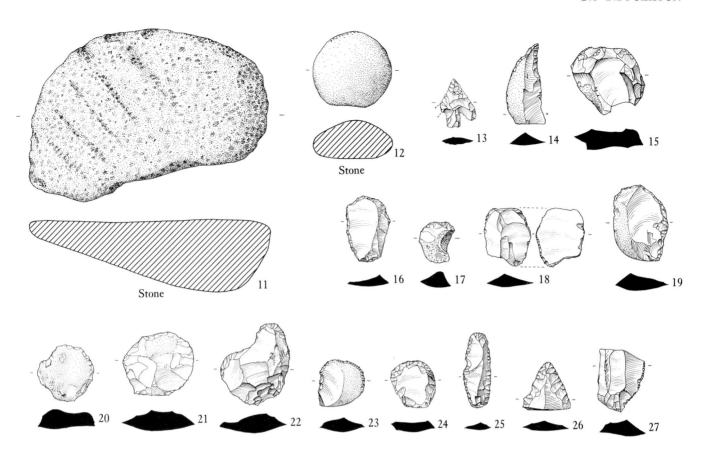

Stone 11

Stone 12

242 FOLKTON

Burial 1

Burial 2

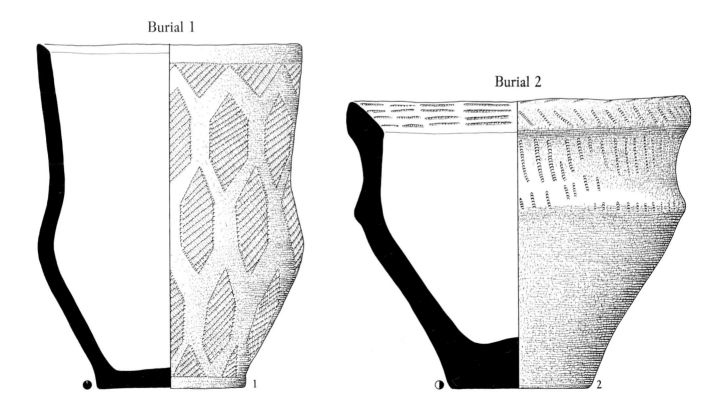

1

2

Burial 6

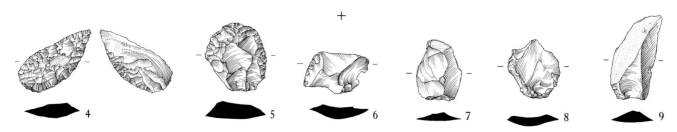

243 FOLKTON

Burial 1

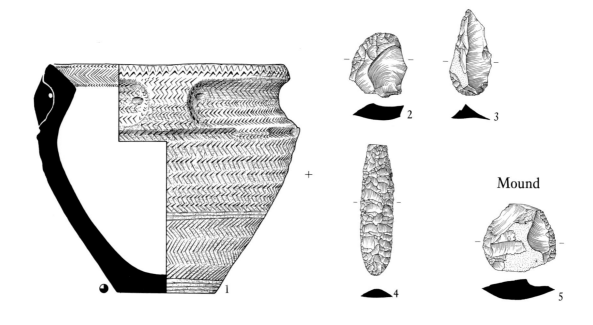

Mound

244 FOLKTON

Burial 2

245 FOLKTON

The chalk drums from Folkton (245:1–3).

Burial 1

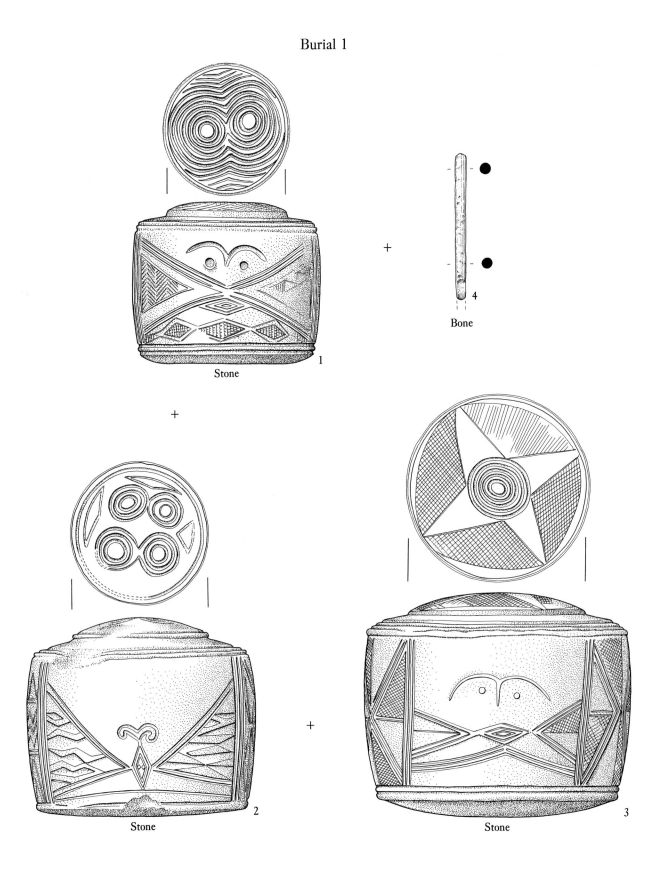

Stone 1

Bone 4

Stone 2

Stone 3

(3:8)

Burial 7

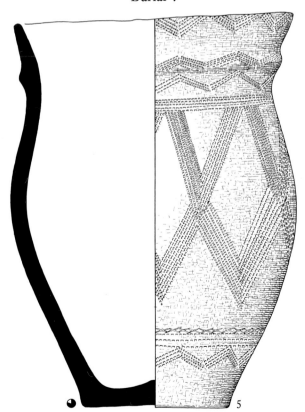

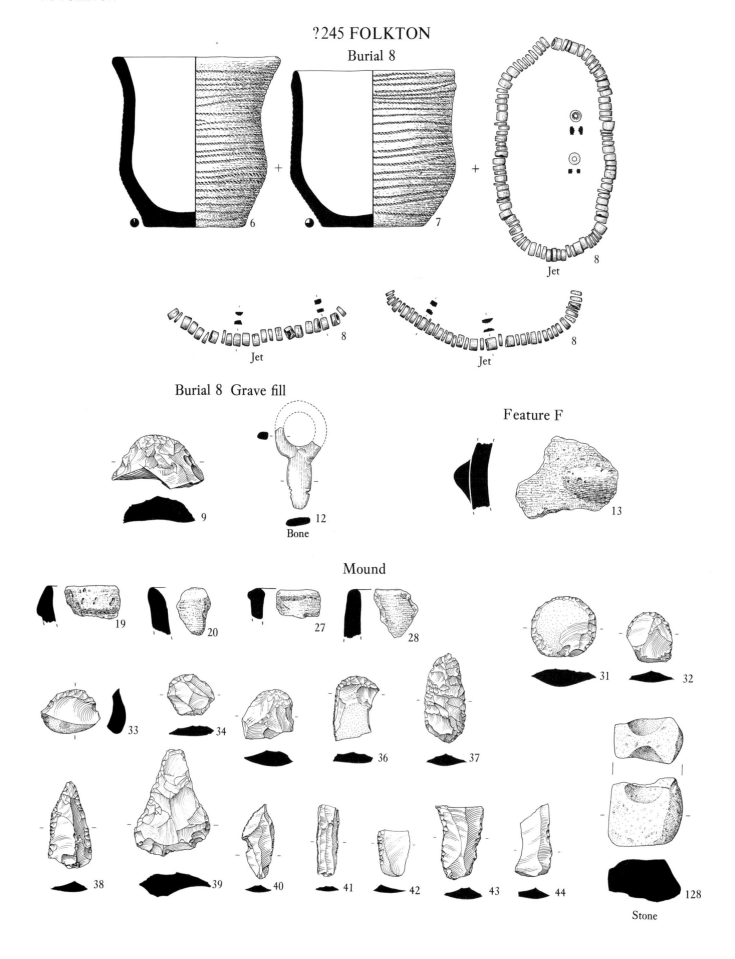

?245 FOLKTON
Burial 8

6 + 7 + 8
Jet

8
Jet

8
Jet

Burial 8 Grave fill

9

12
Bone

Feature F

13

Mound

19   20   27   28

31   32

33   34   36   37

38   39   40   41   42   43   44   128

Stone

247 FOLKTON

Burial 1

Mound

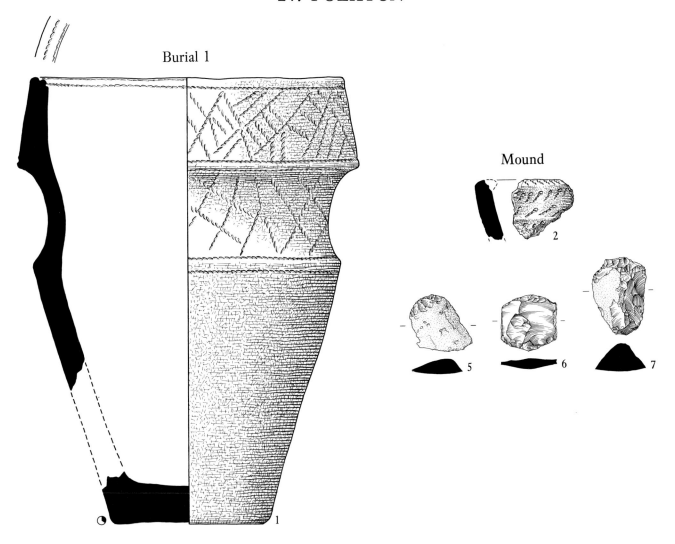

250 HUNMANBY

Burial 1

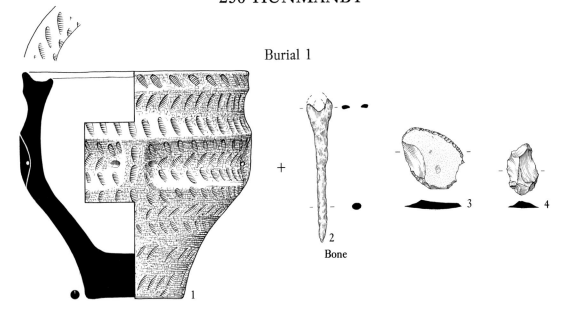

Bone

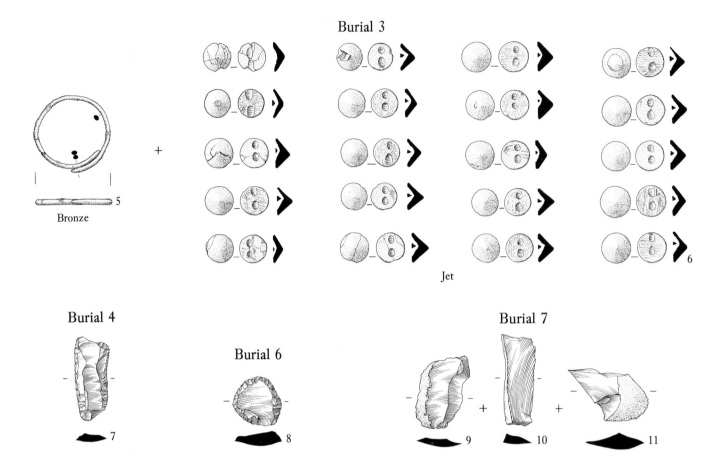

Burial 3

+

Bronze

5

Jet

6

Burial 4

7

Burial 6

8

Burial 7

9 + 10 + 11

253 BEMPTON

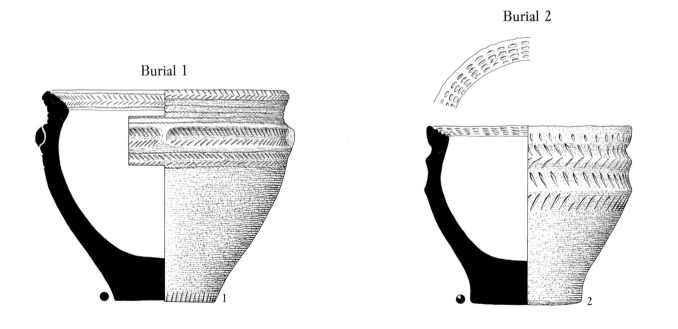

Burial 1

Burial 2

1

2

Mound

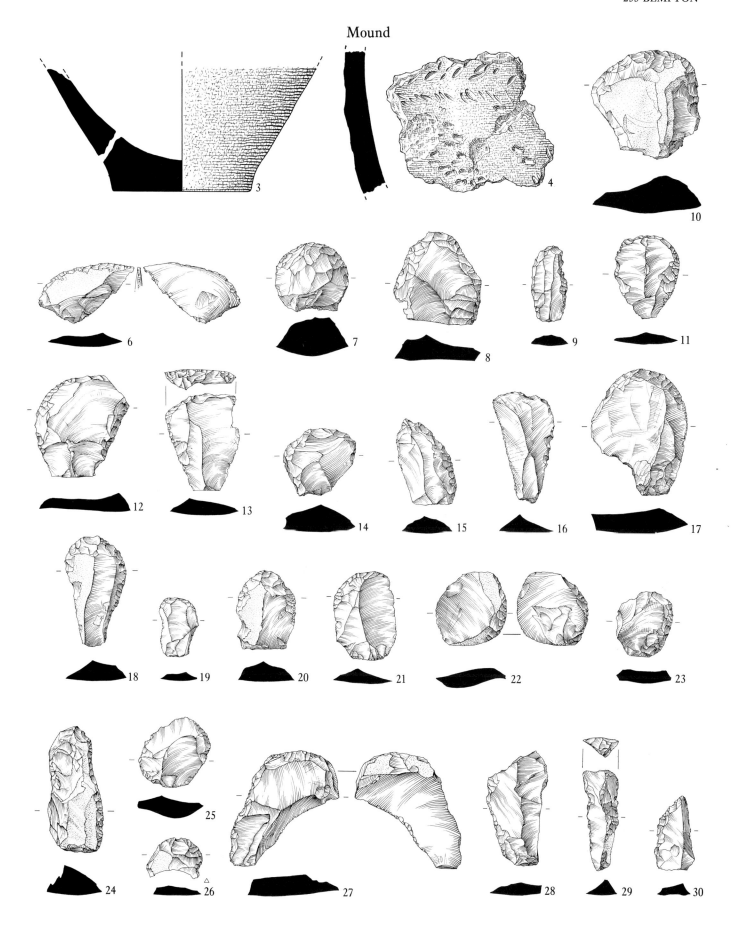

254 HARPHAM

Mound

Burial 1

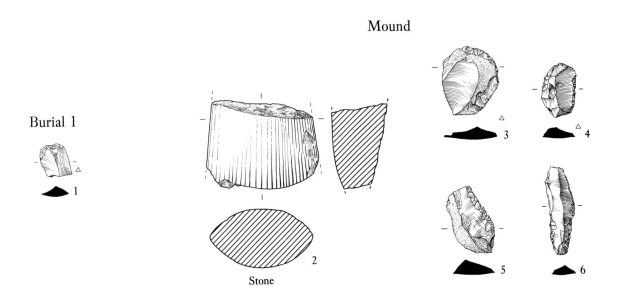

Stone

255 BISHOP BURTON

Burial 2

Burial 3

Burial 1

Backfill

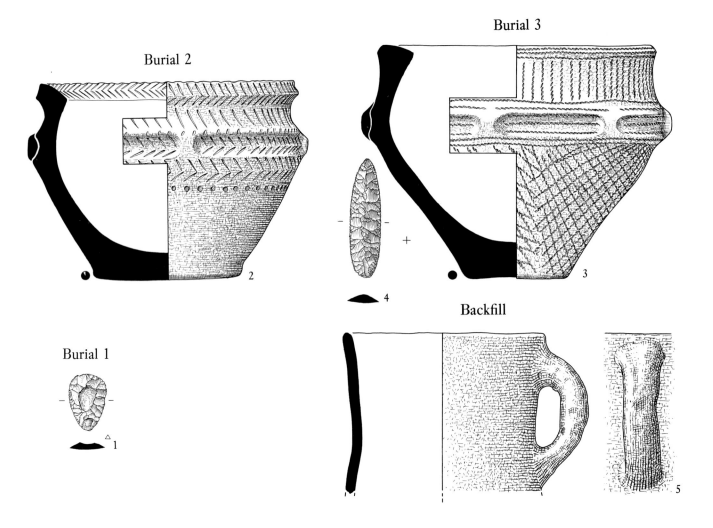

256 BISHOP BURTON

Burial 3   Burial 4   Mound

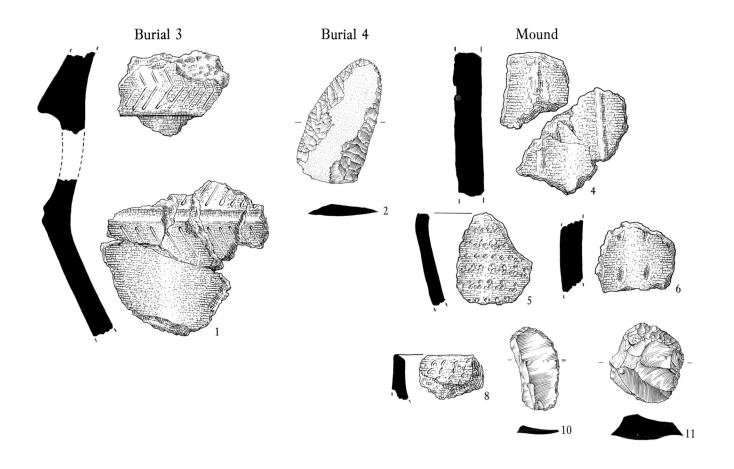

257 BISHOP BURTON

Burial 1   Burial 3

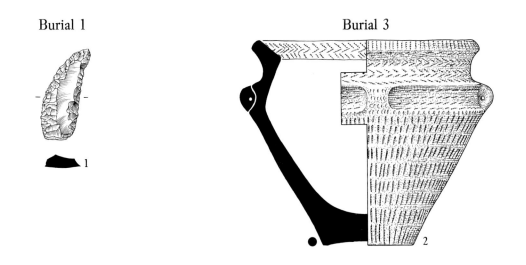

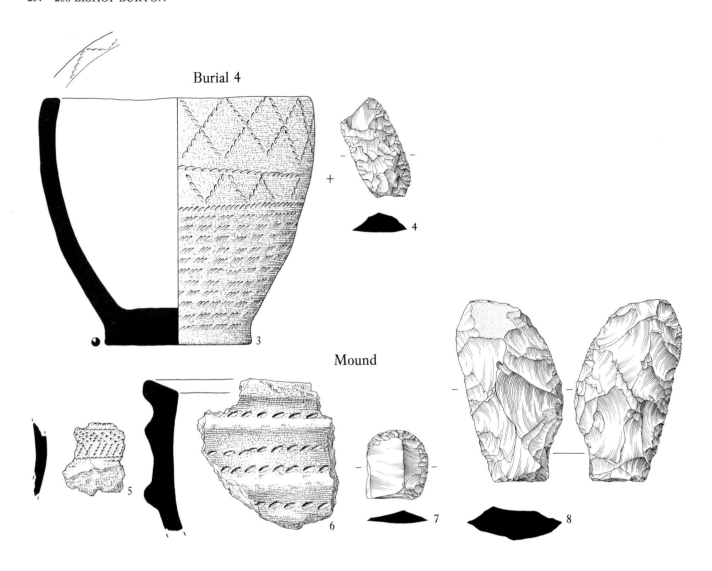

Burial 4

Mound

258 BISHOP BURTON

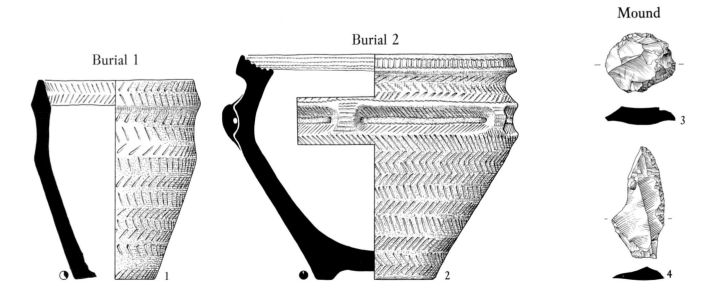

Burial 1

Burial 2

Mound

259 BISHOP BURTON

Mound

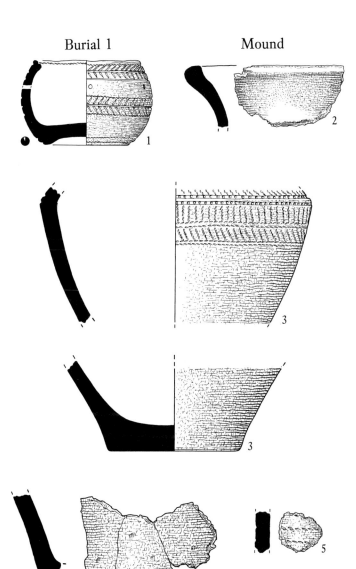

261 BISHOP BURTON

Mound

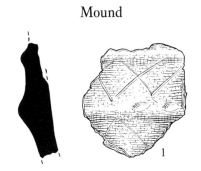

262 BISHOP BURTON

Burial 1

Mound

265 BISHOP BURTON

Burial 1

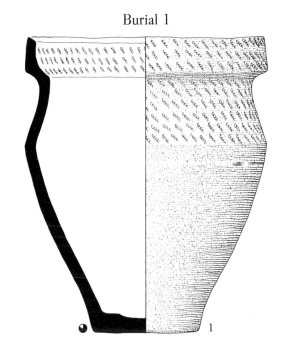

Burial 2   Mound

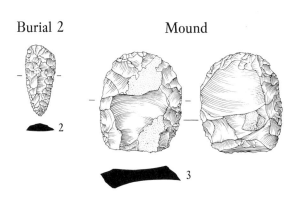

268 FYLINGDALES

271 FYLINGDALES

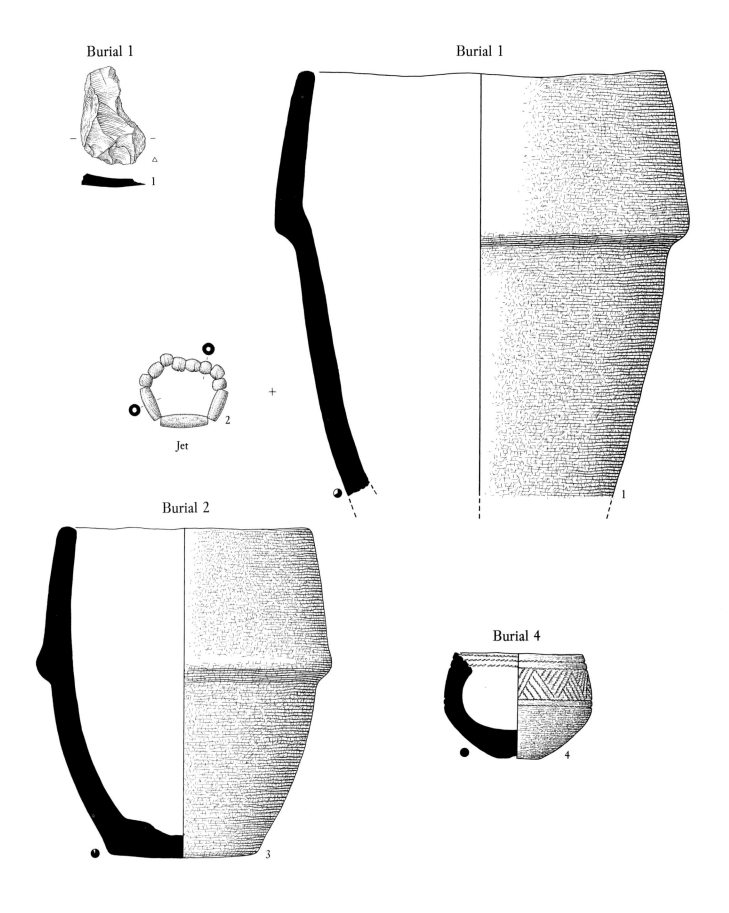

Burial 1

Burial 1

Jet

Burial 2

Burial 4

274 LYTHE

Burial 1

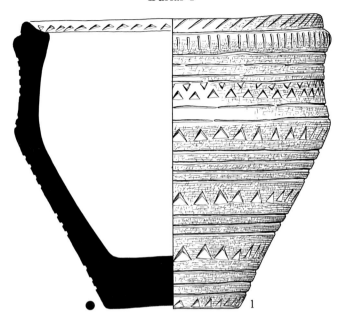

1

Mound

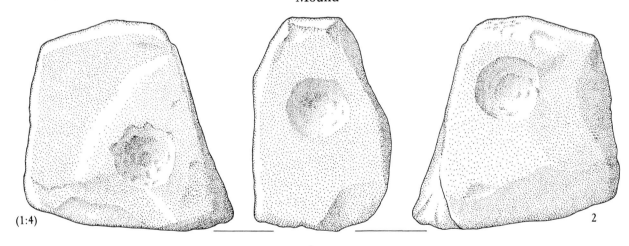

(1:4)

2

Stone

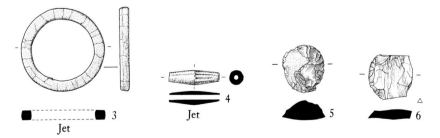

3

Jet

4

Jet

5

6

276 ALDBOURNE

Burial 3

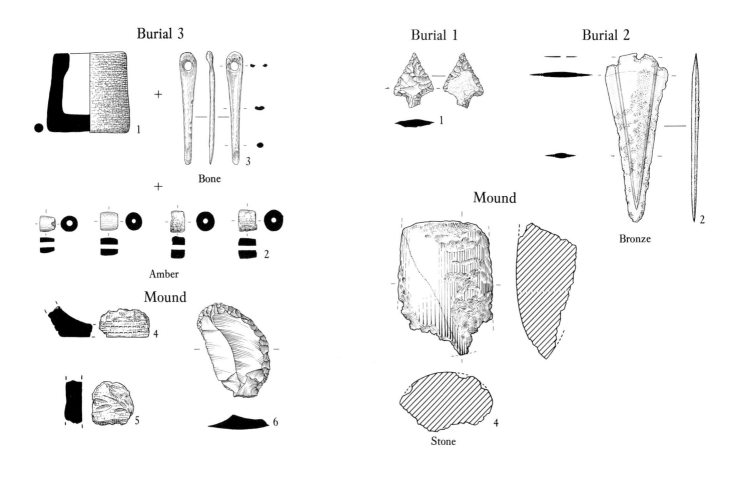

1

+

3

Bone

+

2

Amber

Mound

4

5

6

277 ALDBOURNE

Burial 1

1

Burial 2

2

Bronze

Mound

4

Stone

278 ALDBOURNE

Burial 1

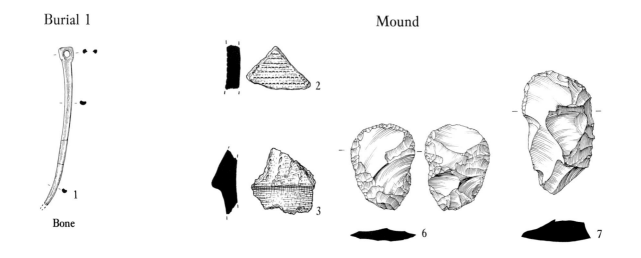

1

Bone

Mound

2

3

6

7

279 ALDBOURNE

Burial 3

1

280 ALDBOURNE

Burial 1

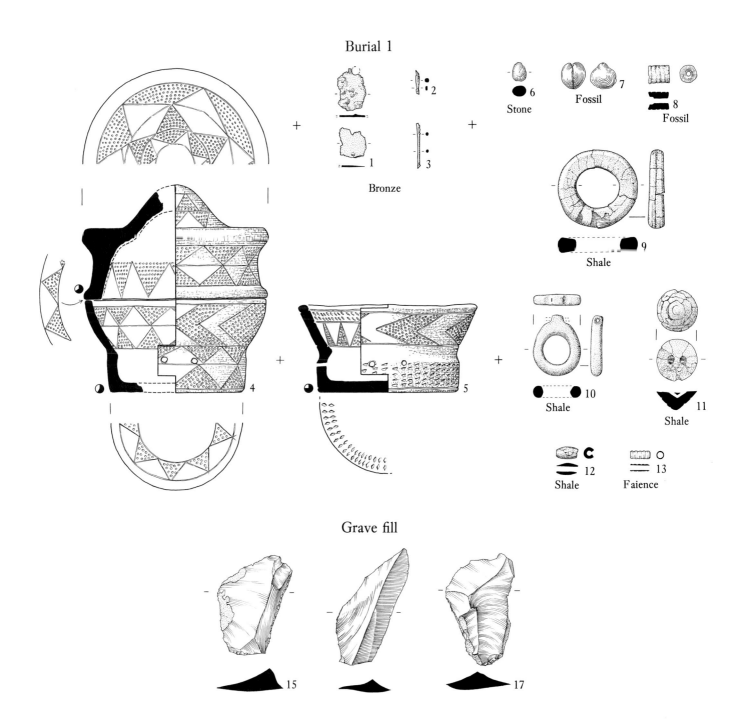

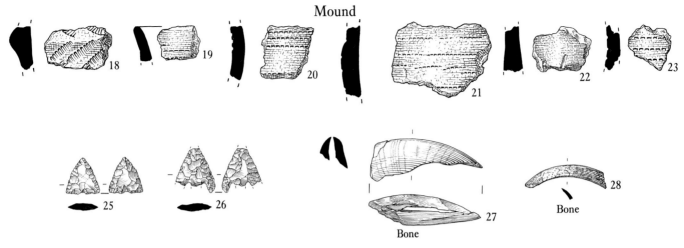

Mound

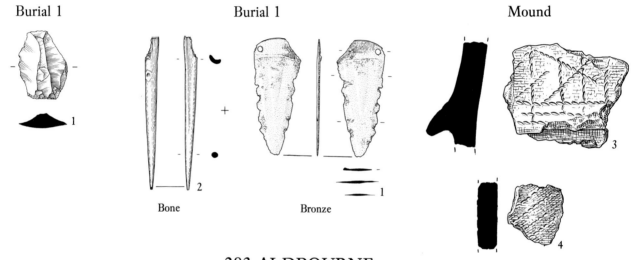

281 ALDBOURNE

282 ALDBOURNE

Bone

Bone

Bone

283 ALDBOURNE

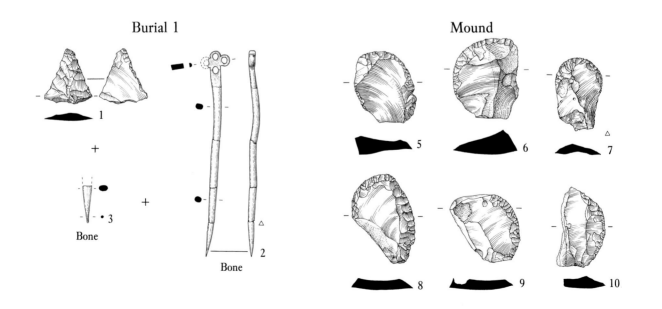

Burial 1

Burial 1

Mound

Bone

Bone

Bronze

Burial 1

Mound

Bone

Bone

284 ALDBOURNE

Burial 1

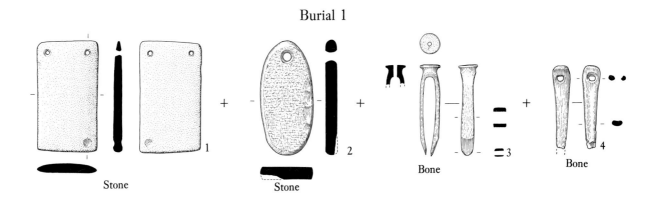

Stone 1

Stone 2

Bone 3

Bone 4

285 ALDBOURNE

Burial 1

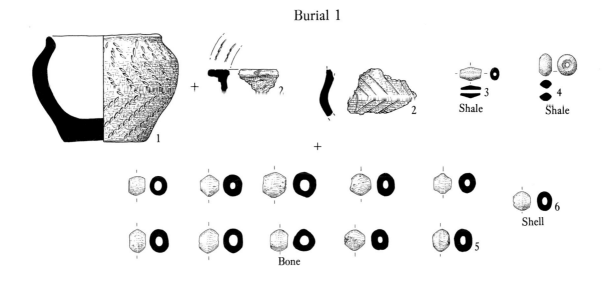

1

2

Shale 3

Shale 4

Bone 5

Shell 6

286 ALDBOURNE

Burial 1

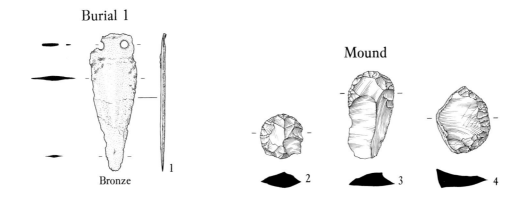

Bronze 1

Mound

2

3

4

287 HINTON

Burial 1

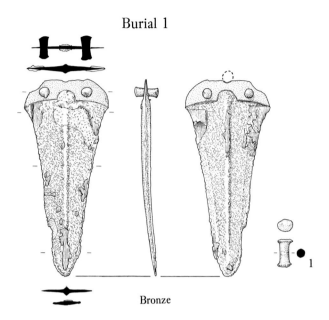

Bronze

1

289 LAMBOURN

Burial 1

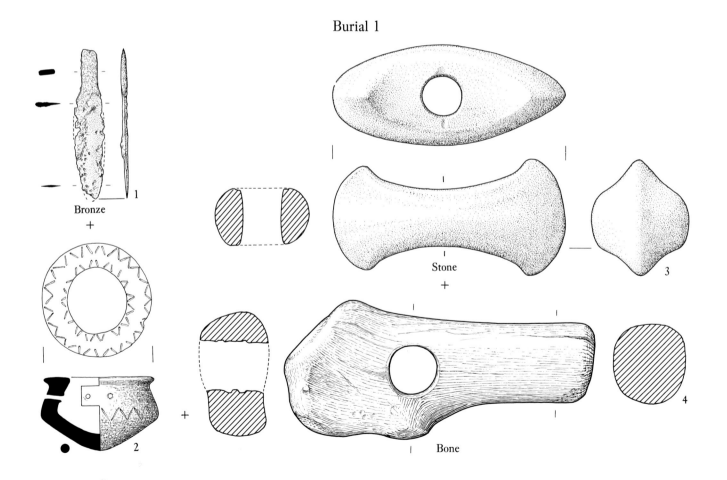

Bronze

+

Stone

+

Bone

2

3

4

Old surface

Mound

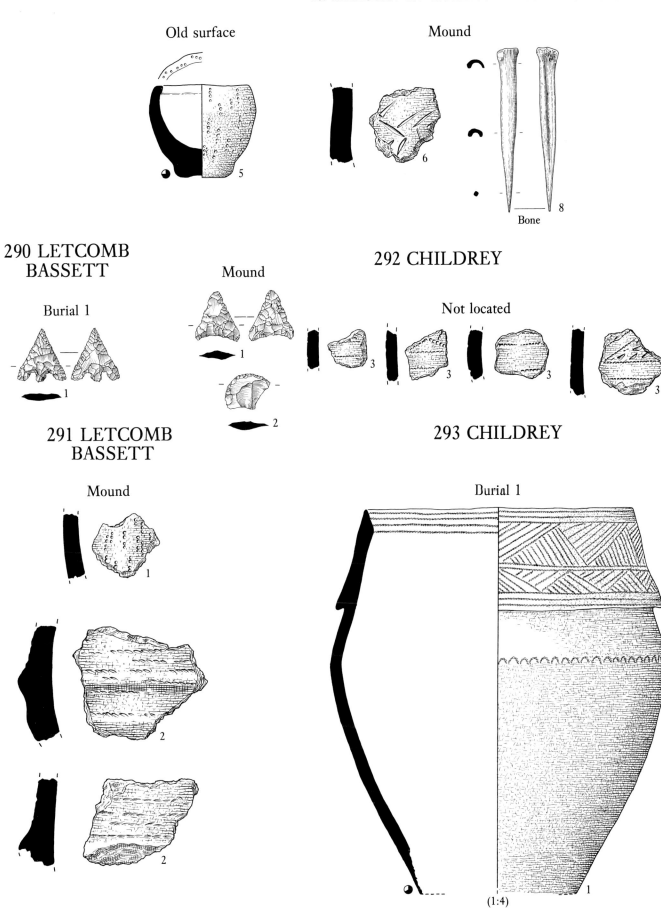

Bone

290 LETCOMB BASSETT

Burial 1

292 CHILDREY

Mound

Not located

291 LETCOMB BASSETT

293 CHILDREY

Mound

Durial 1

(1:4)

296 WARKWORTH

Burial 1

1

Bronze

Burial 5

Burial 9

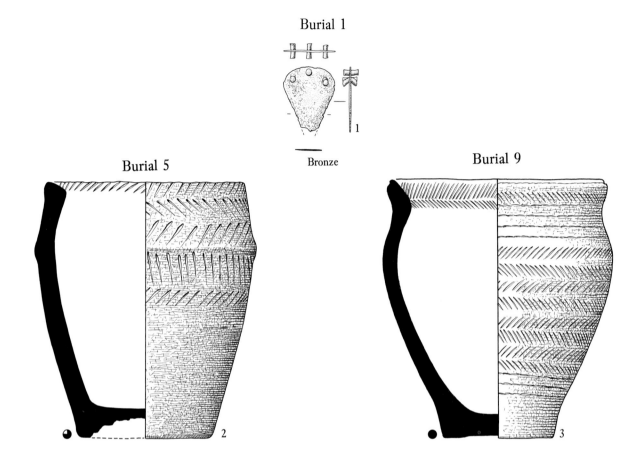

2

3

297 SNOWSHILL

Burial 1

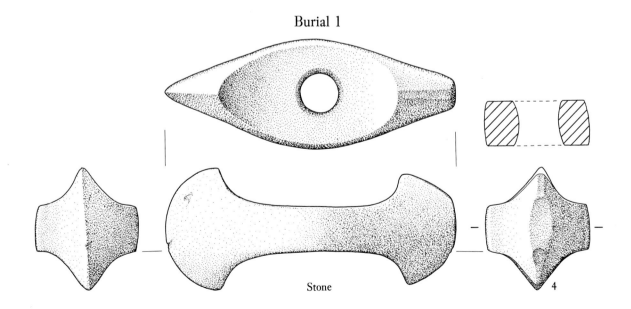

Stone

4

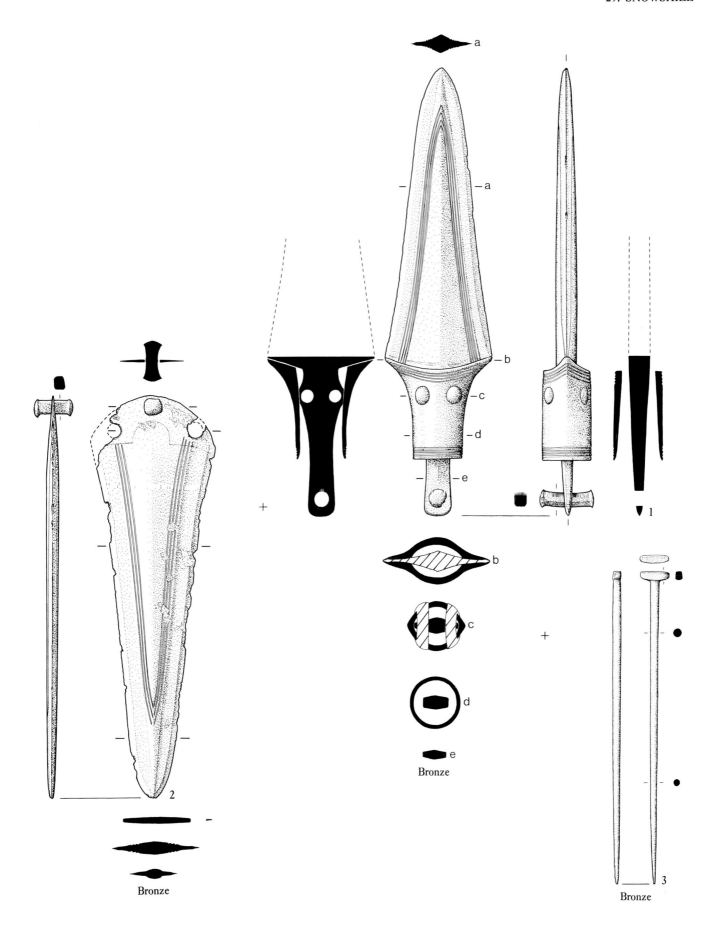

Bronze

Bronze

Bronze

UNNUMBERED BARROWS
DISTRIBUTION MAP

0   50   100 KM

BERKSHIRE, ROWCROFT UN. 1

BERKSHIRE, WYTHAM UN. 2

Burial 1

Burial 1

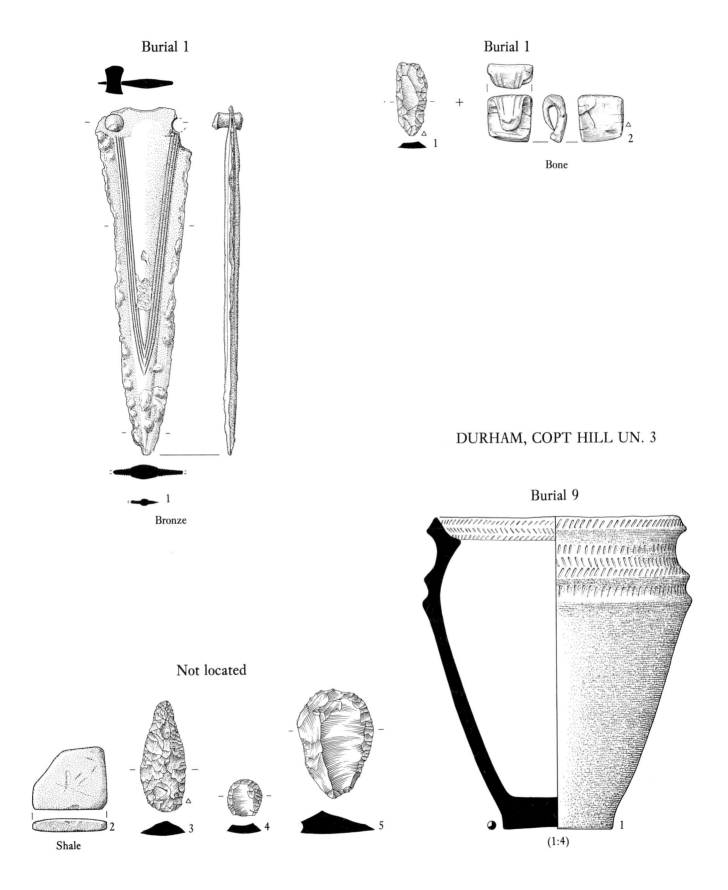

Bone

DURHAM, COPT HILL UN. 3

Bronze

Burial 9

Not located

Shale

(1:4)

DURHAM, SACRISTON UN. 4

Burial 1

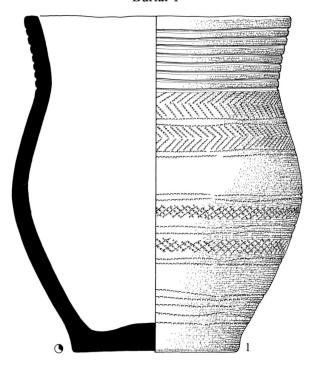

1

DURHAM, STONEBRIDGE UN. 6

Burial 1

Burial 2

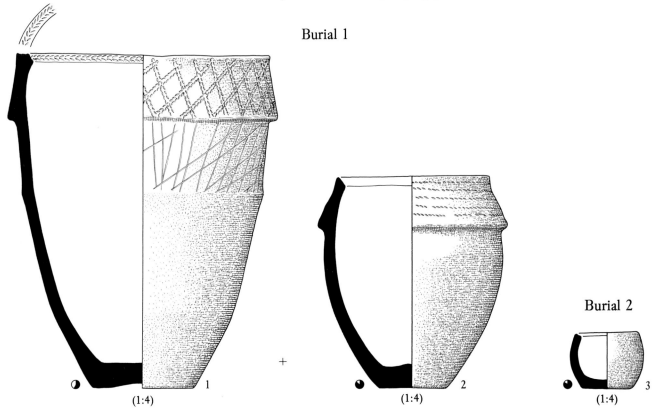

1
(1:4)

2
(1:4)

3
(1:4)

DURHAM, TRIMDON GRANGE UN. 7

Not located

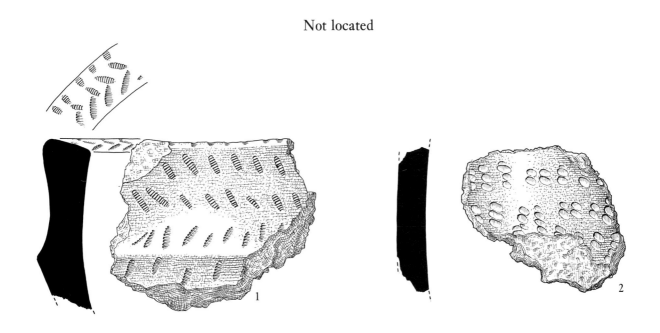

LANCASHIRE, ULVERSTON UN. 8

Burial 1

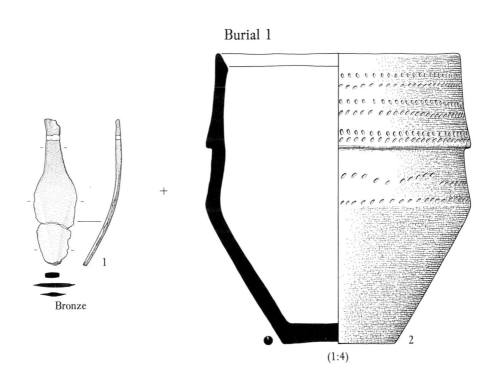

Bronze

(1:4)

Burial 2

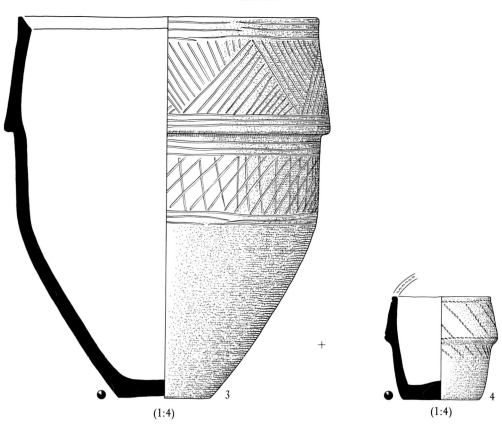

(1:4) 3

(1:4) 4

LINCOLNSHIRE, DENTON UN. 9

Burial 1

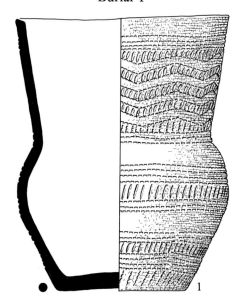

1

NORTHUMBERLAND, ALWINTON UN. 10

Burial 2

Burial 1

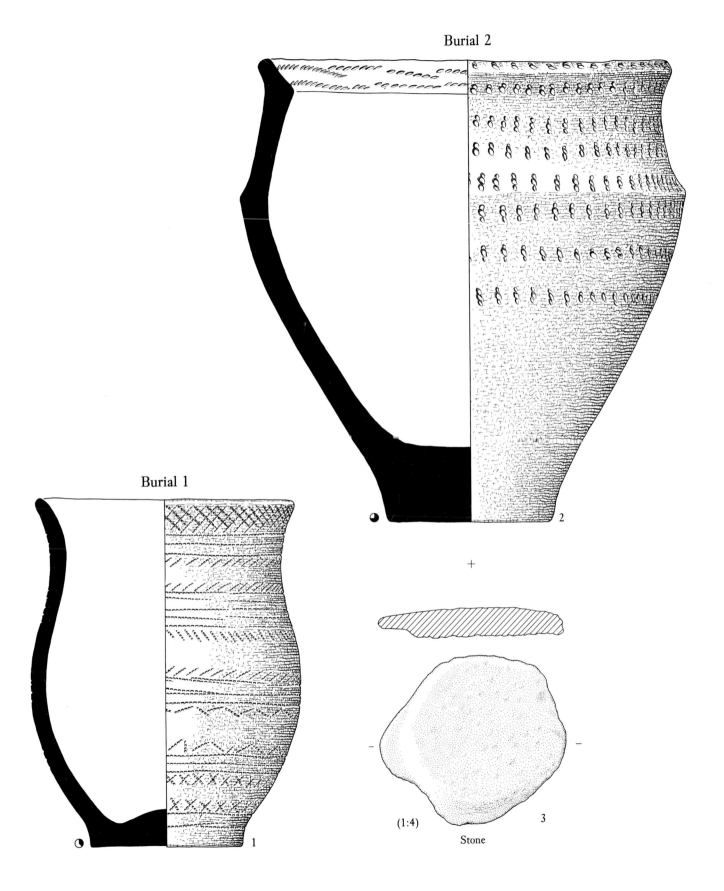

1

2

3

(1:4)

Stone

NORTHUMBERLAND, ANCROFT UN. 11

NORTHUMBERLAND, BEWICK MOOR UN. 12

Burial 1

Not located

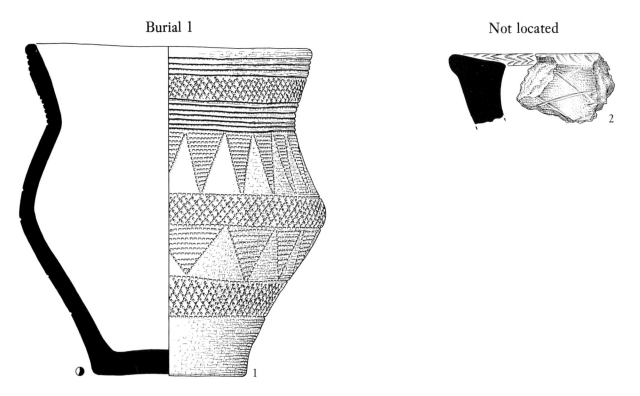

NORTHUMBERLAND, BLUEBELL INN UN. 13

Burial 1

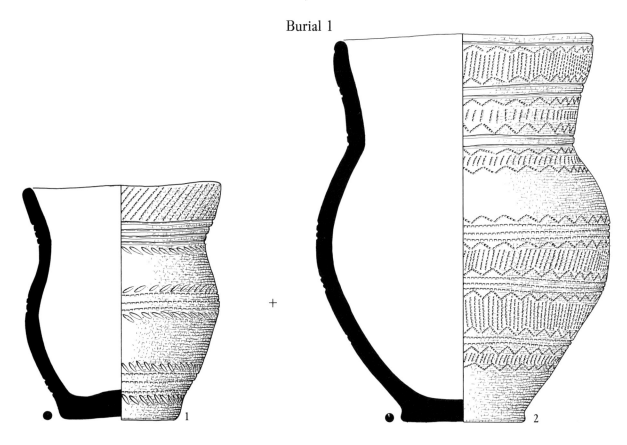

NORTHUMBERLAND, BROOMRIDGE 2 UN. 15

Burial 1

Not located

NORTHUMBERLAND, CHESWICK UN. 16

Burial 1

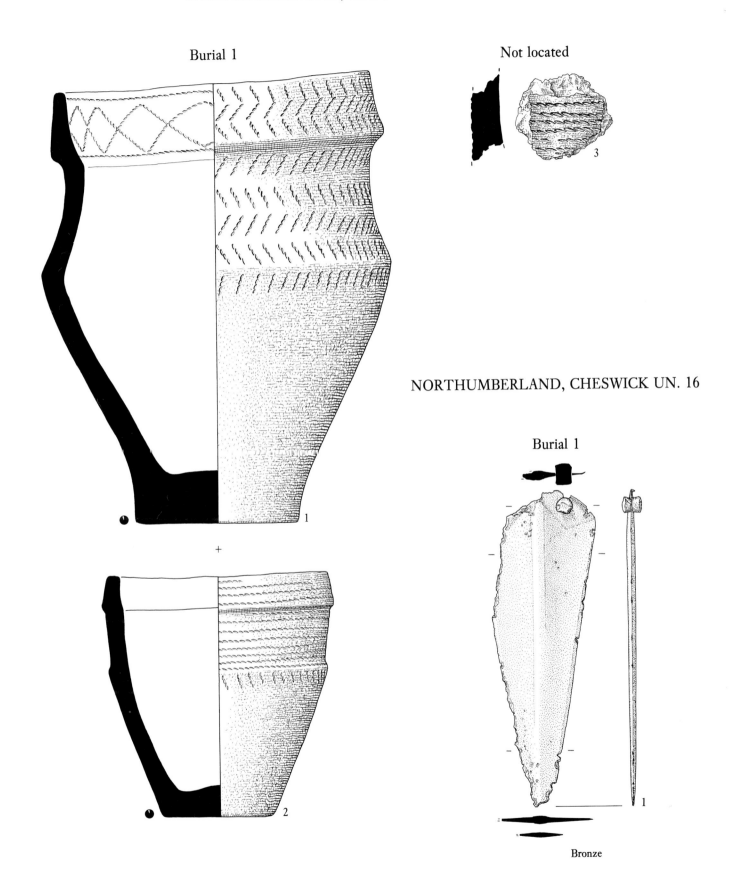

Bronze

NORTHUMBERLAND, CROOKHAM UN. 17

NORTHUMBERLAND, CROOKHAVEN UN. 18

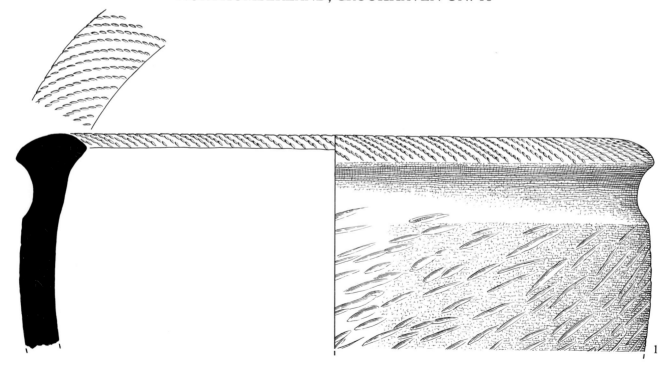

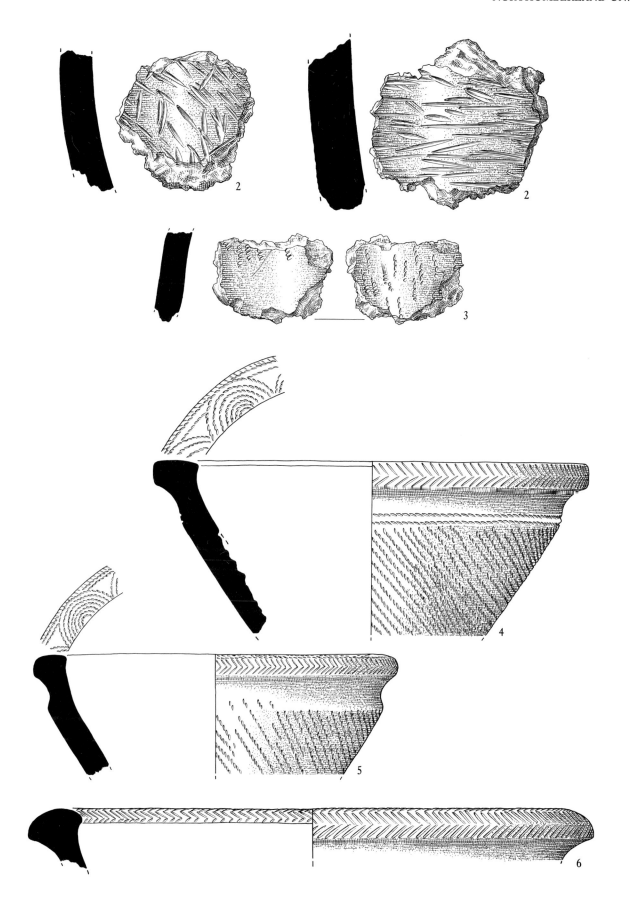

NORTHUMBERLAND, DODDINGTON MOOR UN. 19

Not located

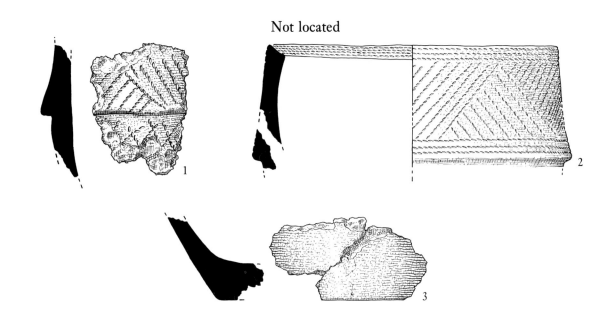

NORTHUMBERLAND, FORD UN. 20

Not located

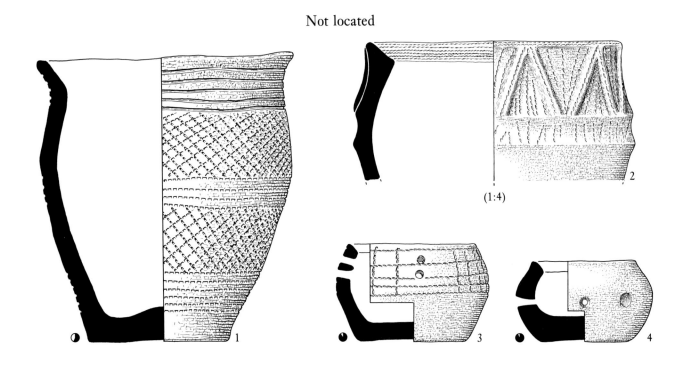

(1:4)

NORTHUMBERLAND, FOWBERRY UN. 21

Burial 1

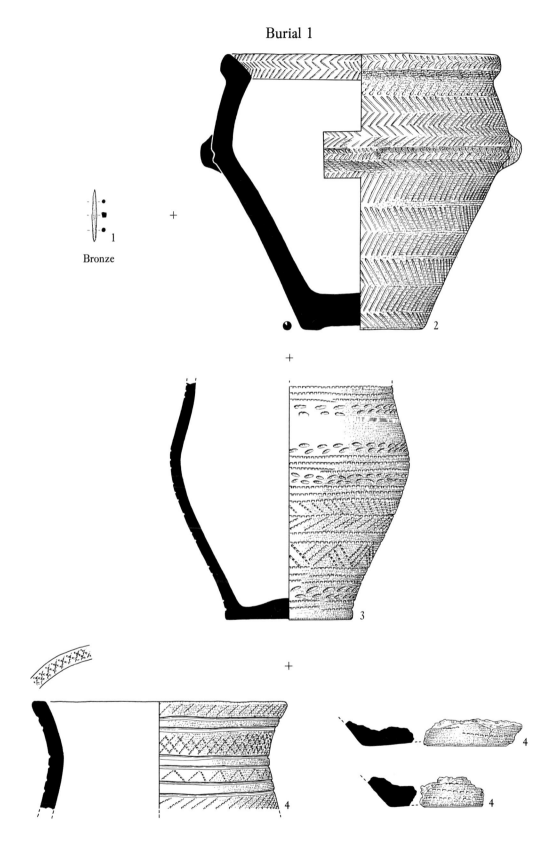

Bronze

NORTHUMBERLAND, GREAT TOSSON UN. 22

Burial 1

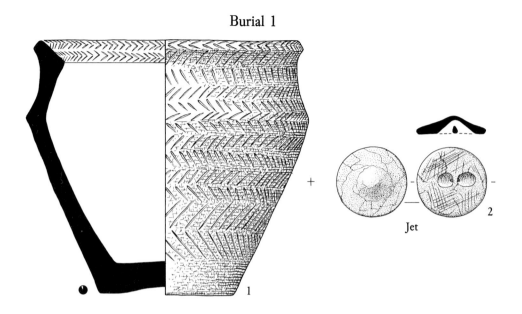

Jet

1

2

Burial 2

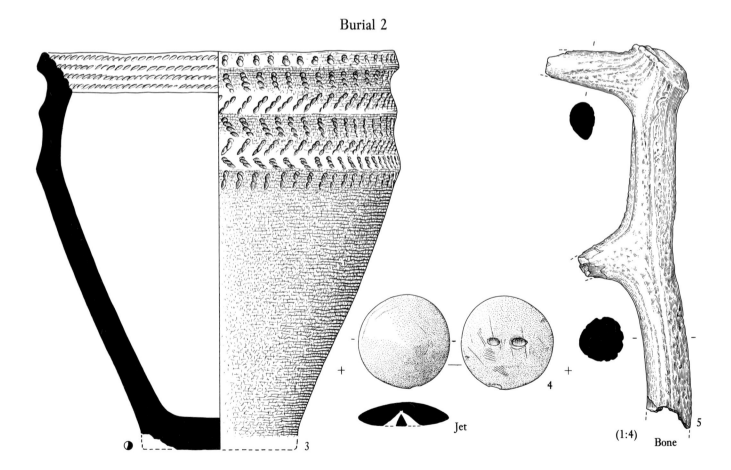

Jet

3

4

(1:4)

Bone

5

NORTHUMBERLAND, GREENHILL UN. 23

NORTHUMBERLAND, GUNNERTON UN. 25

Burial 1

Burial 1

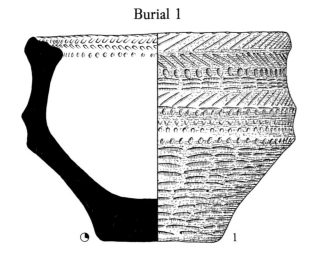

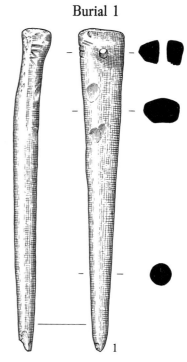

Bone

NORTHUMBERLAND, HEDLEY WOOD UN. 27

Burial 1

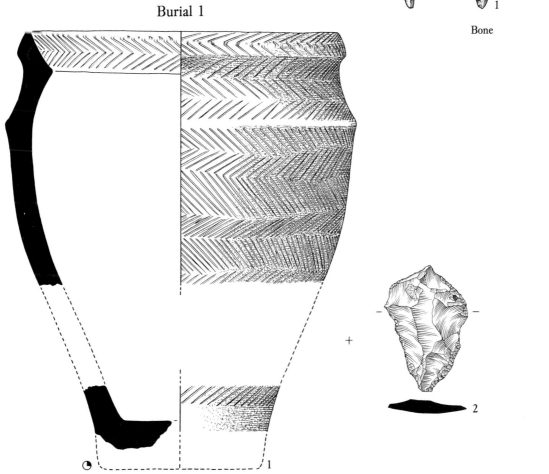

NORTHUMBERLAND, HEPPLE 1 OR FENTON UN. 28

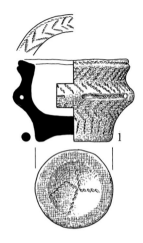

NORTHUMBERLAND, HEPPLE 2 UN. 29

Burial 1

Jet

NORTHUMBERLAND, NORHAM UN. 32

Not located

NORTHUMBERLAND, HOWBURN UN. 30

Burial 1

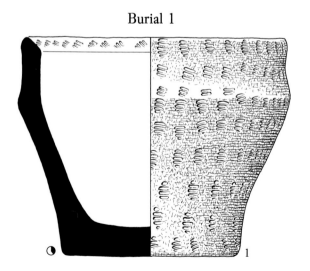

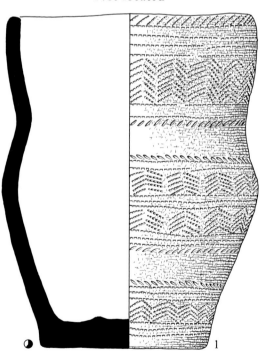

NORTHUMBERLAND, NORTH CHARLTON
UN. 33

NORTHUMBERLAND, OLD BEWICK UN. 34

Burial 2

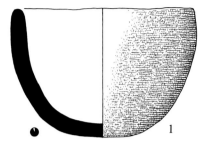

1

Bronze

NORTHUMBERLAND, OLD ROTHBURY UN. 35

Burial 1

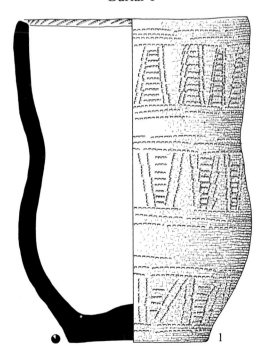

1

NORTHUMBERLAND, PLESSY MILL UN. 36

Burial 1

Burial 2

Burial 3

Burial 1–3

NORTHUMBERLAND, RATCHEUGH UN. 37

Not located

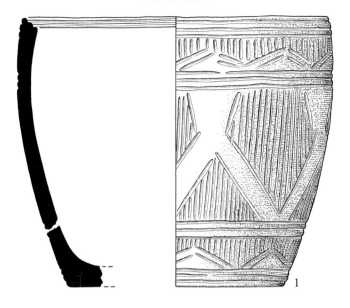

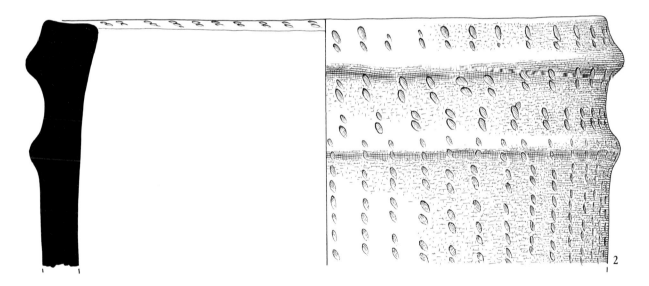

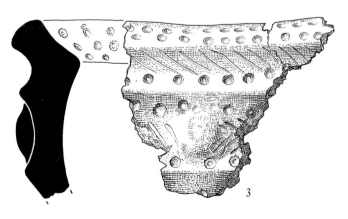

NORTHUMBERLAND, RED SCAR BRIDGE UN. 38

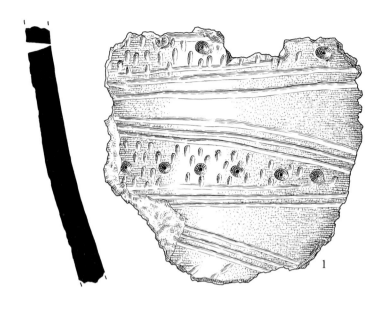

NORTHUMBERLAND, ROSEDEAN UN. 39

Burial 1   Burial 2

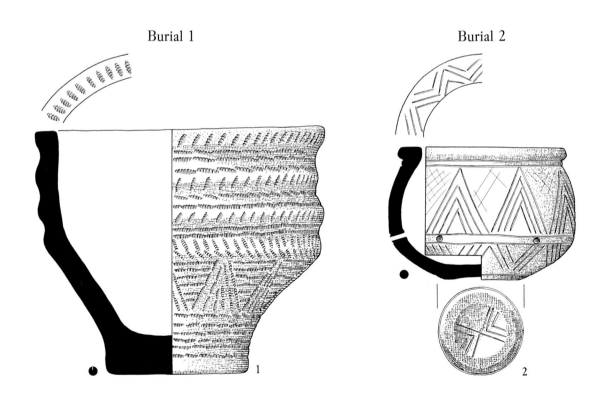

NORTHUMBERLAND, SEGHILL UN. 40

Burial 1

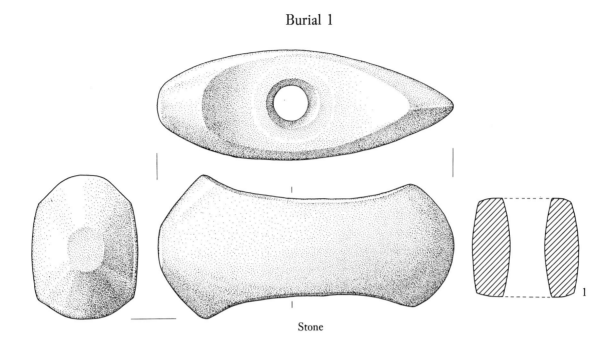

Stone

NORTHUMBERLAND, SMALESMOUTH UN. 41

Burial 1

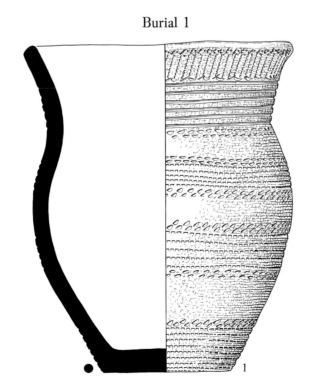

NORTHUMBERLAND, SPINDLESTON UN. 42

Not located

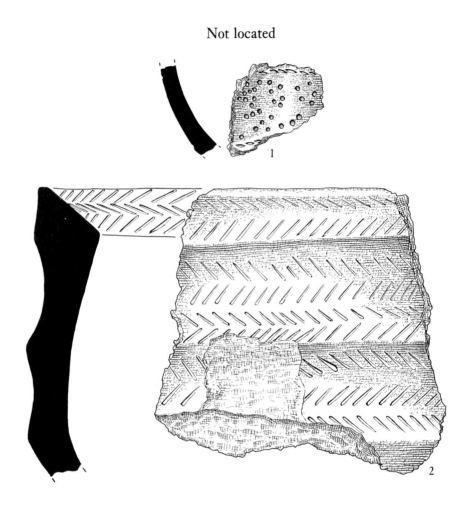

NORTHUMBERLAND, TANTALLON'S GRAVE UN. 43

Not located

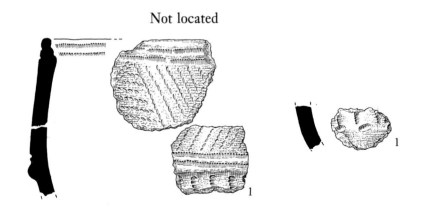

NORTHUMBERLAND, WARKSHAUGH UN. 44

Burial 1

Burial 2

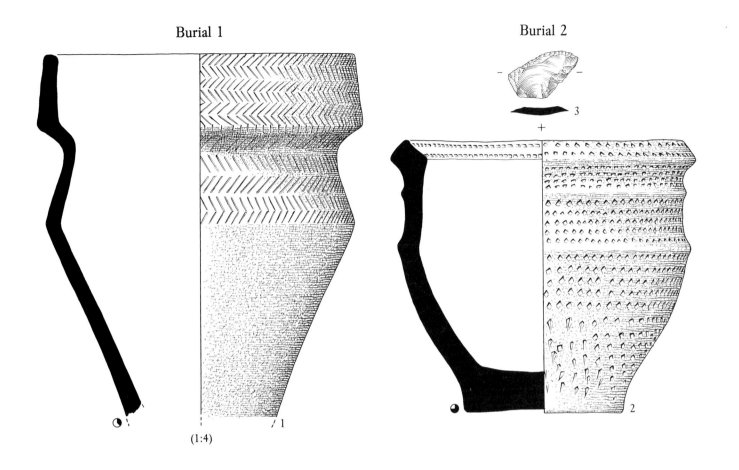

(1:4)

NORTHUMBERLAND, WHITTINGHAM UN. 45

Not located

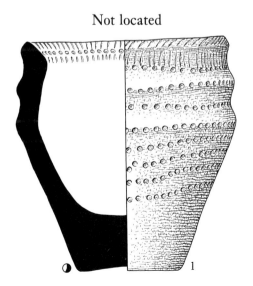

NORTHUMBERLAND, WOODHORN UN. 46

Burial 1

1

NORTHUMBERLAND, WOOLER UN. 47

Burial 1

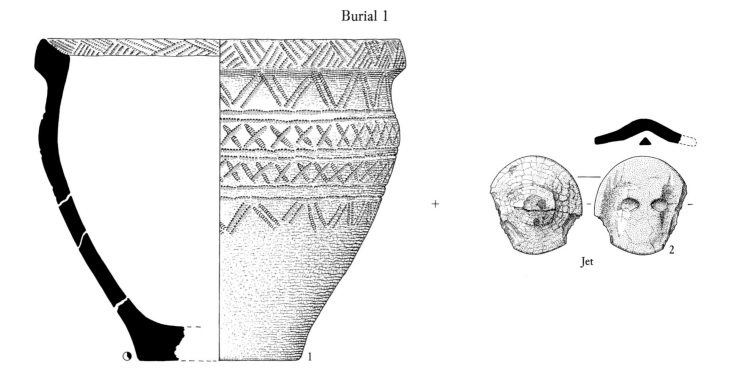

1

+

Jet

2

OXFORDSHIRE, SUMMERTOWN UN. 48

Burial 1

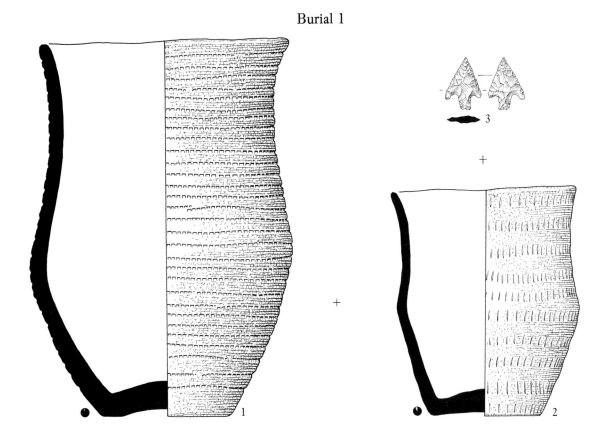

OXFORDSHIRE, YARNTON UN. 49

Burial 1

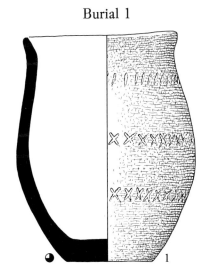

SUFFOLK, AMPTON UN. 50

Burial 4

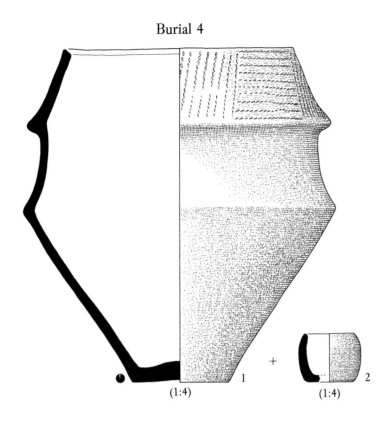

1 (1:4)

+

2 (1:4)

SUFFOLK, BARTON HILLS UN. 51

Mound

1

SUFFOLK, RISBY 1 UN. 54

Mound 1959

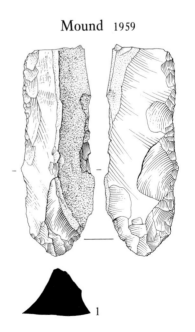

1

SUFFOLK, RISBY 2 UN. 55

Mound 1959

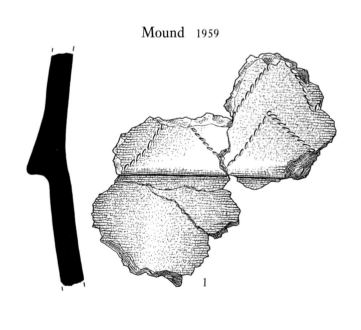

1

SUFFOLK, TUDDENHAM UN. 56

Not located

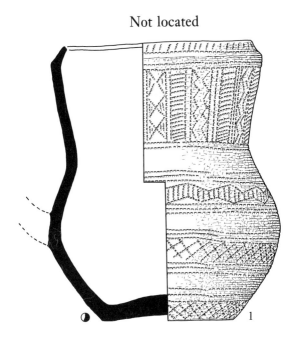

SUFFOLK, UNDLEY BARROW UN. 57

Not located

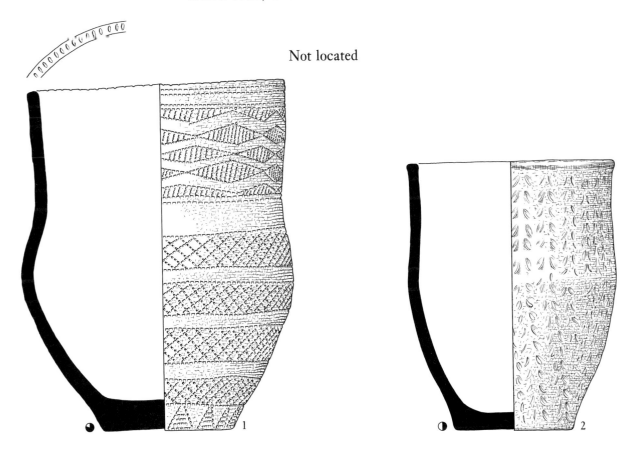

SUFFOLK, WARREN HILL UN. 58

Not located

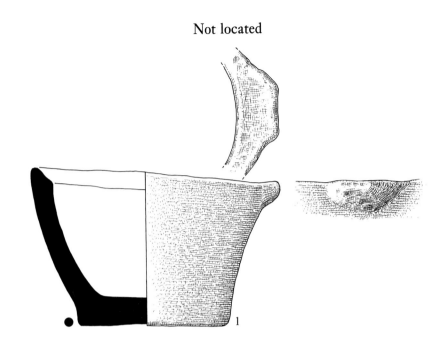

SUSSEX, CISSBURY UN. 59

Burial 1

WILTSHIRE, ALDBOURNE UN. 61

Not located

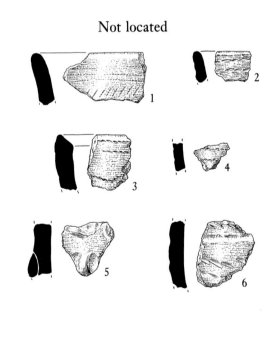

WILTSHIRE, WINTERBOURNE STOKE 1 UN. 63

Burial 1

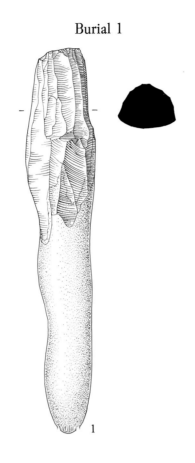

1

Burial 2

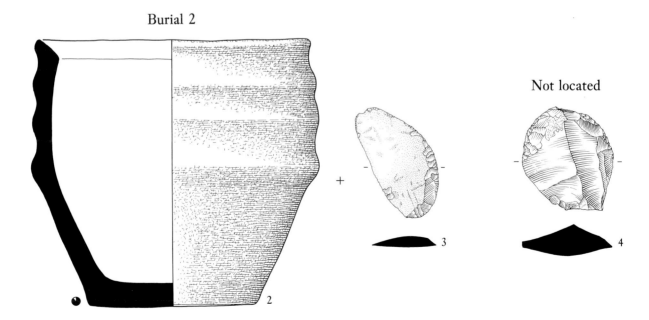

Not located

2

+

3

4

YORKSHIRE E.R., ARRAS UN. 64

Burial 1

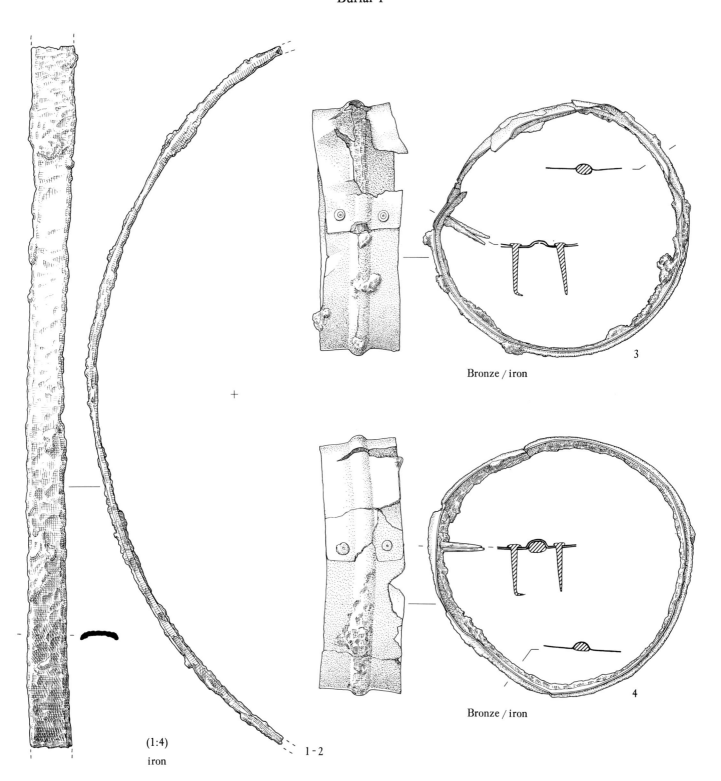

Bronze / iron

3

Bronze / iron

4

(1:4)
iron

1 - 2

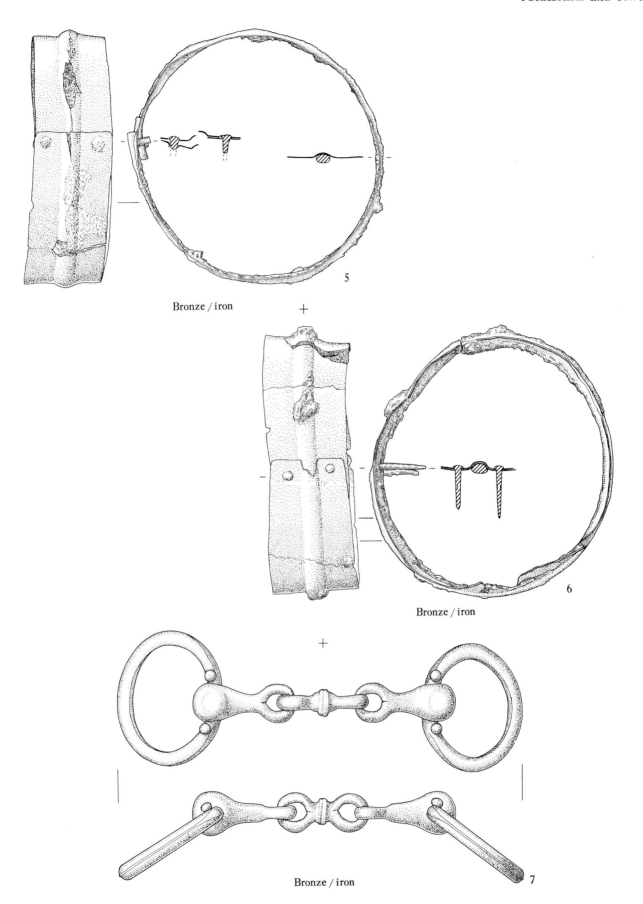

Bronze / iron

5

Bronze / iron

6

Bronze / iron

7

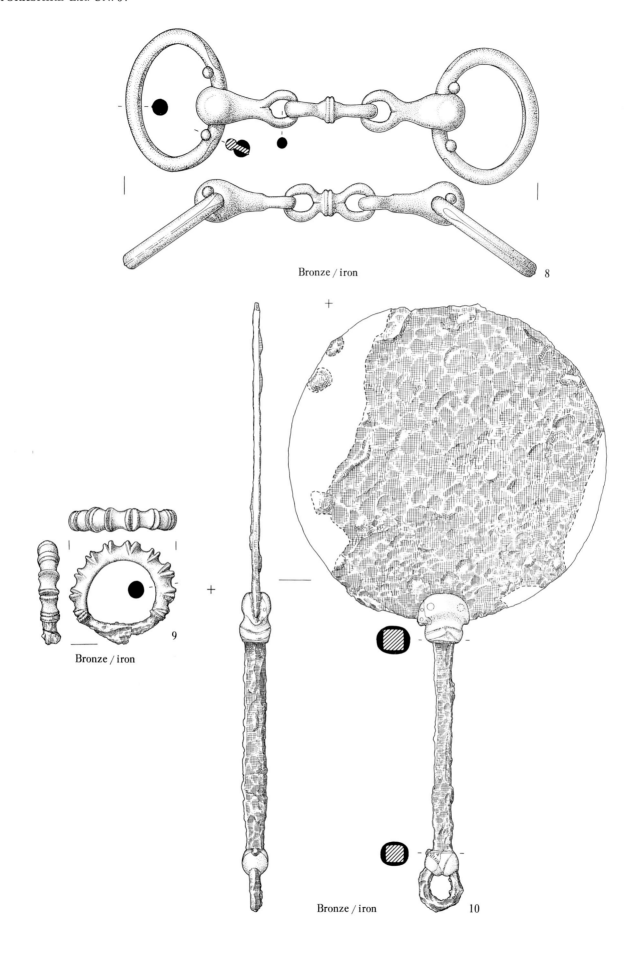

Bronze / iron   8

Bronze / iron   9

Bronze / iron   10

YORKSHIRE E.R., BEVERLEY 1 UN.65

Burial 1

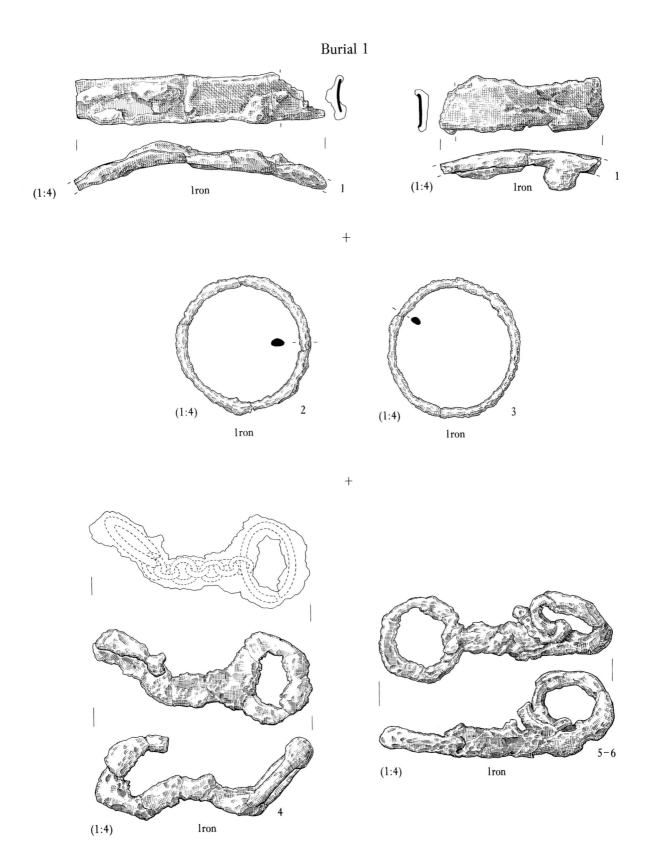

(1:4)   1ron   1

(1:4)   1ron   1

(1:4)   1ron   2

(1:4)   1ron   3

(1:4)   1ron   4

(1:4)   1ron   5-6

YORKSHIRE, E.R. BISHOP BURTON UN. 67

Not located

1

YORKSHIRE, E.R. BLANCH FARM UN. 68

Not located

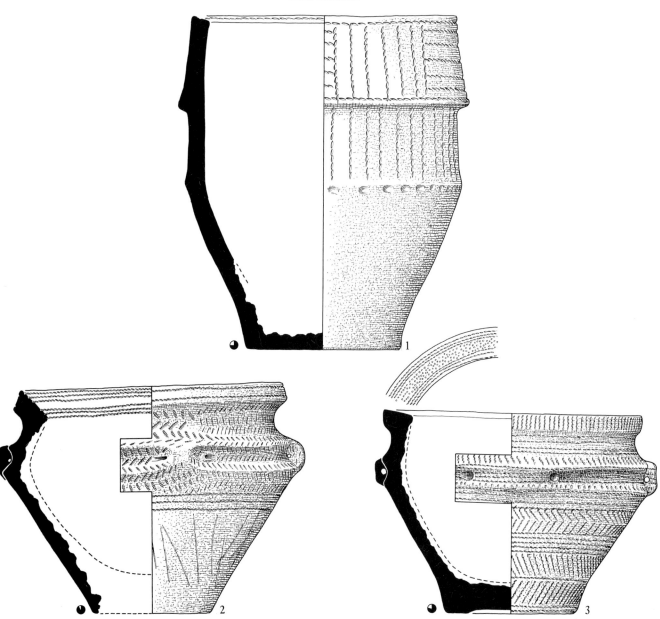

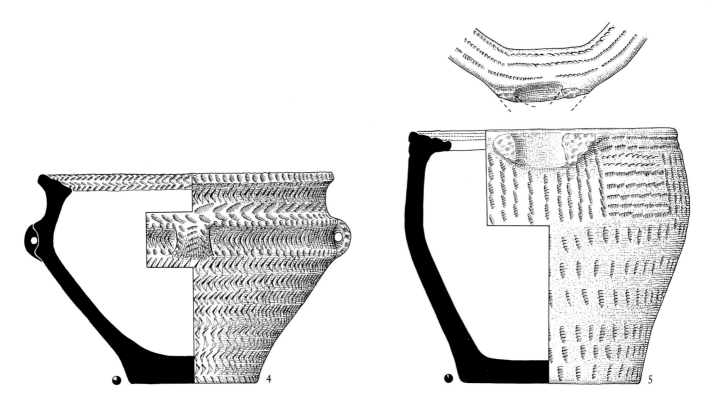

YORKSHIRE E.R., BROUGH UN. 69

Burial 1

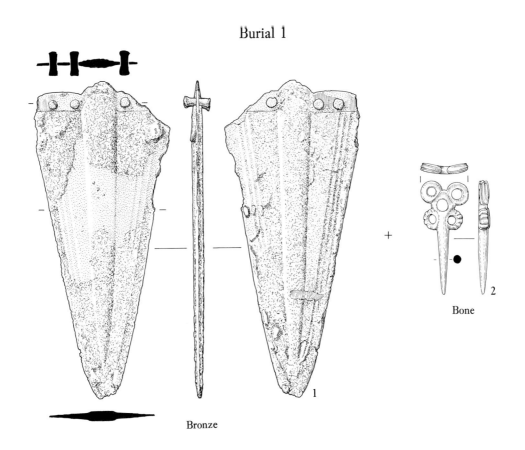

Bronze

Bone

YORKSHIRE E.R., DANES GRAVES 19 UN. 74

Burial 1

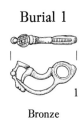

Iron

1

YORKSHIRE E.R., DANES GRAVES 48 UN. 84

Burial 1

Bronze

1

YORKSHIRE E.R., DANES GRAVES 53 UN. 85   YORKSHIRE E.R., DANES GRAVES 54 UN. 86

Burial 1   Burial 1

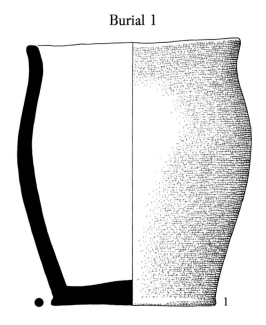

1   1

YORKSHIRE E.R., DANES GRAVES 65 UN. 87

Burial 1

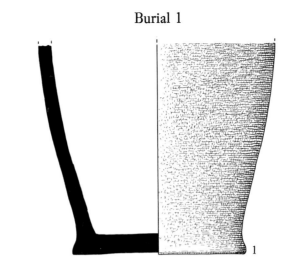

1

YORKSHIRE E.R., DANES GRAVES 70 UN. 88   YORKSHIRE E.R., DANES GRAVES 79 UN. 89

Burial 1   Burial 1

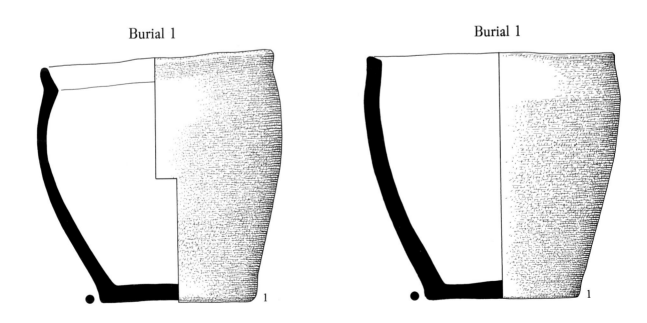

YORKSHIRE E.R., ELF HOWE UN. 90

Burial 5

Not located

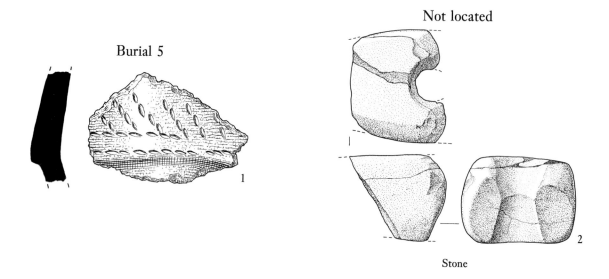

Stone

YORKSHIRE E.R., GOODMANHAM WOLD 1 UN. 93

YORKSHIRE E.R., GOODMANHAM WOLD 2 UN. 94

Burial 1

Burial 1

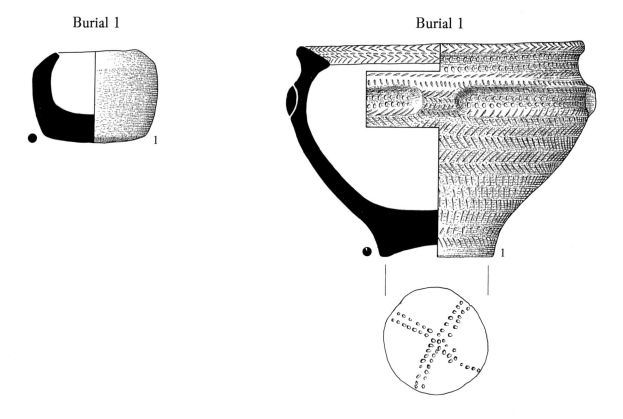

YORKSHIRE E.R., HELPERTHORPE UN. 95

Feature A

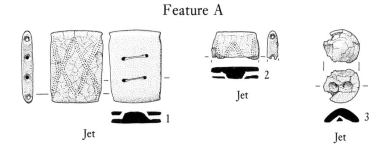

Jet

Jet

Jet

YORKSHIRE E.R., HUGGATE WOLD 1 UN. 98

Not located

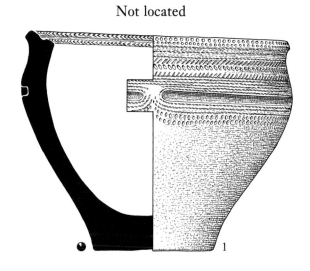

YORKSHIRE E.R., HUGGATE WOLD 2 UN. 99

Not located

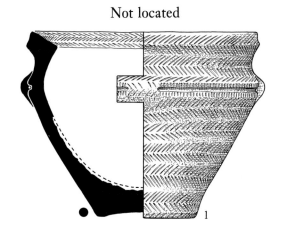

YORKSHIRE E.R., KELLEYTHORPE 1 UN. 100

Burial 1

YORKSHIRE E.R., KELLEYTHORPE 2 UN. 101

Burial 1

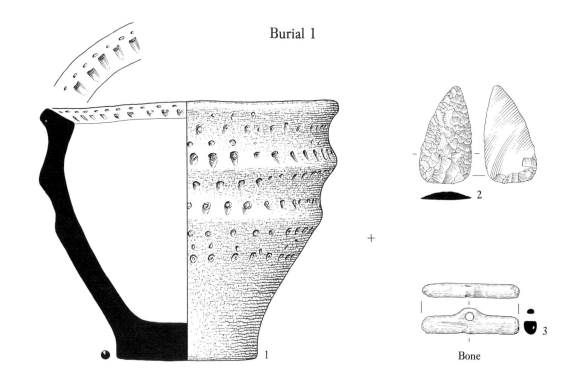

2

Bone

3

Burial 2

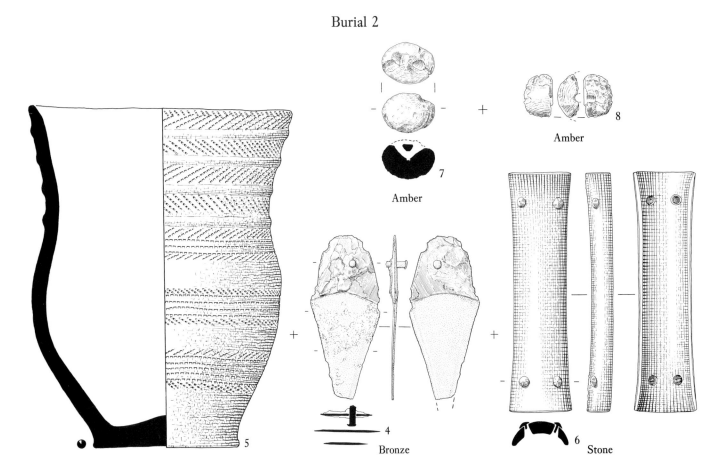

7

Amber

8

Amber

4

Bronze

6

Stone

5

YORKSHIRE E.R., LUND WARREN UN. 102

Not located

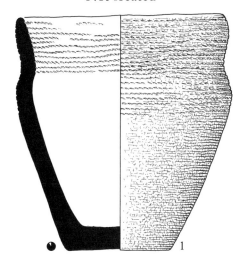

YORKSHIRE E.R., MAIDEN'S GRAVE UN. 103

Old surface

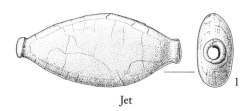

Jet

YORKSHIRE E.R., RUDSTON/BURTON AGNES UN. 104

Not located

Jet

YORKSHIRE E.R., SHERBURN UN. 105

Not located

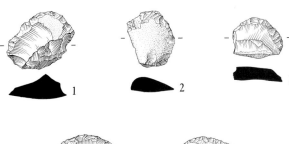

YORKSHIRE E.R., SHERBURN WOLD UN. 107

Not located

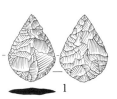

YORKSHIRE E.R., WARTER WOLD 1 UN. 108

Not located

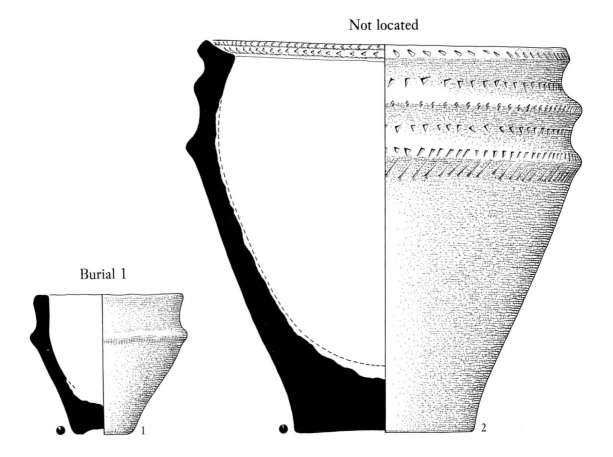

Burial 1

YORKSHIRE E.R., WARTER WOLD 2 UN. 109

Burial 1

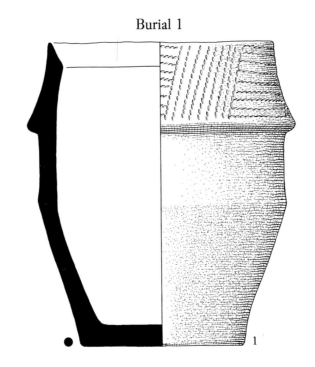

Not located

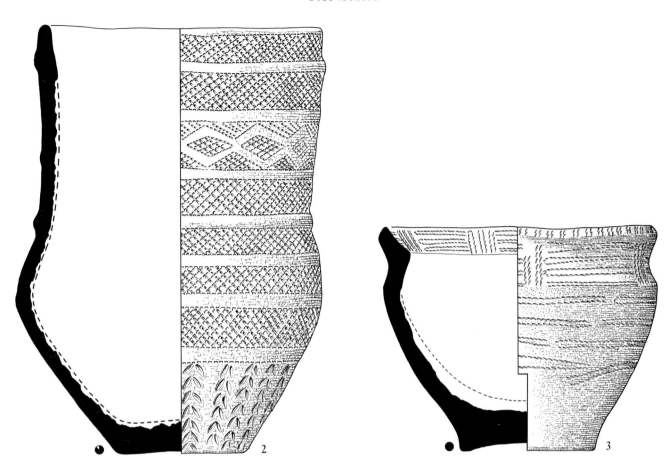

YORKSHIRE N.R., AMOTHERBY UN. 112

Not located

YORKSHIRE N.R., AYTON EAST FIELD UN. 113

Burial 4

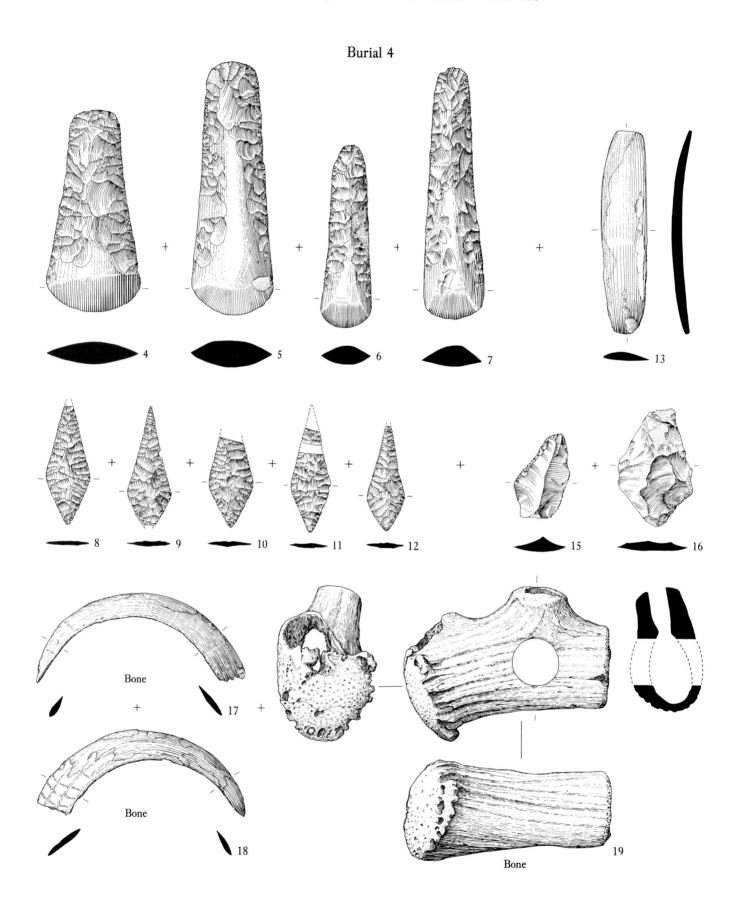

4   5   6   7   13

8   9   10   11   12   15   16

Bone   17

Bone   18

Bone   19

YORKSHIRE N.R., CROSSCLIFFE UN. 116

YORKSHIRE N.R., EGTON MOOR UN. 118

YORKSHIRE N.R., FYLINGDALES UN. 119

Burial 1

Cairn material

Not located

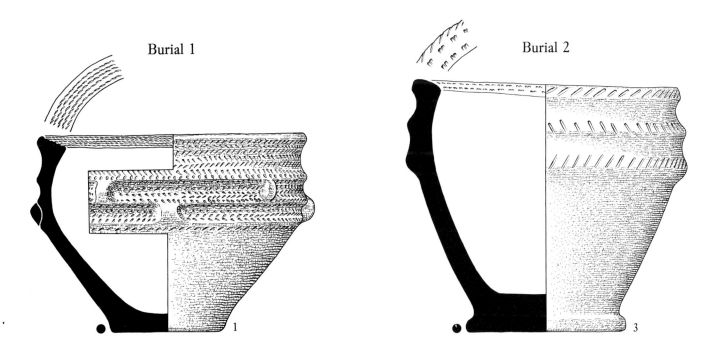

Stone

YORKSHIRE N.R., HAGWORM HILL UN. 120

Burial 1

Burial 2

Feature A

Feature B

Mound

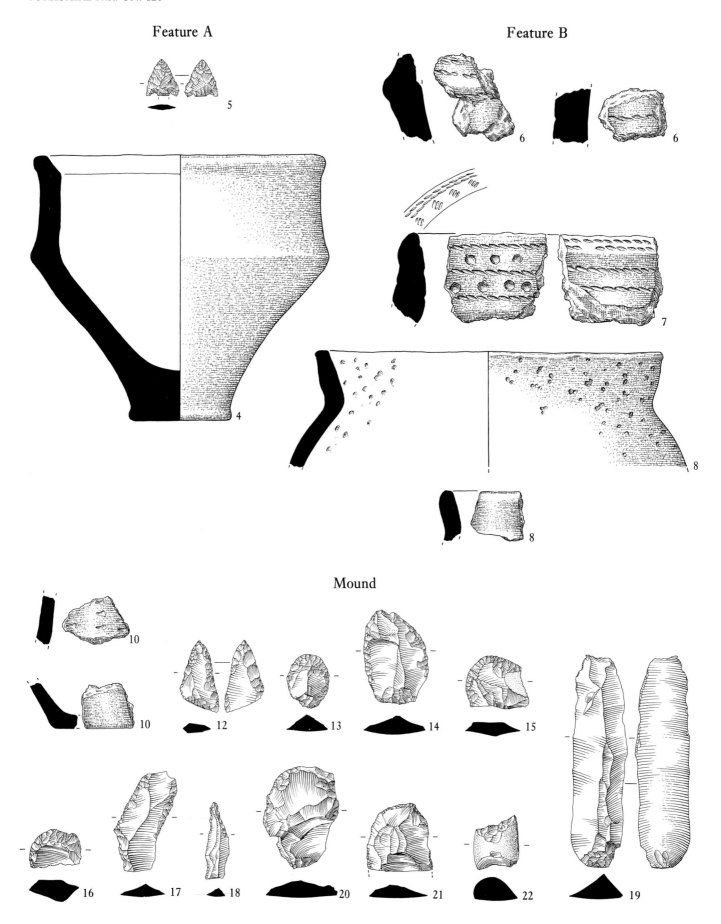

YORKSHIRE N.R., HAWNBY UN. 121

Not located

1

YORKSHIRE N.R., HELMSLEY UN. 122

Burial 1

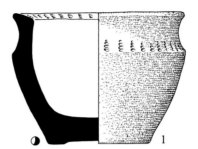

1

YORKSHIRE N.R., HOLWICK IN TEESDALE UN. 123

Not located

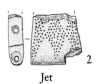

Jet 1   Jet 2

YORKSHIRE N.R., LEVISHAM MOOR UN. 124

Burial 2

Not located

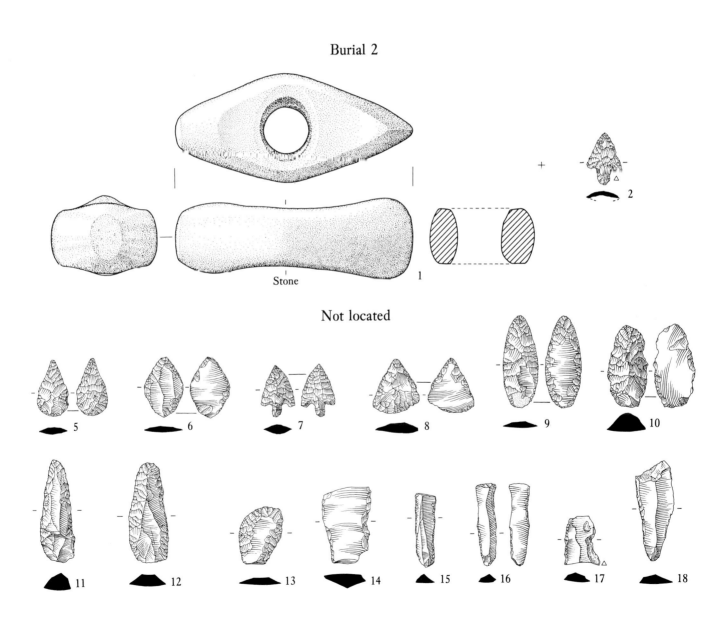

Stone 1

2

5   6   7   8   9   10

11   12   13   14   15   16   17   18

YORKSHIRE N.R., ORCHARD HILLS UN. 126

Burial 1

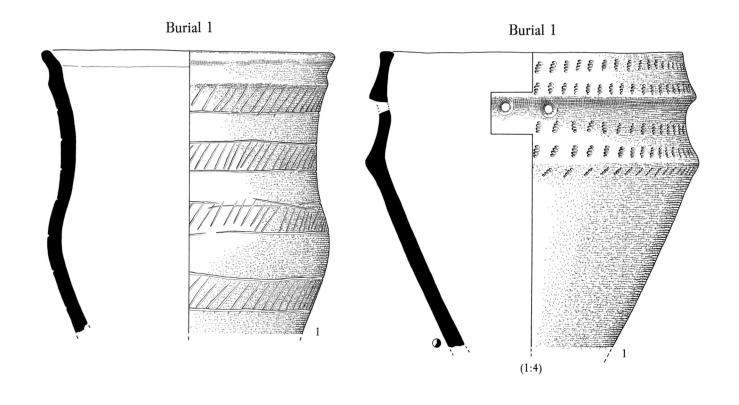

YORKSHIRE N.R., SCALBY UN. 127

Burial 1

(1:4)

YORKSHIRE N.R., SEAMER MANOR HOUSE UN. 129

Burial 2

YORKSHIRE N.R., SEAMER MOOR 2 UN. 131

Burial 1

Burial 1 or 2

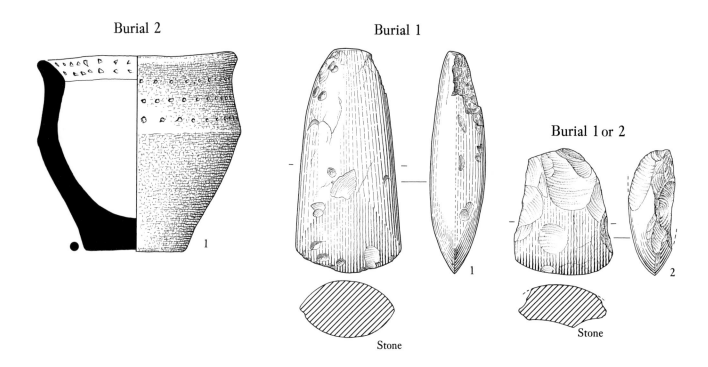

Stone

Stone

YORKSHIRE N.R., WHITBY UN. 132   ARGYLL, BALLYMEANOCH UN. 134

Not located   Burial 1

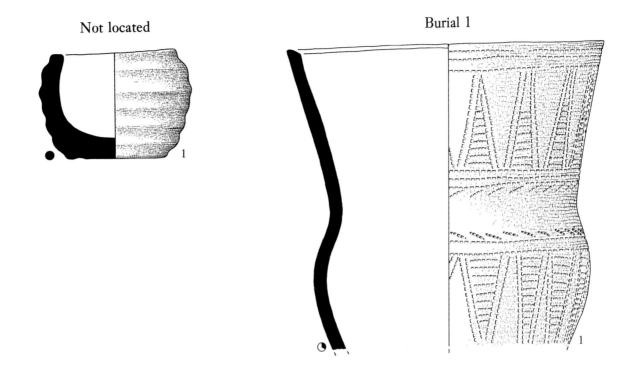

ARGYLL, DUNCRAGAIG UN. 135

Burial 1   Burial 4

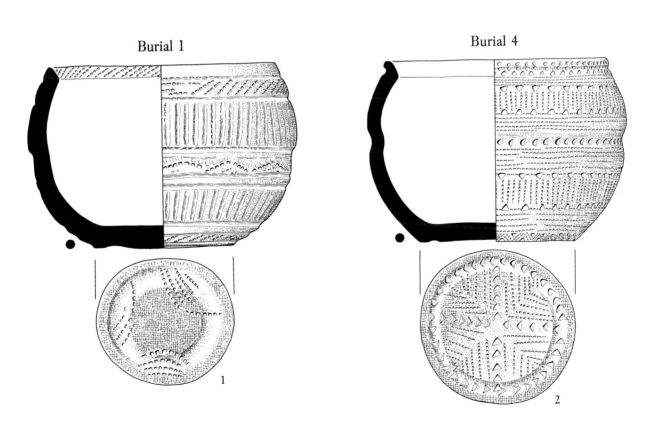

ARGYLL, GLEBE UN. 136

Burial 1

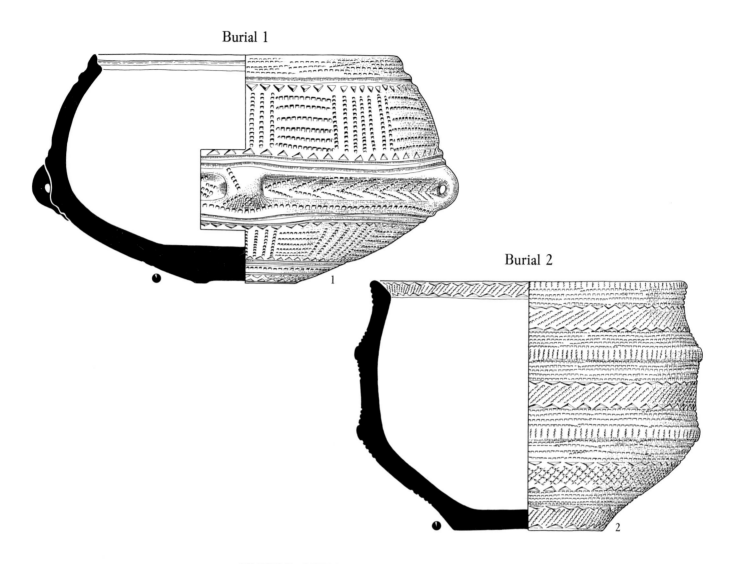

Burial 2

ARGYLL, NETHER LARGIE UN. 137

Burial 5

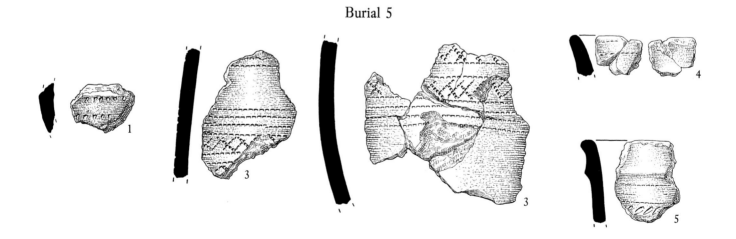

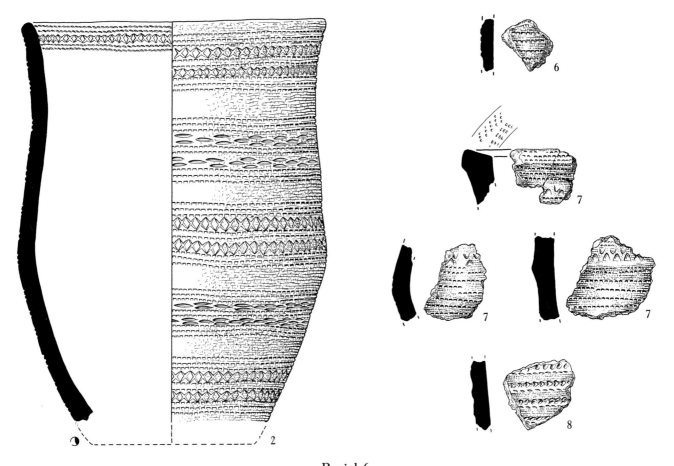

Burial 6

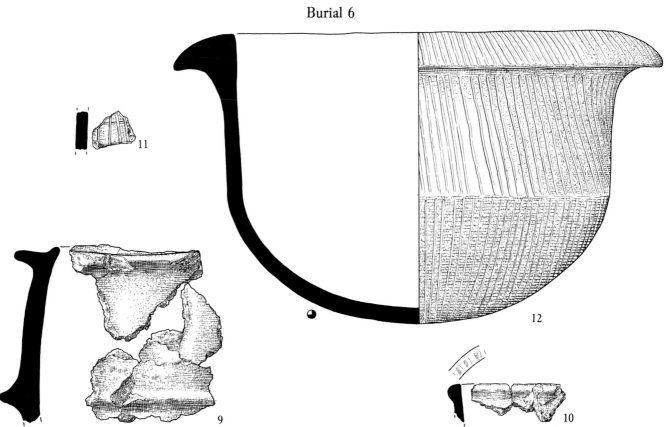

Burial 6

Burial 7

13   14   15   16

19   20

17   18

ARGYLL, RUDLE UN. 138

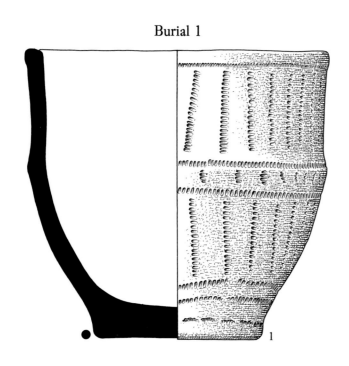

Burial 1

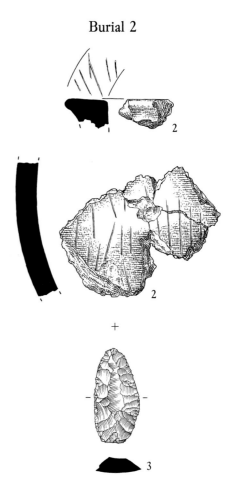

Burial 2

2

2

+

3

1

FORFAR, TEALING HILL UN. 139

Burial 1

Burial 2

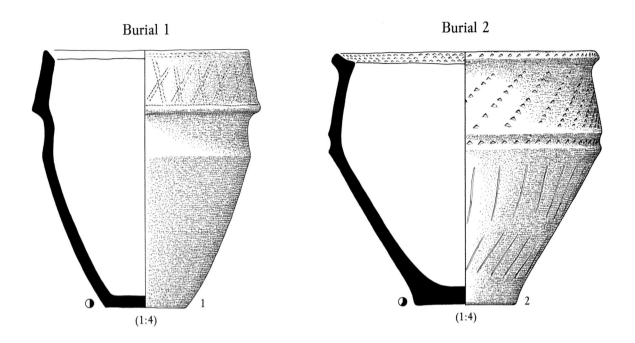

(1:4)   1

(1:4)   2

KIRKCUDBRIGHT, KIRKMABRECK UN. 140

Burial 1

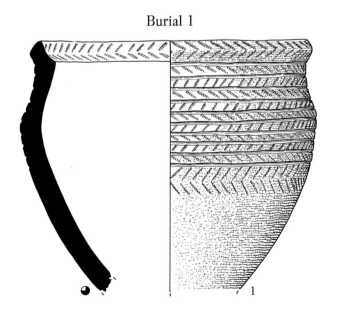

1

MORAY, KENNY'S HILLOCK UN. 141

Burial 1

Burial 2

MORAY, URQUHART UN. 142

Not located

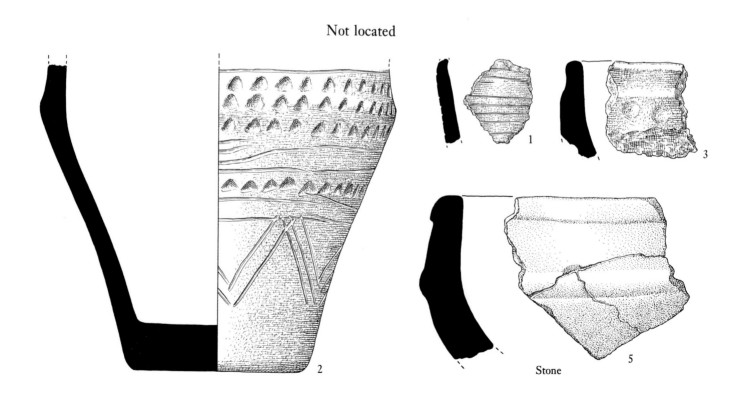

Stone

PERTHSHIRE, BLAIRGOWRIE UN. 143

PERTHSHIRE, HARRIETFIELD UN. 144

Burial 1

Not located

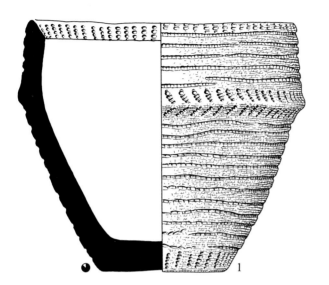

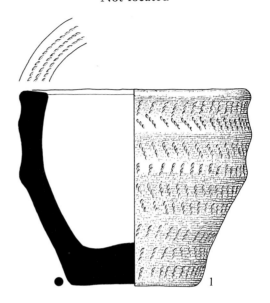

ROXBURGH, BLACKBURN UN. 145

ROXBURGH, LANTON MAINS UN. 146

Burial 1

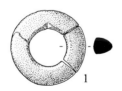

Jet